the International COOKBOOK

Includes over 1,000 recipes from around the world with full color photographs.

MODERN PROMOTIONS
A Division of Unisystems Inc., New York, New York 10022

Contents

VIENNESE

SOUP

BROWN BEEF SOUP
(*Braune Rindsuppe*)
    1 tbls. fat
    2 oz. beef liver
    beef bones, crushed
    2½ qts. water
    2 tsp. salt
    2½ lbs. beef
    soup greens
        2 medium-sized carrots
        ½ parsley root
        ¼ celery root
    1 small onion

Melt fat. Fry crushed bones, diced liver, sliced carrots, parsley, and celery root until slightly yellow. Add sliced onion. When light brown, pour off surplus fat; add mixture to salted cold water. Bring to a boil. Add meat. For strong soup, add meat before boiling. For stronger meat flavor, place meat in boiling water. Proceed as in white beef soup.
    Serves 6.

JULIENNE SOUP
(*Rindsuppe mit Schnittgemüsen*)
    1 cup kohlrabi, cut into strips
    1 cup carrots, cut into strips
    1 cup string beans, Frenched
    1 cup cabbage, shredded
    1 cup green peas
    1 cup cauliflower flowerets
    ½ cup mushrooms sliced and sautéed
    1½ qts. brown beef soup (see Index)

Cook all vegetables except mushrooms separately about 20 minutes in salted water. Add with mushrooms to brown beef soup.
    Serves 6.
    Note: The same soup with ½ cup cooked rice, more cabbage, and 3 tablespoons cubed mutton, is called "Irish Soup."

WHITE BEEF SOUP
(*Weisse Rindsuppe*)
    soup greens
        2 medium-sized carrots
        1 parsley root
        3 stalks of celery
        ½ leek
    1 small onion
    2 oz. liver
    1 lb. bones
    2½ qts. water
    3 tsp. salt
    2½ lbs. beef (chuck, rump, round)

Clean and slice soup greens. Dice liver. Place with bones in slightly salted cold water. Add washed and pounded meat. Bring to boil and cover tightly. Simmer 2-3 hours; don't boil vehemently. When meat is tender, strain soup, cool, and skim off fat. Clear, if necessary, as follows:
    Beat 1-2 egg whites with 1 tablespoon cold water.
    Add to soup. Bring to boil, whipping constantly for 5 minutes or more.
    Strain through linen cloth.
    Serves 5-6
    Note: Serve marrow from bones separately. Remove marrow before cooking, and cook separately in a cup of soup for a few minutes.
    For color and strength, add a piece of tripe, fowl, cauliflower bits, mushroom peelings, cabbage and tomato, to the boiling soup.

5

BEEF CONSOMMÉ WITH FLOUR BISCUITS
(*Rindsuppe mit Mehlsohöberln*)

> **biscuits**
>> 3 tbls. butter
>> 3 egg yolks
>> 1 egg
>> ⅔ cup flour, sifted
>> ¼ cup milk
>> ¼ tsp. salt
>> 3 egg whites, stiffly beaten
> 2½ qts. brown beef soup (see Index)

Cream butter; add egg yolks, egg, flour, milk, salt; fold in egg whites. Bake in greased and floured loaf form in 300° oven for 20-30 minutes until mixture separates from tin. Turn out on wooden board. Cut into bias pieces; reheat before serving. Serve separately from soup.

Serves 8.

OXTAIL CONSOMMÉ
(*Klare Ochsenschleppsuppe*)

> 1 tbls. fat
> 1 parsley root
> 2 carrots
> ½ celery root
> onion (small)
> peppercorns
> 2 small oxtails, split
> ¾ lb. beef bones
> 2 qts. water
> 1 tsp. salt
> 1½ lbs.
>> peas
>> string beans
>> carrots
>> cauliflower
>> asparagus tips
> 1 tbls. butter
> mushrooms

Melt fat. Slice parsley root, carrots, celery root, chop onion, and fry with peppercorns in fat for a few minutes. Cut oxtail in pieces, add beef bones, water, salt, fried soup greens, and cook until tender, about 1½ hours. Remove meat from bones and cut into small pieces. Strain soup and let cool. Remove fat.

Clear soup, if necessary, as follows:

Beat one egg white.

Add to soup and bring to a boil, whipping constantly.

Strain through linen cloth.

Finely cut and cook all vegetables (except mushrooms). Drain. Slice mushrooms and sauté in butter. Add meat, mushrooms, and vegetables to soup stock.

Serves 6.

VIENNESE RAGOUT SOUP
(*Ragoutsuppe*)

> **white sauce**
>> ½ cup butter
>> ¾ cup flour
>> 2½ qts. soup stock mixed with vegetable stock
>> ¼ tsp. salt
> 1 small cauliflower head
> ½ cup green peas
> 3-4 mushrooms
> 1 tsp. parsley, chopped
> 1 tbls. butter
> ⅓ lb. veal, diced

Prepare white sauce (see Index). Cook cauliflower in salted water; divide into flowerets. Cook peas. Sauté mushrooms and parsley in butter. Fry or boil veal. Add vegetables and meat to soup.

Serves 8.

Note: Instead of veal, sweetbread or chicken meat may be used.

HERB SOUP
(*Kräutersuppe*)

> ½ lb. various herbs mixed with spinach
> 1 tbls. butter or fat
> 1 tbls. onion, chopped
> 1 tbls. parsley, chopped
> **white sauce**
>> ½ cup butter
>> ¾ cup flour
>> 2½ qts. water
>> salt, pepper
> ½ cup sour cream
> 1 tsp. lemon juice
> 2 white rolls

Clean and wash herbs. Melt butter or fat. Fry onion and parsley slightly. Add herbs and spinach; simmer until soft. Put through strainer. Prepare white sauce (see Index). Add herb mixture. Stir; bring to a boil. Blend in sour cream and lemon juice.

Garnish: fried diced rolls

Serves 8.

Note: The soup is more nourishing if 1 or 2 egg yolks are added.

EXQUISITE CREAM SOUP
(Feingemischte Einmachsuppe)

    1 carrot, cut into strips
    ½ parsley root, cut into strips
    ¼ celery root, cut into strips
    1½ cups green beans, cut into strips
    ½ cup peas
    1 cup asparagus tips
    ½ head cauliflower, divided into flowerets
    white sauce
        ½ cup butter
        ¾ cup flour
        2½ qts. vegetable stock
        salt, pepper
    6-7 medium-sized mushrooms
    1 tbls. butter
    4 oz. veal, cooked and diced (or any other leftover meat)

Cook carrot, parsley root, celery root, beans, peas, asparagus, and cauliflower 10 minutes in salted water. Prepare white sauce (see Index). Sauté mushrooms in butter. Add, with veal and cooked vegetables. Cook gently 5-10 minutes.

Serves 8.

Note: For stronger flavor, use chicken or beef soup instead of vegetable stock.

SOUP À LA TEGETTHOFF
(Tegetthoff-Suppe)

    1 fowl
    1 parsley root, sliced
    1 carrot, sliced
    ¼ celery root, sliced
    4 tbls. flour
    1 cup soup or vegetable stock
    1 lb. asparagus

    ¼ cup green peas
    2½ qts. water
    1 tbls. salt
    3 tbls. butter
    ½ tsp. chervil, chopped
    1 egg yolk
    ¼ cup milk or cream
    3 mushrooms, sliced
    1 tbls. butter

Cook fowl, parsley, carrot, and celery root in water with salt. Melt butter and fry chervil. Blend in flour; add soup or vegetable stock. Bring to a boil. Cook asparagus and peas in salted water 20 minutes. Rub through strainer and add. Mix yolk with milk or cream; add to soup. Heat, but do not bring to a boil. Add mushrooms, sautéed in butter, and fowl, cut in small pieces, as garnish.

Serves 8.

ENTRÉES AND APPETIZERS

EGGS IN BÉCHAMEL SAUCE
(Kernweiche Eier in Milcheinmach)

    6 eggs
    béchamel sauce
        1 tbls. butter
        1 tbls. flour
        ¾ cup milk
        ¼ tsp. salt
        1 tsp. lemon juice
        Worcestershire sauce
        1 tsp. grated Parmesan cheese

Place eggs in boiling water; cook 5 minutes. Place in cold water; shell. Prepare béchamel sauce (see Index). Pour over eggs before serving.

Serves 3-6.

EGGS WITH LIVER PURÉE
(Eier mit Leberfarce)

    liver purée
        ¼ tsp. onion, chopped
        ¼ tsp. parsley, chopped
        1 tbls. fat
        ¼ lb. calf liver, ground
        2 slices white bread
        1 tbls. butter

1 tbls. flour
½ cup soup stock
salt, pepper to taste
6 eggs, poached
1 tsp. truffles, chopped
1 tsp. tongue, chopped

Sauté onions and parsley in hot fat. Fry liver and bread slices in same fat 5 minutes. (Liver should remain pink). Put through meat grinder. Melt butter; blend in flour; add soup and stir until thick. Add ground liver and bread, salt, and pepper to the liquid. Bring to a boil. (Mixture must be a purée, but not a thin one.) Pour into 6 custard cups. Top each with one poached egg. Sprinkle with truffles and tongue. Serve hot.

Serves 6.

EGGS IN SOUR CREAM
(Eier in Rahm)

1 cup sour cream
¼ tbls. milk
6 eggs
1 tbls. butter, melted
⅓ tsp. parsley, chopped
½ tsp. chives, chopped
4 anchovies, chopped
1 tbls. bread crumbs

Pour sour cream mixed with milk into ovenproof dish. Break eggs gently and drop into mixture. Pour butter over. Sprinkle with parsley, chives, anchovies, and bread crumbs. Bake in 350° oven until eggs are set (not too hard) and a light brown crust appears on top.

Serves 6.

PEASANT OMELET
(Bauernomelette)

3 oz. bacon or salt pork, diced
½ lb. potatoes, cooked and cubed
1 tbls. onions
10 eggs
¼ tsp. salt
½ tsp. parsley, chopped
¼ cup butter

Render bacon or salt pork. Fry potatoes and onions in fat; add crisp rind of bacon or pork. Beat eggs lightly; add salt, parsley, and potato mixture. Bake 3

separate omelets in butter, stirring with fork and shaking pan. Fold over from both sides.

Serves 6.

VEGETABLE SOUFFLÉ
(Gemüseauflauf)

½ cup green peas
1 cup Brussels sprouts
½ medium-sized cauliflower head
4-5 carrots, cut into strips
2-3 medium-sized mushrooms, sliced
2 tbls. butter
béchamel sauce
    3 tbls. butter
    3 tbls. flour
    1¼ cups milk
    5 egg yolks
    5 egg whites, stiffly beaten
    salt

Boil green peas, Brussels sprouts, cauliflower flowerets, and carrots in salted water. Drain; set aside to cool. Sauté mushrooms in butter. Prepare béchamel sauce (see Index). Fold in vegetables and mushrooms. Place mixture in buttered ovenproof glass dish and bake in 300° oven 45 minutes.

Serves 5.

SACHER* CHEESE
(Sacherkäse)

½ lb. farmer or cottage cheese
2 hard-boiled egg yolks
3 anchovies
2 tbls. butter
dash of onion, chopped
1 tsp. oil
1 tsp. mustard
dash of paprika
decoration
    1 parsley sprig
    3 anchovies
    3 hard-boiled eggs, sliced
    2 small sour gherkins
    ½ tsp. paprika

Rub cheese, egg yolks, anchovies, butter, and onion through strainer. Mix with oil, mustard, and paprika. Heap mixture on platter in shape of a pineapple. Decorate with parsley, anchovy strips, egg slices, and pickles. Sprinkle lightly with paprika.

FRIED CHEESE
(Gebackener Käse)
1 lb. Camembert or Swiss cheese
(Emmentaler), domestic or
imported
1½ cups frying batter (see Index)
1 cup fat

Cut cheese into ¾″ slices. Dip into frying batter. Fry in deep fat until golden brown. Place on absorbent paper.

Note: The cheese may be dipped in flour, then in beaten egg, and rolled in bread crumbs.

The frying batter may be wine, beer, or milk, as preferred.

CHEESE DUMPLINGS AU GRATIN
(Käsenockerl, gratiniert)
¼ cup water
1½ tbls. butter
¼ tsp. salt
½ cup grated cheese
½ cup flour
2 eggs
sauce
1-2 eggs
¾ cup milk
¼ tsp. salt
2 tbls. grated cheese

Boil water, butter, and salt. Add grated cheese and flour. Stir until mixture slides from spoon. Cool; add eggs. Form small balls, 1¼″ in diameter. Drop into boiling salted water. Simmer gently for 6-8 minutes. Drain. Place in buttered ovenproof dish. Combine eggs with milk and salt. Pour over dumplings. Sprinkle with grated cheese. Bake in 325° oven until crisp on top (about 25 minutes).

Serves 4.

LIPTAU* CHEESE
(Liptauer Käse)
½ lb. cottage cheese
1 cup butter
¼ tsp. paprika
½ tsp. chives, chopped
½ tsp. caraway seeds
½ tsp. capers, chopped
1 tsp. mustard
1 anchovy, chopped

***City in Czechoslovakia.**

Rub cheese through strainer. Cream butter. Combine cheese, butter, paprika, chives, caraway seeds, capers, mustard, and anchovy. Add salt if needed.

Serves 4.

Note: One chopped sardine may be added.

STUFFED KOHLRABI
(Gefüllte Kohlrabi)
10 kohlrabi
filling
1 tbls. fat
1 tsp. onion, chopped
½ tsp. parsley, chopped
2 mushrooms, chopped fine
3 cups leftover beef, chopped
1 egg
salt, pepper
white sauce
1 tbls. butter
2 tbls. flour
2 cups soup or water
salt, pepper
½ tsp. parsley, chopped
kohlrabi remnants

Peel and wash kohlrabi. Cut off tops and save for covers. Scoop. Boil in salted water about 15 minutes; drain. Fill with meat mixture, prepared as follows:

Melt fat. Fry onions.

Add parsley and mushrooms. Fry a few minutes and add beef.

Add egg, salt, and pepper.

(The cooked and mashed kohlrabi remnants may be added, too.)

Cover stuffed kohlrabi with tops. Place in shallow casserole, one next to the other. Prepare white sauce (see Index). Add parsley. Rub kohlrabi remnants through strainer and stir in. Add some boiled and chopped kohlrabi leaves. Cook until well-blended. Pour over kohlrabi. Simmer 15-30 minutes.

Serves 8-10.

Note: Instead of beef, pork and a soaked and squeezed roll may be used in the filling.

The very small kohlrabi leaves may be used as decoration over tops.

ARTICHOKE BOTTOMS WITH LIVER PURÉE
(Artischokenböden mit Leberbrei)

10 canned artichoke bottoms
stock of artichokes
¼ lb. sliced ham
liver purée (1 cup)
    1 thin slice salt pork
    1 tsp. onion
    1 tsp. fat
    ½ lb. chicken or goose liver, sliced
    dash of salt, pepper, marjoram
    ½ bay leaf
    1 white roll
    ½ cup milk
    1 egg yolk
2 tbls. grated Parmesan cheese
water or soup as needed

Simmer artichokes in canned stock until tender. Cover each with 1 slice of ham. Top with small peak of liver purée, prepared as follows:

Chop salt pork and onions.
Fry slightly in fat.
Add liver, salt, pepper, marjoram, and bay leaf.
Soak roll in milk; squeeze dry. (Use only crust.)
Combine with first mixture; stir over flame.
Add egg yolk and rub through strainer.

Sprinkle artichokes with cheese. Put into casserole with ½ cup soup. Bake in 400° oven 10 minutes before serving.

Serves 5.

Note: Sliced cooked celery may be used instead of artichokes.

MEAT, FISH AND POULTRY DISHES

VEAL RISOTTO
(Kalbfleischrisotto)

    ½ cup butter
    1 tbls. onion, chopped
    3 cups veal or leftover roast, diced
    1¾ cups rice
    3½ cups water or soup
    salt to taste
    ¾ cup cheese, grated

Heat butter. Fry onion. Add meat; brown slightly. Add rice; fry and stir 5 minutes. Pour in soup; add salt; simmer, covered, 30 minutes. Mix in cheese.

Keep warm in double boiler. Sprinkle with more cheese before serving.

Serves 6-8.

HASHED VEAL
(Kalbfleischhaschee)

    3 white rolls
    ⅔ cup milk
    1 tbls. onion, chopped
    1 tsp. parsley, chopped
    4 medium-sized mushrooms, chopped
    1 tbls. butter
    1 egg yolk
    salt, pepper to taste
    4 cups hashed roast of veal
    6 fried eggs

Soak rolls in milk; squeeze dry; hash. Fry onion, parsley, and mushrooms slightly in butter. Add egg yolk, salt, pepper, meat, and rolls. Cook gently 5 minutes. Remove to serving dish. Top with fried eggs.

Serves 6.

FRIED CHICKEN CROQUETTES
(Gebackene Geflügelröllchen)

    1 small chicken or fowl (about 4 lbs.)
    ½ lb. shoulder of veal
    ½ lb. smoked tongue
    1 truffle
    5-6 medium-sized mushrooms
    2 tbls. butter
    white sauce
        2 tbls. butter
        ⅓ cup flour
        veal and chicken stock as needed
        salt, pepper to taste
        2 egg yolks
    ⅓ cup flour
    2 eggs
    ¾ cup bread crumbs
    ¾ cup fat.

Cook chicken, veal, and tongue. Grind meat. Chop truffle; sauté sliced mushrooms. Prepare white sauce (see Index). Combine with meat, mushrooms, truffle. Set aside 45 minutes in a cool spot. Form rolls. Dip in flour, then in beaten egg; roll in bread crumbs. Fry in deep fat.

Serves 7.

HAM CRESCENTS OF POTATO DOUGH
(Schinkenkipfel aus Kartoffelteig)
- ½ cup butter
- 1 cup flour (scant)
- ¾ cup potatoes, cooked and mashed
- ¼ tsp. salt
- 1 egg yolk
- ½ pkg. yeast
- 1 tbls. water
- 1½ cups smoked ham or smoked pork, chopped
- 1 egg white

Work butter, flour, potatoes, salt, egg yolk, and yeast dissolved in water to a dough. Let stand 1 hour. Roll out ¼" thick. Cut into 4" squares. Heap 1 teaspoon ham or pork in center of each square. Form crescents; brush with egg white. Place on greased baking sheet. Let rise in warm place before baking. Bake in 350° oven 25-35 minutes or until yellow.

Serves 4.

FLOURED FRIED "AUGSBURGER" OR KNACKWURST
(Gebratene Augsburger oder Knackwurst mit Mehl)
- 6 sausages
- 1 tbls. flour
- 3 tbls. fat

Skin sausages and split lengthwise. Make 3 bias incisions on round side. Dip in flour. Fry on both sides until golden brown.

Serves 4.

FRENCH BREAD WITH FILLING OF MEAT LEFTOVERS
(Jägerwecken mit Bratenrestenfülle)
- 2 large loaves French bread
- filling
    - 2 tbls. butter
    - 3 cups leftover meat (game, pot roast), minced
    - ½ cup salt pork, minced
    - ½ cup ham, chopped
    - ¼ cup smoked tongue, chopped
    - 1 tsp. pistachios, chopped
    - 2 pickles, chopped
    - 1 hard-boiled egg, chopped
    - salt to taste

Cream butter. Mix in all ingredients. Scoop soft insides from bread. Stuff mixture tightly into bread. Set in refrigerator for 1-2 hours. Slice.

BAKED MEAT STRUDEL
(Gebackener Fleischstrudel)
- strudel dough (see Index)
- filling
    - 2½ cups boiled beef or leftover roast, chopped
    - 1 egg
    - ½ tsp. onion, chopped
    - ½ tsp. parsley, chopped
    - 1½ tbls. fat
    - 1 tbls. butter
    - 2 tbls. flour
    - ½ cup water or soup
    - ½ tsp. salt
    - dash paprika
- 2 tbls. butter, melted

Stretch out strudel dough. Prepare filling:
Mix meat with egg.
Fry onion and parsley in fat and add to meat.
Melt butter; blend in flour; add water or soup, meat mixture, salt, and paprika.
Spread over half of dough. Brush other half with melted butter. Roll strudel, starting from filled side. Bake in 300° oven on greased baking sheet about 30 minutes.

Serves 5.

MEAT PUDDING
(Fleischdunstkoch)
- 3 tbls. butter
- 2 rolls
- ½ cup water
- 3 egg yolks
- ¼ tsp. salt
- dash pepper
- 1 tbls. onion, chopped
- 1½ tbls. fat
- ½ tsp. parsley, chopped
- 1 cup chopped meat
- ¼ cup sour cream
- 3 egg whites, stiffly beaten
- 1 tbls. bread crumbs

Beat butter until creamy. Soak rolls in water; squeeze dry and rub through strainer. Combine butter, egg yolks, rolls, salt, pepper. Fry onion in fat until yellow. Add parsley and meat. Mix in sour cream; add to butter mixture. Fold in egg whites. Butter a pudding mold. Sprinkle with bread crumbs. Pour mixture in. Cook 1 hour in hot-water bath (see Index). Turn out.

Serves 4-5.

MACARONI MILANAISE
(Mailänder Makkaroni)

    1 lb. macaroni
    ½ cup butter
    ⅔ cup flour
    1 cup water or beef soup (see Index)
    ½ cup tomato purée
    ¼ cup red wine
    1⅓ cups smoked pork or ham, cooked and
        sliced
    5 mushrooms, sliced and sautéed
    2 tbls. butter, melted
    ½ cup cheese, grated
    2 tbls. bread crumbs

Break macaroni into small pieces. Cook in boiling salted water 7 minutes. Drain; pour cold water over. Drain again. Melt butter; blend in flour; add water or soup. Mix in tomato purée, wine, meat, mushrooms, and macaroni. Simmer 5-10 minutes. Place in buttered shells or casseroles. Pour butter over. Sprinkle with cheese and bread crumbs. Bake in 350° oven about 10 minutes (until crisp on top).

Serves 5-6.

Note: Fresh tomatoes may be used instead of tomato purée. Simmer with soup greens and ½ cup water until thick; rub through strainer.

BRAIN AU GRATIN
(Überkrustetes Hirn)

    2 pairs calf brains (generous, 1½ lbs.)
    sauce
        2 tbls. butter
        2 tbls. flour
        ½ cup beef soup (see Index)
        2 cups milk
        ½ tsp. salt
        ½ tsp. Worcestershire sauce
        2 tbls. grated Parmesan cheese
        1 tbls. lemon juice
        1 egg yolk
        1 tbls. milk
    2 tbls. butter, melted
    3 tbls. Parmesan cheese, grated
    1 tbls. bread crumbs

Wash brains. Cook in boiling salted water 15-20 minutes. Skin. Dice. Prepare sauce:

Melt butter; blend in flour; add soup and milk. Cook gently until thick.

Add salt, Worcestershire sauce, cheese, and lemon juice.

Mix egg yolk with milk. Add.

Butter 10 shells or casseroles; put diced brains in them and cover with sauce. Pour melted butter over. Sprinkle with cheese and bread crumbs. Bake in 350° oven 10 minutes.

Serves 5 or 10.

Note: To help shells stand better on baking sheet, sprinkle rock salt on sheet.

CALF SWEETBREADS À LA CHEVALIER
(Kavalier-Kalbsbries)

    2 lbs. sweetbreads
    salt to taste
    2 tbls. flour
    ½ cup fat
    2 mushrooms, quartered
    1 tbls. butter
    15 asparagus tips, cooked
    1 head cauliflower, cooked and separated into
        flowerets
    white sauce
        3 tbls. butter
        3 tbls. flour
        1 cup soup or water
        ½ tsp. salt
        1 tsp. lemon juice

Cook sweetbreads 5 minutes in salted water. Slice; salt; dip in flour. Fry in fat. Sauté mushrooms in butter. Prepare white sauce (see Index). Add sweetbreads, mushrooms, cauliflower, and asparagus; simmer 15 minutes.

Serves 4-5.

Note: The white sauce may be bound with egg yolks.

CREAM OF HAM IN ASPIC
(Schinkencreme in Aspik)

    ¼ lb. chicken livers
1 tsp. flour
1 tsp. shallots, chopped fine
1 tsp. fat
salt
pepper
½ lb. ham
1 egg yolk
white sauce
    1 tbls. butter
    2 tbls. flour
    ⅓ cup milk
seasoning
    ½ cup aspic (see Index)
    ½ cup heavy cream, whipped
    1 cup aspic for the mold

Dip chicken livers in flour on one side. Fry with shallots in fat, seasoned with salt and pepper. Rub through strainer. Mix with ham, egg yolk, white sauce (see Index for preparation), seasoning, liquid aspic, and whipped cream. Place in cool spot. Pour aspic into mold; let bottom and sides set in refrigerator; pour off surplus. Put ham mixture into mold and leave in refrigerator about 3 hours to set. Turn out on platter.

Garnish (optional) with parsley, chopped aspic, and small cones of ham filled with caviar.

Serves 4.

CARP IN GELÉE
(Gesulzter Karpfen)

    4 lbs. carp
2 cups parsley root, celery root, and carrots, cut into small sticks
1 small onion, sliced
10 peppercorns
½ cup vinegar

Scrape, clean, and wash carp. Cut in slices 1″ thick. Boil parsley root, celery root, carrots, onion, peppercorns, and vinegar in salted water. Add fish and cook gently for 15 minutes. (Water must cover fish.) Arrange fish in serving dish. Pour fish stock with vegetables on top. Leave in refrigerator to set.

Serves 7-9.

Note: Any other fish may be prepared this way.

BOILED CARP
(Gekochter Karpfen)

    4 lbs. carp
½ cup vinegar
2 cups parsley, celery root, carrots, sliced
1 small onion, sliced
30 peppercorns
thyme, bay leaf
3 tbls. butter, melted

Scrape and wash fish. To facilitate handling, wrap in cheesecloth and tie up. Cook vinegar, soup greens, onion, peppercorns, thyme, bay leaf in salted water, in fish pan, 15-20 minutes. Place fish in the pan. (Water must cover the fish.) Simmer 30 minutes. Remove to platter. Pour melted butter over.

Side Dish: boiled potatoes.

Serves 7.

Note: Any fish may be cooked in this stock, called "court bouillon."

PIKE À LA RADZIWILL
(Schill nach Fürst Radziwill)

    4 lbs. pike
béchamel filling
    ½ lb. cod
    2 tbls. butter
    2 tbls. flour
    ½ cup milk
    ½ cup soup
    salt to taste
    1 egg yolk
⅓ cup butter
2 stalks celery, sliced
1 parsley root, sliced
1 carrot, sliced
peppercorns
2 tbls. butter
½-1 cup water or soup

Clean, wash pike; cut open along stomach. Remove backbone and other bones. Cook cod for filling; bone, hash. Add to béchamel sauce (see Index for preparation). Stuff pike with mixture. Sew slit and roast fish, with vegetables and peppercorns, in 350° oven 1 hour. Baste frequently. Strain gravy; add 2 tablespoon butter, water or soup. Bring to a boil.

Serves 6-8.

HALIBUT SLICES À L'ORLY
(*Heilbuttfilets nach Orly*)

   3 lbs. halibut
salt
frying batter
      1½ cups flour
      1 cup beer
      1 egg
      1 egg yolk
      1 tbls. olive oil
      salt
   1½ cups fat for frying

Skin and bone halibut. Cut into small pieces. Salt; dip into batter, prepared as follows:

Beat flour and beer until well-blended.

Add egg, egg yolk, olive oil, salt.

Fry in deep fat. Place on absorbent paper.

Serves 6-7.

SALMON ROULADE IN ASPIC
(*Lachsrolle in Aspik*)

   10 big slices smoked salmon
filling
      2 medium-sized cans salmon
      10 eggs, hard-boiled
      ½ cup mayonnaise
      ¼ tsp. salt
      dash cayenne pepper
      Worcestershire sauce
      1 tsp. anchovy, crushed
      1 pkg. gelatin
      8 tbls. aspic (see Index)
   sliced truffles for decorating

Spread salmon slices close to each other on parchment. Form a roll of fish filling, prepared as follows:

Drain canned salmon.

Rub through strainer with eggs.

Bind with mayonnaise.

Add salt, cayenne pepper, Worcestershire sauce, mashed anchovy, dissolved gelatin, and dissolved aspic.

Stir.

Place in refrigerator.

Place on top of salmon slices and fold over from each side, or roll. Let set in refrigerator. Brush with aspic. Cut into bias pieces 2″ thick. Decorate with truffles dipped in aspic.

Serves 8-10.

BASS WITH ANCHOVY BUTTER
(*Ungarischer Schill mit Sardellenbutter*)

   4 lbs. bass (or halibut)
   3 anchovies, cut in strips
   ⅓ cup fat
anchovy butter
      ½ cup butter
      2 anchovies, rubbed through strainer

Clean and wash fish. Use larding needle to pull strips of anchovies through surface of fish. Place in hot fat in roasting pan in 325° oven and roast until tender (about 30 minutes). Baste frequently with its own juice. Prepare anchovy butter (see Index). Add to gravy and bring to a boil.

Serves 6.

FLOUNDER IN SHELLS
(*Rot-Zunge in Muscheln*)

   4 lbs. filet of flounder
salt
1 tbls. lemon juice
1-2 tbls. butter
1-2 tbls. melted butter
1 tbls. grated Parmesan cheese
1 tbls. bread crumbs
potato purée (see Index), using 1 lb. potatoes
béchamel sauce
      2 tbls. butter
      2 tbls. flour
      2 cups milk
      1 egg
      1 egg yolk
      salt, pepper, nutmeg
      1 tbls. lemon juice
      1 tsp. Worcestershire sauce

Clean and wash fish; salt. Sprinkle with lemon juice. Fry quickly, or place in buttered pan, cover with buttered paper, and bake 10-15 minutes in 350° oven. Put fish into casserole greased with butter. Pour béchamel sauce (see Index for preparation) on top. Pour melted butter over. Sprinkle with Parmesan and bread crumbs. Decorate with potato purée. Bake in 350° oven 10 minutes before serving.

Serves 8.

Note: Leftover fish may be used, too, for this recipe.

FRIED COD IN HERB SAUCE
(Gebratener Schellfisch)

> **3 lbs. cod**
> **1 cup milk, or water with vinegar**
> **1 tbls. lemon juice**
> **salt**
> **1 tbls. flour**
> **2 tbls. fat**
> **sauce**
>> **1 tbls. shallots, chopped**
>> **2 tbls. butter**
>> **½ tsp. basil**
>> **½ tsp. rosemary**
>> **1 tsp. parsley green**
>> **5-6 mushrooms, chopped**
>> **2 tbls. flour**
>> **¾ cup water**
>> **¼ cup sour cream or more**

Skin fish. Soak in milk or water with vinegar ½ hour. Dry; sprinkle with lemon juice and salt. Cut fish in slices ¾" thick. Dip in flour and fry in hot fat on both sides. Prepare sauce:

Fry shallots (or onion) in butter.

Add herbs and mushrooms and sauté about 8 minutes.

Stir in flour; add water. Bring to a boil; add sour cream.

Add fried fish slices. Simmer 5 to 10 minutes in gravy.

Serves 7.

FILET OF SOLE IN WHITE WINE
(Seezungenschnitten in Weisswein)

> **4 lbs. sole, fileted**
> **salt**
> **2 tsp. shallots, chopped**
> **10 peppercorns**
> **1 cup white wine**
> **stock**
>> **1 cup soup greens**
>> **1 medium-sized onion**
>> **1 tbls. vinegar**
> **sauce**
>> **2 tbls. butter**
>> **2 tbls. flour**
>> **1 cup stock**
>> **2 egg yolks**
>> **¼ cup cream**

Wash and salt filets. (Save bones and skin. See note.) Cover the bottom of a casserole with chopped shallots and peppercorns. Place fish on top. Add white wine. Cover with greased paper; bake in 325° oven 10 minutes. Boil soup greens, onion, and vinegar. Strain. Prepare sauce.

Melt butter, add flour; stir.

Add stock and fish gravy.

Add yolks and cream; stir until thickened.

Serves 8.

Note: To make more stock, if necessary, boil bones and skin in salted water with 1 tablespoon vinegar, peppercorns, and sliced soup greens.

FISH PUDDING
(Fischdunstkoch)

> **filling**
>> **2¼ lbs. fish (any kind with firm meat)**
>> **3 rolls**
>> **½ cup milk**
>> **2 eggs**
>> **1 tbls. Parmesan cheese, grated**
>> **1 tbls. salt**
>> **1 tbls. flour**
>> **2 tbls. butter, melted**
> **sauce**
>> **2 tbls. butter**
>> **3 tbls. flour**
>> **1 small onion, chopped**
>> **2 cups water, or beef soup (see Index)**
>> **3 anchovies, crushed**
>> **½ cup white wine**
>> **1 tbls. lemon juice**
>> **2 egg yolks**

Wash and clean fish. Boil in salted water 5 minutes. Drain. Bone. Chop half of fish. Soak rolls in milk and squeeze dry. Rub rolls and fish through strainer. Mix with eggs, grated cheese, salt, butter, and flour. Cut second half of fish into 1" cubes. Grease pudding form; sprinkle with bread crumbs. Alternate one layer of filling with one layer of fish cubes. Steam pudding in hot-water bath (see Index) 1 hour. Turn out on platter. Prepare sauce:

Melt butter; add flour; stir.

Add chopped onion; cook slightly. Blend in water, soup, or fish stock.

Add anchovies.

Rub mixture through a strainer.

Add white wine and lemon juice.

Stir in egg yolks rapidly.

Pour over fish and serve.

Serves 6.

Note: It is easier to turn out the pudding if the cubed fish is mixed into the filling.

SHRIMP, VIENNESE STYLE
(Skampi auf wienerische Art)

> **2 lbs. shrimp**
> **2 shallots**
> **¼ cup oil**
> **¼ cup brandy**
> **½ cup white wine**
> **dash sugar**
> **1 tbls. tomato purée**
> **salt, cayenne pepper to taste**
> **1 tbls. butter**
> **1 tbls. flour**

Remove shells and veins from shrimp. Fry chopped shallots in oil. Add shrimps. Pour brandy over; set aflame. When flame has burned down, add white wine, sugar, tomato purée, salt, cayenne pepper. Simmer 15 minutes; remove shrimp. Melt butter; blend in flour, add 3 tablespoons shrimp gravy; stir. Combine with rest of gravy. Bring to a boil; strain. Add shrimp; heat.

Serves 4.

ROAST BEEF WITH ANCHOVY FILLING
(Rostbraten mit Sardellenfülle)

> **3 lbs. sirloin, round or hip steak**
> **salt, pepper to taste**
> **filling**
> > **4 oz. salt pork**
> > **6 oz. smoked pork, cooked**
> > **2 pickles**
> > **2 anchovies**
> **sauce**
> > **3 tbls. fat**
> > **1 tbls. flour**
> > **1 cup soup stock or water**
> > **1 cup sour cream**
> > **1 tbls. vinegar**

Cut meat into slices ¼" thick. Pound; season with salt and pepper. Cover each slice with strips of salt pork, smoked pork, pickles, and anchovies. Roll and

tie. Simmer in natural juice, adding water or soup gradually if needed. Remove meat. Prepare sauce as follows:

Add fat to gravy.

Blend in flour; brown slightly.

Add soup, sour cream, vinegar.

Add meat and simmer 5 minutes in sauce.

Serves 6.

SAUTÉED BOILED BEEF
(Gekochtes Rindfleisch, überdünstet)

> **sauce**
> > **4 small onions (cut into rings)**
> > **3 tbls. fat**
> > **¼ tsp. paprika**
> > **1 tbls. vinegar**
> > **2 tbls. flour**
> > **2 cups soup stock**
> > **½ tsp. salt**
> **2-3 lbs. boiled beef (leftover boiled beef may be used)**

Prepare sauce:

Fry onions in fat until light yellow.

Add paprika and vinegar.

Blend in flour.

Add beef soup and salt; cook gently 20 minutes.

Add meat, cut into individual portions. Simmer 30 minutes in sauce.

Serves 5-6.

ESTERHAZY ROAST BEEF
(Esterházy-Rostbraten)

> **¼ celery root**
> **1 small onion**
> **2 carrots**
> **2 tbls. butter (or 1 cup beef soup, see Index)**
> **4 lbs. beef (sirloin, or round steak), cut into 5 slices**
> **dash salt, pepper**
> **1-2 tbls. flour**
> **6 tbls. fat**
> **sauce**
> > **1 tbls. butter**
> > **1 tsp. flour**
> > **water or soup stock**
> > **1 cup sour cream**
> > **salt to taste**
> **½ cup soup greens, chopped**

Cut celery root, onion, and carrots into samll strips. Fry in butter or boil in beef soup until tender. Cut incisions in borders of meat. Pound; season with salt and pepper. Sprinkle one side with flour. Fry quickly on both sides in hot fat. Remove meat. Prepare sauce as follows:

Skim off fat from gravy; thicken with butter and flour.

Add water or soup as needed; bring to a boil.

Add sour cream and salt; blend well and simmer 5 minutes.

Place meat in gravy and reheat. Remove meat to platter. Pour gravy over. Sprinkle with chopped soup greens.

Serves 5-6.

POT ROAST WITH SOUR CREAM SAUCE
(Rindsbraten mit Rahmsoss)

⅛ celery root, sliced thin
½ parsley root, sliced thin
1 carrot, sliced thin
½ onion, sliced thin
4 tbls. fat
3 lbs. beef (top round, brisket, or rump)
salt, pepper to taste
¼ lb. salt pork
½ bay leaf
20 peppercorns
dash thyme
dash nutmeg and ginger
2½ cups water or soup stock
1 tbls. flour
½ cup sour cream

Fry celery root, parsley root, carrot, and onion slightly in 1 tablespoon fat. Wash and pound meat; season with salt and pepper, and lard with salt pork. Place in roasting pan in 400° oven. Melt 3 tablespoons fat; pour over meat. Add fried soup greens, bay leaf, peppercorns, thyme, nutmeg, ginger, and 2 cups water or beef soup. Baste frequently and roast 2½ hours, covered. When nearly tender, remove meat. Add flour and remaining water or soup. Return meat; lower heat. Roast until tender, uncovered, 1 hour or more. Strain and mash gravy; add sour cream. Blend well and bring to a boil.

Serves 6.

SWABIAN BEEF
(Schwäbisches Fleisch; Côte de Boeuf Braisée)

3 lbs. tail of tenderloin
dash salt, pepper
4 oz. salt pork
2 tbls. flour
3 tbls. fat
water or soup stock, as needed
2 tbls. onions, chopped
2 tbls. flour
1 tsp. parsley, chopped
1 cup sour cream
1 tsp. capers, chopped
1 tsp. lemon rind, chopped
2 pickles, chopped
2 anchovies, chopped

Slice meat ¼" thick. Trim edges; pound; season with salt and pepper, and lard with strips of salt pork. Sprinkle one side with flour. Fry gently in 2 tablespoons fat until medium rare. Pour fat into another pan. Add ½ cup water or soup to remaining gravy; bring to a boil. Fry onions in fat in pan, adding 1 more tablespoon fat. Mix in flour. Add parsley, gravy, and sour cream. (If needed, add some more soup.) Place meat in gravy with capers, lemon rind, pickles, and anchovies. Simmer until tender (about 20-30 minutes).

Serves 6.

Note: If another cut of beef is used instead of tenderloin, cook about 1½-2 hours, or until tender, and add sour cream before serving.

MEAT LOAF
(Faschierter Braten)

1 lb. beef, chopped
1 lb. pork, chopped
3 rolls
1 egg
4 strips of bacon, unfried and diced
dash salt, pepper
marjoram
1 tbls. onion, chopped
1 tbls. parsley, chopped
1 tbls. fat
⅓ cup water or soup
1 tbls. bread crumbs

3 tbls. fat, melted
1 cup sour cream

Mix chopped meat with rolls (soaked and squeezed dry). Add egg, bacon, salt, pepper, marjoram, onions and parsley fried in fat, and water. Knead well. Spread bread crumbs on wooden board, so ingredients do not stick. Form a loaf and place in pan. Pour hot fat over. Roast in 375° oven 1½ hours. Add 1 or 2 tablespoons water or soup from time to time and baste. Half an hour before serving, skim off fat and add sour cream.

Side Dishes: salads, vegetables, mashed potatoes.
Serves 5.

STUFFED VEAL ROLLS
(Gefüllte Kalbsvögerl)

   3 lbs. shoulder of veal
   filling
      ½ lb. salt pork
      3 tbls. sour cream
      garlic, lemon peel (grated), thyme to taste
      1½ cups cooked meat, minced
      1 egg yolk
      salt to taste
   1 small onion, sliced
   soup stock as needed
   ½ cup sour cream

Cut meat into small even slices (3" in diameter). Prepare filling as follows:

Fry half of salt pork until yellow.

Add sour cream, garlic, lemon peel, thyme, minced meat, egg yolk, and salt.

Mix well.

Spread filling on each slice of veal; roll and tie. Put onion and remaining salt pork in a pan. Add meat rolls and simmer, covered, until tender (45 minutes), adding a little soup from time to time. About 10 minutes before serving, add sour cream to gravy. Blend well.

   Serves 6-8.

VIENNESE VEAL CUTLETS
(Wiener Schnitzel)

   3 lbs. leg of veal
   salt to taste
   ¾ cup flour
   2 eggs, beaten

   1 cup bread crumbs
   1 cup fat
   1 lemon, sliced

Have your butcher cut and flatten out thin cutlets. Make incisions at borders after trimming. Salt. Dip first in flour, then in eggs, then in bread crumbs. Fry in deep hot fat until golden brown. Drain on absorbent paper. Decorate with lemon slices.

Serves 6-8.

TYROLEAN PORK SHOULDER
(Tiroler Geröstel)

   2 tbls. fat
   2 small onions, chopped
   1 lb. pork shoulder, sliced thin
   salt and pepper to taste
   ¾ cup water or soup stock, or more
   3 lbs. potatoes, cooked and peeled
   3 tbls. butter or fat
   1 tsp. salt

Melt fat. Fry onions until yellow. Add pork, salt, and pepper. Add water or soup and simmer 45 minutes to 1 hour. Slice potatoes; fry in butter; add salt. Mix with meat.

Serves 4-6.

Note: In the Tyrol, beef or other leftover meat is used more often than pork for this recipe. If leftover meat is used, it may be fried with the cooked potatoes.

FILET OF PORK À LA COLBERT
(Schweinslungenbraten nach Colbert)

   3 lbs. boned loin of pork
   2 heads cabbage
   ½ lb. salt pork, sliced
   dash salt, caraway seeds
   1 small onion, chopped
   1 tsp. parsley, chopped
   3 mushrooms, chopped
   2 tbls. pork fat
   1 cup water or soup stock

Wash and skin meat. Pour boiling water over cabbages. Separate leaves and place one beside the next. Top with salt pork slices. Rub meat with salt and caraway seeds. Fry onion, parsley, and mushrooms in fat. Brush meat with this mixture. Place meat on top of salt pork and cabbage leaves. Roll and tie. Roast in 375° oven 1¼ hours, basting frequently, first with pan gravy, then with water or soup stock.

Serves 6.

Note: In Austria the whole roast is wrapped into a pork's net, seldom available in this country.

LEG OF PORK WITH VEGETABLES
(Gedämpfter Schweinsschlegel mit Wurzelwerk)

    3 lbs. leg of pork
    salt, caraway seeds to taste
    1 clove garlic, crushed
    2 cups mixed soup greens, sliced
        parsley root
        celery root
        carrot
    1 small onion, sliced
    ½ cup fat
    2 cups water or soup stock, or more
    ¼ cup white wine
    ½ tsp. flour
    1 cup sour cream

Bone and wash meat. Rub with salt, caraway seeds, and garlic; tie. Fry soup greens and onion in fat. Brown meat. Add water or soup stock and wine; simmer 1½-2 hours. Remove meat. Skim off fat; blend flour into gravy; pour in more soup stock or water if needed. Strain gravy; add sour cream. Bring to a boil.

Serves 5-6.

Note: Pork tenderloin may be prepared the same way.

PORK CHOPS WITH HERBS
(Schweinsrippchen mit Feinen Kräutern)

    3 lbs. pork chops
    salt, caraway seeds to taste
    2 tbls. flour
    3 tbls. fat
    1 tbls. onion, chopped
    ½ tbls. parsley, chopped
    3-4 mushrooms, chopped
    2 tbls. flour
    ½-1 cup water or soup stock
    dash salt
    1 cup sour cream

Clean chops; make incisions at borders. Pound, salt and sprinkle with caraway seeds. Dip one side in flour. Fry quickly on both sides in 2 tablespoons fat until golden brown. Fry onion, parsley, and mushrooms in 1 tablespoon fat. Blend in flour; fry a little; add water or soup stock and fried chops. Simmer, covered, about 30 minutes. Stir in salt and sour cream. Bring to a boil and serve.

Serves 4-6.

Note: Cutlets and tenderloin may be prepared the same way.

STEAMED HAM
(Gedämpfter Schinken)

    4 lbs. ham
    ½ parsley root, sliced
    ¼ celery root, sliced
    ½ carrot, sliced
    ½ onion, sliced
    2 tbls. fat
    white sauce
        2 tbls. butter
        2 tbls. flour
        1 cup water or soup stock, or more
    ¼ cup white wine
    ½ cup sour cream

Cook ham in water 1 hour. Remove skin. Fry parsley root, celery root, carrot, and onion in fat in deep pot. Place skin of ham over soup greens and onion; add ham. Prepare white sauce (see Index). Pour over ham. Simmer 1½ hours, or until tender. Remove ham. Blend wine and sour cream into sauce. Bring to a boil; strain.

Serves 10.

BREADED FRIED LAMB
(Gebackenes Lämmernes mit Mehl und Bröseln)

    4 lbs. lamb (shoulder or leg)
    salt to taste
    1 cup flour
    2 eggs, slightly beaten
    1 cup bread crumbs
    1½ cups fat

Cut meat into small cutlets, Sprinkle with salt. Dip in flour, then in eggs. Roll in bread crumbs. Fry in deep fat. Place on absorbent paper to drain.

Serves 8.

LAMB CHOPS IN PUFF PASTE
(Lammsrippchen in Blätterteig)

        3 lbs. lamp chops (rib)
        salt to taste
        ⅓ cup flour
        ½ cup fat
        stuffing
                ¾ lb. goose or chicken liver
                dash basil, chopped
                5-6 mushrooms, chopped and sautéed
                1 small onion, chopped
                ½ tsp. parsley, chopped
                dash salt, pepper
        puff paste (see Index); prepare ½ recipe
        1 egg, beaten
        gravy
                2 tbls. fat
                meat trimmed from chops
                ½ cup mixed soup greens, diced
                ¼ cup white wine or tomato purée
                ¾ cup soup stock or water

Prepare chops; pound and salt meat; make incisions at borders; trim. Sprinkle one side with flour; fry quickly in fat on both sides. Cool; leave in refrigerator. When completely cold, brush with liver stuffing, prepared as follows:

Run liver through meat grinder; add basil, mushrooms, onion, parsley, salt, and pepper.

Blend well.

Wrap chops in puff paste rolled out thin, leaving the ribs uncovered. Place on wet baking sheet; brush top of chops with egg. Be sure all ribs are facing in the same direction. Decorate chops with small pieces of puff paste cut out with cutter (1 on each chop). Bake in 400° oven until light brown. Prepare gravy as follows:

Melt fat.

Fry meat scraps and soup greens.

Add wine or tomato purée and soup or water.

Bring to a boil and strain.

Pour over chops and serve.

Serves 6.

CHICKEN VILLEROI
(Villeroihühner)

        3 young chickens
        ¼ parsley root, sliced
        ¼ celery root, sliced
        ½ carrot, sliced
        ½ onion, sliced
        2 cups villeroi sauce (see Index)
        ¼-½ cup bread crumbs
        2 eggs, beaten
        1 cup bread crumbs
        1½ cups fat

Wash and clean chickens. Cook in salted water with parsley root, celery root, carrot, and onion until tender (about 50 minutes). Skin and quarter chickens. Cool; dip in sauce. Sprinkle baking sheet with bread crumbs. Place chicken on top. Leave in refrigerator ½ hour. Dip chicken in eggs; roll in bread crumbs. Fry in deep fat. Place on absorbent paper to drain before serving.

Serves 6.

CHICKEN IN TOMATO CREAM SAUCE
(Hühner in Paradeiseinmach-Soss)

        3 fryers
        salt to taste
        ¼ cup oil
        white sauce
                2 tbls. butter
                2 tbls. flour
                ½ cup soup
        2 tbls. butter
        2 shallots, chopped
        ¼ cup white wine
        2-3 tbls. tomato purée
        5 mushrooms, diced
        2 tbls. butter
        baked eggs
                6 eggs
                ¼ cup oil

Clean and wash chickens. Cut into quarters. Salt and fry in hot oil. Prepare white sauce (see Index). Melt butter; add shallots, chicken, wine, white sauce, tomato purée and mushrooms sautéed in butter. Simmer 30 minutes. Decorate with baked eggs, prepared as follows:

Shell and drop eggs, whole, into hot oil.

Fold egg whites over yolks with spoon.

Remove when egg whites are set (about 5 minutes).

Yolks should remain soft.

Serves 6.

Note: Veal à la Marengo is prepared the same way.

RAGOUT À LA PICKELSTEIN
(Münchener Pickelsteine)

        2-3 lbs. chuck or tail of tenderloin, boned
        5 large onions, chopped
        ½ cup fat
        2 tbls. vinegar
        ½ tsp. salt
        1½ cups water or soup stock
        3 tbls. flour
        3 tbls. white wine
        2 tsp. lemon rind, grated
        1 clove garlic, crushed
        ½ tsp. parsley, chopped
        dash capers, chopped
        dash marjoram
        3-4 kohlrabi, cut up
        1 bunch carrots (7 oz.), cut up
        3 lbs. potatoes, cut into balls

Skin and cube meat. Fry onions in fat; add vinegar and meat. Fry meat until slightly browned. Add salt and 1 cup water or soup. Cook gently until tender (chuck takes 3 hours, tenderloin 40-45 minutes). Blend in flour, ½ cup water or soup, and wine. Mix sauce with lemon rind, garlic, parsley, capers, and marjoram. Cook kohlrabi, carrots, and potato balls in salted water. Add to meat dish.

Serves 5-6.

NOTE: For richer flavor, add cooked green peas, sautéed sliced mushrooms, cauliflower flowerets, and tomato chunks.

Potato balls may be cooked until partly done, then fried in hot fat.

BEEF GOULASH
(Rindsgulyas)

        5 tbls. fat
        6 medium-sized onions
        3 lbs. beef (chuck, shin, or end of tenderloin)
        1 tsp. paprika
        1 tbls. vinegar
        caraway seeds, marjoram to taste
        dash salt
        1-2 cups water or soup stock
        1 tsp. flour

Heat fat; fry sliced onion rings until yellow. Cut meat into 2″ cubes; add to fat. Add paprika, vinegar, caraway seeds, marjoram, and salt. Add 1 cup water or soup, or more, gradually, as needed. Simmer until meat is tender (2½-3 hours). Add flour; blend well and boil a few minutes.

Serves 5-6.

Note: For richer color, cook ½ teaspoon paprika in 1 teaspoon fat. Add 1 tablespoon soup. Bring to a boil and pour on top of goulash when ready to serve.

STRASSBURG GOULASH
(Strassburger Gulyas)

        5-6 medium-sized onions, chopped
        ½ cup fat
        1 tsp. paprika
        2 tbls. vinegar
        1 lb. beef, cubed
        ½ bay leaf, chopped
        dash thyme, ginger
        1-2 cups water
        1 lb. pork, cubed
        1¼ lbs. veal, cubed
        1 lb. potatoes
        1 tbls. tomato purée
        ¼ cup red wine
        1 tbls. flour

Fry onions in fat until yellow. Add paprika, vinegar, and beef. Add bay leaf, thyme, ginger, and water. Simmer until meat is half done (about 1 hour). Add pork and veal, potatoes, tomato purée, and wine. Cook gently until gravy is clear. Add flour and salt; simmer until meat is tender (about 1 hour).

Serves 6-7.

TENDERLOIN STEW WITH ONIONS
(Fleisch mit Zwiebeln)

        1 cup onions, chopped
        ⅓ cup fat
        2 tbls. vinegar
        dash lemon rind, chopped
        3 tbls. tenderloin tip, cubed
        1 cup water or soup stock, or more
        dash garlic, thyme
        salt, pepper, marjoram to taste
        2 tbls. flour

Fry onions in fat until slightly yellow. Add vinegar, lemon rind, tenderloin, ½ cup water or soup (or more). Add garlic, thyme, salt, pepper, and marjoram.

Simmer about 1½ hours, adding more liquid gradual-ly. When meat is tender and the gravy has boiled down, stir in flour and add water or soup.

Serves 6.

FISH STEW
(Fischgulyas)

1½ lbs. cod (or any other salt water fish)
1 tbls. lemon juice
2-3 oz. bacon or salt pork
2 tbls. oil
4 small onions, chopped
1 tsp. paprika
1 tbls. vinegar, or more
1 tbls. flour
½ cup water
½ tsp. salt
1-2 tbls. tomato purée
2 lbs. potatoes, quartered

Clean fish; cut into pieces. Sprinkle with lemon juice. Dice bacon or salt pork and fry in oil. Add onions and fry until yellow. Blend in paprika, vine-gar, and flour; cook, stirring constantly. Pour in water and add salt; bring to a boil. Add tomato purée and potatoes. Cook 20 minutes. Add fish. Simmer, co-vered, 15 minutes more.

Serves 5.

FISH RISOTTO
(Fischrisotto)

1 lb. cod (or halibut or pike)
½ tsp. salt
1 tsp. lemon juice
1 tbls. onion, chopped
½ cup oil
¾ lb. rice
3 cups water or soup
1 tbls. tomato purée
2 tbls. cheese, grated

Wash and clean fish. Cut into 1¼" cubes. Salt; sprinkle with lemon juice. Let stand 30 minutes. Fry onion in oil 5 minutes. Add rice; fry slightly. Add fish; brown. Pour water or soup in. Add tomato purée; simmer 30 minutes in 300° oven or on top of stove. Stir occasionally with fork. Mix in half the cheese. Sprinkle with remaining half.

Serves 4-5.

VEGETABLES

VEGETABLE STEW
(Mischgemüse)

1 lb. carrots
2-3 kohlrabi
1 celery root
5 leeks
1 lb. potatoes
3 tbls. fat
1 head cauliflower
salt, pepper to taste
soup stock or water to cover
1 cup cheese, grated
1 tbls. parsley, grated

Clean carrots, kohlrabi, celery root, leeks and pota-toes; slice or cut into strips. Simmer in fat 5-10 mi-nutes. Divide cauliflower into flowerets and add. Add salt and pepper. Cover with soup or water. Simmer 1 hour. Sprinkle with cheese and parsley.

Serves 5.

Note: Vegetables may be varied with season.

VEGETABLE BOUQUET WITH WHITE SAUCE
(Gemüsejardinière, eingemacht)

1 bunch carrots, peeled and diced
2 bunches kohlrabi, peeled and diced
½ cup green peas
1 cup string beans, cut into strips
1 cut Brussels sprouts
1 head cauliflower, cooked
white sauce
   3 tbls. butter
   ¼ cup flour
   ½ tsp. parsley, chopped
   dash salt
   ½ cup soup or vegetable stock, or more

Boil carrots, kohlrabi, green peas, string beans, and Brussels sprouts separately, about 20 minutes each. Drain. Add cauliflower, broken into flowerets. Pre-pare white sauce (see Index). Boil gently 3-4 minutes. Add vegetables.

Serves 6.

GREEN BEANS, VIENNESE STYLE
(Grüne Fisolen auf wiener Art)

        3 lbs. green beans
        3 tbls. fat
        3 tbls. flour
        1 onion, chopped
        1 tbls. dill, chopped
        ½ tsp. parsley, chopped
        ½ cup soup stock or vegetable stock
        1 tbls. vinegar
        dash salt, pepper
        1 cup sour cream

Clean beans; cut off ends; wash. Cut into small pieces. Cook in salted water about 20 minutes. Drain. Melt fat; blend in flour; add onion and brown. Add dill, parsley, and soup or vegetable stock; bring to a boil. Add beans, vinegar, salt, pepper, and sour cream. Bring to a boil again, stirring constantly.

Serves 10.

ASPARAGUS IN WHITE SAUCE
(Eingemachter Spargel)

        3 lbs. asparagus
        2 tbls. butter
        2 tbls. flour
        1 cup soup stock or asparagus stock
        dash salt

Peel asparagus; cut off tough ends. Place in cold water; drain. Cut into small pieces; cook in salted water 10 minutes (or until tender). Drain. Melt butter; blend in flour; add soup or stock. Cook gently 3 minutes, stirring constantly. Add asparagus (except tips) and cook until tender (about 10 minutes). Add tips last to prevent overcooking.

Serves 6.

Note: Cauliflower may be prepared the same way.

RED BEETS, WARM
(Rote Rüben, warm)

        3 lbs. red beets (8-12 roots)
        ½ cup butter
        ½ cup water
        ½ cup red wine
        dash caraway seeds
        2 tbls. flour
        ½-1 cup soup stock or water
        1 tbls. sugar

Peel and wash beets; dice. Simmer with butter, water, wine, and caraway seeds 20 minutes, or until tender. Blend in flour. Add soup or water and sugar. Cook gently 5 minutes.

Serves 6.

STEAMED CABBAGE
(Gedünstetes Kraut)

        ⅔ cup fat
        3 tbls. sugar
        1 small onion, in rings
        2 heads cabbage (3 lbs.), shredded
        ½ tsp. caraway seeds
        ½ tsp. salt
        1-2 tbls. vinegar
        1 cup water or soup stock
        1 tsp. flour

Heat fat; add sugar and onion rings. Add cabbage, caraway seeds, salt, and vinegar. Simmer 10 minutes; add water or soup as needed. Cook until soft (about 25 minutes). Blend in flour; add more water or soup and cook gently 10 minutes more.

Serves 6.

CAULIFLOWER PUDDING
(Karfioldunstkoch)

        3 tbls. butter
        3 egg yolks
        ¼ tsp. salt
        dash pepper
        6 mushrooms, chopped
        1 tbls. butter
        ½ tsp. onion, chopped coarse
        1 tsp. parsley, chopped
        1½ rolls
        3 egg whites, stiffly beaten
        1 head cauliflower
        1 tbls. flour

Cream butter; add egg yolks, salt, pepper. Sauté mushrooms in butter with onion and parsley; add. Soak rolls in water; squeeze dry; add and beat until blended. Fold in egg whites. Cook cauliflower; separate flowerets. Butter a pudding mold; sprinkle with flour. Place flowerets around bottom and sides of mold. Cover with layer of mushroom mixture. Repeat procedure until ingredients are used up. Cook in hot-water bath (see Index) 45 minutes to 1 hour.

Serves 4-5.

23

ARTICHOKE BOTTOMS AU GRATIN with
VEGETABLE FILLING
(Überkrustete Artischokenböden mit Gemüsefülle)
>   10 canned artichoke bottoms
>   filling
>>   2 tbls. butter
>>   ¼ cup flour
>>   ½ cup milk
>>   2 egg yolks
>>   dash salt
>>   ½ cup asparagus tips, cooked
>>   ½ cup green beans, Frenched and cooked
>>   2 mushrooms, diced
>>   1½ tbls. butter
>   white sauce
>>   1½ tbls. butter
>>   2 tbls. flour
>>   ½ cup water or soup stock
>>   1 egg yolk
>>   ¼ cup milk
>>   ¼ tsp. salt
>   1½ tbls. cheese, grated

Cook artichoke bottoms in canned stock 5 minutes. Place in buttered ovenproof dish. Prepare filling.

Melt butter; blend in flour; add milk.

Cool; add egg yolks and salt.

Add cooled asparagus tips, beans, and mushrooms sautéed in butter.

Heat on top of artichoke bottoms. Prepare white sauce (see Index). Pour over filling. Sprinkle with cheese. Bake in 375° oven 10 minutes.

Serves 5-7.

FRIED MUSHROOMS
(Gebackene Pilzlinge)
>   20 mushrooms
>   dash salt
>   ½ cup flour
>   2 eggs, beaten
>   1 cup bread crumbs
>   1 cup fat

Clean mushrooms. Cut into slices ⅓" thick. Season with salt. Dip in flour, then in eggs; roll in bread crumbs; fry in deep fat until golden brown. (Decorate with fried parsley, prepared as follows: wash and dry parsley, fry in hot fat until crisp, and season with salt.)

Serves 6-7.

EGGPLANT AND SQUASH
(Eierfrüchte und grüne Kürbisse)
>   1 tbls. onion, chopped
>   ⅓ cup oil
>   ½ tsp. garlic, crushed
>   1 tbls. parsley, chopped
>   2 eggplants
>   3 squash
>   1 tsp. salt
>   dash pepper
>   3 tomatoes, peeled and sliced

Fry onion in oil; add garlic and parsley. Peel and dice eggplants and squash. Season with salt and pepper. Simmer, covered, 10 minutes. Add tomatoes and cook gently 10 more minutes, or until soft. (Serve with grated cheese if desired).

Serves 6.

SAUERKRAUT WITH WINE
(Weinkraut)
>   ⅓ cup onion, chopped
>   ½ cup butter or fat
>   2 lbs. sauerkraut
>   1¼ cups white wine
>   ¼ tsp. salt (or more)
>   dash pepper
>   ¼ cup sugar

Fry onion in butter. Add sauerkraut, wine, salt, pepper, and sugar. Simmer 1 hour.

Serves 6.

POTATO STEW
(Gulyaskartoffeln)
>   3 oz. salt pork, diced
>   3 tbls. fat
>   4 large onions, sliced
>   1 tsp. paprika
>   1 tbls. vinegar
>   4 lbs. potatoes, peeled and quartered
>   1 tbls. salt
>   2 tbls. tomato purée
>   water or soup stock to cover

Fry salt pork in fat. Add onions. Fry until yellow. Blend in paprika, vinegar, potatoes, salt, and tomato purée; cover with water or soup. Cook gently until soft (20-30 minutes).

Serves 6-8.

PRINCESS POTATOES
(Prinzessinnenkartoffeln)

2 lbs. potatoes
½ cup butter
⅓ cup Parmesan cheese, grated
1 egg
1 egg yolk
salt to taste

Rub potatoes through strainer. Beat butter until creamy. Combine butter with potatoes, cheese, egg, egg yolk, and salt. Press small pointed mounds through pastry tube on greased and floured baking sheet. (Brush with lightly beaten egg if desired). Bake in 300° oven 10-15 minutes.

Serves 5.

Note: To heighten flavor, sprinkle with Parmesan cheese.

POTATO PATTIES
(Kartoffelpuffer)

2 lbs. potatoes
1 white roll
1 cup milk
2 eggs
2 tbls. flour
salt to taste
½ cup fat

Peel potatoes; grate, raw, into cold water. Drain and dry. Cook roll in milk 3 minutes, and cool. Mix with potatoes, eggs, flour, and salt. Heat fat. Drop spoonfuls of mixture into fat; flatten with spatula. Fry patties 3″ in diameter until very crisp. Serve at once.

Serves 4-5.

PURÉE OF LENTILS
(Linsenbrei)

1 lb. lentils
3 tbls. butter
½ tsp. salt
¼ tsp. pepper
1-2 egg yolks (optional)
1 cup light cream

Wash lentils; cook in unsalted water until soft. Rub through strainer. Add butter, salt, and pepper. Blend in egg yolks mixed with cream. Keep in hot-water bath (see Index) until served.

Serves 5-6.

Note: This purée is usually served with game (pheasants, partridges, etc.)

Purées can be made with white sauce, too.

To avoid skin forming on surface, dot purées with lumps of butter.

SALADS

WARM CABBAGE SALAD
(Warmer Krautsalat)

1-2 heads cabbage (3 lbs.)
¼ cup vinegar
¼ cup water
salt, caraway seeds to taste
¼ tsp. sugar
3 oz. salt pork, diced

Wash and shred cabbage; pour cold water over. Drain. Cook vinegar, water, salt, caraway seeds, and sugar. Pour over cabbage; let stand 15 minutes. Remove cabbage. Bring liquid to a boil again. Pour over cabbage. Repeat procedure 3 times. Fry salt pork. When crisp, sprinkle over cabbage and serve.

Serves 6-8.

TOMATO SALAD
(Paradeisäpfelsalat)

3 lbs. tomatoes
½ tsp. salt
dash cayenne pepper
¼ cup oil
½ cup vinegar
¼ tsp. French mustard
¼ tsp. sugar
several drops Worcestershire sauce (optional)
¼ tsp. parsley, chopped

Wash tomatoes. Cut horizontally into thin slices. Mix salt, cayenne, oil, vinegar, mustard, sugar, and Worcestershire sauce. Pour over tomatoes. Sprinkle with parsley. Chill in refrigerator 30 minutes before serving.

Serves 6.

RED BEET SALAD
(Roter Rübensalat)

6 red beets
1 tsp. caraway seeds
½ cup vinegar
2 tbls. sugar
½ tbls. salt

Wash beets. Cook until tender; peel and slice. Put into glass or china bowl. Sprinkle with caraway seeds. Cook vinegar with sugar and salt. Pour over beets. Let stand 2-4 days before using.

Serves 4-5.

OLD VIENNA SALAD
(Alter Wienersalat)

4 oranges
½ cup sugar
2 tbls. orange juice
2 tbls. lemon juice
8 apples
apple stuffing
    jam
    butter lumps

Peel oranges carefully; slice. Arrange layers in glass bowl, sugaring each layer. Moisten with orange and lemon juice. Peel small apples; core. Stuff with jam; sprinkle with sugar and butter lumps. Bake in buttered ovenproof dish in 250° oven until soft; cool. Place on top of orange salad. Keep in refrigerator until ready to use.

Serves 8.

VEGETABLES IN ASPIC
(Gemüse in Aspik)

½ cup green peas
1 cup Brussels sprouts
1 cup green beans, Frenched
1 cup asparagus tips
1 cup cauliflower flowerets
marinade (see Index)
3 tomatoes, peeled and cut in slices ¼″ thick
aspic (see Index)

Cook peas, Brussels sprouts, beans, asparagus tips, and cauliflower separately in salted water about 25 minutes. Drain; leave in marinade 30 minutes. Add tomato slices to marinade. Cover bottom and sides of five small casseroles or forms with thin layer of aspic. Place in refrigerator to set. Add vegetables in layers, so that each layer presents a different color. (Brush each layer with aspic and place in refrigerator to set before adding the next.) Top with aspic; chill. Dip forms in warm water for a second. Turn out on lettuce leaves. (Decorate platter with egg slices, pickle slices, tomato slices, radishes.)

Serves 5.

DESSERTS

STRAWBERRY CAKE
(Ananaserdbeerentorte)

¾ cup butter
1 cup flour
⅓ cup sugar
⅔ cup almonds, grated
½ tsp. lemon rind, grated
1 egg white
1 lb. strawberries (fresh), cleaned (whole)
jelly
    1 cup water
    1 cup strawberries, mashed
    ½ cup sugar
    1 tbls. lemon juice
    few drops red food coloring
    1 pkg. gelatin
    1 tbls. water

Work butter, flour, sugar, almonds, and lemon rind to a dough. Leave in refrigerator 30 minutes. Roll out ⅛″ thick. Press into cake tin. Cut off edges and form roll for the border. Brush with egg white. Bake in 300° oven about 20 minutes. Cool; cover with whole strawberries. Prepare jelly by cooking all ingredients together until thick. Pour over cake while hot. Let it set.

Note: Currants, apricots, or peaches may be used instead of strawberries.

APPLE STRUDEL WITH SHORTCAKE DOUGH
(Apfelstrudel aus mürben Teig)

- 1 cup butter (scant)
- 2¼ cups flour
- ½ cup sugar
- dash salt
- 1 egg yolk
- 2 tbls. milk
- 2 tbls. wine
- filling
    - 1½ lbs. apples
    - ½ cup sugar
    - 2 tbls. raisins
    - 1 few drops lemon juice
- 1 egg white
- 1 tbls. sugar

Work butter into flour. Add sugar, salt, egg yolk, milk, and wine; mix with fork or pastry blender. Knead. Leave in cool place 1 hour. Roll into thin rectangular layer. Scatter peeled, sliced apples over center part. Sprinkle with sugar, raisins, and lemon juice. Fold both sides over filling. Cut small strips of dough, using pastry wheel. Put them over top, crosswise. Brush with egg white. Bake in 300° oven on baking sheet about 30 minutes. Cool. Sprinkle with sugar.

CHEESE CAKE
(Topfen Schnitten)

- 2 cups flour (generous)
- 1 cup butter
- 1 egg
- 1 tbls. rum
- 2 tbls. sour cream
- ¼ cup sugar
- filling
    - 3 tbls. butter
    - 2 egg yolks
    - ¼ cup vanilla sugar
    - ⅓ cup raisins
    - ¼ tsp. lemon rind, grated
    - ⅔ lb. cream cheese, rubbed through strainer
    - ¼ cup sour cream
    - 2 egg whites, stiffly beaten
- 1 egg, beaten

Work flour, butter, egg, rum, sour cream, and sugar to a dough. Let stand 30 minutes. Roll into two rectangles ⅛″ thick. Bake one rectangle on ungreased baking sheet in 300° oven 10-15 minutes, until slightly brown. Cover with cheese filling, prepared as follows:

Cream butter; add yolks, vanilla sugar, raisins, lemon rind, cheese, and sour cream.

Fold in egg whites.

Top with second rectangle; brush with egg. Bake in 325° oven until light brown on top (about 15 minutes). Cool; cut into rectangles about 1½″ × 3″. Sprinkle with sugar.

SMALL POCKETS, VIENNESE STYLE
(Wiener Tascherl)

- 2¾ cups flour
- 1¼ cups butter
- ⅔ cup sugar
- 1 tsp. lemon rind, grated
- 2 hard-boiled egg yolks, rubbed through strainer
- 1 raw egg yolk
- 1 cup currant jam
- 1 egg white

Work flour, butter, sugar, eggs, rum, and lemon rind to a dough. Roll out ⅛″ thick and cut into 3″ squares. Place 1 teaspoon jam in center of each. Gather corners of squares on top of jam and press together. Brush with egg white. Bake in 300° oven 25-30 minutes.

WALNUT STICKS
(Nuss Stangerl)

- 1⅓ cups flour
- 6 tbls. butter
- 2 egg yolks
- 2 tbls. sugar
- 2 tbls. milk
- filling
    - ¾ cup sugar
    - ⅛ cup water
    - ⅔ lb. walnuts, ground
    - 1 tbls. milk
    - 1 tbls. butter
- icing
    - 2 egg whites
    - 1¼ cups finest confectioners' sugar
    - ½ tsp. lemon juice

Work flour, butter, yolks, sugar, and milk to a dough. Roll until a scant ¼" thick. Prepare filling as follows:

Boil sugar and water to a thread. Add walnuts, milk, and butter. Spread even layer over dough. Top with icing, prepared as follows:

Beat egg whites with sugar and lemon juice until thick enough to coat spoon.

(If too thin, add a little more sugar.)

Cut in strips ¾" × 2¼", using knife dipped in cold water. Bake in 325° oven until easily removed from baking sheet.

ALMOND RISSOLES
(*Maultaschen*)
 1¼ cups flour
 ¾ cup butter
 3 egg yolks
 dash salt
 filling
      3 egg whites, stiffly beaten
      3 egg yolks
      ⅓ cup sugar
      ¾ cup almonds, blanched and chopped
 1 egg white
 3 tbls. almonds, grated or chopped

Work flour, butter, egg yolks, and salt to a dough. Leave in refrigerator 20 minutes. Roll out ⅛" thick. Cut out round circles with cutter. Cover half of circles with almond filling, prepared by mixing egg whites, yolks, sugar and almonds together. Cover with remaining dough circles; press borders together with fingers. Brush with egg white. Sprinkle with almonds. Bake on ungreased baking sheet in 275° oven 25-30 minutes.

SMALL RINGS À LA KARLSBAD
(*Karlsbader Ringerl*)
 1½ cups butter
 ⅓ cup sugar
 ½ tsp. lemon rind, grated
 1 raw egg yolk
 3 hard-boiled egg yolks
 2 cups flour
 1 egg, beaten
 1 tbls. cube sugar, crushed
 ⅓ cup almonds, peeled and chopped

Cream butter and work to a dough with sugar, lemon rind, egg yolks, and flour. Leave in cool place 30 minutes. Roll out thin. Cut with cutter in ring form. Brush pastry with beaten egg. Sprinkle with sugar and almonds. Bake in 275° oven about 20 minutes.

SOUFFLÉ À LA SALZBURG
(*Salzburger Nockerl*)
 ½ cup butter
 1 cup sugar
 10 egg yolks
 3 tbls. flour
 10 egg whites, stiffly beaten
 ¼ cup milk, hot
 2 tbls. sugar

Beat butter with sugar and egg yolks until fluffy. Add flour. Fold in egg whites. Cover the bottom of small roasting pan (or ovenproof dish) with milk. Pour mixture in. Bake in 350° oven about 10 minutes, or until slightly yellow on top. Remove in big spoonfuls to a platter. Sugar lavishly. Serve at once.

Note: This specialty may be served with vanilla cream.

CREAM PUFFS OF SPONGE CAKE DOUGH
(*Cremekrapferl aus Biskuitteig*)
 4 egg yolks
 2 tbls. sugar
 8 egg whites
 4 tbls. sugar
 ¾ cup flour
 filling
      1½ cups milk
      3 egg yolks
      dash cornstarch
      ⅓ cup sugar
      1" piece vanilla bean
      ½ cup butter
      3 oz. chocolate, melted
 chocolate icing (see Index)

Stir egg yolks and sugar together. Beat egg whites; add 4 tablespoons sugar, beating until stiff. Add to first mixture; blend in flour. Press small thick cookies onto buttered and floured baking sheet or onto paper. (Sprinkle with sugar.) Bake in 275° oven about 15 minutes. Scoop out and cool. Fill with cream, prepared as follows:

Beat milk, egg yolks, cornstarch, sugar, and vanilla in double boiler until thick.

Remove vanilla bean.

Cream butter with chocolate and combine.

Put cookies together in pairs and cover with chocolate icing.

PALM LEAVES
(Palmenblätter)
puff paste for pastries (see Index)
granulated sugar as needed

Roll out puff paste, on sugared board, ¼" thick or less to form a rectangle 16" × 10". Sprinkle with sugar all over. Roll both 10" sides tightly to meet in center. Dip sharp knife in hot water and cut slices ¼" thick. Place on wet baking sheet. Bake in 450° oven until brown and crisp (about 15 minutes).

MERINGUE COOKIES WITH ALMONDS
(Eiskipferl)
1 cup sugar
7 egg whites
3 cups almonds, peeled and chopped

Beat sugar and egg whites in double boiler until very thick. Cool. Form small round cookies with 2 teaspoons. Sprinkle thickly with almonds. Bake on well-greased and floured baking sheet in 275° oven 10-15 minutes. Do not brown. (Serve with ice cream.)

CONES WITH WHIPPED CREAM
(Schaum Skarnitzen)
5 eggs
1¼ cups sugar
¾ cup flour
filling
1½ cups heavy cream
¼ cup sugar
strawberries, cut up small

Beat eggs and sugar until fluffy, blend in flour. Grease a baking sheet. Spread circles 3" in diameter on it. Bake in 375° oven 8-10 minutes. While hot, remove with flexible knife from sheet. Fold into cones. Cool. Fill with cream, whipped and sugared, before serving; sprinkle whipped cream with strawberries.

LINZER TARTLETS
(Linzer Törtchen)
⅔ cup butter
½ cup flour
⅓ cup sugar
⅔ cup hazelnuts, ground
½ cup bread or cake crumbs, sifted
2 tbls. chocolate, grated
¾ cup jam
chocolate icing (see Index)
1 tsp. pistachios, chopped

Work butter, flour, sugar, hazelnuts, crumbs, and chocolate to a dough. Leave in cool place 30 minutes. Roll out ⅛" thick. Cut circles with cutter. Bake on ungreased baking sheet in 300° oven about 10 minutes. Cool. Put together in pairs filled with jam. Cover with chocolate icing. Sprinkle with pistachios.

CHOCOLATE ALMOND MACAROONS
(Schokoladenmakronen mit Mandeln)
4 egg whites
⅔ cup sugar (generous)
1⅔ cups chocolate, grated
2½ cups almonds, grated and slivered

Beat egg whites until stiff, add sugar, chocolate, and almonds. Form small round cookies. Grease a baking sheet, place cookies on it, and bake in 300° oven about 20 minutes. (The macaroons should be crisp on top and soft inside.)

Note: Macaroons with hazelnuts are prepared the same way.

LADY FINGERS
(Biskotten)
6 egg yolks
2 tbls. sugar
8 egg whites
¾ cup sugar
1 cup flour (generous)
1 tbls. sugar

Beat egg yolks with 2 tablespoons sugar. Beat egg whites; before stiff, add ¾ cup sugar. Continue beating; blend in flour. Combine mixtures. Cover baking sheet with paper. Press mixture through pastry tube onto sheet in shape of lady fingers. Sprinkle with sugar. Bake in 300° oven 10-15 minutes.

FAMILY DELIGHT
(Hausfreunde)

    ¾ cup sugar
    3 egg yolks
    2 cups flour
    1½ cups almonds, peeled and slivered
    1 cup raisins
    3 egg whites, stiffly beaten

Fold sugar, egg yolks, flour, almonds, and raisins into egg whites. Pour into greased loaf form. Bake in 250° oven about 30 minutes. Cool; cut into thin slices. Dry in cool oven.

CHEESE DOUGH CAKE
(Topfenkuchen)

    ⅓ lb. farmer cheese
    ¾ cup butter
    ⅔ cup sugar
    5 egg yolks
    1 tsp. lemon rind, grated
    1½ cups almonds, blanched and grated
    5 egg whites, stiffly beaten

Rub cheese through strainer. Cream butter; add sugar, egg yolks, lemon rind, cheese, and almonds; beat until well-blended. Fold in egg whites. Grease and flour cake form. Pour mixture in. Bake in 300° oven 45 minutes. Sprinkle with sugar.

Note: The same recipe may be prepared with cottage or cream cheese.

DOBOS CAKE
(Dobostorte)

    6 egg yolks
    ¾ cup sugar
    6 egg whites, stiffly beaten
    1 cup flour
    chocolate cream
        1¼ cups butter
        4½ oz. semi-sweet chocolate
        1 cup sugar
        1 egg yolk
    caramel icing
        ¾ cup sugar
        1 tbls. butter
    ⅓ cup hazelnuts

Beat egg yolks and sugar until fluffy. Add flour; blend well. Fold in egg whites. Bake 8-12 layers in well-greased and floured cake tins or spread even circles 8" in diameter on baking sheet. Bake in 300° oven 8-10 minutes. Remove from tin while warm. Cool. Set one layer aside for top.
Prepare chocolate cream as follows:
    Beat butter until creamy.
    Melt chocolate and add, with sugar and egg yolk, to butter.
    Beat until fluffy. Cool in refrigerator.
    Spread between bottom layers. Trim borders. Cover top layer with caramel icing, prepared by melting and browning sugar in skillet, stirring constantly. Butter a wooden board 1" wider than cake. Place top layer of cake on board; pour caramel icing over. While warm, cut with buttered knife into equal segments. Cut off surplus icing on sides. Place on top of cake. Spread chocolate cream over sides of cake and sprinkle with sliced hazelnuts.

SACHER CAKE
(Sachertorte)

    ¾ cup butter
    6½ oz. semi-sweet chocolate
    ¾ cup sugar
    8 egg yolks
    1 cup flour
    10 egg whites, stiffly beaten
    2 tbls. apricot jam
    icing
        1 cup sugar
        ⅓ cup water
        7 oz. semi-sweet chocolate

Beat butter until creamy. Melt chocolate. Add sugar and chocolate to butter; stir. Add egg yolks one at a time. Add flour. Fold in egg whites. Grease and butter 8-9" cake tin. Pour mixture in. Bake in 275° oven about 1 hour. Test with toothpick or straw. Remove to board; cool. Cut top off and turn bottom up. Heat apricot jam slightly and spread over top. Cover with chocolate icing, prepared as follows:
    Cook sugar and water to thin thread.
    Melt chocolate in top of double boiler.
    Add sugar gradually to chocolate.
    Stir constantly until icing coats the spoon.
    Pour on top of cake.
    Note: If desired, split cake into 2 or 3 layers. Fill with apricot jam or whipped cream.

PANAMA CAKE
(Panama-Torte)

¾ cup sugar
7 egg yolks
6 tbls. chocolate, grated
1½ cups almonds, grated
5 egg whites, stiffly beaten
cream
    6 tbls. butter
    ½ cup vanilla sugar
    3 squares semi-sweet chocolate, melted
    2 eggs
⅔ cup almonds, blanched, roasted, and sliced

Beat sugar and egg yolks until fluffy. Add chocolate and almonds. Fold in egg whites. Pour mixture into greased and floured cake tin. Bake in 250°-300° oven 45-55 minutes. Cook completely. Split cake into 2 layers. Between them spread half of cream, prepared as follows:

Beat butter until creamy.

Add vanilla sugar, chocolate, and eggs.

Continue beating until smooth and light.

Cover top and sides with remaining cream. Sprinkle with almonds.

NAPOLEON CAKE WITH WHIPPED CREAM
(Napoleon Schaumtorte)

1 egg
7 egg yolks
¾ cup sugar
1½ cups almonds, grated
8 tbls. chocolate, grated
1 tsp. candied orange peel
2 tbls. cake crumbs
7 egg whites, stiffly beaten
½ pt. heavy cream
2½ tbls. sugar
chocolate icing (see Index)

Beat egg, egg yolks, and sugar until creamy. Add almonds, chocolate, orange peel, and cake crumbs; continue beating. Fold in egg whites. Bake in two greased and floured 8-9″ cake tins in 300° oven 20-25 minutes. Split each cake into 2 layers. Spread cream, whipped and sugared, between layers. Pour chocolate icing over top layer.

TUTTI-FRUTTI CAKE
(Tutti frutti-Torte)

6 egg yolks
⅔ cup sugar
¼ cup dates, pitted and cut up small
¼ cup figs, cut up small
¼ cup raisins
1 tbls. candied orange peel, chopped
7 tbls. chocolate, grated
⅔ cup almonds, grated
1 cup flour (generous)
6 egg whites, stiffly beaten
2 tbls. sugar

Beat egg yolks and sugar until fluffy. Add dates, figs, raisins, orange peel, chocolate, almonds, and flour. Fold in egg whites. Pour mixture into greased and floured cake tin. Bake in 300° oven 50 minutes to 1 hour. Sprinkle with sugar or top with any flavor icing.

WALNUT CAKE WITH COFFEE CREAM
(Nusstorte mit Kaffeecreme)

2 eggs
5 egg yolks
½ cup sugar
¾ cup walnuts, grated
½ cup hazelnuts, grated
1 tbls. almonds, grated
¼ cup cake crumbs
5 egg whites, stiffly beaten
filling
    ½ cup butter
    ½ cup sugar
    1½ cups walnuts, halved
    2 tbls. black coffee
coffee icing (see Index)
⅓ cup walnuts, halved

Beat eggs, egg yolks, and sugar until fluffy. Add walnuts, hazelnuts, almonds, and cake crumbs. Fold in egg whites. Bake in buttered and floured baking tin in 300° oven 35-45 minutes. When cold, split into two layers. Prepare filling as follows:

Beat butter until creamy.

Add sugar, walnuts, and coffee.

Spread between layers. Top with coffee icing. Decorate with halved walnuts.

YEAST DOUGH
(Hefeteig; Germteig)

General Rules

1. Keep butter, milk, and flour lukewarm.
2. Dissolve yeast in 2 tablespoons warm water; add 2 tablespoons flour and 1 tablespoon sugar; stir.
3. Cover and leave in moderately warm place.
4. Mixture must rise to double the amount.
5. Mix milk, melted butter, eggs, 1 tablespoon sugar, and the risen yeast.
6. Add to salted warm flour, or beat butter until creamy.
7. Mix all ingredients and risen yeast.
8. Beat dough until it loosens from beater or wooden spoon and from bowl and makes large bubbles.
9. Sprinkle top with flour; cover with cloth or towel.
10. Leave in warm place.
11. If the batter is light, it takes less time to rise.
12. If the batter is thick or contains much butter, it takes longer to rise.
13. When the batter has risen to double its amount, it is ready for use.
14. Before baking, allow ½ hour more for rising.
15. When baked, test it with toothpick; if it does not stick, it is done.
16. Baked yeast doughs must be turned out or removed from baking sheet immediately after baking and placed on rack or wooden board in order not to lose the crispness on bottom.

RING CAKE WITH RUM
(Germ-Reifkuchen mit Rum; Savarin au Rhum)

>   1 oz. yeast
>   1 tsp. salt
>   3 cups flour
>   1 tbls. lemon peel, grated
>   3 eggs
>   3 tbls. sugar
>   3 tbls. butter, melted
>   1 cup milk, lukewarm
>   sauce
>>   1 cup sugar
>>   1 cup water
>>   ½ tsp. lemon rind, grated
>>   ¼ cup rum

Dissolve yeast as indicated in general rules for yeast dough (see above). Leave in warm place until doubled in size. Mix salt and flour; add grated lemon peel, eggs, sugar, yeast, butter, and milk. Beat until batter loosens from beater or spoon. Pour into 2 buttered and floured ring molds. Let rise until doubled in size. Bake in 350° oven about 20 minutes. Prepare sauce as follows:

Cook sugar with water and lemon rind.

Add rum; strain.

Pour some sauce over warm cake; serve the rest separately.

CHOCOLATE COFFEE RING
(Schokoladengugelhupf)

>   1¾ cups butter
>   2¼ cups sugar
>   6 egg yolks
>   1 cup milk
>   4¼ cups flour, sifted
>   ¼ tsp. lemon rind, grated
>   1 tsp. baking powder
>   6 egg whites, stiffly beaten
>   4 tbls. cocoa
>   4-5 tbls. water
>   2 tbls. sugar

Beat butter until creamy. Add sugar, egg yolks, milk, half the flour, and lemon rind; stir until fluffy. Combine baking powder with remaining flour and add to mixture, together with egg whites. Divide into 2 parts. Stir cocoa with water and sugar until smooth. Add to one part of batter. Blend well. Butter and flour deep-fluted ring mold. Put one layer of white and one layer of dark batter into mold; repeat. Bake in 325° oven 45 minutes to 1 hour.

CAKE MOUSSELINE
(Flaumkuchen)

>   1 pkg. dried yeast
>   2 tbls. flour
>   2 tbls. water
>   dash sugar
>   ⅔ cup butter
>   ¼ cup sugar
>   1 egg yolk
>   1 egg
>   ½ cup almonds, grated
>   dash salt
>   2 cups flour
>   2 cups milk

1¼ cups sugar
½ cup water
4 tbls. orange juice
1 tbls. maraschino
1-1½ cups pineapple cubes
cream
    5-8 egg yolks
    ½ cup sugar
    ⅔ cup light cream
    1 tbls. maraschino
    1-1½ cups pineapple cubes

Prepare yeast mixture with flour, water and sugar; let rise as indicated. Cream butter, sugar, egg yolk, and egg; add almonds and salt. Mix with flour, yeast mixture, and milk. Beat until dough loosens from spoon. Leave in warm place to rise. Pour batter into greased and floured ring form; let rise again. Bake in 325° oven 25-30 minutes. Cool. Cook sugar with water until it spins a light thread. Add orange juice and maraschino. Dip cake in this liquid. Decorate with pineapple cubes. Fill center with cream, prepared as follows:

Beat egg yolks, sugar, cream, and maraschino in double boiler until thick.

Mix with pineapple cubes.

Note: Decorate with sugared whipped cream.

PANCAKES
(Palatschinken)
    1¾ cups flour
    2 cups milk
    2 egg yolks
    ¼ cup sugar
    dash salt
    3 tbls. fat
    apricot jam as needed
    1 tbls. sugar

Beat flour and milk until smooth. Add egg yolks, sugar, and salt; blend well. Cover the bottom of frying pan with fat (or brush with melted butter). Pour in thin layer of batter. Fry over medium flame on both sides. Repeat until batter is used up. Fill each pancake with apricot jam; roll. Sprinkle sugar on top.

Serves 4-5.

DESSERT OMELET
(Biskuit-Omelette)
    5 egg yolks
    ½ cup sugar
    ½ tsp. rum
    ½ cup flour (generous), sifted
    5 egg whites, stiffly beaten
    2-3 tbls. butter
    ½ cup jam
    ¼ cup sugar

Stir egg yolks with sugar until fluffy. Blend in rum and flour. Fold in egg whites. Heat 1 tablespoon butter in pan; pour in half the batter. Bake omelet in 300° oven until slightly brown (about 8 minutes). Fill with jam; fold over; sprinkle with sugar. Keep hot. Prepare second omelet the same way. Serve.

Serves 2-3.

COFFEE PUDDING
(Kaffeedunstkoch)
    ⅓ cup butter
    ⅓ cup sugar
    5 egg yolks
    ¾ cup almonds, grated
    2 white rolls
    2 tbls. black coffee
    5 egg whites, stiffly beaten
    coffee cream
        ½ cup cream
        3 egg yolks
        1 egg
        ½ cup sugar
        3 tbls. coffee, black
        1 cup heavy cream, whipped

Cream butter; add sugar. Add egg yolks gradually; stir in almonds. Soak rolls in coffee; squeeze dry; rub through strainer. Fold in egg whites. Grease a pudding mold; sprinkle with sugar; pour mixture in. Cook in hot-water bath (see Index) 1 hour. Serve with coffee cream, prepared as follows:

Beat cream, egg yolks, egg, sugar, and coffee in double boiler until thick.

Cool.

Fold in whipped cream.

Serves 4-5.

Note: You may substitute plain whipped cream for the coffee cream.

BREAD PUDDING
(Scheiterhaufen; Charlotte de petits pains blancs)

7 rolls
2 eggs
1 cup milk
1 tbls. raisins
½ cup almonds, blanched and slivered
1 lb. apples, peeled and sliced
⅓ cup sugar
3 tbls. butter

Slice rolls. Beat eggs with milk. Pour over rolls; let stand 15 minutes. Grease a deep ovenproof dish. Spread a layer of bread mixture in dish. Sprinkle with raisins, almonds, apples, sugar, and small pieces of butter. Continue until all ingredients are used up. Bake in 300° oven about 30 minutes.

Serves 4-5.

NUTMARZIPAN BALLS
(Nussmarzipankugerl)

1½ cups nuts, ground fine
¾ cup sugar
1-2 egg whites
2 tbls. candied fruit, chopped
chocolate icing (see Index)
2 tbls. nuts, halved

Mix nuts with sugar and egg whites. Add candied fruit. Form small balls (size of a nut). Top with chocolate icing all around. Decorate with halved nuts.

WINE SOUFFLÉ
(Weinkoch)

⅔ cup sugar
7 egg yolks
½ tsp. lemon rind, grated
dash cinnamon
7 egg whites, stiffly beaten
¾ cup cake crumbs
2 tbls. butter, melted
¼ cup white wine
cooked red wine (Gluhwein)
  1½ cups red wine
  ½ cup sugar
  rind of ½ lemon, grated
  2 cloves, crushed
  1 piece cinnamon

Stir sugar, egg yolks, and lemon rind until creamy. Add cinnamon. Fold in egg whites. Blend in cake crumbs and butter. Grease and sugar a pudding mold. Pour mixture in. Cook in hot-water bath (see Index) 30 minutes. Pour white wine over. Continue cooking in hot-water bath 30 minutes longer. Turn out and serve with cooked red wine, prepared as follows:

Cook wine with sugar, lemon rind, cloves, and cinnamon 5 minutes.

Strain and serve hot.

Serves 6.

APPLES À LA MANNHEIM
(Äpfel à la Mannheim)

1 lb. apples
1 cup water
2 tbls. sugar
1″ piece cinnamon stick
2 tbls. butter
¼ cup sugar
5 egg yolks
½ cup almonds, grated
5 egg whites, stiffly beaten
1 tsp. sugar

Peel apples; core; cut in halves. Cook in water with sugar and cinnamon until half done. Place apples in buttered ovenproof dish. Beat butter until creamy. Add sugar and yolks; continue beating. Add almonds. Fold in egg whites. Pour mixture over apples. Bake in 350° oven 30 minutes. Sprinkle top with sugar.

Serves 3.

FRIED PRUNE FRITTERS
(Baweusen)

10 white rolls (2 days old)
2 cups milk
2 eggs, beaten
1¼ cups bread crumbs
1¼ cups fat
prune filling
  1 cup prunes, diced and cooked
  ¼ cup sugar
  dash cinnamon
  1 tsp. lemon rind, grated
  1 tsp. rum

Remove crust from rolls. Cut into slices ⅓″ thick. Dip in milk, then in egg; roll in bread crumbs. Fry in deep fat until golden brown. Place on absorbent paper to drain. Put slices together in pairs filled with prune filling, prepared as follows:

Mix prunes with sugar, cinnamon, lemon rind, and rum.

Stir over heat until well-blended.

Cool.

Serves 6-8.

Note: Rolls may be dipped in white or red wine instead of milk. The fritters are then called "Drunken Knights."

BADEN COFFEE DROPS
(Badener Kaffeebonbons)

 1 cup sugar
 ¾ cup water
 ¾ cup black coffee
 ½″ vanilla bean
 ½ cup heavy cream
 1 tbls. corn syrup
 1 tbls. almond oil or butter

Cook sugar with water (244°) until firm ball is formed when dropped in cold water. Add coffee, vanilla bean, heavy cream, and syrup; cook until one drop thrown in cold water becomes tough substance. Grease marble board with almond oil or butter. Pour mixture on top while still liquid and warm. Shove slightly together. When cool and firm, cut in ¾″ squares with greased thick knife. When cold, break squares apart. Wrap each first in wax paper, then in colored paper.

PEARS À LA MELBA
(Melba-Birnen)

 2 lbs. pears, peeled and halved
 ¼ cup water
 ¾ cup sugar
 1 qt. vanilla ice cream
 1 cup strawberry purée

Cook pears in water with sugar until soft. Put 2 heaping tablespoons ice cream in each glass. Place half a lukewarm pear on top. Pour strawberry purée over.

Serves 6.

CANDIED ORANGE PEEL
(Arancini)

 3¼ cups orange peel, cooked and drained
 1½ cups granulated sugar
 1½ cups water

Cut orange peel with small cutter ¾″ in diameter. Leave in water 5-6 days. Change water every day. Drain; cook until half done. Add sugar and water and cook until liquid gets thick; remove peel. Roll while warm in granulated sugar (or, preferably, in small sugar crystals). Place on platter or board one next to the other. Let dry 2 days.

Note: The peel may be cut into strips instead of circles.

CREAM À LA MERAN
(Meraner Creme)

 ¼″ vanilla bean
 ⅓ cup sugar
 6 egg yolks
 1 tbls. rum
 ½ cup whipped cream
 ¼ cup sugar
 ½ cup whipped cream

Mix seeds of vanilla bean with sugar. Beat egg yolks and vanilla sugar mixture until fluffy. Combine with rum and whipped cream. Cool. Spoon into glasses; decorate with sugared whipped cream.

Side Dish: sliced sponge cake.

Serves 6.

MIXED FRESH FRUIT WITH CHAMPAGNE
(Macedoine von frischen Früchten)

 ½ lb. cherries
 ½ lb. pears
 ½ lb. apricots
 ½ lb. peaches
 ½ lb. strawberries
 ¼ cup maraschino
 2 cups brandy
 1 cup spun sugar (use ¼ cup water
  and ½ lb. sugar)
 1 cup white wine
 1 cup water
 1 cup champagne

Cut fruit into small pieces. Place in glass bowl. Mix maraschino, brandy, spun sugar, white wine, and water. Pour over fruit. Place in refrigerator. Serve in sherbet or champagne glasses. Pour champagne over before serving.

Serves 4-5.

FRUIT GELÉE
(Früchtensulz)
>   3 cups white wine
>   3 cups water
>   1½ cups sugar
>   1 pkg. gelatin
>   2 tbls. water
>   6 egg whites
>   ½ cup water
>   3 cups fresh fruit
>   3 cups stewed dried fruit

Cook white wine with water and sugar 5 minutes. Stir in gelatin dissolved in water; remove from heat. Mix egg whites with ½ cup water; add hot wine mixture. Beat with wire whisk to boiling point. Cool and strain through linen towel (or very fine sieve). Rinse a mold. Cover bottom with layer of gelée; leave in refrigerator to set. Add layers of fresh and stewed fruit, one kind at a time, to achieve color contrasts. Pour in another layer of gelée; leave in refrigerator to set. Repeat procedure until mold is filled. The last layer must be gelée. Leave in refrigerator 2 hours. Dip mold in hot water a second before serving. Turn out.

Note: For pink effect, add few drops of red coloring.

The gelée may also be served in wide champagne glasses with the fruit daintily arranged in the middle.

COLD RICE CREAM
(Kalte Reiscreme)
>   ¾ cup rice (generous)
>   4 cups water
>   ½ cup sugar
>   ½ cup water
>   juice of ½ orange
>   ¼ tsp. orange rind, grated
>   1 cup cream or milk
>   5 egg yolks
>   1 egg
>   ⅓ cup sugar
>   1" vanilla bean

>   ½ pkg. gelatin
>   1 cup heavy cream
>   2 oranges
>   ⅔ cup sugar
>   ¼ cup water

Cook rice in water; drain. Spin sugar in water to heavy thread. Combine rice, sugar, orange juice, and grated orange rind. Cool. Beat cream or milk, egg yolks, egg, sugar, and vanilla bean in double boiler until thick. Remove vanilla bean. Add gelatin and rice mixture. Cool. Whip cream and add. Rinse mold with cold water. Pour in rice and cream mixture. Cover; grease mold around cover. Leave in refrigerator or freezer 2 hours. Turn out before serving. Cut peeled oranges in thin slices. Spin sugar to heavy thread; pour over orange slices and place in refrigerator until ready to serve. Use as decoration for pudding.

BEVERAGES

EGG NOG
(Eierpunsch)
>   2 egg yolks
>   1 tbls. sugar
>   ¼ cup light cream, heated
>   ⅓ cup rum
>   ¼ cup curaçao

Beat egg yolks and sugar until fluffy. Combine with lukewarm cream, rum, and curaçao. Pour into top of double boiler and beat until thick.

HOT WINE
(Glühwein)
>   1 cup red wine
>   1 piece lemon rind
>   4 cloves
>   1 piece cinnamon
>   ⅓ cup sugar, or more

Bring all ingredients to boil. Strain. Serve piping hot.

REFERENCES

WHITE SAUCE
(Weisse Soss; Sauce Blanche)
- **2 tbls. butter or other fat**
- **1½ tbls. flour**
- **1 cup water or chicken soup, or more**

Melt butter; add flour; stir. Add liquid, stirring to boiling point.

Note: White sauce is more digestible if it simmers awhile.

ANCHOVY BUTTER
(Sardellenbutter)
- **¾ cup butter**
- **3 anchovies, rubbed through strainer**

Melt butter. Mix anchovies in. (When butter is browned, add 1 teaspoon water to prevent butter from tasting bitter.)

HOT-WATER BATH

The hot-water bath, used mostly for puddings, although for other specified dishes as well, is performed as follows:

1. Boil water in a deep pan. (In some cases, where the mold to be placed in bath is small, a shallow pan is preferable.)

2. Cover mold containing ingredients under preparation. (Foil paper may be used instead of metal lid.)

3. Place in hot-water bath so that boiled water reaches to ⅔ the height of the mold.

4. Cover hot-water bath (optional).

5. Simmer length of time specified in recipe.

Note: The hot-water bath is a commonly used cooking method, known in French as *bain-Marie.*

POTATO PURÉE
(Kartoffelbrei)
- **2 lbs. potatoes**
- **1 cup milk, boiled (or soup stock)**
- **3 tbls. butter**
- **¼ tsp. salt**
- **1 medium-sized onion**
- **1 tbls. fat**

Peel and quarter potatoes. Cook in salted water until soft. Drain. Rub through strainer. Add milk, butter, and salt; blend well. Cut onions in rings; salt; fry in fat until golden brown. Arrange on top of potato purée.

Serves 4-5.

Note: Instead of onion rings, you may use fried bread crumbs as topping.

VILLEROI SAUCE
(Villeroisoss)
- **3 tbls. butter**
- **5 tbls. flour**
- **3 cups soup stock (beef or chicken)**
- **½ cup cream**
- **2 egg yolks**
- **dash salt, pepper**
- **1 tsp. Worcestershire sauce**
- **1 pkg. gelatin**

Melt butter; blend in flour; add soup; stir. Bring to a boil. Add cream and egg yolks, salt, pepper, Worcestershire sauce, and gelatin (dissolved in water). The sauce must be thick enough to coat a spoon.

Note: If desired, add finely diced, sautéed mushrooms.

ASPIC
(Aspik)
- **1-2 lbs. veal bones**
- **4 pork feet**
- **1 lb. shin of beef, cut up small**
- **1 lb. pork rind**
- **8 qts. water**
- **¼ cup cider vinegar**
- **¼ cup tarragon vinegar**
- **dash salt**
- **thyme, spice to taste**
- **1 bay leaf**
- **20 peppercorns**
- **2 carrots**
- **1 parsley root**
- **½ celery root**
- **1 onion**
- **2 egg whites**
- **3 tbls. lemon juice**

Boil crushed veal bones, pork feet, and beef, with pork rind in water 3 hours. Skim frequently. Add vinegar, salt, thyme, spice, bayleaf, peppercorns, carrots, parsley root, celery root, and onion. Cook gently

4 hours more. Strain. Leave in cool spot. Skim off fat. Reheat and clarify as follows:

 Beat egg whites slightly; add lemon juice.
 Add to soup.
 Bring to boil, stirring constantly.
 When clear, strain through wet linen cloth.
 Pour into glass.
 Note: For aspic mayonnaise, mix mayonnaise with equal quantity of liquid aspic.

BÉCHAMEL* SAUCE
(Béchamel Soss)
 2 tbls. butter
 2 tbls. flour
 1½ cups milk, boiling
 salt to taste
 seasonings as needed for dish in preparation

*Marquis de Nointel Béchamel, Court Chamberlain of Louis XIV, famous gourmet and author of *Sur l'art de cuisine.*

Melt butter. Blend in flour. Add boiling milk. Stir, until well-blended, to boiling point. Add seasonings. Stir.

Note: With recipes requiring little milk, prepare the béchamel as follows: cook butter and milk; stir in flour quickly and continue stirring until it forms a lump. This might be done for puddings and soufflés.

FRYING BATTER
(Backteig)
1. With Milk
(mit Milch)
 1 cup milk
 1⅓ cups flour
 2 eggs
 1 tbls. sugar
 1 tbls. rum
 dash salt

Mix all ingredients to a thick batter.
Note: For salted dishes, omit sugar.

2. With Wine
(mit Wein)
 1 cup white wine
 1½ cups flour
 1 tbls. sugar
 1 tsp. lemon peel, grated

 dash salt
 2 egg whites, stiffly beaten

Mix all ingredients except egg whites until smooth. Fold in egg whites.

3. With Beer
(mit Bier)
 1 full cup beer
 1⅓ cups flour
 1 tbls. oil
 2 egg yolks
 dash salt
 2 egg whites, stiffly beaten

Mix all ingredients except egg whites. Let stand 20 minutes. Fold in egg whites.

STRUDEL DOUGH
(Strudelteig)
 2 cups flour
 1 egg yolk
 ¼ tsp. salt
 ½ tsp. fat or oil
 ¼ cup lukewarm water
 ½ tsp. lemon juice or vinegar
 1 cup butter, melted
 1 tbls. sugar

Place flour on pastry board. Make a hole in the center. Place egg yolk, salt, fat, water, and lemon juice in center. Mix dough quickly with a knife; then knead it until it becomes elastic and leaves the board. Cover with a hot bowl; keep warm ½ hour. Lay dough in center of well-floured tablecloth on big table. Flour dough. Roll a little with rolling pin. Brush dough with ¼ cup melted butter. With hands under dough, palms up, pull and stretch dough all around until it is transparent; cut off thick edges. Spread filling on ⅔ of dough, leaving bare. Sprinkle this part with ¼ cup melted butter. Roll strudel, starting from the end with the filling on it. Hold one side of the cloth high with both hands so strudel will roll over and over. Trim edges. Twist roll into greased pan. Brush with remaining butter. Bake in 350° oven 35-45 minutes (or until brown and crisp). Sprinkle with sugar.

GENERAL RULES FOR PUFF PASTE
(Blätterteig)

Butter Dough: Cut butter in thin slices into flour on board. Work to a dough with roller. Shape to patty or loaf. Leave in refrigerator 30 minutes.

Strudel Dough: Mix flour, lemon juice, egg, salt, cold water, and wine to a smooth dough. Beat like strudel dough (see Index). Cover with cloth; let stand 20 minutes.

1. Roll strudel dough to a square on floured wooden board.

2. Place butter dough on top.

3. Fold two sides of strudel dough over butter dough.

4. *Handle it as one dough.*

5. Roll out into rectangle 16″ long × 10″ wide.

6. Fold over small sides to center.

7. *Brush off flour* and fold dough in two parts, like a book.

8. Let stand 30 minutes.

9. Repeat the same procedure of rolling out, brushing, folding, and letting stand two or three times more.

10. It is now ready for use.

Note: Never prepare puff paste in a warm place. Bake on cold ungreased baking sheet moistened with water. Bake at high heat.

PUFF PASTE FOR PASTRIES
(Blätterteig)

butter dough
1⅓ cups butter
½ cup flour
strudel dough
1½ cups flour
1 tbls. lemon juice
1 egg
dash salt
¼ cup white wine
2 tbls. water
1 egg, beaten

Butter Dough: Work butter with flour to a dough. Shape to a patty. Place in refrigerator.

Strudel Dough: Mix flour with salt, lemon juice, egg, and water to a smooth dough. Beat until it loosens from spoon.

1. Roll strudel dough to a square on floured wooden board.

2. Place butter dough in center.

3. Fold over the four sides like a package.

4. Proceed further as in general directions for puff paste. But do not allow dough to stand. Roll out four times and fold again.

5. Before using, leave in refrigerator 30 minutes.

6. Roll out ¼″ thick.

7. Cut out half moons, stars, etc.

8. Brush with egg.

9. Bake on moist sheet in 500° oven about 15-20 minutes until light brown on top.

MARINADE FOR GAME (or *Beef, Vegetables, etc.*)
(Beize für Wild, Rindfleisch, usw.)

1 carrot
½ parsley root
¼ celery root
1 small onion
2½ qts. water
1 cup vinegar
20 peppercorns
10 whole allspice
1 bay leaf
dash thyme, salt

Clean, wash, and slice carrot, parsley root, celery root, and onion. Cook in water and vinegar, with peppercorns, allspice, bay leaf, and thyme, 30 minutes. Add salt. Let stand ½ hour. When cool, add meat. (Marinade must cover meat). Let stand overnight.

CHOCOLATE ICING
(Schokoladenglasur)

1 cup sugar
½ cup water
4½ oz. chocolate
1 tbls. butter

Cook sugar with water until it spins a heavy thread. Melt chocolate in double boiler; add butter. Add hot syrup gradually, stirring constantly until smooth and until mixture coats spoon.

Italian

CAPONATINA SICILIAN STYLE
>   4 medium eggplants
>   1½ cups olive oil
>   4 onions, sliced
>   ½ cup tomato sauce
>   4 stalks celery, diced
>   ½ cup capers
>   12 green olives, pitted and cut into pieces
>   1 tablespoon pine nuts
>   ½ cup wine vinegar
>   ¼ cup sugar
>   ¾ teaspoon salt
>   ½ teaspoon pepper

Peel and dice eggplants and fry in 1 cup hot olive oil. Remove fried eggplant from skillet, add remaining oil and onions and brown gently. Add tomato sauce and celery and cook until celery is tender, adding a little water, if necessary. Add capers, olives, pine nuts and fried eggplant. Heat vinegar in small saucepan, dissolve sugar in vinegar and pour over eggplant. Add salt and pepper and simmer 20 minutes, stirring frequently. Cool before serving. This caponatina will keep a long time in refrigerator.

FRIED BREAD WITH ANCHOVIES
>   16 slices of bread from a long French loaf, ½ inch thick
>   ½ pound mozzarella cheese, sliced thin
>   8 anchovy filets
>   ½ teaspoon pepper
>   ½ cup flour
>   2 eggs, lightly beaten
>   1 cup olive oil

Place a slice of mozzarella and 1 filet of anchovy on each of 8 slices of bread. Sprinkle with pepper and cover with another slice of bread. Dip into plain cold water, roll in flour, dip into beaten egg and fry in olive oil until golden brown on each side. Serve immediately.

Serves 2 or 4.

ITALIAN ANTIPASTO
>   4 thin slices Italian salami
>   4 thin slices prosciutto
>   4 anchovy filets
>   2 celery hearts, cut in halves lengthwise
>   1 small can Italian tuna fish
>   1 small can imported Italian antipasto (optional)
>   8 large green olives
>   2 teaspoons capers
>   4 artichoke hearts in oil
>   1 small can pimentos
>   4 slices tomato
>   4 vinegar peppers
>   8 black ripe olives

Use a large oval platter. Place tuna fish and imported antipasto in center of dish and arrange all the other ingredients around, making as pretty a pattern as you can. Serve with crusty Italian bread and butter.

Serves 4.

PROSCIUTTO AND HONEY
>   1 small jar honey
>   8 thin slices Italian bread, long loaf
>   8 slices prosciutto (about ¼ pound)

Spread each slice of bread lightly with honey and add 1 slice prosciutto.

Serves 4.

MUSSELS IN PIQUANT SAUCE

 2 pounds mussels, with shells
 2 tablespoons olive oil
 1 clove garlic
 5 anchovy filets, chopped
 1½ cups dry white wine
 1½ cups vinegar
 1 tablespoon chopped parsley
 dash cayenne pepper

Open mussels, wash in salt water and drain. Brown garlic in oil, remove from oil and add mussels and anchovies. Keep fire low and add wine and vinegar. Simmer until liquid is half the original quantity. Add parsley and cayenne pepper. Remove mussels and marinade, place in earthen container and allow to marinate 3 days.

Serves 4.

OYSTERS VENETIAN STYLE

 8 oysters
 2 teaspoons lemon juice
 dash cayenne pepper
 2 teaspoons caviar

Open oysters but keep both shells. Mix lemon juice, cayenne and caviar and spread thinly over each oyster. Close shell and serve on ice.

Serves 2.

SOUPS

BEEF BROTH

 1 pound chuck of beef
 1 good marrow bone
 1 good sponge bone
 3 quarts water
 3 stalks celery
 1 small onion
 2 carrots
 3 fresh tomatoes, cut into pieces, or ½ medium
   can tomatoes
 1 teaspoon salt

Place meat and bones in cold water with salt and bring to a boil. Remove scum that forms on top of water. Add celery, onion, carrots and tomatoes, cover pan and cook about 1¼ hours, or until meat is tender. Remove meat and use as desired. Strain broth. This should make about 2 quarts beef broth. A little water may be added if broth seems too condensed.

SOUP ALLA PAVESE

 8 thin slices French bread
 ½ cup butter
 1 quart broth or bouillon
 4 eggs
 ⅛ teaspoon salt
 2 tablespoons grated Parmesan cheese

Melt butter in frying pan and fry bread in it until golden on both sides. Bring broth to boiling point. Place 2 slices bread in each soup dish, top with whole egg and sprinkle ½ tablespoon cheese on each egg. Pour ¼ of the boiling broth into each dish, taking care that the egg does not break.

Serves 4.

CHICKEN BROTH

 1 4-pound chicken, cleaned and left whole
 1 teaspoon salt
 4 stalks celery
 2 medium carrots
 3 fresh tomatoes, cut into pieces, or ½ medium
   can tomatoes
 3 quarts water

Place cleaned and washed chicken in cold water, add salt and bring to boil. Remove scum that forms on top of water. Add celery, carrots and tomatoes, cover pan and cook from 1½ hours for a tender chicken to 2½ hours for a tough one. Add a little water if soup seems too condensed. Remove chicken whole and serve as you wish. Strain broth. Makes about 2 quarts chicken broth.

RUSTIC MINESTRONE

 ½ pound sweet Italian sausage
 1 pound spareribs
 ½ medium cabbage, shredded
 2 stalks celery, diced
 2 medium onions, sliced
 4 white turnips, diced
 ½ teaspoon salt
 ½ teaspoon pepper

turnip leaves, shredded
½ head chicory, shredded
2 teaspoons chopped parsley
4 stalks Swiss chard, shredded

Mix all vegetables together, divide in half, and place half the quantity in large soup pan. Add enough water to cover, salt and pepper and place sausage and spareribs on vegetables. Cover with remaining vegetables. Cover pan tightly and cook gently 3 hours. Serve sausage, spareribs and vegetables together.

Serves 4.

TAGLIOLINE BOLOGNA STYLE

4 cups flour (scant)
2 eggs
1½ quarts chicken or beef broth

Place 3 cups flour on pastry board, make a well of flour and break eggs into it. Work eggs and flour together until flour has been absorbed and continue working dough 20 minutes, adding more flour if necessary. Cut dough into 2 parts and roll very thin with rolling pin. Let 2 sheets of dough dry ½ hour on floured towels, and when reasonably dry, fold over and cut into strips ¼ inch wide. Unravel. Bring broth to boiling point, add taglioline and cook 5 minutes.

Serves 6.

BRODETTO ROMAN STYLE

1½ quarts lamb broth
6 egg yolks
2 teaspoons lemon juice
¼ teaspoon salt
¼ teaspoon fresh marjoram, crushed
18 thin slices French bread, toasted
6 teaspoons grated Parmesan cheese

Beat eggs with fork in large soup pan 5 minutes; add lemon juice and salt and beat 1 minute longer. Bring lamb broth to boil and pour slowly over eggs, stirring constantly. Place pan over very low flame and continue to stir constantly. Cook soup very slowly 5 minutes, allowing it to become slightly thickened. Do not allow it to boil. Remove from fire. Place 3 slices toasted bread in each soup dish, pour soup over bread, sprinkle with Parmesan and serve.

Serves 6.

FISH BRODETTO ANCONA STYLE

2 pounds mixed fish in season (sole, mullet, mackerel, whiting, dogfish or porgy)
½ dozen Little Neck clams, shelled, with juice
1 small eel, cut into pieces (optional)
2 small squid, skinned, cleaned and cut into small pieces (optional)
½ cup olive oil
1 large onion, sliced thin
½ clove garlic
1 tablespoon chopped parsley
1 small can peeled tomatoes, cut into pieces
2 tablespoons tomato sauce
¾ teaspoon salt
½ teaspoon pepper
small dash cayenne pepper (optional)
1 teaspoon wine vinegar
4 slices Italian bread, 1½ inches thick, toasted

Clean fish and cut into pieces. (This dish should be cooked in an earthen pan, but if this is not available an ordinary soup pan will do.) Brown onion and garlic in olive oil, add parsley, tomatoes, tomato sauce, salt, pepper and cayenne and cook 3 minutes. Add fish and bring to boiling point. Add vinegar and cook, without cover, 20 minutes, adding a little warm water, if more liquid is desired. Place 1 slice toasted bread in each soup dish and pour soup over it.

Serves 4.

MUSSEL SOUP

3 dozen mussels with shells
½ cup olive oil
2 cloves garlic
2 tablespoons tomato sauce
½ teaspoon salt
1 tiny piece red pepper (optional)
8 slices long Italian bread, 1 inch thick
½ teaspoon oregano

Scrub mussels well. Place oil in large pan, add 1 clove garlic and brown. Add tomato sauce, pepper, salt and mussels and cook over very high flame until all mussels are open. Add oregano and cook 1 minute longer. Toast bread slices and, while hot, rub with 1 clove garlic. Place 2 slices toast on each plate, pour mussels over toast and serve.

Serves 4.

FISH SOUP ROMAN STYLE

8 Little Neck clams, with juice
4 oysters, cut into pieces, with juice
½ cup olive oil
1 clove garlic
1 tablespoon chopped parsley
4 anchovy filets, cut into pieces
3 seeds hot pepper, or
1 pinch cayenne pepper
1 cup dry red wine
1 cup canned tomatoes
½ pound cod filet, cut into large pieces
1 lobster tail, cut into pieces
1 small lobster, washed and cut into pieces with shell
½ pound halibut, cut into pieces
½ pound filet of sole, cut into pieces
½ teaspoon salt
4 slices French or Italian bread, toasted

Place clams and oysters in pan and heat until shells open. Cut oysters into pieces and strain juice of oysters and clams, reserving juice. Place olive oil and garlic in large soup pan, add parsley, anchovies and pepper and brown slowly, stirring well. Add wine and cook until it evaporates. Add tomatoes and cook 5 minutes. Add all the fish, clams, oysters, lobster and oyster and clam juice. Add salt and enough water to cover fish and cook 30 minutes, adding more water if necessary, as soup should not be too condensed. Place 1 slice toasted bread in each soup dish and pour serving of soup over it.

Serves 4.

BROCCOLI AND MACARONI SOUP

⅛ pound salt pork, chopped fine
1 tablespoon olive oil
½ clove garlic
1 tablespoon tomato paste, diluted in 3 cups water
¼ teaspoon salt
¼ teaspoon pepper
½ bunch broccoli flowerlets, cleaned and washed
2 cups short macaroni
2 tablespoons grated Roman cheese

Place oil, salt pork and garlic in soup pan and brown. Add tomato paste, diluted in water, salt and

pepper and bring to boiling point. Add broccoli, cover pan and cook 5 minutes. Add macaroni and continue cooking 10 minutes. Sprinkle with grated Roman cheese and serve. Makes 4 large or 6 medium servings.

CACCIUCCO LEGHORN STYLE

½ cup olive oil
1 clove garlic, chopped
1 tiny red pepper
1½ pound shrimps, shelled and cut into pieces
½ pound squid, skinned, cleaned and cut into small pieces
½ cup dry white wine
2 tablespoons tomato paste
3 cups water
½ teaspoon salt
1 pound cod filet, cut into pieces
½ pound scallops, cut into pieces
½ pound halibut, cut into pieces
4 slices Italian bread, toasted and rubbed with clove of garlic.

Place oil, garlic and pepper in soup pan and brown garlic lightly. Add shrimps and squid, cover pan and cook 30 minutes, or until squid is tender. Add wine and continue cooking until it evaporates. Add tomato paste, water and salt and cook 5 minutes. Add other fish and cook 15 minutes longer, adding more water if needed. Place 1 slice toasted garlic bread in each soup dish and pour serving of soup over it.

Serves 4.

CLAM SOUP

40 Little Neck clams
½ cup olive oil
1 clove garlic
3 anchovy filets, chopped
1 tablespoon chopped parsley
½ cup dry red wine
1 tablespoon tomato paste
½ cup warm water
½ teaspoon salt
½ teaspoon pepper
¼ teaspoon oregano
8 thin slices Italian bread, fried in olive oil

Wash clams and scrub shells well with vegetable brush. Place oil in large saucepan, add garlic, brown and remove. Add anchovies, parsley and wine to oil and cook 5 minutes. Add tomato paste, water, salt and pepper and cook 3 to 4 minutes. Add clams, cover pan and cook no more than 5 minutes, or until all the shells are open. Add oregano and cook 2 minutes longer. Place 2 slices fried bread in each soup dish, pour over them serving of clams and juice.

Serves 4.

CECI SOUP ROMAN STYLE

½ cup olive oil
½ teaspoon rosemary
1 clove garlic, chopped fine
3 anchovy filets, chopped
1 tablespoon tomato paste, diluted in
4 tablespoons water
1 can ceci (garbanzo beans or chick peas)
¼ teaspoon salt
1 cup elbow macaroni
½ teaspoon pepper

Place oil, rosemary, garlic and anchovies in soup pan and brown well. Add diluted tomato paste and cook over slow fire 20 minutes. Add ceci beans with liquid and add another can full of water. Add salt and bring to boiling point. Add elbow macaroni and cook 8 minutes longer or until macaroni is tender. Add pepper and serve.

Serves 4.

PEAS AND RICE VENETIAN STYLE

3 pounds fresh peas
¾ pound rice
2 tablespoons olive oil
½ cup butter
1 slice bacon, cut into small pieces
1 small onion, chopped
2½ cups stock or bouillon
¼ teaspoon salt
⅛ teaspoon pepper
2 tablespoons grated Parmesan cheese

Shell peas and wash. Place olive oil, butter, bacon and onion in soup pan and brown lightly. When brown, add peas, cook 5 minutes and add stock. When boiling, add rice and cook about 12 minutes, or until rice is tender. Add salt, pepper and cheese. This makes a very thick soup.

Serves 4.

POTATO SOUP ITALIAN STYLE

4 large potatoes (about 2 pounds)
3 tablespoons butter
1 small onion
2 stalks celery, diced
1 tablespoon chopped parsley
½ clove garlic
2 carrots, diced
1 cup tomato sauce
½ teaspoon salt
¼ teaspoon pepper
4 cups warm water
3 tablespoons grated Parmesan cheese

/1Boil potatoes until thoroughly cooked, peel and put through sieve. While potatoes are cooking, melt butter in soup pan, add onion, celery, parsley, garlic and carrot and brown gently. Remove garlic, add tomato sauce, salt, pepper, warm water and strained potatoes and simmer 15 minutes. Serve with Parmesan cheese.

Serves 4.

NEOPOLITAN MINESTRONE

1½ pounds beef shanks
1 onion, quartered
1 package soup greens (or 2 celery stalks, 1 carrot, 1 potato, 1 turnip and a sprig of parsley, all cleaned and chopped)
1 small bay leaf
2 whole peppercorns
1 clove
1½ teaspoons salt
6 cups water
1 celery root
¼ pound ham
2 ounces penne or elbow macaroni
3 tablespoons tomato paste
1 teaspoon dry chervil
4 tablespoons grated Parmesan cheese

In a large Dutch oven, combine the beef shanks, onion, soup greens, bay leaf, peppercorns, clove, and salt. Add the water and bring to a boil. Skim any foam. Reduce the heat to low and simmer covered 1½ to 2 hours. Remove the meat and cool. Strain the broth and skim the fat. Return the broth to the pot. Clean the celery root and cut into thin sticks. Dice the meat from the beef shanks and cut the ham into thin strips. Boil the macaroni until tender in boiling salted water and drain. Bring the broth to a boil. Combine the tomato paste with 1 cup of the broth and stir until dissolved. Add to the broth in the pot along with the celery root, diced beef and the ham. Cover and cook 15 minutes. Add the macaroni and chervil and heat through. Sprinkle with the Parmesan cheese and serve. Makes 6 servings.

ZUCCHINI SOUP

    8 small zucchini, diced
    1 tablespoon leaf lard
    1 teaspoon olive oil
    ½ teaspoon salt
    ½ teaspoon pepper
    1 quart water
    4 eggs, lightly beaten
    4 tablespoons grated Parmesan cheese
    1 teaspoon chopped parsley
    ½ teaspoon chopped sweet basil

Melt leaf lard in soup pan, add oil, zucchini, salt and pepper and brown lightly. Add water, cover pan and cook 20 minutes. Beat eggs lightly in mixing bowl, add cheese, parsley and basil and blend together well. Remove soup from fire, add egg mixture, stirring it in well, and let stand 3 minutes before serving.

Serves 4.

EGG DISHES

FRIED EGGS WITH POLENTA (Cornmeal)
    ¼ pound polenta (cornmeal)
    3 quarts water
    1 teaspoon salt
    2 tablespoons butter
    8 eggs
    2 tablespoons olive oil
    1 cup tomato sauce (see index)
    2 tablespoons grated Roman cheese

Cook cornmeal in boiling salted water 30 minutes, or until cornmeal comes away from pan. Stir constantly during cooking. Spread in large dish 1½ inches in height and let cool. When cool, cut into 8 rounds and fry in butter until brown on both sides. Fry each egg separately in olive oil and place each egg on a round of fried polenta. Pour warm tomato sauce over all, sprinkle with cheese and serve.

Serves 4.

EGGS FLORENTINE STYLE

    1 pound spinach, cooked, chopped and
       strained
    1 tablespoon butter
    ⅛ teaspoon salt
    ⅛ teaspoon pepper
    8 tart shells, or 8 slices toast
    8 soft fried eggs
    ½ tube anchovy paste
    2 tablespoons grated Parmesan cheese

Place spinach in small pan with butter, salt and pepper and cook 5 minutes. Line shells, or cover toast, with some spinach, place eggs on top of spinach, squirt anchovy paste over eggs, sprinkle with cheese and place in moderate oven (350°F.) 10 minutes.

Serves 4.

ANCHOVY OMELETTE

    4 eggs
    2 tablespoons grated Parmesan cheese
    ¼ teaspoon pepper
    ¼ cup butter
    2 teaspoons anchovy butter

Beat eggs lightly with fork and add Parmesan and pepper. Fry egg mixture in butter in four parts, making 4 small omelettes. Spread each little omelette with a fourth of the anchovy butter and fold. Serve immediately.

Serves 4.

EGGS WITH PROSCIUTTO

    2 cups cream sauce (see index)
    4 slices prosciutto
    4 eggs
    2 tablespoons grated Parmesan cheese
    ½ teaspoon salt
    ½ teaspoon pepper
    1 tablespoon butter

Pour cream sauce into shallow baking dish and place prosciutto slices over it. Break 4 eggs gently over prosciutto, sprinkle with cheese, salt and pepper and dot with butter. Bake in hot oven (400°F.) 10 minutes, or until eggs are set.

Serves 4.

EGGS GYPSY STYLE

2 tablespoons butter
½ tablespoon flour
½ teaspoon meat extract, blended in ½ cup boiling water
1 teaspoon tomato paste
⅛ teaspoon salt
⅛ teaspoon pepper
¼ pound mushrooms, sliced
4 poached eggs
4 slices toast
1 teaspoon chopped parsley
1 tablespoon grated Parmesan cheese (optional)

Melt 1 tablespoon butter in saucepan, blend in flour, add water in which meat extract has been dissolved, tomato paste, salt and pepper and cook 5 minutes. Sauté mushrooms in 1 tablespoon butter 5 minutes and add to sauce. Place 1 poached egg on each slice of toast in serving dish, pour some of mushrooms and sauce over each egg, sprinkle with cheese, if desired, and serve.

Serves 4.

EGG CROQUETTES

4 hard cooked eggs, chopped
1 cup thick cream sauce (see index)
1 tablespoon grated Parmesan cheese
4 slices prosciutto, shredded
¼ teaspoon salt
⅛ teaspoon pepper
½ cup flour
1 egg, lightly beaten
1 cup fine bread crumbs
2 cups oil or leaf lard

Mix together chopped eggs, cream sauce, Parmesan cheese, prosciutto, salt and pepper and let cool thoroughly. When cool, shape into croquettes, flour, dip into beaten egg and roll in bread crumbs. Fry in hot oil or leaf lard until golden in color. Serve hot.

Serves 4.

PROSCIUTTO SOUFFLE

4 egg yolks, lightly beaten with wooden spoon
⅛ teaspoon salt
⅛ teaspoon white pepper
2 tablespoons grated Parmesan cheese
¼ pound prosciutto; sliced and cut into thin strips
4 egg whites, beaten stiff
½ cup butter, melted

Mix egg yolks with salt, pepper, cheese and prosciutto. Fold in egg whites and melted butter. Grease a casserole and pour in egg mixture. The mixture must not be more than ⅓ the height of the casserole. Bake in moderate oven (350°F.) 20 minutes. Serve immediately.

Serves 4.

OMELETTE SARDINIAN STYLE

1 medium zucchini, chopped
1 tablespoon bread crumbs, soaked in ½ cup milk
1 tablespoon grated Parmesan cheese
⅛ teaspoon sugar
½ teaspoon grated lemon peel
4 eggs
2 tablespoons olive oil
½ cup bread crumbs

Mix together zucchini, bread crumbs which have been soaked in milk, Parmesan, sugar and lemon peel. Add lightly beaten eggs and mix well. Grease baking dish with olive oil and coat with bread crumbs. Pour egg mixture into casserole and place in hot oven (400°F) 20 minutes.

Serves 4.

PANDORATO ROMAN STYLE

8 slices white bread
½ cup lukewarm milk
2 eggs, lightly beaten with ¼ teaspoon salt
1 cup butter

Remove crusts from bread and cut slices in half. Sprinkle lightly with milk and dip into egg. Place bread on flat dish, cover and let stand 30 minutes so that the egg will soak through. Fry in hot butter until golden brown.

Serves 4.

OMELETTE WITH ARTICHOKES

- **3 artichokes**
- **2 tablespoons olive oil**
- **¼ teaspoon salt**
- **⅛ teaspoon pepper**
- **2 slices bread, soaked in water and squeezed dry**
- **2 tablespoons grated Parmesan cheese**
- **1 teaspoon chopped marjoram leaves**
- **4 eggs, lightly beaten**
- **½ clove garlic, chopped**
- **¼ teaspoon salt**
- **⅛ teaspoon pepper**
- **2 tablespoons olive oil**

Remove outer leaves of artichokes, cut in half, remove chokes and cut hearts into 8 or 10 slivers. Place artichoke slivers in saucepan with oil, salt and pepper, cover pan and cook slowly, stirring often, for 25 minutes or until tender. Mix together thoroughly bread, cheese, marjoram, eggs, garlic, salt and pepper. To this mixture add cooked artichokes and mix well.

Heat oil in frying pan, add egg and artichoke mixture and cook slowly 10 minutes on one side, turn and cook 8 minutes on other side. Serve immediately.

Serves 4.

KIDNEY OMELETTE

- **1 teaspoon butter**
- **1 tablespoon olive oil**
- **1 veal kidney, sliced thin**
- **⅛ teaspoon salt**
- **⅛ teaspoon pepper**
- **2 tablespoons Marsala or sherry wine**
- **1 teaspoon meat extract, blended in 1 tablespoon warm water**
- **4 eggs, lightly beaten with fork with ¼ teaspoon salt**
- **1 tablespoon butter**

Place butter and olive oil in frying pan, add kidney slices and cook over high flame 10 minutes, turning often. Add salt and pepper, remove kidney from pan and place in warm dish. Add Marsala or sherry to pan gravy and cook until it evaporates. Add meat extract and water, mix well and let cook 2 minutes. Return kidney to pan and turn until sauce covers all sides. Make 1 large omelette, pour kidney slices and sauce over omelette and serve.

Serves 4.

OMELETTE WITH GREENS

- **½ small onion, sliced**
- **2 tablespoons olive oil**
- **½ cup cooked shelled peas**
- **1 medium-size green pepper, cut into small pieces**
- **1 small zucchini, diced**
- **1 small tomato, skinned and sliced**
- **½ teaspoon oregano**
- **⅛ teaspoon salt**
- **⅛ teaspoon pepper**
- **2 tablespoons flour**
- **½ cup milk**
- **4 eggs**
- **¼ teaspoon salt**
- **⅛ teaspoon pepper**

Place onion and oil in small saucepan and sauté lightly. Add peas, green pepper and zucchini and sauté 20 minutes. Add tomato, oregano, salt and pepper and cook 3 minutes longer. Set aside. Mix flour and milk until very smooth, add eggs, salt and pepper and beat well 5 minutes.

Grease a small frying pan, pour into it 1 tablespoon egg mixture and cook slowly until firm. Place 1 tablespoon vegetable mixture in center, cover with another tablespoon egg mixture and cook gently of both sides, turning gently so vegetables do not come out. Repeat procedure until both mixtures are used.

Serves 4.

NEAPOLITAN OMELETTE

- **3 cups leftover spaghetti with sauce**
- **4 eggs, lightly beaten with fork**
- **⅛ teaspoon salt**
- **⅛ teaspoon pepper**
- **1 tablespoon minced parsley**
- **2 tablespoons grated Parmesan cheese**
- **2 tablespoons olive oil**

Cut up spaghetti, add eggs, salt, pepper, parsley and Parmesan cheese and mix very well. Heat oil in frying pan, pour in spaghetti mixture and cook very slowly but thoroughly on both sides. Allow about 15 minutes cooking time for each side.

Serves 4.

CHEESE DISHES

MOZZARELLA CHEESE SANDWICHES WITH AN-CHOVY SAUCE

anchovy sauce:

¼ cup butter

2 anchovy fillets

1 tablespoon drained capers, chopped

2 tablespoons chopped parsley

Juice of ½ lemon

mozzarella cheese sandwiches:

16 thin slices of Italian bread (½ inch thick)

8 thick slices mozzarella cheese (⅜ inch thick)

3 eggs

Salt to taste

½ cup dry bread crumbs

¼ cup butter or margarine

First, prepare the anchovy sauce. Melt the butter in a small skillet. Do not brown. Under cold running water, rinse the anchovies. Chop finely and add with the capers and parsley to the butter. Add the lemon juice and stir well. Keep warm.

Remove the crust from the bread. Lay one slice of cheese between two slices of bread and press together. In a small bowl beat the eggs and a pinch of salt. Dip the bread and cheese sandwiches in the egg and dredge in the bread crumbs. Heat the butter or margarine over moderate heat in a heavy skillet. Add the cheese sandwiches and cook until golden brown on one side and turn and cook on the other side.

Serve immediately topped with the anchovy sauce.

Makes 8 3-inch sandwiches (4 servings).

OLD-FASHIONED CHEESE BALLS

1½ cups fresh bread crumbs

½ pound grated caciocavallo (Parmesan cheese may be substituted)

3 eggs

¼ teaspoon salt

¼ teaspoon pepper

dash nutmeg

½ tablespoon chopped parsley

½ cup flour

1 egg, lightly beaten

2 cups olive oil

Mix together bread crumbs, grated cheese, eggs, salt, pepper, nutmeg and parsley. This mixture should be moderately hard. If too hard, add a teaspoonful milk. Shape into small balls, roll in flour, dip into beaten egg and fry briskly in hot olive oil until golden in color, Serve hot.

Serves 4.

PILLOWS WITH PROSCIUTTO
(Cuscinetti Filanti Al Prosciutto)

8 thin slices white bread

½ pound mozzarella, sliced thin

8 large slices prosciutto, sliced thin

½ cup milk

½ cup flour

1 egg

1 cup lard or oil

Remove crust from bread. Place one slice of cheese and 2 slices prosciutto on each of 4 slices of bread and cover with other bread slices. Cut sandwiches crosswise, making three-cornered sandwiches. Dip into milk, roll in flour, dip into egg and fry in hot oil or lard until golden brown on both sides.

Serves 2 or 4.

FISH AND SHELLFISH

BURIDDA GENOA STYLE

1½ pounds mackerel

½ cup olive oil

2 medium onions, sliced thin

1 tablespoon chopped parsley

8 clams, shelled

½ teaspoon salt

½ teaspoon pepper

1 small can tomatoes, drained

½ cup dry white wine

Wash and dry fish and cut into 2-inch slices. Place ¼ cup olive oil in shallow casserole and place half the fish slices in it. Cover fish with half the onions, parsley, clams, salt and pepper. Repeat, using remaining half and cover top layer with tomatoes, remaining oil and wine. Bake in moderate oven (375°F.) 40 minutes, or until all wine has evaporated.

Serves 4.

BUTTERFISH IN WHITE WINE

1 large onion, sliced
¼ pound mushrooms, sliced
3 anchovy filets, chopped
1 tablespoon chopped parsley
¼ cup butter
1 cup dry white wine
2 tablespoons water
3 pounds butterfish, cleaned
2 tablespoons flour
1 tablespoon butter
juice of ½ lemon

Place onion, mushrooms, anchovies, parsley and ¼ cup butter in large skillet and brown gently. Add wine and water and cook 1 minute. Roll fish in flour and place in skillet. Cover skillet and cook slowly 20 minutes. Remove fish to serving dish. Add 1 tablespoon butter and lemon juice to pan gravy and pour over fish.

Serves 4.

LOBSTER ALLA DIAVOLO

2 medium lobsters (boiled)
2 tablespoons olive oil
2 tablespoons butter, melted
½ cup vinegar
½ teaspoon pepper
5 red pepper seeds (optional)
1 teaspoon meat extract, dissolved in 1 cup boiling water
1 teaspoon tomato paste
1 tablespoon butter
1 teaspoon flour
½ tablespoon prepared mustard

Cut lobster in halves lengthwise and place shell side down in baking dish. Sprinkle with oil and butter and bake in hot oven 20 minutes. Serve with sauce made in the following manner:

Place vinegar, pepper and red pepper seeds together in saucepan and simmer until vinegar is reduced to half quantity. Add meat extract in hot water and tomato paste to vinegar and cook 10 minutes. Mix together butter and flour, blending well, and add slowly to sauce. Mix well, add mustard and pour over baked lobsters.

Serves 2 or 4.

FILET OF COD WITH MUSHROOMS

9 small filets of cod
1 sliced white bread, soaked in water and squeezed dry
1 tablespoon butter
¼ teaspoon salt
¼ teaspoon pepper
½ cup stock
1 tablespoon dry white wine
½ black truffle, sliced thin
1 tablespoon butter
½ tablespoon flour
½ pound mushrooms
2 tablespoons butter

Chop 1 cod filet and mix together with bread, butter, salt and pepper. Spread mixture over 1 side of each filet. Roll filets and spear through with toothpicks. Place in well-greased baking dish. Add stock and wine, cover baking dish and bake in moderate oven (375°F.) 15 minutes.

Remove fish from baking dish and keep warm. Add truffle, 1 tablespoon butter and flour to pan gravy, mix well and cook until slightly thickened. Fry mushrooms in 2 tablespoons of butter 10 minutes and arrange around fish. Pour sauce over all and serve.

Serves 4.

LOBSTER LUCULLUS STYLE

2 large lobsters (boiled)
3 tablespoons butter, melted
½ teaspoon salt
12 oysters
4 anchovy filets, chopped
2 teaspoons bread crumbs
dash powdered mustard
dash cayenne pepper
½ cup butter, melted

Split lobsters in halves and remove parts not wanted. Brush with butter, sprinkle with salt and place under broiler 18 minutes. Place 3 oysters on each half of lobster. Mix together chopped anchovies, bread crumbs, mustard and cayenne pepper and put some of the mixture on each oyster. Brush well with melted butter, return lobsters to hot oven 10 minutes and serve immediately.

Serves 4.

FROG LEGS FRICASSEE

  12 whole frogs, cleaned
  2 tablespoons olive oil
  1 small onion, chopped
  1 clove garlic, chopped
  ¼ cup white wine
  ½ teaspoon salt
  ½ teaspoon pepper
  ¼ cup dried mushrooms, soaked in water for
    half an hour
  2 tablespoons flour
  1 tablespoon parsley, chopped
  2 egg yolks, lightly beaten
  1 tablespoon lemon juice
  12 thin slices French bread, toasted

Skin frogs and remove legs. Place frog legs in cold water and let stand 2 hours. Brown onion and garlic in oil and add wine. When wine has evaporated, add frog bodies, salt, pepper and dried mushrooms. Add just enough water to cover and simmer for 1 hour, keeping pan covered. This will make a delicious broth. Strain broth.

Flour frog legs and add to broth. Cook slowly about 30 minutes, mixing well occasionally. When legs are tender, add chopped parsley to sauce. Remove pan from fire and add 2 egg yolks and lemon juice. Mix well and serve on toasted bread slices. Serves four.

BAKED HALIBUT OR SWORDFISH

  4 medium slices halibut, or 2 large slices, 1 inch
    thick
  ½ cup olive oil
  1 sprig parsley
  ¼ teaspoon thyme
  2 bay leaves
  1 scallion, sliced
  4 peppercorns
  ½ cup flour
  ½ teaspoon salt
  ½ teaspoon pepper
  ½ lemon, cut in wedges

Place fish slices in marinade made of oil, parsley, thyme, bay leaves, scallion and peppercorns and let stand 2 hours, turning fish occasionally. Remove fish from marinade, strain oil and place oil in iron skillet. Roll fish in flour, place in oil in skillet, sprinkle with salt and pepper and brown lightly on both sides. When brown, transfer skillet to moderate oven (375°F.) and cook 30 minutes, basting frequently with oil from bottom of skillet. Serve with lemon wedges.

Serves 4.

FLOUNDER WITH BLACK BUTTER SAUCE

  1 medium onion
  ½ teaspoon thyme
  ½ bay leaf
  1 teaspoon salt
  ½ teaspoon peppercorns
  ½ cup vinegar
  3 quarts water
  3 pounds flounder, cleaned and cut into large
    pieces
  ½ cup butter
  2 tablespoons vinegar
  ¼ teaspoon salt

Place onion, thyme, bay leaf, salt, peppercorns and ½ cup vinegar in water and bring to a boil. Add fish and boil very gently 15 minutes. Remove from fire and drain. Skin and bone fish, place on serving dish and keep warm.

Melt butter, cook slowly until light brown in color and remove from fire. Boil 2 tablespoons vinegar until half the quantity evaporates, add salt and browned butter. Pour this black butter sauce over fish and serve.

Serves 4.

PERCH FILETS MILANESE STYLE

  1 pound perch filets
  1 cup flour
  1 egg, lightly beaten with
  ½ teaspoon salt and
  ½ teaspoon pepper
  1 cup bread crumbs
  ½ cup butter
  1 lemon, cut in quarters

Roll filets in flour, dip into egg mixture, roll in bread crumbs and fry in hot butter until nicely browned on each side (frying time will be about 5 minutes on each side). Serve with lemon quarters.

Serves 4.

PIKE WITH RAISINS
>3 pounds pike
>4 cups dry white wine
>1 large carrot, diced
>1 tablespoon minced parsley
>2 bay leaves
>1 medium onion, chopped
>½ teaspoon salt
>1 cup seedless raisins
>1 tablespoon butter

Clean and wash pike. Place in deep skillet, add wine, carrot, parsley, bay leaves, onion and salt and cook 45 minutes. Remove fish, place in serving dish and keep warm. Strain pan gravy, add raisins and boil gently 15 minutes. Add butter, mix well, pour over fish and serve.

Serves 4.

MACKEREL IN TOMATO SAUCE
>2 tablespoons olive oil
>1 small onion, sliced
>½ clove garlic, chopped
>1 tablespoon chopped parsley
>1 small can tomatoes
>2 tablespoons water
>½ teaspoon salt
>½ teaspoon pepper
>3 pounds mackerel, cut into 4 pieces

Place olive oil, onion, garlic and parsley in skillet and brown. Add tomatoes, water, salt and pepper and cook 5 minutes. Add fish, cover skillet and cook 5 minutes. Turn fish over and cook 10 minutes longer.

Serves 4.

MULLET CALABRAIN STYLE
>½ cup olive oil
>3 pounds mullet, cleaned and washed
>½ teaspoon salt
>juice of 1 lemon
>1 teaspoon oregano

Oil bottom of large skillet and add fish in single layer. Sprinkle with salt, lemo , oregano and remaining olive oil and cook over high flame 8 minutes on each side. Serve immediately.

Serves 4.

BAKED EEL
>½ cup olive oil
>2 tablespoons wine vinegar
>2 bay leaves
>1 teaspoon salt
>½ teaspoon pepper
>1 tablespoon bread crumbs
>2 pounds eel (large variety), skinned and cut into 4-inch pieces
>additional bay leaves

Mix together oil, vinegar, bay leaves, salt, pepper and bread crumbs. Marinate eel pieces in this mixture 3 hours, turning frequently. Place eel pieces on skewers, alternating with bay leaves. Place skewers in greased baking dish and bake in moderate oven (375°F.) 30 minutes, turning often. Brush with remaining marinade while cooking.

Serves 4.

FILET OF SOLE MARGHERITA
>8 shrimp
>12 mussels, scrubbed clean
>5 tablespoons dry white wine
>1 cup clam broth
>¼ teaspoon salt
>¼ teaspoon thyme
>1 bay leaf
>juice of ½ lemon
>1½ pounds filet of sole
>1 tablespoon butter
>2 tablespoons butter
>1½ teaspoons flour
>2 egg yolks, slightly beaten
>1 tablespoon heavy cream
>¼ cup butter

Boil shrimp 10 minutes and shell. Place mussels in small pan with 1 tablespoon wine and cook until all mussels are open. Strain juice from mussels, mix with clam broth, add 2 tablespoons wine, salt, thyme, bay leaf and lemon juice and boil gently 20 minutes. Strain and save liquid. Place sole in well-greased baking dish, add just enough clam liquid to cover dish. Add 2 tablespoons wine. Dot with butter, cover with greased paper and bake in moderate oven (375°F.) 12 minutes. Remove from oven and keep warm.

Blend together 2 tablespoons butter and flour, add

remaining clam liquid and gravy from baking dish and mix well. Add egg yolks and cream and mix with rotary beater until smooth. Place over very low flame and continue mixing until slightly thick. Add ¼ cup butter, a little at a time, mixing constantly. Place mussels and shrimp around filets, pour sauce over all and place in hot oven (400°F.) 3 minutes.

Serves 4.

PORGY WITH RICE
 1 large fish head
 1½ quarts water
 ½ teaspoon salt
 1 small onion
 1 clove
 1 carrot
 1 stalk celery
 1 sprig parsley

Place fish head in water, add salt, onion, clove, carrot, celery and parsley and boil 30 minutes. Strain and save the stock.

 1 medium onion, sliced
 1 carrot, diced fine
 ½ cup butter
 ½ clove garlic, chopped
 1 tablespoon chopped parsley
 1 bay leaf
 ¼ teaspoon thyme
 ½ teaspoon salt
 ½ teaspoon pepper
 ½ cup dry white wine
 1 cup fish stock
 4 anchovy filets, chopped
 ½ pound mushrooms, sliced
 2 tablespoons olive oil
 2 tablespoons flour
 3 pounds porgy
 2 tablespoons olive oil
 1 cup rice
 2 cups fish stock
 1 cup dry white wine
 1 tablespoon butter

Place onion, carrot and butter in saucepan and brown a little. Add garlic, parsley, bay leaf, thyme, salt and pepper and cook 5 minutes. Add ½ cup wine and cook until wine evaporates. Add 1 cup fish stock, anchovies and mushrooms and cook 10 minutes.

Heat 2 tablespoons olive oil in frying pan, flour the fish and fry in oil on both sides. Drain on paper, place in prepared gravy, cover pan and cook 6 minutes. Remove from fire and keep warm.

Place 2 tablespoons oil in another saucepan, heat and add rice. Cook rice in oil 3 or 4 minutes, stirring well, add 2 cups fish stock and 1 cup wine, cover pan and place in heated oven (400°F.) 18 minutes. The rice will then be cooked and dry. Add butter to rice, place on serving dish and place fish and gravy over it.

Serves 4.

SQUID IN MUSHROOM SAUCE
 2 pounds small squid
 ½ cup olive oil
 3 anchovy filets, chopped
 ½ clove garlic, chopped
 1 teaspoon minced parsley
 2 tablespoons dry white wine
 1½ tablespoons tomato sauce
 ¼ teaspoon salt
 ½ teaspoon pepper
 ½ cup water
 2 tablespoons dry mushrooms, well washed and cut into pieces

Skin squid, remove head and insides, cut into small pieces and wash well. Heat oil in saucepan, add anchovies, garlic, parsley and wine and cook 5 minutes. Add tomato sauce, squid, salt, pepper and ½ cup water, cover pan and cook 20 minutes. Add mushrooms and cook over low flame 40 minutes longer, adding water occasionally if needed.

Serves 4.

FRIED FISH SICILIAN STYLE
 ½ cup olive oil
 1 teaspoon salt
 2 pounds fish (porgy, bass, trout, butterfish)
 ½ lemon, cut into wedges

Heat olive oil in frying pan, add salt and let oil become very hot. Add fish, cover pan and cook 15 minutes on each side. Serve with lemon wedges.

Serves 2.

FRESH SARDINES LIGURIAN STYLE

16 fresh sardines
4 slices bread, soaked in water and squeezed dry
2 eggs
1 tablespoon Parmesan cheese
¼ pound mushrooms, sliced and cooked in butter
¼ clove garlic, chopped
¼ teaspoon marjoram
½ teaspoon oregano
½ teaspoon salt
½ teaspoon pepper
½ cup flour
1 egg, lightly beaten
1 cup olive oil

Remove heads from sardines, slit on one side and remove bones. Mix together well bread, eggs, cheese, mushrooms, garlic, marjoram, oregano, salt and pepper. Open sardines, spread with this mixture and do not close fish again. The sardines should somewhat resemble cutlets. Roll in flour, dip into egg and fry in hot oil until golden brown on each side.

Serves 4.

SWORDFISH PUDDING

1½ cups rice
1 small onion, sliced
2 tablespoons olive oil
2 tablespoons tomato sauce
½ teaspoon salt
½ teaspoon pepper
1 egg, lightly beaten
2 tablespoons olive oil
1 clove garlic
2 tablespoons tomato sauce
1½ pounds swordfish, diced
¼ pound mushrooms, sliced
1 cup bread crumbs
1 egg, lightly beaten
2 tablespoons butter

Wash and drain rice. Brown onion in olive oil, add 2 tablespoons tomato sauce, rice, salt, pepper and enough water to cover and cook until rice is almost done, adding a little water if needed. Remove from fire, add beaten egg and let cool.

Brown garlic in oil and remove garlic. Add 2 table-spoons tomato sauce and diced fish and cook 10 minutes. Add mushrooms and cook 3 minutes. Cool. Grease well a 2-quart pudding mold and sprinkle all over with bread crumbs. Brush with beaten egg and sprinkle again with bread crumbs. Line mold with partly cooked rice, leaving a large well in center. Fill the well with fish, cover with additional bread crumbs and dot with butter. Bake in moderate oven (375°F.) 45 minutes. Let cool 5 minutes before turning out on serving dish.

Serves 6.

FRESH SARDINE PIE

1 cup bread crumbs
½ teaspoon salt
½ teaspoon pepper
1 tablespoon chopped parsley
½ cup olive oil
½ clove garlic, chopped
1 tablespoon water
16 fresh sardines, boned and with heads removed
juice of 1 lemon

Mix together well bread crumbs, salt, pepper, parsley, olive oil, garlic and water. Place 1 layer fish in well-oiled casserole, top with some of the bread mixture and repeat layers, ending with bread mixture. Sprinkle with a little more oil and bake in moderate oven (375°F.) 40 minutes. Remove from oven, sprinkle with lemon juice and serve.

Serves 4.

SHRIMP BUONGUSTO

2 pounds shrimp, shelled and veined
½ cup flour
½ cup olive oil
½ cup dry white wine
½ tablespoon tomato paste
4 tablespoons warm water
½ teaspoon salt
½ teaspoon pepper
small dash cayenne pepper
1 tablespoon chopped parsley
1 small scallion, chopped
½ black truffle, sliced thin (optional)
2 teaspoons lemon juice

Wash and dry shrimp and roll in flour. Brown in hot oil on both sides in large skillet. Remove oil from skillet and save. Add wine to shrimp and cook until wine has evaporated. Place oil in small saucepan, add tomato paste, water, salt, pepper and cayenne and cook 3 or 4 minutes. Pour over shrimp, add parsley, scallion and truffle and cook 4 minutes. Remove from pan, add lemon juice and serve.

Serves 4 or 6.

BLUE BROOK TROUT

   3 pounds brook trout
   water to cover fish
   2 teaspoons salt
   ½ cup vinegar
   ½ cup butter, melted
   1 tablespoon minced parsley
   ¼ teaspoon pepper

Clean and wash trout. Bring water to a boil, add salt, vinegar and trout and cook gently 12 minutes. Remove trout from pan and place on serving dish. Mix melted butter with parsley and pepper and serve with fish.

Serves 4.

TROUT SAVOY STYLE

   2 pounds trout
   ¼ teaspoon salt
   ½ teaspoon pepper
   ½ cup flour
   ½ cup butter
   1 tablespoon olive oil
   1 tablespoon butter
   ½ pound mushrooms, sliced
   ¼ teaspoon salt
   ¼ teaspoon pepper
   1 teaspoon minced parsley
   1½ tablespoons fine bread crumbs
   2 tablespoons butter, melted
   ¼ cup butter
   1 scallion, minced

Clean and wash trout and sprinkle with salt and pepper. Roll in flour and fry in ½ cup butter slowly 10 minutes on each side, or until well done. Fry mushrooms in 1 tablespoon butter and oil 10 minutes and add salt, pepper and parsley. Spread mushrooms in baking dish and place trout over them. Sprinkle with butter in which trout was fried and with bread crumbs. Sprinkle with 1 tablespoons melted butter and bake in moderate oven (375°F.) 5 minutes. Heat ¼ cup butter, add minced scallion and simmer 1 minute. Pour over fish and serve.

Serves 2.

WHITING IN BAKING DISH

   4 pounds whiting
   1 small onion, sliced fine
   ½ pound mushrooms, sliced thin
   ½ teaspoon salt
   ½ teaspoon pepper
   2 tablespoons bread crumbs
   1 tablespoon grated Parmesan cheese
   2 tablespoons dry white wine
   ½ cup butter, melted
   1 lemon, quartered

Clean and split fish. Grease a large baking dish. Place sliced onions in bottom of baking dish, cover with mushrooms and place fish on mushrooms, skin side up. Sprinkle with salt, pepper, bread crumbs, cheese, wine and melted butter and bake in hot oven (400°F.) 18 minutes. Serve garnished with lemon quarters.

Serves 6.

EXQUISITE FISH FILETS

   1¼ cups leftover fish or plain boiled fish
   2 tablespoons flour
   1 tablespoon Cream of Wheat
   2 egg yolks
   ½ teaspoon salt
   ½ teaspoon pepper
   dash nutmeg
   2 cups milk
   1 tablespoon grated Parmesan cheese
   ½ cup flour
   1 egg, lightly beaten
   1 cup bread crumbs
   1 cup olive oil
   1 lemon, cut into wedges

Bone fish and chop. Mix together flour, Cream of Wheat, egg yolks, salt, pepper, nutmeg and milk. Place on fire and cook until thickened, stirring constantly. Add fish and Parmesan cheese and mix well. Pour over well-floured board and spread 1 inch thick. Cut into slices 2 inches wide and 4 inches long. Flour slices well, dip into egg, roll in bread crumbs and fry in hot oil until golden brown on both sides. Serve with lemon wedges.

Serves 4.

FISH IN SHELLS
    2 cups leftover fish, or canned fish
    ¼ cup butter
    1 tablespoon flour
    1½ cups milk
    ½ teaspoon salt
    1 egg yolk
    1½ tablespoons grated Parmesan cheese
    4 pastry shells
    ½ cup bread crumbs
    2 tablespoons butter

Bone fish and shred. Melt butter in saucepan, blend in flour and cook 2 minutes. Add milk and salt and cook until slightly thickened, stirring constantly. Add egg yolk, mix well and add cheese, continuing to mix well.

Butter 4 large shells, pour 1 tablespoon sauce into each and fill with shredded fish. Pour remaining sauce over fish, sprinkle with bread crumbs and dot with butter. Bake in hot oven (400°F.) 10 minutes. Serve immediately.

Serves 4.

LAND SNAILS ROMAN STYLE
    4 pounds land snails, alive
    4 slices bread, soaked in water
    1 cup vinegar
    2 tablespoons salt

Put snails in a large vessel with the soaked bread broken into pieces. Leave snails in the pan for two days, covering pan so that they may breathe freely but not escape. After 2 days, make a bath of water, vinegar and salt and place snails in it. Mix well with hands. This will make a lot of foam. Repeat, changing water, salt and vinegar a few times until there is no more foam. Rinse thoroughly in fresh water. Place snails in large pan, with enough water to cover, over slow fire. When snails begin to push heads out of shells, turn fire high and boil about 10 minutes.

Then take:
    3 tablespoons olive oil
    2 cloves garlic, sliced
    6 anchovy filets, chopped
    1 large can tomatoes
    1 sprig fresh mint
    1 pinch red pepper

Brown garlic in olive oil, add anchovies and brown. Add tomatoes and salt and cook about 15 minutes. Add mint, red pepper and snails (drained). Simmer for about half an hour and serve. (Use small oyster fork or nut pick to extract snail.)

Serves 6.

MEATS

BEEF TONGUE IN SWEET-SOUR SAUCE
    3½ pounds tongue
    ½ cup olive oil
    ½ onion, chopped
    1 carrot, chopped
    1 stalk celery, chopped
    1 slice salt pork, ¼ inch thick, cut very fine
    ½ clove garlic, chopped
    2 teaspoons chopped parsley
    salt
    pepper
    1¼ cups wine
    1 cup stock or water
    3 tablespoons sugar
    1 clove garlic
    1 bay leaf
    ⅓ cup vinegar
    2 tablespoons bitter chocolate, grated
    1 tablespoon flour
    ½ cup pine nuts
    1 tablespoon chopped orange peel
    ¼ teaspoon salt

Place tongue in large pan with oil, chopped onion, carrot, celery, salt pork, chopped garlic and parsley. Add salt and pepper and brown well over moderate heat. When tongue and herbs are well browned, add wine and continue cooking until wine has evaporated. Add stock or water, cover pan and cook about 2 hours, until tongue is well done. When tongue is cooked, remove with a spoon some of the fat that forms on top of the gravy. Remove tongue from pan, strain gravy and keep both warm while preparing sweet-sour sauce.

Place sugar, garlic and bay leaf in a small pan, and let sugar melt over low flame. Mix frequently (do not add water) and when sugar is light brown in color, add vinegar. Mix well, scraping bottom of pan, and keep over moderate flame. Add grated chocolate. Add this sauce to strained gravy and if too thin, thicken with flour. Add pine nuts, orange peel and salt. Slice tongue and serve with sauce.

Serves 8.

BEEF ALLA CERTOSINA

2½ pounds eye of the round of beef
1 tablespoon olive oil
1 tablespoon butter
1 slice bacon, chopped
salt and pepper to taste
⅛ teaspoon nutmeg
3 or 4 anchovy filets, chopped fine
2 teaspoons chopped parsley
1 cup stock or water

Put meat in large saucepan with oil, butter, chopped bacon, pepper, salt, nutmeg, and brown slowly but thoroughly. When meat is well browned add the chopped anchovies, parsley and the stock or water. Reduce heat, cover the pan, and cook slowly about 1¼ hours, or until the meat is tender. Slice and serve covered with gravy. Add a little water to the gravy if necessary.

Serves 6.

BEEFSTEAK CACCIATORA
(Hunter Style)

1 tablespoon olive oil
1 porterhouse steak, 1½ inches thick
½ teaspoon salt
½ teaspoon pepper
2 tablespoons Marsala or sherry wine
½ cup dry red wine
½ clove garlic, minced
½ teaspoon fennel seeds
1 tablespoon tomato purée

Heat oil in frying pan, add steak, cook on both sides until done to your taste, add salt and pepper, remove from pan and keep warm. Add Marsala or sherry to pan gravy and cook slowly, scraping bottom of pan with wooden spoon, until wine has almost evaporated. Add garlic, fennel seeds and tomato purée, mix together well with pan gravy and cook 1 minute longer. Pour over steak and serve.

Serves 2.

OXTAIL ROMAN STYLE

4 pounds oxtail, cut into pieces
1 tablespoon leaf lard
2 slices bacon, cut into small pieces
1 small onion, sliced
½ clove garlic
1 carrot, diced
1 teaspoon chopped parsley
½ teaspoon salt
½ teaspoon pepper
1¼ cups dry red wine
3 tablespoons tomato paste
6 celery stalks, cut into large pieces

Place oxtail in large pan with lard, bacon, onion, garlic, carrot and parsley and brown very well. Add salt and pepper. Add wine and cook slowly until wine evaporates. Add tomato paste with enough water to cover meat, lower fire, cover pan and simmer slowly 4½ hours. Add celery pieces and cook 20 minutes longer.

Serves 4.

RIB OF BEEF AL BAROLO

1 bottle of Barolo wine, or any other dry red wine
1 onion, chopped
1 carrot, sliced
1 stalk celery, cut into small pieces
1 bay leaf
4 peppercorns
4 pounds rib roast of beef
2 tablespoons butter
2 slices bacon, chopped
⅛ teaspoon salt

This dish should be started the day before the actual serving.

Mix wine, chopped onion, carrot, celery, bay leaf and peppercorns (no salt). In this mixture, place the beef and marinate for 24 hours, turning the meat once or twice. When ready to cook, remove meat from liquid, dry thoroughly and tie to keep in shape. Place in large pan with butter and chopped bacon and brown well on all sides. Strain wine marinade and place in a small saucepan. Boil until reduced to half. Add salt to the meat. Add wine sauce. Cover pan and simmer for about 2 hours.

The meat must be so well cooked that it will not be necessary to cut it with a knife, but just "spoon it." Pour gravy over meat and serve.

Serves 8.

LARGE MEATBALL HOME STYLE

1¼ pounds chopped beef

⅛ pound prosciutto or lean bacon, chopped

4 slices bread, soaked in water and squeezed dry

1 egg

2 tablespoons grated Parmesan cheese

1 teaspoon chopped parsley

1 teaspoon chopped sweet basil

¼ teaspoon salt

8 cups water

1 onion

1 stalk celery

1 carrot

1 fresh tomato, cut into pieces

1 teaspoon chopped parsley

¼ teaspoon salt

Mix the chopped beef, bacon or prosciutto, bread, egg, Parmesan, parsley, basil and salt together thoroughly, and shape into a large meatball. In a soup pan, put the water, onion, celery, carrot, tomato, parsley and salt and bring to a boil. When the liquid is boiling, immerse the large meatball and lower the heat to a simmer. Simmer for 2 hours. Do not boil at high speed because the meatball would come apart.

After simmering for 2 hours, take the meatball out of the liquid and place on a platter, covering it with another platter so as to press it a little. When cold, slice and serve with mayonnaise sauce. Save the liquid for a tasty soup.

Serves 4.

BRAISED BEEF GENOESE STYLE

2 tablespoons dried mushrooms

1 slice bacon

1 small onion

1 stalk celery

1 teaspoon chopped parsley

1 small carrot

4 pounds eye of the round of beef

1 tablespoon lard

1 cup dry red wine

salt and pepper to taste

2 cups stock or water

Soak mushrooms in cold water for 30 minutes. Chop bacon and vegetables fine. Place meat in large saucepan with lard and chopped ingredients, mushrooms and ¾ of the wine and cook slowly until the wine has evaporated. Add the rest of the wine, salt and pepper to taste, cover the saucepan and continue to cook slowly until the wine has evaporated and the meat and vegetables are well browned. Add the stock or water, cover pan tightly, and cook for 2 hours or until the meat is tender to the fork. Slice the meat and serve with the gravy. Fresh ham may be substituted for beef.

Serves 8.

RABBIT IN EGG SAUCE

1 tablespoon butter

1 medium-sized rabbit, cut into small pieces

1 small onion, chopped

3 slices prosciutto or lean bacon, chopped

2 tablespoons chopped parsley

salt and pepper

½ tablespoon flour

½ cup white wine

2 egg yolks, lightly beaten

1 tablespoon lemon juice

Place butter in large pan, melt, and add rabbit. Cook over hot fire 2 or 3 minutes. Add onion, prosciutto or bacon, 1 tablespoon parsley, salt and pepper. Brown the meat thoroughly, then sprinkle with flour. Mix well and add wine. Cook until wine evaporates, then add enough water to cover. Lower heat, cover pan, and cook until meat is tender (about 1 hour), and the sauce rich and concentrated. Mix egg yolks with lemon juice and rest of parsley. Remove rabbit from stove, add egg mixture to sauce and mix well. Cover pot and let stand in warm place 5 minutes before serving.

Serves 4.

VEAL CUTLETS PARMESAN

- 1 pound veal cutlets
- ½ cup butter
- ¼ cup grated Parmesan cheese
- ½ pound Mozzarella cheese
- 1 cup dry bread crumbs
- 2 eggs, beaten
- 1 can tomato sauce
- ¼ teaspoon salt
- dash of pepper

Dip cutlets in beaten eggs combined with seasoning, then in mixture of Parmesan cheese and bread crumbs. Fry in butter until brown (about 8 minutes). Then place cutlets in baking dish, pour tomato sauce over them and add slices of Mozzarella cheese. Bake in moderate oven 10-15 minutes.

Serves 4.

MILANESE VEAL ROLLS

- 1½ pounds rump roast of veal or veal cutlet
- salt and pepper
- ground sage
- 4 slices prosciutto
- 8 thin slices mozzarella cheese
- 3 tablespoons olive oil
- 1 small onion, chopped
- 1 clove garlic, minced
- 1 16-ounce can Italian-style peeled tomatoes
- ½ cup white wine
- salt and pepper
- 8 thin strips mozzarella cheese
- parsley sprigs

Pound the meat with a mallet to ⅛ inch thickness. Sprinkle with salt, pepper and a little sage. Cut into 8 rectangular pieces. Cut the slices of prosciutto in half. Top the veal pieces with a piece of ham and a slice of mozzarella. Roll jelly-roll fashion and tie with string. In a large skillet, heat the oil and sauté the veal rolls until browned. Remove from the pan. Add the onion and garlic and sauté until tender. Break the tomatoes up with a fork and add to the skillet, with the white wine and salt and pepper. Mix

well. Add the veal rolls and cover. Simmer 1½ hours or until tender. Top with the mozzarella strips, cover and melt the cheese.

Serve on a bed of hot cooked spaghetti, topped with the sauce and garnished with the parsley sprigs.

Makes 4 servings.

SALTIMBOCCA

- 2 pounds veal cutlets, sliced very thin (Italian style)
- 1 teaspoon sage
- ¼ pound prosciutto or ham, sliced thin
- 3 tablespoons butter
- salt and pepper
- 2 tablespoons water

Cut veal cutlets into pieces about 5 inches square. On each piece sprinkle a little of the sage and place a slice of prosciutto or ham on top. Keep the prosciutto or ham in place on veal with a toothpick. Melt 2 tablespoons butter in frying pan and place meat in it. Sprinkle with salt and pepper. Cook over a high fire for a few minutes on each side until the veal is well browned.

Place the slices of cooked meat on serving dish with prosciutto or ham facing up. Add water to contents of frying pan and scrape bottom well. Add rest of butter and mix well over low fire. Pour gravy over meat.

Serves 6.

VEAL CHOPS MILANESE

- 4 large veal chops, ½ inch thick
- ½ teaspoon salt
- ½ teaspoon pepper
- 1 egg, well beaten with fork
- 1 cup bread crumbs
- 4 tablespoons butter
- 1 lemon, cut into wedges

Sprinkle veal chops with salt and pepper, dip into beaten egg and roll in bread crumbs. Melt butter in frying pan, add chops and fry slowly 10 minutes on each side. The meat must cook well but slowly. Remove chops to platter, pour butter from pan over them, and serve garnished with lemon wedges.

Serves 4.

SCALOPPINE AL MARSALA

1½ pounds veal cutlets, sliced thin (Italian style)
salt and pepper
1 tablespoon flour
2 tablespoons butter
½ cup Marsala wine
2 tablespoons stock or water

Have butcher pound cutlets very thin. Cut veal into pieces about 6 inches square. Sprinkle with salt and pepper and flour lightly. Melt butter in large frying pan, and when hot, put in veal and brown thoroughly on both sides over high heat. When well browned, add the Marsala and, keeping the flame high, let meat cook 1 minute longer. Place meat in serving dish. Add stock or water to pan, scraping bottom and sides, and pour over meat.

Serves 4.

LAMB BRODETTATO

1½ pounds lamb for stew, cut into pieces
2 slices prosciutto or lean bacon, minced
1 very small onion, chopped
1 tablespoon leaf lard
½ teaspoon salt
½ teaspoon pepper
2 tablespoons flour
¼ cup dry white wine
water to cover meat
2 egg yolks
1 tablespoon lemon juice
1 tablespoon chopped parsley
½ teaspoon marjoram

Place lamb, prosciutto or bacon, onion and leaf lard in frying pan and brown thoroughly over slow fire. Add salt and pepper, sprinkle with flour and blend in well. Add wine, cook until wine evaporates, add enough water to cover meat and cook 45 minutes or until meat is tender, adding more water if needed.

Beat the egg yolks and lemon juice together lightly with fork, and when mixed well, add parsley and marjoram, mixing well. Lower flame as much as possible under meat, pour egg mixture over meat, mix well, shut off flame and let stand on stove 5 minutes before serving.

Serves 4.

LAMB HUNTER STYLE
(Roman)

1½ pounds lamb for stew (lean), cut into pieces
1 tablespoon leaf lard
½ teaspoon salt
¾ teaspoon freshly ground pepper
½ clove garlic
½ teaspoon rosemary
1 sage leaf, chopped
1½ teaspoons flour
½ cup wine vinegar
½ cup water
2 anchovy filets, chopped

Place lamb in large skillet with leaf lard, and brown well on all sides over high flame. Add salt, pepper, garlic, rosemary and sage and continue browning a little longer. Sprinkle meat with flour and press in flour well with wooden spoon. Add vinegar and water, mix all together well, scraping bottom of pan. Lower flame and cook slowly 45 minutes until meat is almost done. If gravy becomes too dry, add a little water from time to time during cooking. Mix anchovies with 1 teaspoon water, add to meat, and cook 1 minute.

Serves 4.

LEG OF LAMB IN GALANTINE

1 small tender leg of lamb, boned
1¼ cups Marsala or sherry wine
¼ pound tongue, diced
¼ pound prosciutto, diced
1 tablespoon shelled pistachio nuts
1 black truffle, diced (optional)
2 tablespoons Marsala or sherry wine
½ pound lean veal, chopped
½ pound lean pork, chopped
½ pound salt pork, chopped
½ teaspoon pepper
½ teaspoon salt

Place leg of lamb in earthen bowl with wine and let stand over-night. Mix together diced tongue, prosciutto, pistachio nuts and truffle. Soak in 2 tablespoons Marsala or sherry wine for 3 hours. Add chopped veal, pork, salt pork and pepper and mix together well.

With this stuffing fill the leg of lamb in opening left by removal of bone and close together. Wrap leg in towel and tie around as for roast beef. Place in large Dutch oven and add enough water to cover meat. Add 1 teaspoon salt to water, cover pot and simmer gently 2 hours.

Remove meat from pot and let stand 10 minutes. Remove string and towel and rinse towel in cold water. Again wrap lamb in rinsed towel and tie again with string, this time more tightly. Put dish over meat and put something heavy over the dish to press meat down. Let stand until following day. Remove string and towel, slice and serve.

Serves 8 to 10.

PORK CHOPS WITH MUSTARD

    4 pork loin chops, ½ inch thick
    1 tablespoon butter
    1 small onion, chopped
    1 tablespoon flour
    ½ cup dry white wine
    ½ cup stock
    ½ teaspoon prepared mustard
    1 teaspoon capers
    ½ teaspoon salt
    ⅛ teaspoon pepper

Braise pork chops in skillet with butter, browning nicely about 20 minutes on each side. Remove chops from skillet. Place onion in skillet, brown slowly, blend in flour, add white wine and stock and boil gently until mixture is slightly thickened. Return chops to skillet and simmer 10 minutes. Add mustard, capers, salt and pepper, mix well and serve.

Serves 4.

FRESH HAM AL MARSALA

    3-pound slice fresh ham
    1¾ cups Marsala or dry sherry wine
    2 tablespoons olive oil
    2 medium onions, chopped
    2 carrots, chopped
    1 stalk celery, chopped
    2 teaspoons minced parsley
    ¼ teaspoon salt
    ⅛ teaspoon pepper
    ½ cup stock or bouillon
    1 teaspoon flour
    1 tablespoon butter, melted

Place ham in casserole about the same size as the slice. Pour 1 cup wine over it. Let it stand about 6 hours, turning meat occasionally.

Place the oil and chopped vegetables in a large frying pan. Remove meat from wine sauce, drain well and place in frying pan. Add salt and pepper and brown meat slowly on both sides, taking care that the vegetables do not burn. When meat is brown, add the wine in which the meat was marinated 1 tablespoon at a time, browning after each addition. Add ¼ cup stock or bouillon and cook slowly for about an hour, turning meat often.

Place meat on serving dish, slicing it as you wish. Remove some of the fat from the pan gravy, add flour and mix thoroughly. Place on fire and when gravy starts to thicken remove from fire and add remaining Marsala or sherry, ¼ cup stock or bouillon and butter. Mix well and serve on meat.

Serves 6.

PIG'S FEET WITH BROCCOLI

    4 pig's feet
    1 bunch broccoli
    ½ pound Italian sausage, cut into 1-inch lengths
    1 tablespoon olive oil
    1 tablespoon leaf lard
    ½ teaspoon pepper
    ½ pound mozzarella cheese, cut into very thin slices
    4 tablespoons grated Roman cheese
    2 eggs

Cook pig's feet in boiling water 1½ hours, or until tender. Remove from fire and reserve the broth. Clean broccoli, cut into small pieces, and boil in slightly salted water 10 minutes. Fry sausage in oil and leaf lard, adding 1 or 2 tablespoons water, if necessary, until sausage is tender.

In a casserole place 3 tablespoons broth obtained from boiling pig's feet, add 2 pig's feet cut into pieces, half the broccoli, half the pepper and cover with half the mozzarella and half the grated Roman cheese. Repeat the procedure and pour over it another 2 tablespoons broth. Break eggs into bowl, add 1 tablespoon grated cheese and beat with fork 5 minutes. Pour egg and cheese mixture over broccoli and pig's feet and bake in moderate oven (350°F.) 45 minutes.

Serves 4.

PORK CUTLETS WITH CAPERS

8 small pork cutlets
3 tablespoons flour
¼ teaspoon salt
⅛ teaspoon pepper
1 egg, lightly beaten
½ cup bread crumbs
3 tablespoons oil
1 small onion, chopped
1 tablespoon butter
2 anchovy filets, cut into small pieces
2 tablespoons capers, chopped
1 tablespoon parsley
¼ teaspoon flour
2 tablespoons vinegar
½ cup stock or water
½ tablespoon butter

Dredge cutlets in flour, sprinkle with salt and pepper, dip into egg, roll in crumbs and fry in oil 15 minutes on each side or until well browned. Place onion in saucepan with butter, and brown. Add anchovies, capers, parsley and flour and cook 2 minutes, stirring well. Add vinegar and stock and cook 10 minutes longer. Add butter. Pour sauce over cutlets and serve.
Serves 4.

LAMB BRAINS NEAPOLITAN STYLE

4 lamb's brains
3 tablespoons olive oil
¼ teaspoon salt
⅛ teaspoon pepper
1 teaspoon capers
12 ripe black olives, pitted and diced
2 tablespoons bread crumbs

Put brains in small pan, cover with cold water and let stand 10 minutes. Change water and place pan with brains and fresh water over flame. Allow water to reach boiling point, then remove brains and rinse them in clear, cool water. Dry with towel.

Put 1½ tablespoons olive oil in shallow casserole, add brains, sprinkle with salt and pepper, cover with layers of capers, then a layer of olives. Sprinkle with bread crumbs, pour remaining 1½ tablespoons olive oil over crumbs, and place casserole in hot oven for 10 minutes. Serve in casserole.
Serves 4.

VEAL KIDNEYS TRIFOLATI

4 veal kidneys
1 clove garlic
2 tablespoons olive oil
¼ teaspoon salt
⅛ teaspoon pepper
½ teaspoon butter
2 filets of anchovies, chopped
1 tablespoon chopped parsley
1 teaspoon lemon juice

Slice kidneys thin as possible and remove all fat. Brown garlic in oil over gentle fire, and when brown, remove garlic from pan. Add slices of kidney, season with salt and pepper, increase flame and cook briskly 5 minutes. Add butter and chopped anchovies, mix well, remove from fire, add parsley and lemon juice and serve immediately.
Serves 4.

SWEETBREADS WITH ARTICHOKES

1 pound sweetbreads
4 artichokes
2 tablespoons olive oil
salt and pepper
1 tablespoon butter
2 thin slices prosciutto, minced
2 tablespoons Marsala or sherry
¼ teaspoon salt
⅛ teaspoon pepper

Place sweetbreads in cold water for 15 minutes. Change water, place in saucepan over fire and bring water to boiling point. Remove sweetbreads and place again in cold water, drain, dry and remove skin.

Remove outer leaves and chokes from artichokes and cut each into 8 pieces. Place in frying pan with oil and cook until tender. Add salt and pepper and a few drops of water if artichokes become too dry.

Place butter in another frying pan, add sweetbreads and cook over high flame 3 minutes on each side or until golden brown in color. Add prosciutto and cook 2 minutes longer. Add Marsala or sherry, season with salt and pepper and cook 1 minute more. Remove from fire and serve.
Serves 4.
Variation: 1 pound shelled fresh peas may be substituted for artichokes if desired.

BEEF LIVER FLORENTINE STYLE

1 pound beef liver, sliced thin
2 tablespoons flour
2 tablespoons olive oil
2 cloves garlic, chopped
6 fresh sage leaves
½ teaspoon salt
½ teaspoon pepper
1 tablespoon olive oil
2 tablespoons tomato purée

Dredge liver in flour. Place 2 tablespoons olive oil, garlic and sage leaves in frying pan, add liver and fry 4 minutes on each side. Add salt and pepper and remove liver from pan. Add 1 tablespoon oil and tomato purée to pan gravy and cook 1 minute. Return liver to pan, cook 3 or 4 minutes longer and serve.

Serves 4.

ITALIAN SAUSAGE WITH ENDIVE

¾ pound Italian sausage, sweet or hot
1 head endive
¼ teaspoon salt
¼ teaspoon pepper (omit if hot sausage is used)

Prick sausage with needle, place in large frying pan with 1 tablespoon water and brown slowly. When well browned, remove from frying pan. Add endive, which has been washed and chopped fine, to pan gravy, add a little water if necessary and cook 20 minutes. Add salt and pepper. Cut sausage into 3-inch pieces and serve with endive.

Serves 4.

LIVER TRIESTE STYLE

2 tablespoons olive oil
1 onion, chopped
1 stalk celery, chopped
1 carrot, sliced
1 pound beef or calf's liver, in 1 piece
1 clove
¼ teaspoon salt
⅛ teaspoon pepper
6 slices toast
1 tablespoon bread crumbs
2 teaspoons lemon juice
1 sprig parsley, chopped

Place olive oil and vegetables in saucepan. Re-move skin from liver, stick clove in liver, and place over vegetables. Add salt and pepper, enough water to cover, cover pan and bring to boiling point. When boiling, remove cover, lower flame and simmer 2 hours, turning liver occasionally.

Cut toast into triangles and place on serving plate. Slice liver thin, place on toast and pour gravy and vegetables over it. Sprinkle with bread crumbs and lemon juice, garnish with parsley and serve.

Serves 4.

GOLDEN TRIPE ALLA BOLOGNESE

1 tablespoon olive oil
1 thin slice salt pork, chopped
1 small onion, chopped
½ clove garlic, chopped
1 tablespoon chopped parsley
½ teaspoon salt
¼ teaspoon pepper
2 pounds parboiled tripe, cut into 2-inch squares
3 egg yolks, lightly beaten with fork
1 teaspoon meat extract, dissolved in ½ cup warm water
2 tablespoons grated Parmesan cheese

Place olive oil, salt pork, onion, garlic and parsley in a large frying pan and brown together slowly. Add salt and pepper and tripe and cook slowly 1 hour, mixing frequently.

In a mixing bowl combine egg yolks with meat extract, dissolved in water. Lower flame under tripe as much as possible and add egg and meat extract mixture. Mix well, cover pan and let simmer very slowly 5 minutes. Remove from fire, add Parmesan and mix well. Serve with additional Parmesan sprinkled over tripe, if desired.

Serves 6.

FRIED ITALIAN SAUSAGE

1 pound Italian sausage sweet or hot
water to cover

Prick sausage all over with a needle and place in frying pan. Cover with cold water and cook over moderate fine 45 minutes. After all water has been evaporated, there will be enough fat in pan to brown sausage nicely and give it a delicious brown crust.

Serves 4.

POULTRY

CHICKEN CACCIATORA

4-pound spring chicken, cut into pieces
½ cup flour
1 teaspoon salt
½ cup fat
¼ cup chopped onion
1 clove garlic, chopped fine
¼ chopped carrot
3 sprigs parsley
1 basil or bay leaf
4 cups tomatoes
1 teaspoon salt
dash pepper
¼ cup Marsala, sherry or white wine

Dredge chicken in flour, sprinkle with salt and brown in fat until golden on all sides. Place in covered dish in warm place. Brown onion, garlic, carrot, parsley and bay leaf or basil in fat left in frying pan.

Strain tomatoes (when strained you should have 2 cups pulp). Add tomato pulp to browned vegetables in frying pan, add 1 teaspoon salt and dash of pepper and bring to a boil. Add chicken and wine and simmer 30 minutes, or until chicken is tender.

Serves 4.

FRIED CHICKEN, ITALIAN STYLE

2½ pounds chicken parts (drumsticks, thighs, breasts and wings)
⅓ cup flour
½ teaspoon seasoned salt
¼ teaspoon pepper
2 eggs
2 tablespoons milk
⅔ cup dry bread crumbs
⅓ cup grated Parmesan cheese
oil for frying
parsley
lemon slices

Wash the chicken and pat dry. Combine the flour and seasoned salt and pepper in a paper bag and shake the chicken a few pieces at a time in the flour mixture until lightly coated. Beat the eggs and milk together in a shallow bowl. On a piece of waxed paper combine the bread crumbs and Parmesan cheese. Dip the floured chicken pieces in the egg and then the bread crumb mixture, coating well. Heat 1½ inches of oil in a heavy skillet over moderate heat. Fry the chicken a few pieces at a time until golden brown. Drain on paper towels. Place on a baking sheet and bake at 350°F for 15 to 20 minutes or until the juices run clear when pierced with a knife.

Garnish with parsley and lemon slices and serve with basil flavored tomato sauce if you wish.

Makes 4 servings.

CHICKEN TETRAZZINI

5- to 6-pound stewing chicken
2 teaspoons salt
¼ teaspoon pepper
1 pound spaghetti
3 slices bacon, shredded
1 large sweet onion, chopped
4-ounce can roasted peppers, chopped
1 large green pepper, chopped
1 pound grated cheese
1 8-ounce can mushrooms

Cut chicken into pieces, cover with water, add salt and pepper and cook slowly 3 hours, or until meat loosens from bones. Remove meat from bones and cut into small pieces. Cook spaghetti in boiling chicken broth until tender, and drain. Brown bacon in large pot, add onion, brown lightly, add roasted peppers, green pepper, cheese and mushrooms and mix thoroughly. Add chicken and spaghetti and keep over low flame until thoroughly heated. If needed, moisten with a little chicken broth.

Serves 12.

STUFFED TURKEY LOMBARDY STYLE

10-pound turkey
1 pound chopped beef
½ pound sweet Italian sausage, skinned and chopped
2 eggs
½ cup grated Parmesan cheese
⅛ teaspoon nutmeg
15 boiled peeled chestnuts, mashed
2 slices fat bacon, diced
heart, liver and gizzard, boiled and chopped
⅛ teaspoon salt
⅛ teaspoon pepper
½ cup butter
2 slices prosciutto
1 sage leaf

½ teaspoon rosemary
½ cup wine
1 teaspoon flour
1 cup stock or water

Mix the beef, sausage, eggs, Parmesan, nutmeg, chestnuts, bacon, heart, liver and gizzard together and add half the salt and pepper. Stuff turkey and sew up opening. Melt butter in a large iron pot or Dutch oven, place turkey in it, and place prosciutto, sage and rosemary over turkey. Brown turkey well on all sides. When well browned, add wine. Cover pot, lower fire and continue cooking for 3 hours. Occasionally add a little stock or water. Baste frequently.

When turkey is tender, remove from pan and place on serving dish. Blend 1 teaspoon flour with pan gravy and add 1 cup stock or water. Serve this gravy over turkey.

Serves 8.

TURKEY BALLS

2 cups cooked turkey, chopped
½ teaspoon salt
¼ teaspoon pepper
⅛ teaspoon cinnamon
2 tablespoons grated Parmesan cheese
1 egg yolk
3 slices bread
1 tablespoon butter
1 teaspoon tomato paste
2 cups stock
1 tablespoon butter, melted
1 tablespoon flour

Mix turkey meat with salt, pepper, cinnamon, cheese and egg yolk. Soak bread in water, squeeze dry and add to mixture. Blend all together until mixture is smooth. Make about 12 balls. Place 1 tablespoon butter in large saucepan, melt, add tomato paste and stock and cook 5 minutes. Place turkey balls in stock and simmer 20 minutes. Remove balls from broth and place on serving dish.

Boil broth rapidly until reduced half in quantity. Blend together 1 tablespoon melted butter and 1 tablespoon flour, add to stock, stirring in well, and cook until thickened. Pour this sauce over balls and serve.

Serves 4.

DUCK IN SALMI

1 medium-sized duck, cut into pieces
1 large onion, spiked with 3 cloves
2 sage leaves
1 bay leaf
liver, heart and gizzard, chopped very fine
½ cup olive oil
½ cup wine vinegar
¼ teaspoon salt
⅛ teaspoon pepper

Place duck in large pan with onion, spiked with cloves, sage leaves, bay leaf, liver, heart and gizzard. Add oil, vinegar, salt and pepper. Cover pan with a double sheet of brown paper, tucking in edges of paper. Put pan cover on and cook over a very moderate fire about ½ hour. When meat is done, place in serving dish, strain gravy and serve on toasted bread.

Serves 4.

MACARONI, SPAGHETTI AND RICE

MANICOTTI
(Little Muffs)

2 cups flour
1 tablespoon butter
3 eggs
½ teaspoon salt
1 cup lukewarm water
1 pound ricotta
2 cups tomato sauce (see index)
1 tablespoon fresh chopped basil
½ cup grated Roman cheese

Combine flour, butter, eggs and salt, add water gradually and mix to form a medium soft dough. Knead until smooth and roll on floured board until thin. Cut into rectangles 4 by 6 inches. Place 1½ tablespoons ricotta in center of each rectangle, roll dough and close, moistening and pressing edges carefully to prevent ricotta from falling out.

Boil manicotti gently 10 minutes in extra large pan in about 8 quarts water. Remove carefully with flat strainer and place in 1 large casserole, or 2 each in individual casseroles. Cover with tomato sauce, sprinkle with fresh basil leaves and place in hot oven (400°F.) 10 minutes. Serve with grated Roman cheese.

Serves 6.

Italian antipasto (see recipe page 40)

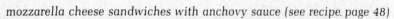

mozzarella cheese sandwiches with anchovy sauce (see recipe page 48)

(see recipe page 72) macroni with sauce amatrice

Picture on opposite page: fried chicken italian-style
(see recipe page 63)

neopolitan minestrone (see recipe page 44)

milanese veal rolls (see recipe page 58)

(see recipe page 79) florentines

cannoli (see recipe page 79)

LASAGNE NEAPOLITAN STYLE

1 pound Ronzoni curly edge lasagne (#80)
1 pound pork shoulder
1 tablespoon olive oil
½ onion, minced
1 clove garlic, sliced
1 teaspoon minced parsley
½ teaspoon salt
½ teaspoon pepper
1½ cans tomato paste
2 cups warm water
5 quarts water
3 teaspoons salt
1 pound ricotta (Italian pot cheese)
1 tablespoon hot water
4 tablespoons grated Parmesan cheese

Place pork in saucepan with oil, onion, garlic, and parsley and brown thoroughly on all sides. Add salt, pepper and tomato paste, diluted in 2 cups warm water. Cover pan and cook 2 hours, adding a little water from time to time, if necessary. This should make about 2 cups of tomato sauce. Remove pork from sauce, and keep warm.

In another pan bring water to boil, add salt, and drop in lasagne.

Cook 15 minutes, or until tender, stirring almost constantly to prevent lasagne from sticking together. Drain. Mix ricotta with 1 tablespoon warm water, making a soft paste.

In a casserole, arrange lasagne in layers, alternating with sauce, ricotta and Parmesan, until lasagne is all used, and ending with a layer of sauce, ricotta and Parmesan. Bake in moderate oven 20 minutes and serve. Serve pork as second course.

Makes 6 large or 8 medium servings.

GREEN LASAGNE MODENA STYLE

3 cups flour
½ pound spinach, cooked drained and strained
2 eggs
¼ teaspoon salt

Make a mound of the flour on large pastry board and scoop out a well in the mound. Place strained spinach, eggs and salt in well and work into flour, knead for 20 minutes, adding a little more flour if necessary. Divide the kneaded dough into two parts and roll each part paper thin. Stretch dough sheets on clean towels to dry. Let dry 1 hour. Fold each sheet and cut across dough with sharp knife, making ribbons ¾ inch wide. Shake ribbons loose and cook in boiling salted water ½ hour, or less, to taste. Drain. Have ready:

3 cups chopped meat sauce (see index)
6 tablespoons grated Parmesan cheese
½ cup butter

In large casserole place a layer lasagne, cover with sauce and Parmesan and dot with butter. Repeat until lasagne is all used, ending with sauce, cheese and butter. Bake in moderate oven ¾ hour. Sprinkle with additional Parmesan and serve.

Serves 4.

PENNONI WITH MUSHROOMS

4 tablespoons olive oil
½ clove garlic, chopped
1½ pounds mushrooms, cut into pieces
⅛ teaspoon salt
⅛ teaspoon freshly ground pepper
2 teaspoons parsley, chopped
1 pound pennoni (type of macaroni)
4 quarts boiling water
2 teaspoons salt
4 tablespoons grated Parmesan cheese

Place oil, garlic and mushrooms in saucepan and cook gently 15 minutes. Add salt, pepper and parsley and cook 5 minutes longer.

Cook pennoni in salted water 15 minutes and drain. Pour mushroom mixture over pennoni, sprinkle with grated cheese and serve.

Serves 4.

RAVIOLI WITH RICOTTA

4 cups flour
3 eggs
1 tablespoon water

Mix the above ingredients together, making a dough, and work until firm. Cut in two and roll into 2 thin sheets. Now take:

1 pound ricotta
1 egg
2 tablespoons grated Parmesan cheese

½ teaspoon salt
5 quarts boiling water
3 teaspoons salt

Mix together thoroughly ricotta, egg, Parmesan and salt, and place 1 teaspoon of mixture on one of the dough sheets at 2-inch intervals. Place second sheet over the first and press with fingers around each ricotta mound. Cut into 2-inch squares, making sure that edges are well closed. Cook about 20 minutes, according to taste, in salted boiling water. Serve with meat sauce (see index) or with butter and grated Parmesan cheese.

Serves 4.

SPAGHETTI WITH CHICKEN LIVERS

1 pound spaghetti
2 tablespoons olive oil
1 onion, chopped fine
2 cups tomato purée
½ teaspoon salt
¼ teaspoon pepper
½ cup grated Parmesan cheese
½ pound mushrooms, washed and peeled, or 1 large can mushrooms
1 pound chicken livers
¼ pound butter

Cook spaghetti in rapidly boiling salted water until tender, and drain. Heat olive oil in large frying pan, add onion and brown until golden in color. Add tomato purée, salt and pepper. Add grated cheese, a little at a time, blending thoroughly. Add spaghetti and keep over low flame, stirring constantly until thoroughly heated. Sauté mushrooms and chicken livers in butter. Place spaghetti mixture on serving dish, pour over it the mushrooms and chicken livers and serve with a sprinkling of Parmesan cheese.

Serves 4.

SPAGHETTI ALLA NOVELLI

3 medium onions, chopped
1 tablespoon olive oil
8 anchovy filets, minced
2 tablespoons chopped parsley
1 stalk celery, chopped fine
1 teaspoon rosemary
1 teaspoon sage
1 pound fresh ripe tomatoes, peeled and cut into pieces

½ cup dry white wine
½ teaspoon salt
¼ teaspoon pepper
4 quarts water
3 tablespoons salt
1 pound spaghetti
2 tablespoons grated Roman cheese
2 tablespoons grated Parmesan cheese

Brown onions gently in olive oil. Add anchovies, parsley, celery, rosemary and sage and continue browning 5 minutes. Add tomatoes and cook 30 minutes. Add wine and seasoning, cook 1 minute longer and remove from fire.

While sauce is cooking, put water on to boil, adding salt. When water is boiling, put in spaghetti, cut in half, and boil 15 minutes, or until spaghetti is cooked to your taste. Drain, serve with sauce and sprinkle with grated cheeses.

Makes 4 large or 6 medium portions.

POLENTA WITH SAUSAGE GRAVY

1 pound Italian sausage (hot or sweet, according to taste)
2 tablespoons water
1 small onion, chopped
1 clove garlic, sliced
¼ teaspoon salt
⅛ teaspoon pepper (omit if using hot sausage)
1 medium can tomatoes
2 small cans tomato purée

Place sausage in large saucepan with 2 tablespoons water. Prick sausage with needle and let brown in its own fat. Add onion, garlic and salt, brown a little longer. Add tomatoes and tomato purée and simmer 1½ hours. When gravy is ready, take:

1 pound cornmeal
1¼ quarts boiling water
2 teaspoons salt
3 tablespoons grated Roman cheese

Pour cornmeal slowly into boiling salted water, stirring constantly with wooden spoon. Continue cooking and stirring 30 minutes or until cornmeal leaves sides of pan easily. Pour cornmeal onto large platter, pour gravy over it and place sausage around it. Sprinkle with cheese and serve.

Serves 4 or 6.

ARANCINI SICILIAN STYLE

1 cup rice
4 cups boiling salted water
¼ pound chopped beef
2 chicken livers
2 tablespoons olive oil
1 clove garlic
½ small onion, minced
¼ pound mushrooms, sliced
2 tablespoons tomato paste
1 cup warm water
¼ teaspoon salt
¼ teaspoon pepper
½ cup butter
3 tablespoons grated Parmesan cheese
2 egg yolks
1 egg, lightly beaten
1 cup bread crumbs
1 cup olive oil

Wash rice and cook in boiling salted water until tender.

Meanwhile, place chopped beef, chicken livers, oil, garlic and onion in saucepan and brown gently. Add mushrooms and cook 1 minute. Add tomato paste and water and cook 30 minutes. Add salt and pepper.

Drain rice, add butter and Parmesan and cool a little. To this, add egg yolks and the tomato gravy, holding aside the meat and mushrooms. Mix rice well. Make little balls of rice, placing inside each ball some of the meat, livers and mushrooms. Dip rice balls into egg, roll in bread crumbs and fry in hot olive oil until golden brown all over.

Serves 4 or 6.

GREEN GNOCCHI

1 pound spinach, boiled, squeezed dry and strained
2½ pounds potatoes, boiled and mashed
2 egg yolks
2 tablespoons grated Parmesan cheese
¼ teaspoon salt
5 tablespoons flour
5 quarts boiling water
3 tablespoons salt
¼ pound butter
3 cups tomato sauce (see index)
3 tablespoons grated Parmesan cheese

Mix together spinach, potatoes, egg yolks, Parmesan cheese, salt and flour. Roll on floured board in long finger-thin roll and cut into pieces 2 inches long. Cook 10 pieces at a time in boiling salted water. When pieces rise to surface, remove with strainer. Keep water boiling and repeat procedure until all gnocchi are cooked. Place in serving dish, add sauce, sprinkle with grated Parmesan and serve.

Serves 4.

NEAPOLITAN STUFFED CALZONE

1 recipe bread dough for pizza (see recipe below)
¼ cup leaf lard
½ pound mozzarella cheese, diced
¼ pound sliced prosciutto, cut into slivers
⅛ pound Italian salami, cut into slivers
⅛ teaspoon salt
¼ teaspoon pepper
2 cups tomato sauce (see index)
2 tablespoons grated Roman cheese

Cut dough into 4 parts and press and roll each part until you get 4 large disks about ¼ inch thick. Coat each disk with leaf lard and place on each a quarter of the mozzarella, prosciutto, salami, salt and pepper. Fold each disk in half, pressing around the edges and making sure that the stuffing is well closed in. Coat each calzone with more leaf lard and place on pie plate in hot oven for about 20 minutes.

Remove, pour sauce over all, sprinkle with grated cheese and serve.

Serves 4.

BREAD DOUGH FOR PIZZA

4⅔ cups sifted flour
2 tablespoons leaf lard
¼ teaspoon salt
¼ teaspoon pepper
1¼ envelopes yeast
1⅛ cups warm water

Place flour on pastry board, add lard, salt, pepper, yeast and warm water and work well until smooth. Place in large pan, cover and let rise in warm place 2 hours, or until double in bulk. Place on floured board and pound lightly to deflate it. Divide into 2 pieces and stretch each piece on bottom of greased 12-inch pie plate. Dough may be prepared in this manner, may be purchased from a baker, or a prepared dough mix may be used.

MACARONI WITH SAUCE AMATRICE

sauce

2 tablespoons olive oil

2 cloves garlic, peeled and minced

¼ pound salt pork, diced

1 small onion, chopped

¼ cup dry white wine

1 28-ounce can Italian plum tomatoes, drained and minced

1 teaspoon sugar

1 teaspoon chili powder

½ teaspoon paprika

½ teaspoon dried sweet basil, crumbled

½ teaspoon dried oregano, crumbled

Salt and pepper

pasta

3 quarts water

1 tablespoon salt

1 tablespoon cooking oil

12 ounces penne or other macaroni

Grated Parmesan cheese

Heat the olive oil in a large saucepan. Add the garlic, salt pork, and onion and sauté until the onion is tender. Add the white wine and cook until it has evaporated. Add the tomatoes and spices and simmer 20 minutes, uncovered.

Meanwhile, heat the water to boiling. Add the salt and float the oil on the surface of the water. Add the penne and cook until al dente. Drain. Place in a serving bowl, top with the sauce and serve with Parmesan cheese.

Makes 4 servings.

RICE WITH SHRIMPS

1½ pounds shrimps

3 cups salted water

¼ cup butter

½ medium onion, sliced

1 carrot, diced fine

1 teaspoon chopped parsley

⅛ teaspoon thyme

1 bay leaf

2 tablespoons cognac

½ medium onion, minced

1 tablespoon olive oil

½ cup butter

1 pound rice

1 cup dry red wine

2 cups stock from shells

Shell shrimps. Boil shrimp shells 20 minutes in salted water.

Place ¼ cup butter, onion, shrimps, carrot, parsley, thyme and bay leaf in saucepan and sauté until golden brown. Add cognac and cook until evaporated.

In another larger pan place minced onion, olive oil and ½ cup butter. Brown onion a little and add rice. Let rice brown a little, stirring frequently, then add wine. Let wine evaporate, add stock and cook until rice is tender, about 15 minutes. Remove from fire. Pour shrimps and sauce over rice and serve.

Serves 4.

PIZZA WITH SAUSAGE

This pizza may be made with sweet or hot sausage, according to your taste. If hot sausage is used, omit pepper.

1 envelope dry yeast

1 cup lukewarm water

3⅛ cups flour

2 tablespoons olive oil

½ pound Italian sausage, cut into thin slices

1 large can tomatoes, drained

½ teaspoon basil

½ cup grated Roman cheese

2 tablespoons olive oil

½ teaspoon salt

½ teaspoon pepper

Blend yeast with 2 tablespoons lukewarm water and let stand 5 minutes. Place flour on pastry board, add yeast and remaining lukewarm water and knead well 15 minutes, or until dough is soft and malleable. Add olive oil and work into dough. Let rise in warm place 2 hours, or until dough is doubled in bulk.

Place sausage in saucepan with a few drops water and brown lightly. Add tomatoes, basil and cheese and simmer 15 minutes. Stretch dough as thin as possible over large baking sheet or pie plate. Sprinkle with olive oil, spread tomato and sausage over dough and sprinkle with salt and pepper. Bake in hot oven (400°F.) 15 minutes. Lower heat to 375°F. and continue baking 30 minutes.

Serves 4.

VEGETABLES

ARTICHOKES PARMESAN STYLE

4 artichokes
3 tablespoons flour
1 egg, lightly beaten
1 cup olive oil
2 slices bacon, chopped
1 very small onion, sliced
3 tablespoons tomato paste
1 cup warm water
½ teaspoon salt
½ teaspoon pepper
4 tablespoons grated Parmesan cheese
2 tablespoons butter

Cut off stalks and tips of artichokes and remove tough outer leaves. Cut into very thin slices, roll in flour and in egg and fry a few slices at a time in olive oil until golden brown.

Brown bacon and onion in small saucepan, add tomato paste, water, salt and pepper and cook 10 minutes. Place a layer of fried artichoke slices in greased casserole, cover with some of the sauce, sprinkle with some of the Parmesan cheese, dot with butter and repeat layers until all artichokes are used, ending with a layer of Parmesan. Bake in moderate oven (375°F.) 20 minutes.

Serves 4.

ARTICHOKES SICILIAN STYLE

4 artichokes
½ small onion, chopped
1 clove garlic, chopped
1 tablespoon chopped parsley
2 tablespoons grated Roman cheese
1 cup bread crumbs
½ teaspoon salt
½ teaspoon pepper
¼ cup olive oil
2 tablespoons olive oil

Cut off stalks and tips of artichokes and remove some of the tough outer leaves. Spread remaining leaves open. Mix onion, garlic, parsley, cheese, bread crumbs, salt and pepper, moisten with ¼ cup olive oil and 2 tablespoons water and fill each leaf with a tiny bit of this mixture. Fill the center of each artichoke with this mixture also.

Place artichokes in baking dish, sprinkle with olive oil and pour a little water in bottom of the dish. Bake in slow oven (325°F.) 45 minutes, or until the bottoms of the artichokes are soft to the fork.
Serves 4.

ASPARAGUS WITH EGGS MILANESE

1 small bunch asparagus
4 poached eggs
½ cup butter, melted
4 tablespoons grated Parmesan cheese
1 teaspoon salt
½ teaspoon pepper

Clean asparagus and cut off tough part of stalk. Boil briskly about 15 minutes, or until tender. Exact time for boiling depends on thickness and tenderness of the asparagus. Drain very well. Place poached eggs in center of baking dish, arrange asparagus around eggs, sprinkle with melted butter, Parmesan, salt and pepper and bake in very hot oven (450°F.) 3 or 4 minutes.
Serves 4.

BEANS TUSCAN STYLE

¾ pound white beans
2 tablespoons olive oil
½ teaspoon sage
2 cloves garlic, sliced
4 cups water
1 large fresh tomato, peeled and cut into pieces
1 teaspoon salt
½ teaspoon pepper
2 tablespoons olive oil

Place well-washed beans in large saucepan with oil, sage, garlic, water and tomato. Cover pan, and cook over low flame 3 hours, or until tender. Add salt, pepper and olive oil before serving.
Serves 4.

BROCCOLI WITH PROSCIUTTO

1 medium bunch broccoli
1½ tablespoons leaf lard
½ clove garlic
½ teaspoon salt
½ teaspoon pepper
3 thin slices prosciutto or ham, shredded

Remove all tough leaves and stems from broccoli. Cut into pieces and boil in salted water 15 minutes, or until tender. Drain. Melt leaf lard in skillet, add garlic and brown a little. Add cooked broccoli and mash with fork. Add salt and pepper and cook 5 minutes. Add prosciutto or ham and cook 2 minutes longer.

Serves 4.

EGGPLANT PARMIGIANA

    1 large eggplant, or 2 small ones
    1 cup olive oil
    1¼ cups tomato sauce (see index)
    3 tablespoons grated Parmesan cheese
    ½ pound mozzarella cheese, sliced thin

Peel eggplant and cut into thin slices. Fry in oil until brown and drain well on paper. Place 1 layer fried eggplant in casserole, cover with sauce, sprinkle with Parmesan and cover with layer of mozzarella. Repeat procedure until all eggplant is used, ending with mozzarella. Bake in hot oven (400°F.) 15 minutes and serve hot.

Serves 4.

EGGPLANT PROVENZALE

    4 small eggplants
    1 tablespoon chopped salt pork
    ¼ clove garlic, chopped
    1 small onion, chopped
    2 slices bread, soaked in water and squeezed dry
    ¼ pound mushrooms, sliced thin
    1 slice prosciutto, minced
    2 anchovy filets, cut into pieces
    1 egg
    ½ teaspoon salt
    ½ teaspoon pepper
    3 tablespoons bread crumbs
    ¼ pound butter, melted
    1½ teaspoons lemon juice

Cut eggplants into halves and scoop out some of the insides. Mix together well the salt pork, garlic, onion, bread, mushrooms, prosciutto, anchovies, egg, salt and pepper and stuff eggplant halves with this mixture. Sprinkle with bread crumbs and melted butter. Place eggplants in well-greased baking dish and bake in moderate oven (375°F.) 40 minutes. Remove from oven, sprinkle with lemon juice and serve.

Serves 4.

CELERY PARMIGIANA STYLE

    1 very large bunch celery
    2 quarts stock or water
    1 small onion
    1 clove
    2 slices bacon
    1 cup tomato sauce (see index)
    ½ cup grated Parmesan cheese

Clean celery, remove leaves and cut stalks into 5-inch pieces. Cook in boiling stock or water with onion, clove and bacon 15 minutes, or until celery is tender. Place 1 layer celery in greased shallow casserole, top with tomato sauce, sprinkle with Parmesan and repeat layers until celery is all used, ending with tomato sauce and cheese. Bake in hot oven (400°F.) 10 minutes.

Serves 4.

STUFFED MUSHROOMS GENOA STYLE

    12 large mushrooms
    1 tablespoon olive oil
    ½ clove garlic, chopped
    1 veal brain, parboiled and chopped
    1 pork brain, parboiled and chopped
    ½ teaspoon salt
    ½ teaspoon pepper
    ½ teaspoon marjoram
    2 egg yolks
    1 tablespoon grated Parmesan cheese
    2 tablespoons olive oil

Cut off stems of mushrooms and wash well. Chop stems and brown in olive oil with garlic 5 minutes. Add chopped parboiled brains, salt, pepper and marjoram and cook 5 minutes longer. Remove from stove, add egg yolks and Parmesan and mix very well.

Fill the mushroom caps with this mixture. Place in shallow baking dish, sprinkle with olive oil and bake in moderate oven (375°F.) 40 minutes.

Serves 4.

SOUFFLE OF CHESTNUTS
1½ pound chestnuts
¼ teaspoon salt
1 tablespoon butter
1½ cups stock
2 egg whites, beaten stiff

Peel chestnuts, boil 30 minutes, or until tender, remove from fire and remove second skin. Force through strainer. Place in saucepan, add salt, butter and stock and cook, stirring well, until stock has evaporated. Cool. Fold in stiff egg whites and pour mixture into greased casserole. Bake in moderate oven (375°F.) 20 minutes.
Serves 4.

PEPPERS AU GRATIN
4 large green peppers
1 tablespoon capers
4 anchovy filets, cut into pieces
8 black olives, pitted and cut into pieces
4 tablespoons olive oil
2 tablespoons fine bread crumbs
½ teaspoon salt
½ teaspoon pepper

Roast peppers in very hot oven (450°F.) 10 minutes, or until skin is easily removed. Peel, remove seeds and cut into wide slices. Place in oiled baking dish, dot with capers, anchovies, olives and sprinkle with oil, bread crumbs, salt and pepper. Bake in moderate oven (375°F.) 20 minutes and add more olive oil. This dish can be served either hot or cold.
Serves 4.

EGGPLANT WITH ANCHOVIES
2 medium eggplants
1 cup oil, olive or cooking
½ clove garlic
3 tablespoons olive oil
6 anchovy filets, cut into pieces
1 tablespoon chopped parsley
1 tablespoon vinegar

Remove stem and peel eggplant. Cut into ½-inch slices and fry in oil until golden brown. Drain well on paper. Place 3 tablespoons oil and garlic in frying pan and brown garlic. Remove garlic when brown and add anchovies. Cook gently 3 minutes. Add

parsley and vinegar and cook 1 minute. Pour sauce over fried eggplant and serve either hot or cold.
Serves 4.

SPINACH PARMESAN
1 pound spinach, washed and chopped, or 1 package frozen chopped spinach
2 tablespoons butter
¼ teaspoon salt
⅛ teaspoon nutmeg
2 eggs, lightly beaten
3 tablespoons grated Parmesan cheese

Cook spinach in 1 cup water 5 minutes, drain, and chop fine. Place in saucepan with butter, salt and nutmeg and cook 4 minutes, stirring well. Shut off flame and keep pan on hot stove plate. Add eggs, mix well, add Parmesan cheese and continue stirring 2 or 3 minutes. Serve immediately.
Serves 4.

ITALIAN YELLOW SQUASH SICILIAN STYLE
1 pound squash, sliced thin
2 tablespoons olive oil
½ clove garlic, chopped
1½ tablespoons wine vinegar
½ teaspoon salt
½ teaspoon sugar
1 teaspoon chopped mint leaves

Place squash in skillet with oil and garlic and cook gently until squash is tender. Add vinegar, salt, sugar and mint leaves and cook 2 minutes longer.
Serves 4.

STRING BEAN PUDDING
1 pound string beans
2 tablespoons butter
¼ teaspoon salt
1 cup cream sauce (see index)
2 eggs, lightly beaten with 2 tablespoons grated Parmesan cheese
2 tablespoons fine bread crumbs
2 tablespoons butter

Wash string beans and cut into very small pieces. Boil in water 18 minutes and drain. Place beans in saucepan with butter and salt and cook gently 5 minutes. Remove from fire and add cream sauce, eggs and Parmesan.

Grease a 1-quart mold and sprinkle with bread crumbs. Pour in bean mixture, top with more bread crumbs and dot with butter. Bake in hot oven (400 F.) 45 minutes, or until mixture is firm. Remove from oven and let stand 4 minutes before unmolding.
Serves 4.

POTATOES PIZZAIOLA

2 pounds potatoes
2 tablespoons olive oil
1 clove garlic
3 fresh tomatoes, peeled and cut into pieces, or ½ large can tomatoes
½ teaspoon salt
½ teaspoon pepper
½ teaspoon oregano

Parboil potatoes 15 minutes, drain, peel and cut into thin slices. Brown garlic in olive oil. Remove garlic from oil, add tomatoes, salt, pepper and oregano and cook 5 minutes. Add sliced potatoes and cook 10 minutes. Serve immediately.
Serves 8.

TOMATO SOUFFLE

2 pounds ripe tomatoes, or 2 large cans tomatoes.
¼ cup butter
1 small onion, sliced
1 teaspoon crushed basil leaf
½ teaspoon salt
¼ teaspoon pepper
½ cup butter
4 tablespoons flour
2 cups milk
2 tablespoons grated Parmesan cheese
¼ pound Swiss type cheese, diced
4 egg yolks
4 egg whites, beaten stiff

Peel fresh tomatoes and cut into pieces. Melt butter, and onion and brown lightly. Add basil, tomatoes, salt and pepper and cook until tomatoes are thick.

Make a cream sauce as follows: Melt butter, blend in flour, add milk and cook slowly until thick and creamy, stirring constantly. Remove from fire, add grated and diced cheese, the tomato sauce and egg

yolks and mix well. Fold in gently the egg whites which have been beaten stiff but not dry. Pour into a 1-quart buttered form and bake in moderate oven (375°F.) 1 hour. Remove and serve immediately.
Serves 4.

ONIONS BORDOLESE

4 very large onions
8 chicken livers, chopped
¼ teaspoon pepper
½ teaspoon salt
½ black truffle, diced fine (optional)
½ cup butter
1 tablespoon flour
1½ cups water
½ teaspoon meat extract
1 jigger cognac

Peel onions, cut in halves and scoop out centers to make room for stuffing. Mix together chicken livers, pepper, salt, truffle and ¼ cup butter and stuff onion halves with this mixture. Place onions in well-buttered, covered baking dish and bake in moderate oven (375°F.) 20 minutes.

Melt rest of butter in small saucepan, blend in flour, add water and meat extract and cook 1 minute. Pour sauce over onions and continue baking in moderate oven 15 minutes longer, or until onions are tender. Remove from oven, sprinkle onions with cognac and serve.
Serves 4.

ZUCCHINI PIE

4 large zucchini
2 tablespoons flour
1 cup olive oil
3 tablespoons grated Parmesan cheese
1 cup tomato sauce (see index)
½ pound mozzarella, sliced thin

Cut zucchini into 1-inch slices, sprinkle with flour and fry in olive oil until light brown. In greased casserole place 1 layer of fried zucchini, sprinkle with Parmesan cheese, add a little of the sauce, cover with thin layers of mozzarella and repeat procedure until zucchini and other ingredients are all used, ending with mozzarella. Bake in moderate oven (375°F.) 30 minutes.
Serves 4.

SALADS

SALAD MUSETTA
 ½ cup olive oil
 ¼ teaspoon salt
 ¼ teaspoon pepper
 1 tablespoon wine vinegar
 1 tablespoon mayonnaise
 1 celery heart, in pieces
 1 fennel heart, in pieces
 2 small boiled potatoes, diced
 ⅛ pound Swiss cheese, diced
 4 artichoke hearts in oil
 4 mushrooms in oil
 head of 1 head chicory, shredded fine
 2 anchovy filets, in pieces
 1 teaspoon capers
 1 hard cooked egg, sliced

Mix olive oil with salt, pepper, vinegar and mayonnaise. Place other ingredients in salad bowl, pour oil mixture over them and mix gently but thoroughly.
Serves 4.

SICILIAN OLIVE SALAD
(Olive Schiacciate)
 2 pounds green Sicilian olives (imported)
 1 head celery, diced
 1 cup capers
 2 cloves garlic, sliced
 1 small onion, sliced
 1 cup olive oil
 1 teaspoon freshly ground black pepper
 2 large red vinegar peppers, in pieces
 1 carrot, sliced thin
 salt, if needed
 ½ teaspoon fennel seed
 1 tablespoon wine vinegar, if desired

Pound each olive until broken so that the pits show, but do not remove the pits. Place in large bowl and add all ingredients. The salt must be added only if needed, because the olives vary in saltiness. Mix well and long, cover and let stand in cool place at least 24 hours before serving.

These olives are a fine addition to an antipasto, or will be welcomed with meats, poultry and vegetables. A cup of these olives added to any Italian salad will do wonders. They keep in jars in the refrigerator for an indefinite time.

TYPICAL ITALIAN SALAD
 1 clove garlic
 ¼ cup olive oil
 ½ teaspoon salt
 ½ teaspoon pepper
 1 tablespoon wine vinegar
 1 small head crisp lettuce, shredded
 2 firm tomatoes, cut into pieces
 ½ cucumber, peeled and sliced
 4 radishes, sliced
 ¼ green pepper, cut into small pieces

Rub garlic over sides of salad bowl. Mix together oil, salt, pepper and vinegar. Place greens in salad bowl and pour dressing over them. Mix very well 5 minutes.
Serves 4.

SAUCES

CREAM SAUCE
 ½ cup butter
 6 tablespoons flour
 1 quart milk
 1 teaspoon salt

Melt butter over very low flame, blend in flour, cook 2 minutes, stirring well, add milk gradually and salt and bring to boiling point. Cook at a simmer until thickened, stirring constantly.
Makes 5 cups.

THICK CREAM SAUCE
 ¼ cup butter
 ¼ cup flour
 1¼ cups milk
 ¼ teaspoon salt
 dash nutmeg

Melt butter and blend in flour until smooth. Add milk gradually, salt and nutmeg and simmer, stirring constantly, until thickened. Makes 1¾ cups thick cream sauce.

CAPER SAUCE FOR FISH

- 2 tablespoons butter
- 1 tablespoon flour
- ¼ teaspoon salt
- ¼ teaspoon pepper
- 2 tablespoons stock
- 2 tablespoons capers in vinegar
- 1 teaspoon vinegar

Melt 1 tablespoon butter, blend in flour, cook until slightly brown and add remaining butter. Add salt, pepper and stock and cook until slightly thickened. Add capers and vinegar and mix well. Makes enough sauce for 1 pound of fish.

CHOPPED MEAT SAUCE FOR SPAGHETTI

- ½ pound each of beef and pork, chopped together
- 1 tablespoon olive oil
- 1 clove garlic
- ½ medium onion, chopped
- 1 teaspoon chopped parsley
- 1 medium can tomatoes
- 2 small cans tomato purée
- ⅛ teaspoon salt
- ⅛ teaspoon pepper
- ½ teaspoon chopped basil
- 2 bay leaves
- 1 tablespoon butter

Place chopped meat, oil, garlic, onion and parsley in saucepan and brown slowly, stirring frequently to prevent meat from cooking in lumps. Remove garlic as soon as browned. Add tomatoes, tomato purée, salt and pepper, cover pan and simmer 1 hour. Add basil, bay leaves and cook 1 minute longer. Remove from fire and add butter. Makes enough sauce for 1 pound spaghetti or other forms of macaroni.

TOMATO SAUCE

- 3 tablespoons olive oil
- ½ stalk celery, finely chopped
- 1 small onion, chopped
- 1 teaspoon parsley, minced
- 1 clove garlic
- 1 large can Italian tomatoes
- 1 medium can tomato purée
- ½ teaspoon salt
- ½ teaspoon pepper
- ½ teaspoon basil leaf, minced
- ½ teaspoon oregano
- 1 bay leaf

Place oil, celery, onion, parsley and garlic in saucepan and brown lightly. Add tomatoes and tomato purée, salt and pepper and simmer gently for about 45 minutes. Add the basil, oregano and bay leaf. Cook for 10 minutes longer. Makes sufficient sauce for 1 pound of spaghetti or macaroni.

Variation: ⅛ pound butter may be substituted for the olive oil, if preferred.

SPAGHETTI SAUCE WITH MEATBALLS

- ½ pound each of beef and pork, chopped together
- 1 tablespoon grated Roman cheese
- 4 slices bread, soaked in water and squeezed dry
- 1 tablespoon chopped parsley
- 1 egg
- ½ teaspoon grated onion
- ¼ clove garlic, chopped
- ¼ teaspoon salt
- ⅛ teaspoon pepper
- 3 tablespoons lard or olive or vegetable oil
- 1 medium can tomatoes
- 2 small cans tomato purée
- ¼ teaspoon salt
- ⅛ teaspoon pepper
- 2 bay leaves
- ½ teaspoon chopped sweet basil
- ¼ cup butter

Place chopped meat, cheese, bread, parsley, egg, grated onion, garlic, salt and pepper in mixing bowl. Mix together thoroughly and shape into small balls. Place lard or oil in frying pan and fry meat balls over brisk fire 5 minutes on each side or until well browned.

Place tomatoes and tomato purée in saucepan, bring to a boil and add meat balls. Add salt and pepper and simmer 1 hour. Add bay leaves, basil, and butter. Pour sauce over spaghetti or other macaroni, place meat balls around spaghetti and serve. Makes enough for 1 pound spaghetti or macaroni.

DESSERTS

CANNOLI

pastry:
- 2 cups flour
- 1 teaspoon salt
- 2 tablespoons sugar
- 2 tablespoons soft butter, cut into small pieces
- 1 egg, beaten
- 10 tablespoons white wine
- Oil for frying
- 5-inch long × 1-inch diameter cannoli forms or pieces of dowel

filling:
- ⅔ cup sugar
- ½ cup flour
- ⅛ teaspoon salt
- 2 cups scalded milk
- 2 eggs, lightly beaten
- ½ teaspoon vanilla extract
- ¼ teaspoon almond extract
- 1 pound ricotta cheese
- ½ cup powdered sugar
- ½ cup finely chopped candied fruit
- 1 1-ounce block semisweet chocolate, grated

Combine the flour and salt in a mixing bowl. Make a well in the center and add the sugar, butter and egg. Add the wine and stir with a fork until the liquid is absorbed. Turn out on a floured board and knead until smooth. Divide the dough into four equal parts. Roll out on a floured surface until 1/16th of an inch thick. Cut into 3½ inch squares. Roll the squares diagonally onto the forms, overlapping the corners. Seal with a little water. Heat ¾ of an inch of oil in a heavy skillet to 375°F. Fry the cannolis, 3 at a time, in the hot oil. When light golden, remove from the oil and slip off of the forms as soon as they are cool enough to handle. Allow to cool completely.

Next make the cream filling. Combine the sugar, flour and salt in the top of a double boiler. Slowly stir in the scalded milk. Cook the mixture over boiling water until the mixture thickens. Combine 1 cup of the custard mixture with the eggs and beat well. Pour the mixture back into the double boiler and continue to cook, stirring, 3 minutes. Cool, then stir in the flavoring (filling must be cold before adding the ricotta). Beat the ricotta and powdered sugar until the ricotta is smooth. Fold in the custard, mixed fruit and chocolate.

Fill the cannoli with a small spatula, carefully packing the filling. Refrigerate until serving time.

Makes 30 to 35.

Note: Shells can be made ahead and frozen and filled as needed.

FLORENTINES

- ½ cup butter
- ¾ cup sugar
- 3 eggs
- ¾ teaspoon almond extract
- 1 teaspoon grated orange peel
- 2½ cups all-purpose flour
- 1½ teaspoons baking powder
- ¼ teaspoon salt
- 1 cup ground almonds
- 1 cup semisweet chocolate chips
- 2 tablespoons hot water

Cream the butter and sugar. Add the eggs one at a time, beating well after each addition. Beat in the almond extract and the orange peel. Sift together the flour, baking powder, and salt and add to the creamed mixture and stir well to combine. Add the almonds and stir well.

Refrigerate the dough for several hours. Lightly grease a cookie sheet. Form the dough into loaves 1½ inches wide and ½ inch thick. Make sure the loaves are several inches apart as the cookies spread in baking. Make the loaves as long as your cookie sheet allows, but leave at least an inch space between the end of the loaf and the edge of the cookie sheet to prevent burning. Bake at 375°F for 12 to 15 minutes or until lightly browned and a toothpick inserted in the center of the loaf comes out clean. While still warm, cut the loaves into ¾-inch strips and cool on a cake rack.

Melt the chocolate chips over hot water, stirring occasionally. When completely melted, stir in just enough boiling water to make a thick mixture with consistency of layer-cake icing. Dip both ends of the cookie strips in the chocolate and allow to dry on a rack until the chocolate has hardened.

Makes 3½ to 4 dozen cookies.

Polish

SOUPS

PICKLED BEET SOUP
(Barszcz Kwaszony z Buraków)

    6 large or 10 small beets
    1 slice sour rye bread or buttermilk rye
    4 cups lukewarm water
    salt and pepper to taste
    dash of sugar (optional)

Scrape and dice the beets. Cover with water and place slice of bread on top. Cover loosely and let stand for 4 days in the warmest spot in the kitchen. The liquid should be sufficiently sour and tasty by that time (depending on the weather). Should mold appear, carefully skim it off. Discard bread, and season soup to taste. May be served hot or cold, with topping of sour cream if desired. Tightly covered, it may also be stored in refrigerator for later use.

Serves 4.

CAULIFLOWER SOUP
(Zupa Kalafjorowa)

    6 cups light soup stock
    1 med. cauliflower
    1 tbs. butter
    1 tbs. flour
    2-3 egg yolks
    ½ cup cream
    6 fresh mushrooms (optional) cut into strips and sautéed in butter
    salt and pepper to taste

Cook cauliflower in salted boiling water until tender—about 20 minutes. Reserve 6 to 8 flowerets. Mash the rest, combine with hot meat stock, thicken with the flour and butter stirred to a paste and diluted until smooth. Let simmer another few minutes. In the meantime beat the egg yolks with cream. Add, a little at a time, stirring constantly to avoid cur-

dling. Season to taste. Add the whole flowerets, mushrooms if desired, and serve with croutons.

Serves 6 to 8.

BRUSSELS SPROUT SOUP
(Zupa z Brukselki)

    ¼ lb. smoked pork
    1 med. onion
    1 leek
    1 celery stalk
    1 celery root
    1 parsnip
    few sprigs fresh parsley
    1 pt. Brussels sprouts
    7-8 cups water
    salt and pepper to taste
    1 tbs. flour
    1 tbs. bacon fat

Start pork and vegetables in cold water; simmer until done—about 45 minutes. Reserve half the sprouts (choosing the most tightly closed ones) and put remaining vegetables through sieve or ricer. Dice the meat. Return to pot, add the whole sprouts, and heat through. Brown the flour, make paste of flour and bacon drippings, add a little soup, and stir until smooth. Add to soup, let bubble up, and serve.

Serves 6.

WINE SOUP
(Polewka z Wina)

    1 cup water
    6 cloves
    1 stick cinnamon
    2 cups white table wine
    2-3 egg yolks (depending on size)
    sugar, 1 tbs. to each egg yolk

Boil water with cloves and cinnamon, covered, for 15 minutes. Add wine, and bring to boil and strain.

Combine egg yolks and sugar, and cream thoroughly. Place on asbestos over low heat and slowly add the boiling wine mixture, beating constantly with whisk or rotary beater until foamy and thick, taking care not to let eggs curdle. Serve in cups with dry biscuits or Melba toast.

Serves 3 to 4.

CLEAR BERRY SOUP
(Zupa Jagodowa Czysta)

1 qt. blueberries (huckleberries or blackberries may be substituted)
1½ qts. water
sugar to taste
1 tbs. potato flour

Clean berries and bring to a boil. When fruit is soft—about 10 or 15 minutes—press through a sieve and then return to liquid. Add sugar to taste and the potato flour dissolved in cold water. Stir thoroughly. Serve hot or iced.

Serves 6.

VEGETABLE PURÉE
(Zupa Jarzynowa)

1 large marrow bone, cut and split
2 med. onions
1-2 med. carrots
1 celery root
1-2 celery stalks with leaves
1 parsley root
1 parsnip
½ head savoy cabbage or 1 cup Brussels sprouts (optional)
other vegetables to taste
small bunch fresh parsley and, if available, fresh dill
salt and pepper to taste
1 tbs. butter
½ tbs. flour
8 cups cold water

Cover soupbones with cold water and simmer one hour, skimming as necessary. Add salt. Peel and cook vegetables separately, tightly covered, using just enough water to cook without scorching. When thoroughly done, chop and put through meat grinder or sieve together with cooked bone marrow, saving all the juices. Moisten with soup stock as needed to make sure all vegetable pulp is utilized. Combine with strained soup stock. Melt butter in heavy skillet; blend in flour, stirring constantly; dilute with a few spoonfuls of stock and return to pot. Season to taste and serve with croutons and grated Parmesan.

Serves 6.

BREAD SOUP
(Zupa Chlebowa)

2 cups stale dark bread (rye, whole wheat, etc.) moistened with water
2 med. onions
1-2 carrots
1 leek
few sprigs parsley
6 green beans or 2-3 tbs. Lima beans or peas
1 celery stalk
1 celery root or parsnip
5 cups salted water
dash of nutmeg
1 cup milk
3 egg yolks
salt and pepper to taste

Make light broth of all the vegetables and the bread. When vegetables are soft (30 to 45 minutes), put through sieve or ricer and return to broth. Add nutmeg and milk; stir thoroughly and bring to a simmer but do not boil. Dilute beaten egg yolks with a few spoonfuls of the broth and blend into soup, being careful not to curdle. Season to taste and serve with croutons or slices of hard-cooked egg.

Serves 6.

SWEET-AND-SOUR BEER SOUP
(Kalteszal)

3 pts. beer
1 cup sugar, or less, to taste
4 egg yolks
juice of 2 lemons
grated rind of 1 lemon
2″ stick cinnamon
1 jigger rum
2 tbs. seedless raisins

Beat egg yolks and half the sugar until very light. Add lemon juice and rind. Bring beer to a boil, covered, with cinnamon and the rest of the sugar. Let cool slightly. Then place in double boiler over boiling water and stir in eggs, stirring constantly. Add rum and raisins and chill. Serve with croutons.

Serves 6.

FISH AND SHELLFISH

BAKED PIKE
(*Szczupak z Pieca*)
> 3- to 4-lb. pike
> ⅛ lb. butter
> 1 lemon
> ½ tbs. flour
> 2 cups sour cream
> salt and pepper

Parboil fish in court bouillon. Place belly-down in an oblong baking dish, spreading with butter. Bake in a moderate oven until it begins to brown. Sprinkle with juice of a whole lemon. Beat the flour into the sour cream until smooth, and spread over the fish. Continue baking, basting frequently with the cream, for another 30 minutes.

Serves 6 to 8.

PERCH IN WINE SAUCE
(*Sandacz na Winie*)
> 1 med. or 2 small perch
> 1 cup white wine
> 2 tbs. butter
> 1½ tsp. flour
> salt and pepper to taste
> 2 egg yolks
> lemon juice to taste

Clean and salt the perch, either whole or cut into serving pieces. Steam in wine with 1 tbs. butter, covering dish with sheet of greased paper. (Time will depend on whether fish is cooked whole or in pieces.) Keep fish hot over steam, and strain liquid in which it cooked, adding a little more wine if necessary. Blend 1 tbs. butter with the flour, dissolve with wine sauce, and stir until smooth. Boil up once, season, and at the very last, stir in beaten egg yolks and add lemon juice to taste. Serve very hot.

Serves 4 to 5.

MARINATED TROUT
(*Pstragi Marynowane*)
> 5 to 6 ½-lb. trout
> 1 large onion
> 2 carrots
> 1 celery root
> 1 parsley root
> few sprigs parsley
> 2 qts. water
> 1 cup very dry white wine
> 2 tbs. vinegar *or* juice 1 lemon
> 1-2 bay leaves
> 6 peppercorns
> salt to taste

Dice the onion and vegetables, and cook in water alone until half done, about 10 minutes. Add wine, vinegar, salt, and spices. Cut fish into slices, add to pot, and cook at a slow boil for another 10 to 15 minutes, or until fish and vegetables are done. Allow to cool, put into jars together with vegetables and liquid, cover tightly, and store in refrigerator. Marinated fish may be preserved for a considerable time.

Serves 5 to 6.

Note: This recipe may be used for marinating carp, pike, etc.

EEL IN ASPIC
(*Wjegorz w Galarecie*)
> 1 med. eel, with head
> 1 onion, sliced
> 1-2 carrots, diced
> 1 celery root, diced
> 1 parsley root, diced
> 1 stalk celery and celery leaves
> 6 peppercorns
> 1 bay leaf
> few sprigs parsley
> 1 raw egg
> 2-3 hard-cooked eggs, sliced
> 1 lemon, sliced thin
> 12-16 cooked crayfish or shrimp
> 1 envelope gelatin

Clean and skin eel. Cook diced vegetables and spices in enough water to make stock for aspic—4 to 6 cups. When vegetables are nearly done, add fish and simmer, tightly covered, for 30 minutes. Remove fish from broth, add the raw egg with crushed shell and let broth boil up once. Allow to stand until broth clears, then strain. Cut fish into serving pieces. Arrange in mold, together with slices of egg and lemon and the cooked shrimp. Dissolve gelatin in a little cold water, add to broth, season to taste, and fill the mold. Chill thoroughly. Allow a half-pound of fish per serving.

CARP WITH MUSHROOMS
(Karp z Grzybami)
    3-lb. carp
    3-4 tbs. butter
    salt and pepper to taste
    Fresh Mushroom Sauce (see Index)

Have carp cleaned, leaving head and tail intact. Wash, drain, rub with salt and pepper, and bake in shallow buttered pan in medium-hot oven, allowing 15 to 20 minutes per inch of thickness. Baste frequently with butter. After half an hour cover generously with Fresh Mushroom Sauce and continue baking another 20 minutes or until sauce browns on top. Serve with parsley potatoes.
    Serves 6.

BAKED SALMON WITH MADEIRA
(Łosoś Pieczony z Maderja)
    1 med. salmon, whole, or 3- to 4-lb. piece cut
        from larger fish
    salt and pepper to taste
    few strips bacon or salt pork, cut thin
    1 truffle (optional)
    3 tbs. butter for basting
    juice ½ lemon
    ½ cup Madeira wine
    1 tbs. butter
    1½ tsp. flour

Season fish and lard with the bacon strips and, for added delicacy, thin strips of truffle. Arrange in buttered shallow baking dish, cover with sheet of greased paper, and bake in moderate oven, basting frequently. When half done, sprinkle with lemon juice, add wine, and continue baking until slightly brown. Thicken sauce with butter and flour stirred to a paste and thoroughly blended in. Garnish with sprigs of parsley and slices of lemon. Allow a half-pound per serving.

FISH SOUFFLÉ
(Soufflé z Ryb)
    2 lbs. boned fish
    1 tbs. butter
    dash of pepper
    dash of nutmeg
    salt to taste
    6 egg whites, beaten stiff
    4-6 tbs. grated Parmesan

Chop fish fine or put through meat grinder. Add creamed butter and seasoning, combine with beaten egg whites, and continue beating until thoroughly mixed and stiff. Pour into well-greased baking dish, leaving mixture in a mound rather than spreading evenly. Sprinkle thickly with grated Parmesan and bake in medium-hot oven for 25 minutes. Test with straw for doneness. Serve with melted brown butter or Anchovy Sauce (see Index).
    Serves 7 to 8.
    (A good way to utilize leftover egg whites.)

CRAYFISH POLISH-STYLE
(Raki po Polsku w Śmietanie)
    30 large crayfish
    1 tbs. butter
    salt to taste
    2 cups sour cream
    1 heaping tbs. bread crumbs
    1 heaping tbs. chopped fresh dill

Scrub the crayfish thoroughly and throw into boiling unsalted water for a minute or two. Drain and rinse. Put into saucepan with melted butter and simmer for 10 minutes, until crayfish turn red. Salt lightly, add sour cream, bread crumbs, and dill. Simmer, tightly covered, for another 15 minutes. (Overcooking kills the taste.) Serve at once.
    Serves 5 to 6.

RAGOUT OF FROG LEGS
(Żabki w Potrawce)
    16 pairs frog legs
    flour for dusting
    3 tbs. butter
    4 med. mushrooms, sliced thin
    ¼ lb. sweetbreads
    ½ cup white wine

¼ cup bouillon
salt and pepper to taste
3 egg yolks, lightly beaten
lemon slices

Wash, dry, and salt the frog legs. Dust with flour and fry in half the butter to a light, golden brown. Arrange tightly in saucepan, add sliced mushrooms, the sweetbreads cut in small pieces, the rest of the butter, the wine, and bouillon. Season to taste and simmer, tightly covered, for 30 minutes. Arrange frog legs on a hot platter. Combine pan liquid with egg yolks, stirring in a little at a time and taking care not to curdle. Pour this sauce over the frog legs and garnish with lemon slices.

Serves 4.

SOLE IN WHITE WINE
(Sola na Białem Winie)
1 tbs. butter
1 cup strong vegetable broth
1 cup dry white wine
4-5 mushrooms, sliced
salt and pepper to taste
¼ tsp. tarragon (optional)
2 lbs. sole (or flounder)
2 tsp. butter
1½ tsp. flour } for thickening
2 egg yolks, lightly beaten

Combine 1 tbs. butter, broth, wine, mushrooms and seasonings in heavy saucepan. Add fish and simmer, tightly covered, for 20 to 30 minutes. Melt remaining butter without browning, stir in flour, and dilute with enough of the cooking liquid to blend thoroughly. Slowly add egg yolks, taking care not to curdle sauce. Add more broth, until sauce is the desired thickness. Pour over fish arranged on a hot platter.

Serves 6.

STUFFED SNAILS
(Ślimaki Nadziewane)
4 doz. snails
½ onion, minced
6 mushrooms, sliced
4 tbs. butter
1 white roll, moistened with milk
2 eggs
salt and pepper to taste

dash of fresh-ground nutmeg
2 tbs. bread crumbs
clove of garlic (optional)

Rinse snails in several waters. Then put into enough hot salted water to cover, and bring to a boil. When snails come out of their shells, drain; rinse shells again and let dry. Combine snails, onion, and mushrooms with 1 tbs. butter and simmer, tightly covered, for half an hour. Add roll and chop fine. Combine with slightly-beaten eggs, another tablespoon of butter, and seasoning. Mix thoroughly and fill snail shells with the mixture. Arrange in shallow baking dish, and over each shell pour melted butter and bread crumbs which may be flavored with garlic. Put into hot oven or under broiler for 10 minutes to allow to brown.

Serves 4 to 6.

POULTRY

CAPON OR CHICKEN IN CREAM
(Kapłon lub Kura z Kremem z Pieca)
capon (5-6 lbs.)
court bouillon to cover (see Index)
4 egg yolks
1 heaping tbs. butter
1 tbs. flour
2 cups sour cream
salt and pepper to taste
½-1 cup very strong bouillon

Rub bird with salt an hour beforehand. Simmer for an hour in court bouillon, taking care not to overcook. Allow to cool. In the meantime, cream egg yolks and butter, add flour, blend thoroughly, and combine with sour cream. Season lightly and whip until stiff. Allow to thicken in top of a double boiler, stirring constantly to keep from curdling or sticking (handle like Hollandaise Sauce). Cool. Make incisions in capon as for carving, without cutting through. Fill these with cream, and then spread rest over the whole surface of the bird. Roast in shallow baking pan in very hot oven for 20 minutes, allowing cream to brown. When done, pour hot bouillon over it. Serve with Potato Croquettes and cauliflower, or with salad.

Serves 6 to 7.

POULTRY LIVERS SMOTHERED IN MADEIRA
(Watróbki z Drobiu Duszone w Maderze)

    ½ lb. chicken, turkey, or goose livers
    milk for soaking
    2 tbs. butter
    1 small or ½ med. onion, minced
    salt and pepper to taste
    flour for dredging
    ¼ cup bouillon
    ¼ cup Madeira (or sherry or Marsala)

Soak livers in milk for several hours. Drain, and cut large ones in half. Cook onion in butter until transparent, increase heat, and add livers. Brown quickly on both sides. Season, dredge with flour, and when this too browns, reduce heat. Add bouillon and wine and allow to boil up a couple of times. (Livers should never cook longer than 6 to 8 minutes and should be faintly pink inside; otherwise they will be tough.)

Serves 2 to 3.

ROAST CAPON OR CHICKEN WITH ANCHOVIES
(Kapłon lub Pularda Pieczone z Sardelami)

    capon or chicken (5-6 lbs.)
    salt and pepper
    butter for roasting

Soak bird for a couple of hours in cold water if possible. Wipe, rub well with salt inside and out, and allow to stand an hour.

    stuffing
      ¼ lb. bacon
      1 lb. veal
      chicken liver
      1-2 tbs. butter
      1 med. onion, minced
      6 peppercorns
      6 allspice
      few sprigs parsley
      1 hard roll, moistened with milk and mashed (or equivalent amount of bread crumbs)
      8-10 anchovies
      3 eggs, separated
      ½ tsp. lemon rind
      dash of grated ginger
      salt and pepper to taste

Combine bacon, veal cut in pieces, and liver with onion and spices. Smother in butter, tightly covered, for about half an hour or until tender, taking care that mixture does not brown or stick. (It is best to add liver only during the last 10 minutes.) Then put mixture through meat grinder, along with the roll. Chop anchovies very fine, cream with egg yolks, add lemon rind, ginger, and salt and pepper to taste. Combine with meat mixture. Beat egg whites stiff and fold in last. Stuff bird and roast as directed, first in slow, then hot oven, for 1½ to 2 hours.

Serves 6.

DUCK BRAISED IN RED WINE
(Kaczka Duszona na Czerwonym Winie)

    1 duckling (about 5 lbs.)
    salt
    garlic (optional)
    2 tbs. butter
    2 tsp. flour
    1 cup dry red wine
    lemon juice to taste
    1 tsp. lemon rind
    pinch of sugar

Rub duck with salt and garlic 2 hours before cooking. Brown duck quickly in very hot butter. Separately, brown the flour lightly in a dry pan, stirring to prevent sticking or burning. Remove from heat and add wine, a little at a time, stirring constantly to prevent lumps. Add to duck, cover tightly, and braise over low heat about 1½ hours, or until thoroughly tender. At the end of the first hour add lemon juice and rind and a pinch of sugar. Continue braising. Serve with beet purée or with red cabbage.

Serves 5.

BEEF

STEAMED BEEF
(Sztuka Mięsa w Parze)

    3-4 lbs. rump or eye of round
    salt and pepper to taste
    1-2 onions, sliced and blanched
    ½ cup each diced carrot, celery root, parsley root, parsnip, green peas
    2-3 celery stalks

½ cup asparagus stems (optional)
cauliflower core (optional)
1 tbs. butter

Pound the meat to tenderize, and salt a half-hour before cooking. Place in top of double boiler, cover with onions and vegetables, add butter, and steam over briskly-boiling water, tightly covered, for at least 3 hours. Test with fork for doneness. Vegetables may be varied according to what is available, and proportions need not be exact. Lower stems of asparagus may be utilized when tips are to be served as a vegetable; broccoli stems, cauliflower parings, etc., may be similarly used. Serve meat thinly sliced, together with the vegetables which have steamed with it. Serve with parsley potatoes and the juice in which meat has steamed.

Serves 6 to 8.

MOCK VENISON POT ROAST
(Pieczeń Wolowa na Dziko)
   3 lbs. rump, round, or eye of round
   marinade to cover
      1 qt. water
      1½ to 2 cups wine vinegar
      1 carrot
      ½ parsley root
      ½ celery root
      1 onion
      20 peppercorns
      10 juniper berries
      1 bay leaf
      dash of thyme or marjoram
      salt to taste

Slice vegetables, add spices, and cook in water and vinegar for 30 minutes. Season. Allow to cool. Add meat and let stand at least 24 hours, turning occasionally. If a more seasoned taste is preferred, meat may marinate under refrigeration for as long as eight days.

When ready to use, wipe meat dry and salt a half-hour before cooking.

   to pot-roast:
      2-3 tbs. butter
      1 large or 2 small onions, diced
      3-4 dried mushrooms
      ½ celery root, diced

½ parsley root, diced
few sprigs parsley
dash of thyme and marjoram (optional)
1 cup sour cream
1½ tsp. flour

Brown meat on all sides in hot butter, using heavy skillet. Transfer to casserole. Add onions, vegetables, butter in which meat browned, spices, and seasoning. Simmer tightly covered, basting occasionally with cold water. When tender—after about 2 hours—add sour cream blended with flour and simmer another 30 minutes. Slice thin, strain the sauce, and serve with pan-fried potatoes, buttered noodles or spaghetti.

Serves 6.

SMOTHERED ROAST BEEF
(Roastbeef Duszony)
   3-4 lbs. rib roast, boned
   2 tbs. butter
   ½ cup soup stock or prepared bouillon (scant)
   ¼ cup Madeira or ½ cup red wine
   salt and pepper to taste
   pinch of marjoram (optional)
   1 tbs. flour

Sear the meat on all sides in hot butter and transfer to casserole. Add soup stock, wine, and seasoning, and simmer, tightly covered, for at least 2 hours or until tender. Dust with flour and baste, allowing a few minutes for the flour to cook and sauce to thicken. Slice thin and serve with potatoes and vegetables.

Serves 6 to 8.

ROAST DONE ON A SPIT
(Pieczeń z Rożna)
   3-4 lbs. sirloin roast
   2-3 tbs. olive oil
   juice ½ lemon
   3-4 onions, sliced
   salt and pepper to taste
   melted butter for basting
   1 tbs. flour

Rub meat with olive oil, sprinkle with lemon juice, and cover top and bottom with onion slices. Let stand 3 hours. An hour before cooking season the meat. Preheat rotisserie and cook on spit at very high temperature, brushing frequently with melted butter. (Be sure to catch all the dripping in a gravy pan.) When meat is well browned, dust with flour, allow to dry out, and again brush with butter. The roast should be ready in not less than 35 or 40 minutes, not more than 40 or 50 minutes, depending on size and how well done one prefers it. Slice thin and serve with potatoes or vegetables. Thicken sauce with flour if desired, or serve plain.

Serves 6 to 8.

ROLLED BEEF WITH ANCHOVIES
(Pieczeń Wołowa z Sardelami)

    3 lbs. top or bottom round, cut in a long thin slice and pounded thin
    4 large anchovies, soaked and boned, or 8 anchovy fillets
    1 egg
    2 heaping tbs. sour cream
    1 white roll or ½ cup bread crumbs, moistened in milk
    salt and pepper to taste
    ½ lb. fat pork meat, ground twice
    butter for frying
    1 med. onion, chopped
    1 tbs. flour
    1 cup soup stock or prepared bouillon

Chop anchovies fine and combine with egg, sour cream, roll or bread crumbs, and seasoning. Then mix thoroughly with ground pork. Spread meat with this stuffing, roll tightly, and secure with string. Brown on all sides in very hot butter. Transfer to casserole, add onion and the butter in which meat has browned. Simmer, tightly covered, occasionally sprinkling with cold water, until tender (about 1½ hours). Dust with flour and add soup stock. Allow to simmer another 15 minutes.

Serves 8.

TENDERLOIN À LA KREJCIK
(Polędwica)

    3-lb. tenderloin
    salt and pepper to taste
    2 tbs. French mustard
    ½ stick of butter
    1 lb. roast veal or pork

    6 mushrooms, coarsely chopped
    1 small onion, chopped
    2 small or 1 med. head savoy cabbage
    1 tbs. chopped fresh parsley
    1 egg
    6 slices bacon

Rub meat with salt, pepper, and mustard and return to refrigerator for 2 hours. Brown in very hot butter, and allow to cool. In the meantime, chop roast fine or put through meat grinder. Sauté mushrooms and onion in butter; reserve outside leaves of the savoy cabbage and shred the centers. Combine roast meat, mushrooms, onions, and chopped cabbage, add chopped parsley and whole raw egg, season, and mix thoroughly. Spread mixture over the meat, wrap in cabbage leaves, and cover with bacon slices. Secure with cotton string. Add any remaining butter drippings and bake in hot oven for 30 to 35 minutes. Remove string, slice with very sharp knife, and serve with its own juice.

Serves 8.

BEEF SLICES PEASANT-STYLE
(Rozbratle po Chłopsku)

    2¼ lbs. rib steak, boned and cut into 6 slices
    1 cup ham, coarsely chopped
    2 cups raw potatoes, diced or sliced thin
    1 tbs. butter
    1 med. onion, coarsely chopped
    1 carrot
    1 parsley root
    1 celery root
    1 leek
    1 parsnip
    few sprigs parsley
    10 peppercorns
    1 bay leaf (optional)
    10 allspice
    salt to taste
    1 cup beef stock for basting
    3-4 tbs. sour cream
    1 tsp. flour

Pound the meat until very thin. Combine raw potatoes and ham, season to taste, and spread over meat slices. Roll up meat slices and secure each with cotton thread, tying tight. Brown the butter and onion in a heavy casserole. Brown the meat on all sides and push aside. Arrange the vegetables, which have been thinly sliced, in bottom of casserole. Arrange the meat on top, and add the spices, which are best tied in a piece of cheesecloth so that they can be easily discarded. Season, and simmer tightly covered for 2 hours, basting occasionally with beef stock. When meat is done, remove the thread. Discard the spices. Press the vegetables through a sieve, thicken sauce with sour cream and flour, and return the meat to casserole. Simmer 10 minutes more. Serve with noodles.

Serves 6.

BIGOS FROM LEFTOVER ROAST
(Bigos z Pieczeni)

    2 cups diced leftover meat—beef, veal, pork, lamb, or a combination
    2 lbs. sauerkraut
    3-4 dried mushrooms
    liquid in which mushrooms cooked
    1 onion, minced
    4 ozs. salt pork or bacon, diced
    1 tbs. flour (less if desired)
    1 tsp. Maggi sauce
    salt, pepper, and dash of sugar to taste
    ¼ cup Madeira (optional)

Cook the mushrooms until soft, cut into strips, and combine with sauerkraut and liquid in which the mushrooms cooked. Render the diced salt pork or bacon, add onion, and cook until transparent. Add flour and blend until smooth. Combine with sauerkraut, season, and simmer about 45 minutes longer. Dice the meat and add to the kraut. Meat and sauerkraut should simmer together, tightly covered, for 30 minutes.

Serves 4 to 5.

BEEF BIRDS RADECKI
(Zrazy Zawijane à la Radecki)

    2 lbs. tenderloin or sirloin
    ½ lb. mushrooms
    2 large onions
    2 tbs. butter
    2 tbs. chopped dill
    2 tbs. bread crumbs
    salt and pepper to taste
    butter for frying

    1 scant tbs. flour
    1 cup soup stock or bouillon
    ½ cup Madeira or 1 cup red wine

Slice meat thin and flatten further by pounding. If sirloin is used, cut pieces about 4 inches square. Season and spread with the following stuffing: Chop fine about two-thirds of the mushrooms and the onions and brown lightly in butter. Add chopped dill and bread crumbs, season, and mix thoroughly. After spreading each piece of meat with a little of the stuffing, roll tightly and tie securely with cotton thread, which should be removed before serving. Brown the birds in hot butter, searing quickly on all sides. Arrange tightly in casserole, add the butter in which they browned, and dust with flour. Slice and add the remaining mushrooms, the soup stock, and wine, and simmer slowly until soft, 45 minutes to 1 hour, depending on cut of meat.

Serves 6 to 7.

BEEF TONGUE À LA POLONAISE, IN GRAY SAUCE
(Ozór po Polsku w Szarym Sosie)

    1 beef tongue, about 3 lbs.
    1 large carrot
    2 med. onions
    3 stalks celery with leaves
    10 peppercorns
    1 bay leaf (optional)
    few sprigs parsley
    salt to taste (about 1 tsp.)

The recipe is for a fresh tongue, but corned or smoked tongue may be substituted. The basic recipe remains the same, with slight variations. A corned tongue should be soaked in cold water for about 2 hours before cooking. Average cooking time for a fresh tongue is about 3 hours; a smoked tongue may need from 2 to 4 hours, depending on how tender the meat is.

Place tongue in an open kettle together with vegetables and spices. Add just enough boiling water to cover. Simmer until tender, allow to cool enough in the water to handle and skin. Reserve the liquid for soup and/or sauce. Slice the tongue and serve with Gray Sauce (see Index).

Serves 6 to 7.

Serve with potatoes or spaghetti.

OXTAIL RAGOUT
(Potrawa z Ogona)

  2 oxtails
  3 tbs. butter
  2 med. onions, sliced
  2 carrots, sliced
  1 celery root, diced
  1 parsnip, diced
  3 stalks celery, cut in pieces
  1 leek
  few sprigs parsley
  2-3 dried mushrooms
  salt and pepper to taste
  1 bay leaf (optional)
  water or beef bouillon merely to cover (about 3 cups)
  1 tsp. Maggi sauce
  lemon juice to taste

Wash oxtails, dip in boiling water, and cut at each joint to separate into pieces. Brown quickly in very hot butter, add vegetables, and cover with water or soup stock. Season, and simmer, tightly covered, until thoroughly done (about 3 hours). Remove meat, discard bay leaf, and purée vegetables by mashing or putting through sieve. Return to liquid in which they cooked, add the Maggi sauce and lemon juice to taste, stir thoroughly, and pour over meat.

Serves 6.

VEAL

VEAL ROASTED IN OVEN
(Pieczeń Cielęca z Pieca)

  leg or shoulder of veal (4-5 lbs.)
  salt and pepper
  juice ½ lemon
  2 tbs. butter
  flour for dusting

Dip meat in boiling water for a minute or two. This will make it more tender and also seal the juices inside. Wipe dry, rub with salt, and sprinkle with lemon juice. Let stand for 2 hours. Place in shallow roasting pan, preferably on a rack. Rub with butter, and roast in hot oven (at least 400°), basting frequently, until skin begins to crisp and brown. Reduce heat to 300° and continue roasting for 2 to 2½ hours, still basting. When nearly done, dust with flour and baste again.

Serves 8 to 10.

ROAST STUFFED LOIN OF VEAL
(Nerkówka Cielęca Nadiewana)

  4 lbs. loin of veal with or without kidney
  salt and pepper to taste
  2 tbs. butter

A stuffed roast will stretch the meat by several servings. Have butcher separate meat from bone underneath the ribs and prepare a pocket for stuffing. Season a half-hour before putting into oven, or before starting to prepare the stuffing.

  stuffing
  4 tbs. butter
  1 cup bread crumbs, moistened with milk
  2 eggs, separated
  1 tbs. chopped fresh parsley
  1 tbs. chopped fresh dill
  salt and pepper to taste
  dash of nutmeg (optional)

Cream butter, combine with bread crumbs and lightly-beaten egg yolks, add the chopped herbs, and season to taste. If fresh dill is unavailable, substitute more parsley. Beat egg whites until stiff and fold in. Fill meat pocket with stuffing, and secure with toothpicks or sew with white cotton thread. Rub meat with butter and roast in open pan, starting at 400° and reducing heat to 300° when meat begins to brown. Baste frequently with pan drippings, alternating with cold water. Cook about 1½ hours.

Serves 8 to 10.

FRICANDEAU OF VEAL
(Fricandeau z Cielęciny)

  4 lbs. rump or shoulder veal, boned
  ¼ lb. salt pork for larding
  juice ½ lemon
  salt and pepper to taste
  1 celery root
  2 carrots
  1 parsley root
  1 kohlrabi or parsnip
  2 stalks celery with leaves

½ cup snap beans
¼ to ½ cup peas
1 onion (optional)
1 tbs. butter
1 cup soup stock or commercial bouillon
flour for dusting
few sprigs fresh parsley

Lard meat with the salt pork, sprinkle with lemon juice, season, roll tight, and secure with cotton string. Dice vegetables. Arrange meat in a heavy casserole and cover with vegetables. Add butter and simmer, tightly covered, basting frequently with bouillon, until meat is nicely brown and vegetables soft. Dust lightly with flour and continue basting until sauce thickens. Slice thin and serve with the vegetables.

Serves 8.

CALF'S LIVER SMOTHERED IN SOUR CREAM
(Watróblka Duszona ze Śmietana)

1 whole liver
milk or buttermilk to cover
4 ozs. salt pork for larding
salt and pepper to taste
2-3 tbs. butter
1 small or ½ med. onion, chopped
3-4 tbs. cold bouillon or water
1 cup sour cream
1 tsp. flour

Soak liver in milk or buttermilk for 3 to 4 hours. Wipe, lard with thin strips of salt pork, and season just before putting into skillet. Brown quickly on both sides in hot butter, adding the onion and taking care not to scorch either meat or onion. Reduce heat. cover, and simmer for 15 minutes, basting with cold water or bouillon. Blend sour cream and flour and add to meat. Allow to bubble up. Slice liver and serve on hot platter, covered with the sauce. The cooking process should not take more than 30 minutes. Serve with potatoes.

Serves 6.

Note: Sliced liver may be prepared the same way, but the over-all cooking time should be no more than 10 to 15 minutes; otherwise the meat will be dry. Larding may be omitted. Liver, like steak, should never be salted until the last minute, or meat will be tough.

FRIED CALF'S LIVER AU NATUREL
(Watróbka Smażona Naturalna)

2 lbs. calf's liver, sliced
milk or buttermilk to cover
salt and pepper to taste
flour for dredging
butter for frying

Soak liver slices in milk or buttermilk for 3 to 4 hours, remove membranes, season, dust with flour and fry at once in hot butter, browning quickly on both sides. Liver should be pink inside: cooking time should be 5 to 10 minutes, depending on thickness of slices.

Makes 6 servings.

FRIED SWEETBREADS
(Mleczko Cielęce Smażone)

2 pairs sweetbreads
milk to cover
court bouillon to cover (see Index)
salt and pepper to taste
flour for dusting
1 egg, lightly beaten
bread crumbs (about ½ cup)
3-4 tbs. butter or lard for frying
lemon slices

Soak sweetbreads in milk for 2 to 3 hours (water may be substituted). Drop into boiling court bouillon and parboil for 10 to 15 minutes. Allow to cool for convenient handling; then remove membranes and slice. Season with salt and pepper, dust with flour, dip in egg, roll in bread crumbs, and fry in hot fat to a golden brown, taking care to brown evenly on all sides. Decorate each slice with sliver of lemon, and serve with green peas, spinach, or cauliflower.

Serves 4.

BRAISED SWEETBREADS
(Mleczko Cielęce w Potrawie)

2 pairs sweetbreads
bouillon to cover
White Lemon Sauce (see Index)

Dip sweetbreads in boiling water for 2 to 3 minutes. Remove membranes, and simmer in just enough strong bouillon to cover for about 20 minutes. Drain, reserving bouillon. Make a White Lemon

Sauce, using the bouillon in which meat has cooked. Garnish with Veal Croquettes, whole broiled mushrooms, and croutons.

Serves 4.

SMOTHERED VEAL KIDNEYS
(Cynaderki Duszone)

- **2 veal kidneys with most of the fat removed**
- **flour for dredging**
- **salt and pepper to taste**
- **2-3 tbs. butter**
- **½ cup bouillon**
- **¼ cup sour cream**
- **¼ tsp. paprika**
- **½ tsp. marjoram**
- **lemon juice to taste**

Slice the kidney diagonally, season, and dust with flour. Brown quickly on both sides in hot butter. Using the butter in which kidneys browned, make a sauce as follows: Add ½ tbs. flour to the butter and stir to a paste. Blend in bouillon, and add sour cream, paprika, and marjoram. Season with lemon juice, salt, and pepper. Return kidneys to sauce, cover tightly, and allow to simmer for about 10 minutes.

Serves 3.

VEAL CUTLET ZINGARA
(Kotlety Cielęce à la Zingara)

- **6 loin veal chops about ¾″ thick**
- **piece of salt pork**
- **6 slices boiled ham, the same size as chops and about ¼″ thick**
- **2-3 tbs. butter**
- **1 med. onion**
- **1 carrot**
- **1 parsley root**
- **½ celery root**
- **1-2 stalks celery**
- **¼ cup snap beans**
- **1 cup strong bouillon**
- **1 cup dry white wine**
- **salt and pepper to taste**

Bone the chops and pound lightly. Season and lard heavily with strips of salt pork and ham (use scraps of ham cut from edges). Brown the meat lightly in hot butter. Dice vegetables and onion and braise in the butter until half done. Arrange veal and ham

slices alternately in a heavy casserole and cover with vegetables, using all the butter in the pan. Add bouillon and wine and cover tightly. Place the casserole in another, larger dish half-filled with boiling water, and simmer for half an hour. Purée the vegetables, return to sauce, and boil up once.

Serves 6 generously.

LAMB

BRAISED LAMB WITH GARLIC
(Pieczeń Duszona z Czosnkiem)

- **4-lb. piece leg of lamb**
- **salt and pepper**
- **1 clove garlic, mashed**
- **2 tbs. butter**
- **10 peppercorns**
- **10 juniper berries**
- **pinch of thyme**
- **½ med. onion**
- **flour for dredging**
- **1 cup soup stock or bouillon**

Rub meat with salt and garlic and let stand an hour. Sear in butter, and when brown on all sides, add spices and onion. Simmer, tightly covered, for about 2 hours, sprinkling frequently with cold water. When nearly done dredge with flour, baste with soup stock, and allow gravy to thicken. Slice thin. Strain gravy.

Serves 6.

BRAISED LAMB WITH TOMATOES
(Potrawka Barania z Pomidorami)

- **3-4 lbs. lean breast or shoulder lamb, boned**
- **1 clove garlic (optional)**
- **2 tbs. butter**
- **soup stock as needed, no more than 1 cup**
- **salt and pepper to taste**
- **12 shallots**
- **2-3 tomatoes or 2 tbs. tomato purée**
- **10 peppercorns**
- **1 bay leaf (optional)**
- **10 juniper berries**
- **dash of allspice**
- **1 cup red wine**
- **1 tbs. flour**

½ tsp. each of Maggi and Soy sauce
sugar to taste

Sear meat in butter with or without garlic. Add a couple of tablespoons of soup stock and simmer, tightly covered, until meat is nicely brown and half done. Cut into serving pieces, return to pot, add peeled shallots, the tomatoes or tomato paste, spices, and red wine. Continue simmering until thoroughly done. Dredge with flour, add more soup stock, and allow another 15 minutes so that sauce will thicken. Add Maggi and Soy sauce and a dash of sugar. Let bubble up and serve with potatoes. Total cooking time should not be more than 2 hours.

Serves 6 to 8.

ROAST LAMB MUSCOVITE
(Pieczeń Barania à la Moscovite)

leg of lamb (4-lb. piece or whole small leg)
2 tbs. butter
salt and pepper to taste
3 onions, diced
3 carrots, diced
2 stalks celery
1 celery root
1 tsp. Maggi extract
4 cups marinade, made with
    2 cups water
    2 cups vinegar
    1 onion
    1 bay leaf
    10 peppercorns
    6 cloves
    1 stalk celery with leaves

Remove excess fat from meat, pound well, and blanch with boiling marinade. Reserve marinade. Wipe off meat, rub well with salt, and sear in hot butter. Roast in hot oven, basting frequently with pan drippings. Cook the vegetables in marinade, allowing liquid to simmer down so that there will be no more than 2 cups of sauce. When vegetables are thoroughly done (about ½ hour), add Maggi extract and pour everything over meat. Reduce heat to 300° and continue basting. Meat should be pink inside when ready to serve. Put vegetables through sieve and add to pan drippings. Slice meat, arrange back on the bone, and pour sauce over it.

FRICASSEE OF LAMB
(Fricassée z Baraniny)

3-4 lbs. lean shoulder or breast of lamb, boned
boiling water
salt and pepper to taste
1 clove garlic, mashed
2 tbs. butter
½ med. onion, minced
1 heaping tbs. chopped fresh parsley
6 med. mushrooms, sliced
3 anchovies, chopped
1 tsp. grated lemon rind
lemon juice to taste
2 cups soup stock
2 tsp. butter
2 tsp. flour
1 tsp. Worcestershire sauce

Blanch meat, cut into serving pieces, and rub with salt and garlic. Season with pepper. Sear in hot butter. When all the meat is brown, add onion, parsley, and other ingredients, and about ½ cup soup stock. Simmer, tightly covered, until tender (about 1½ to 2 hours), adding stock as needed. When meat is done, cream butter and flour, add to meat, and allow to melt. Add Worcestershire sauce, boil up once.

Serves 6 to 8.

PORK

ROAST FRESH HAM
(Pieczeń Wieprzowa z Szynki)

1 whole fresh ham (7-8 lbs.)
light marinade to half-cover
½ stick butter
caraway seeds (optional)
salt and pepper to taste
1 large onion, sliced

Make a marinade of water, wine vinegar, onion, bay leaf, spices to taste, taking care not to have it too sour (⅓ vinegar to ⅔ water, at most), and bring it to a boil. Pour the boiling liquid over meat and let stand for 24 hours, turning occasionally. Wipe meat dry. Rub well with salt, sprinkle with pepper and caraway seed, and roast in 500° oven, basting first with butter. When meat fat begins to melt, baste with the pan drippings. Once meat begins to brown on top, add onion, reduce heat to 300°, and continue to roast until thoroughly done, basting occasionally. Allow 25 to 30 minutes per pound or use an oven thermometer. Serve with red cabbage, beets, or puréed split peas.

Serves 8 to 10.

Leftover meat may be served cold or used in a casserole dish.

Note: If time does not permit marinating for 24 hours, meat may be prepared in the morning for use the same night. Unmarinated meat will give good results, although it will be less tender. A smaller piece may be used for roasting if using a whole ham is not practical, but anything less than 3 to 4 pounds will produce a dry roast and would be better braised or pot-roasted.

PORK GOULASH
(Gulasz Wieprzowy)

1

> 2 lbs. fresh pork butt or shoulder, cut in pieces
> 4-6 med. onions, chopped
> 2 tsp. paprika
> salt and pepper
> flour for dusting
> 1½ cup soup stock
> 1-2 tbs. tomato purée
> 6 large or 12 small potatoes, peeled, cut, and parboiled

Use cheaper cuts of meat. Have butcher bone and cut meat into serving pieces. Combine in heavy casserole the meat, onions, seasoning, and paprika, and simmer, tightly covered, turning occasionally, until meat browns. Dust with flour, add soup stock, tomato purée, and the parboiled potatoes. Cover and continue to simmer until meat and potatoes are done, about 1 hour.

Serves 6.

2

Prepare the same as 1, but instead of potatoes, add the following:

> 2 lbs. sauerkraut
> ½ celery root, sliced
> ½ parsley root, sliced

This Goulash, known in Hungary as *Szèkély Gulyas*, is especially good with beer.

PORK POT ROAST
(Pieczeń Wieprzowa Duszona)

> 3-4 lbs. fresh ham or boned loin
> salt and pepper
> 1 tbs. butter
> 1 med. onion
> 1 carrot
> ½ celery root
> ½ parsley root
> 1-2 stalks celery
> few sprigs parsley
> 2 fresh tomatoes or 2 tbs. tomato paste (optional)
> spices to taste: peppercorns, allspice, pinch of marjoram, caraway seed
> flour for dusting
> ½ cup bouillon
> ½ tsp. Maggi extract

Pound meat and rub well with salt an hour before using. Sear in hot butter in the pan in which it will cook (preferably heavy cast-aluminum or cast-iron). Add diced vegetables and onion, spices, and seasoning to taste, and simmer, tightly covered, until brown and tender. Do not add water. Allow about 30 minutes per pound. When done, dust with flour, baste with a little bouillon, add Maggi extract, and allow sauce to thicken. Slice thin, strain sauce, and pour over meat.

Serves 6 to 8.

SMOTHERED PORK CHOPS
(Kotlety Wieprzowe Duszone)

> 6 loin chops
> juice ½ lemon
> salt and pepper to taste
> 2 tsp. caraway seed
> ¼ cup soup stock
> flour for dusting
> ½ cup white wine (optional)
> 1 tbs. butter

Sprinkle chops with lemon juice and let stand 2 hours. Season, sprinkle with caraway seed, and simmer with soup stock, tightly covered, until fat on the meat has melted and most of the stock is gone. Remove cover and brown lightly on both sides. Dust with flour, cover again, and continue cooking until tender, about 45 minutes in all. Add butter after taking pot off the heat and let stand, covered, until butter melts. For a more subtle flavor, add white wine to sauce after browning chops.

Serves 6.

SPARERIBS AND CABBAGE
(Boczek Duszony z Kapustą)

    3 lbs. spareribs
    2 small heads cabbage or savoy cabbage
    1 onion, diced
    1 carrot, diced
    ¼ celery root, diced
    1 parsley root, diced
    salt and pepper to taste
    1 tbs. butter
    2 tsp. flour
    ½ bouillon cube (optional)

Start meat in enough cold water to cover. When water begins to simmer, remove scum. Simmer, uncovered, for a half-hour. Cut cabbage into quarters and parboil in salted water. Drain, add to meat, and add diced onion and vegetables. Season to taste and continue simmering, tightly covered, until meat is tender—about 1 hour. Discard vegetables. Melt butter, blend in flour, and dilute with a little of the stock in which meat has cooked. If stock has not cooked down enough and seems too thin, enrich with bouillon cube. Pour over meat and cabbage and simmer another half-hour. Serves 4 to 5.

SAUSAGE IN POLISH SAUCE
(Kiełbasa w Polskim Sosie)

    1 Polish sausage ring (about 1½ lbs.)
    2 cups beer
    2 cups water
    2 onions, sliced
    1 tbs. butter
    1 tbs. flour
    ½ tsp. Maggi extract
    2 tbs. vinegar
    1 tsp. to 1 tbs. sugar (according to taste)

Simmer sausage and onion in combined water and beer for 20 minutes. Brown the butter and blend in flour, then slowly add 1 cup of liquid strained from the meat. Stir until thoroughly blended. If sauce is too thick, add more liquid. Add Maggi extract, vine-

gar, and sugar to taste (brown sugar may be substituted). Slice the sausage, pour the sauce over it, and serve with boiled potatoes.

Serves 4.

SAUSAGE SMOTHERED IN RED CABBAGE
(Kiełbaski Duszone w Czerwonej Kapuście)

    1 sausage ring or 6 frankfurters or knockwurst
    1 small head red cabbage
    vinegar or lemon juice
    1 tbs. butter
    1½ tsp. flour
    1 cup red wine (or strong broth)
    salt and pepper
    1½ tsp. Maggi extract
    sugar and lemon juice to taste

Shred cabbage, blanch, and sprinkle with lemon juice or vinegar to restore color. Brown the butter, blend in flour, and slowly add the wine, stirring until smooth. Add cabbage, season with salt, pepper, Maggi extract, sugar and lemon juice to taste, and simmer tightly covered for about half an hour. When nearly done add the sausage, cover, and continue simmering for another 15 minutes.

Serves 4.

(Meat may be added in greater proportion to cabbage, if desired.)

FRIED SAUSAGE
(Kiełbasa Smażona)

    1 Polish sausage ring (about 1½ lbs.)
    1-2 tbs. butter or bacon fat
    1 onion, minced

Perforate the sausage casing with a pin to prevent its bursting in cooking. Half-cover with water, bring to a boil, and simmer, covered, for 20 minutes. Drain, allow to cool slightly, and fry slowly in butter or bacon fat until lightly brown on both sides. Add onion and continue frying until onion browns lightly. Slice the meat and serve with cooked cabbage or potatoes, using butter and onion as garnish.

Serves 4.

VENISON, GAME AND GAME BIRDS

VENISON CUTLETS
(Zrazy z Jelenia)

> **2 lbs. cutlets from loin or rump (no more than ½″ thick)**
> **3-4 ozs. salt pork for larding**
> **salt and pepper**
> **flour for dredging**
> **2-3 tbs. butter**
> **1 med. onion, chopped**
> **6 med. mushrooms, sliced**
> **1 cup dry red wine**
> **2 bay leaves**

Pound the cutlets, lard generously, season, and brown quickly on both sides in hot butter, adding the onion. Add mushrooms, wine, bay leaves, and simmer, tightly covered, for 1½ hours. Discard bay leaves.

Serves 5 to 6.

Note: Another way of preparing these is with sour cream, in which case substitute bouillon for wine and add ½ cup sour cream.

HARE OR RABBIT
(Zając z Naturalnym Sosem)

Hare is a gamier meat than rabbit and more of a delicacy. If it is to be prepared unmarinated, it should be well-seasoned as well as young. Have the butcher dress and clean the carcass, then cut off neck, shoulders, and front legs, all of which may be used for paté dishes (see Index). For roasting and stewing, the best meat is the lower two-thirds of the animal, behind the shoulders. Hare should be washed thoroughly in running water but never soaked. Remove membranes and tendons as much as possible.

> **2 hares**
> **6 ozs. salt pork for larding**
> **juice 1 lemon**
> **ground pepper, thyme, and juniper berries**
> **slices of onion, carrot, celery root, and parsley root (about 2 cups in all)**
> **salt to taste**
> **3 tbs. butter**
> **flour for dredging**

Prepare hares as directed above. Lard generously, sprinkle with lemon juice, rub with spices, and cover with sliced vegetables. Allow to refrigerate for several hours, overnight if possible. Season with salt a half-hour before roasting. Discard vegetables. Arrange meat in shallow baking dish; cover with dabs of butter. Roast in hot oven for 1 to 1½ hours, depending on size, basting frequently with pan drippings. When nearly done, dredge lightly with flour and baste again.

Serves 6 to 8.

Serve with a tart jelly or preserves and a salad.

ROAST PHEASANT
(Bażant Pieczony)

> **2 pheasants**
> **salt and pepper to taste**
> **6 ozs. salt pork for larding and covering**
> **3 tbs. butter**

Singe and wash pheasants. Wipe dry, and salt inside and out an hour before using. Lard breast and drumsticks generously. Use remaining salt pork or bacon in slices to cover bird while roasting. Baste frequently with butter. Roast in medium-hot oven for 1 to 1½ hours, depending on size. During the final 15 minutes, discard bacon slices and continue basting with pan drippings so that skin will be brown and crisp. Carve like chicken and serve with pan drippings, a salad, and tart jelly or preserves.

Serves 6.

Note: The traditional way to serve pheasant is to reassemble bird after it has been carved and decorate it with its own colorful feathers to simulate a live pheasant.

GAME PÂTÉ
(Pasztet z Dziczyny)

> **1½ lbs. shoulder of venison**
> **1 whole small hare or large rabbit**
> **2 onions**
> **2 carrots**
> **1 parsley root**
> **1 celery root**
> **1 bay leaf**
> **2-3 cloves**
> **10 peppercorns**

10 juniper berries
water and vinegar in equal parts for marinade
   (about 2 qts.)
2 tbs. olive oil
½ lb. salt pork or bacon
¼ lb. corned or pickled tongue
½ cup red wine
4 eggs, slightly beaten
salt and pepper
bacon slices for lining mold

Boil vegetables and spices in enough of the water and vinegar mixture to half-cover meat. Pour boiling mixture over the meat, add olive oil, and let stand in the marinade for 2 to 3 days, turning occasionally. Add half the salt pork and simmer, tightly covered, in the marinade until the meat is very tender and comes away from the bones (about 1½ hours). Let cool for easy handling. Then bone meat and put through meat grinder, together with the marinated salt pork. Press through a sieve, dice, and add the rest of the salt pork and the tongue, the wine, and the eggs. Season and mix thoroughly. Line a mold with bacon strips, pour in paté mixture, cover, and cook over steam or in a kettle of boiling water for a full 2 hours. Let cool before unmolding. Chill and cut into thin slices.

VEGETABLES

EGGPLANT À LA PROVENÇALE
(Bałtarzany à la Provençale)

6 small eggplants
6 small shallots or 1 small onion, chopped fine
olive oil
1 heaping tbs. bread crumbs for stuffing
bread crumbs for topping
1 heaping tsp. each chopped dill and parsley
salt and pepper to taste
2 egg yolks

Cut tops off eggplants and scoop out as much of the meat as possible without injuring skin. Parboil shells in salted water. Drain. Chop eggplant meat. Combine with shallots, bread crumbs, herbs, and olive oil, taking care not to make stuffing too greasy. Season and sauté until transparent and tender. Allow to cool, and then add egg yolks and mix thoroughly. Fill eggplants with stuffing, cover with their own tops, arrange tightly in a shallow baking dish, top with bread crumbs and olive oil, and bake in moderately hot oven for 30 minutes.
Serves 6.

GLAZED SHALLOTS
(Cebulka Glasowana)

1 lb. shallots (or very small white onions)
2 tbs. butter
2 level tbs. sugar
bouillon to cover (about 1 cup)
salt and pepper to taste

Blanch onions, and when cool enough to handle, peel and brown lightly in butter. In a shallow casserole melt the sugar and allow to brown. Add onions, bouillon, salt and pepper, and more sugar if necessary—for a sweet-salty taste. Simmer, tightly covered, until onions are tender, 25 to 30 minutes. There should be almost no liquid left. If too much liquid remains, remove cover and allow to simmer, open, until sauce has been reduced to consistency of honey.
Serves 4.

SWEET-SOUR SNAP BEANS
(Fasolka na Kwaśno)

1 lb. snap beans
juice ½ lemon or a few spoonfuls wine vinegar
sugar to taste
1 heaping tbs. butter

Steam beans 10 minutes in a little salted water. Drain. Combine all the ingredients and simmer 10 minutes more. Excellent served with fillet steak or with roast lamb.
Serves 3 to 4.

TURNIPS
(Brukiew)

Choose yellow, round turnips and peel like carrots. Dice and cook, covered, in salted water or in light broth. When half-done—after about 15 minutes—add a pinch of sugar. Make manié with 1 tbs. each of butter and flour, dissolve with liquid in which turnips have cooked, add to pot, and continue simmering until thoroughly done. Allow 2 pounds for 6 portions. Especially good with ham or lamb.

SMOTHERED PUMPKIN
(Dynia Duszona)

1

    2 lbs. pumpkin
    1 tbs. butter
    ½ tsp. sugar
    salt and pepper
    1 tbs. chopped herbs—fresh dill, parsley, chives, tarragon
    1 tsp. flour

Dice the parboiled pumpkin and simmer with butter and other ingredients, tightly covered, until tender. Use no water.

Serves 6.

2

Prepare as for 1. Simmer in 2 cups of milk blended with 1 tbs. flour, omitting herbs. When done, blend in 2 egg yolks, taking care not to let eggs curdle.

KOHLRABI
(Kalarepka)

    6-8 young kohlrabies, pared and diced or sliced thin
    salted water to cover
    sugar to taste
    1 tbs. butter
    2 tsp. flour

Simmer in salted water with a little sugar until tender (45 to 50 minutes). Thicken gravy with *manié* of butter mixed with flour.

Serves 6.

SNAP BEANS WITH SOUR CREAM
(Fasolka na Kwaśno ze Śmietana)

    2 lbs. snap beans
    1 cup court bouillon (see Index)
    1 tbs. butter
    1 cup sour cream
    1 tsp. flour
    lemon juice, salt, and pepper to taste

Blanch beans, season, then simmer in court bouillon until tender (about 10 minutes). Add other ingredients and simmer another 5 minutes.

Serves 6.

SMOTHERED GREEN PEAS
(Groszek Zielony Duszony)

    2 lbs. peas, shelled
    water to half-cover
    salt
    1 heaping tbs. butter
    ½ tsp. sugar
    1 tsp. flour
    2 tsp. chopped fresh dill (optional)

Simmer peas, tightly covered, with salt and butter for about 10 minutes. Add sugar, dust with flour, and continue simmering until tender—another 10 to 15 minutes. Add chopped dill, mix thoroughly, and serve.

Serves 6.

CAULIFLOWER ITALIAN-STYLE
(Kalafjory po Włosku)

    1 large cauliflower
    6-8 med. mushrooms
    butter
    grated Parmesan
    1-2 slices boiled ham or Canadian bacon, shredded
    ½ to 1 cup Tomato Sauce

Boil or steam cauliflower. Break into flowerets. Slice mushrooms and cook in butter until limp. Arrange cauliflower in shallow buttered baking dish; sprinkle generously with Parmesan, then with shredded ham and mushrooms. Cover with Tomato Sauce and bake in hot oven (450°) for about 15 minutes, or until brown on top.

Serves 4 to 5.

SWEET CABBAGE WITH CARAWAY SEED
(Kapusta na Słodko z Kminkiem)

    2 small heads white cabbage
    salted boiling water
    2-3 ozs. salt pork or bacon, minced
    1 med. onion, minced
    2-3 tsp. caraway seed
    3 tbs. bouillon
    salt and pepper to taste
    2 tsp. flour
    ½ tsp. Maggi extract or Kitchen Bouquet

Cut cabbage into small sections, core, and parboil in salted water for 10 minutes. Drain. Heat salt pork until transparent, add onion, and continue cooking until onion is lightly brown. Add cabbage, caraway, bouillon, and seasoning. Simmer, tightly covered, stirring occasionally, until soft—about 1 hour. Dust with flour and add Maggi extract, stir, and let simmer another 5 minutes.

Serves 6 to 7.

POTATOES STUFFED WITH MUSHROOMS
(Kartofle Nadziewane Grzybami)

1

6 baked Idaho potatoes
stuffing
2-3 tbs. cooked dried mushrooms, chopped fine
1 small or ½ med. onion, minced
1 tbs. butter
2 whole eggs, lightly beaten
1 tsp. each of chopped fresh dill and parsley
2-3 tbs. of the mushroom cooking liquid
sauce
1 cup Mushroom Sauce (see Index) or 1 cup sour cream thickened with 1 tsp. flour
grated Parmesan
bread crumbs and melted butter for topping

Bake potatoes until skins are crisp (45 to 60 minutes). Cut each lengthwise in half or cut off a thin top layer to use later as a cover. Scoop out centers and mash. Brown onion lightly in butter, combine with chopped mushrooms, mashed potato, eggs, herbs, mushroom liquid, and seasoning, and refill the shells. Cover with their own tops, arrange in shallow baking dish, and pour Mushroom Sauce or sour cream over them. Sprinkle with grated Parmesan and melted butter, and dot generously with bread crumbs. Bake in hot oven for 5 to 10 minutes.

Serves 6.

An excellent Lenten dish.

2

May also be prepared with the addition of 2 tbs. sour cream to the stuffing. Omit Parmesan and Mushroom Sauce. Top only with melted butter and bread crumbs. Bake 5 minutes.

STUFFED SAVOY CABBAGE
(Kapusta Włoska Faszerowana)

2 small heads savoy cabbage, quartered
salted boiling water
1 med. onion, minced
1 tbs. butter
1 lb. ground meat (pork or lamb)
1 white roll, moistened in milk and mashed
salt, pepper, and a dash of nutmeg
2 whole eggs, lightly beaten
bacon strips for lining casserole

Parboil cabbage for 5 minutes in salted boiling water. Drain, and when cool enough to handle, spread the leaves with stuffing made as follows: Brown onion lightly in butter. Mix thoroughly with meat, roll, seasoning, and eggs. After spreading the leaves, roll up and secure each roll with cotton thread. Then arrange tightly in a casserole lined with bacon strips. Add ½ cup water and simmer, tightly covered, until almost dry. Bake, still covered, in a 375° oven for 1½ hours, so that cabbage looks baked and brown.

Sauce:

To pan drippings, add:

1 tbs. butter
1½ tsp. flour
1 tsp. Maggi extract or Kitchen Bouquet
water or bouillon to taste (½ to 1 cup)

Place cabbage in sauce and simmer another 10 minutes.

Serves 8.

POTATOES SMOTHERED IN SOUR CREAM
(Kartofle Duszone ze Śmietana)

2 lbs. potatoes, peeled and sliced
2 med. onions, chopped
1 tbs. butter
½ cup sour cream
1 heaping tbs. chopped dill
salt and pepper to taste

Parboil potatoes in salted water 5 minutes. Drain. Brown onions lightly in butter and add to potatoes, with sour cream, dill, and seasoning. Cover tightly and simmer until done, about 30 minutes.

Serves 6.

SWISS POTATOES
(Kartofle po Szwajcarsku)

    2 med. onions, chopped
    2 tbs. butter
    4 cups peeled, sliced potatoes
    1 carrot, sliced thin
    1 celery root, sliced thin
    1 parsley root, sliced thin
    salt and pepper to taste
    1 cup sour cream
    1 tsp. lemon rind
    lemon juice to taste

Brown onions lightly in butter. Blanch the sliced vegetables, drain, and add to onions. Season, mix thoroughly, add sour cream, lemon rind, and a little lemon juice. Bake uncovered in medium-hot oven for about 1 hour. Top should be crisp.

Serves 6.

SMOTHERED CARROTS
(Marchew Duszona)

    2 bunches very young carrots, washed and blanched
    2 tbs. butter
    salt and pepper to taste
    dash of sugar
    ½ cup bouillon
    flour for dusting

Very young carrots (3 inches long) need not be peeled or scraped. Wash carefully and cut off tops and tips. Blanch in salted water and simmer, tightly covered, with butter, bouillon, and seasoning until tender. When done, dust with flour and stir. Let cook a few minutes uncovered to reduce liquid. Older carrots should be scraped, sliced, and parboiled; then they may be prepared the same way. Allow ½ cup per portion.

FRIED CARROTS
(Marchew Smażona)

    2 bunches carrots, blanched
    1-2 tbs. butter
    salt and pepper to taste
    ¼ cup bouillon or water
    sugar to taste (lemon juice optional)

Very young carrots may be used whole, unpeeled; older ones should be scraped and cut in halves or quarters. Blanch, then simmer tightly covered with butter, seasoning, and bouillon. When steamed through, add sugar for a sweetish taste, lemon if desired, and cook uncovered, stirring constantly, until sauce thickens and carrots begin to brown.

Serves 6.

ARTICHOKES
(Karczochy)

Artichokes should be freshly picked; leaves and stems should be green, not brown, and the leaves tight together. The secret of good artichoke cooking is to be sure they are very well done; unlike other vegetables, they should be almost mushy. Trim stems, cut top leaves off with a sharp knife (about 1 inch) since tops are not edible, and if possible scoop out chokes before cooking. This, however, is not essential. Cook in boiling water to cover. Add juice of half a lemon, a teaspoon of sugar, and salt to taste. Stand upside down to drain before serving. Artichokes are also excellent if, in addition to lemon and sugar, the following are added to cooking water: 1 tbs. olive oil, 1 clove garlic, 1 tsp. thyme, marjoram or oregano. Cook 30 to 40 minutes. Serve artichokes hot with drawn butter, butter and lemon, Mayonnaise.

Serve artichokes cold with Mayonnaise or French Dressing.

ARTICHOKES IN WINE
(Karczochy na Winie)

    4 med. artichokes
    2 tbs. melted butter
    1 cup dry white wine
    salt and pepper to taste

Cook artichokes 20 minutes according to directions in above recipe. Drain half-cooked artichokes, and when cool enough to handle, cut in quarters, scoop out hairy centers, and arrange tightly in casserole. Add butter and wine, season lightly, and simmer tightly covered another 20 minutes. Serve with olive oil and vinegar, or other sauce according to preference.

Serves 4 to 8.

STUFFED CUCUMBERS
(Ogórki Faszerowane)

6-8 cucumbers
thin bacon strips to cover
1 cup strong bouillon
2 tsp. flour
½ tsp. Maggi extract
3 ozs. Madeira or sherry
stuffing
> **½ onion, grated**
> **1½ tsp. butter**
> **½ lb. ground veal, raw or leftover roast, or ½ lb. raw boned fish**
> **1 stale white roll, moistened in milk and mashed (or bread crumbs)**
> **salt and pepper to taste**
> **1 egg, lightly beaten**

Pick out medium, even-sized cucumbers. Peel, cut in half lengthwise, and scoop out seeds. Blanch in boiling salted water. To make stuffing, brown onion lightly in butter. Combine all the stuffing ingredients, mix thoroughly, and fill cucumber halves. Arrange tightly in casserole, cover with bacon strips, and add bouillon. Simmer, tightly covered, until transparent and completely done, about 30 minutes. Brown flour in a dry skillet, taking care not to burn. Dilute with a little of the sauce, add Maggi extract and Madeira, and pour over cucumbers. Allow to bubble up and serve.

Serves 6 to 8 as main dish.

SMOTHERED CELERY ROOTS
(Selery Duszone)

3-4 celery roots, cleaned and par-boiled in salted water
1 cup bouillon
lemon juice to taste
salt and pepper
1 tbs. butter
2 tsp. flour

Slice parboiled celery roots thin. Cover with bouillon, add a little lemon juice, season, and simmer tightly covered until tender. Combine butter and flour, dilute with the bouillon, and when smooth add to the celery roots. Let bubble up and then serve with croutons.

Serves 4.

LEAF CELERY
(Selery Liściaste)

2 bunches white or Pascal celery
salt and pepper
water or light bouillon for cooking

Cut off leaves, clean celery stalks, and cut into serving pieces. Simmer in salted water or bouillon until transparent, about 12 to 15 minutes. Serve like asparagus.

Serves 6 to 8.

SMOTHERED TURNIPS WITH SAUSAGE
(Rzepa Duszona z Kiełbaskami)

3-4 young turnips
1 cup White Sauce (see Index) made with bouillon
1 tsp. caraway seed
salt and pepper to taste
1 tbs. chopped fresh parsley
1 sausage ring or 6 frankfurters

Peel, dice, and parboil turnips in salted water for 5 minutes. Simmer in White Sauce with caraway seed and seasoning. When tender, add parsley. Serve with hot frankfurters or with Polish sausage (kiełbasa) heated in boiling water or pan-broiled.

Serves 3 to 4.

SMOTHERED SALAD GREENS
(Sałata Duszona)

4 young heads lettuce or escarole or endive
3-4 strips bacon, diced
1 tsp. chopped fresh dill and parsley
salt and pepper to taste
2-3 tbs. sour cream
½ tsp. flour

If small heads of salad greens are not available, discard the outside green leaves of larger heads and cut in halves or quarters. Blanch with salted water and drain. Heat diced bacon until transparent, together with a little extra bacon fat. Add salad greens and herbs. Season and simmer, tightly covered, until limp and transparent—about 10 minutes. Blend sour cream with flour. Add to sauce, let bubble up, and serve.

Serves 4.

RHUBARB
(Rzewień)

Combined with potatoes, rhubarb makes an excellent vegetable. Prepare as follows:

    10 stalks rhubarb, with leaves cut off
    2 cups new potatoes or potato balls
    1 tbs. butter, lightly browned
    1 tbs. flour
    1 heaping tbs. chives
    1 clove garlic
    ½ tsp. Maggi extract or Kitchen Bouquet
    salt and pepper
    broth
        2 cups water
        6 dried mushrooms
        1 onion, peeled and sliced
        1 bay leaf
        few sprigs dill
        salt and pepper

Allow broth to simmer about half an hour so that mushrooms will cook and lend it their special flavor. Clean rhubarb, cut into 1 inch pieces, and cover with boiling broth. Simmer until tender. Then drain, reserving liquid, and rinse in cold water. In the meantime, cook the potatoes separately. Brown the butter, add flour, and blend well. Add about 1 cup of the rhubarb broth. Stir until smooth. If too thick add more broth. Add chives, garlic, and Maggi, and season to taste. Return rhubarb and potatoes to the sauce and simmer together until thoroughly heated.

Serves 6.

SPINACH WITH SWEET CREAM
(Szpinak ze Śmietanka)
    3 lbs. spinach, cleaned and par-boiled in salted
        water for 5 minutes
    white sauce, made with:
        1 tbs. butter
        1 tbs. flour
        ½ cup sweet cream (milk if preferred)
        salt and pepper to taste
        dash of sugar

Drain parboiled spinach and rinse under cold water to restore color. Chop fine and press through a sieve. Melt butter, blend in flour, add cream, and stir

until smooth. Season, add spinach, and simmer tightly covered for 15 to 20 minutes.

Serves 6.

Note: Serve garnished with slices of hard-cooked egg if desired.

SPINACH CROQUETTES
(Kotlety ze Szpinaku)
    2 rolls or 2 slices bread
    1 tbs. butter
    2 cups chopped cooked spinach
    2 cups bread crumbs
    2 eggs, lightly beaten
    1 tbs. creamed or melted butter
    salt and pepper to taste
    bread crumbs for rolling
    butter for frying

Cube the rolls or bread and make croutons by frying cubes in 1 tbs. butter. Combine with the spinach (preferably cooked in bouillon), the bread crumbs, eggs, creamed butter, and seasoning. Shape into oval croquettes, roll in bread crumbs, and fry in butter to a golden brown.

Serves 6.

BAKED TOMATOES
(Pomidory Pieczone)
    12 small, even-sized tomatoes
    6 lumps butter
    salt and pepper to taste
    1 tbs. chopped dill or chives

Cut tops off tomatoes and scoop out seeds. Fill with butter and herbs, season, and cover again with the tops. Bake in shallow dish, uncovered, in medium-hot oven for about 30 minutes.

Serves 6.

VEGETABLE MACÉDOINE
(Macédoine z Jarzyn)
    ½ cup each diced carrots, kohlrabi, celery root,
        parsnip, and parsley root
    salt and sugar to taste
    2 tbs. butter
    1 scant cup bouillon
    ½ cup green peas, cooked separately

½ cup snap beans or asparagus tips, cooked
  separately
1½ tsp. flour

Combine carrots, kohlrabi, celery root, parsnip, and parsley root with 1 tbs. butter, sugar, seasoning, and bouillon. Simmer, tightly covered, until tender. Combine with peas, snap beans and/or asparagus tips. Dust in the flour and simmer a few minutes longer or until sauce thickens. Remove from heat. Add remaining butter and allow to melt. Serve garnished with croutons as a side dish.

Serves 6.

PURÉE OF BEETS AND APPLES
(Purée z Buraków z Jabłkami)

5-6 med. beets
2 sour apples
1 tbs. bacon fat
salt and pepper to taste
lemon juice to taste
sugar to taste
2-3 tbs. sour cream
1½ tsp. flour

Peel beets and apples and grate coarsely, reserving all the juices. Melt bacon fat, add grated beets and apples, together with all their juices. Season with salt and pepper, and add lemon juice and sugar to taste. Simmer, covered, for half an hour. Reduce liquid, add sour cream combined with flour, and let bubble up. Simmer a few more minutes. Excellent with roasts.

Serves 5 to 6.

BREADED MUSHROOMS
(Grzyby Panierowane)

15-20 mushrooms of even size
½ minced onion
4 tbs. butter
salt and pepper
1 egg, lightly beaten
bread crumbs

Cook onion in a little butter until limp. Add mushrooms, season, and simmer tightly covered until transparent. Dip in egg, roll in bread crumbs, and fry evenly in hot butter. Serve with another vegetable in lieu of meat during the Lenten season.

Serves 3 to 4.

STUFFED MUSHROOMS
(Pieczarki Faszerowane)

12-16 large mushrooms and 4-6 smaller ones
½ med. onion, chopped fine
butter
1 heaping tbs. chopped fresh dill or parsley, or
  combination of both
2 tbs. bread crumbs
1 veal kidney with surplus fat removed, or
  equivalent amount roast veal
salt and pepper to taste
1 egg, lightly beaten
bread crumbs and butter for topping
½ cup strong bouillon

Clean and wash mushrooms. Cut out stems from the large ones, leaving only caps for stuffing. Simmer mushroom caps in salted boiling water for about 5 minutes. In the meantime, chop stems and remaining small mushrooms and simmer with the onion, tightly covered, until transparent and limp. Add chopped dill, bread crumbs, and slightly-cooked kidney or roast veal, chopped fine. Season, add beaten egg and mix thoroughly. Fill mushroom caps with the mixture, sprinkle with bread crumbs, and dot with butter. Bake in 375° oven for 15 to 20 minutes, taking care not to dry out too much. Bread crumbs should be nicely brown on top. Add bouillon to pan after removing mushrooms. Allow to boil up once and use as gravy. Serve with meat or on toast as a luncheon dish.

Makes 3 to 4 servings.

MUSHROOM RAMEKINS
(Pieczarki w Muszelkach)

12-15 med. mushrooms
lemon juice
½ med. onion, minced
butter
salt and pepper to taste
1 heaping tsp. flour
2 tbs. grated Parmesan cheese
1 cup sweet cream
2 egg yolks, lightly beaten
butter and bread crumbs for topping

Wash and clean mushrooms, slice thin, and sprinkle with lemon juice. Simmer, tightly covered, with the onion and a little butter until transparent. Season, dust with flour, add grated Parmesan, cream, and egg yolks. Mix thoroughly. Pour mixture into buttered ramekins, sprinkle with bread crumbs, and dot with butter. Bake in hot oven 5 minutes.

Makes 3 to 4 servings.

MUSHROOMS AU GRATIN
(Grzyby au Gratin)

    1 lb. mushrooms of even size
    3 tbs. butter
    ½ onion, minced
    salt and pepper
    1 cup sour cream blended with 1 tsp. flour
    grated Parmesan
    bread crumbs for topping

Wash and clean mushrooms. Simmer with a little butter and the onion and seasoning, tightly covered, until transparent—about 10 minutes. Arrange in oven-proof *gratin* dish, cover with sour cream with the flour blended into it, sprinkle generously with grated Parmesan, then with bread crumbs, and top with remaining butter. Brown under broiler or in very hot oven for a few minutes.

Serves 4.

MAYONNAISES AND ASPICS

MAYONNAISE OF PIKE, SALMON, OR PERCH
(Szczupak, Łosoź lub Sandacz w Majonezie)

The recipe below is a traditional one for serving at large parties and receptions. We give it in its full glory, but the modern hostess can easily reduce it to modern kitchen and table proportions.

    1 whole fish, 9-12 lbs., cleaned and salted down
        the day before
    4-5 onions
    2 leeks
    1 bunch parsley
    3 bay leaves
    20 peppercorns
    3-4 carrots
    2 celery roots
    3 parsley roots
    2 lemons
    3-4 stalks celery
    water

Make a court bouillon of all the vegetables with enough water to cover the fish. When vegetables are soft, immerse the fish (complete with head and tail) in the boiling water, belly down. Reduce the heat. Let simmer 10 minutes, counting from the time the water begins to boil again. Remove from heat and let stand, covered, in the water for another 30 minutes. Remove carefully (using a rack facilitates this), drain, and place on a platter when cool, belly down. Spread thickly with mayonnaise.

    Garnish
        10 sweet and sour pickles, sliced colored
            aspic made with beet juice, tomato
            juice, etc.
        ¼ lb. each of red and black caviar
    30 crayfish tails or shrimp
        1 can lobster meat
        salad greens (watercress, romaine, Boston
            lettuce, iceberg lettuce, endive, etc.)
    4-6 cups Vegetable Macédoine
    oil and vinegar

Garnish as follows: Put a sprig of watercress in the mouth, decorate the back with thin slices of pickle, slices of colored aspic, capers, dabs of red and black caviar, crayfish tails (or shrimp), and canned lobster meat. Along the edges of the platter arrange various kinds of green salad leaves. Refrigerate until thoroughly chilled.

Serves 18 to 24.

PULLET OR CAPON ASPIC
(Pularda lub Kaplon w Auszpiku)

    1 capon or 2 pullets
    salt
    juice of 1 lemon
    2 onions
    3 carrots
    1 leek
    1 parsley root
    1 celery root
    2 stalks celery
    few sprigs parsley
    6 peppercorns
    salt

Wash and dry the capon, rub with salt inside and out, and sprinkle with lemon juice. Let stand 2 hours. Add all the giblets from the bird and place in enough salted boiling water to cover, together with vegetables and spices. Reduce to a simmer when the water begins to boil again. Cook until meat separates easily from the bones, about 1½ hours. Drain, reserving liquid and carrot. Skin, bone, and cut into small pieces.

gelatin:
  3 cups broth in which capon was cooked
  1 cup white wine
  2 egg whites and shells
  lemon juice to taste
  ½ tsp. Maggi extract
  2 tbs. (2 envelopes) gelatin to 4 cups liquid

Strain soup stock, add white wine, beaten egg whites and shells, lemon to taste, and Maggi extract. Bring to a boil and let stand half an hour. Strain, and then add dissolved gelatin and pour over chicken in individual molds, lined as follows:

slices of lemon
slices of hard-cooked egg
slices of gherkin
slices of marinated mushrooms
slices of cooked carrot (from broth)

Arrange lemon and egg slices, augmented with any of the other ingredients, according to taste, in bottom and on sides of molds. Follow with pieces of chicken, using best pieces for the top. Pour in liquid, filling molds full. Chill. Unmold just before serving and garnish with lemon slices and parsley sprigs.
Serves 8.

MOCK SALMON MADE WITH VEAL
(Fałszywy Łosoś)
  3 lbs. boned veal, rolled as for roasting
  veal bones, split in several pieces
  1 large onion
  1-2 carrots
  1 celery root
  2 celery stalks
  1 parsley root
  few sprigs fresh parsley
  10 peppercorns
  1 bay leaf
  1-2 cloves
  salt and pepper to taste
  3 cups water
  1 cup vinegar

Peel and cut up onion and vegetables, and boil with veal bones, spices, and salt and pepper in water and vinegar. (Proportions of water and vinegar may be varied according to taste. There should be just enough liquid to cover meat.) When water comes to a boil, put in the meat and simmer for 3 hours. Cool and leave in the liquid until the following day. Drain, slice, and arrange on platter. Pour the following sauce over the meat.

sauce
  3 hard-cooked egg yolks
  1 cup olive oil
  juice of 2-3 lemons
  1 tbs. capers
  1 tin anchovy fillets, chopped fine
  salt and pepper to taste
  dash of sugar

Mash the egg yolks and beat in one cup olive oil, a spoonful at a time, beating constantly until all the oil has been absorbed. Add the lemon juice, continuing to beat. Add capers and anchovies. Season to taste and mix thoroughly.
Serves 6 to 8.

SALADS

POTATO SALAD WITH HERRING OR ANCHOVIES
(Salata z Kartofli ze Śledziem lub z Sardelami)
  6 med. potatoes, cooked in salted water in jackets
  1 matjes herring or 6 anchovy fillets
  ½ med. onion, blanched and chopped fine
  1 heaping tsp. each of chopped chives, dill, and parsley
  ¼ cup olive oil
  3 tbs. vinegar
  pepper

Peel potatoes and slice thin. Chop herring. Mix with other ingredients, then add olive oil and vinegar and a little pepper. Mix thoroughly and refrigerate for about an hour. Salad will probably not need salt, since herring or anchovies are salty in themselves.
Serves 6.

POTATO SALAD
(Salata z Kartofli)
1
>   6 med. potatoes
>   salt and pepper to taste
>   ½ med. onion, minced, *or* equivalent amount
>   chopped chives
>   ¼ cup olive oil
>   3 tbs. vinegar

Potatoes for salad should be cooked in their jackets, peeled, and allowed to cool. Avoid Idahos and other mealy potatoes-new potatoes are excellent. Slice thin, season, add minced onion or chives and olive oil and vinegar. Mix and refrigerate for 1 hour. Serves 6.

2
>   Prepare potatoes as in 1.
>   **dressing:**
>   2-3 hard-cooked egg yolks
>   ¼ cup olive oil
>   salt and pepper to taste
>   ¼ cup white wine
>   lemon juice to taste
>   1 heaping tbs. chopped chives or chopped
>   dill and parsley

Cream egg yolks and olive oil, season, add wine and lemon juice to taste. Mix with potatoes. Sprinkle with chopped chives or herbs. Refrigerate until cold. Serves 6.

POTATO, APPLE, AND CAPER SALAD
(Salata z Kartofli z Jablkami i Kaparami)
>   6 med. potatoes, cooked in salted water in jackets
>   2 med. apples
>   1 heaping tbs. capers
>   ¼ cup olive oil
>   ¼ cup dry white wine
>   lemon juice to taste
>   salt and pepper

Peel potatoes and allow to cool. Core and peel apples. Slice potatoes and apples very thin, mix with capers, olive oil, wine, and lemon juice to taste. Season with salt and pepper. Refrigerate 1 hour. Serves 6 to 7.

TOMATO SALAD
(Salata z Pomidorów)
>   4 med. tomatoes
>   salt and pepper to taste
>   ½ med. onion, blanched and minced
>   1-2 tbs. chopped fresh dill and parsley, or either
>   herb separately
>   4 tbs. olice oil
>   lemon juice or vinegar (preferably wine vine-
>   gar) to taste

Slice tomatoes, season, and sprinkle with minced onion and fresh herbs. Add olive oil and lemon juice or vinegar-the proportion should be considerably more oil than lemon juice, not the usual French dressing. Allow to refrigerate for 1 to 2 hours. Serves 4 to 5.

SALAD WITH POLISH SOUR CREAM DRESSING
(Salata po Polsku ze Śmietanq)
>   green salad in any combination desired—
>   enough for 6 portions
>   2-3 hard-cooked eggs
>   1 cup sour cream
>   ½ tsp. sugar (optional)
>   lemon juice or white vinegar to taste
>   salt and pepper to taste

Cream 2 egg yolks with sour cream. Add sugar, lemon juice, salt, and pepper to taste and stir thoroughly. Add to salad and toss. Chop remaining egg whites and use for garnish, together with the third egg, cut into thin slices. Omit sugar if desired. Serves 6.

SAUERKRAUT SALAD
(Salata z Kiszonej Kapusty)
>   1 lb. sauerkraut
>   3-4 tbs. olive oil
>   salt and pepper to taste
>   1 tsp. sugar
>   lemon juice to taste (optional)
>   1 apple, cored, pared, and shredded

Mix all the ingredients together, adding sufficient sugar and lemon juice to give sauerkraut a sweet-and-sour taste. Serve chilled. Serves 4 to 6.

RED CABBAGE SALAD
(Salata z Czerwonej Kapusty)
    1 med. head red cabbage, shredded
    salted, boiling water
    juice of 1 lemon
    salt and pepper to taste
    sugar to taste
    olive oil

Throw shredded cabbage into boiling water. As soon as the water boils again, drain and allow cabbage to dry off. Sprinkle with lemon juice to restore bright red color. Chill. An hour before serving, season with salt and pepper. Add sugar to taste and several tablespoons of olive oil, depending on one's preference.
    Serves 6.

CELERY ROOT SALAD
(Salata z Selerów)
    3-4 celery roots
    salted, boiling water to cover
    salt and pepper to taste
    ½ med. onion, minced, or 1 tbs. chopped chives
    1 tbs. chopped fresh dill
    olive oil and vinegar (preferably wine vinegar)
        to taste

Pare or scrape celery roots, cook in boiling water until tender, drain, and cool in cold water. Slice thin, season with salt and pepper, and mix with chopped chives or minced onion and fresh dill. Add 3 to 4 tbs. olive oil and 2 to 3 tbs. vinegar.
    Serves 3 to 4.

JAPANESE SALAD
(Salata Japónska)
    4 med. potatoes, cooked in jackets, peeled, and
        diced
    10 mussels or steamer clams, cooked and diced
        (canned may be used)
    1 tsp. each chopped parsley, dill, chives, and
        tarragon
    olive oil to taste (about ¼ cup)
    ¼ cup white wine
    lemon juice to taste
    salt and pepper to taste
    lettuce leaves
    2 hard-cooked eggs, quartered

    1-2 cooked truffles, cut in thin strips

Combine potatoes, clams, and herbs with olive oil, wine, and lemon juice. Season to taste. Toss, arrange on a bed of lettuce leaves, and garnish top with strips of truffle and hard-cooked egg sections. Refrigerate about 2 hours.
    Serves 6.

DIPLOMAT SALAD
(Salata "Diplomate")
    2-3 tomatoes, peeled and diced
    2-3 slices fresh or canned pineapple, cut in
        pieces
    1 large or 2 small bananas, sliced
    2 truffles, cut in thin strips
    1 cup mayonnaise (preferably homemade)
    ¼ cup Rhine wine
    1 large, or 2 small apples, cored, pared, and
        diced
    3 medium potatoes, cooked in jackets, peeled,
        and sliced thin
    Worcestershire sauce to taste (1 tsp. or less)
    dash of cayenne pepper

Combine fruits, potatoes, and truffles. Dilute mayonnaise with wine (add according to taste), season with Worcestershire sauce and cayenne pepper, and add to mixture. Toss lightly and refrigerate for 3 to 4 hours.
Serves 6.

BLACK RADISH SALAD
(Salata z Rzodkwi)
    3-4 large black radishes (white may be substi-
        tuted)
    ¼ cup sour cream
    lemon juice to taste
    salt and pepper to taste

Peel radishes and grate coarsely. Mix with sour cream, and add lemon juice and seasoning to taste. Serve with cold meats as one would horseradish.

REFERENCES AND SAUCES

BOILING:

Fish may be cooked whole or cut into serving pieces, depending on convenience. A large fish served whole looks best when appearance counts. For easiest handling, cooking should be done in a large oblong pan on a rack (a roasting pan with cover can double for a fish kettle); for additional ease, the fish may be wrapped in cheesecloth.

Prepare a court bouillon, using per quart of water:

1 large onion
2-3 carrots
½ celery root
½ parsley root
2-3 celery stalks with leaves
slice of lemon
½ bay leaf (optional)
salt and pepper to taste
other spices according to personal preference; thyme, oregano, tarragon, etc.

Boil the water and vegetables until vegetables are done. Strain. (The other vegetables may later be used to strain for sauce, the carrots for garnish.) Place fish on rack, belly down, and immerse in the liquid, of which there should be enough to cover. Simmer very slowly until done, about 5 minutes per inch of thickness. Remove with rack and drain; cut cheesecloth and remove carefully. Broth may be used as the basis of a fish chowder.

STEAMING:

1st Method:

Place fish, whole or cut into serving pieces, on rack over enough court bouillon (see No. 1) to allow plenty of steam throughout cooking time, which is a very little longer than boiling time. Cover very tightly and simmer. Remove with rack, drain, and proceed as in No. 1.

2nd Method:

Place fish, whole or cut into serving pieces, directly in bottom of pan, adding (per pound):

1 tbs. butter
2-3 tbs. broth
½ cup white wine
salt and pepper to taste

Simmer very slowly, tightly covered, until done.

In both boiling and steaming, care should be taken not to let fish fall apart.

FRYING:

Small fish may be fried whole, with or without the heads, according to preference. Large fish are cut into serving pieces for frying.

Wash and drain the fish, dust with seasoned flour, and fry either in deep fat or in a skillet. Use butter, olive oil, a combination of both, or vegetable oil, according to personal taste. Fish may also be fried seasoned but without being dredged in flour. Another method is to dip them in beaten egg and bread crumbs. In all cases frying should be done over medium heat and the fish turned once carefully. Fry until a light, golden brown.

BROILING:

Brush whole fish or serving pieces with butter or other fat, and place under preheated broiler for about 10 minutes. Large fish takes longer. It is important to preheat the broiler and have temperature high, since turning is awkward. Baste frequently. Larger fish should be split for broiling and done skin-down. Many people prefer the newer method of broiling at medium temperature for a longer time. This results in less shrinkage, but the fish will have a slightly "steamed" taste.

BAKING:

For baking, first parboil fish in court bouillon, or dust with flour and fry lightly in butter. Then arrange tightly in a buttered shallow pan. Spread with butter or whatever sauce is recommended, and bake in medium-hot oven (350° or less), allowing 20 minutes per inch of thickness. Fish should be lightly browned on top.

ANCHOVY SAUCE FOR FISH OR VENISON
(Sos Sardelowy do Ryp i Dziczyzny)

4 chopped anchovy fillets
3 hard-cooked eggs
1 tsp. dry mustard
1 tsp. olive oil (or more)

juice ½ lemon

salt, pepper, and sugar to taste

Press the chopped anchovies and cooked egg yolks through a sieve. Combine with mustard, oil, and lemon juice until blended. Mix and stir thoroughly, season to taste, and sprinkle with chopped egg whites. (Excellent for beef roasts as well.)

POLISH GRAY SAUCE
(Sos Polski Szary)

1 tbs. browned flour
1 tbs. butter
1 cup beef or fish broth, depending on whether
    serving over meat or fish
1½ tsp. Maggi extract
2 tbs. seedless raisins
2 tbs. chopped almonds
1-2 bitter almonds (optional)
juice ½ lemon
2 tsp. sugar
1 tsp. caramelized sugar (see No. 3)
salt and pepper to taste
¼ cup red table wine or half as much Malaga
    wine

Combine flour and butter and stir until smooth. Add broth, stir until thoroughly blended, and let simmer 10 minutes. Blanch, peel, and chop the almonds. Combine all ingredients, stir thoroughly, and let simmer another 5 to 10 minutes. Serve with fresh or smoked tongue or with carp.

About 1½ cups.

WHITE LEMON OR POULETTE SAUCE
(Sos Bialy Cytrynowy)

2 tbs. butter
1 tbs. flour
1 cup soup stock
juice ½ lemon
grated lemon rind to taste
4-6 mushrooms, chopped and sautéed in a little
    butter
1 tbs. chopped fresh parsley
salt and pepper to taste
2 egg yolks

Cream flour and butter without cooking. Blend

with soup stock over very low heat. Add lemon juice (less if preferred), lemon rind, and the sautéed mushrooms. Let bubble up, and add the chopped parsley and salt and pepper to taste. Cream egg yolks with remaining butter and add slowly to sauce, taking care not to curdle.

About 1½ cups.

BUTTER MANIE
(Zaprażka na Surowo)

1 tbs. flour
1 tbs. butter
½ cup soup stock

Cream butter and flour, dilute with cold soup stock, and then simmer over low heat for 10 to 15 minutes, adding a little stock if necessary. For fish, veal, or ragout of poultry.

BROWN SAUCE THICKENING FOR STORING
(Zaprażka Rumiana do Przechowania)

½ lb. unsalted butter
1 cup flour

Melt the butter, stir in the flour, and brown lightly. Store, tightly covered, in refrigerator. Heat and use in sauces as necessary. If dark sauce is called for, brown further.

DRIED MUSHROOMS
(Suche Grzyby)

Imported dried mushrooms are tangier than domestic ones. Polish mushrooms, now readily available in the United States, are particularly recommended, since they are wild European mushrooms specially prepared. In Europe, where they are cheaper and more abundant, they are used as a vegetable. Here, however, this would be an impossible luxury, since good imported mushrooms cost about $12.00 a pound. But they are excellent in sauces and soups, for an ounce or even a half-ounce can "make" a dish. Dried mushrooms are best soaked overnight in milk or a little water, then simmered half an hour in the soaking liquid. If a recipe does not call for milk, be sure to soak in water. This water can then take the place of bouillon in sauce.

FRESH MUSHROOM SAUCE
(Sos Pieczarkowy)

        8 large fresh mushrooms
        ½ med. onion
        2 tbs. butter
        1 tbs. flour
        salt and fresh-ground pepper to taste
        1 cup broth
        ¾ cup white wine
        2-3 tbs. sweet cream
        lemon juice to taste
        2 egg yolks (optional)

Chop mushrooms, using both stems and caps. Chop onion fine, and sauté together with mushrooms in butter until onions are a golden brown and mushrooms soft (about 15 minutes). Add flour and seasoning, and continue cooking, stirring constantly and taking care not to brown the flour, until thoroughly blended. Slowly add the broth, and when sauce is smooth, add the wine and cream. Season with lemon juice to taste and let simmer another 5 to 10 minutes. For richer texture add beaten egg yolks, taking care not to curdle. Serve at once.

Makes 2 cups of sauce.

BREAD-CRUMB SAUCE
(Maslo z Rumianą Bułką)

        3 tbs. butter
        2 tbs. bread crumbs

Melt butter and brown lightly. Add bread crumbs and cook over medium heat for another 2 to 3 minutes, just long enough to let the crumbs brown to the color of toast. For vegetables and dairy dishes.

DILL SAUCE
(Sos Koperkowy)

        1 tbs. butter
        1½ tsp. flour
        1 cup broth
        1 cup sour cream
        salt to taste
        2 tbs. chopped fresh dill
        2 egg yolks (optional)

Melt butter, stir in flour, blend thoroughly, and dilute with broth. Combine with sour cream, stirring constantly until smooth. Add dill, season to taste, and let bubble up once. For a more delicate taste add the beaten egg yolks, taking care not to let sauce curdle.

Makes 1¼ to 1½ cups. Excellent for boiled beef, or boiled steak fish such as sturgeon, salmon, or cod.

TARTARE SAUCE
(Sos Tatarski)

        6 egg yolks
        ¾-1 cup olive oil
        ¼ cup cold water
        2 tsp. dry English mustard
        2-3 sharp relish pickles, chopped
        pinch of sugar

Follow directions given in No. 38. When thickened, place in top of double boiler over low heat and continue beating, adding the cold water and remaining ingredients. If not tart enough, add a few drops of lemon juice. Take care not to let the sauce boil. Chill before serving. If the sauce is too thick, add more cold water while still beating over the heat.

TARTARE SAUCE WITH HARD-COOKED EGGS
(Sos Tatarski z Jaj na Twardo)

        6 hard-cooked egg yolks
        6-8 tbs. olive oil
        2 tbs. prepared French mustard
        salt, pepper, and sugar to taste
        1 tsp. vinegar
        ½ tsp. Worcestershire sauce

Mash egg yolks thoroughly or press through a sieve. Slowly add the olive oil, beating constantly. When thick and thoroughly blended, add mustard, seasoning, and vinegar. Add sharp sauce. Continue beating a minute or two more. Chill. This sauce is traditional with cold meats at Easter.

WHITE THICKENING OR SAUCE
(Zaprażka Biala)

        1 tbs. butter
        1 tbs. flour

Melt the butter in a heavy skillet and heat until it bubbles. Add the flour, a little at a time, stirring constantly and taking care not to brown. Add water or stock a little at a time, and continue to stir the consistency of a loose paste. Stir out all lumps. Use as thickening for soups and stews, or season as necessary and use as a sauce.

Czechoslovak

SOUPS

CARAWAY SOUP
(Kmínová Polévka)
¼ cup butter
¼ cup flour
5 cups water or soup stock
salt to taste
1 teaspoon caraway seeds
1 cup cooked noodles

Brown butter in flour. Add water or stock, salt, and caraway seeds. Simmer for 20 to 30 minutes. Add noodles before serving.

Serves 4 to 5.

GIZZARD SOUP
(Polévka Z Drůbežích Drubků)
6 cups cold water
gizzard, neck, wings, and back of chicken, duck, turkey, or goose
salt to taste
2 carrots, cut up
1 parsnip, cut up
½ medium celery root, cut up
1 medium onion, cut up
¼ cup very thin noodles or rice
dash of mace
1 tablespoon minced parsley

Put well-cleaned gizzard, neck, wings, and back into water. Add salt and vegetables. Simmer for 2 to 3 hours or until tender. Strain soup, purée vegetables through strainer, remove meat from bones, dice. Return vegetables and meat to soup. Thicken soup by adding noodles or rice, and cooking until done. Add mace and parsley before serving.

Serves 4.

CREAMED MEAT SOUP
(Masitá Polévka Bílá)
½ pound beef
6 cups water
2 cups diced vegetables (carrot, parsnip, celery root, cauliflower, peas, onion)
¼ cup butter
¼ cup flour
1 egg yolk
½ cup milk or cream
salt to taste
1 tablespoon minced parsley

Simmer beef in salted water until tender (about 2 hours). Strain. Melt butter, blend in flour, and add to soup. Simmer for 20 minutes more. Add vegetables, and simmer for 10 minutes more. Beef can be diced and returned to soup, or served, sliced, to 2 persons, with a sauce or creamed vegetables as a main course. Before serving soup, add egg yolk, beaten with the milk or cream, and parsley. Do not boil again. Serves 4 to 6.

LEGUME SOUP
(Luštěninová Polévka)
½ pound legumes (lentils, beans, or dried peas)
6 cups water
1 cup grated vegetables (carrot, onion, parsnip, celery root)
3 tablespoons flour
4 tablespoons butter
salt to taste
1 clove minced garlic
½ cup milk croutons

Simmer legumes slowly in water until tender (1½ to 2 hours). Rub through strainer. Brown flour in butter, add to soup. Add vegetables. Simmer for 10 to 20 minutes. Stir in salt, garlic, and milk. Serve with croutons.

Serves 4 to 6.

CREAMED SWEETBREADS SOUP
(Brzlíková)

Make like Creamed Meat Soup, but use ½ pound sweetbreads in place of beef. Wash and skin sweetbreads; dice, and put into prepared soup.

Serves 4 to 6.

LIVER DUMPLINGS
(Járové)

- ¼ pound liver, ground or scraped
- 2 tablespoons butter
- dash of salt
- dash of pepper
- 1 egg
- ½ clove garlic, crushed, or pinch of marjoram
- 1½ cups (approximately) bread crumbs

Cream butter with salt and egg; add balance of ingredients; mix into a stiff dough. Form into balls, each the size of a walnut. Test dough by boiling just one dumpling at first to make sure it does not fall apart; if dough is not thick enough to adhere, add more bread crumbs and make another test dumpling. Simmer dumplings for 3 to 5 minutes.

MARROW DUMPLINGS
(Morkové)

- ¼ pound marrow
- 1 egg
- salt to taste
- 2 tablespoons milk or cream
- dash of mace
- 1⅓ cups (approximately) bread crumbs

Prepare like Liver Dumplings (above).

DOUGH DROPS
(Kapání)

- ⅓ cup instantized flour
- 1 egg
- 2 tablespoons milk

Beat egg and milk. Add flour; mix until smooth. Pour over a fork into boiling soup. Simmer for 4 minutes. Dough Drops can also be poured over a fork into hot fat and fried until golden. Add to soup before serving.

FRIED FARINA SOUP
(Polévka Z Pražené Krupice)

- 1 cup chopped soup greens
- ¼ cup butter
- ½ cup farina
- 4 cups water
- salt to taste
- 1 teaspoon soy sauce
- 1 tablespoon minced parsley

Fry vegetables in butter. Add farina, and fry until golden. Add water and salt. Simmer for about 20 minutes. Before serving, add soy sauce and parsley.

Serves 4 to 6.

RYE BREAD SOUP
(Chlebová Polévka)

- 1 pound stale rye bread, diced
- 6 cups water or soup stock
- salt to taste
- ½ teaspoon caraway seeds
- ½ cup sour cream
- 1 egg yolk, beaten
- 1 cup diced cooked smoked meat (optional)
- 1 cup sliced frankfurters (optional)

Simmer bread in water or soup stock for 20 to 30 minutes, or until soft enough to rub through strainer. Add salt, butter, and caraway seeds. Before serving, blend in sour cream and egg yolk. Add smoked meat or frankfurters, if desired.

Serves 4 to 6.

MEATS

LARDED ROAST BEEF
(Hovězí Pecéné Prírodní)

- 2 pounds beef (top round)
- 2 ounces bacon
- 1 large onion, chopped
- ¼ cup lard
- salt to taste
- dash of pepper
- 2 cups water
- 1 tablespoon flour

Lard meat with ½-inch-thick bacon strips. Fry onion in lard until golden; add meat, brown quickly. Sprinkle with salt and pepper, and add ½ cup of water. Cover, and simmer for about 1 hour. Transfer meat to a preheated 350° oven and cook, uncovered, until tender (1 to 1½ hours). Remove meat from pan. Dust the drippings with flour, stir until brown, add remaining water, simmer for 5 to 10 minutes. Slice meat, return to gravy, serve with dumplings or potatoes.

Serves 4 to 6.

BEEFSTEAKS
(Bifteky)
    2 pounds tenderloin of beef
    salt to taste
    pepper to taste
    6 tablespoons lard
    1 tablespoon flour
    1 cup water or soup stock
    3 tablespoons butter

Cut tenderloin into 6 slices, sprinkle with salt and pepper. Brown in hot lard about 4 to 5 minutes on each side. Arrange on a hot serving platter. Skim fat from pan, dust drippings with flour, stir until brown; add water or stock and bring to a boil; add butter. Pour gravy over meat.

Serves 6.

BRAISED BEEFSTEAK WITH VEGETABLES AND SOUR CREAM
(Roštěnsky Dušené Na Zelenině Se Smetanou)
    4 slices ¾-inch-thick round steak
    ¼ pound lard
    salt to taste
    2 tablespoons flour
    1 medium onion, chopped
    ½ carrot, chopped
    ½ parsnip, chopped
    ¼ celery root, chopped
    3 peppercorns
    1 allspice
    ½ bay leaf
    1 cup water
    1 tablespoon vinegar
    1 cup sour cream
    1 tablespoon flour
    ¼ cup white wine

Pound steak, slash borders. Sprinkle with salt; roll in 2 tablespoons flour. Fry quickly on both sides in

half the fat. Brown vegetables lightly in remaining fat; add peppercorns, allspice, bay leaf, water, vinegar, and meat. Simmer until tender (30 to 45 minutes). Remove the meat from pan. Mix sour cream with 1 tablespoon flour; pour into the gravy and blend well. Simmer for 5 minutes. Strain. Return meat to pan and add wine. Serve with dumplings, potatoes, noodles, or rice.

Serves 4.

BRAISED BEEF
(Hovězí Dušené Přírodní)
    2 pounds beef (brisket or round)
    ¼ pound lard or bacon fat
    1 or 2 medium onions, chopped
    salt to taste
    dash of pepper
    2 cups water
    1 tablespoon flour

Pound meat. Brown onion in fat; add meat, salt, and pepper to it. Brown meat well on both sides. Pour ¾ cup of water over meat, cover, and simmer until tender (about 2 to 2½ hours). When tender, remove meat. Dust drippings with the flour, stir until brown, add the remaining water. Simmer for 5 minutes. Slice meat and return it to the gravy. Serve with noodles, potatoes, rice, or dumplings.

Serves 4.

TENDERLOIN WITH VEGETABLES
(Svíčková Na Zelenině)
    3 pounds tenderloin of beef
    3 ounces bacon
    2 cups sliced vegetables (onion, carrot, parsnip, celery root)
    ¼ cup butter
    salt to taste
    1 cup boiling water
    5 peppercorns
    2 allspice
    1 bay leaf
    pinch of thyme
    1 tablespoon flour

Lard meat with ½-inch-thick bacon strips. Brown vegetables in butter, add meat, and brown on all sides. Pour in ½ cup of water, salt, and seasonings.

Roast in a 325° oven until tender (1 to 1½ hours), basting frequently. Remove meat from pan, dust drippings with flour, stir until brown. Add remaining water and simmer for 5 minutes. Rub gravy through a strainer and pour over sliced meat.

Serves 4 to 6.

BEEF GOULASH
(Hovězí Guláš)

2 pounds beef (shank or chuck)
¼ cup lard
1 large onion, chopped
¼ teaspoon paprika
dash of pepper
pinch of marjoram
salt to taste
1 clove garlic, mashed
1 tablespoon flour
2 cups (approximately) water

Fry onion in lard until yellow; add paprika and meat; brown. Add seasonings; pour in ½ cup water. Cover, and simmer until tender, adding more water as it evaporates. When meat is done, uncover it, and let all of the water evaporate. Dust with flour; stir until brown. Add 1 cup more water; simmer for 10 to 15 minutes longer.

Serves 4 to 6.

ROLLED BREAST OF VEAL WITH FRANK-FURTERS
(Telecí Hrudí Jako Ruláda S Párky)

2 pounds boned breast of veal
salt to taste
1 teaspoon paprika
8 frankfurters
3 ounces butter
1 cup water
1 tablespoon flour

Pound breast of veal lightly; sprinkle with salt on both sides. Sprinkle paprika on one side and arrange frankfurters on top; roll up meat and tie. Brown on all sides in melted butter; pour in ⅓ cup water, and roast in a 350° oven for about 2 hours. Remove meat from pan. Mix flour in the remaining water, add to drippings; simmer for 5 to 10 minutes. Slice meat, and serve, either hot with gravy, or cold (without gravy), with salads.

Serves 4 to 6.

MUTTON WITH MARJORAM
(Skopové Maso S Majoránkou)

1½ pounds shoulder of mutton, cubed
¾ cup sliced vegetables (onion, carrot, parsnip, celery root)
6 tablespoons butter
salt to taste
1 or 2 cloves garlic, crushed
½ teaspoon marjoram
2 cups water
3 tablespoons flour

Fry vegetables in 3 tablespoons of butter; add meat, salt, garlic, and marjoram; brown well. Add 1 cup water, cover, and simmer until tender (1½ to 2 hours). Brown flour in remaining butter, add rest of water, and bring to a boil; add to meat. Simmer for 5 minutes.

Serves 4 to 6.

VEAL ROAST KARLSBAD
(Karlovarský Kotouč)

2½ pounds veal shoulder
salt to taste
¼ pound sliced bacon
4-6 ounces ham, sliced
2-3 eggs, scrambled in 2 tablespoons butter
1 pickle, chopped
6 tablespoons butter
1 tablespoon flour
1½ cups water

Have meat cut in a slice about ¾ inch thick. Pound lightly; sprinkle with salt. Cover with layers of sliced bacon, sliced ham, cooled scrambled eggs, and chopped pickle. Roll up meat and tie tightly. Brown on all sides in butter, add ½ cup water, and roast in a 350° oven for about 1½ to 2 hours, basting frequently. Dust drippings with flour, stir well; add remaining water, simmer for 5 minutes.

Serves 6 to 8.

PARISIAN VEAL CUTLETS
Telecí Řízky Pařížské)

1½ pounds leg of veal, cut into 4 slices
dash of salt
2 tablespoons flour
2 eggs, beaten
1 tablespoon milk

3 tablespoons flour
1 tablespoon minced parsley
1 cup shortening
2 tablespoons butter

Pound meat, sprinkle with salt, dip in flour. Mix eggs, milk, flour, parsley, and dash of salt in a bowl into a smooth batter. Dip meat into batter, then put into hot shortening. Keep moving the pan so cutlets do not stick to it. When batter sets on one side, turn and brown cutlet on the other side; then turn again and brown first side. (This method prevents peeling of crust from meat.) Remove cutlets to platter and spread butter over them.

Serves 4.

QUICK PORK CHOPS OR CUTLETS
(Vepřové Řízky Nebo Kotlety Rychlé)

4 pork chops or cutlets, cut ½ inch thick
salt to taste
1 tablespoon flour
¼ cup lard
⅓ cup water
½ teaspoon caraway seeds

Pound meat and loosen partially from bone. Dust with salt and flour. Melt lard in an iron skillet and brown meat about 3 minutes on each side. Remove to a warm plate. Skim off half of the lard, add water and caraway seeds to drippings, stir in well, bring to a boil, and serve over meat. Serve with hard rolls or rye bread, and a green salad.

Serves 2.

ROAST PORK PIQUANT
(Vepřová Pečeně Pikantní)

2 pounds fresh picnic or butt, boned
2 ounces bacon   } cut into wedges 2 inches
2 ounces cooked ham } long and ¾ inch wide
1 pickle, cut into 2-inch by ½-inch strips
2 ounces bacon, chopped
1 medium onion, chopped
salt to taste
pepper to taste
1½ cups water
1 carrot, chopped
1 pickle, chopped
1 tablespoon flour

Sprinkle meat with salt and pepper. Cut slits in it big enough to hold the wedges of bacon, ham, and pickle, and push them in. Fry chopped bacon; add onion, let it brown. Add meat, and brown on all sides. Pour in ½ cup water. Cover, and simmer for 45 minutes. Remove cover from pan, add ½ cup water; roast in a 350° oven for 45 minutes. Remove meat from pan, add carrot, chopped pickle, and flour mixed well with remaining ½ cup water. Simmer for 5 minutes. Serve over sliced meat.

Serves 4 to 6.

RAZNICI
(Ražniči)

1½ pounds tenderloin of pork or lean fresh ham
salt to taste
¼ cup oil
1 cup chopped onion

Cut meat into small pieces (about 2½ inches by 2½ inches and ⅜ inch thick), crossgrain. Pound lightly, sprinkle with salt, and brush with oil. Broil on a hot open grill for 6 minutes on each side (or cook in a greased iron skillet). Serve with chopped onion and dark bread.

Serves 4 to 6.

QUICK PORK KIDNEYS
(Vepřové Ledvinky Narychlo)

1½ pounds kidneys
1 medium onion, chopped
¼ cup lard
¼ teaspoon caraway seeds
dash of pepper
1 tablespoon flour
⅔ cup water
salt to taste

Split kidneys lengthwise. Remove inner and outer membranes. Wash well under running water and pat dry. Slice. Fry onion in lard, add kidney slices, caraway seeds, and pepper; brown for about 7 minutes or until done. Remove meat from pan. Dust drippings with flour and stir until brown; add water. Bring to a boil, stir in salt; serve gravy over kidneys.

Serves 3 to 4.

MEAT LOAF
(Sekaná Pečeně)

    1½ pounds ground beef
    ¾ pound ground pork
    salt to taste
    pepper to taste
    2 eggs
    3 rolls
    ¾ cup milk
    ½ cup diced bacon
    1 medium onion, chopped
    ½ cup lard
    1 cup stock

Mix meats together, add salt and pepper; add eggs. Soak rolls in milk and squeeze almost dry, then chop them and add to mixture with half the bacon. Fry the rest of the bacon, add onion, and brown. Cool, and add to meat. Mix well. Form into a roll with floured hands. Melt lard in a roasting pan and place meat roll on top. Roast in a 350° oven for 1 to 1½ hours, adding stock as needed and basting frequently.

Serves 6 to 8.

FRIED MEAT PATTIES
(Karbanáky)

    ¾ pound ground pork
    ¾ pound ground beef
    salt to taste
    pepper to taste
    1 small onion, chopped
    1 tablespoon chopped bacon
    1 egg
    1 tablespoon minced parsley
    1 roll
    ¼ cup milk
    1 egg white
    1 tablespoon water
    ¾ cup bread crumbs
    ¾ cup shortening

To meat add salt and pepper. Fry onion with bacon. Add to meat with egg and parsley. Soak the roll in milk and squeeze almost dry. Mince, and add to meat mixture. Mix well, and form into patties about 3½ inches in diameter and ¾ inch thick. Brush with egg white beaten with water; roll in bread crumbs. Fry slowly in hot shortening until golden brown.

Serves 4 to 6.

BREADED BEEF BRAIN
(Hovězí Mozeček Smažený)

    1 pound beef brain
    salt to taste
    ½ cup flour
    2 eggs, beaten
    1 cup bread crumbs
    ¾ cup shortening

Scald brain and place it in cold water; remove membranes. Slice; sprinkle with salt. Dip slices first in flour, then in eggs, then in bread crumbs; fry in hot shortening until golden brown.

Serves 3 to 4.

BREADED CALF'S LIVER
(Telecí Játra Smažená)

    1½ pounds calf's liver, sliced ½ inch thick
    salt to taste
    2 tablespoons flour
    2 eggs, beaten
    1 cup bread crumbs
    ¾ cup shortening

Pound liver lightly; sprinkle with salt. Dip first in flour, then in beaten eggs; roll in bread crumbs. Fry in hot shortening until golden brown.

Serves 4.

BOILED BEEF TONGUE
(Hovězí Jazyk Vařený)

    1 fresh beef tongue (about 4 pounds)
    1 medium onion
    1 carrot
    1 parsnip
    water to cover
    salt
    ½ celery root
    beaten egg
    bread crumbs   optional

Simmer tongue in salted water until tender (3 to 4 hours). Add vegetables during last ½ hour of cooking. Remove tongue from pot, place it in cold water, and skin. Slice, and serve with Polish Sauce (see Index), or fry the pieces, dipped first in beaten egg and then in bread crumbs. Reserve stock for use in sauces or roasting.

Serves 6.

ROASTED BEEF TONGUE WITH ANCHOVY BUTTER
(Hovězí Jazyk Pečený Se Sardelovým Máslem)

1 fresh beef tongue, boiled and skinned
¼ pound butter
6 anchovies, mashed
1 medium onion, chopped
½ teaspoon lemon juice
1 cup stock
1 cup bread crumbs

Cream half the butter with anchovies; spread over cooked tongue. Brown onion in the remaining butter, add meat; brown. Pour in ½ cup stock. Roast in a 350° oven for about 1 hour or until tongue is brown on both sides. Sprinkle with lemon juice and bread crumbs, add remaining stock, and bake until bread crumbs are golden brown.

Serves 6.

CREAMED TRIPE
(Zadělávané Drštky)

3 pounds tripe
1 medium onion
1 carrot
1 parsnip
½ celery root
salt
½ cup flour
¼ pound lard or butter
½ teaspoon paprika
2 cups (approximately) stock
dash of pepper
dash of marjoram
1 clove garlic, mashed
1 cup diced, cooked, smoked meat or ham
1 tablespoon chopped parsley

Wash tripe thoroughly in scalding water and clean well. Simmer in salted water until tender (about 2 hours). During the last ½ hour add vegetables. Strain; cool tripe. Brown flour in lard or butter and add paprika. Pour in stock, a little at a time, stirring constantly to make a smooth sauce. Add seasonings, and simmer for 10 to 15 minutes. Cut tripe in thin strips and put into sauce with diced smoked meat and parsley. Serve with onion or salt rolls.

Serves 6 to 8.

BRAISED SWEETBREADS
(Brzlík Dušený)

1 pair sweetbreads
1 tablespoon chopped bacon
1 small onion, chopped
salt to taste
pepper to taste
1 cup vegetable stock or water
2 teaspoons flour

Wash sweetbreads in cold water. Simmer for 5 minutes in boiling salted water; drain. Plunge into cold water, slip off the thin membrane, and cut out thick connective tissue and fat. Break into small pieces. Put bacon into hot frying pan, add onion, and brown. Add sweetbreads, salt, and pepper. Brown well. Pour in ½ cup stock and simmer until tender (about 20 minutes). Dust with flour; stir until brown. Add remaining stock and simmer 5 minutes longer.

Serves 2.

POULTRY AND GAME

CHICKEN WITH MUSHROOMS
(Kuře S Houbami)

1 chicken (3-4 pounds)
½ cup butter
1 large onion, chopped
1 cup sliced mushrooms
salt to taste
1½ cups water
1 cup sour cream
1 tablespoon flour

Cut chicken into small pieces and brown in butter. Add onion; wilt; add mushrooms, salt, and water. Cover, and simmer until tender (about 45 minutes). Remove chicken from pan. Mix sour cream and flour together, blend into pan juices, and bring gravy to a boil. Serve with chicken.

Serves 4 to 5.

ROAST STUFFED CHICKEN
(Nadívané Kuře Pečené)
> **1 roasting chicken (3-4 pounds)**
> **salt to taste**
> **¼ cup butter**
> **1 recipe Bread Crumb Stuffing (see below)**
> **1 cup water**

Clean and stuff the chicken. Sprinkle with salt and rub with butter, and add any remaining butter to roasting pan. Roast bird in 350° oven for 45 to 60 minutes. Baste frequently with water, adding it as needed.

Serves 4 to 5.

BREAD CRUMB STUFFING
(Nádivka)
> **½ cup butter**
> **3 eggs, separated**
> **1 chicken liver, chopped**
> **1⅓ cups bread crumbs**
> **½ cup light cream or milk**
> **salt to taste**
> **1 tablespoon minced parsley**

Cream butter; add egg yolks, 1 at a time, blending in thoroughly. Mix in liver, bread crumbs soaked in cream or milk, salt, and parsley. Fold in stiffly beaten egg whites. Pack lightly into cavity of bird.

CHICKEN FRICASSEE
(Kuře Zadělávané)
> **1 chicken (3-4 pounds)**
> **salt to taste**
> **7 tablespoons butter**
> **½ carrot**
> **½ parsnip**
> **½ celery root**
> **1 medium onion**
> **dash of pepper**
> **dash of nutmeg**
> **piece of lemon peel**
> **1½ cups water**
> **3 tablespoons flour**
> **½ cup sliced mushrooms**
> **1 tablespoon minced parsley**
> **2 tablespoons heavy cream**
> **1 egg yolk**
> **lemon juice to taste**

Sprinkle chicken with salt; brown with vegetables in 3 tablespoons butter. Add spices, lemon peel, and water. Cover, and simmer until tender (about 45 minutes). Remove chicken from pan. Brown flour in 3 tablespoons butter, and stir into pan. Simmer gravy for 5 to 10 minutes; strain over chicken. Add mushrooms browned in 1 tablespoon butter, parsley, and cream, and bring to a boil. Just before serving, blend in egg yolk and lemon juice.

Serves 4 to 5.

DUCK WITH PEAS
(Kachna S Hráškem)
> **1 duck**
> **salt to taste**
> **2 tablespoons butter**
> **½ cup water**
> **2 tablespoons diced bacon**
> **10 small onions, whole**
> **1 pound fresh peas**

Cut duck in serving pieces and sprinkle with salt. Sauté in butter until almost tender (about 1 hour). Add water as needed. Add bacon, onions, and peas, and cook until vegetables are tender (about 20 minutes).

Serves 4.

STUFFED ROAST SQUAB
(Holoubata S Nádivkou)
> **3 squabs**
> **salt to taste**
> **¼ cup butter**
> **1 cup water**
> **stuffing**
> > **¼ cup butter**
> > **2 eggs, separated**
> > **salt to taste**
> > **chopped livers**
> > **1¼ cups bread crumbs**
> > **¼ cup milk**
> > **dash of mace**
> > **1 tablespoon minced parsley**

Clean squabs; loosen skin from breasts. Stuff body and neck cavities, and tie with thread. Sprinkle with salt and rub with butter. Melt any remaining butter in roasting pan, lay in squabs, and roast in a 325°

oven for 30 to 45 minutes, adding water as needed. Remove thread before serving.

To prepare stuffing, cream butter thoroughly with egg yolks and salt. Add livers, bread crumbs soaked in milk, and seasonings. Mix well. Fold in stiffly beaten egg whites. Pack lightly into cavities.

Serves 3.

RABBIT PAPRIKA
(Králík Na Paprice)

1 rabbit
salt to taste
1 large onion, chopped
6 tablespoons butter
1 teaspoon paprika
2 cups water
2 tablespoons flour
1 cup sour cream

Clean rabbit, cut into serving pieces, and sprinkle with salt. Fry onion in butter, add paprika and meat, and brown on all sides. Pour in water; cover and simmer until tender (about 1 hour). Remove meat from pan. Mix flour with sour cream, add to gravy, and simmer for 5 minutes.

Serves 6 to 8.

LEG OF VENISON WITH RED WINE
(Srnčí Maso S Červeným Vínem

2 pounds leg of venison, boned
4 ounces bacon, cut in ½-inch strips
salt to taste
¾ cup sliced vegetables (parsnip, celery root, carrot)
1 medium onion, chopped
5 tablespoons butter
2 cups water
4 peppercorns
2 allspice
½ bay leaf
strip of lemon peel
1 tablespoon flour
½ teaspoon sugar
lemon juice to taste
¼ cup red wine

Lard meat with bacon and sprinkle with salt. Fry vegetables and onion in butter, add meat, and brown

on all sides. Pour in 1 cup of water, add spices and lemon peel; simmer until tender (about 1 hour). Remove meat from pot. Mix flour with remaining cup of water, add to drippings, and simmer for 5 minutes. Add sugar, lemon juice, and wine. Rub through a sieve.

Serves 4 to 6.

FISH

FRIED FISH
(Smažené Ryby V Těstíčku)

2 eggs
1 cup milk
1 cup flour
3 pounds fish fillets
salt to taste
¾ cup butter
lemon wedges

Mix together well eggs, milk, and flour. Sprinkle fish with salt, and dip in batter. Fry in hot butter, about 7 minutes on each side. Serve with lemon.

Serves 6.

FISH WITH ANCHOVIES
(Ryba Na Sardeli)

3 pounds fish
salt to taste
⅓ cup butter
2-3 anchovies, boned and chopped
1 onion, chopped
1 tablespoon chopped
parsley
¼ cup flour
1 cup water or fish stock
1 cup sour cream

Cut cleaned fish into serving pieces; sprinkle with salt. Sauté in half the butter for 4 to 5 minutes on each side. Melt the remaining butter, add anchovies, onion, and parsley, and fry. Blend in flour, stir in water or fish stock, and simmer for 5 minutes. Strain. Add sour cream, blend well. Reheat sauce and pour over fish.

Serves 6 to 8.

STEWED FISH IN WINE
(Ryba Na Víně)

> 6 tablespoons butter
> 1 onion, chopped
> 1 bay leaf
> 5 peppercorns
> 2 whole cloves
> 3 pounds fish (carp or pike)
> salt to taste
> 1 cup red wine
> ½-1 cup water or fish stock
> ¼ cup flour
> lemon juice to taste

Wilt onion in half the butter. Add bay leaf, peppercorns, cloves, and fish sprinkled with salt. Add wine, and simmer for about 15 minutes. Remove fish to a heated platter. Melt the remaining butter; blend in flour. Blend in wine sauce, and water or fish stock. Simmer for 5 minutes. Strain sauce over fish, and sprinkle with lemon juice.

Serves 6 to 8.

BLUE CARP
(Kapr Na Modro)

> 3 pounds carp
> 3 cups water
> salt to taste
> 1 cup sliced vegetables (celery root, parsnip, carrot)
> 2 medium onions, sliced
> 10 peppercorns
> 4 allspice
> ½ bay leaf
> dash of thyme
> ½ cup boiling vinegar
> ¾ cup butter, melted
> parsley
> lemon wedges

Carp is a traditional Christmas Eve dish.

Clean carp, cut lengthwise. Cook vegetables and spices in salted water for 20 minutes. Put carp in a large vessel, skin side up, and slowly pour vinegar over it. (Skin will turn blue.) Pour in vegetables with water, but not directly over the fish. Cover, and simmer for 15 to 20 minutes. Remove carp to a warm plate. Garnish with parsley and lemon wedges, and serve with butter.

Serves 4 to 6.

MARINATED FISH
(Ryby Marinované)

> 3 pounds fish (carp, pike, eel, trout, salmon, tuna, or mackerel)
> salt to taste
> ¼ cup butter
> marinade
> > 1½ cups water
> > ½ cup vinegar
> > ½ cup fish stock
> > 2 medium onions, sliced
> > 5 peppercorns
> > 2 allspice
> > 1 clove
> > ½ bay leaf
> > 1 large pickle, chopped
> > 2 teaspoons chopped capers
> > ¼ cup oil

Sprinkle fish with salt; bake in butter in a 350° oven for about 20 minutes. Boil together water, vinegar, stock, onion, and spices for 20 to 30 minutes; cool. Add pickle, capers, oil. Pour over fish; refrigerate for 24 hours.

Serves 6.

BAKED FISH
(Pečené Ryby)

> 3 pounds fish
> salt to taste
> ¼ teaspoon caraway seeds
> 1 tablespoon lemon juice
> ⅔ cup butter

Split a large fish lengthwise, or use a small whole fish. Sprinkle with salt, caraway seeds, and lemon juice. Bake in butter in a 350° oven for 20 to 30 minutes.

Serves 4 to 6.

FISH WITH MUSTARD
Ryba Na Hořčici)

> 2 pounds fish (in 1 piece)
> salt to taste
> 4 teaspoons mustard
> ¼ cup butter
> 1 onion, chopped
> 2 tablespoons flour

lemon juice to taste
water
stock
    2 cups water
    1 cup diced soup greens
    1 bay leaf
    5 peppercorns
    5 allspice

Cook ingredients for stock together for 20 minutes. Sprinkle fish with salt; spread mustard over it. Wilt onion in butter, add fish; brown. Add stock. Simmer for 15 minutes. Remove fish to a heated platter. Mix flour in enough water to make a paste, and blend into stock. Simmer again for 5 minutes. Add lemon juice to taste. Strain sauce over fish.

Serves 4 to 5.

HERRING CASSEROLE
(Zapečený Slaneček)
    2 pounds potatoes, boiled, sliced
    1 medium onion, chopped
    ½ cup butter
    1 pound herring
    2 cups milk
    1 egg

Brown onion in 2 tablespoons butter; mix with potatoes. Soak herring in 1 cup milk; remove skin and bones, dice. Put half the potatoes in a greased pan, top with the herring, cover with the rest of the potatoes. Melt the remaining butter; pour over potatoes. Beat egg with 1 cup milk and pour over casserole. Bake in a 350° oven for 30 minutes.

Serves 4 to 6.

SAUCES

CREAM SAUCE
(Smetanová Omáčka)
    2 cups light cream
    ¼ cup flour
    ½ cup milk
    salt to taste
    2 tablespoons chopped blanched almonds

Bring cream to a boil. Pour in milk mixed with flour. Stir constantly. Simmer over low heat for 15 minutes. Add salt and almonds.

WHITE TOMATO SAUCE
(Rajská Omáčka Bílá)
    1 medium onion, chopped
    2 tablespoons butter
    ½ pound tomatoes, diced
    salt to taste
    1 cup water
    ¼ cup flour
    1 cup sour cream

Wilt onion in butter; add tomatoes, salt, and water. Simmer for 10 minutes. Rub through a sieve, bring to a boil. Mix flour with sour cream; add to tomatoes. Bring to a boil. Makes about 3 cups.

WHITE ONION SAUCE
(Cibulová Omáčka Bílá)
    2 large onions, sliced
    2 tablespoons butter
    1 cup boiling water
    ¼ cup flour
    1 cup milk
    salt to taste
    1 egg yolk

Wilt onions in butter, pour in boiling water. Bring to a boil. Mix flour with milk and salt and pour into sauce. Simmer for 20 minutes. Rub through a sieve, then add egg yolk, mixed well in ¼ cup of cooled sauce. Do not boil. Makes about 2 cups.

SAUERBRATEN SAUCE
(Svíčková Omáčka)
    1 carrot, chopped
    1 parsnip, chopped
    ½ celery root, chopped
    1 medium onion, chopped
    3 tablespoons butter
    2 cups stock
    4 peppercorns
    2 allspice
    ½ bay leaf
    salt to taste
    vinegar to taste

Fry vegetables in butter. Add stock, peppercorns, allspice, bay leaf. Simmer for 30 minutes. Rub through a sieve. Add salt and vinegar.

POLISH SAUCE
(Polská Omáčka)

1 medium onion, chopped
2 tablespoons butter
¼ cup flour
1½ cups stock
¼ teaspoon grated lemon peel
⅓ cup raisins
⅓ cup blanched almonds, sliced
2 teaspoons prune butter
2 teaspoons currant jam
salt to taste
½ cup red wine

Fry onion in butter, add flour, and brown. Add stock, and simmer for 30 minutes. Strain. Add all other ingredients and simmer for 5 to 10 minutes.

This is very good with Boiled Beef Tongue (see Index).

HORSERADISH WITH BREAD CRUMBS
(Houskový Křen)

2 tablespoons grated horseradish
¼ cup bread crumbs
½ cup hot stock
salt to taste
sugar to taste
vinegar to taste

Mix together all ingredients. Serve with boiled beef or pork.

EGGS, CHEESE AND NOODLE DISHES

CZECH OMELET
(Trhanec)

4 eggs, separated
¼ cup sugar
dash of salt
2 cups milk
2¼ cups flour
4 tablespoons butter for pan

Beat together egg yolks, sugar, salt, and half the milk. Add flour and the remaining milk. Beat until smooth. Fold in stiffly beaten egg whites. Melt 1 tablespoon butter in a pan, pour in one-quarter of the batter. Fry on both sides until golden brown. Tear with two forks into bite-size pieces; sprinkle with sugar. Serve with fruit syrup. Repeat to make three more omelets.

Serves 4.

POTATO OMELETS
(Bramborový Trhanec)

1 cup grated boiled potatoes
¼ cup sugar
dash of salt
2 eggs
1 cup milk
2 cups flour
¼ cup butter for pan, melted

Mix all ingredients to a smooth batter. Brush a frying pan with butter; fry omelets to a golden brown. Tear into small pieces, and sprinkle with sugar.

Serves 4.

EGG TOADSTOOLS
(Muchomurky)

6 hard-cooked eggs
3 anchovies
¾ cup (approximately) butter
3 tomatoes
2 cups finely chopped lettuce

Peel eggs. Slice a piece off the wider end of each so the yolk can be removed with a small spoon. Mash anchovies with butter and egg yolks; stuff mixture into hollowed egg whites. Arrange lettuce on a serving dish; stand the eggs, cut side down, on it. Cut tomatoes into halves, and place a half on each egg as a "cap." Dot with additional creamed butter.

Serves 6.

BAKED EGGS WITH CHICKEN LIVERS
(Vejce V Kelímcích S Kuřecími Játry)

4 chicken livers, chopped
¼ cup butter
salt to taste
pepper to taste
4 tablespoons cooked green peas
4-8 eggs

1 teaspoon minced parsley
2 teaspoons grated cheese

Brown chicken livers in half the butter. Divide into 4 greased custard cups; sprinkle with salt. Place 1 tablespoon peas in each cup, and break in 1 or 2 eggs. Sprinkle with salt and pepper. Top with remaining butter; sprinkle with parsley and cheese. Place cups in a pan of boiling water and bake in a preheated 350° oven until eggs are set (about 20 minutes).

Serves 4.

NOODLE SOUFFLÉ
(Nudlový Nákyp)

2⅔ cups milk
dash of salt
½ pound wide egg noodles
5 tablespoons butter
5 tablespoons sugar
3 eggs, separated
1 teaspoon vanilla
1 pound apples, peeled, cored, and sliced

Bring milk and salt to a boil. Add noodles. Cook until thick, stirring constantly. Cool. Cream butter with sugar, add egg yolks, and beat until foamy. Add cooked noodles and vanilla. Fold in stiffly beaten egg whites. Pour half the mixture into a greased baking dish, arrange apples on top, then pour in the remaining mixture. Bake in a preheated 350° oven 30 to 45 minutes. Sprinkle with sugar.

Serves 4 to 6.

RICE SOUFFLÉ
(Rýžový Nákyp)

3 cups milk
½ cup butter
½ cup plus 2 tablespoons sugar
1 cup rice
3 eggs, separated
1 teaspoon grated lemon peel
1 teaspoon vanilla
⅓ cup grated nuts
3 apples, peeled, cored, and sliced

Bring milk to a boil. Add ¼ cup of the butter, ¼ cup of the sugar, and rice. Cook until rice is done (about 14 minutes). Cool. Cream remaining butter and sugar, add egg yolks, beat until foamy. Add lemon peel, vanilla, nuts, and the cooked rice. Fold in stiffly beaten egg whites. Pour half the mixture into a greased soufflé dish. Arrange apples on top. Pour the remaining mixture over all. Bake in a preheated 350° oven for about 1 hour.

Serves 4 to 6.

HARD ROLL SOUFFLÉ
(Žemlový Nákyp)

6 hard rolls, sliced
2 cups hot milk
¼ cup butter
½ cup plus 2 tablespoons sugar
3 eggs, separated
½ teaspoon grated lemon peel
3 apricot kernels, grated
1 tablespoon farina
1 tablespoon cocoa

Pour milk over rolls; cool. Rub through a strainer. Cream butter with sugar and egg yolks until foamy. Add lemon peel, apricot kernels, and rolls. Fold in stiffly beaten egg whites and farina mixed with the cocoa. Grease a baking dish, and sprinkle with fine bread crumbs. Pour in the mixture, and bake in a preheated 350° oven for 35 to 45 minutes. Serve with Stewed Fruit or a fruit sirup.

Serves 4 to 6.

NOODLES
(Nudle)

3 cups instantized flour
2 eggs, lightly beaten
½ cup water

Mix eggs and water. Heap flour on a pastry board and make a well in the center. Pour egg mixture into the well. Mix with a fork at first, then knead into an elastic shiny dough. Cut into 3 pieces, cover with a napkin, and let stand for 30 minutes. Roll each piece out as thin as possible without tearing. Let dry for a few minutes. Cut into strips about 2 to 3 inches wide, or roll up and slice for longer noodles. Cut into desired width (⅛ inch for soup, ¾ inch for wide noodles). Cook in 4 quarts of salted boiling water for 4 to 5 minutes, stirring often. Drain.

Serves 3 to 4.

NOODLES WITH POPPY SEEDS OR GINGERBREAD
(Nudle S Mákem Nebo Perníkem)
>   **1 recipe Noodles (see Index)**
>   **½ cup butter, melted**
>   **½-¾ cup ground poppy seeds or grated ginger-bread**
>   **⅓ cup sugar**

Prepare noodles. Mix half the butter with cooked, drained noodles. Arrange on a plate. Mix poppy seeds or gingerbread with sugar, and sprinkle over the noodles. Pour the remaining butter over all.

Serves 3 to 4.

NOODLES WITH SPINACH
(Nudle Se Špenátem)
>   **⅛ recipe Noodles (see Index)**
>   **1 small onion, chopped**
>   **¼ cup butter**
>   **1 pound spinach, cleaned, cooked, and chopped**
>   **salt to taste**

Prepare noodles. Wilt onion in butter, add spinach and salt. Sauté for 5 minutes, add cooked noodles. Mix.

Serves 3 to 4.

DUMPLINGS AND PANCAKES

NAPKIN DUMPLING
(Třený Knedlík)
>   **⅔ cup butter**
>   **4 eggs, separated**
>   **1 teaspoon salt**
>   **¾ cup milk**
>   **4 cups instantized flour**
>   **4 cups diced stale white bread**
>   **2 tablespoons butter**

Cream ⅔ cup butter. Add egg yolks, 1 at a time, mixing well. Dissolve salt in milk and add liquid, alternately with flour, by spoonfuls to butter-egg mixture. Add the bread cubes, which have been fried in the 2 tablespoons butter, and mix in well. Fold in stiffly beaten egg whites.

Wet a large napkin; wring out. Place in sieve; pour in dough. Pull napkin up around dough and tie in 2 places with a thread: first right above mound of dough, then ¾ inch above that. Tie napkin corners over a wooden spoon and place this across a deep pot containing boiling water. Dumpling must be completely submerged but must not touch the bottom of the pot, and it should hang about 2 inches below water surface. Cook for 20 minutes, then untie the first thread. Continue to cook 40 minutes longer. Remove dumpling from napkin, and slice with thread. Slide a piece of thread about 20 inches long under dumpling; to slice dumpling, switch ends from one hand to the other, and pull.

Serves 6 to 8.

FARINA DUMPLINGS
(Krupicové Nočky)
>   **½ cup milk**
>   **salt to taste**
>   **¼ cup farina**
>   **2 tablespoons butter**
>   **1 egg**
>   **dash of mace**

Bring milk, salt, and farina to a slow boil, stir until thick. Cool. Add butter, egg, and mace. Drop in small amounts from a wet spoon into boiling soup; simmer for 3 to 5 minutes.

(POTATO DUMPLINGS (COLD POTATOES)
(Bramborové Knedlíky Ze Studených Brambor)
>   **2 pounds potatoes**
>   **salt to taste**
>   **3¼ cups instantized flour**
>   **2 eggs**
>   **boiling salted water**

Boil potatoes, let stand until the next day. Peel and grate. Add salt, flour, and eggs. Knead into firm dough. Do not let dough stand too long because it will get thin. Form into 4 rolls about 2½ inches in diameter. Boil in water for 15 to 20 minutes. Make sure dumplings do not stick to the bottom of the pan. Remove from water and slice.

Serves 4 to 6.

CHEESE FRUIT DUMPLINGS
(Těsto Tvarohové)

> **2 tablespoons butter**
> **1 egg**
> **½ cup pot cheese**
> **dash of salt**
> **2 cups instantized flour**
> **½ cup milk**
> **1-1½ pounds fruit (fresh prunes, apricots, cherries, apples, or any other firm fruit)**

Cream butter, egg, and cheese together thoroughly. Add salt, flour, and milk to make a medium-firm dough. Break off pieces and wrap around fruit (dough should be 3/16 inch thick), sealing edges well. Cook in boiling water for 5 to 8 minutes, turning once. When dumplings are done, remove with a skimmer and tear open with 2 forks. Serve with melted butter, more cheese, and sugar.

Serves 4 to 6.

THIN PANCAKES
(Palačinky)

> **2 eggs**
> **pinch of salt**
> **3 tablespoons sugar**
> **2 cups milk**
> **2 cups flour**
> **¼ cup butter for pan**
> **jam**

Beat together eggs, salt, sugar, milk, and flour until smooth. Heat a frying pan; brush with butter. Pour in a thin layer of batter, and spread by tilting the pan. Pancakes must be very thin-almost transparent. Fry on both sides to a golden brown. Spread with jam, roll up, and keep warm until served. Dust with sugar.

Serves 4 to 6.

PLAIN PANCAKES
(Lívance)

> **1 tablespoon compressed yeast (see Index)**
> **2 tablespoons sugar**
> **2½-2¾ cups flour**
> **2 cups (approximately) milk**
> **1 egg or 2 egg yolks**
> **pinch of salt**
> **½ teaspoon grated lemon peel**

> **⅓ cup butter (for pan)**
> **½ cup jam (optional)**
> **cinnamon sugar (½ cup sugar mixed with 1 teaspoon cinnamon-optional)**

Stir yeast and sugar together until mixture liquifies, and to it add 1 tablespoon flour and 1 or 2 tablespoons lukewarm milk. Let rise for 5 to 10 minutes (until mixture is bubbly). Add eggs, salt, and lemon peel; beat until well blended. Add flour and milk, and mix until batter is smooth. Let rise in a warm place for about 30 minutes or until doubled in bulk. Heat a heavy frying pan or griddle and brush with butter. Spoon in batter. Make pancakes about 4 inches across; turn to brown on both sides. Spread with jam, or dip in cinnamon sugar.

Serves 4.

VEGETABLES

BAKED ASPARAGUS
(Chřest Zapékaný)

> **3 tablespoons flour**
> **¼ cup butter**
> **1 cup milk or water**
> **salt to taste**
> **dash of nutmeg**
> **1 pound asparagus, boiled**
> **½ cup grated cheese**

Brown flour in half the butter. Add milk, salt, and nutmeg. Simmer sauce for 5 minutes. Arrange asparagus in a greased casserole in layers with sauce, and sprinkle with cheese. Dot with the remaining butter and bake in 350° oven for 30 minutes.

Serves 2.

CREAMED BRUSSELS SPROUTS
(Kapustová Poupata Na Smetaně)

> **1½ pounds Brussels sprouts**
> **boiling water to cover**
> **¼ cup butter**
> **1½ tablespoons flour**
> **1⅔ cups cream**
> **salt to taste**
> **pepper to taste**

dash of mace
dash of nutmeg

Soak cleaned Brussels sprouts in cold water for 15 minutes. Drain, then place in boiling water for 5 minutes. Drain again. Melt butter, blend in flour; add cream, and stir until smooth. Add Brussels sprouts, salt, and pepper. Simmer for 10 minutes or until tender. Add mace and nutmeg to taste.

Serves 6 to 8.

SAUTÉED CARROTS
(Mrkev Dusená)

3 cups sliced carrots
1 cup water
½ cup butter
salt to taste
½ teaspoon sugar
3 tablespoons flour
1 cup milk
juice of ½ lemon
1 tablespoon minced parsley or chives

Cook carrots in water with butter, salt, and sugar until tender (15 to 25 minutes). Dust with flour, add milk, and simmer for 5 minutes. Before serving, add lemon juice and parsley or chives. Or cook carrots with green peas, kohlrabi, asparagus tips, or fresh mushrooms.

Serves 4 to 6.

CAULIFLOWER SOUFFLÉ
(Květákový Nákyp)

1 cup butter
salt to taste
4 eggs, separated
1 cup sautéed mushrooms
2 cups cooked cauliflower, separated into flowerets
1 cup cooked and chopped veal or ham
¼ teaspoon nutmeg
2 tablespoons minced parsley
2 cups (approximately) bread crumbs

Cream ½ cup butter; add salt and egg yolks, mix well. Add mushrooms, cauliflower, meat, nutmeg, parsley, and 1⅔ cups bread crumbs; blend well. Fold in stiffly beaten egg whites. Pour into a greased baking dish lightly dusted with bread crumbs. Bake in a hot-water bath in a preheated 350° oven for 45 minutes. Brown ¼ cup bread crumbs in remaining ½ cup butter and sprinkle over casserole before serving.

Serves 4 to 6.

CUCUMBER STUFFED WITH MEAT
(Okurky Plněné Masem)

½ pound veal, cut up
1 medium onion
1 bay leaf
3 peppercorns
1 tablespoon butter
1 egg
½ cup bread crumbs
4 cucumbers
¼ cup chopped bacon

Simmer meat with onion seasonings until tender. Remove meat from pan and grind. Add butter, egg, and bread crumbs. Blend. Pare and cut cucumbers lengthwise into halves. Hollow out centers, fill with meat mixture, and cook in bacon until tender (about 30 minutes).

Serves 3 to 4.

STUFFED KALE ROLLS
(Kapustové Závitky)

2 small heads of kale, boiled
¼ cup butter
½ cup stock
filling:
    1 pound cooked pork, ground
    ½ pound cooked smoked meat, ground
    2 cups cooked rice
    salt to taste
    marjoram to taste
    1½ cups chopped mushrooms
    2 tablespoons butter

Sauté mushrooms in 2 tablespoons butter. Blend together all ingredients for filling. Pull off kale leaves carefully; chop the hearts and add to filling. Put 2 tablespoons filling on each kale leaf; roll up. Arrange in a greased baking dish, dot with butter, pour in stock. Bake in a preheated 375° oven for 30 to 45 minutes.

Serves 4 to 6.

KALE WITH EGGS (MOCK BRAINS)
(Kapusta S Vejci (Nepravý Mozeček))

> 1 medium onion, chopped
> ¼ cup butter
> 1 (1-pound) head of kale, cut into strips
> salt to taste
> 4 eggs, lightly beaten

Fry onion in butter; add kale, sprinkle with salt, and sauté until tender (10 to 15 minutes). Add eggs and stir until set.

Serves 2 to 4.

CABBAGE PATTIES
(Zelné Karbenátky)

> 3 slices bacon, chopped
> 2 cups chopped cooked cabbage
> 2 knockwursts or 4 frankfurters, sliced
> salt to taste
> 1 egg
> bread crumbs as needed
> ¼ cup flour
> ½ cup shortening for frying

Fry bacon and add to it cabbage, knockwurst or frankfurters, salt, egg, and enough bread crumbs to make a medium firm dough. Shape into patties, roll in flour, and brown in hot shortening.

Serves 4.

MORAVIAN CABBAGE
(Moravské zelí)

> 1½ pounds cabbage, shredded
> 1 cup water
> 1 medium onion, chopped
> ½ cup lard
> ⅓ cup flour
> ½ teaspoon caraway seeds
> salt to taste
> 4 teaspoons sugar
> ⅓ cup vinegar

Simmer cabbage in water for 5 minutes. Brown onion in lard, add flour, and stir until brown. Pour in the liquid from cabbage, and stir until smooth. Add cabbage, caraway seeds, salt, sugar, and vinegar. Simmer for 20 minutes.

Serves 4.

GREEN BEANS PAPRIKA
(Fazolové Lusky Na Paprice)

> 1 medium onion, chopped
> ¼ cup butter
> ¼ teaspoon paprika
> 1 pound green beans cut into 1-inch pieces (3 cups)
> salt to taste
> ½ cup water
> 2 tablespoons flour
> ½ cup sour cream

Fry onion in butter, add paprika, beans, salt, and water. Simmer until tender (20 to 30 minutes). Mix flour with sour cream, stir into beans. Simmer for 5 minutes. Serve with meat or hard-cooked eggs and potatoes.

Serves 4.

LENTILS
(Čočka Na Kyselo)

> 1½ cups lentils
> 3-4 cups water
> 1 medium onion, chopped
> ¼ cup lard
> 2 tablespoons flour
> salt to taste
> 2 tablespoons vinegar

Wash lentils and soak in water overnight. Cook until soft (about 1 hour). Fry onion in half the lard; add flour, and stir until brown. Add 1 cup water, bring to a boil, and add to lentils. Salt to taste. Simmer for 5 to 10 minutes. Add vinegar and the remaining lard. Serve with poached or boiled eggs.

Serves 4 to 6.

PEAS WITH BARLEY
(Hrách A Kroupy)

> 2 cups cooked dried peas
> 2 cups cooked barley
> ¼ cup lard
> 1 medium onion, chopped
> 8-12 slices bacon, fried

Mix freshly cooked peas with barley and lard. Brown onion in bacon drippings. Sprinkle crumbled bacon and onion over the peas with barley. Serve with boiled smoked meat and pickles.

Serves 4 to 6.

KOHLRABI KRAUT
(Brukvové Zelí)

> 1 medium onion, chopped
> ¼ cup butter
> 8 kohlrabi (2 pounds), peeled and cut into thin
>   strips
> pinch of caraway seeds
> salt to taste
> 1 tablespoon flour
> ½ cup water
> vinegar to taste
> sugar to taste

Fry onion in butter; add kohlrabi, caraway seeds, and salt. Sauté for 10 to 15 minutes. Dust with flour; add water, vinegar, and sugar; bring to a boil, and serve.

Serves 6 to 8.

POTATO AND MUSHROOM CASSEROLE
(Brambory ZapéKané S Houbami)

> 1 medium onion, chopped
> ½ cup butter
> 2 pounds mushrooms, sliced
> salt to taste
> ¼ teaspoon caraway seeds
> 2 pounds cooked potatoes, peeled and sliced
> 1 cup milk
> 2 eggs, lightly beaten

Sauté onion in butter, add mushrooms, salt and caraway seeds. In a greased casserole arrange alternate layers of potatoes and mushrooms. Repeat layering, ending with potatoes. Mix together milk and eggs, and pour over casserole. Bake in a preheated 350° oven for 20 to 30 minutes, or until eggs are set.

Serves 4 to 6.

POTATO GOULASH WITH PAPRIKA
(Bramborovy Guláš Na Paprice)

> 2 medium onions, chopped
> ½ cup lard or chopped bacon
> ½ teaspoon paprika
> dash of pepper
> ¼ teaspoon caraway seeds
> 2½ pounds potatoes, peeled and sliced
> salt to taste
> water as needed

> ½ cup cream
> 1 tablespoon flour

Fry onions in lard or bacon; add paprika, pepper, caraway seeds, potatoes, and salt. Half cover with water. Cook until potatoes are tender. Mix cream with flour, stir into potatoes, and simmer for 5 minutes. Serve as is, or with any leftover diced meat, fish, vegetables, or hard-boiled eggs added.

Serves 6.

POTATOES WITH TOMATOES
(S rajskými jablíčky)

> 1 medium onion, chopped
> ¼ cup oil
> 1 pound potatoes, peeled and diced
> 1 pound tomatoes, peeled and sliced
> salt to taste
> pepper to taste
> 1 tablespoon minced parsley

Fry onion in oil, add potatoes, and sauté for 10 minutes. Add tomatoes, salt, and pepper; cover, and simmer until tender. Before serving, add parsley.

Serves 2 to 4.

SOUR POTATOES
(Brambory Na Kyselo)

> 2½ pounds potatoes, peeled and sliced
> salted water to cover
> ½ teaspoon caraway seeds
> ¼ cup flour
> ¼ cup shortening
> 1 cup sour cream
> 1 tablespoon vinegar
> ½ teaspoon sugar
> 1 tablespoon chopped dill or chives
> 1 or 2 egg yolks

Boil potatoes in salted water with caraway seeds. Drain, and reserve liquid. Brown flour in shortening, stirring constantly, and stir in 1 to 1½ cups of potato water. Simmer for 10 to 15 minutes. Add the remaining ingredients and potatoes. Serve as is, or add diced boiled meat.

Serves 6.

PICKLED MUSHROOMS
(Houby V Octě)

2 pounds mushrooms
⅓ cup vinegar
1 cup water
salt to taste
1 teaspoon sugar
3 peppercorns
2 allspice
1 small bay leaf
pinch of mustard seeds

Simmer small whole or large quartered mushrooms in salted water for 3 minutes. Drain. In another pot, simmer vinegar, the cup of water, salt, sugar, peppercorns, allspice, and bay leaf for 5 minutes. Cool. Arrange mushrooms in a screw-top jar and sprinkle with mustard seeds. Pour the strained vinegar mixture over them. Cover, and store in a cool place for about 1 week.

Serves 20.

STUFFED GREEN PEPPERS
(Papriky Plněné)

8 green peppers, cleaned
filling:
    1 medium onion, chopped
    2 tablespoons shortening
    1 pound ground pork, or pork and beef
    1 tablespoon minced parsley
    salt to taste
    pepper to taste
    1 cup cooked rice
sauce:
    2 large onions, chopped
    ⅓ cup oil
    1 pound tomatoes, chopped
    salt to taste
    ½ cup sour cream

To prepare filling, sauté onion in shortening. Add meat, parsley, salt, and pepper. Brown meat. Remove from heat and add rice. Stuff the peppers with the mixture.

To prepare sauce, sauté onion in oil. Add tomatoes. Cook for 20 minutes. Rub through a sieve and add salt. Place stuffed peppers in the sauce, cover, and simmer for 30 minutes. Before serving, add sour cream to sauce.

Serves 4 to 6.

SPINACH PANCAKES
(Špenátové Lívanečky)

1 pound spinach, cleaned
¼ cup butter
2 eggs, separated
salt to taste
⅓ cup flour

Steam spinach 3 to 5 minutes. Drain and chop very fine. Cream butter with egg yolks, add salt, spinach, and flour. Mix well. Fold in stiffly beaten egg whites. Bake on a greased griddle. Make pancakes small (about 3 inches in diameter).

Serves 4 to 6.

SPINACH SOUFFLÉ
(Špenátový Nákyp)

3 eggs, separated
½ cup butter
salt to taste
2 hard rolls
½ cup milk
3 cups cooked spinach, chopped
½ pound ham or smoked meat, chopped
pepper to taste
1 clove garlic, mashed
melted butter
grated cheese

Cream egg yolks with butter and salt. Soak rolls in milk, and rub through a sieve. Add to butter mixture. Add remaining ingredients. Fold in stiffly beaten egg whites. Bake in a greased soufflé form in a preheated 350° oven 30 to 35 minutes, or until eggs are set. Serve with melted butter and grated cheese.

Serves 6 to 8.

TOMATOES FILLED WITH EGGS AND CHEESE
(Rajská Jablíčka Plněná Vejci A Sýrem)

8 tomatoes
salt to taste
pepper to taste
1 cup grated Swiss or American cheese
¼ cup butter
8 eggs
1 tablespoon minced parsley

Cut out a circle at the stem end in tomatoes. Scoop out insides carefully, sprinkle with salt, pepper, and

half of the cheese. Put in a bit of butter, and drop an egg into each tomato. Sprinkle with more salt, the remaining cheese, and parsley. Bake in a preheated 350° oven for 30 minutes or until eggs are set. Excellent as a meatless dish with potato or legumes purée.
Serves 4 to 8.

TOMATOES WITH EGGS
(Opečená Rajčata S Vejci)

4-6 slices Canadian bacon
1 medium onion, sliced
1 pound tomatoes, sliced
4-6 eggs
salt to taste
pepper to taste

Brown bacon in a frying pan. Top each slice with onion and tomatoes. Cook 10 to 15 minutes, or until all the liquid evaporates. Place an egg on each slice; cover, and cook slowly until eggs are set.
Serves 4 to 6.

VEGETABLE SOUFFLÉ
(Zeleninový Nákyp Pečený)

2½ cups diced vegetables (cauliflower, asparagus, green peas, carrots, kohlrabi, etc.)
1 cup diced cooked potatoes
½ cup sliced mushrooms
1 cup diced ham or smoked meat
2 tablespoons grated cheese
½ cup butter, melted
1 cup cream or milk
1 egg
1 tablespoon flour

In a greased casserole, place a layer each of vegetables, potatoes, mushrooms, and ham. Sprinkle with cheese and butter. Repeat. Bake in a preheated 350° oven for 10 minutes. Mix together egg and flour; add cream. Pour over the casserole. Bake 20 minutes longer.
Serves 6 to 8.

SALADS

RUSSIAN SALAD
(Ruský Salát)

3 cups diced ham
2 cups diced cooked potatoes
1 cup peas
1½ cups diced pickles
1 cup diced onion
1 pickled herring, diced
1 tablespoon capers
salt to taste
pepper to taste
Homemade Mayonnaise (see Index)

Mix all ingredients with salt and pepper. Bind with mayonnaise and chill for several hours.
Serves 8 to 10.

GREEN BEAN SALAD
(Salát Z Fazolových Lusku)

3 cups cooked green beans, cut into 1-inch pieces
1 large onion, chopped
dressing:
½ cup water
2 tablespoons vinegar
1 tablespoon oil
salt to taste
½ teaspoon sugar
or
⅔ cup mayonnaise
lemon juice to taste

Toss together all ingredients, chill, and serve.
Serves about 4.

PRAGUE SALAD
(Pražský Salát)

1½ cups thin strips of roast veal
1½ cups thin strips of roast pork
1½ cups thin strips of pickles
1 cup thin strips of onion
1 cup thin strips of sour apples
salt to taste
pepper to taste
1 tablespoon lemon juice
Homemade Mayonnaise (see Index)

Mix together cut-up ingredients. Sprinkle with lemon juice, salt, and pepper; bind with mayonnaise. Chill for several hours.

Serves 8.

CAULIFLOWER SALAD
(Salát Z Květáku)

salad:

3 cups cauliflower, broken into flowerets

4 cups water

salt to taste

1 bay leaf

3-4 peppercorns

dressing:

½ cup water

3 tablespoons vinegar

salt to taste

½ teaspoon sugar

1 small onion, grated

3 tablespoons oil

Boil cauliflower in salted water with bay leaf and peppercorns for about 10 minutes. Drain. Mix dressing, pour over flowerets, and chill.

Serves about 4.

PARSNIP SALAD
(Salát Z Pastináku)

1⅓ cup water

⅔ cup vinegar

2 peppercorns

2 allspice

2 cloves

1 bay leaf

salt to taste

1 pound parsnips, pared and sliced

boiling water to cover

1-2 tablespoons oil

1 large onion, chopped

Bring water with vinegar, spice, and salt to a boil. In another pot, pour fresh boiling water over parsnips; simmer for 2 minutes. Drain parsnips, place in boiling vinegar water, cover, and simmer for about 30 minutes. Remove spice, add oil. Chill. Before serving, sprinkle onion over top.

Serves 4 to 6.

LETTUCE WITH BACON
(Hlávkový Salát Se Slaninou)

2-3 heads Boston lettuce

½ cup water

½ teaspoon sugar

¼ teaspoon salt

2 tablespoons vinegar

3-4 strips bacon, chopped and fried

Wash lettuce and break up into a bowl. Dissolve sugar and salt in water, add vinegar, and pour over lettuce. Before serving, pour warm, not hot, bacon and fat over the salad.

Serves 4 to 6.

POTATO SALAD WITH MEAT (OR FISH)
(Saláty Bramborové Masité)

2 pounds potatoes, cooked and diced

1 large onion, chopped

3 sour-sweet pickles, diced

salt to taste

vinegar to taste

½ pound (1½ cups) diced meat (any kind) or fish

¾-1 cup mayonnaise, to taste

Mix all ingredients well. Chill.

Serves 6 to 8.

BREAD, ROLLS AND COFFEE CAKES

SINGLE-ACTING BAKING POWDER

Phosphate type, is not very successfully interchanged with double-acting (sodium aluminium sulphate) baking powder. If a recipe calls for single-acting baking powder, and you want to substitute double-acting baking powder for it, use ¼ less.

COMPRESSED (FRESH) YEAST

Compressed yeast seems to give more satisfactory results in the recipes in this book than does granular yeast, but if you cannot obtain compressed yeast, use granular, bearing in mind that 2 ounces (4 tablespoons) compressed yeast is equal to 4 packages dry or granular yeast. Follow the directions on the package for dissolving granular yeast (remember that a warmer liquid—110° to 115°—is needed to dissolve granular than fresh yeast); then proceed as directed in the recipe.

Whether you are using compressed or granular yeast, be sure it is fresh. Always dissolve compressed yeast before using to test its freshness; fresh yeast will foam and bubble in 5 to 10 minutes. Granular yeast carries on the package a date beyond which it should not be used for best results. Note that in many of the recipes here, sugar is crumbled over the yeast and the two mixed together until the sugar liquefies.

To be successful with yeast dough, you must give it special attention. Not only must the yeast be fresh, but the ingredients—and even the bowl in which you mix the dough—must be lukewarm or at least at room temperature. And, finally, let the dough rise in a warm place, free from drafts.

SOFT YEAST DOUGH
(Polotuhé Těsto Kynuté)
- 1 tablespoon compressed yeast (see Index)
- 1 tablespoon sugar
- 2 tablespoons flour
- 2 tablespoons lukewarm milk
- 4 cups flour
- ¼ cup sugar
- 1 teaspoon salt
- 1 cup lukewarm milk
- ¼ cup butter, melted
- 1 egg
- ½ teaspoon grated lemon peel
- 1 teaspoon vanilla

Place yeast in a bowl, sprinkle yeast with sugar, and stir until mixture liquefies. Add 2 tablespoons flour and 2 tablespoons milk; blend. Cover with a cloth and let rise in a warm place for 5 to 10 minutes. Add all other ingredients; mix well with a wooden spoon. Remove dough from bowl, put on a floured pastry board, and knead until it is smooth and does not stick. Return to bowl, sprinkle with flour, and cover with a cloth. Let it rise in a warm place (about 80°F.) 30 to 60 minutes or until it is almost doubled. Punch down, form into desired shapes and let rise again for about 30 minutes. Bake in a preheated oven at 400° for 15 to 20 minutes.

FIRM YEAST DOUGH 1
(Tuhé Kynuté Těsto)
- 5½ teaspoons compressed yeast (see Index)
- 1 tablespoon sugar
- 2 tablespoons flour
- 2—3 tablespoons lukewarm milk
- 4½ cups flour
- ½ cup sugar
- 1 teaspoon salt
- 1 cup lukewarm milk
- ½ cup butter, melted
- 2 egg yolks
- ½ teaspoon grated lemon peel
- 1 teaspoon vanilla
- ¼ cup raisins
- ⅓ cup Blanched Almonds (see Index), sliced
- 2 tablespoons chopped citron

Follow directions for making Soft Yeast Dough. This dough will take longer to rise because it is much richer. Add raisins, almonds, and citron after dough has been kneaded. Form into desired shapes and bake in a preheated oven at 400° for 15 to 20 minutes.

FIRM YEAST DOUGH 2
(Tuhé Kynuté Těsto)
- 2 tablespoons plus ½ teaspoon compressed yeast (see Index)
- 1 tablespoon sugar
- 2 tablespoons flour
- 2-3 tablespoons lukewarm milk
- 4½ cups flour
- ⅔ cup sugar
- 1 teaspoon salt
- 1 cup (approximately) lukewarm milk
- ⅔ cup butter, melted
- 3-4 egg yolks
- ½ teaspoon grated lemon peel
- 1 teaspoon vanilla
- ½ cup raisins
- ½ cup Blanched Almonds (see Index), sliced
- ⅓ cup chopped citron

Follow directions for making Soft Yeast Dough (see Index). This dough will take longer than Soft Yeast Dough to rise because it is much richer. After kneading the dough, add raisins, almonds, and citron. Form into desired shapes and bake in a preheated oven at 400° for 15 to 20 minutes.

SALT ROLLS
(Housky)

> 2 tablespoons plus 1 teaspoon compressed yeast (see Index)
> 1 tablespoon sugar
> 2 tablespoons flour
> 2-3 tablespoons lukewarm milk
> 4¼ cups flour
> 2 teaspoons salt
> 1 egg
> ½ cup lukewarm milk
> ¼ cup butter, melted
> topping:
>> 1 egg, beaten
>> coarse salt
>> whole poppy seeds or caraway seeds (optional)

Prepare dough as in recipe for Soft Yeast Dough (see Index), and, after it has risen, punch down and shape into long sticks or small rolls. Or roll dough out and cut it into strips ½ inch wide and 6 inches long; braid 3 strips and press ends together. Place on a greased baking sheet and let rise. Brush with egg and sprinkle with coarse salt, and add poppy seeds or caraway seeds, if you like. Bake in a preheated 400° oven for 15 to 20 minutes.

CABBAGE ROLLS
(Zelníky)

> 1 recipe Soft Yeast Dough (see Index)
> ¼ cup butter, melted
> filling:
>> 4 cups shredded cabbage
>> 2 tablespoons butter
>> salt to taste
>> sugar to taste
>> ½ teaspoon vanilla
>> ¼ cup milk

Stew cabbage in butter for about 10 minutes. Add the remaining ingredients, and cook for 10 minutes longer or until all liquid has evaporated. Cool. Roll out dough about ¾ inch thick, and cut into 4-inch squares. Place a spoonful of filling in the center of each. Bring dough edges together and pinch to seal in filling. Place rolls on a buttered baking sheet, and let rise. Brush with melted butter. Bake in a preheated 350° oven for about 30 minutes.

BRIOCHES
(Briošky)

> 1 recipe Firm Yeast Dough 1 or 2 (see Index)
> 1 egg, beaten

Knead raised dough on lightly floured board and shape into buns. Place on a well-greased baking sheet and let rise again. Cut a cross in top of each with scissors; brush with egg. Bake in a preheated 400° oven for 15 minutes; reduce heat to 375° and bake for 10 to 15 minutes longer.

YEAST PUFF DOUGH
(Překládané Těsto Kynuté (Plundrově))

> butter dough:
>> 1¼ cups butter
>> 1 cup flour
> yeast dough:
>> 4½ teaspoons compressed yeast (see Index)
>> 1 tablespoon sugar
>> 2 tablespoons flour
>> 3 tablespoons lukewarm milk
>> 3 cups flour
>> 1 teaspoon salt
>> ¼ cup sugar
>> 2 eggs
>> 1 egg yolk
>> ½ cup lukewarm milk

Prepare Butter Dough first. Cut butter into flour; work to a dough. Shape into a rectangle ½ inch thick. Put into refrigerator.

To make Yeast Dough, mix yeast with sugar until it liquefies. Add flour and milk; mix well. Let rise in a warm place for 5 to 10 minutes (until bubbly). Add other ingredients and beat with a wooden spoon until dough loosens from spoon. Cover with a cloth and let rise in a warm place for about 1 hour. Place Yeast Dough on a floured pastry board and roll out into a square. Place Butter Dough in the center of Yeast Dough and fold Yeast Dough over it, like an envelope, pinching corners together in the center. Fold in half and roll out into a rectangle about ½ inch thick. Fold lower third up over center third, and fold remaining third down over first third. Fold in half again, bringing the 2 shorter sides together. Cover and let rest for 1 hour in a cool place, then roll out and repeat folding process. Let rest for another 30 minutes. Roll out and form into desired shapes, place on a greased baking sheet, and let rise again. Bake in a preheated oven at 400° for 15 to 20 minutes.

EASTER CAKE
(Bochánek Velikonoční)

    1 recipe Firm Yeast Dough 1 or 2 (see Index)
    1 egg, beaten
    2 tablespoons sliced Blanched Almonds (see Index)

Knead prepared raised dough on lightly floured board and shape into a large round loaf. Put on a well-greased baking sheet and let rise. Brush with egg. Cut a cross in top of loaf with scissors; sprinkle with almonds. Bake in a preheated 400° oven for 15 minutes; reduce heat to 375°, and bake 30 to 45 minutes longer.

CROWN CAKE
(Bábovka)

    1 recipe Soft Yeast Dough (see Index)
    ⅓ cup raisins
    ⅓ cup sliced Blanced Almonds (see Index)
    2 tablespoons chopped citron or candied orange peel

Prepare dough, and after it has been kneaded, mix in raisins, almonds, and citron or orange peel. Butter and flour a large fluted tube pan. Place dough in it, cover with a cloth, and let rise in a warm place. Bake in a preheated 350° oven for 45 to 60 minutes. Test cake with a toothpick before removing from oven. When it is done, let it stand in pan for 5 minutes, then turn out on a wire rack to cool. (If cake sticks to pan, wrap outside of pan in a damp towel for a few minutes.) Sprinkle with sugar.

JELLY DOUGHNUTS
(Koblihy)

    4½ teaspoons compressed yeast
    1 tablespoon sugar
    2 tablespoons flour
    3 tablespoons lukewarm milk
    3 tablespoons butter
    ¼ cup sugar
    4-5 egg yolks
    4¼ cups flour
    pinch of salt

    1-2 tablespoons rum
    1 cup (approximately) milk or cream
    1 cup jam (apricot, raspberry, or currant)
    1½-2 cups oil for frying
    confectioners' sugar

Blend yeast and the tablespoon of sugar together until mixture liquefies, add flour and milk, and beat well. Put in a warm place, cover, and let rise 5 to 10 minutes. Beat butter with sugar and egg yolks until foamy. Mix in raised yeast. Add flour, salt, rum, and enough milk to make a medium firm dough. Beat with a wooden spoon until smooth; dough will then loosen from spoon. Dust with flour, cover, and let rise in a warm place for about 45 minutes. On a lightly floured board, roll out dough lightly about 1/5 inch thick. Cut out circles with a 3-inch cutter. Put 2 teaspoons of jam in the center of half the dough circles, cover with the remaining circles; press edges together with fingertips, and cut doughnuts again with cutter to trim dough. Place doughnuts on a warm floured cloth, cover with a napkin, and let rise for about 15 minutes. Turn over, and let rise again for 15 minutes. Heat ¾ inch of oil in a skillet, put doughnuts in, and cover immediately. Shake skillet slightly a few times during cooking so doughnuts do not stick to bottom. Fry about 2 or 3 minutes, turn with a spatula, and fry on the other side, uncovered. Remove from pan and drain on absorbent paper. A light border should show around the middle. Dust with sugar.
Makes about 2 dozen doughnuts.

DESSERTS

BLACK-AND-WHITE LINZ DOUGH
(Linecké Těsto Dvoubarevné)

    2¼ cups flour
    ½ cup sugar
    ¾ cup butter
    1-2 egg yolks
    1 teaspoon vanilla
    2 tablespoons (approximately) cocoa
    1-2 egg whites, lightly beaten (optional)

Sift flour with sugar. Cut in butter. Add egg yolks and vanilla. Work into a smooth dough. Add cocoa to half the dough. Shape cookies as follows:

CHECKERBOARD COOKIES
(Šachovnice)

On a floured board roll out each portion of Linz Dough (opposite) ½ inch thick. Cut into ½-inch-wide strips. Lay 5 strips alternately on a piece of waxed paper (first a light strip, then a dark, another light, another dark, then a light). The strips must touch each other. Over the first layer place a second layer of strips, this time starting and ending with a dark strip, and top this with a third layer, starting with a light strip. Wrap dough in waxed paper, keeping it flat, and chill for 2 to 3 hours. Slice into ¼-inch-thick cookies, place on a greased baking sheet, and bake in a preheated 350° oven for 10 to 15 minutes.

CRISP CHEESE DOUGH STICKS
(Křehké Těsto Tvarohové)
- **⅔ cup farmer cheese**
- **1⅓ cup flour**
- **¾ cup shortening**
- **salt to taste**
- **1 egg, lightly beaten**
- **coarse salt**
- **caraway seeds** } **(optional)**
- **grated cheese**

Mix cheese, flour, shortening, and salt into a smooth dough. Roll out about ¼ inch thick. Cut into sticks with a pastry wheel. Brush with egg, and sprinkle with coarse salt and caraway seeds, or grated cheese. Bake in a preheated 400° oven for about 15 minutes.

KARLSBAD RINGS
(Věnečky Z Vařených Žloutku)
- **¾ cup butter**
- **½ cup sugar**
- **2 hard-cooked egg yolks, rubbed through a sieve**
- **2 raw egg yolks**
- **1 teaspoon vanilla**
- **1 teaspoon grated lemon peel**
- **2½ cups flour**
- **1 egg, lightly beaten**
- **½ cup chopped filberts or chopped candied fruit**

Cream butter; mix in sugar, egg yolks, vanilla, and lemon peel thoroughly. Add flour. Work into a smooth dough. Roll out on a lightly floured board ⅛ inch thick. Cut into small rings, sprinkle with nuts or fruit. Bake in a preheated 350° oven for 15 to 20 minutes.

CARPENTER'S CURLS
(Hoblovačky)
- **½ cup sugar**
- **½ cup flour**
- **2 eggs**
- **1 tablespoon anise seeds**

Beat together sugar, flour, and eggs with a wire whisk for about 10 minutes. Grease and flour a baking sheet. With a pastry tube, make 3 or 4 strips of the batter, ½ inch wide, the length of the baking sheet. Sprinkle with anise seeds. Bake in a preheated 350° oven for 5 to 10 minutes. Cut strips into halves or thirds, and curl over the handle of a wooden spoon while still warm. Repeat until all batter is used up.

COCOA BALLS
(Kakaové Dulkové Koláčky)
- **1 cup flour**
- **2 tablespoons cocoa**
- **5 tablespoons sugar**
- **5 tablespoons lard, melted**
- **1 teaspoon vanilla**
- **⅓ cup jam**

Mix together all ingredients except jam into a smooth dough. Form into 1½-inch balls. With the handle of a wooden spoon make an indentation in the center of each. Bake in a preheated 275° oven for 20 to 30 minutes. Fill centers with jam.

CHOCOLATE CAKE
(Dort Čokoládový)
- **½ cup butter**
- **½ cup sugar**
- **4 eggs, separated**
- **1 teaspoon vanilla**
- **3½ ounces (squares) chocolate, melted**
- **1 cup flour**

Cream together butter, sugar, and egg yolks until foamy. Add vanilla and chocolate. Gently fold in stiffly beaten egg whites alternately with flour. Pour into greased and floured spring form or 9-inch deep cake pan, and bake in a preheated 325° oven for 30 to 45 minutes. When cake is cool, split into 2 layers and fill with Whipped Cream, or Cocoa or Vanilla Butter Cream.

BREAD CHERRY CAKE
(Housková Bublanina)

- ½ cup butter
- ½ cup sugar
- 4 eggs, separated
- 2⅓ cups (3½ ounces) fresh fine bread crumbs
- 2 teaspoons single-acting baking powder (see Index)
- ¼ teaspoon cinnamon
- 1-1½ pounds sour or sweet cherries
- confectioners' sugar

Cream butter thoroughly with sugar and egg yolks. Blend in bread crumbs mixed with baking powder and cinnamon. Fold in stiffly beaten egg whites. Spread 1 to 1½ inches high on a greased and floured 4-sided baking sheet. Arrange cherries on top of batter. Bake in a preheated 320° oven for 20 to 30 minutes. Cool. To serve, cut in squares and sprinkle with sugar.

CHEESE CAKE
(Tvarohový Koláč Třený)

- ½ cup butter
- ½ cup sugar
- 3 eggs, separated
- ½ cup cottage cheese, rubbed through a strainer
- 1 cup ground nuts
- ⅓-½ cup bread crumbs
- jam
- grated chocolate
- nuts

Cream butter with sugar and egg yolks thoroughly. Blend in cheese and nuts. Fold in stiffly beaten egg whites and bread crumbs. Butter a spring form and sprinkle with bread crumbs. Spread in cake mixture. Bake in a preheated 320° oven for about 30 minutes. When cake is cool, spread with jam and sprinkle with grated chocolate and nuts.

MERINGUE PORCUPINE
(Sněhový Ježek)
  cake:
- 5 eggs, separated
- 5 tablespoons sugar
- 5 tablespoons instantized flour
- ½ teaspoon vanilla
- 1 cup jam
- confectioners' sugar (optional)

  meringue:
- 3 egg whites
- ¾ cup sugar

Beat egg whites until very stiff. Add egg yolks, 1 at a time, sprinkling each with sugar, and blending in gently. Fold in flour and vanilla. Spread batter on a greased and floured 4-sided baking sheet. Bake in a preheated 325° oven for 15 to 20 minutes. Turn out onto waxed paper or a damp cloth sprinkled with confectioners' sugar. Spread with jam while still warm, and roll up.

To prepare meringue, beat egg whites until stiff; beat in half the sugar, then fold in the other half. Meringue will be very stiff and glossy.

Place jelly roll on a baking sheet, and with a pastry tube, cover the roll with tiny rosettes of meringue. Bake in a 350° oven for 15 to 20 minutes. Slice to serve.

SPECIAL CROWN CAKE
(Jemná Bábovka)

- 1 cup butter
- 1¼ cups sugar
- 5 eggs, separated
- 2¼ cups instantized flour
- 1 cup milk
- 2 teaspoons single-acting baking powder (see Index)
- ½ teaspoon grated lemon peel
- 1 teaspoon vanilla
- ⅓ cup chocolate pieces, melted
- 2 tablespoons (approximately) oil for pan

Cream butter and sugar, add egg yolks, beat until light and creamy. Mix in flour and milk alternately by spoonfuls. Add the baking powder mixed into the last ½ cup flour. Blend in lemon peel and vanilla. Fold in stiffly beaten egg whites. Pour half the batter into another bowl and add the chocolate to it. Brush a fluted tube pan with oil, and pour in batter in four alternating light and dark layers. Cut through batter with a spoon to get a marbled effect. Bake in a preheated 350° oven for 60 to 75 minutes. Cool in pan for 15 minutes, then turn cake out onto a wire rack. Sprinkle with Vanilla Sugar (see Index) when cool.

SPONGE CAKE
(Piškot Šlehaný)

        4 eggs, separated
        ¾ cup sugar
        1 cup flour
        ½ teaspoon lemon juice
        ½ teaspoon grated lemon peel
        fine bread crumbs

Beat egg whites to soft peaks. Add ⅓ cup sugar, beat until whites are very stiff and glossy. Fold in egg yolks, 1 at a time, sprinkling each before blending with part of the remaining sugar and flour. Gently blend in lemon juice and peel. Grease a spring form and sprinkle with bread crumbs; pour in batter. Bake in a preheated 325° oven for 30 to 45 minutes. Cook cake for 15 minutes, then remove from pan.

YOLK FLOWER BOXES
(Žloutkové Rakvičky)

        "boxes" pastry:
            2⅓ cups confectioners' sugar
            5 egg yolks
            1 egg
            1 tablespoon instantized flour
            1 teaspoon vanilla
        filling:
            Whipped Cream (see Index)

Beat all ingredients for "boxes" in an electric mixer or with a wire whisk until thick and foamy (about 45 minutes). Prepare the tiny loaf pans used for these (or éclair molds) by brushing with melted butter and sprinkling with flour; fill two-thirds full with batter. Bake in a preheated 375° oven for 10 minutes or until "boxes" are puffed up, then reduce heat to 325° and bake 10 to 15 minutes longer. Cool in pans. With the point of a knife, make small openings in both ends of pastry. Force in whipped cream with a pastry tube, and decorate top with a line of cream.

WALNUT CAKE
(Dort Ořechový)

        6 eggs, separated
        ½ cup sugar
        ⅔ cup ground walnuts
        ½ cup flour
        ⅔ cup fine bread crumbs

Beat egg whites until very stiff. Carefully blend in egg yolks, 2 at a time, sprinkling each with sugar before blending. Mix nuts, flour, and bread crumbs together; fold lightly into batter. Pour into a greased and floured spring form. Bake in a preheated 325° oven for 45 to 60 minutes. Cover with Whipped Cream, Vanilla Cream Filling, or Coffee Cream Filling. (See Index)

MALAKOV CAKE
(Dort Malakov)

        ½ cup butter
        ½ cup plus 2 tablespoons sugar
        3 egg yolks
        ¾ cup grated Blanched Almonds (see Index)
        1 cup heavy cream
        40-50 (approximately) ladyfingers

Cream butter thoroughly with sugar and egg yolks. Add almonds, mix well. Pour in cream slowly, beating continuously. Line a spring form with waxed paper, and line the sides and bottom with ladyfingers. Fill pan with alternate layers of batter and ladyfingers, ending with ladyfingers. Cover form with waxed paper and place on it another cake pan holding a weight. Put in refrigerator overnight. Remove cake from form, and decorate with Whipped Cream.

MERINGUE CRESCENTS WITH NUTS
(Oříškové Pěnové Rohlíčky)

        4 egg whites
        1 cup superfine sugar
        1 cup ground filberts or almonds

Beat egg whites and sugar in a double boiler until thick. Place by spoonfuls on a board sprinkled with the nuts. Roll in nuts and shape into crescents. Bake on a greased baking sheet in a preheated 200° oven until crisp (about 40 to 50 minutes).

QUICK CRUMB PIE
(Drobenkový Koláč Rychlý)

- 2¼ cups instantized flour
- ½ teaspoon baking powder
- ½ cup sugar
- ½ cup butter
- 1 egg, lightly beaten
- ½ teaspoon vanilla
- ½ teaspoon grated lemon peel
- 1 pound apples, pared and sliced
- ¼ cup sugar
- ¼ cup butter, melted
- 1 tablespoon sugar (for top)

Mix together dry ingredients, and rub in butter to form crumbs. Mix in egg, vanilla, and lemon peel. Crumble again with your fingers. Put half the crumbs in a buttered and floured cake pan. Spread on apples, sprinkle with the ¼ cup sugar and half the melted butter. Cover with the remaining crumbs, and sprinkle with the tablespoon sugar and the rest of butter. Bake in a preheated 400° oven for 30 to 45 minutes.

Serves 4 to 6.

STRETCHED STRUDEL DOUGH
(Závin Tažený)

- 2⅔ cups flour
- pinch of salt
- 1 egg, lightly beaten
- ½ cup lukewarm water
- ½ teaspoon vinegar
- 1 tablespoon lard, melted

Sift flour onto a pastry board and make a well in the center. Mix together salt, egg, water, vinegar, and lard, and add gradually to flour, stirring with a fork until flour is completely moistened. Knead dough until smooth and elastic. Shape into a ball, and let it rest, covered with a warm, inverted bowl, on lightly floured board for 30 minutes.

Cover a table with a clean cloth and sprinkle with flour. Place dough in the center, dust with flour, and roll out ⅛ inch thick. Slide hands under dough, and with the backs of your clenched fists, start stretching it, working from center in all directions, and being careful not to tear it. When center of dough becomes paper thin, concentrate the stretching closer to dough edges. Stretched dough should finally be as thin as tissue paper. Fill as directed in one of the following recipes.

APPLE STRUDEL
(Jablkový závin)

- 1 recipe Stretched Strudel Dough (above)
- ½ cup butter, melted
- 2 pounds apples, pared and sliced
- 1 cup bread crumbs
- 3 tablespoons butter
- ½ cup sugar
- 1 teaspoon cinnamon
- ⅓ cup raisins
- confectioners' sugar

Brush prepared dough generously with part of the melted butter and sprinkle with bread crumbs browned in the 3 tablespoons butter. Spread apples evenly over dough; sprinkle with sugar mixed with cinnamon, raisins, and more melted butter. Grasp cloth holding dough on one side with both hands. Lift slowly, and start rolling up dough, brushing underside with butter as you roll. Roll strudel from the cloth onto a greased baking sheet. Brush top with butter and bake in a 350° oven for about 30 minutes. Dust with confectioners' sugar. Slice to serve.

CHERRY STRUDEL
(Třešňovy závin)

- 1 recipe Stretched Strudel Dough (above)
- ½ cup butter, melted
- 1 cup bread crumbs
- 3 tablespoons butter
- 2 pounds sour (or sweet) cherries, pitted
- ½-1 cup sugar
- confectioners' sugar.

Follow instructions for making Apple Strudel (above). The amount of sugar used will depend on tartness of the cherries.

"MIRACLE" TORTE
(Levný Dort "Zázrak")

torte:
- 1 tablespoon honey
- ½ cup sugar
- 2½ tablespoons butter
- 1 teaspoon vanilla
- 1 egg
- 1 teaspoon baking soda
- 2 cups flour

filling:

2 cups milk

⅓ cup potato starch

½ cup sugar

¼ cup butter

1 tablespoon cocoa

¼ cup chopped nuts

To make torte, put honey, sugar, butter, vanilla, and egg into top of double boiler. Beat with a wire whisk over medium heat until foamy. Add soda; beat in well. Remove from heat. Blend in flour. Turn out on a floured pastry board and divide into 5 parts. Roll out each into a 9-inch circle (use a cake pan as a guide). Place tortes on a greased baking sheet; bake 2 at a time in a preheated oven at 350° for 15 to 20 minutes or until light golden.

To prepare filling, mix potato starch in ½ cup milk. Put the remaining milk and sugar into a pan and bring to a boil. Beat in potato starch mixture with a wire whisk. Bring to a full boil; remove from heat. Cool completely. Cream butter with cocoa in a separate bowl; blend into first mixture. Spread filling between torte layers, and spread additional filling over sides. Decorate top and sides with chopped nuts. Refrigerate for 6 to 8 hours.

FRUIT MERINGUE CREAM

(Ovocný Krém Sněhový)

6 apples

1 cup water

2 tablespoons raspberry or strawberry jam

⅓ cup sugar

1 lemon, juice only

2 egg whites, stiffly beaten

Bake apples in water in a 300° oven for about 1 hour. Rub through a sieve; cool. Mix sauce with jam, sugar, and lemon juice. Add beaten egg whites. Beat until thick. Chill.

Serves 4 to 6.

ORANGE GELÉE

(Pomerančový Rosol)

1 cup sugar

6 tablespoons white wine

2 oranges, juice only

1 lemon, juice only

1 tablespoon grated orange peel

4 egg yolks

2½ tablespoons gelatin

2 tablespoons rum

5 egg whites, stiffly beaten

Sprinkle sugar with wine, add orange juice, lemon juice, orange peel, and egg yolks. Beat over low heat until thickened. Stir in gelatin softened in rum, and cool. Fold in egg whites. Pour into a rinsed mold, and chill until firm.

Serves 6 to 8.

STRAWBERRY CREAM

(Jahodový Krém)

1 cup milk

2 egg yolks

¼ cup sugar

1 tablespoon cornstarch

2 tablespoons cognac

3 cups Whipped Cream (see Index)

3 cups strawberries

Mix together milk, egg yolks, sugar, and cornstarch. Bring to a full boil, stirring constantly. Let mixture cool, then add cognac and 2 cups Whipped Cream. Place 1 cup strawberries in a mold, pour in half the cream; repeat process. Chill until firm. Decorate with the remaining strawberries and Whipped Cream.

Serves 8.

FRUIT CREAM

(Ovocný Krém)

1 cup milk

2 egg yolks

¼ cup sugar

1 tablespoon cornstarch

2 tablespoons cognac

2 cups Whipped Cream (see Index)

⅔ cup chopped toasted nuts

1 orange, sliced

½ cup candied cherries

½ cup grapes

Mix together milk, egg yolks, sugar, and cornstarch. Bring to a full boil, stirring constantly. Cool. Add cognac and half the Whipped Cream. Fold in nuts and fruit. Pour into a mold, and chill until firm. Decorate with the remaining Whipped Cream.

Serves 6.

RUM CHARLOTTE RUSSE
(Rumový Krém)
1 cup milk
4 eggs, separated
1 cup sugar
2½ tablespoons gelatin
½ cup rum
30 ladyfingers

Mix together milk, egg yolks, and sugar. Beat over low heat until thickened. Add gelatin softened in rum, and chill. Fold in stiffly beaten egg whites. Line bottom and sides of a form with ladyfingers. Pour in cream mixture, and chill until firm.

Serves 6 to 8.

NUT PUDDING
(Oříškový Pudink)
2 cups milk
½ cup sugar
1 teaspoon vanilla
5 tablespoons cornstarch
1 egg, separated
⅔ cup ground toasted nuts
whole or halved nuts for decoration

Pour 1½ cups of the milk, sugar, and vanilla into a saucepan and bring to a boil. Mix remaining milk thoroughly with cornstarch and egg yolk. Pour into hot mixture, stirring constantly. Bring to a boil again. Cool. Fold in ground nuts and stiffly beaten egg white. Pour into serving dishes; decorate with nuts, and chill.

Serves 4 to 6.

FRUIT SHERBET
(Ovocná Zmrzlina)
2 cups water
1¼ cups sugar
1 tablespoon gelatin
2 cups fruit juice or puréed fruit
1 cup Whipped Cream (see Index; optional)

Soften gelatin in 2 tablespoons water. Pour balance of water over sugar; cook for 5 minutes. Stir in softened gelatin; cool. Add fruit juice (or puréed fruit) and Whipped Cream. Freeze until firm.

Serves 8 to 10.

APRICOT MOUSSE
(Zmrzlý Meruňkový Krém)
6 tablespoons sugar
½ cup white wine
10 large apricots, peeled and pitted
1 egg white
½ cup ground Blanched Almonds (see Index)
2 tablespoons gelatin
2 cups Whipped Cream (see Index)
apricot halves (for decoration; optional)

Sprinkle sugar with 6 tablespoons of white wine and bring to a boil. Add apricots. Cook for about 10 minutes, or until soft. Rub through a sieve; cool. Add egg white, and beat to a thick foam. Blend in almonds. Dissolve gelatin by heating it in the remaining wine, and add to fruit mixture. Blend in cream. Pour into a mold rinsed with cold water and freeze for 2 to 3 hours. Dip bottom of mold into hot water, and turn out on a platter. Decorate with additional apricot halves, if desired.

Serves 4 to 6.

CANDIED ORANGE OR LEMON PEEL
(Kandování Pomerancové A Citrónové Kůory)
orange or lemon peel
granulated sugar
water

Soak thick orange or lemon peel in water for 5 or 6 days, changing water daily. Drain. Cut into strips or desired small shapes. Weigh the peel and add to it equal amount of sugar. Add enough water to cover peel. Cook slowly until peel is transparent. Roll pieces in granulated sugar while still warm. Place on a baking sheet and let dry for about 24 hours on each side.

STEWED FRUIT
(Rychlý Kompot)
⅓-¾ cup sugar (depending on tartness of fruit)
1 cup water
½ lemon, juice only
fruit (see below)

Pour water over sugar and bring to full boil. Add lemon juice and fruit. Cook as directed below. Remove fruit from liquid, continue to cook liquid until sirupy, then pour over fruit. Chill.

Blueberries, cranberries, gooseberries, strawberries, raspberries, blackberries, red currants, sweet or sour cherries, or fresh prunes: Use 2 to 3 cups. Cook for 2 minutes.

Peaches and apricots: Use 3 peaches (peel first by dipping in boiling water), cut in half and pitted, or 8 to 12 apricots. Cook for 2 to 3 minutes.

Apples and pears: Use 3 to 4, peeled, cored, and quartered. Add a strip of lemon peel or piece of cinnamon stick, or 1 whole clove during cooking. Cook for 3 minutes.

REFERENCES

HOMEMADE MAYONNAISE
(Majonéza)
- 2 egg yolks
- salt to taste
- 1 cup oil
- 1 tablespoon lemon juice

Beat egg yolks well with salt until creamy. Add oil, drop by drop, stirring vigorously all the while. Add lemon juice; blend well. (If mayonnaise curdles, correct as follows: Put 1 egg yolk into a clean bowl, add salt, beat until creamy. Add curdled mayonnaise by spoonfuls, stirring constantly.)
Makes 1½ cups mayonnaise.

VANILLA SUGAR
(Tlučení Vanilky)
Wrap a vanilla bean in foil and dry in the oven until brittle. Break into small pieces and beat in a mortar with 2 or 3 sugar cubes to a fine powder. Sift. Keep in an airtight jar. Mix with confectioners' sugar, and use for dusting over cakes and pies.

VANILLA CREAM FILLING
(Vanilkový Krém)
- 2 egg yolks
- ½ cup plus 2 tablespoons superfine sugar
- ½ teaspoon ground vanilla bean
- 2 tablespoons milk
- 1 cup butter

Beat egg yolks with sugar until foamy. Add vanilla and milk. Bring almost to a boil, but do not boil, stirring constantly. Pour into a bowl and cool. Cream butter, and to it add egg mixture, a spoonful at a time.

COFFEE CREAM FILLING
(Kávový Krém)
Prepare Vanilla Cream (above), but add ½ cup very strong black coffee with the milk.

CHEESE FILLING
(Tvarohová Nádivka)
- 1 pound farmer cheese
- ¼ cup butter
- ½ cup sugar
- 2 eggs, separated
- 1-2 teaspoons vanilla
- ½ cup raisins
- 1-2 tablespoons milk or cream

Rub cheese through a sieve. Cream butter, sugar, and egg yolks. Add cheese, vanilla, and raisins, and blend well. If mixture is too thick, add milk or cream. Fold in stiffly beaten egg whites.

WHIPPED CREAM
(Šlehaná Smetana)
- 2 cups heavy cream
- 3-4 tablespoons confectioners' sugar

Chill bowl and beater. Pour in cream, and whip until it stands in rounded peaks. Sift sugar over top, and fold in.

BLANCHED ALMONDS
(Spařování Mandlí)
Plunge almonds into boiling water to cover. Bring to full boil. Cover, and let stand for 5 minutes. Drain. Slip off skins. Let almonds dry.

Chinese

Appetizers

WRAPPING SKIN FOR EGG ROLLS AND WON TONS
(Chwin Guen Won Ton Pei: General)

A. **2 cups flour**
B. **½ teaspoon salt**
C. **1 egg**
D. **½ cup water**

PREPARATION:

I. Sift A, B together.

II. Beat C, add D, and mix well. Blend thoroughly with A, B; knead until dough is smooth.

III. Roll dough on floured board until paper-thin. Be sure board is well dusted with flour.

IV. For egg rolls, make about 18 6-inch-square wrappings. If won ton wrappings are desired, cut each 6-inch square into four pieces. (If wrappings are not to be used immediately, they may be stacked together, but each piece should be well floured. Wrap stack in aluminum foil, and place in refrigerator. This will keep about a week. If skins become too hard and dry, place a wet dishcloth around them to remoisten.)

Serves 4

FUN GOH DOUGH (SKIN)
(Fun Goh Pei: Canton)

A. **1 cup wheat starch**
B. **½ cup tapioca flour**
C. **1 cup, 2 tablespoons boiling water**
D. **1 teaspoon peanut oil**

PREPARATION:

I. Sift A, B together in bowl.

II. Add C gradually. Stir with fork.

III. Grease hands with D.

IV. Knead dough until firm, about 4 minutes. Let stand 10 to 12 minutes.

V. Divide dough into 36 balls, 1 inch in diameter.

VI. Grease rolling pin and table, roll out balls as thin as possible to form patties 3 inches in diameter. This is a basic recipe for a pastry that is to be filled with meats and then steamed.

FUN GOH
(Fun Goh: Canton)

A. **36 fun-goh skins (see recipe above)**
B. **6 Chinese mushrooms**
C. **1 cup chopped roast pork**
D. **½ cup chopped Chinese celery cabbage (stem only) or ½ cup chopped bamboo shoots**
E. **1 scallion**
F. **½ teaspoon salt**
G. **½ teaspoon sugar**

PREPARATION:

I. Wash B, soak in warm water 15 minutes, drain, and chop.

II. Chop E very fine.

III. Mix B-G thoroughly.

IV. Prepare A.

COOKING:

1. Fill center of each A patty with 1 teaspoon B-G.
2. Fold over, shape in half-moon.
3. Arrange single layer on greased plate.
4. Steam 10 minutes.

FRIED WON TONS
(Tza Won Ton: Canton)

A. **peanut oil for deep frying**
B. **6 precooked won tons (see recipe next page)**

COOKING:

1. Heat A to 375°, deep-fry B a few at a time 2 to 3 minutes. Serve hot or cold.

WON TONS
(Won Ton: General)

A. 1 egg
B. ½ lb. ground pork
C. 1 tablespoon chopped scallion
D. 8 water chestnuts, chopped
E. 1 teaspoon salt
F. ⅛ teaspoon pepper
G. 12 won ton skins (see Wrapping Skin for Egg Rolls and Won Tons)

PREPARATION:

I. Beat A.
II. Mix A, B, C, D, E, F well.
III. Cut each G into quarters.

COOKING:

1. Fill each G with ½ to 1 teaspoon A-F mixture. Shape each into a cap to make won tons by drawing the four corners together and seal by pressing gently at juncture.

2. Boil 2 qts. water, add won tons, bring to boil, and cook 5 minutes. Drain won tons in colander, run cold water over won tons to cool. Cooked won tons can be frozen or left in refrigerator for a few days.

STEAMED LITTLE BAO TZE WITH BEEF
(Niu Ro Tong Bao: Shanghai)

A. 2 cups flour
B. ¾ cup water
C. 1 cup ground beef chuck
D. 1 cup chopped water chestnuts
E. 2 tablespoons Chinese parsley
F. 1 teaspoon light soy sauce
G. ½ teaspoon sesame oil
H. ½ teaspoon sugar
I. ½ to 1 teaspoon salt (to taste)

PREPARATION:

I. Combine A, B, mix well. Knead into a soft dough. Cover, let stand at room temperature 30 to 60 minutes, while preparing filling, as follows:
II. Combine C, D, E, F, G, H, I; mix.
III. Knead dough, then divide into 24 parts. Roll as thin as possible. Place 1 to 2 teaspoons of filling in center of each piece; then wrap each.

COOKING:

1. Steam 15 to 20 minutes. Serve hot.

EGG ROLLS

You can purchase ready-made egg roll skins in supermarkets or Oriental specialty stores.

dipping batter

A. 1 egg
B. 1 tablespoon cornstarch
C. 1½ teaspoons baking powder
D. 1 cup flour
E. 1 tablespoon sugar
F. 2 teaspoons salt
G. ½ teaspoon MSG
H. 1¼ cups milk
I. 1¾ cups water

filling

J. 1 cup shredded bamboo shoots
K. ½ pound bean sprouts, rinsed and well-drained
L. 1½ cups shredded water chestnuts
M. 3½ cups slivered cooked chicken
N. ¾ cup slivered barbecued pork
O. ¾ cup finely chopped fresh parsley
P. 1 cup chopped fresh mushrooms
Q. ½ cup finely chopped scallion
R. Salt and freshly ground black pepper to taste
S. Oil

Beat A slightly. Sift together dry ingredients. Mix with A. Slowly stir in H and I and stir until smooth.

All filling ingredients should be cut finely. Mix filling ingredients (except S) together and sauté in a little S for about 10 minutes, stirring occasionally. Let mixture cool. Spoon about ½ cup onto egg roll skin. Fold like an envelope. Dip in batter and fry in hot oil for about 5 minutes, turning carefully to brown both sides. Serve with Chinese mustard and/or duck sauce.

Makes approximately 2 dozen.

SHRIMP DUMPLINGS
(Har Gow: Canton)

A. 1 lb. fresh shrimp
B. 1 scallion, chopped
C. ¼ lb. ground pork
D. 2 teaspoons light soy sauce
E. 1½ teaspoons salt
F. ¼ teaspoon sesame oil

G. dash pepper

H. 36 fun-goh skins (see Index)

PREPARATION:

I. Shell and devein A and cut into small pieces.

II. Mix A, B, C, D, E, F, G thoroughly.

III. Fill center of each H with 1 teaspoon A-G mixture.

IV. Gather edges of each H, squeeze tight, and press toward one side.

COOKING:

1. Arrange dumplings in single layer on greased plate.

2. Steam over boiling water 12 minutes.

3. Serve with hoisin sauce.

SHRIMP TOAST

(Sha Tze Mein Bao: Shanghai)

A. peanut oil to fill deep-fat fryer

B. ½ lb. small shrimp

C. 12 water chestnuts, minced

D. 1 egg white

E. 1 tablespoon light soy sauce

F. ½ teaspoon salt

G. 1 teaspoon sherry

H. 1 tablespoon cornstarch

I. 6 slices white bread

PREPARATION:

I. Shell, devein, wash, and mince B.

II. Mix B, C, D, E, F, G.

III. Remove crust from I and cut into 1-inch squares.

IV. Liberally spread each square of I with B-G mixture.

COOKING:

1. Heat A in deep fryer.

2. Deep fry B-I face down in A at 350° until light brown.

3. Remove, drain well; serve with duck sauce.

STUFFED PORK PASTRY

(Shu Mai: Canton)

A. ½ lb. ground pork

B. 2 scallions (white part only), chopped

C. 1 cup chopped Chinese celery cabbage (stem only)

D. 1 teaspoon salt

E. 1 teaspoon light soy sauce

F. 1 teaspoon cornstarch

G. 6 egg roll skins, prepared or purchased (see Wrapping Skins for Egg Rolls or Won Tons)

PREPARATION:

I. Mix A, B, C, D, E, F.

II. Quarter each G, round corners, add 1 portion of filling to each skin; gather skin at top.

COOKING:

1. Steam in steamer over boiling water 8 to 10 minutes.

Soups

CELESTIAL SOUP (SOUP FOR THE GODS)

(Ching Tong: General)

A. 6 cups water

B. 2 tablespoons light soy sauce

C. 1 scallion, sliced

D. 1 teaspoon peanut oil

E. 1 teaspoon salt

F. 3 drops sesame oil

PREPARATION:

I. Boil A.

II. Place B. C. D. E. F in large serving bowl.

COOKING:

1. Pour A over B-F mixture in bowl.

2. Serve. Clears the palate and refreshes taste.

SIMPLE EGG DROP SOUP

(Dan Hwa Tong: General)

A. 13¾-oz. can chicken broth

B. 2 tablespoons cornstarch mixed with ¼ cup water

C. 1 egg

D. 1 tablespoon chopped scallion

PREPARATION:

I. Dilute A with 1 can water.

II. Beat C.

COOKING:

1. Bring diluted A to boil.

2. Thicken with B.

3. Turn off heat, slowly stir in C.

4. Garnish with D.

VELVET MUSHROOM SOUP
(Fu Yong Sien Ku Tong: General)

   A. 8-oz. can chicken broth
   B. ¼ cup diced Smithfield ham
   C. ¼ cup green peas
   D. ¼ cup diced bamboo shoots
   E. ¼ lb. fresh mushrooms, sliced
   F. 1 tablespoon cornstarch mixed with ¼ cup water
   G. 1 tablespoon wine
   H. salt, pepper to taste
   I. 2 to 3 egg whites
   J. ½ teaspoon salt
   K. 2 teaspoons wine

PREPARATION:

   I. Beat I slightly, add J, K and ½ cup A. Mix well.
   II. Steam over boiling water until set (about 12 minutes).

COOKING:

   1. Add enough water to rest of A to make 2½ cups liquid; bring to a boil.
   2. Add B; cook 2 minutes.
   3. Add C, D; cook 2 minutes.
   4. Add E; cook 1 minute. Thicken with F.
   5. Add G. H; pour over I-K mixture; serve hot.

RED-IN-SNOW FISH SOUP
(Shieh Tsai Yu Tong: Ninpo)

   A. ¼ cup peanut oil
   B. 1 scallion
   C. 2 slices ginger
   D. 1 porgy (about 1 lb.)
   E. 1 tablespoon sherry
   F. ¼ cup preserved red-in-snow
   G. ½ cup sliced bamboo shoots
   H. 1 teaspoon salt

PREPARATION:

   I. Clean and wash D, dry between paper towels. Make 2 diagonal slashes on each side.
   II. Tie B into a knot.

COOKING:

   1. Heat A, add B, C, stir-fry 1 to 2 minutes.
   2. Add D, brown on both sides; discard B, C; add E and cover for a few seconds.
   3. Add 1 qt. cold water, bring to boil, cook 1 minute.

   4. Spread F, G over fish, add salt, cover and simmer 15 minutes or until fish is done.
   5. Turn heat high and cook 1 more minute. Remove oil that floats to top of soup.
   6. Serve hot.

CHICKEN, MUSHROOM, AND BAMBOO SHOOT SOUP
(Gee Pien Dung Gu Tong: General)

   A. 13¾-oz. can chicken broth
   B. 1 small chicken breast
   C. 1 teaspoon cornstarch
   D. ¼ teaspoon salt
   E. ¼ lb. fresh mushrooms
   F. ¼ cup canned bamboo shoots, sliced as in preparation
   G. 2 teaspoons sherry

PREPARATION:

   I. Bone B, slice meat into pieces ⅛ to ¼ inch thick. Add C, D, mix well.
   II. Wash E well, cut each in half.
   III. Cut F into slices ⅛ to ¼ inch thick and 2 inches long.

COOKING:

   1. Empty A into saucepan, add 1½ cans water, bring to boil.
   2. Add B-D mixture, stir well, add E, F, G. Cook 3 to 5 minutes. Serve hot.

CURRY SOUP WITH NOODLES
(Ga Li Tong Mien: Canton)

   A. 5 cups soup stock
   B. ½ lb. fresh noodles
   C. ¼ to ½ teaspoon curry powder
   D. ½ teaspoon salt
   E. 3 tablespoons peanut oil
   F. ½ cup finely chopped onions
   G. ½ lb. beef tenderloin, sliced, or ground beef
   H. ½ teaspoon sugar
   I. ½ teaspoon salt
   J. ¼ cup soup stock

PREPARATION:
   I. Parboil B. Set aside.
   II. Mix C, D. Set aside.
   III. Mix H, I. Set aside.

COOKING:

1. Heat A to boiling.
2. Add B, C, D and bring to boiling point again.
3. Place in large serving bowl. Set aside.
4. Put E in very hot skillet and bring to high heat.
5. Add F; stir-fry until brown.
6. Add G; stir-fry until just done.
7. Add H-I with J. Stir 15 seconds.
8. Spread E-J mixture over A-D mixture.

TRADITIONAL CONGEE
(Shi Fan: General)

A. 20 cups water
B. 2 cups rice
C. kettle of boiling water (add as necessary for desired consistency)
D. 4 tablespoons light soy sauce
E. 3 slices ginger, minced
F. 2 teaspoons heavy soy sauce
G. 1 tablespoon peanut oil
H. 1 teaspoon salt
I. 4 dried Chinese black mushrooms
J. ½ cup ginkgo nuts (optional)
K. 9 tablespoons water
L. 3 tablespoons cornstarch
M. 6 scallions, chopped

PREPARATION:

I. Wash B.
II. Soak I in warm water 15 minutes. Add water to A.
III. Mix D, E, F, G, H. Set aside.
IV. Mix K, L. Set aside. Stir well before using.

COOKING:

1. Bring A to boil.
2. Add B. Simmer 90 minutes or more until a thin paste is formed. Stir every 10 minutes, avoiding the very bottom.
3. Add C to thin congee toward completion of Step 2.
4. Add D-H mixture. Add I, J. Continue to simmer 30 minutes.
5. If necessary, add K-L slowly to thicken.
6. Serve congee in individual bowls with liberal sprinkling of M over each.

Serves 8 to 10.

WONTON SOUP
dumpling dough

A. 4 ounces flour
B. Salt
C. 1 tablespoon milk
D. 2 tablespoons oil
E. 1 small egg

filling

F. 4 ounces fresh spinach, chopped
G. 4 ounces ground pork
H. ½ tablespoon soy sauce
I. ⅛ teaspoon ground ginger

soup

J. 5 cups chicken broth
K. 2 tablespoons chopped chives

Stir together A and B in bowl. Add C, D, and E. Knead dough until smooth. Roll out dough on floured board until paper-thin. Cut into 3-inch squares. Cover with kitchen towel while preparing filling.

Thoroughly wash F; remove coarse stems. Place in bowl; barely cover with boiling water. Let stand 3 minutes; drain well. Coarsely chop. Add G, H, and I; blend thoroughly. Place 1 teaspoon filling on each dough square, giving filling lengthy shape. Fold over dough from one side; roll up jelly-roll fashion. Press ends of roll together to seal.

Bring J to boil. Add wontons: simmer over low heat 20 minutes. Spoon into bowls. Garnish with K.

Makes 6 servings.

HOT AND SOUR SOUP
(Swan La Tong: Szechuan)

A. 13¾-oz. can chicken broth
B. ¼ cup shredded preserved kohlrabi
C. ½ cup shredded roast or fresh pork
D. ½ cup shredded bamboo shoots
E. 2 dried Chinese mushrooms
F. 2 soybean cakes
G. 2 tablespoons cider vinegar
H. 1 teaspoon light soy sauce
I. 2 tablespoons cornstarch

PREPARATION:

I. Wash red powder off B before shredding.
II. Soak E in warm water 20 minutes, remove and discard stems, shred.

III. Slice F very thin.

IV. Mix G, H, I until there are no lumps.

COOKING:

1. Dilute A with 1 can water, boil, add B, and cook 5 minutes.

2. Add C, D, E and boil 1 minute.

3. Add F.

4. When soup boils again, thicken with G-I.

FRIED NOODLES WITH SHREDDED MEAT SOUP
(Yoke Si Yee Fu Mein: Adapted)

A. 3 tablespoons peanut oil

B. ¼ lb. beef (pork or chicken), shredded

C. 1 carrot

D. 1 stalk celery, shredded

E. 1 cup shredded cabbage

F. 1 teaspoon salt

G. 2 pkgs. noodles (Yee fu mein) with soup base (or water and canned chicken broth to make qt.)

H. pepper to taste

I. 2 teaspoons chopped scallion

J. 2 slices ginger, chopped

K. 1 teaspoon cornstarch

L. 2 teaspoons light soy sauce

M. ¼ teaspoon sugar

N. few drops sesame oil

PREPARATION:

I. Mix B with I, J, K, L, M, N.

II. Peel C. slice, then shred.

III. Bring 1½ cups water to boil; add G, stir until noodles are loosened; add soup base and cook 3 to 4 minutes.

COOKING:

1. Heat 2 tablespoons A, add B mixture, stir-fry 1 to 2 minutes; remove to dish.

2. Heat 1 tablespoon A, add C, D, E, stir-fry 2 minutes; add F, and 1 to 2 tablespoons water, if necessary.

3. Add B mixture, stir well, cook ½ minute longer.

4. Add G, mix well.

5. Add H and serve hot.

Eggs

SIMPLE SHRIMP OMELET
(Sha Mi Tsao Don: Adapted)

A. ¼ cup vegetable oil

B. 5 eggs

C. 1 oz. dried shrimp (about 30) or 3 dried scallops

D. 1 teaspoon salt

E. 2 scallions, minced

PREPARATION:

I. Soak C in hot water 20 minutes. Drain, save water; chop.

II. Break B. Add C, D, E, and whip. Add 2 tablespoons water from Step I.

COOKING:

1. Heat A in hot skillet.

2. Add B-E mixture to A. Stir-fry 3 to 7 minutes (according to preference).

FANCY OMELET
(Gee Don Bing: General)

A. ¼ cup vegetable oil

B. 4 oz. pork (or leftover chicken or white turkey meat), shredded

C. 2 teaspoons light soy sauce

D. 2 slices ginger, shredded

E. 6 dried Chinese mushrooms

F. 10-oz. pkg. frozen peas

G. 6 eggs

H. 1 teaspoon salt

PREPARATION:

I. Defrost F.

II. Soak E in hot water 20 minutes, drain, save water. Slice each E into 3 pieces.

III. Break G into bowl, beat, and add H.

IV. Marinate B with C, D.

COOKING:

1. Using high heat, add 2 tablespoons A to hot skillet. Add B-D mixture, stir-fry 1 minute. If water is needed, add some from soaking mushrooms. Add E, F, continue stir-frying 1 to 2 minutes. Remove to bowl.

2. Add remaining A to cleaned skillet. Use high heat. Add G-H mixture to pan without stirring. Allow skin to form. Lower heat when skin thickens.

3. Add A–F mixture to half of pan. Fold over G–H skin so that it forms a pouch. Serve hot.

PLAIN EGG FU YONG
(Ru Ee Fu Yong Don: Canton)

    A. 4 tablespoons peanut oil
    B. 2 scallions, minced
    C. 6 Chinese black mushrooms
    D. 2 cups bean sprouts
    E. ¼ cup shredded canned water chestnuts
    F. 6 eggs
    G. ½ teaspoon salt
    H. ¼ teaspoon pepper
    I. 2 teaspoons light soy sauce

PREPARATION:

I. Wash and soak C 15 minutes in warm water, drain, and slice into long, thin strips.

II. Wash D thoroughly. Drain.

III. Beat F; mix with G, H, I thoroughly.

COOKING:

1. Heat 1 tablespoon A, stir-fry B, C about a minute.

2. Add D, E, stir constantly 1 to 2 minutes.

3. Add cooked B–E mixture to F–I mixture, emptying frying pan contents.

4. Heat remaining A in frying pan. Cook egg-vegetable mixture over medium heat until one side is brown. Turn over, press, and fry until second side is brown. Serve hot.

Note: To serve as pancake (Fu Yong Don Bang) with oyster sauce, combine ¼ cup oyster sauce, ½ cup water, and 1 teaspoon cornstarch in a saucepan. Cook until thickened. Pour sauce over egg fu yong pancake and serve hot.

PORK EGG FU YONG
(Chai Shu Fu Yong Don: Canton)

    A. 3 tablespoons peanut oil
    B. 4 eggs
    C. 1 cup shredded roast pork
    D. 1 scallion, minced
    E. 2 slices ginger, minced
    F. 1 teaspoon light soy sauce
    G. ½ teaspoon sugar
    H. ¾ teaspoon salt
    I. ⅛ teaspoon pepper

PREPARATION:

I. Beat B, mix thoroughly with C, D, E, F, G, H, I.

COOKING:

1. Heat A in frying pan.

2. Add B–I mixture, brown one side over medium heat until golden brown. Then turn over and brown second side.

PEKING CUSTARD
(Kao Don: Peking)

    A. 4 eggs
    B. 4-oz. can mushrooms (drained)
    C. ¼ cup chopped frozen shrimp
    D. ¼ cup ground pork
    E. 1 teaspoon salt
    F. ⅛ teaspoon sherry
    G. 1 cup chicken broth
    H. 1 teaspoon sesame oil

PREPARATION:

I. Beat A.

II. Chop B into small pieces.

III. Combine A, B, C, D, E, F, G; mix well.

IV. Pour A–G mixture into well-greased baking dish.

COOKING:

1. Preheat oven to 375°.

2. Bake A–G mixture until golden brown (about 35 minutes).

3. Sprinkle with H and serve.

SCRAMBLED EGGS WITH SOY SAUCE AND TO-MATOES
(Fan Chieh Tsao Don: General)

    A. 4 tablespoons peanut oil
    B. 1 clove garlic, minced
    C. ½ teaspoon salt
    D. 8 eggs
    E. 1 tomato
    F. 1 tablespoon light soy sauce
    G. 1 tablespoon heavy soy sauce
    H. 1 scallion, sliced

PREPARATION:

I. Beat D.

II. Cut E into 8 wedges.

III. Mix B, C.

IV. Mix F, G.

COOKING:

1. Put A in very hot skillet and bring to high heat.

2. Add B, C, stir-fry rapidly 15 seconds to brown garlic slightly.

3. Add D. Scramble until almost firm.

4. Add E. Stir-fry 1 minute.

5. Add F, G. Mix well.

6. Serve with garnish of H.

STEAMED EGGS
(Tzing Don: Canton)

    A. 10 dried shrimp

    B. 6 Chinese mushrooms

    C. 1 scallion

    D. 2 slices ginger

    E. 6 eggs

    F. ¼ cup ground pork

    G. 2 teaspoons sherry

    H. 2 tablespoons peanut oil

    I. 1½ teaspoons salt

PREPARATION:

I. Wash and clean A, B. Soak in warm water 30 minutes; drain, saving ½ cup of the water.

II. Chop A, B, C, D very fine.

III. Beat E; combine with A-D, F, G, H, I, ½ cup mushroom and shrimp water; mix well.

IV. Place A-I mixture in a bowl.

COOKING:

1. Steam over boiling water in steamer 20 to 25 minutes.

Fish

CANTONESE FRIED FISH
(Jien Yu: Canton)

    A. 1 cup peanut oil

    B. 1-to 1½-lb. sea bass

    C. 2 teaspoons salt

    D. dash pepper

    E. 1 egg

    F. 2 tablespoons cornstarch

PREPARATION:

I. Cut B into quarters or use whole.

II. Mix C, D. Rub B thoroughly inside and out with C mixture, let B stand 15 minutes.

III. Beat E with 1 tablespoon F. Dip prepared B in E mixture, then roll in remaining portion of F.

COOKING:

1. Heat A to 350° and fry B-F mixture until golden brown (about 5 to 7 minutes each side).

2. Serve with Chinese hot sauce (optional).

ABALONE WITH MUSHROOMS AND BAMBOO SHOOTS
(Tsao Bao Yu: Canton)

    A. 4 tablespoons peanut oil

    B. 8 Chinese dry mushrooms

    C. 1 scallion

    D. 4 slices ginger

    E. 1-lb. can abalone

    F. 2-stalks Chinese cabbage heart

    G. ½-can (8 oz.) bamboo shoots

    H. salt and pepper to taste

PREPARATION:

I. Slice E into small pieces.

II. Wash B and soak in hot water ¼ hour; cut each into 4 pieces.

III. Wash F and cut diagonally same size as E. Put into boiling water 1 minute; drain and let cold water run through.

IV. Slice G into small pieces.

V. Cut C into 1-inch pieces.

VI. Slice D into strips.

COOKING:

1. Heat A.

2. Stir-fry B, C, D one minute.

3. Add E, F, G. Mix well.

4. Add H, cover and cook 2 minutes and serve.

BOILED FISH WITH SZECHUAN SAUCE
(Sao Yu: Szechuan)

    A. 1-to 1½-lb. sea bass

    B. 2 tablespoons peanut oil

    C. ¼ cup shredded bamboo shoots

    D. 4 Chinese mushrooms

    E. 1 tablespoon chopped scallion

    F. 1 teaspoon chopped ginger

    G. 1 clove garlic, minced

    H. 2 teaspoons light soy sauce

    I. 2 teaspoons brown bean sauce

    J. ½ teaspoon salt

K. 2 teaspoons sherry
L. 2 teaspoons vinegar
M. 1 teaspoon sugar
N. 2 teaspoons cornstarch mixed with ½ cup mushroom water

PREPARATION:

I. Wash A, make 3 or 4 diagonal slashes on each side.

II. Wash and soak D in warm water 15 minutes. Drain (save water for N) and shred.

III. Mix H, I, J, K, L, M, N.

COOKING:

1. Place A in frying pan, cover with boiling water and cook over low heat 3 minutes. Remove from heat but leave in water 12 to 15 minutes, remove to plate.

2. Heat B, add C, D, E, F, G, stir-fry 1 minute, add H-N mixture, stir until gravy is thickened; pour over fish and serve.

STEAMED HOT AND SPICED FISH
(Wong Yo Tsen Yu: Szechuan)
A. 1½-lb. bass
B. 1½ teaspoons salt
C. 1 tablespoon sherry
D. 2 cloves garlic, chopped
E. 1 red-hot pepper
F. 3 tablespoons salted black beans
G. 1½ teaspoons sugar
H. 1 tablespoon light soy sauce
I. 1 piece caul fat 8 by 12 inches
J. 1 tablespoon cornstarch

PREPARATION:

I. Clean and wash A, dry between paper towels. Make 2 slashes diagonally on both sides. Rub inside and outside with B.

II. Sprinkle A with C and marinate 10 minutes.

III. Discard stem and seeds of E, chop.

IV. Soak F in a cup of water 1 minute so that any sand will settle on bottom; remove F, wash, drain, and mash.

V. Mix D, E, F, G, H well with 1 tablespoon water. Stuff A with 1 tablespoon of D-H mixture.

VI. Wash I in warm water, dry between paper towels, sprinkle lightly with J.

VII. Spread ½ of D-H mixture over I, J.

VIII. Place A on top of D-H mixture and place the other half of D-H mixture over A.

IX. Wrap I over fish and place in a dish.

COOKING:

1. Steam in a steamer 15 minutes or until fish is done.

RED-COOKED MANDARIN FISH
(Hung Sao Yu: Peking)
A. 6 tablespoons peanut oil
B. 2-lb. sea bass
C. ¼ cup sliced bamboo shoots
D. 8 Chinese mushrooms
E. 1 scallion
F. 2 slices ginger, chopped
G. 1 clove garlic, chopped
H. ¼ cup light soy sauce
I. 1 tablespoon sherry
J. 1 teaspoon sugar
K. 2 teaspoons cornstarch
L. ½ cup chicken broth

PREPARATION:

I. Wash B well, dry with paper towels, and diagonally slash on each side about 2 inches apart.

II. Wash D, soak in warm water 15 minutes, drain. Cut each into 4- to 5-inch pieces.

III. Cut E into pieces 1½ inches long.

IV. Mix H, I, J, K, L.

COOKING:

1. Heat A. Brown B on both sides. Discard A, reserving 1 to 2 tablespoons.

2. Add C, D, E, F, G, H,-L mixture to B. Bring to boil, cover, and cook over low heat about 30 minutes. During this time, baste B two or three times with sauce. Serve hot.

PORK-COOKED WHOLE FISH
(Chuan Cheh Gwa: Fukien)
A. 1 to 2 cups peanut oil
B. 1-lb. sea bass
C. 2 teaspoons cornstarch
D. ¼ lb. pork
E. 10 dried shrimp
F. 1 scallion
G. 3 slices ginger
H. 1½ tablespoons light soy sauce
I. 1½ tablespoons vinegar
J. 2 teaspoons sugar

K. 2 teaspoons white wine

L. ½ teaspoon salt

M. ½ cup water

N. 2 teaspoons cornstarch mixed with 2 tablespoons water

O. pepper to taste

PREPARATION: I. Clean and wash B; dry between paper towels. Make two diagonal slashes on each side; coat with C.

II. Cut D into thin slices, then into shreds.

III. Wash and clean E, then soak in cold water 15 minutes; drain and chop.

IV. Cut F into 1-inch pieces.

V. Mix H, I, J, K, L, M.

COOKING:

1. Heat A to 350°; deep fry B-C until golden brown (about 4 to 5 minutes on each side); remove to a dish.

2. Remove 2 tablespoons A to a pan, heat; add D, E, F, G, stir-fry about two minutes.

3. Add H-M mixture; mix well and cook 1 more minute.

4. Thicken with N. Pour sauce over fish, add O and serve.

SWEET AND SOUR FISH
(Tang Tsu Yu: Shanghai)

A. 3 cups peanut oil

B. 1- to 1½-lb. porgy or bass

C. ½ cup shrimp, diced

D. ½ cup peas

E. 1 tablespoon light soy sauce

F. 1 tablespoon sherry

G. 3 tablespoons catsup

H. 1 tablespoon sugar

I. 1½ tablespoons vinegar

J. 2 tablespoons cornstarch

K. 1 tomato

L. 1 teaspoon cornstarch mixed with 2 tablespoons water

M. 1 teaspoon salt

N. dash pepper

PREPARATION:

I. Mix L, M, N thoroughly.

II. Slash both sides of B diagonally at 2-inch intervals, rub with L-N mixture. Roll in J so that B is coated with a thin layer.

III. Mix E, F, G, H, I and 1 tsp. J.

IV. Mix C with additional ½ teaspoon cornstarch and dash of salt.

V. Place K in boiling water for a few seconds, remove, peel, and cut into cubes.

COOKING:

1. Heat A to 325°; deep fry B until golden brown (about 5 minutes). Remove to dish.

2. Heat additional 1 tablespoon oil, stir-fry C 1 to 2 minutes, add D, stir for 1 minute.

3. Add E, K, J mixture, stir until thickened.

4. Pour over B and serve. Garnish with K.

FLOUNDER FILLET WITH CHINESE BROCCOLI
(Gai Lan Yu Pien: Canton)

A. ½ cup peanut oil

B. 4 slices ginger

C. ½- to 1-lb. fillet of flounder

D. 4 teaspoons cornstarch

E. 1 teaspoon salt

F. 6 Chinese mushrooms

G. ½ lb. Chinese (or American) broccoli or cabbage

H. 2 teaspoons sherry

I. 2 tablespoons oyster sauce

J. 1 teaspoon sugar

K. salt, pepper to taste

PREPARATION:

I. Cut C into pieces 1 inch wide, scoring each piece twice before severing.

II. Wash F, soak 15 minutes in warm water. Drain (saving water to mix with D) and quarter each.

III. Mix D with ¼ cup F water.

IV. Mix C, half of D mixture, and E.

V. Cut G into 2- to 3-inch diagonal segments.

VI. Mix H, I, J; add remaining D mixture.

COOKING:

1. Heat A, add B, stir-fry several seconds.

2. Add C-E mixture, stir 1 to 2 more minutes, and remove to a dish, leaving only 3 tablespoons A in pan.

3. Add F, G to remaining A in pan, stir-fry 3 minutes.

4. Add ¼ cup water and H-J mixture, stir until thick.

5. Return C-E mixture to pan, add K, mix well, and serve hot.

BUTTERFISH IN BEER SAUCE
(Go Sao Gih Yu: General)

- A. ¼ cup peanut oil
- B. 1½ lbs. butterfish (about 5)
- C. ¾ teaspoon salt
- D. 3 scallions, shredded
- E. 4 slices ginger, shredded
- F. 1 teaspoon sugar
- G. 1 tablespoon brown bean sauce
- H. 1 tablespoon cider vinegar
- I. 1 teaspoon light soy sauce
- J. 1 tablespoon sherry
- K. ¾ cup beer
- L. 2 teaspoons cornstarch

PREPARATION:

I. Scale and clean B. Rinse in cold water, then dry with paper towels. Slash skin diagonally 1 inch apart across the width of the fish on both sides. Rub C over B and inside cavity.

II. Mix D, E, F, G, H, I, J.

COOKING:

1. Heat frying pan. When hot, add A.
2. Brown B in A 3 to 4 minutes on each side.
3. Pour off excess A and add D-J.
4. Add ½ cup K, cover and simmer 15 minutes.
5. Mix L with rest of K so that no lumps remain. Add to frying pan to thicken sauce. Mix well and serve hot.

STUFFED RED SNAPPER
(Yu Riong Ro Bing: Shanghai)

- A. 2-lb. red snapper
- B. 1 teaspoon salt
- C. 4 oz. ground pork
- D. 2 slices ginger, minced
- E. 2 scallions, minced
- F. 2 teaspoons sherry
- G. 2 teaspoons light soy sauce
- H. 1 teaspoon cornstarch
- I. 1 teaspoon brown sugar
- J. 3 slices ginger
- K. 2 scallions
- L. 1 tablespoon cornstarch
- M. 1½ cups water
- N. 2 tablespoons light soy sauce
- O. 5 stalks Chinese parsley (optional)

PREPARATION:

I. Clean A. Make diagonal slashes in skin, one inch apart. Rub B over skin.

II. Mix C, D, E, F, G, H and stuff A with mixture.

III. Mix I, J, K, L, M, N for sauce.

COOKING:

1. Fry A-H in skillet with ½ cup hot oil, until browned on both sides. Pour off excess oil.

2. Add I-N sauce to skillet; cover tightly, Simmer A 15 to 20 minutes on each side. Add small amount of water, if needed. Serve hot. O may be sprinkled on top, if desired.

STIR-FRIED FROGS' LEGS
(Tsao Tien Gee Twei: Shanghai)

- A. ⅓ cup peanut oil
- B. ½ teaspoon sesame oil
- C. ¼ cup sherry
- D. 1 teaspoon salt
- E. 2 teaspoons vinegar
- F. 2 teaspoons sugar
- G. 1 tablespoon light soy sauce
- H. 1 lb. frogs' legs
- I. 2 tablespoons cornstarch
- J. 6-oz. can fried vegetable steak
- K. 1 scallion, minced
- L. 6 slices ginger, minced

PREPARATION:

I. Cut J into ½ inch chunks.

II. Clean H and cut each into 2 to 3 small pieces.

III. Mix B, C, D, E, F, G.

IV. Marinate H in B-G mixture ½ hour.

V. Place I in paper bag, add H and shake.

COOKING:

1. Heat A in skillet until hot.

2. Brown B-I in A. Add J, K, L, and cook additional 3 minutes with small amount of water.

Shrimp

FRIED SHRIMP

(Tza Sha: Shanghai)

A. 1 lb. large shrimp

B. 2 eggs

C. 1 teaspoon salt

D. dash pepper

E. ½ cup flour

F. peanut oil for deep frying

G. cocktail sauce or Tabasco

PREPARATION:

I. Shell A, except end part. Devein.

II. Cut lengthwise until back is connected slightly.

III. Beat B lightly.

IV. Sprinkle A with C, D; dip first in B, then in E.

COOKING:

1. Put several inches of F in deep fryer or sauce-pan. Heat.

2. Fry prepared A in hot F until golden brown.

3. Eat with G.

STIR-FRIED SHRIMP WITH VEGETABLES

(Ching Do Dung Gu Sha Ren: Peking)

A. 3 tablespoons peanut oil

B. 1 tablespoon chopped scallion (white part only)

C. ½ teaspoon chopped ginger

D. 1 clove garlic, chopped

E. 1 small egg white

F. 1 teaspoon sherry

G. 1 teaspoon salt

H. 1½ teaspoons cornstarch

I. ½ lb. medium shrimp

J. 10-oz. pkg. frozen peas, defrosted

K. 6 to 8 Chinese mushrooms

PREPARATION:

I. Shell, and cut open the backs of I, devein, and wash.

II. Beat E, mix well with F, G, H.

III. Add I and mix well.

IV. Wash K and soak in warm water 15 minutes, drain, dice.

COOKING:

1. Heat A, and B, C, D, stir-fry ½ minute; add E-I mixture, stir-fry 1 minute, remove to a dish, return oil to pan.

2. Heat pan, add J and K, stir-fry 1 minute.

3. Add B-I, stir-fry with J-K 2 more minutes and serve.

GLAZED SHRIMP

(Gahn Tsao Sha: Shanghai)

A. 3 tablespoons vegetable oil

B. 1 lb. medium shrimp

C. 1 egg white

D. 1 tablespoon cornstarch

E. dash baking soda

F. 1 tablespoon sherry

G. 3 slices ginger, chopped

H. 2 tablespoons light soy sauce

I. 2 scallions, minced

PREPARATION:

I. Shell B, devein, and wash in 1 pt. water containing 1 teaspoon salt. Drain, then dry on paper towels.

II. Mix B, C, D, E, F, G, H. Marinate for 30 minutes.

COOKING:

1. Place A in hot skillet. When oil is hot, add B-H mixture and stir continuously 1 minute. Lower heat, simmer 5 more minutes.

2. Add I, cover and cook on low heat for additional 5 minutes.

CURRIED SHRIMP WITH BAMBOO SHOOTS

(Yeh Jiong Ga Li Har: Canton)

A. 2 tablespoons peanut oil

B. 1 medium-size onion

C. 1 to 2 cloves garlic

D. 1 to 2 teaspoons curry powder

E. 1½ teaspoons salt

F. 1 cup cubed bamboo shoots

G. 1 cup coconut flakes

H. 1½ cups hot water

I. 1 lb. large shrimp

J. 2 teaspoons cornstarch mixed with 2 tablespoons water

PREPARATION:

I. Peel skin of B and C; chop into fine pieces.

II. Mix D, E.

III. Mix G, H and let stand 1 hour. Stir well, then squeeze out juice through a colander. Reserve juice; discard coconut.

IV. Shell, devein, and wash I. Dry between paper towels.

COOKING:

1. Heat A, add B, C; stir-fry over medium heat until onion is transparent (about 2 minutes).

2. Add D, E mixture; mix well.

3. Add F and G juice. Bring to a boil, then lower heat and simmer 10 minutes.

4. Turn up heat, add I and cook 5 minutes.

5. Thicken with J; serve with rice.

SHRIMP WITH WATER CHESTNUTS
(Har Gow: Canton)
   A. ½ lb. medium shrimp
   B. ¼ cup water chestnuts
   C. 1 scallion
   D. 1 teaspoon salt
   E. ⅛ teaspoon pepper
   F. ¼ teaspoon sesame oil
   G. 36 fun goh skins (see Fun Goh Dough)
   H. 2 teaspoons light soy sauce

PREPARATION:

I. Shell, devein, wash, dry, and chop A.

II. Chop B, C.

III. Mix A, B, C, D, E, F, H thoroughly.

IV. Fill each piece of G with 1 teaspoon A-H mixture.

V. Gather dough edges, pinch lightly, and press toward one side.

COOKING:

1. Arrange single layer of dough on greased plate.

2. Steam over boiling water 10 to 12 minutes.

3. Serve with hoisin sauce.

SHRIMP BALLS IN OYSTER SAUCE
(Ho Yow Har Kew: Canton)
   A. 2 cups peanut oil
   B. 1 lb. large shrimp
   C. 6 water chestnuts, chopped
   D. ¼ cup bamboo shoots, chopped
   E. 1 egg white
   F. 2 teaspoons lard (optional)
   G. 2 tablespoons cornstarch
   H. 1 tablespoon sherry
   I. 1 teaspoon salt
   J. dash pepper

   K. ¼ cup oyster sauce
   L. 1 scallion, chopped, or Chinese parsley

PREPARATION:

I. Shell, devein, and wash B. Chop fine.

II. Mix B, C, D, E, F, G, H, I, J, let stand 30 minutes.

COOKING:

1. Heat A in 2-qt. saucepan to about 350°.

2. Scoop B-J with a large soup spoon, drop balls gently into A. Deep fry until golden brown. When balls float, remove and drain.

3. Place B-J on plate. Pour hot K over them. Garnish with L.

Other Seafood

LOBSTER CANTONESE
(Tsao Lung Ha: Canton)
   A. 2 tablespoons peanut oil
   B. 2 cloves garlic, minced
   C. 1 slice ginger, minced
   D. 2 tablespoons salted black beans, mashed
   E. ½ teaspoon salt
   F. ½ lb. ground pork
   G. 1 teaspoon sugar
   H. 1½ tablespoons light soy sauce
   I. 2 tablespoons sherry
   J. 2 cups soup stock
   K. 2 tablespoons heavy soy sauce
   L. 2 tablespoons cornstarch
   M. 1- to 1½-lb. lobster
   N. 2 eggs
   O. 2 tablespoons soup stock
   P. 2 tablespoons peanut oil
   Q. 4 scallions, sliced

PREPARATION:

I. Chop M (crosswise) into bite-sized (1-inch) pieces. Remove and crack claws. Discard gills (white), head shell, legs.

II. Mix B, C, D, E. Set aside.

III. Mix G, H, I. Set aside.

IV. Mix K, L. Set aside.

V. Mix beaten N slightly. Add O. Set aside.

COOKING:

1. Put A in very hot skillet and bring to high heat.

2. Add B-E mixture. Stir-fry rapidly 15 seconds to brown B slightly.

3. Add F. Stir-fry 2 minutes, add M. mix well.

4. Add G-I mixture. Stir-fry 1 minute.

5. Add J. Cover. Bring to boil. Cook 5 to 7 minutes.

6. Add K-L mixture slowly. Stir-fry until sauce thickens and coats all ingredients well.

7. Cover and cook 2½ minutes or until lobster is tender. Make certain lobster is well coated with sauce.

8. Turn off heat and add ¾ of N-O mixture all at once. Do not stir, but let N-O set 30 seconds.

9. Remove entire contents of skillet at once to serving dish. Pour remainder of N-O mixture over dish.

10. Heat P to smoking. Pour over lobster and sauce.

11. Serve with garnish of Q.

SHRIMP WITH LOBSTER SAUCE
(Ha Tzee Lung Ha Joing: Canton)

Substitute 1 lb. large shelled, washed, drained shrimp for M. Split along back but do not cut through completely. Cook 3 to 5 minutes in Step 7.

SAVORY STEAMED LOBSTER WITH PORK
(Tsing Lung Ha Yoke Bang: Canton)

A. 1 egg
B. ½ teaspoon salt
C. ½ teaspoon sugar
D. 1 tablespoon light soy sauce
E. 1 teaspoon sherry
F. 1 tablespoon peanut oil
G. 1 slice ginger, minced
H. 1 dash garlic powder
I. 1 teaspoon light soy sauce
J. 6 water chestnuts, chopped
K. ¼ lb. ground pork
L. 1- to 1½-lb. lobster
M. 1 tablespoon peanut oil
N. 3 scallions, sliced

PREPARATION:

I. Boil water in steamer.

II. Clean L, freshly killed; cut or chop into easily handled pieces; reassembly and place on serving platter suitable for steaming. Discard gills, head shell, and legs.

III. Mix B, C, D, E, F, G, H, I, J and set aside.

COOKING:

1. Beat A lightly. Add B-J mixture. Add K. Stir thoroughly.

2. Spread B-K over L.

3. Place A-L on platter in steamer.

4. Cover and steam over steady moderate heat 35 minutes.

5. Remove platter. Set aside.

6. Bring M to smoking heat. Pour over steamed lobster.

7. Serve with garnish of N.

BRAISED SOFT-SHELLED CRABS
(Yo Mun Shiao Sha: Shanghai)

A. 4 tablespoons peanut oil
B. 8 soft-shelled crabs
C. 1 teaspoon wine vinegar
D. 2 tablespoons minced ginger
E. 1 tablespoon light soy sauce
F. 1 teaspoon heavy soy sauce
G. 2 teaspoons sugar
H. ¼ cup chicken broth

PREPARATION:

I. Wash B well, and cut each in half.

II. Mix C, D; stuff into cut side of crab and let stand 15 minutes. Drain.

III. Mix E, F, G, H.

COOKING:

1. Heat A, brown both sides of B.

2. Add E-H and bring to boil. Cover and cook over low heat 3 minutes; turn over and cook another 2 to 3 minutes. Serve hot.

STIR-FRIED CRAB
(Tsao Hai: Canton)

A. 2 tablespoons peanut oil
B. 1 scallion, chopped
C. 2 slices ginger, chopped
D. 2 cloves garlic, chopped
E. 3 to 4 medium crabs
F. 2 tablespoons sherry
G. 1 tablespoon yellow bean sauce
H. 1 tablespoon light soy sauce
I. 1 teaspoon sugar
J. ¼ teaspoon salt
K. ⅓ cup water

PREPARATION:

I. Wash E well; remove claws (crack with back of cleaver), legs, shell. Cut each E into quarters.

II. Combine F, G, H, I, J; mix well.

COOKING:

1. Heat A, stir-fry B-D a few seconds.

2. Add E, stir-fry 1 minute.

3. Add F-J mixture, continue stirring 1 to 2 more minutes.

4. Add K, mix well, bring to boil. Lower heat, simmer 10 minutes.

5. Serve hot with rice.

STEAMED SCALLOPS WITH CHINESE CABBAGE
(Gahn Bei Bai Tsai: Peking)

A. 6 dried scallops

B. 1 Chinese cabbage or celery cabbage (1 to 2 lbs.)

C. 1 teaspoon salt

PREPARATION:

I. Wash A, soak in ½ cup hot water 30 to 45 minutes until soft. Drain, saving water.

II. Discard few outside tough leaves of B. Wash, clean whole B, then cut into 2-inch cross-section pieces (try not to separate leaves). Put into a bowl.

III. Sprinkle B over A. Add ½ cup A water or chicken broth and C.

COOKING:

1. Steam in steamer over boiling water 30 minutes. Serve hot.

CRAB MEAT WITH CELERY CABBAGE
(Sha Ro Bai Tsai: Peking)

A. 3 tablespoons vegetable oil

B. 2 scallions

C. 3 slices ginger

D. 1 clove garlic

E. 6 oz. canned crab meat

F. 1 teaspoon sherry

G. ½ teaspoon sugar

H. 2 teaspoons cornstarch

I. 2 tablespoons water

J. 1 cup chicken broth

K. 1½ lbs. celery cabbage

L. ½ cup thinly sliced bamboo shoots

M. salt to taste

PREPARATION:

I. Chop B, C, D and mix.

II. Cut K diagonally into 1-inch segments.

III. Mix F, G, H, I.

COOKING:

1. Heat A in frying pan; add B-D and stir-fry ½ minute.

2. Add E and stir-fry 2 minutes.

3. Add F-I mixture, simmer 2 to 3 minutes.

4. Heat J to boiling in large (11-inch) frying pan.

5. Add K, L; bring to boil; simmer 5 minutes; add M. Place in bowl and top with B-I mixture.

SQUID WITH GREEN PEPPERS
(Ching Jao Yo Yu: Shanghai)

A. 4 tablespoons vegetable oil

B. 1 medium onion, shredded

C. 1 large pork chop

D. 3 dried squid

E. 1 large green pepper

F. 2 pieces pressed bean curd

G. 1 tablespoon sherry

H. 2 teaspoons light soy sauce

I. 1½ teaspoons cornstarch

J. ½ teaspoon sugar

K. dash pepper

L. ½ teaspoon baking soda

M. salt to taste

PREPARATION:

I. Soak D overnight. Remove soft bones and membranes. Change water. Add L and boil 30 minutes, covered. Then soak ½ hour, drain and rinse. Cut into thin shreds.

II. Bone C and cut into ¼- to ½-inch-wide strips.

III. Remove seeds from E and shred into ¼-inch-wide strips.

IV. Cut F into ¼-inch-wide strips.

V. Mix G, H, I, J, K with D and soak 20 minutes.

COOKING:

1. Heat A in frying pan. Add B, C, stir-fry 1 to 2 minutes.

2. Add E and D mixture, stir-fry 1 to 2 minutes.

3. Add F and a small amount of water or meat stock. Cover for a total cooking time of 6 minutes. Adjust with M.

SWEET AND SOUR SCALLOPS WITH PINEAPPLE
(Tiem Shwin Kong Yu-Chu: Canton)

A. 2 cups peanut oil
B. ½ lb. bay scallops
C. ½ teaspoon minced ginger
D. 1 tablespoon chopped scallion
E. 1 teaspoon light soy sauce
F. 1 teaspoon sherry
G. 1 egg white
H. 2 tablespoons water chestnut flour
I. 1 tablespoon light soy sauce
J. 1 tablespoon vinegar
K. 2 teaspoons sugar
L. 1 tablespoon cornstarch
M. ¾ cup pineapple juice
N. 1 green pepper
O. 1 cup pineapple chunks
P. salt to taste

PREPARATION:

I. Place B in a colander and rinse under cold water a few seconds; drain.

II. Mix B, C, D, E, F; marinate ½ hour.

III. Mix G, H well; stir into B-F mixture.

IV. Mix I, J, K, L, M together in a saucepan.

V. Wash N, discard stem and seeds, and cut into 1-inch cubes.

COOKING:

1. Heat A to 325°; deep fry B-H 2 to 3 minutes, drain on paper towel.

2. Heat I-M mixture, stir until it thickens.

3. Add N and cook 1 minute; add B-N and O; stir well; add P.

SQUID WITH PICKLED MUSTARD GREENS
(Sien Tsai Tsao Yo Yu: Shanghai)

A. 2 tablespoons vegetable oil
B. 3 dried squid
C. ½ teaspoon baking soda
D. 1½ tablespoons sherry
E. 1½ teaspoons cornstarch
F. 1½ teaspoons sugar
G. 1 large pork chop
H. 1 cup chopped bamboo shoots
I. 1 cup pickled mustard greens
J. ½ cup meat stock
K. 4 slices ginger
L. salt to taste

PREPARATION:

I. Soak B overnight. Remove soft bones and membranes. Change water, add C, and boil 30 minutes, covered. Then soak ½ hour, drain and rinse. Cut into ¼-inch shreds.

II. Shred K.

III. Bone G and cut into pieces ¼-inch wide. Discard bone.

IV. Mix D, E, F with ¼ cup water and mix with B.

COOKING:

1. Heat A in frying pan, add B, D-F mixture, stir-fry 1 to 2 minutes.

2. Add G, H, I, J, K, cover, allow to simmer 5 minutes. Stir-fry 1 to 2 minutes.

3. Adjust with L and serve.

FRIED FRESH OYSTERS
(Tza Sun How: General)

A. 2 cups peanut oil
B. ½ pint oysters (about 12)
C. 1 teaspoon salt
D. 1 teaspoon dry sherry
E. 1 teaspoon light soy sauce
F. ¼ teaspoon ground pepper
G. 1 scallion, chopped
H. ½ teaspoon chopped ginger
I. ½ cup flour
J. ½ teaspoon baking powder
K. 1 teaspoon salt
L. 1 egg
M. ¼ cup water

PREPARATION:

I. Rub B lightly with C; place in colander and rinse under cold water ½ minute.

II. Put B into 2 cups boiling water, stir 30 seconds, drain.

III. Mix D, E, F, add B and marinate 10 minutes, turning once.

IV. Sift I, J, K together.

V. Beat L.

VI. Mix G, H, I, J, K, L, M well.

VII. Mix B with egg batter.

COOKING:

1. Heat A to 350°, add B-M a tablespoonful at a time; deep fry until golden brown (about 2 to 3 minutes) on each side. Serve with lemon or Szechuan pepper salt.

CORNMEAL CLAM CAKES
(Jien Ga Li Chio: Tientsin)

    A. peanut oil 1½ inches deep in deep-fat fryer
    B. ¾ cup cornmeal
    C. ¾ cup flour
    D. ¼ cup minced scallions
    E. ¼ teaspoon baking soda
    F. 1½ teaspoons baking powder
    G. 1½ teaspoons salt
    H. 1 qt. fresh clams
    I. 1 egg
    J. 1½ cups buttermilk

PREPARATION:

    I. Mix B, C, D, E, F, G in large bowl.
    II. Grind H or chop very fine.
    III. Combine H, I, J with B-G mixture in bowl; mix well.

COOKING:

    1. Heat A to 325°.
    2. Drop 1 tablespoon batter at a time into oil, turning until formed cakes are browned (cooking time: 2 to 3 minutes).
    3. Drain cakes on absorbent paper. Serve with catsup, optional.

TARO EEL

(Yu Tow Mun Wong Hien: Canton)

    A. 3 tablespoons vegetable oil
    B. 2 cloves garlic
    C. 2 lbs. eel
    D. 6 small taro roots
    E. 2 teaspoons salted black beans
    F. 3 slices ginger
    G. 1 tablespoon sherry
    H. 1 oz. Virginia ham, minced
    I. 2 cups pork or chicken soup
    J. 2 scallions, minced
    K. salt to taste

PREPARATION:

    I. Skin C, cut into 1-inch sections.
    II. Skin D, cut each in quarters.
    III. Crush B, remove outside skin.
    IV. Soak E in hot water until soft, then mash.

COOKING:

    1. Heat A in large, heavy pot. Add B, then C, stir-fry 7 minutes.

    2. Add D, E, F, G, H, I. Cook until C and D are tender. Add water as needed, simmer covered 25 minutes. Sauce will thicken as taro softens.
    3. Add J, adjust with K.

RED-COOKED SNAILS

(Hung Shiu Tien Lo: Canton)

    A. 3 tablespoons vegetable oil
    B. 10-oz. can snail meat
    C. 6 dried mushrooms
    D. ½ lb. pork, shredded
    E. 2 tablespoons diced ham
    F. 2 tablespoons sherry
    G. 1 cup sliced bamboo shoots
    H. 1 tablespoon light soy sauce
    I. 4 slices ginger, minced
    J. 1 tablespoon minced scallions
    K. ½ cup pork or chicken stock
    L. 2 teaspoons corn flour

PREPARATION:

    I. Slice B into thin, bite-size pieces. Marinate in F.
    II. Soak C in hot water 20 minutes. Drain, saving water, and cut each C into thirds.
    III. Mix L with ¼ cup C water.

COOKING:

    1. Place A in large frying pan. Stir-fry B 5 minutes over high heat.
    2. Add C, D, E, G, H, I, J; continue stir-frying.
    3. Add K. Lower heat, simmer covered 25 minutes.
    4. When B is tender, add F, thicken with L mixture. Serve hot.

SEA CUCUMBER IN MUSHROOM SAUCE

(Hai Sun Sao: Shanghai)

    A. 4 tablespoons peanut oil
    B. 2 teaspoons light soy sauce
    C. 1 teaspoon salt
    D. 1 cup dried sea cucumber
    E. 2 cups clear chicken soup
    F. ½ lb. Chinese white cabbage or celery cabbage
    G. 8 dried black mushrooms
    H. 1 tablespoon cornstarch
    I. 2 scallions, minced

J. 2 slices ginger

K. 1 teaspoon sesame oil

L. 3 tablespoons water

PREPARATION:

I. Soak D in water 48 hours. Discard water, then boil D in 2 cups of fresh water with ½ I and J 15 minutes.

II. Cut each D into 2 to 4 pieces.

III. Cut F into ½-by 2-inch pieces.

IV. Soak G in hot water 20 minutes. Cut off stems, then cut each into 3 pieces.

COOKING:

1. Place A in skillet. Heat, then add B, C, D. Bring to boil.

2. Add E, then F, G. Keep stirring over high heat.

3. Mix H, remaining I, J, K, L. Add to sauce, keep stirring. When sauce thickens, it is ready to serve.

Chicken

CHICKEN IN RED BEER
(Jiu Tzao Gee: Fukien)

A. 1½ cups peanut oil

B. 1½-to 2-lb. roasting chicken

C. 1 tablespoon peanut oil

D. 1½ teaspoons garlic salt

E. 1 teaspoon sugar

F. 1½ cups beer

G. 1 to 2 drops red food coloring

H. 1 scallion

I. 1 slice of ginger (about size of a nickel and ½ inch thick)

J. 1 tablespoon cornstarch mixed with 2 table-spoons water

K. salt to taste

PREPARATION:

I. Cut B into bite-size pieces. Rub with D and let stand 15 minutes.

II. Tie H into a knot and pound with side of cleaver.

COOKING:

1. Heat A to 375°; deep fry B 1 to 2 minutes. Drain.

2. Heat C in another pot, add B, stir-fry a few seconds, then add E, F, G, H, I; bring to a boil.

3. Lower heat and simmer 15 minutes or until B is tender.

4. Remove H and I and thicken with J.

5. Add K and serve.

BOILED CHICKEN WITH PORK AND GLUTINOUS RICE STUFFING
(No Mai Ju Yoke Gai: Canton)

A. 2 tablespoons peanut oil

B. ¼ lb. lean pork, diced

C. ¼ cup canned bamboo shoots, diced

D. 3 dried black mushrooms

E. 1 tablespoon gin

F. 2 tablespoons light soy sauce

G. 1 cup glutinous rice

H. 3-lb. chicken

PREPARATION:

I. Wash G and cook in rapidly boiling water 5 minutes. Drain. Rinse with cold water. Drain.

II. Soak D in warm water 15 minutes. Drain and slice into slivers.

III. Mix C, D, E, F. Set aside.

COOKING:

1. Put A in very hot skillet and bring to high heat.

2. Add B and stir-fry 1 to 2 minutes.

3. Add C-F mixture and stir-fry 1 minute.

4. Add G. Mix well.

5. Stuff H with this mixture. Fasten opening with skewers.

6. Wrap H in cheesecloth and immerse in water (just enough to cover) at the simmering point. Simmer 30 to 40 minutes or until tender.

7. Remove from water. Unwrap. Carve at table and serve with a spoonful of stuffing.

DEEP-FRIED SWEET-AND-SOUR CHICKEN

A. 2 tablespoons cornstarch

B. 2 tablespoons soy sauce

C. 1 teaspoon salt

D. 2 eggs

E. Oil for cooking

F. 1 4-pound cooked chicken, boned, skinned, meat cut into 1-inch cubes

Combine A and B: mix well.

Combine C and D in mixing bowl: beat with whisk until light. Stir in A mixture until just mixed.

Heat E in deep-fryer to 375°F or until small ball of flour mixed with water dropped into E floats to top immediately.

Dip F into D mixture: drain slightly. Drop F, several cubes at a time, into E. Fry until lightly browned; drain on paper toweling. Place F in individual serving dishes. Spoon Sweet-and-Sour Sauce over F. Makes 4 to 6 servings.

Sweet-and-sour Sauce
- **G. ¾ cup sugar**
- **H. 2 tablespoons soy sauce**
- **I. 1 tablespoon dry white wine**
- **J. 3 tablespoons wine vinegar**
- **K. 3 tablespoons catsup**
- **L. 2 tablespoons cornstarch**
- **M. ½ cup water**

Combine G, H, I, J, and K in saucepan; bring to boil.

Dissolve A in water; add to sauce. Cook over low heat, stirring, until sauce has thickened. Makes 1 to 1¼ cups.

CHICKEN WITH DATES
- **A. 1 chicken, approximately 3 to 3½ pounds**
- **B. Salt**
- **C. Pepper**
- **D. Curry powder**
- **E. 2 tablespoons oil**
- **F. 1 medium onion, chopped**
- **G. 2 green peppers, cut into thin strips**
- **H. 1 cup beef bouillon**
- **I. ½ pound rice**
- **J. 1 teaspoon cornstarch**
- **K. 12 dates, pitted, cut into halves**
- **L. 1 cup yogurt**
- **M. 3 tablespoons toasted sliced almonds**

Divide A into 8 pieces. Remove all except wing and leg bones.

Rub A with B, C, and D.

Heat E in heavy skillet. Add A; cook until golden on all sides.

Add F, cook until golden. Add G. Pour in H; simmer over low heat 30 minutes.

Meanwhile cook I according to package directions.

Remove A from sauce; keep warm. Strain sauce.

Blend J with small amount cold water. Slowly stir into sauce; cook until thick and bubbly. Add K.

Beat L with fork; stir into sauce. If necessary, correct seasonings.

Heat through, but do not boil. Spoon I into bowl or platter; arrange A on top. Pour sauce over A; top with M.

Makes 4 or 5 servings.

BARBECUED CHICKEN
(Jiang Yo Sao Gee: Shanghai)
- **A. 2 chickens (2 to 3 lbs. each)**
- **B. ½ cup light soy sauce**
- **C. 2 tablespoons sherry**
- **D. ¼ teaspoon paprika**
- **E. ¼ cup peanut oil**
- **F. 1 teaspoon sugar**

PREPARATION:

I. Wash A; dry with paper towels. Cut into 8 pieces.

II. Mix B, C, D, E, F; marinate A in mixture 1 hour.

COOKING:

1. Get coals red-hot on horizontal grill. Put on A. Cover A with aluminum foil to retain juices. If half hood is on grill, place one end of foil on top of hood (with weights) and allow foil to hand extended over edge of grill. When A browns, turn over. Cooking time: 25 to 40 minutes.

Serves 6 to 8.

CURRIED CHICKEN CANTONESE
(Yea Tsup Ga Li Gai: Canton)
- **A. 3 tablespoons peanut oil**
- **B. 1 medium onion, chopped**
- **C. 2 slices ginger, chopped**
- **D. 2 teaspoons curry powder**
- **E. 2 cups chicken broth**
- **F. 1½ teaspoons salt**
- **G. 2-lb. chicken**
- **H. 1 cup milk**
- **I. ½ cup coconut flakes**
- **J. 1 tablespoon flour**

PREPARATION:

I. Cut G into bite-size pieces.

II. Mix H, I in a pan, warm 30 minutes over low heat (do not boil), stirring occasionally.

III. Pour H-I from pan through a wire strainer, squeeze I, discard coconut residue, and mix liquid with J.

COOKING:

1. Heat A, brown B, C 1 minute.

2. Add D, stir 2 minutes more.

3. Add E, F, bring to boil. Lower heat, cook 5 minutes. Remove B, C.

4. Add G, cook 30 minutes.

5. Thicken with H-J mixture. Serve hot with rice.

CHICKEN IN OYSTER SAUCE

(Ho Yow Gai: Canton)

   A. 3 tablespoons peanut oil
   B. 2-lb. frying chicken
   C. 1 scallion
   D. 4 slices fresh ginger
   E. 4 tablespoons oyster sauce
   F. salt to taste

PREPARATION:

   I. Cut B into small pieces.

   II. Cut C into 1-inch pieces.

COOKING:

1. Heat A. Add B, C, D. Sauté until golden brown.

2. Add E. Cook, covered, 25 minutes over low heat.

3. Add F.

4. Serve hot or cold.

PAPER-WRAPPED CHICKEN

(Tze Bao Gee: Shanghai)

   A. 2 cups vegetable oil
   B. 3 lbs. breast meat of frying chickens
   C. 1 tablespoon light soy sauce
   D. 1 tablespoon gin
   E. 1 teaspoon salt
   F. ½ teaspoon ground white pepper
   G. 1 to 3 teaspoons sesame oil (to taste)

PREPARATION:

   I. Slice B into pieces 2 inches long by ¼ inch wide. Place in bowl.

   II. Mix C, D, E, F, G and pour over B in bowl. Mix well and let stand 1 hour.

   III. Wrap each piece of B in wax paper.

COOKING:

1. Heat A to 375°, and deep fry packages 1 minute on each side.

2. Serve hot in wrapping (to be unwrapped at the table).

SPICY SMOKED CHICKEN

(Woo Siang Shwin Gee)

   A. 3-lb. roasting chicken
   B. 2 tablespoon sherry
   C. 2 teaspoons salt
   D. ¼ teaspoon cinnamon
   E. 2 cloves star anise
   F. ½ cup sugar
   G. 1 tablespoon molasses
   H. 2 scallions
   I. 3 tablespoons light soy sauce
   J. ¼ teaspoon sesame oil
   K. 7 drops tabasco sauce

PREPARATION:

   I. Clean A, dry thoroughly with paper towels.

   II. Mix B, C; rub on A.

   III. Stuff A cavity with H. Refrigerate overnight.

   IV. Mix D, E, F, G.

COOKING:

1. Steam prepared A over boiling water 30 minutes. Remove from heat, let A stand in steamer 15 more minutes.

2. Line a Dutch oven with aluminum foil. Spread D-G uniformly over foil. Place a rack above D-G mixture.

3. Place prepared A on rack, cover, and cook over low heat 10 to 15 minutes. Remove from heat.

4. When Dutch oven is cool remove prepared A and cut into bite-size pieces.

5. Mix I, J, K, paint on A. Serve hot or cold.

KUNG BAO CHICKEN DING

(Kung Bao Gee Ding: Szechuan)

   A. ¼ cup peanut oil
   B. 2 chicken breasts
   C. 1 egg white
   D. 2 teaspoons cornstarch
   E. 1 to 2 scallions, chopped
   F. 2 to 4 slices ginger, chopped
   G. 2 to 3 red-hot peppers (dried hot or pepper flakes)
   H. ¼ cup water chestnuts (optional)
   I. 1 tablespoon soy bean sauce (mien see)
   J. 1 teaspoon sugar
   K. 2 teaspoons light soy sauce
   L. 2 teaspoons sherry
   M. 2 teaspoons vinegar

N. ¼ teaspoon sesame oil
O. salt to taste

PREPARATION:

I. Bone B, discard skin, dice and mix with C, D.

II. Split G into halves, discard stem and seeds, cut each into ½-inch pieces.

III. Mix I, J, K, L, M, N.

COOKING:

1. Heat A, stir-fry B-D mixture for 1 to 2 minutes, remove to dish.

2. Leave excess oil in same pan, and heat. Add E, F, G, H, (drained and diced); stir-fry 1 to 2 minutes.

3. Add B-D mixture, stir-fry 1 to 2 minutes.

4. Add I-N mixture, continue stirring until well mixed. Add O.

CHICKEN WINGS AND LEGS WITH SOY SAUCE
(Jiang Yo Gee)

A. 1 cup light soy sauce
B. 1 scallion
C. 1 slice ginger (½ inch thick) about size of a nickel
D. ¼ cup of wine
E. ¼ cup water
F. 2 tablespoons brown sugar
G. wings and legs from 2- to 3-lb. fryer
H. 1 to 2 teaspoons sesame oil
I. 1 scallion, chopped

PREPARATION:

I. Tie B in a bundle.

II. Peel C and pound lightly with side of cleaver.

COOKING:

1. Place A, B, C, D, E, F in a saucepan, bring to a boil.

2. Add G spread out in a single layer; when mixture boils again, lower heat, cover, and simmer 5 minutes.

3. Turn G pieces over, turn up heat until sauce boils again; then lower heat, cover and simmer 5 minutes. Turn G, bring to boil, lower heat, and simmer 15 minutes.

4. Remove saucepan from heat. Keep covered and let stand 10 minutes.

5. Remove G from pan, brush with H, and let cool completely.

6. With cleaver, cut G into bite-size pieces.

7. Place on platter and garnish with I. Pour 2 to 3 tablespoons of the sauce over G. Serve. (The remaining sauce can be used over again as a sauce for hard-cooked eggs, gizzards, or any red-cooked dish.)

CHICKEN CHOW MEIN

A. 1 green sweet pepper, cut into slices
B. 1 red sweet pepper, cut into slices
C. 1 cup boiling water
D. 1½ tablespoons butter
E. 1 small onion, chopped
F. 2 stalks celery, sliced
G. 1 tablespoon flour
H. 1 cup chicken broth
I. 2 tablespoons soy sauce
J. Freshly ground pepper to taste
K. 1 4-ounce can sliced mushrooms, drained
L. 8 ounces cooked chicken breast, cut into bite-size pieces
M. 6 cups water
N. 8 ounces egg noodles
O. Salt
P. 1 tablespoon butter
Q. Oil for frying
R. 4 ounces sliced almonds, toasted and slightly salted

Cut A and B into slices. Blanch in C for 5 minutes. Remove and drain. Heat D in saucepan. Add E and F and saute;a until E are transparent. Sprinkle with G, pour in H and bring to a boil while stirring constantly. Simmer for 10 minutes. Season with I and J. Add A and B, drained K, and L pieces. Cover and simmer for 15 minutes.

Meanwhile, bring 6 cups of slightly salted M to a boil and add N and cook for 15 minutes. Drain and rinse with cold water. Set aside ⅓1 of the N. Place rest of N in heated bowl, add 1 tablespoon P, cover and keep warm.

Heat Q in skillet until very hot. Cut N that were set aside into approximately 2-inch-long pieces. Add to hot Q and fry until golden. Drain on paper towels. To serve, spoon L mixture over buttered N; top with fried noodles and R.

Makes 4 servings.

PEKING CRISPY DUCK

(Go Sao Ya Tze: Peking)

A. 3-lb. duck
B. 1½ tablespoons salt
C. 2 tablespoons sherry
D. 1 tablespoon chopped scallion
E. 1 teaspoon chopped ginger
F. ¼ cup flour
G. 2 small eggs
H. 2 teaspoons light soy sauce
I. 1 tablespoon cornstarch mixed with ¼ cup water
J. 2 cups peanut oil

PREPARATION:

I. Wash A thoroughly.
II. Mix B, C, D, E.
III. Rub A inside and out with B-E.
IV. Beat G, mix with H, I.

COOKING:

1. Place A in dish, steam over boiling water 1 to 2 hours or until tender.
2. Bone A or simply dry between paper towels. Coat lightly with F.
3. Rub A with G-I.
4. Deep fry A in J at 350° until golden brown (about 3 minutes each side).
5. Cut into strips, arrange on plate in a row or cut into bite-size pieces and serve.

ROASTED DUCK WITH ORANGE PEEL

(Chan Pei Pei Shiu Op: Canton)

A. 3- to 4-lb. duck
B. 2 to 3 pieces dried orange peel
C. 1 tablespoon yellow bean sauce
D. 5 slices ginger
E. 1 clove garlic
F. 2 tablespoons light soy sauce
G. 1 teaspoon sugar
H. 2 tablespoons whiskey
I. 1 teaspoon salt

PREPARATION:

I. Wash A well, remove fat from cavity, dry with paper towels.
II. Wash B, soak in warm water until soft (about 30 minutes). Rinse, chop fine.
III. Mash C into a paste.

IV. Chop D, E, very fine.
V. Mix B, C, D, E, F, G, H, I with a fork.
VI. Rub A thoroughly with B-I mixture, inside and out.

COOKING:

1. Place A in large pot; braise each side 2 minutes, or until very little sauce remains.
2. Line roasting pan with foil. Place A on top, roast 20 minutes each side in 450° oven.
3. Reduce heat to 325°, roast each side 30 more minutes. Serve.

PRESSED DUCK

(Ban Yah: Nanking)

A. 4- to 5-lb. duck
B. 1 teaspoon saltpeter (obtained in drugstore)
C. 6 tablespoons salt
D. 2 teaspoons anise pepper

PREPARATION:

I. Wash A thoroughly, remove fat from cavity, dry with paper towels.
II. Mix B, C, D well. Rub A with B-D mixture inside and out thoroughly.
III. Place a rack in large pan. Place A on rack; refrigerate 3 days. Hang A in sun 1 day.

COOKING:

1. Cut A in halves or quarters. Wash away salt under cold water.
2. Place A pieces in deep plate; steam 1 hour.
Note: Hung or pressed duck can be refrigerated several weeks. Cook when needed. (When processed for commercial sale, it is flattened, or pressed.)

SOY SAUCE DUCK

(Jiang Yo Yah: Shanghai)

A. 3-lb. duck
B. ½ teaspoon five spices powder
C. ½ teaspoon salt
D. 3 scallions
E. 4 slices ginger
F. ¼ cup light soy sauce
G. 2 tablespoons sherry

COOKING:

1. Place A in Dutch oven, adding enough water to half cover it. Cover pan and simmer 1 hour.

2. Drain, saving soup; let stand and remove grease from top; return A to Dutch oven. Rub B and C over A; place D, E in A cavity.

3. Add F, G, and 4 cups soup. Boil 30 minutes, or until duck is tender.

SOY SAUCE DUCK WITH GRAPES (ONE DUCK, TWO FLAVORS)
(Yet Op Liang Mei (Pu To Op): Canton)
   A. 3-lb. duck, cooked (see Soy Sauce Duck)
   B. 40 seedless grapes
   C. ½ teaspoon sesame oil
   D. 2 teaspoons light soy sauce

PREPARATION:
   I. Split A lengthwise. Bone, shredding meat with grain. Skin B and cut each in half.

SERVING:
   1. Place A on platter.
   2. Mix B, C, D and neatly cover A. Serve cold.

Pork

SLICED PORK WITH VEGETABLES
(Er Dung Ro Pien: Peking)
   A. 3 tablespoons peanut oil
   B. ½ lb. pork tenderloin
   C. 1 small egg white
   D. 1 teaspoon cornstarch
   E. few drops sesame oil
   F. ½ teaspoon chopped ginger
   G. 1 tablespoon chopped scallion (white part only)
   H. 1 cup sliced bamboo shoots
   I. ½ cup button mushrooms
   J. 1 tablespoon light soy sauce
   K. 2 teaspoons sherry
   L. ½ cup chicken broth
   M. ½ teaspoon salt
   N. 2 teaspoons cornstarch mixed with I liquid

PREPARATION:
   I. Slice B into 1- by 2-inch thin pieces, mix well with C, D, E.
   II. Drain I and save liquid for N.
   III. Mix, J, K, L, M.

COOKING:
   1. Heat A, add B-E mixture, stir-fry 1 to 2 minutes, remove to dish; leave oil in pan.
   2. Heat oil in pan, stir-fry F, G a few times; add H, I, continue frying 1 minute.
   3. Add J-M mixture, bring to boil, thicken with N.
   4. Add B mixture, cook 1 minute and serve.

JADE GREEN MEAT DING
(Fei Chwee Yoke Ding: Canton)
   A. 3 tablespoons peanut oil
   B. ½ lb. pork tenderloin, diced
   C. 1 teaspoon light soy sauce
   D. 1 teaspoon cornstarch
   E. 1 teaspoon peanut oil
   F. 1 cup diced bamboo shoots
   G. ¼ lb. snow peas
   H. 1 teaspoon salt
   I. 1 tablespoon water
   J. ½ teaspoon sugar

PREPARATION:
   I. Mix B, C, D, E.
   II. Discard tips of G. Wash G, drain.

COOKING:
   1. Heat A, stir-fry B-E mixture 2 minutes.
   2. Add F, continue stir-frying 30 seconds.
   3. Add G, H, I, J, stir-fry 1 to 2 more minutes.

STEAMED MINCED PORK WITH WATER CHESTNUTS (OR WATER CHESTNUT MEATCAKE)
(Ma Ti Tsen Tsu Ro: General)
   A. ½ lb. ground pork
   B. 9 canned water chestnuts, chopped fine
   C. 1 teaspoon cornstarch
   D. 2 tablespoons water
   E. 1 tablespoon light soy sauce
   F. ½ teaspoon sugar
   G. ½ teaspoon salt

PREPARATION:
   I. Mix A, B, C, D, E, F, G, well.

COOKING:
   1. Flatten A-G in a flat serving dish suitable for steaming.
   2. Place dish in steaming utensil and steam 25 minutes.
   3. Remove from steaming utensil and serve.

DOUBLE-COOKED PORK WITH HOISIN SAUCE
(Hwei Gwo Ro: Szechuan)

A. 3 tablespoons peanut oil
B. 1 tablespoon chopped scallion
C. 2 tablespoons hoisin sauce
D. ½ lb. pork
E. 2 small green peppers
F. 1 to 2 small sweet red peppers
G. salt to taste
H. 1 tablespoon water

PREPARATION:

I. Cover D with water, bring to boil, lower heat, cook 30 minutes. Broth may be saved for soup.

II. Discard E seeds, cut each E into eighths, each eighth into quarters.

III. Discard F seeds, cut each same as E.

IV. Cut cooked D in slices 1½ by ¾ inches.

COOKING:

1. Heat A, add B, stir-fry a few seconds.
2. Add C, mix well.
3. Add D slices, stir a few times.
4. Add E, F, G, H. Continue stir-frying 1 minute.

SZECHUAN PORK WITH ASPARAGUS
(Lu Sun Tsu Ro: Szechuan)

A. 3 tablespoons peanut oil
B. ½ lb. pork
C. 2 teaspoons light soy sauce
D. 1 teaspoon cornstarch
E. 1 bunch asparagus (½ lb.)
F. 1 tablespoon chopped scallion
G. 1 teaspoon chopped ginger
H. 1 clove garlic, minced
I. 2 teaspoons light soy sauce
J. 2 teaspoons brown bean sauce
K. ½ teaspoon salt
L. 2 teaspoons sherry
M. 2 teaspoons vinegar
N. 1 teaspoon sugar
O. 2 teaspoons cornstarch mixed with ¼ cup water
P. Chinese hot sauce or anise pepper to taste (optional)

PREPARATION:

I. Slice B thin, shred, mix with C, D and 1 teaspoon A.

II. Cut E into 1- to 1½-inch-long pieces.

III. Bring 1 qt. water to boil, add asparagus and parboil 2 to 4 minutes depending on thickness of pieces. Drain. Mix I, J, K, L, M, N, O.

COOKING:

1. Heat remaining A, add B-D mixture, stir-fry 1 to 2 minutes. Remove to a dish, pour excess oil back to pan.
2. Add E, F, G, H, stir-fry 1 minute.
3. Return B-D to pan, stir-fry 1 to 2 minutes.
4. Add I-O mixture, stir until thickened.
5. Add P to taste.

PORK LO MEIN
(Tsu Ro Lo Mein: General)

A. 3 tablespoons peanut oil
B. 4 Chinese mushrooms
C. 1 tablespoon chopped scallions
D. ¼ lb. pork (or beef or chicken)
E. 2 tablespoons light soy sauce
F. 1 teaspoon salt
G. 1 cup shredded celery cabbage
H. 1 cup thinly shredded bamboo shoots
I. 1 cup thinly shredded celery
J. ¼ cup mushroom water
K. 10 snow peas
L. 1 teaspoon cornstarch mixed with 1 table-spoon water
M. ½ lb. fresh or dried thin noodles

PREPARATION:

I. Cook M in 2 qts. boiling water 5 to 8 minutes. Drain and run under cold water a few seconds; drain again.

II. Mix cooked M with ½ E, ⅓ A, and ½ teaspoon F. Put mixture in baking dish and bake in 375° oven 25 minutes.

III. Wash B and soak in warm water 15 minutes. Cut in thin shreds 2 inches long.

IV. Cut D in thin shreds 2 inches long.

COOKING:

1. Heat A in frying pan until hot, stir in B, C, add D and stir-fry 2 minutes. Add E, F, stir-fry 1 minute.
2. Add G, H, I and mix well. Add J, cover and cook 2 minutes. Add K and continue to stir-fry 1 minute.
3. Add L, stir well.
4. Pour over baked crispy M and serve.

chicken with dates (see recipe page 159)

wonton soup (see recipe page 145)

egg rolls (see recipe page 142)

deep-fried sweet-and-sour chicken (see recipe page 158)

chicken chow mein (see recipe page 161)

deep-fried crispy noodles
soft-fried noodles with mushrooms (see recipe page 178)

chinese fruit salad (see recipe page 179)

chop suey (see recipe page 170)

SHREDDED PORK WITH BEAN SPROUTS AND
SCALLIONS
(Nying Ya Ro Si: Hunan)
    A. 4 tablespoons peanut oil
    B. 1 lb. bean sprouts
    C. 2 scallions
    D. 4 slices ginger, shredded
    E. 1 teaspoon salt
    F. ½ lb. pork (or veal or beef), shredded
    G. 1 tablespoon light soy sauce
    H. 1 teaspoon sherry
    I. 1 teaspoon cornstarch
    J. ½ teaspoon sugar

PREPARATION:
  I. Mix F thoroughly with G, H, I, J.
  II. Wash B, drain. Trim and discard tail roots.
  III. Slice C into 1½-inch pieces

COOKING:
  1. Heat 1 tablespoon A. Add B, C, D, stir-fry a few seconds.
  2. Add E, stir-fry 1 minute. Drain off liquid, place B-E mixture on plate for later use.
  3. Heat remaining A until very hot. Add F-J, stir-fry 2 minutes.
  4. Add B-E mixture, mix well, and serve hot.

PORK IN PLUM SAUCE
(Mwei Jiong Yoke: Canton)
    A. ¼ cup vegetable oil
    B. 1 clove garlic
    C. 1 lb. boned pork
    D. ⅓ cup plum sauce
    E. 2 celery stalks, diced
    F. 4 slices ginger
    G. 1 tablespoon sherry
    H. 2 carrots
    I. 2 teaspoons sugar
    J. 1 teaspoon salt
    K. ⅓ cup Chinese pickled scallions
    L. ¼ cup water
    M. 2 teaspoons cornstarch
    N. 2 tablespoons water

PREPARATION:
  I. Cut C into bite-size pieces.
  II. Peel H, cut into cubes.
  III. Crush B with flat side of cleaver; remove skin.

COOKING:
  1. Place A, B in skillet. Using high heat, brown C. Stir 5 minutes.
  2. Add D, E, F, G, H, I, J, K, L. Simmer, covered, 12 minutes.
  3. Add M mixed with N to thicken gravy.

STEAMED SPARERIBS
(Swan Tsai Tsen Pai Gu: Szechuan)
    A. 1 lb. spareribs
    B. 3 teaspoons brown bean sauce
    C. 1 tablespoon water
    D. ½ teaspoon salt
    E. 1 cup shredded pickled mustard greens
    F. ½ teaspoon sugar
    G. ½ cup rice flour
    H. 1 or 2 red-hot peppers (optional)

PREPARATION:
  I. Cut A into 1-inch pieces.
  II. Mix A, B, C, D, marinate 30 to 60 minutes.
  III. Chop E, mix with F and 1 tablespoon G. Add H.
  IV. Place rest of G in paper bag. Add marinated A, and shake, coating each piece with G.
  V. Line soup dish with E, top with A mixture.

COOKING:
  1. Steam A over boiling water in steamer 1 hour, or until meat is tender.

ONION SPARERIBS
(Yang Tsung Tsu Pai: Wushih)
    A. ⅓ cup peanut oil
    B. 1 lb. spareribs
    C. 1 lb. onions
    D. 1 tablespoon sherry
    E. ¼ cup catsup
    F. 1½ tablespoons vinegar
    G. 1½ tablespoons sugar
    H. 1 tablespoon light soy sauce
    I. ¼ cup water

PREPARATION:
  I. Pound B with back of cleaver several times; cut each rib into 2-inch pieces.
  II. Peel C and slice into ½-inch pieces.
  III. Mix E, F, G, H, I.

COOKING:

1. Heat A, add B and brown 1 to 2 minutes; remove B to dish.

2. Heat 2 tablespoons A, add C, and brown 1 minute.

3. Return B, add D, stir well.

4. Add E-I, bring to boil, lower heat and simmer for 10 to 15 minutes, depending on the tenderness of the ribs.

MEATBALLS WITH VEGETABLES
(Ju Yoke Yuan Ju Shiu Tsoi)
    A. ¼ cup vegetable oil
    B. ½ lb. ground pork
    C. 1 egg
    D. 7 water chestnuts, chopped (or 4 tablespoons bread crumbs)
    E. 2 teaspoons sherry
    F. ½ cup chicken broth
    G. 6 dried mushrooms
    H. 3 slices fresh ginger
    I. ¾ lb. Chinese celery cabbage
    J. 2 tablespoons minced scallions
    K. salt to taste

PREPARATION:

I. Mix B, C, D, E. Make spoon-size balls.

II. Soak G in hot water 20 minutes. Drain, saving water. Remove stems; shred.

III. Cut I into 2-inch pieces.

COOKING:

1. Heat A in deep frying pan, add B-E mixture. Stir-fry 1 to 2 minutes.

2. Add F, G, H, simmer covered 10 to 15 minutes.

3. Add I, J. Cook 5 minutes covered. Add K. Serve hot.

SWEET AND PUNGENT SPARERIBS
(Tiem Shwin Pai Gwut: Canton)
    A. 2 lbs. spareribs
    B. 1 tablespoon light soy sauce
    C. 1 tablespoon sherry
    D. 1 teaspoon cornstarch
    E. peanut oil for deep frying
    F. 2 tablespoons peanut oil
    G. 1 green pepper
    H. 1 large tomato
    I. 8-oz. can pineapple chunks, with juice
    J. 3 tablespoons sugar
    K. 3 tablespoons vinegar
    L. 1 tablespoon light soy sauce
    M. 2 teaspoons cornstarch

PREPARATION:

I. Cut A into 1½-inch pieces; cook 10 minutes with just enough water to cover; salt to taste; drain.

II. Mix B, C, D.

III. Add A, let stand 1 hour.

IV. Cut G into small pieces.

V. Cut H into 8 wedges.

VI. Mix I, J, K, L, M and set aside in bowl.

COOKING:

1. Deep-fry A-D mixture in E until golden brown; drain.

2. Heat F; stir-fry G 1 minute.

3. Add H, stir-fry 1 minute.

4. Add A, I-M and stir well; cook until mixture thickens.

5. Serve hot with rice.

CHOP SUEY
    A. 1 pound lean pork, cut into thin slices
    B. 2 tablespoons sherry
    C. 2 tablespoons soy sauce
    D. Salt to taste
    E. Freshly ground pepper to taste
    F. Pinch of powdered ginger
    G. 2 ounces transparent noodles, broken into small pieces
    H. 1 stalk celery, cut into thin slices
    I. 4 tablespoons dried Chinese mushrooms, soaked in water for 30 minutes
    J. 8 tablespoons oil
    K. 2 medium onions, thinly sliced
    L. ¼ cup bamboo shoots, thinly sliced
    M. 1 cup fresh bean sprouts
    N. ½ pound fresh mushrooms, sliced
    O. 3 tablespoons soy sauce
    P. 1 teaspoon sugar
    Q. ⅛ teaspoon MSG
    R. 1 tablespoon cornstarch
    S. 2 jiggers sherry
    T. Cooked rice

Cut A into thin slices and mix with 2 tablespoons B, 2 tablespoons C, D, E, and F. Place in glass or ceramic bowl. Press down meat and cover. Let marinate for 1 hour. Break G into small pieces and boil in salted water for 5 minutes. Drain and set aside. Cut H in thin slices; blanch for 5 minutes. Drain and set aside. Slice I into bite-size pieces.

Heat J in skillet until very hot. Add marinated A and fry for 2 minutes. Remove and keep warm. Add K, L, M, and N. Simmer for 3 minutes. Fold in A, H and G. Season with 3 tablespoons O, P, and Q. Stirring carefully, cook for an additional 3 minutes. Blend R with S and slowly stir into sauce until sauce is thick and bubbly. Correct seasonings if necessary and serve immediately with T.

Makes approximately 3 servings.

RED-COOKED FRESH HAM
(Hung Sao Bing Tang Ti Pong: Shanghai)

A. ½ cup heavy soy sauce
B. 2 tablespoons sherry
C. 1 star anise
D. 1 tablespoon rock sugar
E. 2½ lbs. fresh ham
F. salt to taste

PREPARATION:

I. Clean and wash E thoroughly.

COOKING:

1. Bring 3 cups water in cooking pan to boil.
2. Add A, B, C, D. Keep boiling.
3. Add E, bring back to boil and cook in bubbling A-D sauce 5 to 10 minutes; lower heat and simmer 2 hours (or until E is tender).
4. Turn E over 2 or 3 times during cooking so that it will absorb A-D sauce evenly. Add boiling water if necessary.
5. Add F, if necessary, after first hour of cooking.

BRAISED PORK TONGUE WITH BAMBOO SHOOTS
(Tsu Suh Sao Sun Pien: General)

A. 1 pork tongue (about ½ lb.)
B. 1 tablespoon whiskey
C. 2 tablespoons peanut oil
D. 1 cup sliced bamboo shoots
E. 3 slices ginger
F. 1 scallion
G. 1 tablespoon sherry

H. 1 teaspoon sugar
I. 2 tablespoons light soy sauce
J. ¼ cup tongue stock

PREPARATION:

I. Place A in cold water and clean. Drain; place in pot; add boiling water to cover. Bring to boil, add B, boil 5 to 7 minutes. Drain and let stay in cold water 1 minute. Slice off white skin. Wash and drain.

II. Set aside J.

COOKING:

1. Cover prepared A with water, bring to boil, lower heat and simmer 1 to 1¼ hours. Remove A from pot and cut into thin slices. Serve soup.
2. Heat C, add sliced A, and D, E, F, G, H, I, stir well.
3. Add J, mix well, cover and cook over low heat 25 to 30 minutes. Serve hot.

HOT SPICED FRESH HAM
(Swan La Ti Pong; Szechuan)

A. 3 tablespoons peanut oil
B. 3 slices ginger
C. 1 or 2 cloves garlic
D. 1 or 2 red-hot peppers
E. 2 green peppers
F. 2½-lb. fresh ham, with skin (or ½ ham)
G. ¼ cup light soy sauce
H. 1 teaspoon salt
I. 1 cup chicken soup
J. 1 scallion (white part only), chopped
K. 3 tablespoons sugar
L. ¼ cup vinegar
M. 2 teaspoons cornstarch mixed with ¼ cup water

PREPARATION:

I. Place F in 2 qts. boiling water, bring back to boil, lower heat and simmer 1½ hours or until skin is tender. Remove from pot and cool.

II. Bone cooked F and cut into ½-inch pieces with skin on.

III. Cut each B into 4 pieces.

IV. Pound C with side of cleaver, discard skin and chop.

V. Wash D, E, split open, discard seeds and cut into cubes.

VI. Mix J, K, L, M.

COOKING:

1. Heat A to smoking, add B, C, stir-fry ½ to 1 minute.

2. Add D, E, stir-fry ½ minute, then remove to dish.

3. Heat excess oil, stir-fry F pieces, add G, H, stir 2 to 3 minutes longer.

4. Add I, bring to boil, cover and cook 3 to 5 minutes.

5. Return B-E mixture, mix well.

6. Thicken with J-M; serve hot.

Beef

STEAK KEW

(Ngo Pa Kew: Canton)

A. 3 tablespoons peanut oil
B. 8 to 10 Chinese mushrooms
C. ½ lb. filet mignon or other steak (if less expensive cut is used, sprinkle with ¼ teaspoon meat tenderizer and let stand for 5 minutes before cutting)
D. 1 clove garlic, chopped
E. 2 slices ginger, shredded
F. 1 tablespoon chopped scallion
G. 1 tablespoon oyster sauce
H. 1 tablespoon light soy sauce
I. ½ teaspoon sugar
J. 2 teaspoons cornstarch
K. ¼ lb. snow peas
L. ½ teaspoon salt

PREPARATION:

I. Cut C into 1-inch cubes, mix with D, E, F, G, H, I, J; marinate 15 to 30 minutes.

II. Rinse B; cover with warm water and soak for 15 minutes or until soft. Drain and quarter.

III. Remove and discard tips of K; wash and drain.

IV. Add K to 1 quart of boiling water, stir well. When water boils again, remove from heat, drain, and run cold water over pea pods.

COOKING:

1. Heat A, add B, stir-fry ½ to 1 minute.
2. Add C-J, stir-fry 1 to 2 minutes.
3. Add K, mix well.
4. Stir in L.
5. Pour onto dish and serve hot.

STIR-FRIED BEEF WITH SAUCE

(Tsao Niu Ro: General)

A. 2 tablespoons peanut oil
B. 1 clove garlic, minced
C. ½ slice fresh ginger, minced
D. ¼ teaspoon salt
E. ½ lb. flank steak
F. 1 teaspoon light soy sauce
G. 1 teaspoon sugar
H. 2 tablespoons sherry or gin
I. 1 tablespoon water
J. 1 tablespoon cornstarch
K. 1 tablespoon heavy soy sauce
L. 1 cup soup stock
M. 2 scallions, sliced

PREPARATION:

I. Slice E very thin.
II. Mix B, C, D. Set aside.
III. Mix F, G, H. Set aside.
IV. Mix I, J, K, L. Set aside. Stir well before using.

COOKING:

1. Put A in very hot skillet and bring to high heat.
2. Add B-D. Stir-fry rapidly 15 seconds to brown B slightly.
3. Add E. Stir-fry 1 minute.
4. Add F-H and stir-fry 1 minute.
5. Add I-L slowly. Stir-fry until sauce thickens and coats all ingredients well. Do not cover.
6. Serve, garnish with M.

PEPPER STEAK

(Ching Jao Tsao Niu Ro: General)

A. 3 tablespoons peanut oil
B. 1 lb. flank steak
C. 2 green peppers
D. 2 tablespoons water
E. 1 tablespoon light soy sauce
F. 1 teaspoon oyster sauce
G. 1 tablespoon sherry
H. 2 teaspoons cornstarch
I. ½ teaspoon sugar
J. 1 scallion, chopped
K. 4 slices ginger, shredded

PREPARATION:

I. Cut B into narrow strips about 2 inches by ¼ inch, against the grain.

II. Cut C into strips. Discard seeds.

III. Mix B with E, F, G, H, I, J, K. Let stand 15 minutes.

COOKING:

1. Heat A in skillet until hot.

2. Add B and stir-fry 1 minute. Remove and set aside.

3. Using the same pan, add C and stir.

4. Add D, cover and simmer ½ minute.

5. Add E-K mixture, stir 1 minute and serve.

RED-COOKED BEEF WITH CELLOPHANE NOODLES
(Hung Sao Hgo Yoke Fun See: Canton)

    A. 4 lbs beef shin (including bone)
    B. 6 tablespoons light soy sauce
    C. ¼ cup sherry
    D. 5 slices ginger, minced
    E. 1 cup water
    F. water to cover ⅓ of meat
    G. 2 oz. cellophane noodles

PREPARATION:

I. Precook G by soaking in hot water 20 minutes.

II. Mix B, C, D, E. Set aside.

COOKING:

1. Place A in heavy cooking utensil with cover.

2. Add B-E mixture. Cook over high heat 10 minutes. Stir.

3. Add F. Bring to boil. Turn heat to low and cook until tender (about 2½ hours). Stir occasionally to prevent sticking.

4. Add G. Simmer 10 minutes. Serve.

BEEF WITH GINGER
(Jiang Sih Niu Ro: General)

    A. 2 tablespoons peanut oil
    B. 1½ cloves garlic, mashed
    C. 1 lb. flank steak
    D. 2 tablespoons peanut oil
    E. ½ cup thin slices fresh ginger root
    F. 1 tablespoon salt
    G. 2 tablespoons light soy sauce
    H. 1 teaspoon rice wine or 1 tablespoon sherry
    I. 2 teaspoons sugar
    J. 2 teaspoons cornstarch
    K. ⅔ cup soup stock

    L. 2 teaspoons heavy soy sauce
    M. 4 scallions, sliced

PREPARATION:

I. Slice C into thin, bite-size pieces.

II. Mix E and F. Stir well. Let mixture stand 15 minutes. Wash ginger thoroughly under cold water (to remove "hotness"). Drain. Set aside.

III. Mix G, H, I, J, K, L. Set aside. Stir well before using.

COOKING:

1. Put A in very hot skillet and bring to high heat.

2. Add B. Stir-fry rapidly 15 seconds to brown B slightly.

3. Add C. Stir-fry until nearly done—leaving center rare.

4. Remove B-C from skillet to another container. Set aside.

5. Add D and heat well.

6. Add E-F. Stir-fry 3 minutes.

7. Add G-L mixture and stir until sauce thickens.

8. Replace B-C and mix well to be sure sauce coats all ingredients well.

9. Garnish with M.

BEEF TONGUE WITH TOMATO SAUCE
(Cheh Tze Niu Suh: Shanghai)

    A. 3 tablespoons peanut oil
    B. 2 large onions
    C. 1 cup catsup
    D. 3 teaspoons salt
    E. ½ to 1 teaspoon black pepper
    F. 6 cloves
    G. 2 tablespoons white vinegar
    H. 4- to 5-lb. beef tongue (fresh, not pickled)
    I. 2 qts. soup stock

PREPARATION:

I. In Dutch oven, boil water. Add H, boil 10 to 15 minutes. Remove, cool in cold water. Trim gristle and bone off thick end. H may now be skinned easily. Discard water.

II. Peel B and shred.

III. Mix C, D, E, F, G.

COOKING:

1. Put A into Dutch oven and heat; stir-fry B until brown.

2. Add C-G, simmer 1 minute.

e. Add H and half of I; cover tightly and simmer 3 to 3½ hours or until H is chopstick tender. Add more soup when needed.

4. Slice and serve.

BEEF WITH BEAN SPROUTS
(Niu Ro Loh Do Ya: General)

A. 4 tablespoons peanut oil
B. 1 clove garlic
C. ½ teaspoon salt
D. 1 slice ginger, minced
E. 1 lb. flank steak
F. 2 tablespoons sherry
G. 1 tablespoon light soy sauce
H. 1 teaspoon sugar
I. 1 tablespoon cornstarch
J. ½ cup cold water
K. 2 scallions, sliced
L. 1½ teaspoons heavy soy sauce
M. 1 lb. fresh bean sprouts
N. 2 scallions, sliced

PREPARATION:

I. Cut E into very thin bite-size slices.
II. Mix B, C, D. Set aside.
III. Mix F, G, H, I, J, K, L. Set aside. Stir well before using.

COOKING:

1. Put A in very hot skillet and bring to high heat.
2. Add B-D and stir-fry rapidly 15 seconds to brown slightly.
3. Add E and brown lightly, leaving center of meat rare.
4. Remove E from skillet and set aside.
5. Add F-L to skillet, stir continuously and heat until sauce thickens.
6. Add M. Stir-fry in sauce 1 minute.
7. Return E to skillet and cook 1 minute, mixing well to be sure that it is well coated by sauce.
8. Serve with garnish of N.

SWEET AND SOUR MEATBALLS
(Tien Swan Ro Jieu: General)

A. 2 tablespoons peanut oil
B. 1 large onion, sliced
C. 1 green pepper
D. 2 tomatoes
E. ½ cup canned pineapple chunks
F. ½ cup sweet pickles
G. ½ cup pineapple juice
H. ¼ cup sweet pickle juice
I. 2 tablespoons vinegar
J. 2 tablespoons sugar
K. 1 tablespoon light soy sauce
L. 1 tablespoon cornstarch, dissolved in 3 tablespoons water
M. 2 slices ginger
N. 1 scallion
O. 1 lb. ground chuck
P. 1 egg
Q. 1 tablespoon light soy sauce
R. ½ teaspoon salt
S. ½ teaspoon sugar
T. 1 tablespoon cornstarch
U. salt to taste

PREPARATION:

I. Chop M, N very fine. Mix thoroughly with O, P, Q, R, S, T.
II. Make M-T into balls 1 inch in diameter. Brown in frying pan with 1 tablespoon A. Remove to bowl.
III. Cut C in 16 pieces. Cut D in 8 pieces. Mix C, D, E, F.
IV. Mix G, H, I, J, K; add C-F.

COOKING:

1. Heat 1 tablespoon A in frying pan. Stir-fry B 2 minutes. Add C-K mixture and bring to boil. Thicken with L.
2. Add M-T. Add U. Mix well and serve hot.

Lamb

MONGOLIAN BARBECUED LAMB (OR BEEF)
(Kow Yang Ro: Adapted)

A. 2 lbs. boneless lamb (or beefsteak)
B. 2 or 3 leeks or scallions
C. 2 or 3 stalks Chinese parsley
D. 3 tablespoons light soy sauce
E. 2 teaspoons sugar
F. 2 tablespoons mashed fermented bean cake
G. 2 tablespoons sherry

PREPARATION:

I. Slice A into very thin slices 4 inches long.
II. Mix all ingredients and marinate 6 hours.

COOKING:

1. Cook on grill 3 to 5 minutes, turning frequently. Each person may grill his own pieces.

SPICED LEG OF LAMB
(Wei Yang Ro: Shanghai)

A. ½ leg of lamb (about 2 lbs.)
B. 1 star anise
C. ½-inch piece cinnamon
D. 1 scallion
E. 3 slices ginger
F. 1 tablespoon sherry
G. 2 cups water
H. ¼ tablespoon heavy soy sauce
I. 2 tablespoons light soy sauce
J. 1 teaspoon sugar
K. ½ teaspoon sesame oil
L. 1 tablespoon chopped scallion

PREPARATION AND COOKING:

I. Bone A, clean and wash. Place in Dutch oven.

II. Wrap B, C in cloth, tie tightly with string, add to A.

III. Add D, E, F, G to A, bring to boil; skim froth off top and discard.

IV. Lower heat and simmer 1 hour.

V. Add H, I, J, bring to boil, simmer another hour or until meat is tender and gravy becomes thick. Turn meat over once or twice during cooking and add more water if necessary.

VI. Discard B, C, D, E; add K, stir in well.

VII. Slice A on platter, pour gravy over slices, garnish with L and serve.

LAMB CHAFING DISH (FONDUE)
(Sa Yang Ro: Peking)

A. 10 cups chicken stock
B. 2 lbs. leg of lamb
C. 1 lb. celery cabbage
D. 10-oz. package spinach
E. 10 to 20 cakes bean curd (optional)
F. 1 oz. cellophane noodles
G. 2 or 3 scallions, minced
H. 3 tablespoons light soy sauce
I. ½ teaspoon sesame oil (optional)
J. vinegar*
K. peanut butter*
L. 2 slices ginger

M. 3 tablespoons Chinese parsley, minced (optional)
N. 4 cups soup stock from lamb bones or additional chicken stock

PREPARATION:

This recipe requires a fondue dish or an electric hot plate or an electric deep frying pan. (Each guest is supplied with a porcelain spoon and chopsticks, and will cook his own food at the table.)

I. Cut lamb off bone and slice paper thin.

II. Cut C into 1½-inch strips.

III. Cut E into 1-inch squares.

IV. Soak F in hot water 20 minutes.

V. Place each of the above ingredients in separate bowls on the table.

VI. Prepare sauces by mixing G, H, I or by using J or K, individually or blended together, in any desirable mixture.

COOKING:

1. Place A in deep frying pan or fondue dish as described above. Add L, cover with lid and use high heat to bring to boil.

2. Each guest cooks his own ingredients in a corner of the cooking utensil. When the soup boils again, the cooked food and some of the soup should be ladled out into a bowl and garnished with M.

3. Whenever required, N should be added to cooking utensil.

*Amounts to be determined by individual preference at the table. However, one cup of each should suffice.

Veal

VEAL CUTLET WITH SPINACH
(Bo Tsai Shiao Niu Ro Pien: Shanghai)

A. 10 oz. fresh spinach
B. few drops sesame oil
C. 2 tablespoons peanut oil
D. ½ lb. veal cutlet
E. 1 teaspoon chopped ginger
F. 1 tablespoon chopped scallion
G. 1 clove garlic, chopped
H. 2 teaspoons light soy sauce
I. 2 teaspoons cornstarch
J. ½ teaspoon sugar

K. **2 teaspoons sherry**
L. **1 teaspoon peanut oil**

PREPARATION:

I. Slice D into thin pieces, then shred. Mix with E, F, G, H, I, J, K, L.

II. Wash and clean A, drain.

COOKING:

1. Add 1 teaspoon salt to 2 qts. boiling water; stir.

2. Add A, turn off heat, stir well, and drain A in colander immediately.

3. Mix drained A with B; place on plate.

4. Heat D, add E-L and stir-fry 2 to 3 minutes; add 1 to 2 tablespoons water, if necessary.

5. Arrange on top of A and serve.

DICED VEAL CUTLET WITH SWEET SAUCE
(Jiang Bao Shiao Niu Ro: Adapted)

A. **3 tablespoons peanut oil**
B. **½ lb. veal cutlet**
C. **1 egg white**
D. **2 teaspoons cornstarch**
E. **dash salt**
F. **1 cup diced asparagus**
G. **1 sweet red pepper**
H. **2 tablespoons brown bean sauce**
I. **1 teaspoon sugar**
J. **2 teaspoons sherry**
K. **1 teaspoon light soy sauce**
L. **2 teaspoons chopped scallions**
M. **1 teaspoon chopped ginger**
N. **1 teaspoon cornstarch**

PREPARATION:

I. Dice B and mix with C, D, E.

II. Cut G in halves, remove seeds and stem and dice.

III. Mix H, I, J, K, L, M, N.

COOKING:

1. Heat A, add B-E, stir-fry 3 minutes.

2. Add F, G; continue stirring 2-3 minutes.

3. Add H-N, stir few seconds to mix well, serve.

CALF BRAIN WITH FRESH MUSHROOMS
(Shien Gu Niu Nao: General)

A. **2 tablespoons lard**
B. **¼ cup thin sliced Smithfield ham**
C. **1 calf brain**
D. **2 teaspoons whiskey**
E. **¼ cup sliced bamboo shoots**
F. **6 oz. fresh mushrooms**
G. **4 slices ginger**
H. **2 teaspoons light soy sauce**
I. **¼ cup chicken broth**
J. **¼ teaspoon sugar**
K. **2 teaspoons cornstarch mixed with 2 tablespoons water**
L. **1 scallion, chopped**

PREPARATION:

I. Place C in cold water, remove thin membrane and blood vessels with a toothpick; rinse until water is clear. Drain and mince.

II. Add D and mix well.

III. Wash F and cut each into 2 or 3 slices.

IV. Mix H, I, J.

COOKING:

1. Heat A, add B, stir-fry a few seconds; add C-D and stir-fry ½ minute.

2. Add E, F, G, H-J, stir well, bring to boil; lower heat and cook 10 minutes.

3. Thicken with K.

4. Garnish with L and serve hot.

Vegetables

CHINESE CABBAGE IN CREAM SAUCE
(Nye Yow Box Tsoi Sum: Canton)

A. **2 tablespoons butter**
B. **2 tablespoons flour**
C. **1 cup milk**
D. **1 teaspoon salt**
E. **½ teaspoon sugar**
F. **1 lb. Chinese cabbage hearts**
G. **1 cup chicken broth**

PREPARATION:

I. Cut F lengthwise. Parboil until tender (about 1 minute). Drain, dry between paper towels.

II. Cut F into still thinner strips lengthwise, soak in G 30 minutes.

COOKING:

1. Melt A, add B slowly, and make into a paste.

2. Add C, D, E; heat until thickened.

3. Remove F from G, add to sauce, cook ½ minute.

BRAISED BAMBOO SHOOTS
(Hung Mun Sun: Szechuan)
   A. 2 tablespoons peanut oil
   B. 1 cup sliced bamboo shoots
   C. 1½ tablespoons brown bean sauce
   D. 1 teaspoon sugar
   E. ½ cup chicken broth
   F. 2 teaspoons sherry
   G. 1 teaspoon cornstarch mixed with 2 table-
      spoons water
   H. sesame oil
   I. salt to taste

COOKING:
   1. Heat A, add B, stir-fry 1 to 2 minutes.
   2. Add C, D, E, continue stirring 1 minute.
   3. Add F, mix well, cover and cook 2 to 3 minutes.
   4. Thicken with G, add H, I.

ONE-MINUTE BEAN SPROUTS
(Ching Tsao Do Ya)
   A. 3 tablespoons peanut oil
   B. 4 slices ginger, shredded
   C. 1 scallion
   D. 1 lb. bean sprouts
   E. 1 teaspoon salt
   F. ½ teaspoon sugar

PREPARATION:
   I. Remove tail part of D. Wash well, drain.
   II. Cut C into 1-inch pieces.

COOKING:
   1. Heat A, add B, C, and stir-fry several seconds.
   2. Add D, stir-fry 30 seconds.
   3. Add E, F, stir well several times. D will be crisp
and ready to serve in exactly 1 minute.

MARINATED BROCCOLI STEMS
(Pao Gai Lan)
   A. 3 to 4 broccoli stems
   B. 1 teaspoon salt
   C. 1 clove garlic, minced
   D. 1 teaspoon olive oil
   E. 2 teaspoons distilled white vinegar

PREPARATION:
   I. Peel skin from A; slice thin, diagonally.
   II. Place A, B in a jar and shake well. Let stand
overnight.

III. Mix C, D, E.
IV. Drain salt water from A.
V. Add C-E mixture. Shake well.
VI. Let stand several hours before serving.

HOT AND SOUR CELERY CABBAGE
(Swan La Tsai: Szechuan)
   A. 4 tablespoons peanut oil
   B. 1 teaspoon anise pepper
   C. 3 red-hot peppers
   D. 1 lb. center portion celery cabbage
   E. ⅓ cup white vinegar
   F. ½ teaspoon salt
   G. 1 tablespoon light soy sauce
   H. ½ to 1 teaspoon sesame oil
   I. 1 teaspoon cornstarch

PREPARATION:
   I. Cut D into pieces 1 to 1½ inches wide.
   II. Cut C endwise, discard seeds and stem, then
slice diagonally in thin pieces.
   III. Mix E, F, G, H, I.

COOKING:
   1. Heat A. Add B, stir-fry 1 minute, remove B from
pan. Discard.
   2. Add C, stir-fry a few seconds, add D. Continue
stir-frying 2 to 3 minutes.
   3. Add E-I, mix well. Cover, cook 2 minutes. Serve
hot.

CARROTS WITH SHRIMP SAUCE
(Har Yung Ju Hung Lo Ba: Canton)
   A. 13¾-oz. can chicken broth
   B. 1 bunch carrots
   C. ¼ lb. shrimp
   D. 2 teaspoons sherry
   E. 2 tablespoons cornstarch mixed with ¼ cup
      water

PREPARATION:
   I. Wash, peel B; grate.
   II. Shell C, devein, wash. Mince, mix with D.

COOKING:
   1. Empty A into saucepan. Add B, bring to boil,
cook 5 minutes.
   2. Add C-D, cook 2 to 3 minutes.
   3. Add E to thicken. Serve with rice.

Noodles, Pancakes, Bread

SOFT-FRIED NOODLES WITH MUSHROOMS

A. 1 5-ounce package fine egg noodles
B. 2 tablespoons safflower oil
C. 1 cup bamboo shoots
D. 1 cup sliced fresh mushrooms
E. 1 cup sliced almonds
F. ½ cup chicken broth
G. 3 tablespoons soy sauce
H. Salt to taste

Cook A in large pot in boiling, lightly salted water 8 minutes; drain well.

Heat B in wok or skillet over low heat. Add A; stir-fry 4 minutes. Stir in C, D, and E; mix thoroughly. Stir in F, G, and H. Reduce heat to low; simmer, covered, 20 minutes or until liquid is almost absorbed.

Makes 8 servings.

DEEP-FRIED CRISPY NOODLES

A. 1 5-ounce package fine egg noodles
B. Vegetable oil

Place A in large saucepan in enough water to cover; bring to boil.

Cook, stirring occasionally, 5 minutes; drain well.

Fill deep-fat fryer half full with B; heat to 350°F. Drop A into basket in B; cook 2 minutes. Remove from B; drain well on paper toweling.

Heat B to 375°F. Return A to fryer; cook until golden brown and crisp. Drain well on paper toweling; separate noodles if necessary.

Makes 4 to 5 cups A.

Rice

STIR-FRIED RICE STICKS
(Chao Mi Fun: Fukien)

A. 2 tablespoons peanut oil
B. 1 scallion
C. 8 Chinese mushrooms
D. 12 dried shrimp
E. ½ lb. pork
F. 2 tablespoons light soy sauce
G. ½ teaspoon sugar
H. 13¾-oz. can chicken broth
I. 1 lb. rice sticks
J. 1 scallion, chopped, or Chinese parsley

PREPARATION:

I. Slice E, shred.

II. Wash C, soak in warm water 15 minutes. Drain, saving mushroom water, and shred.

III. Wash D under cold water, soak 15 minutes.

IV. Soak I in cold water a few minutes. Drain, just before adding to A, B, C, D, E, F, G, H below.

COOKING:

1. Heat A, add B, stir-fry a few seconds.
2. Add C, D, stir-fry 1 minute.
3. Add E, stir-fry 2 minutes.
4. Add F, G, mix well.
5. Add H plus 1 can water and mushroom water, bring to boil. Cover, cook over low heat 5 minutes.
6. Add I, cook until all liquid is absorbed. Stir with chopsticks or fork.
7. Garnish with J.

FRIED RICE
(Chao Fan: General)

A. 3 tablespoons peanut oil
B. 6 cups cold cooked rice
C. 2 tablespoons cold water
D. 2 tablespoons light soy sauce
E. 1 tablespoon heavy soy sauce
F. 1 tablespoon sherry
G. 1 tablespoon brown bean sauce
H. 2 eggs
I. 3 scallions, sliced
J. 1 slice ginger, minced
K. 2 tablespoons peanut oil
L. 3 scallions, sliced
M. 1 tablespoon peanut oil

PREPARATION:

I. Beat H lightly. Fry 1 ladleful at a time, spreading thin in skillet with M until set. Repeat until all is used up. Allow to cool. Sliver into thin shreds. Set aside.

II. Separate grains of B, adding C if necessary.

III. Mix D, E, F, G. Set aside.

COOKING:

1. Put A in very hot skillet and bring to high heat.
2. Add B. Stir-fry 2 minutes, stirring continuously.
3. Add D-G mixture and stir-fry 1 minute.
4. Add H. Stir-fry 15 seconds.
5. Add I, J. Stir well 15 seconds.
6. Heat K in separate saucepan until smoking hot. Pour over fried B-J. Stir well 30 seconds.
7. Serve with garnish of L.

Salads

SWEET AND SOUR COLD RADISHES
(Lun Ban Shiao Lo Bo: Peking)
    A. 30 radishes
    B. 3 tablespoons vinegar
    C. 3 tablespoons light soy sauce
    D. 1 tablespoon sugar
    E. sesame oil to taste

PREPARATION:

I. Remove tops and tails of A.
II. Crush each A with blow from the side of a cleaver.
III. Mix B, C, D.
IV. Place A in deep serving bowl.
V. Add B-D. Mix well.
VI. Refrigerate 1 to 2 hours.
VII. Add E to taste (several drops to ½ teaspoon). Serve.

PEKING SALAD
(Ban San Si: Peking)
    A. 1 large kohlrabi
    B. 1 carrot
    C. ½ cup shredded celery cabbage
    D. 1½ teaspoons salt
    E. ½ teaspoon anise pepper
    F. ½ teaspoon sesame oil
    G. ½ cup chopped Chinese parsley

PREPARATION:

I. Peel A, B, slice very thin, then shred.
II. Wash G.
III. Mix A, B, C, D, E thoroughly, marinate vegetables 30 to 45 minutes.
IV. Pour off excess water, add F, G. Mix well and serve.

CHINESE FRUIT SALAD

All the fruits in this recipe are available at Oriental food stores. Some may be available at your supermarket.

    A. 1 4-ounce jar ginger in syrup, drained
    B. 1 11-ounce can lichees in syrup, drained
    C. 1 8-ounce can kumquats, drained
    D. 1 20-ounce can longans, drained
    E. 1 12-ounce can water-lily roots, drained
    F. 1 16-ounce can mangos, drained
    G. 1 round watermelon, chilled, cut in half, meat and seeds removed, meat cut into balls or cubes
    H. 1 18-ounce can white nuts
    I. 1 lemon, sliced

Place A, B, C, D, E, and F in large bowl; mix well. Chill until cold.

Cut slice off base of each G half; place each half on serving dish. Place melon balls or cubes back into shells. Spoon mixed fruit on watermelon balls. Serve with H and I.

Makes about 12 servings.

BEAN SPROUT SALAD
(Lun Ban Dow Ya: Shanghai)
    A. 1 lb. bean sprouts
    B. 3 scallions, chopped
    C. 1 teaspoon salt
    D. ¼ cup vinegar
    E. ¼ cup sugar
    F. 1 teaspoon sesame oil

PREPARATION:

I. Wash A thoroughly.
II. Combine C, D, E, F, mix well.

COOKING:

1. Put A into 1 qt. boiling water. Let stand 30 seconds. Drain.
2. Rinse A under running cold water until thoroughly cold. Drain well.
3. Mix A, B. Just before serving, add C-F; mix well.

GREEK

Note: Items marked with an asterisk (*) in the various recipes are explained in the Glossary.

APPETIZERS

ROQUEFORT CANAPÉ
(Kanape Me Tyri Rokfor)
> 6 tablespoons Roquefort cheese
> 2 or more tablespoons sweet butter
> sliced white bread or assorted crackers
> pickle slices
> capers

Soften the butter and gradually add the cheese to it; cream to make a smooth paste. Trim the crusts from the bread and cut to desired shapes. Spread the bread (or crackers) with the cheese mixture. Top each canapé with a slice of pickle and a caper.

ZAMPON* CANAPÉ
(Kanape Me Zampon)
> 6 slices zampon
> 2 hard-cooked eggs, chopped
> 1 tablespoon mayonnaise or sweet butter
> 1 small pickle, chopped, or 1 tablespoon relish
> 6 buttered bread rounds, crusts removed

Roll the zampon into horn shapes. Add the mayonnaise (or butter) to the chopped eggs, then add the chopped pickle or relish; mix well. Stuff the zampon horns with the filling, and place the horns on the bread rounds.

Serves 6.

RADISH CANAPÉ
(Kanape Me Rapanakia)

Clean and wash some radishes and cut them into rectangular slices. Cut a few radishes into round slices with the red skin showing. Place some green mayonnaise (see index for Green Sauce) on bread rounds. Put a round radish slice on each and surround with white radish slices, to suggest petals or rays. Between the "rays," place slices of black olives.

EGG-CHEESE PUFFS
(Orektika Me Avga Ke Tyri)
> 5 eggs
> ½ cup flour
> 1½ teaspoons baking powder
> 1 teaspoon salt
> 1 teaspoon minced parsley
> 1½ cups cubed kefalotiri* cheese
> butter for frying

Beat the eggs well; add the flour sifted with the baking powder and the salt. Add the parsley and the cubed cheese. Mix together well. Brown the butter in a frying pan, and drop in the batter, a spoonful at a time, to fry. Keep the heat regulated so the puffs do not burn. When they are lightly brown, turn them carefully, with a slotted spoon, without piercing, and drain on absorbent paper. Serve hot.

FETA* OR PARMESAN PUFFS
(Orektika Me Sfoliata Kai Tyri Feta E Parmezana)
> 1 recipe Puff Paste (see index)
> 1 pound crumbled feta or grated Parmesan cheese
> 3-4 eggs
> 2 tablespoons minced onion
> oil for frying

Prepare the puff paste. Beat the eggs lightly, and to them add the cheese and onion. Cut off small pieces from the puff paste and roll into rounds. Place a small amount of the cheese mixture in the center of each round and enclose the filling in the dough. Seal well. Deep-fat fry; drain. Serve hot.

SALTY BISCUITS WITH ANCHOVIES
(Almirah Biscota Me Antsougia)
> 4 cups flour
> 5 teaspoons baking powder
> 3 teaspoons salt
> ½ cup shortening or sweet butter

1 cup milk
2 cans caper-stuffed anchovies
paprika

Sift the flour, salt, and baking powder into a bowl. Add the butter and knead lightly with the fingertips. Add the milk; knead to a soft dough. Lightly flour a bread board or marble-top table and rolling pin. Roll out the dough about ¼ to ½ inch thick. Cut out the biscuits with a floured cutter or glass. On each biscuit place an anchovy stuffed with a caper. Sprinkle with paprika. Place on a lightly buttered baking sheet and bake in a preheated 375° oven for 15 minutes.

Makes 24 to 30 biscuits.

SALTY BRIOCHE
(Mprios Almirah)
    3 tablespoons butter
    6 eggs, separated
    ¾ pound kefalotiri*, grated
    1 teaspoon baking powder
    ½ teaspoon salt
    3 cups (approximately) flour

Cream the butter until very light in color. Add the egg yolks and beat well. Mix in the cheese, baking powder, flour, and salt. Beat the egg whites until stiff but not dry; add to the mixture and knead well. Pinch off small walnut-size pieces. Place on a lightly buttered baking sheet. Bake in a preheated 350° oven for 10 to 15 minutes. Serve hot. These may be reheated.

VOL-AU-VENTS WITH SWEET BUTTER
(Volovan Me Voutiro Fresko)
    1 recipe Puff Paste (see index) or use half the recipe if smaller pastry containing more filling is desired)
    1½ sticks sweet butter
    4-5 hard-cooked eggs, chopped
    5 slices zampon,* minced
    1 teaspoon dry mustard
    salt and pepper to taste
    1 egg white, beaten

Prepare the puff paste, and roll out about ¼ inch thick. Cut into small circular shapes, 2½ to 3½ inches in diameter; place on a baking sheet. Cut out a second group of circles for the tops. In the center of these tops, make a small circular depression, being careful not to cut the dough all the way through. (These inside circles of dough will be removed later.) Brush the edges of the bottom circles with the egg white, but be careful not to spread the egg white all over, as it will prevent the dough from rising correctly. With the tines of a fork, carefully make ridges around the edges of both the top and bottom layers. Join the circles carefully.

While the patty shells are baking (in a preheated 350° oven until golden), cream the butter with the mustard, salt, and pepper. Add the chopped eggs and zampon, and mix well. When the shells are baked and partially cooled, carefully remove the centers from the top (this is the part that was indented earlier). Fill the shells and replace the centers, as lids for the shells.

PIROSKI
(Piroski)
    The Crust
        ⅓ cup milk
        3 packages granular yeast
        4 cups flour
        ⅓ cup vegetable oil
        4 egg yolks
        1 teaspoon salt
        oil for frying
    The Filling
        1 pound chopped meat
        2 tablespoons butter
        1 small onion, chopped
        ½ cup (approximately) tomato sauce
        4-5 tablespoons grated Parmesan cheese
        1 egg white, beaten with a few drops water
        chopped parsley

Heat the milk to lukewarm, pour into a bowl; add the yeast. Mix with your fingers. Add a cup of the flour, and mix to form a ball. Cover the bowl, and set in a warm place. Let the sponge rise until double in bulk. Punch down. Add the vegetable oil, egg yolks, salt, and the remaining flour, mix well, then knead to make a stiff dough. (Add more water or flour, if necessary.) Cover and let rise again.

Meantime, brown the meat in the butter. Add the onion, and cook until light brown. Mix in the tomato sauce and parsley, and cook about 15 to 20 minutes. Stir in the grated cheese.

Lightly flour a bread board and turn the dough out

onto it; knead until elastic. Divide into small pieces. Flatten these with your hands, or roll into thick round shapes. In the center of each, place a table-spoon of the meat mixture. Fold over the dough to form a half-moon shape. Brush the edges with a little egg white, and pinch to seal. Flatten the piroski slightly and place on a buttered baking sheet. Set aside in a warm place to rise again, but for less time. Deep-fat fry until a deep golden color. Remove with a slotted spoon, drain, and serve hot. Makes about 15 to 18 piroski.

Note 1: These can be baked instead of fried. To bake, follow the directions above to the final rising, then brush the tops with egg white, and bake in a preheated 350° oven until golden brown.

Note 2: The filling can be of chicken, ham, fish, or hard-cooked eggs. For any of these, chop the filling and mix with Béchamel Sauce (see index), or mashed potatoes.

Note 3: You can also make sweet piroski by adding 3 tablespoons sugar when you add the salt. Fill the dough with marmalade and chopped glazed fruit. Bake as in Note 1 (above), and top with confectioner's sugar.

SALADS

CABBAGE-TOMATO SALAD
(Salata Lahano-Domates)

   ½-1 head cabbage
   3-6 tomatoes
   black olives
   sprig parsley
   ⅓-½ cup oil
   ¼ cup (or less) vinegar or lemon juice

Clean the cabbage. Cut it in half. Shred. Place in a strainer and wash under running water for several minutes; drain well. Wash and slice half the toma-toes; cut the others into wedges. Mound the cabbage in the center of a round platter; surround with to-mato slices. Place an olive in the center of the cab-bage and circle it with tomato wedges. Place a sprig of parsley in the olive and scatter other olives on the cabbage. Just before serving, pour oil-and-vinegar dressing or oil-and-lemon dressing over it. Salt lightly.
Serves 6.

Note: For an individual salad, wash a small to-mato. Partially cut it into 4 wedges (do not cut all the way through). Place it on a small plate and surround with shredded cabbage. Top with parsley and an olive. Serve with oil-and-vinegar or lemon-and-vinegar dressing.

COUNTRY SALAD
(Salata Horiatiki)

   10-12 small plum tomatoes
   2-3 cucumbers
   2 small onions
   1 green pepper
   ½ pound feta cheese (more or less to taste)
   salt and pepper to taste
   olives

Clean and cut the tomatoes into bite-sized pieces. Cut the cucumbers. Mince the onions and peppers. Cut up the feta cheese. Place all these in a bowl, add olives. Season. Toss well. Serve with oil-and-vinegar dressing.
Serves 6 to 8.

SQUASH SALAD
(Kolokithakia Salata)

   3 pounds (approximately) small squash
   oil
   lemon
   salt

Buy small, fresh, tender squash. Clean and place in lightly salted rapidly boiling water. Cover and boil over a high heat for 30 to 45 minutes (or until tender). Remove from the pot with a slotted spoon. Arrange on a round platter or in a bowl. Serve whole. Pass the oil and lemon.
Serves 6.

EGGPLANT SALAD
(Melitzanosalata)

   2-3 large eggplants
   1 onion, finely grated
   salt and pepper to taste
   lemon juice or vinegar to taste
   1 (or more) cups olive oil, as needed

Wash the eggplants and put into a pan (or wrap in aluminum foil) and bake until soft. Put the onions into cold water to soak and remove some of the strength. Remove the skins from the cooked eggplant and mash the pulp thoroughly. Drain the onion well and add to the eggplant. Add salt and pepper, and beat. Add lemon or vinegar alternately with the oil, and beating all the while, until you have a thick mixture. Serve in a bowl or as a side dish.

GREEN-BEAN SALAD
(*Ampelofasolia Salata*)

    3 pounds (approximately) green beans
    ½ cup parsley
    1 tablespoon chopped garlic
    1 cup oil
    ½ cup vinegar

Clean the green beans and wash them well. Drop into boiling water. Cover and cook over a high heat for about 20 to 30 minutes (or until tender). Remove from the heat; drain. Place in a bowl with the remaining ingredients; mix together and serve.

Serves 6 to 10.

SOUPS

BEAN SOUP
(*Soupa Fassolia*)

    3 cups dried white beans
    2 medium onions
    2-3 stalks celery
    3-4 medium carrots
    1 tablespoon chopped celery root
    1 cup oil
    1 tablespoon tomato paste
    salt and pepper to taste

Wash the beans and soak them overnight in cold water. Rinse well. Place in a large pot and pour in enough water to cover the beans by about 1 inch. Bring to a boil. Pour off this water and replace it with fresh hot water. Chop the onions and the celery stalks, and cut the carrots into rounds. Add all the vegetables to the beans. Add the oil. Simmer for about 45 minutes. Add the tomato paste diluted with some of the liquid from the pot. Season to taste. Boil 20 minutes longer. Serve hot.

Serves 6 to 8.

Note: This soup is thick, but it can be thinned with hot water if desired.

LENTIL SOUP
(*Soupa Fakez*)

    3 cups lentils
    12-15 cups hot water
    1 cup oil
    4-5 cloves garlic
    1 onion, minced
    2 stalks celery
    2 medium carrots, minced
    1 sprig rosemary
    1½ pounds tomatoes, peeled and strained (or 1
        1-pound-14-ounce can of tomatoes)
    salt and pepper to taste
    vinegar (optional)

Soak the lentils overnight in cold water. Rinse and place in a large pot with plenty of water. Bring to a boil. Drain off this water and replace it with the 12 to 15 cups hot water. Add the remaining ingredients except the tomatoes and salt and pepper. Simmer for 45 minutes, then add the tomatoes and cook for about 20 minutes longer (until the lentils are soft). Season. Serve hot.

Serves 6 to 8.

Note: If the soup is too thick, add more water before adding the tomatoes. If the soup is too thin, add 1½ tablespoons flour mixed with 3 tablespoons vinegar, and cook for 5 minutes to thicken.

CHICK PEA SOUP
(*Soupa Revethia*)

    5 cups chick peas (garbanzos)
    water
    2 tablespoons baking soda
    2-3 onions, chopped
    1 cup oil
    salt and pepper to taste
    lemon slices

Soak the beans overnight in warm water in a ceramic bowl. Strain; dust with baking soda. Let stand for 15 minutes. Rinse with hot water. Rub a few at a time between your fingers to remove the skins (unless you have bought them without the skins). Wash well, put into a strainer; let the water run through them for several minutes. Put into a large pot with water to cover and bring to a boil. Skim off the froth as it rises. Add the onion, oil, salt, and pepper. Half cover; simmer until the beans split (about 1 to 2 hours). Serve hot with lemon slices.

Serves 6 to 8.

GREEK EASTER SOUP
(Mayeritsa)

>   entrails (liver, heart, lungs, intestines) of a very
>   young spring lamb
>   4 tablespoons butter
>   1 medium onion, chopped
>   2 tablespoons chopped scallion
>   2 tablespoons chopped dill
>   salt and pepper to taste
>   meat broth
>   ½ cup raw rice
>   2-3 eggs
>   2 lemons, juice only

Wash the entrails in plenty of water. Scald them in boiling water for about 2 to 3 minutes. Cool, then cut into small pieces. Melt the butter in a pot. Sauté the onion until a very light golden color, then add the scallion and the cut-up meats, turning the latter 5 or 6 times. Add the dill, salt and pepper, and enough broth to cover. Bring the whole to a boil and cook, covered, until the meat is tender (1½ to 3 hours). About 20 minutes before it is done, add the rice, and more broth if necessary. When the rice is tender, remove the pot from the heat.

Beat the eggs as in Avgolemono Soup; add the lemon juice, beating it in well. Slowly add some of the hot liquid from the pot, stirring constantly. After the egg-lemon mixture is well-blended, pour it into the soup; stir. Serve hot.

Serves 4.

Note: The broth is usually made from the lamb's head, breast, or shoulder, but you can use any meat stock.

AVGOLEMONO SOUP
(Avgolemono Soupa)

>   6-8 cups any meat stock
>   2-3 whole eggs (or yolks only)
>   1-2 lemons, juice only
>   1 tablespoon cornstarch or flour (optional)

Heat the stock. Beat the eggs well. (Egg whites bind faster than the yolks, and they may be eliminated.

However, we have always used whole eggs; when well-beaten, they are no trouble. Or you may, if you prefer, beat the yolks and whites separately, then mix them together and proceed as follows.) Slowly add the lemon juice to the eggs, beating constantly (about 3 to 5 minutes). To this mixture, slowly add about 1 cup hot stock, mixing constantly, then pour into the pot of soup. Continue to stir the soup or gently shake the pot until the soup thickens slightly (about 3 minutes longer). Serve hot.

Serves 6 to 8.

Note: If you prefer a thicker soup, slowly add the cornstarch or flour to the eggs while you are beating them. The addition of the thickener is not recommended for any soup made with pasta or rice.

TRIPE SOUP
(Soupa Patsas)

>   2 pounds honeycomb tripe
>   4-8 lamb's feet
>   4-6 cloves garlic (optional)
>   coarse salt
>   2-3 eggs
>   2 lemons, juice only
>   pepper to taste
>   vinegar (optional)
>   oil (optional)

Clean, scrape, and wash the tripe and feet. Scald in boiling water; cool. Cut the tripe into small pieces, place in a large pot with the feet, cover with plenty of water; bring to a boil, skimming off the froth as it rises. Lower the heat. Add the garlic, and cook at a slow boil for 1 to 2 hours, adding a little coarse salt just before the meat is tender. Remove the pot from the heat; strain the broth and reserve. Remove and discard the bones from the feet; cut the meat into 3 or 4 pieces; return to the broth.

Prepare the avgolemono as follows: Beat the eggs very well. Slowly add the lemon juice to them, beating all the while. Add a little hot broth from the pot, stirring constantly, then pour the mixture back into the soup. Add pepper just before serving.

Serves 6 to 8.

Note: This soup, very light in color, can be served not only hot but cold. For the latter, let it jell, then cut into squares or diamonds for serving. When it is served hot, some people prefer it mixed with oil and vinegar, instead of avgolemono.

TRAHANA* SOUP
(Soupa Trahanas)

12 cups water
coarse salt
3 cups trahana
3-4 tablespoons butter

Put the water and a little salt into a large pot and bring to a boil. Slowly add the trahana, stirring constantly until the water boils again. Lower the heat and cook until the trahana are soft and the soup is thick (about 45 minutes). Remove from the heat. Stir in the butter, and serve hot.

Serves 6 to 8.

BORSCHT
(Bors Soupa)

3 pounds soup beef
2½ quarts water
⅓ cup butter
1½ cups finely sliced onions
½ cup vinegar
1 tablespoon tomato paste diluted with 1 cup water
½ cup chopped carrots
1 cup diced potatoes
1 tablespoon chopped parsley
2 cups shredded cabbage
coarse salt
salt and pepper to taste
1 cup cooked cubed beets

Wash the meat. Simmer in enough water to cover. Add a little coarse salt and cook about 1½ hours or until tender. Remove from the heat. Remove the meat from the bones and cut the meat into walnut-size pieces. Meanwhile, keep the broth hot. Put the butter in a deep pot, and sauté the onions in it until they are a light golden color. Add the vinegar and the tomato paste to the onions, and bring to a boil. Add all the vegetables except the beets, and cook for 10 minutes. Then add the broth and the meat chunks, and salt and pepper to taste, and simmer, covered, over low heat until the vegetables are half tender (about 15 minutes). Add the beets; cook 15 minutes longer. Serve hot.

Serves 6 to 8.

EGGS AND EGG SPECIALTIES

EGGS AU GRATIN
(Avga O Graten)

8-10 hard-cooked eggs
salt and pepper to taste
1 recipe Béchamel Sauce (see index)
1 cup grated kefalotiri* cheese
3-4 tablespoons toasted bread crumbs
3-4 tablespoons butter, melted

Cut each egg into 8 pieces. Lightly salt and pepper them. Prepare the béchamel. Mix together half of the sauce, the eggs, and ¾ cup of the cheese. Butter a small pan. Spread a thin layer of béchamel over the bottom and sprinkle this with a little cheese. Add the egg mixture and spread evenly. Add the remaining sauce and spread this carefully over the eggs. Sprinkle with the remaining cheese and then the bread crumbs. Drizzle melted butter over the top. Bake in a preheated 350° oven 15 to 20 minutes, or until golden brown. Let stand 10 minutes before serving.

Serves 6.

CHEESE-POTATO OMELET
(Omeleta Me Patates)

1 pound potatoes
½ cup butter
5 eggs
3 tablespoons milk or water
dash of pepper
½ cup grated Parmesan cheese
1 tablespoon chopped parsley

Pare the potatoes and cut into thin, even slices; wash and drain. Melt half the butter in a large frying pan and spread the potato slices in an even layer in it. Fry gently but do not let brown. Add the remaining butter. Beat the eggs with the milk (or water), add the pepper and cheese; mix well. Pour over the potatoes. Lower the heat and cook slowly, stirring very little, until the eggs are set. Remove from the heat. Turn a platter upside down on the pan and turn the pan over quickly so the whole omelet drops onto the platter. Garnish with parsley. Serve immediately.

Serves 2 to 3.

SAUSAGE OMELET
(Omeleta Me Loukanika)

> 5 sausages (any kind)
> 4 tablespoons butter (approximately)
> 5 eggs
> 6 tablespoons milk or water
> salt and pepper to taste

Dip the sausages into hot water and dry them; cut into ½-inch-thick slices; fry until they are cooked but not dry and hard, using butter as needed. Break the eggs into a bowl, add salt and pepper, and milk (or water); mix well. Remove the frying pan from the heat and add the well-beaten eggs; stir gently. Return the pan to low heat, and cook until the eggs are set. Turn out onto a round platter. Serve immediately.

Serves 2 to 3.

Note: The kind of sausage used will determine how much water you will need. If pork sausage is used, pour off the fat as it accumulates and use less butter for frying the eggs. Frankfurters may take more butter.

HAM SOUFFLÉ
(Soufle Zampon)

> 5 tablespoons butter
> 8 tablespoons flour
> 1½ cups milk, scalded
> 1 cup chopped ham
> 1 teaspoon salt
> 6 eggs, separated

Melt the butter in a small saucepan. Add the flour and stir to make a smooth paste. Slowly add the scalded milk, stirring constantly until the sauce thickens. Remove from the heat. Cool. Add the ham and the salt; mix well. Beat the egg yolks until very thick. Beat the whites until stiff. Fold the yolks, then the whites, into the sauce, and pour immediately into a buttered form. Bake in a preheated 350° oven about 30 minutes.

Serves 6.

FISH SOUFFLÉ
(Soufle Psari)

> 5 tablespoons butter
> 7 tablespoons flour
> 1⅓ cups milk, scalded
> 1 teaspoon salt

> 1 cup chopped cooked fish
> 7 eggs, separated

Melt the butter in a small pot; add the flour. Stir to blend well. Slowly add the milk, and stir until you have a thick, creamy sauce. Remove from the heat. Add the salt and fish and blend in well. Beat the egg yolks until very thick; add to the fish mixture. Beat the egg whites until stiff, then fold gently into the sauce. Pour into a buttered mold and bake immediately in a preheated 350° oven for about 30 minutes. Serve immediately.

Serves 8.

SQUASH SOUFFLÉ
(Kolokithakia Soufle)

> 1½ pounds squash
> ½ cup butter
> ½ cup milk, scalded
> ½ cup toasted bread crumbs
> 1 teaspoon baking powder
> 4 eggs, separated
> ¼-½ pound grated Parmesan
> salt and pepper to taste

Wash and peel the squash. Bring to a boil in a pot of water; cook about 10 minutes or until tender. Chop finely or mash. Brown the butter in a pot. Add the squash and mix well; mix in the hot milk. Mix together the bread crumbs and baking powder; add to the squash. Beat the egg yolks and add them with the cheese to the squash. Season with salt and pepper. Beat the whites until stiff, and fold gently into the mixture. Pour immediately into a buttered mold. Bake in a preheated 350° oven for 30 minutes. Serve immediately.

Serves 6 to 8.

VANILLA SOUFFLÉ
(Soufle Vanilias)

> 4 tablespoons butter
> 6 tablespoons flour
> 6 tablespoons sugar
> 1½ cups milk
> 5 eggs, separated
> 2 teaspoons vanilla

Melt the butter. Slowly add the flour, and blend it in with a wooden spoon. Put the sugar into a pot with the milk and heat to scalding but do not boil.

Remove from the heat and pour into the flour; stir quickly to make a thick cream (this may be returned to the heat for a few minutes if necessary). Partially cool. Beat the egg yolks with the vanilla until very thick. Beat the egg whites until stiff but not dry. Add the yolks to the cream mixture; stir well. Fold in the beaten whites. Pour into a buttered glass baking dish or into 6 or 8 individual buttered ramekins.

Bake immediately in a preheated 300° oven for about 20 minutes. Serve hot, sprinkled with powdered sugar.

Serves 6 to 8.

RICE

BOILED RICE
(Pilafia)
There are two methods of cooking rice:

1. Pour the rice into a large pot of boiling water, stir with a fork to separate the grains; cover. Cook, uncovered, over high heat until the rice is done (12 to 20 minutes). Pour in a cup of cold water to stop the cooking; drain, rinse with cold water.

2. Measure the rice and liquids to be used—allow 1 cup rice for each 2½ cups liquid—and put the rice and cold liquid into the pot together. Cook, covered, until the rice is tender (12 to 20 minutes). Remove from the heat. Uncover the pot, put a clean towel over it, and put the lid back over the towel. Let stand for 10 minutes, or until all the liquid has been absorbed.

Note: 1 cup uncooked rice will make 3 cups cooked rice.

PILAF WITH TOMATO SAUCE
(Pilafi Me Saltsa Domata)
1-2 onions, chopped
¾ cup butter
2 cloves garlic, chopped
1½ pounds ripe tomatoes, peeled and strained
1 tablespoon chopped celery
1 tablespoon chopped parsley
3 cups raw rice
salt and pepper to taste

Sauté the onions in half the butter until a light-golden color. Add the garlic, and cook until soft but not brown. Add the tomatoes, celery, parsley, and salt and pepper. Simmer for half an hour. Pass the sauce through a strainer, or purée in a blender, then return it to the pot. Cook until thick. Prepare the rice as directed in Boiled Rice (see index). Brown the remaining butter and pour it over the rice, mixing it in. Pack the rice into a mold, then turn it out onto a platter. Serve hot, with the sauce poured over the rice.

Serves 8 to 10.

PILAF TAS KEBAB
(Pilafi Tas Kebab)
2 pounds leg of lamb or veal
1¼ cups butter
3 medium onions, chopped
½ cup white wine
1½ pounds ripe tomatoes, peeled and strained
or
1 tablespoon tomato paste diluted with 1 cup water
salt and pepper to taste
1 cup water
3 cups raw rice

Cut the meat into 2-inch cubes. Wash and wipe dry. Brown the meat in two-thirds of the butter. Add the onions and brown these too. Add the wine, tomatoes (or tomato paste), salt, and pepper. Cook for about 5 minutes. Add the water. Cook until the meat is tender and about 1 cup sauce remains.

Cook the rice as directed in Boiled Rice (see index). Melt the remaining butter and add it to the rice. Place the meat and the sauce in the bottom of a tube pan or solid mold. Add the rice and pack lightly. Turn out onto a platter so the meat is on top; the sauce will run down the sides of the rice.

Serves 6 to 10.

RICE AU GRANTIN
(Rizi O Graten)
3½ cups chicken or beef broth
4 tablespoons butter
1½ cups raw rice
salt and pepper to taste
1½ cups grated kefalotiri* cheese
3-4 eggs
1 cup chopped ham
2-3 tablespoons toasted bread crumbs

Boil the broth with 2 tablespoons of the butter. Add the rice, stirring it so it doesn't stick. Add salt and pepper. Cover the pot and simmer until the liquid is absorbed (about 15 minutes). Add two-thirds of the cheese, mix well, then remove from the heat. Half cool. Beat the eggs lightly and add to the rice. Add the ham and mix in well with a fork. Butter a baking pan. Put the rice in and spread it evenly. Sprinkle with the remaining cheese and then the bread crumbs. Melt the remaining butter and drizzle it over the top of the rice. Bake in a preheated 350° oven about 15 minutes, or until golden brown.

Serves 4 to 6.

MAKARONIA, SPAGETO, PASTITSIOS

MACARONI AND SPAGHETTI (BASIC RECIPE)
(Makaronia Ke Spageto)

> packaged macaroni or spaghetti
> ¼-½ pound butter for each pound

Cook the macaroni (or spaghetti) according to the directions on the package. Place the butter in a medium-size pot (it will rise and spill over if the pot is too small); heat until it is brown and smoking. Pour over the macaroni. Serve with grated cheese and tomato sauce.

MACARONI WITH TUNA SAUCE
(Makaronia Me Saltsa Tonnou)

> 2 pounds macaroni
> 5-6 Pastés Sardines
> 1¼-1½ pounds ripe tomatoes, peeled and strained, or 1½ tablespoons tomato paste diluted with 2 cups water
> 1 cup oil or ¾ cup butter
> 2 cloves garlic, chopped
> salt and pepper to taste
> 1 bay leaf
> ½ cup canned tuna
> 2 tablespoons chopped parsley
> ½ cup grated Parmesan cheese

Prepare the macaroni according to the directions on the package.

Wash the sardines thoroughly, first in cool water, then in vinegar. (These sardines are packed in salt.) Remove the skins and fins, if any, by rubbing gently with the finger tips. Remove the center bone. Cut

sardines into small pieces (the bones are very small and many Greeks leave them in.) Put the tomatoes or diluted tomato paste into a pot with the oil or butter. Bring to a boil, and add garlic, salt, pepper, and bay leaf. Cook until the sauce thickens. Remove the bay leaf. Add the tuna, sardines, and parsley and cook 5 to 8 minutes longer. Remove from the heat, add cheese. Stir well. Pour over the macaroni and serve.

Serves 6.

SPAGHETTI WITH ZAMPON
(Spageto Me Zampon)

> 1 pound spaghetti
> ¾ cup butter
> 3 eggs
> ¾ cup undiluted evaporated milk
> 1 cup grated kefalotiri* or Parmesan cheese
> 1½ cups chopped zampon*
> 1 cup cooked peas
> bread crumbs
> pepper

Cook the spaghetti as directed on the package; drain. Brown the butter and pour two-thirds of it over the spaghetti. Sprinkle with half of the cheese; mix in the ham and peas. Butter a baking pan. Pour in the spaghetti and spread evenly. Beat the eggs in a deep bowl. Slowly add the milk, beating continuously. Mix in the remaining cheese. Pour this over the spaghetti. Sprinkle with toasted bread crumbs. Season with pepper to taste. Drizzle on the remaining butter. Bake in a preheated 350° oven about 30 minutes or until golden brown in color.

Serves 6.

Note: If you are using canned peas, drain and rinse them well before adding.

SPAGHETTI AND CHICKEN LIVERS
(Spageto Me Sikotakia Poulion)

> ½ pound chicken livers
> 4 tablespoons shortening
> 1 pound spaghetti
> 3 tablespoons sweet butter
> ¾ cup grated Parmesan cheese
> 3 eggs
> ¾ cup grated gravieri or Gruyère cheese
> pepper

Wash the chicken livers and cut into small pieces. Place in a small pot or frying pan with the shortening to brown, and cook for about 3 to 4 minutes. Cook the spaghetti as directed on the package, drain. Return to the pot and mix the spaghetti with half of the butter. Butter a baking pan. Spread half of the spaghetti in it. Sprinkle half of the Parmesan cheese on top. Put the livers on the cheese, cover with the remaining spaghetti, and sprinkle with the rest of the Parmesan cheese.

Beat the eggs in a small bowl. Add the gravieri or Gruyére cheese and pepper to taste. Pour this over the spaghetti. Melt the remaining butter and drizzle over the top. Bake in a preheated 350° oven for about 20 minutes or until golden.

Serves 6.

MACARONI PASTITSIO WITH CHOPPED MEAT
(Makaronia Pastitsio Me Kima)

1½ pounds macaroni
1 cup butter or oil
2 eggs, separated
1¾ pounds chopped meat
½ pound kefalotiri* or Parmesan cheese, grated
1 medium onion, chopped
½ cup white wine
1½ pounds ripe tomatoes, peeled and sieved, or 1 tablespoon tomato paste, diluted with 1 cup water
salt and pepper to taste
1 piece of stick cinnamon
1 cup bread crumbs
1 recipe Béchamel Sauce (see index)

Parboil the macaroni in a generous amount of salted water for 6 minutes; drain. Brown half of the butter and pour it over the macaroni. Beat the egg whites (reserve the yolks for the béchamel), and add to the macaroni. Sprinkle with half of the cheese. Brown the remaining butter (but keep about 2 tablespoons aside to use later), with the chopped meat and onion. Add the wine, the tomatoes (or diluted tomato paste), salt, pepper, and cinnamon, and simmer until all the liquid is absorbed. Remove from the heat, remove the cinnamon, and add half of the remaining cheese and half of the bread crumbs. Mix well.

Prepare the béchamel. Butter a pan and sprinkle with bread crumbs. Spread half of the macaroni evenly in it, and cover with the chopped meat. Add

the remaining macaroni. Pour the béchamel over the top. Sprinkle with the remaining cheese, then with the rest of the bread crumbs. Dizzle the remaining melted butter over the top. Bake in a preheated 350° oven for 30 minutes, until golden brown.

Serves 6 to 8.

LASAGNA PASTITSIO
(Lazania Pastitsio)

1 pound lasagna (flat variety)
1 cup butter
2 egg whites
½ pound Parmesan cheese, grated
1 pound chopped veal
1 onion, chopped
salt and pepper to taste
1 pound ripe tomatoes, peeled and strained
the béchamel sauce
4 tablespoons butter
5 tablespoons flour
4 cups milk, scalded
salt and pepper to taste
2 egg yolks

Set a large pot of water to boil with a little coarse salt. Add the whole lasagna (do not break). Stir and cook until just tender (about 9 minutes; they must be undercooked). Remove from the heat. Add 3 to 4 cups cold water; drain. Return to the pot. Melt ½ cup butter and pour over the lasagna. Beat the egg whites lightly and add to the lasagna. Sprinkle with 3 tablespoons cheese; mix again. Set aside 3 tablespoons of the remaining butter and brown the balance of the butter with the chopped meat and onion. Stir to break up the meat well. Add salt and pepper; add the tomatoes; simmer until all the liquid has been absorbed.

To make the béchamel, melt the butter, add the flour slowly, stirring constantly. Blend the scalded milk slowly into the butter and flour and stir over low heat until it becomes a smooth sauce. Remove from the heat. Add salt and pepper. Beat the egg yolks very well and blend into the sauce. Stir again until smooth.

Divide the macaroni, chopped meat, and sauce into 2 portions each. Butter a baking pan and sprinkle with bread crumbs. Spread in half the lasagna and sprinkle with some of the cheese. Add half the chopped meat; spreading it evenly. Spread on the rest of the lasagna. Sprinkle with cheese, add the remaining chopped meat, and finally the béchamel. Sprinkle the top with cheese, then with bread crumbs. Drizzle the remaining butter over the top. Bake in a preheated 350° oven for 30 minutes, or until the crust is a deep golden brown.

Serves 6 to 8.

STUFFED AND ROLLED SPECIALTIES

STUFFED EGGPLANTS
(Melitzanes Yemistes)

eggplants (allow 1 per serving)
grated cheese (1 tablespoon per eggplant)
½ cup melted butter
¾ pound ripe tomatoes, peeled and strained

Clean the eggplants and boil for 15 minutes in lightly salted water. Remove from the pot and drain well. Cut a thin slice from the side of each eggplant and carefully scoop out the pulp; cut this into small pieces and measure it.

For each cup eggplant pulp use the following:

the filling
½ cup toasted bread crumbs
¼ cup chopped parsley
½ cup pine nuts
1 cup grated cheese
¼ cup butter, melted, or oil
3 eggs
salt and pepper to taste

Mix the filling ingredients with the eggplant pulp and blend well. Carefully stuff the eggplant shells. Sprinkle with cheese and a few bread crumbs. Pour on the ½ cup melted butter, and then pour on the tomatoes. Bake in a 350° oven for 30 to 45 minutes.

STUFFED ARTICHOKES
(Anginares Yemistes)

12-15 large, tender artichokes
3 tablespoons butter
2 pounds chopped meat
2 onions, minced
1 tablespoon tomato paste diluted with 1½ cups water
salt and pepper to taste
½ cup grated kefalotiri* cheese

1 recipe Béchamel Sauce (see index smaller recipe)
2 zweiback, crushed, or bread crumbs as needed
melted butter as needed

Cut the stems from the artichokes so they can stand up. Peel off any bruised outer leaves; cut the tips off all the remaining leaves. Scoop out each 'choke, leaving a small hole in the center. Rub the cut portions with lemon. Boil the artichokes in salted water until tender but not soft (about 35 to 40 minutes). Drain well and place on a platter.

To make the stuffing, melt the butter in a pot; add the meat and onions. Stir to break up the meat; brown well. Add the tomato paste and salt and pepper. Simmer until all the juices are absorbed (about 30 minutes).

Fill the artichokes and place in a buttered pan, and pour the béchamel sauce over them (allowing about 1 tablespoon of sauce for each filled 'choke). Sprinkle with the cheese, and the bread crumbs or zweiback. Brush with melted butter; bake for 15 to 20 minutes in a 350° oven. Allow 1 or 2 'chokes per serving.

TOMATOES STUFFED WITH CHOPPED MEAT
(Domates Yemistes Me Kima)

10 large tomatoes
salt and pepper to taste
1½ pounds chopped meat
2 onions, chopped
½ cup butter
½ cup wine
2 tablespoons chopped parsley
½ cup water
½ cup bread crumbs
½ cup grated kefalotiri* cheese

Wash the tomatoes and cut off the tops, but reserve them. Scoop out the centers and pass the pulp through a strainer. Salt and pepper the tomato cases. Put the chopped meat, onion, and half the butter into a pot, mix well, and brown. Add the wine, tomato pulp, salt, pepper, parsley, and water. Cover and simmer for 1 hour or until all the liquids have been absorbed. Remove from the heat. Add three-fourths of the bread crumbs and three-fourths of the cheese. Mix well. Stuff the tomatoes with this mixture. Cap with the tops. Place the stuffed tomatoes in a shallow pan. Drizzle with the remaining butter; sprinkle with a little grated cheese, bread crumbs, and more butter. Bake 20 to 30 minutes in a preheated 350° oven.

Serves 10.

Note: If you wish, fill the tomatoes only three-quarters full, top them with Béchamel Sauce (see index) and sprinkle with cheese and bread crumbs. Drizzle with butter; bake as above.

STUFFED GRAPE LEAVES
(Dolmathes Yalantzi)

> **1-1½ pounds tender grapevine leaves**
> **1½ pounds onions**
> **1 cup oil**
> **1¼ cups raw rice**
> **½ cup chopped parsley**
> **2 tablespoons chopped dill**
> **½ teaspoon chopped fresh mint leaves**
> **salt and pepper to taste**
> **1 lemon, juice only**
> **water as needed**
> **lemon wedges (optional)**
> **pine nuts (optional)**
> **raisins (optional)**

If possible, buy the prepared grapevine leaves, wash them in clear cold water before using. If you are using fresh leaves, tenderize them first, as follows:

Cut the stems from the leaves with a sharp knife or scissors. Wash the leaves thoroughly, then throw them into a pot of rapidly boiling water. Boil for about 2 to 3 minutes, or until the leaves soften. Remove from the water and spread on a platter or table-top.

To prepare the filling, peel and chop the onions. Put in a strainer and run cold water through them; drain. Sauté in the oil to a very light golden color. Add the rice; brown lightly. Add 1½ to 2 cups water, and the parsley, dill, mint leaves, salt, and pepper. Cook for 5 to 7 minutes, until the rice absorbs the liquid but is only half cooked (watch it carefully so it does not stick to the pot).

When filling the leaves, keep the shiny side of the leaf on the outside. Put 1 teaspoonful of filling in the center of the leaf and fold the sides up over it, covering it, then roll it up like a cigar. Lay the stuffed leaves in a pot (open side down so they do not swell open) in even, tight rows. When one layer is completed, make a second layer on top of the first, or a third layer, if necessary. Lay a plate directly on the top layer of dolmathes. Add enough water to the pot to half cover the stuffed leaves, and add the lemon juice. Cover the pot; cook until the liquid has been absorbed and only a slight amount of oil remains (this should take about 45 minutes).

Serves 6 to 8.

Note: Although these are usually served cold with wedges of lemon, they can also be served hot with Avgolemono Sauce (see index). During the cooking, you may add pine nuts, and/or raisins.

CABBAGE DOLMATHES WITH AVGOLEMONO SAUCE
(Lahano Dolmathes Me Saltsa Avgolemono)

> **5-6 pound cabbage**
> **2¼ pounds chopped pork**
> **½ cup raw rice**
> **2 medium onions, chopped**
> **1 tablespoon chopped parsley**
> **2 tablespoons chopped dill**
> **2 eggs, separated**
> **salt and pepper to taste**
> **½ cup butter**
> **the avgolemono**
> > **1 tablespoon cornstarch**
> > **1 cup cold milk**
> > **1-2 lemons, juice only**
> > **1 cup liquid from the pot**

Select cabbage with leaves suitable for stuffing. Clean carefully, and separate the leaves. Bring a pot of water to a boil and add the leaves, a few at a time; boil for 5 minutes (just to soften the leaves). Remove from the water and set aside.

Mix together the meat, rice, onions, parsley, dill, egg whites, salt, and pepper; knead well. Put 1 teaspoonful of the mixture into the center of each leaf (if the leaf is too large, cut it in half, or even in thirds, if necessary), bring the sides up over the filling, and roll the leaf up like a cigar. Place the dolmathes, open sides down, in closely packed layers in a pot; season lightly with salt and pepper. Melt the butter and pour it in, add enough hot water to cover the dolmathes, and lay a plate on top of them. Cover the pot. Cook over medium heat for 1 hour or until 1 cup of liquid remains. Remove the pot from the heat; strain off the liquid and reserve it.

Prepape the avgolemono. First mix the cornstarch with the milk. In a separate bowl, beat the egg yolks; add lemon juice to taste, beating it in well. Add the milk slowly, beating continuously, then slowly add the hot liquid from the dolmathes. Pour the sauce back into the pot and shake it over low heat for 2 to 3 minutes (until the mixture cooks). Serve hot.

Serves 6 to 8.

LETTUCE DOLMATHES WITH CHOPPED LAMB
(*Dolmathes Me Filo Maroulion Kai Kima*)

2-3 heads lettuce
1½ pounds chopped lamb
2 medium onions, chopped
2 tablespoons chopped parsley
1 tablespoon chopped dill
½ cup raw rice
2 eggs, separated
½ cup butter
salt and pepper to taste
water
1-2 lemons, juice only
1 cup milk

Select lettuce with leaves suitable for stuffing. Clean carefully and separate the leaves. Bring a pot of water to a boil, add the leaves, a few at a time, cook just until they wilt. Remove immediately and spread on a platter. If they are too large, cut them in half before stuffing.

Place the chopped meat, onions, parsley, dill, rice, egg whites, 2 tablespoons of the butter, salt, and pepper in a bowl. Knead well to mix. Place about 1 teaspoon of the mixture on a leaf and bring up the sides toward the center, then roll up like a cigar. Place the stuffed leaves, the open side down, in layers in a pot. Add a little salt and pepper and the rest of the butter, and enough water to half cover. Lay a plate on the dolmathes; cover the pot. Simmer slowly and when they have absorbed almost all the water, add the milk. Allow to cook a few minutes longer until approximately 1 cup liquid remains. Beat the egg yolks, add the lemon juice to them, then blend in the liquid from the pot. Return the sauce to the pot. Shake over low heat for 2 to 3 minutes. Serve hot.

Serves 6 to 8.

SQUASH STUFFED WITH RICE
(*Kolokithakia Yemista Me Rizi*)

3 pounds medium zucchini squash
1 cup chopped onions
1⅓ cups oil or 1 cup butter
1 cup water
1 cup chopped parsley
1 cup raw rice, washed
salt and pepper to taste
½ cup grated cheese
¼ cup toasted bread crumbs
2 eggs, separated
2 lemons, juice only
water as needed

Cut the stems from the squash, and scrape off the skins. Wash and scoop out the flesh, leaving a quarter-inch shell. Brown the onions with half the butter or oil, and add 1 cup water, the parsley, rice, salt, and pepper. Cook slowly until all the liquid is absorbed (about 15 to 20 minutes). Remove from the heat. Add the cheese and bread crumbs, and cool slightly. Fold in the lightly beaten egg whites. Stuff the squash with this mixture; put in the pot. Pour over them the remaining oil or butter and another 1 to 2 cups water. Cover, and simmer until only a small amount of liquid remains.

Beat the egg yolks very well. Add the lemon juice, and beat continuously. Slowly add the liquid from the squash to the egg-yolk mixture and pour it over the squash. Cook over very low heat, shaking the pot gently, until the mixture thickens. Serve hot.

Serves 6 to 8.

BAKED SPECIALITIES

ARTICHOKES BÉCHAMEL
(*Anginares Besamel*)

8-10 artichokes
½ pound feta* cheese
1 cup chopped cooked ham or chicken, or mortadella
1 recipe Thick Béchamel Sauce (see index)
1 cup grated Parmesan cheese
⅓ cup melted butter
2-3 tablespoons toasted bread crumbs

Clean the artichokes as you would for stuffing them. Rub with lemon and place in salted water. Boil until tender (about 45 minutes). Drain. Prepare the béchamel. Break up the feta cheese and mix it with the meat. Add ½ cup of the béchamel; mix well. Sprinkle the mixture with half of the Parmesan cheese and mix in. Line up the artichokes in rows in a buttered baking pan, and drizzle some of the melted butter over them; fill them with the meat-and-cheese mixture. Cover the top with the remaining béchamel, then sprinkle with the rest of the Parmesan. Top with the bread crumbs, drizzle on the melted butter, and bake in a preheated 350° oven for about 20 minutes or until the cheese and sauce take on a golden color.

Serves 4 to 5 or 8 to 10, depending on the size of artichokes.

SPINACH AU GRATIN
(Spanaki O Graten)

3 pounds spinach
7 tablespoons butter
¼-½ pound kefalotiri* cheese, grated
toasted bread crumbs
3 eggs either hard-cooked or raw (optional)
the béchamel sauce
    1 can evaporated milk
    1 can water
    ¼ cup butter
    ½ cup flour
    1 egg, beaten
    salt and pepper to taste

Clean and wash the spinach; cut each leaf into 3 or 4 pieces, and drop into rapidly boiling water. Let the spinach boil for 3 or 4 minutes, then strain it; press out all excess fluid and return it to the pot. Melt 5 tablespoons of the butter, pour it over the spinach.

To prepare the sauce, pour the evaporated milk and water (measured in the milk can) into a pot; scald and keep hot. Melt the ¼ cup butter in another pot. Blend in the flour. Add the hot milk, stirring constantly until the mixture is smooth and thick. Season with the salt and pepper. Cool slightly, then stir in the beaten egg, blending it in well.

Spread a thin layer of the béchamel in a buttered pan; sprinkle with a little cheese. Spread in the spinach; sprinkle with more cheese. Spread the rest of the béchamel over all; sprinkle with the remaining cheese and then with the bread crumbs. Melt the remaining 2 tablespoons butter and drizzle over the

casserole. Bake in a preheated 400° oven for about 20 minutes.

Note: You may add the hard-cooked eggs to this, if you like. Slice them and place them on the spinach before adding the final layer of sauce. Or beat the uncooked eggs and mix them with the spinach before you layer that into the casserole.

SQUASH AU GRATIN
(Kolokithakia O Graten)

3 pounds small squash (zucchini)
1 cup vegetable or olive oil
flour
1 recipe Thick Béchamel Sauce (see index)
1½ cups grated kefalotiri* cheese
toasted bread crumbs
3 tablespoons butter, melted
salt and pepper to taste

Select tender squash. Scrape the skin, wash. Cut into small slices. Season with salt and pepper. Heat the oil in a frying pan. Dip the squash into the flour, shaking off the excess, and fry until rosy. Prepare the béchamel.

Butter a medium pan. Spread in it a thin layer of béchamel, sprinkle with cheese. Cover with a layer of squash. Continue to spread these layers alternately, ending with a thick layer of béchamel. Sprinkle with the cheese and then the bread crumbs. Drizzle the melted butter over the top, and bake in a preheated 325° oven for 20 to 30 minutes.

MOUSSAKA POTATOES
(Mousakas Patates)

3 pounds potatoes
1⅔ cups oil
salt and pepper to taste
½ cup chopped onion
1½ pounds tomatoes, peeled and strained, or
    1½ tablespoons tomato paste diluted with 1
    cup water
½ head garlic (6-8 cloves)
½ cup chopped parsley
1 cup grated cheese
bread crumbs

Clean and peel the potatoes; cut them into thin round slices. Fry in the oil, then season with salt and pepper. Sauté the onions to a light golden color in the pan in which you fried the potatoes, and add to them the tomatoes (or diluted tomato paste), garlic, parsley, and salt and pepper; cook for about 20 minutes, until you have a thick sauce. Remove from the heat. Add to the sauce ¾ cup of the cheese and 3 tablespoons bread crumbs.

Oil a medium-size baking pan lightly. Spread a layer of the potatoes in it; cover them with part of the sauce. Top with another layer of potatoes and another layer of sauce. Continue this process until all the potatoes and sauce are used; sprinkle with the remaining cheese and additional bread crumbs; dribble a little oil over the top, and bake in a preheated oven at 375° for about 30 minutes.

Serves 6 to 8.

EGGPLANT MOUSSAKA
(Mousakas Melitzanes)
> ½ cup butter or vegetable oil
> 1½ pounds chopped meat
> 2 tablespoons chopped onions
> ½ cup white wine
> 1½ pounds ripe tomatoes, peeled and strained
> 2 tablespoons chopped parsley
> salt and pepper to taste
> 3 pounds eggplants
> oil for frying
> 1 recipe Béchamel Sauce (see index)
> 1 cup bread crumbs
> ½ cup grated Parmesan cheese
> 2-3 tablespoons melted butter

Place half the butter (or oil) in a frying pan. Add the chopped meat and the onions. Stir to crumble the meat; brown. Add the wine, tomatoes, parsley, salt, and pepper, and bring to a boil. Lower the heat and simmer until the liquids are absorbed. Wash and dry the eggplant. Cut into thin slices. Fry in the remaining butter (add oil if needed). Place the fried eggplant slices on a platter. Prepare the béchamel.

Arrange half of the eggplant slices in even rows in a medium-size baking pan. Sprinkle with half the bread crumbs. Add half of the cheese to the chopped meat, mixing it in well; spread this on top of the eggplant. Add another layer of eggplant, then cover with the béchamel. Sprinkle the remaining cheese on top, then the remaining bread crumbs. Drizzle with melted butter. Bake for 30 to 40 minutes in a preheated 350° oven until lightly browned.

Serves 6.

Note: This can also be made in individual baking dishes.

ARTICHOKES WITH CHOPPED MEAT
(Anginares Me Kima)
> 1½ pounds chopped meat
> 1 onion, chopped
> 3 tablespoons butter
> 1½ pounds ripe tomatoes, peeled and strained, or 1 tablespoon tomato paste, diluted with 1 cup water
> salt and pepper to taste
> 6-8 artichokes
> 1 lemon, juice only
> ¾ pound fresh peas
> 3 tablespoons butter
> ¼-½ pound grated Parmesan cheese
> ¾ pound phyllo* pastry
> butter for brushing the phyllo
> the béchamel sauce
> > 1 can evaporated milk
> > 1 can water
> > 3 tablespoons butter
> > 1 cup flour
> > 2 egg yolks

Put the chopped meat, onions, and butter together in a pot to brown, stirring with a wooden spoon to break up the meat. Add the tomatoes (or diluted tomato paste), and salt and pepper; simmer, covered, until all the liquid is absorbed.

Clean the artichokes and rub them with lemon juice; boil in salted water for about 15 minutes, then add the peas, and cook until tender (about 30 minutes). Drain; remove the artichokes, and cut them into small pieces; mix these with the peas. Melt the butter and pour it over these vegetables.

To prepare the béchamel, mix together the evaporated milk and water; scald but do not boil. Melt the butter in another pot, and add the flour, stirring constantly. Slowly pour in the hot milk, stirring continuously until the sauce becomes smooth and thick. Remove it from the heat and cool it slightly. Beat the egg yolks and add them to the sauce, blending well.

Butter a medium-size pan and spread 6 to 8 phyllo sheets (see index: About Phyllo) over it, one at a time, brushing each with melted butter. Do not trim the overhang. Spread half the artichoke mixture onto these, then sprinkle with part of the cheese and cover with half the béchamel. Spread the chopped meat evenly over this layer, and cover with the rest of the artichoke mixture. Sprinkle with the remaining cheese, and then spread the balance of the béchamel on it. Fold the phyllo up over this, buttering the sheets well so they do not stick. Spread 4 to 5 phyllo sheets over all, one at a time, brushing each with butter before adding the next; trim off the excess. Brush the top phyllo sheet with more butter. Score the pastry into square-or diamond-shaped serving pieces. Bake in a preheated 350° oven for 40 minutes.

Serves 6 to 8.

VEGETABLE SPECIALTIES

EGGPLANT IMAM BALDI
(Melitzanes Imam Baldi)

3 pounds small oblong eggplants
salt
2½ cups (approximately) oil
3 cups thinly sliced onions
5-6 cloves garlic, chopped
1½ pounds ripe tomatoes, peeled and strained
1 cup chopped parsley
salt and pepper to taste
2 tablespoons Parmesan cheese
2 tablespoons toasted bread crumbs

With a sharp knife, slash each eggplant lengthwise, being careful not to cut all the way through and leaving at least a half inch on both ends uncut. (Do not cut away the stem). Salt the cut and place the eggplants in a pot of salted water for 15 minutes. Drain, and rinse in clear water. Wipe dry. Fry the eggplants in ample oil and place them, split side up, side by side in a baking pan.

In the oil used for the frying, sauté the onions until golden. Add the garlic, tomatoes, parsley, salt, and pepper. Cook for 20 minutes, or until all the liquids are absorbed. Remove from the heat. Stuff this mixture into the cut in the eggplants; sprinkle with cheese and bread crumbs. Drizzle a little oil over them and bake for 30 minutes in a preheated 350° oven.

Serves 6.

Note: This can also be made on top of the stove. After the eggplants are stuffed, place them side by side in a wide pot, add 2 to 3 tablespoons oil and 1 cup water, and cook over low heat for about 45 minutes.

EGGPLANT POTTED WITH BUTTER
(Melitzanes Katsarolas Voutirou)

3 pounds eggplant
¾ cup butter
3-5 cloves garlic, chopped
3 tablespoons parsley, chopped
1½ pounds ripe tomatoes, peeled and strained, or 1 tablespoon tomato paste diluted with 1 cup water
salt and pepper to taste
1 cup water

Peel the eggplants, cut into 1½-inch cubes, and soak in lightly salted water for 15 minutes. Drain, and squeeze gently. Brown the butter in a large pot. Add the eggplant cubes and turn 2 to 3 times, to brown lightly on all sides. Add the garlic; cook until golden. Add the parsley, the tomatoes (or diluted tomato paste), salt, pepper, and 1 cup water. Cover. Simmer until all the liquid is absorbed and only the oil remains (30 to 45 minutes).

Serves 6.

CAULIFLOWER STIFADO
(Kounoupithi Stifado)

6 pounds cauliflower
6 small white onions
1¼ cups oil
3-4 cloves garlic, split lengthwise
1 tablespoon tomato paste diluted with 2 cups water
½ cup vinegar
½ tablespoon rosemary
1 bay leaf
6 peppercorns

Wash the cauliflower and break into flowerets. Skin and wash the onions; drain. Heat the oil in a pot and lightly brown the whole onions. Add the garlic and cook until golden. Add the diluted tomato paste, vinegar, rosemary, and bay leaf, and cook for 30 minutes. Bring a large pot of salted water to a boil; add the cauliflower. Cook for 5 minutes, then drain and add the cauliflower to the sauce. (Add a little water if necessary.) Add the peppercorns. Cover the pot.

Simmer until all the liquid has been absorbed and only the oil remains (about 30 to 45 minutes).

Serves 6 to 8.

PEAS LATHEROS
(Arakas Latheros)

 4½-5 pounds peas
 4 scallions
 1¼ cups oil or 1 cup butter
 1½ pounds ripe tomatoes, peeled and strained, or 1 tablespoon tomato paste diluted with 2 cups water
 3 tablespoons chopped dill
 salt and pepper to taste
 water as needed

Shell, wash, and drain the peas. Chop the white part of the scallions into small pieces and the green part into large pieces. Heat the oil in a large pot. Add the scallions and cook until soft but not browned. Add the peas and brown very lightly. Add the tomatoes (or the diluted tomato paste), dill, salt, and pepper. Add enough water to half cover the peas. Cover the pot. Cook over medium heat until only the oil remains and the liquid has been absorbed (about 45 minutes)

Serves 6 to 9.

Note: You can make this without the tomatoes, if you wish. In that case, add just enough water to half cover the peas.

OKRA IN OIL
(Bamies Latheres)

 3 pounds okra
 salt and pepper to taste
 ½ cup vinegar
 1¼ cups oil or butter
 4-5 cloves garlic
 1 medium onion, chopped
 1¼ pounds ripe tomatoes, peeled and strained, or 1 tablespoon tomato paste diluted with 2 cups water
 water as needed

Wash the okra several times; clean carefully and remove the stems without cutting into the okra. Place them in a pan. Salt lightly, add the vinegar, and place in the sun for about 2 hours.

Heat the oil in a frying pan. Add the garlic and onion, and sauté until golden. Add the tomatoes (or tomato paste). Cook for 5 minutes. Rinse the okra well; discard the vinegar. Add okra, salt, pepper, and about 1 cup water to the tomatoes. Cover the pot. Simmer until the sauce is absorbed and the oil remains (45 minutes to 1 hour).

Serves 6 to 8.

Note: After soaking the okra, you may rinse and fry it in half of the oil; use the rest of the oil as above. Then add the okra and 1 cup water to the sauce and cook for about 30 minutes.

POTATOES YAXNI
(Patates Yiahni)

 3 pounds potatoes
 ¾ cup oil
 2 onions, chopped
 1¼ pounds tomatoes, peeled and sieved, or 1 tablespoon tomato paste diluted with 1 cup water
 2-3 carrots, scraped and sliced
 2-3 cloves garlic
 2 tablespoons chopped celery
 salt and pepper to taste
 water as needed

Peel and wash the potatoes, and cut them into pieces (4 if the potatoes are large; 3, if medium; 2, if small). Place in a bowl of cold water. Heat the oil in a pot and add the onion; sauté to golden brown. Add the tomatoes (or diluted tomato paste), the carrots, garlic, celery, salt, pepper, and 1 cup water. Cook for 5 minutes, then add the potatoes. They should be half covered with the liquid; add water if necessary, to reach the proper level. Cover. Simmer until all the sauce has been absorbed and only the oil remains (about 45 minutes).

Serves 6.

SQUASH CROQUETTES OR PATTIES
(Kolokithokeftethes)

 2 pounds small squash
 1 tablespoon butter
 3 tablespoons chopped onion
 1 cup grated kefalotiri* or Parmesan cheese
 1 cup toasted bread crumbs
 1 tablespoon chopped parsley
 2 eggs

salt and pepper to taste
flour
oil for frying

Clean and wash the squash. Boil in lightly salted water until soft; drain well. Mash and set aside. Melt the butter in a pan, and sauté the onions until limp and golden but not browned. Add the onions, cheese, bread crumbs, parsley, eggs, and salt and pepper to the squash, and mix well. If the mixture is too soft, add more bread crumbs. Let it stand for 10 minutes, then shape into croquettes or patties. Roll in flour, fry until golden.

OVEN-BAKED GIANT BEANS
(Fasolakia Yiyantes Sto Fourno)
  2 pounds dried giant white beans
  2 cups oil
  1 head garlic, cleaned
  3 medium onions, chopped
  1 tablespoon chopped celery
  ½ cup minced parsley
  salt and pepper to taste
  1 cup hot water
  1¾ pounds ripe tomatoes, peeled and strained, or 1 tablespoon tomato paste diluted with 1½ cups water
  water as needed

Wash the beans, place in water, and soak them overnight. Drain them, then place in a pot of fresh cold salted water; cook for 45 minutes; drain. Meanwhile, place the oil, garlic, and onions in a baking pan and bake in a preheated 350° oven until golden. Add the beans, celery, parsley, salt, pepper, and hot water. Bake 30 minutes longer. Remove from oven, stir the beans, pour in the tomatoes (or diluted tomato paste). Return to oven and bake until only the oil remains.

Serves 6.

BRAIM
(Briam)
  2 pounds tomatoes
  1 pound potatoes
  1 pound small squash
  1 pound eggplant
  1 pound okra
  vinegar
  salt and pepper to taste

½ cup chopped onion
1 tablespoon chopped garlic
2 tablespoons chopped green pepper
2 tablespoons chopped parsley
1½ cups oil

Wash and peel the tomatoes and chop them into small pieces; spread half of them in a baking pan. Peel and wash the potatoes; and slice them into rounds. Do the same to the squash and eggplant. Clean the okra and sprinkle with a little vinegar. Lightly salt and pepper the tomatoes in the pan; spread the potatoes, squash, eggplant and okra over them. Add a little more salt and pepper. Mix the onion, garlic, green pepper, and parsley together and sprinkle over the vegetables. Top with the remaining tomatoes. Pour the oil over the surface. Bake in a 250° oven for 1½ to 2 hours, adding a little water if necessary.
Serves 6 to 8.

PHYLLO ENTREES

SPINACH PIE WITH EGGS
(Spanakopitta Me Avga)
  3 pounds spinach
  1 medium onion, chopped
  ½ cup chopped scallions
  1 cup butter
  ½ cup chopped dill
  ½ cup chopped parsley
  salt and pepper to taste
  ½ cup evaporated milk
  4-5 eggs
  ¾ pound phyllo* pastry
  melted butter as needed
  ½ pound feta* cheese, coarsely crumbled

Wash the spinach in plenty of water and cut it into small pieces; place in a bowl. Salt it lightly; stir to spread the salt evenly. Take the spinach, a handful at a time, and squeeze out the excess water; place it in another bowl. Sauté the onion in half the butter until it is a light, golden color; add the scallions and cook until they wilt. Add the spinach; stir until all the vegetables take on a light color. Stir in the dill, parsley, salt and pepper; cover the pot and cook until all the water thrown off by the spinach is absorbed. Remove from the heat; turn into a bowl, and immediately add the milk (to cool the spinach). Beat the eggs in another bowl and add the cheese to them; add to the cooled spinach; mix well.

Line a pan with 8 sheets of phyllo (see index: About Phyllo), brushing each sheet with the melted butter before topping it with the next sheet. Do not trim the overhanging sections. Pour in the spinach mixture, spreading it evenly over the phyllo. Fold the part of the phyllo that extends out of the pan back over the filling. Lay the remaining phyllo on top, again brushing each sheet with melted butter before adding the next. Now trim off the overlap. Brush additional melted butter on top of the pie and score it into square- or diamond-shaped serving pieces. Bake for 30 to 45 minutes in a preheated 300° oven; let it stand for 30 minutes before serving.

Serves 6.

Note: This can also be made without precooking the spinach. In that case, squeeze the spinach free of as much water as possible, mix it with the seasonings, and proceed as above, baking it for 1 hour.

LEEKS IN PHYLLO PASTRY
(*Prassopitta*)

3 pounds leeks
1 cup butter
7 eggs
1 tablespoon farina
¾ pound feta* cheese, crumbled
salt and pepper to taste
1 pound phyllo*
butter for brushing the phyllo

Clean the leeks, discarding the green parts and leaves; use only the white part. Cut into quarters, then chop into small pieces; place in a strainer and wash under running water for several minutes. Melt the butter in a pot. Add the leeks, cook until they soften and the water from them has evaporated. Cool.

Beat the eggs in a bowl until light. Put the leeks into another bowl, and add the farina, cheese, salt, and pepper; mix well. Butter a pan the size of the phyllo sheets. Put 4 to 5 sheets of phyllo (reserve 4 for the top) on the bottom of the pan, brushing each with melted butter before adding it. Spread a layer of leeks on the phyllo (see index: About phyllo) and top it with 3 or 4 tablespoons of the beaten egg. Spread 2 sheets of phyllo, again brushing each one with but-

ter. Spread in a second layer of leeks and top with more egg. Continue layering in the leeks and eggs in this manner until all are spread in the pan. Spread the last 4 sheets of phyllo carefully over the top layer, brushing each one with butter. Pour any remaining butter over the top. Score the phyllo with a sharp knife into serving-size pieces. Bake in a preheated 350° oven for about 30 minutes.

Serves 6 to 8.

CHICKEN PIE
(*Kotopitta*)

1 6-pound stewing chicken
water as needed
1 pound onions, thinly sliced
½ cup milk
1 cup grated Parmesan cheese
5 eggs
salt and pepper to taste
½ teaspoon nutmeg
¾ pound phyllo
melted butter for brushing the phyllo

Clean the chicken and put into a pot with enough water to cover. Bring to a boil; remove the froth as it rises. Add the onions and cook until the chicken is tender (1½ to 2 hours). Remove the chicken from the broth and continue to cook the onions until they become pulpy. When the chicken is cool, remove the skin and the bones, and cut the meat into thin strips. Pass the stock through a strainer to purée the onions and return to the pot. Add the chicken slices and the milk, and cook for about 5 minutes. Remove from the heat. Add the cheese and stir well. Beat the eggs lightly with a little salt and pepper and the nutmeg and add to the pot.

Butter a pan which is smaller than the phyllo sheets (see index: About Phyllo). Line the bottom of the pan with 8 sheets of phyllo, buttering each sheet before you add it; do not trim the phyllo. Pour in the filling and fold the overhanging edge of the phyllo up toward the center, to cover part of the filling; brush well with butter. Cover with the remaining phyllo, first brushing each sheet with butter, and trim the edges with a sharp knife. Score through the top layers. Pour any remaining butter over the pie, and sprinkle with a little water. Bake in a preheated 350° oven for 1 hour. Cool, cut into portions, and serve.

Serves 8.

CHEESE PIE
(Tyropitta Roumeliotiki)

2 pounds feta cheese
10 eggs, lightly beaten
1¼ pounds phyllo
½ cup (approximately) melted butter for brushing the phyllo

Crumble the feta into small particles. Mix the eggs with the cheese. Butter a baking pan the size of the phyllo (see index: About Phyllo) sheets (cut the phyllo to fit, if necessary). Put four sheets of phyllo into the pan, brushing each one with butter. Spoon in some of the cheese mixture; top with 2 phyllo sheets, brushing each with butter before adding it. Add another layer of cheese and another layer of phyllo, again brushing it with butter. Continue in this manner until all the cheese mixture is used. Plan to have 4 sheets of phyllo left for the top layer; add these, first buttering each, then pour the rest of the butter over the top. Score lightly in long strips. Bake in a preheated 300° oven for about 45 minutes. Cut the scored strips into 2-inch pieces and serve hot.

Serves 6 to 8.

CHOPPED MEAT PIE
(Pitta Me Kima)

2 pounds chopped meat
½ cup butter
2 onions, chopped
1¼ pounds ripe tomatoes, peeled and strained, or 1 tablespoon tomato paste diluted with 1 cup water
1 piece of stick cinnamon
1 tablespoon chopped parsley
salt and pepper to taste
2 slices toast
2 cups milk
1 cup grated Parmesan cheese
5 eggs, lightly beaten
¾ pound phyllo*

Brown the meat, half the butter, and the onions in a large pot, stirring with a wooden spoon to bread up the meat. Add the tomatoes (or diluted tomato paste), cinnamon, parsley, salt, and pepper. Simmer until all the liquid is absorbed (about 30 minutes.) In the meantime, soak the toast in the milk, then mash it with a fork. Remove the cinnamon stick and add the milk-toast mixture to the meat; remove from the heat. Add the cheese and eggs, and mix well.

Melt the remaining butter; butter a pan about 2 inches smaller than the phyllo (see index: About Phyllo). Put 7 to 8 phyllo sheets, buttering each before adding it, in the pan, letting the phyllo extend on all sides. Pour in the meat mixture and spread it evenly. Fold the overlapping phyllo back onto the meat. Butter these well. Carefully cut the remaining sheets of phyllo to fit the top of the pan. Brush each with butter and lay it on the filling to make the top of the pitta. Pour on any remaining butter and sprinkle the top very lightly with a little water (to keep the phyllo from rising too high). Bake in a preheated 350° oven for 30 to 40 minutes. Cool about 30 minutes and cut into squares to serve.

Serves 6 to 8.

Note: It is easier to cut this if you score it lightly before baking.

BOUREKIA WITH FRANKFURTERS
(Bourekia Me Loukanika Frankfourtes)

¾ pound phyllo*
½ cup (approximately) melted butter for brushing the phyllo
the béchamel sauce
1 tablespoon butter
4 tablespoons flour
1 cup milk, scalded
1 egg yolk, well-beaten
salt and pepper to taste
the filling
4 frankfurters
½ cup grated Parmesan cheese

Prepare the béchamel (see index for method), using the ingredients indicated above. Remove the skin from the frankfurters and cut them into small pieces. Add the franks and the cheese to the béchamel, and mix well.

Cut the phyllo (see index: About Phyllo) into 3 lengthwise strips. Take 1 strip at a time, brush it with butter, and place 1 teaspoonful of the filling at one end. Fold it over and over to make a triangle. Brush the triangles with butter, place in a pan, and bake in a preheated 350° oven for about 20 minutes. Serve hot. Makes about 30 pieces.

BOUREKIA WITH CHOPPED MEAT
(*Bourekia Me Kima*)

> 1½ pounds chopped meat
> 1 cup butter
> 1 onion, chopped
> 1 tablespoon tomato paste diluted with
> 1 cup water
> 1 tablespoon parsley
> salt and pepper to taste
> 1 piece stick cinnamon
> ½ cup grated Parmesan cheese
> 1¼ pounds phyllo*

Put the meat, 4 tablespoons of butter, and the onion into a pot, brown thoroughly, mixing with a wooden spoon to crumble the meat. Add the diluted tomato paste, parsley, salt, pepper, and cinnamon. Simmer until the liquid is absorbed. Remove from the heat and add the cheese. Discard the cinnamon stick. Cut the phyllo sheets (see index: About Phyllo) in half across the width. Take one sheet at a time (keep the others covered so they do not dry out), brush with melted butter, put a little of the filling on one edge. Fold over two sides to enclose the filling; roll up like a cigar. Brush on all sides with melted butter. Place in a pan. Continue until all the filling is used. Bake in a preheated 350° oven for about 15 minutes.

Serves 6.

Note: These bourekia may be fried in butter or oil instead of being baked.

MEATS

LAMB WITH ARTICHOKES IN AVGOLEMONO SAUCE
(*Arni Me Anginares Avgolemono*)

> 3 pounds boned shoulder of lamb
> 6-8 small artichokes
> 2 lemons
> 5 tablespoons butter
> 2 scallions, chopped
> salt and pepper to taste
> 2 eggs
> water as needed

Cut the meat into 1½-inch cubes. Clean the artichokes, cut off the tips of the leaves. Rub the cut parts with lemon juice. Soak in salted water with the juice of half a lemon.

Brown the butter in a large pot. Add the meat and brown it well. Add the scallions and sauté until soft but not brown. Add 2 cups water, salt, and pepper, and cook over medium heat for about 45 minutes. Rinse the artichokes and add them to the meat. Add the juice of half a lemon, and salt and pepper, and cook slowly until the artichokes are tender (30 to 45 minutes). Remove from the heat.

Beat the eggs in a bowl; add the juice of the second lemon, and beat it in well. Add about ¾ cup of the broth, slowly, beating constantly. Pour the sauce over the meat and artichokes, and shake the pot gently over low heat until the sauce thickens. Serve hot.

Serves 6.

RAGOUT OF LAMB WITH FRESH TOMATOES
(*Arni Me Freskes Domates*)

> 3 pounds shoulder of lamb
> salt and pepper to taste
> flour
> ¾ cup butter or margarine
> ½ cup chopped onion
> 2 teaspoons chopped garlic
> ½ cup white wine
> 4 pounds ripe tomatoes, peeled
> water as needed
> 2 teaspoons sugar

Cut the meat into 6 to 8 pieces; wash, and drain. Salt and pepper it and dust very lightly with flour. Place half the butter in a frying pan. Brown it, then add the meat. When that is well-browned, put it into a large pot; add the onions to the butter in the pan and sauté them. Add the garlic; cook until it softens but does not brown. Pour the onions, garlic, and butter over the meat, and add the remaining butter and put the pot over medium heat. When the butter browns, add the wine, a little at a time (to form a vapor), and half the tomatoes passed through a strainer. Add ½ cup hot water. Cover the pot. Simmer 1½ hours.

Slice the remaining tomatoes and remove their seeds. Salt and pepper them and sprinkle with 2 teaspoons sugar; set aside to drain. Remove the pot with the meat from the heat. Put the meat on a platter.

Arrange the tomatoes on the bottom of the pot and place the meat on top of them. Return to low heat and cook about a half hour. The meat should be in a thick sauce. Serve with rice. Place the meat in the center of the platter and surround with the rice. Put the tomatoes on the rice and pour the sauce over the top. The sauce need not be strained as the onions and garlic will have been reduced to a pulp.

Serves 6.

LAMB WITH ASSORTED VEGETABLES
(Arni Me Thiafora Horta)

    3 pounds lamb
    salt and pepper to taste
    1 pound small potatoes
    4-5 medium carrots
    1 pound small zucchini squash
    4-5 scallions
    1 pound peas, shelled
    1 cup vegetable oil or butter
    2 tablespoons chopped parsley
    3-4 small round ripe tomatoes

Cut the lamb into 6 to 8 portions. Wash, wipe dry, and season. Clean the potatoes and cut each into 2 or 3 pieces. Scrape the carrots and cut into 2-or-3 inch lengths. Clean the squash and cut these into round slices. Clean and chop the scallions. Mix the vegetables together and season lightly. (Reserve the tomatoes until the end.)

Brown the meat in a pan, using half the butter. Add the vegetables and brown lightly. Put the meat and vegetables into a roasting pan, sprinkle with the parsley, pour in all the butter from the browning pan, and add to this the remaining butter. Tuck in the tomatoes. Bake in a preheated 250° oven 1½ to 2 hours.

Serves 6.

LAMB FRICASSEE WITH ONIONS AND LETTUCE
(Arni Fricase Me Kremmithakia Ke Maroulia)

    4-5 pounds shoulder or back of lamb
    ¾ cup butter
    10 scallions
    water as needed
    coarse salt
    3 heads lettuce
    2-3 tablespoons chopped dill
    salt and pepper to taste

    2 egg yolks
    2 lemons, juice only

Cut the lamb into serving-size strips. Place in a pot with the butter. Clean the scallions; chop the white part into small pieces and the greens into larger ones (about 1½- to 2-inches long); add to the meat. Add ½ cup water and a little coarse salt; cook over medium heat for about 1 hour.

Clean the lettuce and cut into 2-inch pieces.

As soon as the meat has absorbed the water it will begin to brown in the butter but do not let the scallions brown. Add the dill, lettuce, salt, and pepper. Cover the pot and simmer over low heat for about 15 minutes. If it is needed, add a little water toward the end of the cooking time (not in the beginning, because then the lettuce will exude water).

Beat the egg yolks with 2 tablespoons of water, add the juice from the lemons, and beat it in well. Add a little of the liquid from the pot, beating constantly. Pour this sauce back into the pot and shake the pot gently to mix the sauce with the food. Serve immediately.

Serves 6.

STUFFED LEG OF LAMB
(Bouti Arnisio Yemisto)

    3 pounds leg of lamb
    salt and pepper to taste
    2 tablespoons chopped parsley
    4 slices zampon*
    ¼ pound kefalotiri* cheese
    1 cup butter
    1 cup white wine
    2 cups (or more) hot water
    3⅔ pounds small, round potatoes

Have the butcher bone and flatten the lamb. Wash and dry the meat. Sprinkle with salt, pepper, and the parsley. Put the slices of ham on top of the lamb. Cut the cheese into thin slices and place these on the top of the ham. Carefully roll the lamb into a compact roll and tie. Put the roll into a pan, add the butter, and place in a preheated 300° oven. Cook until brown on all sides (about 30 minutes). Add the wine; baste the roll with the pan sauces. Add the water; cook an additional 30 minutes. Peel the potatoes, wash them, salt and pepper them, and place them in the pan. Lower the heat to about 225° and cook another 1 to 1¼ hours. Add more hot water if necessary during the cooking. Remove from the oven. Cool slightly to make the carving easier, and serve with a fresh green salad.

Serves 6.

VEAL OR LAMB WITH OKRA
(Mosxhari E Arni Me Bamies)
    3 pounds (approximately) veal or leg of lamb
    3 pounds okra
    ½ cup vinegar
    salt and pepper to taste
    ¾ cup butter
    1 medium onion, chopped
    1½ pounds tomatoes, peeled and strained
    water as needed

Put the okra into a bowl of water and wash it well. Cut off the stems carefully so as not to cut the okra. Place in a pan, sprinkle with vinegar, and salt lightly. Cut the meat into 1½- to 2-inch cubes, wash and drain it; salt and pepper lightly. Put into a pot with the butter to brown. While the meat is browning, add the onion and brown this too. Add the tomatoes and 2 cups of water and cook over medium heat for 20 minutes. Drain the okra and add to the meat in neat layers. Cover the pot and simmer until all the liquid has been absorbed and only the butter remains.

Serves 6.

Note: If you wish, use half of the butter to brown the meat and use the other half to lightly fry the okra. In this case, add only 1 cup water to the meat as the okra will cook more rapidly and less water will be needed.

TAS KEBAB
(Tas Kebàb)
    3 pounds lamb or veal
    ½ pound butter
    1½ pounds onions, peeled and sliced
    2 tablespoons chopped parsley
    ½ cup white wine
    1 tablespoon tomato paste diluted with 1 cup
        water, or 1¼ pounds ripe tomatoes, peeled
        and strained
    salt and pepper to taste

Cut the meat into 1½- to 2-inch pieces. Wash, and put into a pot with the butter into a frying pan,

brown it; add the meat, a few pieces at a time, and brown well. Place the browned pieces in a pot. Add the onions to the butter in which you browned the meat, and sauté lightly but do not brown. Pour the onions and butter over the meat. Place over low heat, and as soon as the meat begins to sizzle, add the wine and then the diluted tomato paste (or tomatoes), the parsley, salt, and pepper. Cover the pot; simmer for 1½ hours. Add a little water only if necessary. This recipe calls for the onions to be cooked almost to the melting point so the meat remains in a thick sauce.

Serves 6.

VEAL OR BEEF WITH EGGPLANT
(Mosxhari E Vothino Me Meltizanes)
    3 pounds veal or beef
    3 pounds long eggplants
    2-3 medium onions
    ½ pound butter
    1½ pounds ripe tomatoes
    salt and pepper to taste
    water as needed

Clean the eggplants and cut each one into 3 or 4 round slices; place in a bowl of salted water to soak for 20 minutes. Cut the meat into serving-size pieces; wash and drain. Clean the onions, chop them and rinse well in a strainer.

Brown half the butter in a pot. Salt and pepper the meat and brown it with the butter; add the onions, and brown them. Pass the tomatoes through a strainer and add to the meat, and bring them to a boil. Add 2 cups of water; simmer about 1 hour for veal, or 1½ hours for beef. The meat should be tender and there should still be a little sauce left.

After the eggplant has soaked for 20 minutes, remove the slices from the bowl, rinse well, wipe with a towel, and fry in the remaining butter, then place carefully on top of the meat; add a little salt and pepper. Cook the meat over medium heat for another 20 minutes, or until all the liquid has been absorbed and only the oil remains.

Serves 6.

Note: If you wish, cook the meat for 1 hour, then add the eggplant without frying it. Add 1 to 2 cups water and cook another hour, until only the oil remains.

VEAL WITH PURÉED VEGETABLES
(Mosxhari Me Poure Apo Thiafora Horta)

> **3 pounds veal steak**
> **¾ cup butter**
> **1½ pounds tomatoes, peeled and strained, or 1 tablespoon tomato paste diluted with 2 cups of water**
> **2¼ pounds potatoes, peeled and washed**
> **1 pound carrots**
> **¾ pound onions**
> **salt and pepper to taste**
> **water as needed**

Tie the meat with a white thread, rinse it, and dry it well. Put the butter into a wide pot to brown, and add the meat; brown it carefully on all sides. Add the tomatoes (or the diluted tomato paste), salt, and pepper. Cover the pot; cook for ½ hour. Clean the onions, peel the carrots; cut them into small pieces and add to the meat. Add 1 to 2 cups water, as needed, and cook an additional 45 minutes. Add the potatoes and cook until they are tender. With a slotted spoon, remove the vegetables and put them through a food mill or whirl in the blender. If there is any liquid remaining, cook the meat a little longer until all of the liquid is absorbed and only the butter remains. Remove the meat to a platter, let it cool partially. Remove the string and cut the meat into thin slices. Return the sliced meat to the pot and heat it. Place the puréed vegetables in the center of a platter. Put the meat slices around the edge and serve with the butter poured over the top.

Serves 6.

MEAT WITH DRIED BEANS
(Kreas Me Fasolia Xsira)

> **1¼-1½ pounds dried beans**
> **3 pounds pork, veal, lamb, or beef**
> **½-¾ cup butter (depending on the amount of fat in the meat)**
> **1 medium onion**
> **1 tablespoon tomato paste diluted with 1 cup water, or 1 2-pound can whole tomatoes**
> **salt and pepper to taste**
> **2 tablespoons chopped parsley**
> **water as needed**

Clean the beans and soak them overnight. Drain; boil them partially (for 30 minutes). Meantime, cut the meat into large cubes and place them in a large pot. Add the diluted tomato paste or canned tomatoes (the latter rather than fresh tomatoes are specified because this is a winter dish) passed through a strainer; add the salt, pepper and parsley, and bring to a boil. Add 1 to 2 cups water. Drain the beans and add to the meat. Cook another half hour or until the beans are soft and all the liquid has been absorbed so only the butter remains.

Serves 6.

FRIED MEATBALLS
(Keftaides Tiganiti)

> **2 pounds chopped meat**
> **1 large onion, chopped**
> **3 tablespoons chopped parsley**
> **1½ cups bread cubes, trimmed of crusts and soaked**
> **1 teaspoon chopped, bruised mint**
> **2 teaspoons lemon juice**
> **2 eggs**
> **1 teaspoon oregano**
> **salt and pepper to taste**
> **oil for frying**
> **flour**

Mix together all the ingredients except the oil and flour; shape into patties or meatballs. Heat the oil in a deep frying pan. Roll the meatballs in flour and shake off any excess. Fry until browned on all sides. Serve hot or cold.

Serves 6 to 8.

MEATBALLS WITH RICE AND TOMATO SAUCE
(Yovarlakia Me Rizi Ke Saltsa Domatas)

> **1 pound ripe tomatoes, peeled and strained, or 1 tablespoon tomato paste diluted with 2 cups water**
> **½ cup melted butter**
> **1¾ pounds chopped meat**
> **½ cup raw rice**
> **½ cup chopped onion**
> **1 egg**
> **½ cup chopped parsley**
> **salt and pepper to taste**

Put the tomatoes (or the diluted tomato paste) into a large pot with the butter. Mix together the meat, rice, onion, egg, half the parsley, and a little salt and pepper; shape into meatballs and put them into the pot with the sauce. Add the remaining parsley and cook over medium heat for about 45 minutes, or until most of the sauce is absorbed.

Serves 6.

SMYRNA MEATBALLS
(Soudzoukakia)

- 1½ pounds chopped meat
- 2-3 slices white bread, trimmed of crusts
- 2-3 cloves garlic, finely chopped
- pinch of cumin seed, pounded, or ½-1 teaspoon cumin powder
- flour
- butter or oil for frying
- 1 pound ripe tomatoes, peeled and seeded, or 1 tablespoon tomato paste, diluted with 1½ cups water
- salt and pepper to taste
- 1 egg (optional)
- ¼-½ cup red wine (optional)

Have the meat ground twice. Soak the bread in cold water and squeeze out the excess well. Mix the meat, bread, garlic, and cumin together; form egg-shaped meatballs; roll lightly in the flour. Heat the butter or oil in a deep frying pan. Fry the soudzoukakia until brown on all sides. Remove them from the pan with a slotted spoon and put them into a pot. Pour the tomatoes (or diluted tomato paste) into the pan with the butter or oil and cook together for 3 to 5 minutes. Pour the sauce over the soudzoukakia and cook another 10 to 15 minutes. Serve with rice.

Serves 6.

Note: If you are using the egg and wine, add both to the meat mixture, and use 1 more slice of bread.

STIFADO
(Stifado)

- 3 pounds lean beef
- 3 pounds small white onions even in size
- 1 cup oil
- ½ head garlic, peeled
- ⅓-½ cup vinegar (to taste)
- 1 tablespoon tomato paste diluted with 1 cup water, or 1½ pounds ripe tomatoes, peeled and strained
- 2 bay leaves

- 1 sprig rosemary
- salt and pepper to taste
- water as needed

This can be made two ways:

1. Wash the meat and cut it into 1½-inch cubes; place in a pot. Add the remaining ingredients and enough water to cover. Bring to a boil, then lower the heat and simmer for 2 to 3 hours. During this time, do not uncover the pot or stir the food; it should absorb all the liquid and only the oil remains.

2. Prepare meat as above, then brown it in oil in a frying pan. Place in a pot, add the tomatoes, and bring to a boil, cook for 5 minutes. Sauté the whole onions in the oil in the frying pan, and add to the meat along with the remaining ingredients. Cover the pot; simmer undisturbed for about 1 to 2 hours until all the liquid is absorbed and only the oil remains.

Serves 6.

MEATBALLS FRICASSEE
(Keftaides Fricase)

the meatballs
- 1 cup white bread, trimmed of crusts
- 2 pounds lean chopped meat
- 3 tablespoons chopped onion
- 1 tablespoon chopped parsley
- 1 tablespoon chopped mint
- 2 eggs, separated
- salt and pepper to taste
- flour
- oil or butter or lard for frying

the sauce
- ⅓ cup butter
- 2-3 bunches scallions, white parts only, cleaned and chopped
- ½ cup white vinegar
- 2 cups hot water
- ½ cup cold milk
- 1 tablespoon cornstarch

Wet the bread with cold water and squeeze out the excess; mix well with the chopped meat. Add the onion, parsley, mint, egg whites, salt, and pepper. Shape the meatballs, and flour them lightly; fry in the oil (or butter or lard).

To make the sauce, brown the butter in a saucepan; add the scallions; sauté until golden. Add the vinegar and water, and cook for 10 minutes. Add the meatballs, and cook until only half the liquid remains. Beat the egg yolks very thoroughly in a bowl. In another bowl, mix the cornstarch in the milk, add this mixture to the egg yolks, then blend in some liquid from the pot, beating all the while. Pour the egg mixture over the meatballs, shaking the pot gently until the sauce thickens.

Serves 6.

GRILLED BEEFSTEAK
(Brizoles Vothines Sti Skara)
> **½ pound steak per person**
> **salt and pepper to taste**
> **1-2 teaspoons oregano**
> **oil for basting**
> **lemon juice or basting**

Remove all excess fat from the steaks. Season with pepper and oregano. Brush with a little oil and let stand for 1 hour, then season with salt. Grill over high heat to sear the meat and retain the juices. Move from high heat to medium heat, brush with oil and lemon, and cook to taste (rare, medium, or well done).

PORK AND CELERY AVGOLEMONO
(Hirino Me Selino Avgolemono)
> **4½-5 pounds celery (with leaves)**
> **salt and pepper to taste**
> **3 pounds pork**
> **½ cup butter**
> **3 medium onions, chopped**
> **water as needed**
> **2 lemons, juice only**
> **2 eggs**
> **1 tablespoon cornstarch**

Clean the celery and cut each stalk into 2 or 3 pieces. Fill a large pot with water and bring it to a boil. Add a little salt and parboil the celery for about 15 minutes; drain and set aside. Cut the meat into cubes, wash, and season with salt and pepper. Put the butter into a pot to brown; add the meat and brown it lightly. Add the onions; cook until soft but not browned. Add 2 to 3 cups of water. Cook about 1 hour or until the meat is half cooked. Add the celery and cook until the liquid is reduced to 1 cup and the celery is tender (about 30 minutes longer).

Beat the eggs in a bowl. Dilute the cornstarch in ¼ cup water and add to the eggs. Add the lemon juice, and beat it in well. Slowly add some of the hot liquid from the meat to the egg-and-lemon mixture, beating it in thoroughly. Pour the sauce back over the meat and shake the pot gently until the sauce thickens slightly. Serve hot.

Serves 6.

BOILED HAM
(Hirino Bouti Vrasto)
> **5-7 pounds fresh ham**
> **water as needed**
> **course salt**
> **5-8 cloves of garlic**
> **salt and pepper to taste**
> **several peppercorns**
> **2-3 bay leaves**

Wash the ham. Pierce it in several places and insert the garlic cloves and peppercorns in these holes. Place the ham in a large pot and cover it with plenty of water. Add some coarse salt and the bay leaves; skim off the froth as it appears. Simmer for 3 to 4 hours, then remove from the heat. Allow the ham to cool thoroughly. Slice and serve as is for cold hors d'oeuvres, or serve it garnished with boiled or fried potatoes and a salad.

Serves 6 to 8.

Note: If you decide to make a soup from the broth, first remove most of the fat.

FOIE GRAS EN GELEE
(Foia Gra An Zele)
> **2 tablespoons unflavored gelatin**
> **3-4 hard-cooked eggs**
> **2 cooked carrots, cooled**
> **10 Calamata olives**
> **1 8-9-ounce can foie gras**
> **3 cups water or clear meat broth**
> **2 tablespoons retsina***
> **salt and pepper to taste**
> **sweet butter**
> **parsley**
> **lemon wedges**

Refrigerate the can of foie gras for 3 hours. Soak the gelatin as directed on the package. Slice the eggs, carrots, and olives; slice the chilled foie gras. Bring the water (or broth) to a boil and add the wine to it; pour into the gelatin. Strain through a cheesecloth and place in the refrigerator until partially set (about 1 hour). Season with salt and pepper, and also season the eggs and carrots.

Rinse out a rectangular mold and line the bottom and sides with the slices of eggs, carrots, and olives. Pour in a layer of gelatin, then place a layer of foie gras slices on it. Cover that with another layer of gelatin, and then a layer of the remaining egg and olive slices. Pour on another layer of gelatin; add a final layer of foie gras; cover with a last layer of gelatin. Place in the refrigerator until set (2 to 3 hours). Before serving, dip the mold into warm water to loosen, then turn it out onto a platter. Garnish with lemon wedges, pats of sweet butter, and a few sprigs of parsley.

Serves 6 to 8.

LIVER WITH TOMATO SAUCE
(Sikotakia Me Saltsa Domatas)

2-2½ pounds calf's liver
½ cup butter
½ cup white wine
1 tablespoon tomato paste diluted with 1 cup water, or 1½ pounds ripe tomatoes, peeled and strained
½ cup water
2 tablespoons chopped parsley
salt and pepper to taste

Cut the liver into small, narrow strips; wash, and drain well. Brown the butter in a pan, add the liver; sauté well. Add the wine slowly, so it steams; add the tomatoes (or diluted tomato paste), water, parsley, and salt and pepper. Cover the pot; cook until only a little sauce remains. Serve hot.

Serves 6 to 8.

MARINATED LIVER
(Sikotakia Marinata)

2-2¼ pounds calf's or lamb liver
oil or butter for frying
½ cup excellent-quality oil
2 tablespoons flour plus flour for dipping
⅓ cup vinegar
½ tablespoon tomato paste diluted with 1 cup water

½ teaspoon sweet rosemary (optional)
1 bay leaf
salt and pepper to taste
1-2 cups water

Slice the liver, dip the slices into flour, fry in hot oil (or butter), and place on a platter. Add the ½ cup oil to the oil in which you fried the liver, and when it is hot, slowly add the 2 tablespoons flour, stirring constantly with a wooden spoon until well-blended. When the mixture is lightly browned, add the vinegar, tomato paste, and water. Add the rosemary, bay leaf, and salt and pepper. Cook the sauce for 5 to 10 minutes (but do not let it become too thick). Add the liver to the sauce; cook for 2 to 3 minutes longer. Serve hot or cold.

Serves 6 to 8.

Note: Liver prepared in this fashion will keep for several days, especially during the winter.

BOILED BRAINS
(Miala vrasto)

1 pair lamb or beef brains
coarse salt
water to cover
1-2 tablespoons vinegar

Brains must be parboiled before they can be used. To prepare, first soak them in cold water for about 30 to 45 minutes, so the blood drains and the membranes soften. Remove the membranes with the point of a sharp knife. Add the vinegar to a pot containing the water and salt, and bring to a boil; add the brains. Cook lamb brains for 10 minutes; cook beef brains 15 to 20 minutes. Remove from the liquid and cool. Serve in any of the ways suggested in the recipes below. One pair of brains serves 2.

BRAINS WITH BÉCHAMEL SAUCE
(Miala Me Besamel)

2 pairs cooked brains
2 tablespoons butter
2 tablespoons flour
1¼ cups scalded milk
1 egg yolk, well-beaten
1 tablespoon lemon juice
½ cup grated Parmesan or Gruyère cheese
1 teaspoon chopped capers
salt and pepper to taste

4 slices day-old bread
butter for frying the bread
8 olives
parsley

Prepare the brains as in Boiled Brains (see index), and cut them, while they are still hot, into 2 to 4 pieces (depending on the size of the brains). Keep hot.

Melt the 2 tablespoons butter over low heat, add the flour; blend well. Add the milk, a little at a time, stirring constantly so the mixture does not lump, and cook until thickened. Remove from the heat. Slowly add the beaten egg yolk and lemon juice, stirring until well-blended, than add half the cheese and the capers.

Cut the slices of bread in half and remove the crusts. Fry lightly in butter until golden. Place the bread on a platter, top each slice with a piece of the brains, and cover with the sauce. Sprinkle the remaining cheese over the top and garnish with finely chopped parsley. Surround with the olives and serve with pieces of parsley tucked between the bread slices.

Serves 4.

POULTRY AND GAME

CHICKEN WITH OKRA
(Kottopoula Me Mpamiez)
    2 broiler-fryers (about 1½ pounds each) or 3
        pounds chicken parts
    salt and pepper to taste
    3 pounds okra
    ½ cup vinegar
    ¾ cup butter
    1 medium onion, chopped
    1½ pounds ripe tomatoes, peeled and strained
    2 cups water

Wash the chickens. (If they are whole, cut them into sections). Season lightly with salt and pepper, and set them aside to drain. Wash the okra. Remove the stems carefully, without cutting the okra. Line them up in a large flat pan and sprinkle with the vinegar; place in the sun for 30 minutes to 1 hour.

Brown the butter in a pot, add the chicken, and sauté until brown, then add the onion and let it

brown. Add the tomatoes and boil for 3 to 5 minutes. Add the water. Simmer for 30 minutes. Add the okra and continue to simmer, covered, until tender. Watch carefully as this may need a little more water. The okra will have abosrbed the liquid and only the oil should remain when the dish is cooked.

Serves 6 to 8.

CHICKEN WITH WALNUT SAUCE
(Kottopoula Me Saltsa Karithia)
    3 broiler-fryers (about 1½ pounds each)
    salt and pepper to taste
    ½ cup butter or oil
    1 cup white wine
    1 cup hot water
    ½ cup chopped walnuts

Thoroughly clean and wash the chickens. Truss them, and allow to drain. Sprinkle lightly with salt and pepper. Melt the butter in a frying pan. Brown the chickens, one at a time, well on all sides, then place them in a wide pot. Pour in the fat remaining in the frying pan, and place this pot over heat. Pour in wine slowly, so it steams, and add the water. Cover. Simmer, adding more water if needed, for about 30 minutes. When the chickens are tender, remove from the heat and cool partially, then cut into quarters. Add walnuts to the sauce, stir, and bring the sauce to a boil, cook for 2 to 3 minutes longer. Add the quartered chickens, and serve hot with fried potatoes and a raw salad.

Serves 6.

RABBIT WITH TOMATO SAUCE
(Kounelli Me Saltsa Domatas)
    1 3- to 6-pound rabbit
    vinegar
    water as needed
    1-2 bay leaves
    8 cloves garlic
    ¼ pound butter
    ¾ cup oil
    ½ cup white wine
    1½ pounds ripe tomatoes, peeled and strained,
        or 1½ tablespoons tomato paste diluted with
        1 cup water

Clean and wash the rabbit. Put it into a ceramic bowl with enough liquid to cover (half water and half vinegar). Add the bay leaves and half the garlic. Marinate overnight, then remove the rabbit from the marinade and cut it up. Heat the butter and oil in a frying pan, and brown the rabbit, a few pieces at a time, well on all sides. Put the rabbit into a large pot. Sauté the garlic in the oil in the pan, add the wine and the tomatoes (or diluted tomato paste). Cook for 3 to 5 minutes. Add this sauce to the pot with the rabbit, add 1 to 2 cups water. Cover the pot, and simmer over medium heat until the rabbit is tender (1½ to 2½ hours). Add water from time to time, as needed. The rabbit should absorb all the liquid; only the oil will remain when the dish is cooked.

Serves 4 to 8.

RABBIT WITH LEMON
(Kounelli Me Lemoni)
    1 rabbit, cut into pieces
    water as needed
    vinegar
    butter for frying
    oil for frying
    3 lemons, juice only

Clean and wash the rabbit; place in a ceramic bowl. Add enough liquid (half water and half vinegar) to cover the rabbit, and marinate overnight. Remove the rabbit from the marinade; wash; drain well. Heat equal amounts of butter and oil in a large pot. Brown the rabbit, a few pieces at a time, on all sides, then return the pieces to the pot and pour the lemon juice over them. Steam until the lemon is absorbed. Add 1 to 2 cups water and simmer, covered, until tender. You may have to add a little water from time to time. The rabbit should absorb all the liquid; only the oil remains when the dish is cooked (about 1½ to 2 hours).

Serves 4.

THRUSH OR PIGEONS IN TOMATO SAUCE
(Tsihles E Pitsounia Me Saltsa Domatas)
    3-6 birds, plucked, singed, and cleaned
    butter or oil for browning
    salt and pepper to taste
    1 cup white wine
    1½ pounds ripe tomatoes, peeled and strained
    1 cup (or more) water

Wash and drain the birds; season lightly with salt and pepper. Heat the butter (or oil) in a frying pan, and add the birds. Brown them well on all sides; transfer to a pot. Add the wine and tomatoes to the fat in the pan; cook for about 5 minutes. Pour the sauce over the birds. Add the water. Cover the pot; simmer until tender (about 1 hour; the birds are done when the meat separates easily from the bones). Add a little more water, if needed, during the cooking. Serve the birds with the sauce, which will thicken during the cooking.

Serves 3 to 6.

FISH

MARINATED FISH
(Psari Marinata)
    3 pounds fish (red mullet or similar fish)
    salt to taste
    1 lemon, juice only
    flour for dipping the fish
    1½ cups oil
    3-4 tablespoons flour
    ½ cup white vinegar
    1 teaspoon tomato paste diluted with 2 cups water
    1 teaspoon sugar
    2 cloves garlic, chopped
    1 teaspoon rosemary
    2 bay leaves
    4-5 peppercorns

Clean, wash, and salt the fish; place on a platter. Squeeze the lemon juice over it. Let it stand for a few minutes, then cut it into pieces suitable for frying. Heat the oil, dip the fish in flour, and fry it, a few pieces at a time. Place on a plate to cool. If the oil has become too black from the frying, strain it and wash the frying pan, then return the strained oil to it. Heat. Add 3 to 4 tablespoons flour, and stir until blended. Add the vinegar, diluted tomato paste, garlic, rosemary, sugar, bay leaves, and peppercorns. Bring to a boil. As soon as the sauce begins to thicken, add the fish, and cook for 3 to 5 minutes. Remove the fish to a platter, pour the sauce over. Cook and refrigerate. Serve cold.

Serves 6.

BAKED FISH
(Psari Plaki Sto Fourno)

    3 pounds fish, whole or cut into pieces
    salt and pepper to taste
    1 lemon
    1⅓ cups oil
    1½ pounds onions
    ½ cup chopped parsley
    1 head garlic, peeled and chopped
    ½ cup white wine
    1½ pounds ripe tomatoes, or 1 tablespoon to-
        mato paste diluted with 2 cups water

Clean and wash the fish; season with salt and pepper, squeeze the juice of the lemon over it, and let it
stand for 1 hour. Clean the onions and slice them
thinly; rinse with cold water. Pour half of the oil into
a pan. Spread the onions in the bottom; sprinkle
with half the parsley and half the garlic. Lay the fish
on this and sprinkle with the remaining parsley and
garlic; pour the remaining oil over it, then the wine
and the tomatoes. Bake in a preheated 350° oven for
30 minutes.

Serves 6.

Note: Using the same ingredients, you can make a
potted version of this recipe by following these
directions:

Cut the fish into slices if it is large; use whole if it
is small. Heat the oil in a wide pot; add the onions,
and brown them lightly. Add the wine, then the tomatoes, garlic, and parsley. Season to taste with salt
and pepper, and add ½ cup water. Cook the stock for
20 minutes, then add the fish. Cover; simmer for 15
to 25 minutes.

You may also add 1½ pounds potatoes, sliced. In
that case, eliminate half the onions, and add the potatoes before the fish. Continue as above. (This may
require a little more water.)

BAKED MACKEREL
(Kolio Fourno)

    3 pounds mackerel
    salt and pepper to taste
    1 lemon
    4 teaspoons chopped garlic
    4 teaspoons chopped onion
    2 tablespoons chopped parsley
    2 teaspoons chopped green pepper

    1 cup oil
    1 pound ripe tomatoes, peeled and strained
    ½ cup white wine

Clean and wash the fish; season with salt and pepper. Place in a pan. Squeeze the lemon over the fish,
then refrigerate for 30 minutes. Sprinkle the garlic
over the fish, then the onion, parsley, and green pepper. Pour the oil over it, then add the tomatoes. Bake
in a preheated 250° oven for 15 minutes. Add the
wine. Baste the fish with the pan sauce, and bake 30
minutes longer, until most of the liquid is absorbed.

Serves 6.

FISH BOURYETO
(Psari Bouryeto)

    3 pounds fish (any type)
    salt and pepper to taste
    2 lemons
    1 cup oil
    6 cloves garlic, chopped
    ½ teaspoon oregano

Clean the fish and slice it into serving-size pieces.
Sprinkle with salt and pepper, and place in a bowl.
Squeeze the juice of the lemons over it.

Put the oil and garlic into a large pot, add the fish
and lemon juice; simmer over low heat until the fish
is cooked (30 to 45 minutes) and only the oil remains
as a sauce. During the last 5 to 10 minutes, add the
oregano.

Serves 6.

Note: Fish will exude some water while cooking
but will reabsorb it.

CODFISH STEW WITH ONIONS, CALAMATA
STYLE
(Bakaliaros Pastos Me Kremmithia, Kalamatianos)

    3 pounds salt cod
    water as needed
    flour for dipping
    1½ cups oil
    2 pounds onions, sliced
    1½-2 pounds ripe tomatoes, peeled and
        strained
    pepper to taste

Cut the cod into small pieces. Skin it, and soak it overnight in enough water to cover, changing it 2 or 3 times. Remove from the water; take out the bones; rinse and dry the fish well. Dip it in flour, shaking off the excess, and fry in hot oil until golden. In the same oil, sauté the onions until they are soft but not brown. Put them in a wide pot, together with the oil from the pan and any of the 1½ cups oil not used in the frying. Add the tomatoes and pepper. Simmer for 30 to 45 minutes, or until the onions dissolve. Add the codfish (and ½ cup hot water if needed), cover the pot, and cook for 10 minutes, until the liquid is abosorbed and only the oil remains.

Serves 6.

Note: This dish is usually made in the summer, when ripe tomatoes are readily available.

SAUCES

BÉCHAMEL SAUCE 1 [REGULAR]
(Saltsa Besamel Kanoniki 1)

> **6 tablespoons butter**
> **7-8 tablespoons flour**
> **4 cups milk, scalded**
> **1-2 egg yolks**
> **salt and pepper to taste**

Melt the butter, but do not brown. Add the flour slowly, mixing constantly. Remove from the heat. Slowly mix in the scalded milk. Return to the heat and stir until the sauce thickens. Beat the egg yolks well, and add them with salt and pepper to the mixture, stirring constantly until blended. If you do not serve the sauce immediately, stir it occasionally to prevent a crust from forming.

BÉCHAMEL SAUCE 2 [THICK]
(Saltsa Besamel Pikti 2)

> **8 tablespoons butter**
> **10-12 tablespoons flour**
> **4 cups milk, scalded**
> **1-2 egg yolks**
> **salt and pepper to taste**

Melt the butter and add the flour slowly to it, blending thoroughly. Remove from the heat and slowly add the milk, mixing constantly. Return to the heat. Stir until the mixture thickens. Beat the egg yolks well; add with the salt and pepper, stirring all the while until well-blended. If you do not serve the sauce immediately, stir occasionally to prevent a crust from forming.

BÉCHAMEL SAUCE 3 [LIGHT]
(Saltsa Besamel Aeri 3)

> **3 tablespoons butter**
> **4 tablespoons flour**
> **4 cups milk, scalded**
> **1-2 egg yolks**
> **salt and pepper to taste**

Melt the butter, but do not brown it. Add the flour slowly, blending it in thoroughly. Remove from the heat. Add the milk slowly, mixing all the while. Return to the heat and stir until the mixture thickens. Beat the egg yolks well and add with the salt and pepper, mixing constantly until well-blended. If you do not serve the sauce immediately, stir occasionally to prevent a crust from forming.

BÉCHAMEL SAUCE 4 [SMALLER RECIPE-THICK]
(Saltsa Besamel Se Mikroteri Analogia)

> **3 tablespoons butter**
> **4 tablespoons flour**
> **1 cup milk**
> **1-2 egg yolks**
> **salt and pepper to taste**

Melt the butter, but do not brown it. Add the flour slowly, blending it in thoroughly. Remove from the heat. Slowly add the milk, mixing constantly. Return to the heat and stir until the sauce thickens. Beat the egg yolks well and add with salt and pepper to the mixture, stirring all the while until well-blended. If you do not use immediately, stir occasionally to prevent a crust from forming.

GREEN SAUCE
(Saltsa Prasini)

> **1 teaspoon parsley juice**
> **2 cups mayonnaise**

Dice the leaves of fresh parsley, then put them into a mortar and pound to a pulp. Pass through a strainer. Mix the juice well with the mayonnaise.

COMPOTES

APPLE COMPOTE
(Komposta Mila)

1½ pounds cooking apples
lemon juice
1 cup sugar
water as needed
1 piece of stick cinnamon
1 lemon peel

Clean the apples and cut them into 2 to 4 pieces. Remove the seeds and the hard section near the core and place in a bowl of cold water with a little lemon juice. Rinse the apples, then put them in a wide pot with the sugar and 2 cups water; bring to a boil. Add the cinnamon stick and lemon peel. As soon as the apples are soft, remove them carefully with a slotted spoon and place in a compote dish. Cook the syrup a few minutes longer to thicken it slightly. Remove the cinnamon and lemon peel, and pour the syrup over the apples.

STRAWBERRY COMPOTE
(Komposta Fraoula)

1½ pounds strawberries
1 cup sugar
½ cup water
½-1 cup sweet dark-red Samos wine (to taste)

Remove the leaves and stems from the berries and wash and drain them thoroughly. Boil the sugar and water together until the syrup thickens (as for jellies), then add the strawberries; cook for 3 to 5 minutes. Remove them with a slotted spoon and place in compote dish. Continue to boil the syrup until quite thick. Add the wine. Remove from the heat, cool, and pour over the strawberries.

QUINCE COMPOTE
(Komposta Kithoni)

1½ pounds quince, cleaned
water as needed
lemon juice
1½ cups sugar
1 lemon rind

Wipe the quince and cut into quarters, then cut each quarter into thin slices. Remove the skin, pits, and hard core. Put the quince into a bowl of water with a little lemon juice added to prevent discoloring. Rinse; drain well; place in a pot and cover with the sugar. Add 2 cups water and the lemon rind, and bring to a boil. Cook for 15 to 20 minutes, or until the quince are soft and turn color. Remove from the heat, cool, and serve in a compote dish.

Note: If you prefer a thicker syrup, remove the quince with a slotted spoon and continue to boil the syrup a little longer. Pour over the quince and serve.

MISCELLANEOUS DESSERTS AND BREADS

PUFF PASTE
(Zimi Sfoliatas)

5 cups flour
2 teaspoons baking powder
1 teaspoon salt
2 cups (approximately) water
2¾ cups butter

Sift the flour with the baking powder and the salt. Place on a marble surface or bread board. Make a well in the middle of the flour and pour in a little of the water. Begin to mix the water into the flour with the fingertips, adding just enough water to make a stiff dough. Do not knead at this point. Shape the dough into a large ball and set it aside in a covered bowl to rest for 30 minutes. While the dough is resting, work the butter in your hands and shape it into a ball. Lightly flour your board. Place the dough in the center and carefully roll with a lightly floured rolling pin into a square about ¼ to ½ inches thick. Place the butter in the center of the dough and bring up the sides of the dough to enclose the butter completely. Lightly flour your hands and begin to work the dough, squeezing it to spread the butter evenly. Shape and pat into a rectangle, and cover with waxed paper; let stand for 10 minutes. Lightly flour the board, rolling pin, and your hands. Place the dough on the board; lightly sprinkle it with flour. Roll the dough into a rectangle (about three times as long as it is wide) about ¼ to ½ inch thick. Fold this over 3 times and lightly press the folds with the rolling pin to join and seal the layers. Let stand for 15 minutes (if it is a very hot day, place in the refrigerator for this time.) Press one finger into a corner of the dough to mark the number of times it has been worked. Again flour the mixing surface lightly and place the dough in the center. Also flour the rolling pin and the surface of the puff paste. Give the dough a quarter turn from its last position and again roll it into a long rectangle, as before. Fold over in three and press lightly with the rolling pin. Let stand for 15 minutes. Repeat this process 3 more times for a total of 6 workings of the dough from the addition of the butter to the end. Remember to give the dough a quarter turn each time. Proceed to make the puffs according to the recipe you are following.

This dough will hold for one day in the refrigerator.

ABOUT PHYLLO (Also spelled fillo, phylo, filo)

Phyllo is a special dough, rolled as thin as tissue paper, and used to make pastries, or coverings for many meat and cheese dishes. Phyllo is very difficult to make at home, but—fortunately—it is available, prepared commercially, wherever Greek food products are sold. It is packed and sold in 1-pound packages, and the average package contains about 20 to 24 12- x 18-inch sheets. Phyllo must be kept well wrapped and refrigerated to keep it from drying out. It can be stored about a month.

Using phyllo: It is important to use just one sheet of phyllo at a time, and keep the rest carefully covered with a piece of paper and a damp towel. Phyllo can be cut as desired. However, if it tears, use the torn sheet between whole sheets; do not attempt to patch it with water, for it will only become pasty and sticky.

The secret to using phyllo is *butter.* Melt the butter and brush it on each sheet as you use it. Do not skimp on the amount of butter you use, or skip spreading it on some of the sheets, or your pastry will emerge thick and heavy, instead of flaky and crisp.

Use from 4 to 9 sheets of phyllo for the bottom layer of any recipe requiring it-even more, if the filling is very moist. If you are preparing a large "pie," or *pitta,* as these dishes are called, select a pan smaller than the phyllo sheets so that about 2 inches

of phyllo extends over the pan on all sides. *Do not cut the phyllo to fit the pan.* Pour in your filling and fold the overhanging phyllo back over the filling to partially enclose it. Brush each sheet with butter as you turn it toward the middle of the pitta. Finally, cover the filling with more layers of phyllo, trimming these to fit the pan so that they completely seal the filling. Some recipes tell you to sprinkle the top of the pitta with a little water. The best way to do this is to wet your hands and shake them over the surface of the pitta. The amount of water that falls from them will be just right.

Score the surface of the pitta with a sharp knife just before baking. This will allow you to cut through the baked pitta cleanly when serving it.

To make triangles, or "turnovers," as we call them, the phyllo is cut into long strips 2 to 4 inches wide. The narrower strips are just right for making hors d'oeuvres and appetizers; the wider ones are suitable for main-course individual portions. Use this technique to prepare the turnover: Place the strip horizontally on the table, with the wide part parallel to you and the narrow ends to your left and right. Put a little filling in the middle of the left corner. Fold the corner over the filling to make a triangle. Continue to turn the triangle over and over until you reach the end of the strip. The filling will be completely enclosed in a triangular strudel-like pastry. Place the turnover, open edge down (to prevent it from opening during the baking), on a baking sheet. Make all the turnovers the same way.

Avgolemono—The best-known Greek sauce. Made of eggs and lemon juice, and used to flavor soups, meats, and vegetables.

Baklava—A favorite Greek pastry. Crisp phyllo pastry filled with nuts and dripping with honey syrup.

Bourekia—Meats or vegetables wrapped in phyllo pastry. Smaller versions are called *bourekakia*.

Copenhagen—A dessert named in honor of King George I of Greece; who had been a Danish prince.

Dolmathes—Stuffed grape leaves. Filled with either meat or rice and served hot or cold, with or without avgolemono.

Feta—Best known of the Greek cheeses. Made of goats' milk.

Fide (Fidelo)—A very fine egg noodle. Sold here as fidelo, fidilini, etc.

Floyeres—Phyllo pastry having a long, flutelike shape.

Giouvetsi—Greek casserole.

Glyko—The word means "sweet" and is used to refer to spoon sweets.

Grapevine leaves—Used for preparing dolmathes. Sold in this country in jars, already prepared for use, just rinse before using.

Halvah—Dessert made with farina.

Imam baldi—A real treat of eggplant and trimmings. Legend has it that the *imam* (high priest) fainted in delight when served this. Other legends say he fainted at the cost of the amount of oil used.

Kasseri—A firm table cheese. Used as a grating cheese. You may substitute Parmesan or Romano cheeses, but these have a stronger flavor.

Kataife—Available in Greek pastry or specialty shops. Some people substitute shredded wheat for it with fairly good results.

Kefalotiri—A hard cheese very similar to Parmesan.

Kimino—Cumin seed. Not too well-known but easily available in this country. You will find many uses for its unusual flavor.

Lathera—Foods braised in oil, and served in the same oil.

Mahlepi—An unusual spice. Must be ground before using. Found in specialty shops.

Mastiha—Mastic. Sometimes refers to the liqueur of the same name.

Mavrodaphne—A dessert wine. Available at most liquor shops.

Mizithra—A mild cheese similar to cottage and ricotta cheeses.

Mortadella—A salami.

Ouzo—A clear liquor flavored with aniseed. Very potent—few can drink it straight. Mix with cold water and it becomes cloudy.

Pantespani—Greek sponge cake.

Pastes Sardelis—Salt-packed anchovies, served cleaned, and with oil and vinegar.

Paximadia—Biscuits served with coffee or tea.

Phyllo—A strudel-like pastry dough available in specialty shops (see introduction to Phyllo chapter: "about Phyllo").

Pilafi—Cooked rice.

Renga—Smoked herring.

Retsina—National wine of Greece. Resinated drinks are quite unusual and one must acquire a taste for them. Don't feel bad if you cannot.

Rizi—Raw rice.

Skordalia—Famous Greek garlic sauce. Very, very powerful. Not to be eaten before a theatre engagement or any social event—unless everyone else has eaten it, too.

Tarama—Carp roe.

Trahana—A homemade noodle used in soups and stews. Now available commercially in specialty shops. Substitute semolina if trahana is unobtainable.

Vissino—Sour cherries in a delicious preserve.

Vissinada—Sour-cherry preserves mixed with iced water for a cool summer drink.

Zampon—Ham.

GERMAN

EGG DISHES

SCRAMBLED EGGS WITH HAM
(Rühreier mit Schinken)

    4 eggs
    1 tbls. milk
    salt and pepper
    ½ cup cooked ham, diced
    1 tbls. butter

Beat eggs, milk and seasoning until frothy. Add ham and mix in. Melt butter in frying pan, pour in mixture, and over slow heat, stir until just set. Serve.
Serves 2.

SPIEGELEIER WITH CHEESE

    2 slices Swiss cheese
    1 tsp. butter
    2 eggs
    salt and pepper

Place thin slices of Swiss cheese in a buttered skillet. Break eggs over each slice. Cook until set. Or bake in a buttered pan 10 minutes in a moderate (350°) oven. Season and serve.
Serves 2.

"LOST" EGGS
(Verlorene, Pochierte, Eier)

    6 cups of water
    2 tsp. vinegar
    4 eggs
    1 tsp. salt (for warm water)

Bring water and vinegar to a boil. Remove from heat and carefully break and slide in eggs, keeping them near surface. Put back on heat and cook 3 to 5 minutes, depending on desired consistency. Remove eggs and place in cold water. Trim ragged edges. Put into warm salt water until ready to serve.
Serves 4.

"LOST" EGGS WITH BERNAISE SAUCE

    6 "Lost" Eggs (see index)
    Tomato sauce or ketchup
    sauce bernaise:
        3 egg yolks
        3 tbls. olive oil
        2 tbls. hot water
        ¾ tbls. vinegar
        ¼ tsp. salt
        few grains cayenne pepper

Prepare eggs. Place on a platter and cover, alternately, with red and yellow sauce.

Beat egg yolks lightly with olive oil, hot water, vinegar, salt and cayenne. Put into a double boiler over hot, not boiling, water and whip until thick. Blend half the sauce with the Tomato Sauce to make the "red sauce."
Serves 6.

OMELETTE SOUFFLÉ

    4 eggs
    3 tbls. sugar
    juice of ½ lemon
    peels of ½ lemon, grated
    2 tbls. cornstarch
    1½ tbls. butter
    confectioner's sugar
    ¾ tbls. jam or marmalade
    ⅓ cup cherry brandy

Separate eggs. Stir until frothy the egg yolks, sugar, lemon juice and peels. Add cornstarch. Beat egg whites stiffly and carefully fold in. Butter a pan or mold. Pour mixture into it and bake in a hot (400°) oven until nicely browned, about 12 minutes. Turn out on oiled paper well covered with sugar, spread on jam or marmalade, and fold in two. Place on hot platter. Sprinkle with more sugar. Pour on cherry brandy. Light and serve flaming.
Serves 2.

SALZBURG "NOCKERLN"
(Salzburger Nockerln)
4 eggs
4 tsp. sugar
1 tbls. butter
½ cup cherry brandy, optional

Separate eggs. Stir the egg yolks and sugar until frothy. Beat egg whites until stiff and fold in. Melt butter in a frying pan, and with the pan very hot, brown mixture quickly, or place briefly in a hot oven (425°). "Nockerln" is sometimes cut in strips and served with flaming cherry brandy.
Serves 2.

HAZELNUT OMELET
(Hazelnussomeletten)
3 tbls. flour
1 cup milk
1 egg, separated
1 tbls. sugar
2 tbls. hazelnuts, grated
salt
2 tbls. butter

Combine flour and milk. Stir in egg yolk, fold in sugar, hazelnuts and stiffly beaten egg white. Add salt to taste. Melt butter and fry omelet golden brown on both sides. Serve with stewed fruits or berries.
Serves 2.

SANDWICHES AND CANAPES

LOBSTER CANAPÉS
(Hummersandwiches)
1 cup lobster meat
2 hard-cooked egg yolks
2 tbls. butter
½ tsp. mustard, prepared
salt and pepper
1 bouillon cube or soup stock
buttered toast

Chop lobster meat and egg yolks and put through food mill. Cream butter. Add mustard, seasoning and enough soup stock or diluted bouillon cubes to moisten. Mix well with lobster and egg. Spread on buttered squares of toast.
Makes 12-16.

GOOSE LIVER CANAPÉS
(Gänsleberbrötchen)
1 goose liver
3 tbls. butter
1 truffle (save a little for garnish)
1 shallot
1 tbls. Madeira
salt and pepper
toast or French bread truffle
aspic (see index)

Sauté liver in 1 tablespoon of the butter. Cool and chop. Cream remaining butter and mix in finely chopped liver, truffle and shallot. Add Madeira and seasonings to taste and mix well. Heap mixture on squares of toast or pieces of French bread. Garnish each piece with a touch of truffle and a dot of aspic.
Makes about 8.

EGG PASTE CANAPÉS WITH ANCHOVY
(Eiercremebrötchen mit Sardellen)
3 hard-cooked eggs
2 tbls. butter
1 tbls. sweet cream
salt and pepper
toast or French bread
flat anchovy fillets
cucumbers or tomatoes
parsley

Mash eggs through strainer. Cream butter and add cream, seasoning and the eggs. Spread generously on squares of toast or pieces of French bread and garnish with a criss-cross of anchovies. Or use on top of sliced cucumbers or tomatoes. Decorate with finely chopped parsley.
Makes about 10-12.

CHEESE AND OLIVE CANAPÉS
(Käse und Olivencanapés)
day-old bread
½ cup butter
6 ozs. cream cheese
salt
olives
red or green peppers

Slice day-old bread and trim into ovals ½ inch thick. Cream butter and mix well with cream cheese. Season, and spread on bread. Garnish with finely chopped olives and small pieces of red or green peppers.

Makes 18-20.

STUFFED DARK BREAD
(Gefülltes Kapselbrot)
  1 square loaf dark bread
  2 hard-cooked eggs
  ½ cup anchovies
  6-8 tbls. butter
  1 cup chopped ox tongue or 1 cup chopped ham
  ½ cup Swiss cheese
  1 tbls. capers
  1 tbls. mustard
  salt and pepper
  aspic (see index)
  1 tomato, sliced
  parsley

Remove crusts from bread and from the top, scoop out most of the insides. Chop eggs finely. Put anchovies through a strainer. Cream butter. Mix all together with the tongue or ham, cheese, capers and seasoning. Stuff into hollow loaf and chill in refrigerator. To serve, slice, and garnish with aspic, slices of tomato and parsley.

Serves 4.

APPETIZERS

LOBSTER MAYONNAISE
(Hummermayonnaise)
  1 lobster
  juice of lemon
  salt and pepper
  1 cup mayonnaise
  1 hard-cooked egg, sliced
  ½ can anchovy fillets
  6 capers
  1 sliced tomato

Remove cooked lobster (see below) from shell. Sprinkle chunks with lemon juice, salt and pepper. Arrange neatly on a glass salad plate between mounds of mayonnaise. Pour remaining mayonnaise over lobster pieces and serve garnished with sliced hard-cooked eggs, anchovies, capers and sliced tomato.

This same recipe may be used for salmon, crabmeat, and most varieties of cooked or canned fish.

Serves 4.

LOBSTER
(Hummer)
  1 lobster
  salt and other seasoning:
    vinegar
    onions
    peppercorns
    parsley

Lobster may be bought already cooked and is then red. If bought alive, clean in cold water with a brush. Half fill a large pot with water. Add salt and other desired seasoning such as vinegar, onions, peppercorns, and parsley. Bring to a boil and plunge lobster in head-first. Boil 20 to 30 minutes depending on size of lobster. When done, carve with shears lengthwise through the center of the body and tail, and crack claws. Leave meat in shell, and arrange attractively on a platter. Serve lukewarm or cold. Serve with mayonnaise and bread or, if desired, a vegetable salad garnished with mayonnaise.

Serves 2.

TOMATOES LUCULLUS
(Tomaten Lukullus)
  2 large, or 4 small tomatoes
  1 hard-cooked egg
  1 cup cooked chicken
  1 stick celery
  2 anchovies
  4 olives
  4 capers
  ¼ cup mixed nuts
  ½ cup mayonnaise
  1 tbls. lemon juice
  lettuce

Wash and polish tomatoes. Cut off a little of the top and save. Hollow out tomatoes. Chop up egg, chicken, celery, anchovies, olives, capers and nuts. Moisten with mayonnaise, and season with salt and pepper. Sprinkle with lemon juice and fill tomato shells. Replace top and serve with lettuce on salad plates.

Serves 2.

HUNGARIAN GOOSE LIVER PATÉ
(Gänseleberpastete, Ungarisch)

   1 truffle
   1 large goose liver
   3 tbls. Madeira wine or milk
   8 tbls. goose fat
   1 onion
   salt and pepper

Slice a truffle and lard a large, fat goose liver with it. Be very careful. Let it soak briefly in Madeira or milk. Brown onion in goose fat, add liver and cook until well done, about 15 minutes. Remove liver and season well. Place in deep china bowl, pour fat over it through a fine strainer. Let cool and serve.

Serves 2-3.

SOUPS

ASPARAGUS SOUP
(Spargelsuppe)

   1 lb. asparagus
   1 qt. water, salted slightly
   4 tbls. flour
   4 tbls. butter
   1 egg yolk
   2 tbls. cream

Clean the asparagus and cut into inch-long pieces. Cook until tender in slightly salted water. Make white sauce by stirring flour into melted butter, adding dashes of asparagus water until flour is completely dissolved. Add to soup and thicken with beaten egg yolk and cream.

Serves 4.

FLOUR DUMPLINGS
(Schwemmklösschen)

   ½ cup milk
   2 tbls. butter
   salt and nutmeg
   6 tbls. flour
   2 eggs

Bring the milk, butter and seasoning to a boil. Sprinkle in flour and form into a loaf. Let cool; then, singly, mix in eggs. From a spoon, slip dumplings into boiling soup stock and cook 4 to 6 minutes.

Serves 4.

CAULIFLOWER SOUP
(Blumenkohlsuppe)

   1 head cauliflower
   1 qt. water, salted
   4 tbls. butter
   4 tbls. flour
   1 egg yolk
   2 tbls. cream
   nutmeg to taste

Clean cauliflower, pluck apart into "bouquets" and soak for one hour in cold salt water. Cook in one quart of salted water. Melt butter, and flour, and half a cup of cooking water and stir until completely dissolved. Add to soup and bring to a boil once more. Thicken with beaten egg yolk and cream. Season with nutmeg. Return bouquets and serve.

Serves 4.

GREEN POTATO SOUP
(Grüne Kartoffelsuppe)

   1 lb. raw potatoes
   1-2 tomatoes
   1 yellow turnip
   1 piece of celery
   1 onion
   2 tbls. butter
   1 tbls. flour
   1½ qts. water or stock
   ½ tsp. salt
   1-2 tbls. sour cream
   parsley
   2 slices toasted dark bread

Dice potatoes and vegetables. Melt butter and heat potatoes and vegetables in it. Do not brown. Sprinkle with flour. Add water or beef stock and salt. Cook thoroughly 25 to 35 minutes. Before serving enrich with cream and garnish with parsley. Cube toast to make croutons and sprinkle over top.

Serves 4-6.

COLD FRUIT SOUP—APPLE, CHERRY, RHUBARB, GOOSEBERRY
(Apfel, Kirsch, Rhabarber, Stachelbeerkaltschale)

   1 lb. any fruit
   2 qts. water
   1 tbls. cornstarch or 4 tbls. tapioca
   2 tbls. sugar

½ **lemon, juice and chopped peels**
½ **cup white wine, optional**

Cook fruits in two quarts of water until soft. Drain, reserving liquid. Put through a fine strainer. Replace pulp in liquid and cook briefly again. Dissolve cornstarch (or tapioca) in ½ cup water or fruit juice and add to liquid. If tapioca is used, cook until it is transparent. Flavor with sugar and lemon to taste. White wine may be added. Garnish with cut fruit or whole berries; chill and serve cold.

Serves 4-6.

FARINA DUMPLINGS
(Griessklösschen)
½ **cup milk**
2 **tbls. butter**
salt and nutmeg
4 **tbls. farina**
2 **eggs**

Bring the milk, butter and seasoning to a boil. Sprinkle in farina and form into a lump. Remove from heat and, singly, mix in eggs. Cool. Cut into small dumplings. Place in boiling soup stock until dumplings rise to the surface.

Serves 4.

LENTIL, PEA OR BEAN SOUP
(Linsen, Erbsen, Bohnensuppe)
½ **lb. legumes**
salt
1-2 **tbls. butter or fat**
4 **tbls. flour**
2 **strips of bacon or Vienna sausage or toasted bread**
marjoram or vinegar or garlic

Soak legumes overnight in cold water. Drain, cover with 2 quarts salted water and cook until tender, about 2 hours. Put legumes through a strainer. Melt butter, add flour and 1 cup of cooking water and stir, over low heat, to smooth consistency. Add to strained legumes. Chop bacon finely, fry it lightly, and add to soup. Or cut Vienna sausage into it. Season pea soup with a little marjoram; lentil soup with a little vinegar; bean soup with a trace of garlic, each, to taste. Croutons of toast may be added before serving.

Serves 4-6.

HOMEMADE SOUP NOODLES
(Nudeln)
1 **egg**
½ **cup water, iced**
1 **cup flour**

Beat egg and water. Gradually add flour until a firm dough is formed. Strew flour on a bread board, turn out dough and knead until very pliable. The dough, when cut, should have small bubbles in it. Roll out to desired thickness and let stand to dry out. Roll up and cut into fine ribbons. Spread out for further drying. Toss into soup stock and boil for not over 5 minutes.

Serves 4.

FISH

BAKED FILLET OF GOLDEN PERCH
(Goldbarschfilet, gebacken)
2 to 3 **lbs. perch**
salt
juice of 1 lemon
1 **beaten egg or** ½ **cup milk**
bread crumbs

Sprinkle fillets of perch with salt and lemon juice. Let stand a short time. Dip into egg or milk, roll in bread crumbs and fry in deep fat until golden brown. The same procedure may be followed with pike or sole. Serve with Potato Salad (see index) and Remoulade Sauce (see index).

Serves 4.

GRILLED EEL
(Aal nach Trentiner Art)
2½ **lbs. eel**
olive oil
lemon juice
marjoram
salt and pepper
Parmesan cheese, grated

Skin eel and cut in 2-inch slices. Sprinkle with oil and lemon juice; add seasoning to taste. Spear on large toothpicks. Grill under high heat for 15 minutes, until golden-brown. To serve sprinkle with salt and grated Parmesan cheese.

Serves 4.

TROUT IN WHITE WINE
(Forellen in Weisswein)

    4 trout
    4 tomatoes
    1 banana
    estragon
    4 shallots
    ½ cup white wine
    salt and pepper
    1 cup Hollandaise Sauce

Clean fish and put in a saucepan. Surround with tomatoes, quartered, and bananas, finely sliced, a little estragon, and chopped shallots. Pour wine over this, season and cook slowly over moderate heat. When half done (about 6 minutes) turn fish over and finish cooking. Carefully remove fish, skin and keep hot until ready to serve. Let sauce boil down somewhat. Prepare Hollandaise Sauce and blend in over moderate heat. Pour over fish to serve.

Serves 4.

HOLLANDAISE SAUCE
(Holländische Sauce)

    2 egg yolks
    1 tbls. lemon juice
    1 tbls. water
    salt and pepper
    nutmeg
    pinch of sugar
    7 tbls. butter

Mix all ingredients, except butter, in top of double boiler. Do not let water in bottom boil. Beat well, over moderate heat. Add butter, by spoonfuls, and keep beating until sauce is rich and thick.

GRILLED SALMON
(Lachs, gegrillt)

    2½ lbs. salmon (center cut)
    lemon juice
    olive oil
    1 large onion, sliced
    salt and pepper

Slice salmon in finger-width slices. Sprinkle with lemon juice and olive oil. Cover with sliced onion and let stand one hour. Remove onions, and grill fish under moderate heat, turning as it browns for 20 minutes. Add seasoning to taste. Serve with Salted Potatoes (see index), raw sliced cucumbers and Sauce Bernaise (see index).

Serves 4.

FRIED SOLE
(Seezunge, gebacken—Soles frites)

    2¼ lbs. fillet of sole
    salt and pepper
    1 whole egg, beaten
    3 tbls. flour
    bread crumbs
    fat
    lemon wedges
    parsley

Cut sole in long, thin, diagonal strips. Rub in salt and pepper. Dip in beaten egg. Tumble in flour. Dip again in egg and then in bread crumbs, to achieve a crunchy crust. Fry in deep fat until brown. Garnish with lemon wedges and parsley.

Serves 3-4.

HUNGARIAN CODFISH
(Kabeljau, ungarische Art)

    1 large onion
    2 tbls. butter
    2½ lbs. codfish
    salt
    lemon juice
    1 tsp. paprika
    1 cup sour cream
    1 tsp. cornstarch
    ½ cup beef stock
    extra seasoning

Chop onion and brown in melted butter. Cut fish in portions. Sprinkle with lemon juice, salt and paprika and add to onions. Fry briefly on each side. Pour in cream and cook over low heat for 10 minutes, basting frequently and moving pan gently to prevent sticking. Be careful not to overcook, as this fish tends to break apart. Place on hot platter. Dissolve cornstarch in beef stock and add to drippings. Season well and bring to a boil. Pour over fish to serve. Serve with Salted Potatoes (see index), buttered rice or macaroni.

Serves 4.

BLUE HERRING
(Heringe, blau)
- **8 herring**
- **½ cup vinegar, hot**
- **2 qts. water**
- **1 tsp. salt**
- **lemon slices**

Clean herring and scald with hot vinegar. Bring salt water to a boil and immerse herring. Lower heat and let simmer for 10 minutes. Place carefully on hot platter and serve garnished with lemon slices.
Serves 4.

CREAMED FISH
(Fisch à la Crème)
- **2 cups cold cooked fish (boned)**
- **1 cup Butter Sauce (see index)**
- **1 bay leaf, chopped**
- **parsley**
- **½ onion**
- **salt and pepper**
- **½ cup bread crumbs**

Prepare sauce and add bay leaf, parsley and onion. Cook briefly together. Butter oven-proof dish and put in it alternate layers of fish seasoned with salt and pepper and sauce. Cover with bread crumbs and bake in a hot oven (400°) until bread crumbs are well browned.
Serves 2.

FRIED LOBSTER
(Gebratener Hummer)
- **1 2-lb. lobster, cooked (see index)**
- **salt and pepper**
- **lemon juice**
- **bread crumbs**
- **2 egg yolks, beaten**
- **fat**

Remove lobster meat, cutting tail section in quarters and leaving claws whole. Season and sprinkle with lemon juice. Dip in bread crumbs, egg yolks, and bread crumbs again. Fry in deep fat. Drain on absorbent paper and serve.
Serves 2.

BUTTER SAUCE
(Buttersauce)
- **3 tbls. flour**
- **4 tbls. butter**
- **2 cups water**
- **salt and pepper**
- **2 egg yolks, beaten, or ½ cup cream**

Brown flour in butter over medium heat. Add water gradually, stirring constantly to form a smooth sauce. Season and continue stirring until sauce thickens. The sauce may be enriched by adding egg yolks or cream which should be well blended.

POULTRY

CHICKEN FRICASSEE
(Hühnerfrikassee)
- **1 5-lb. stewing chicken**
- **salt**
- **lemon juice**
- **salted water**
- **4 tbls. butter**
- **1 cup beef stock**
- **2 tbls. flour**
- **1 cup mushrooms**
- **salt and pepper**
- **1 tsp. lemon juice**
- **4 tbls. white wine**
- **1-2 egg yolks**
- **3 tbls. cream**

Clean chicken and rub with salt and lemon juice. Boil for five minutes in salted water. Remove and dry with towel. Melt 2 tablespoons of the butter and fry chicken lightly. Add beef stock, cover and steam until tender, 1½ to 2 hours. Add water, if needed. Remove, carve, skin if desired and keep warm. Melt remaining butter, add flour and blend, add stock and stir until thickened. Add finely chopped mushrooms, seasoning, lemon juice and wine. Thicken with egg yolks and cream. Put chicken slices in this sauce and cook briefly over low flame. Serve with noodles, or rice, and asparagus.
Serves 4-6.

FRIED CHICKEN LIVERS
(Gebratene Hühnerleber)

    1 slice bacon
    2 tbls. butter
    1 onion, chopped
    6 chicken livers
    2 tbls. flour
    1 cup Brown Sauce (see below)
    1 tsp. lemon juice
    ¼ cup mushrooms, sliced
    parlsey

Chop up bacon and fry for 5 minutes in butter. Scoop out bacon and save. Add onion and fry for 2 minutes more. Add chicken livers and fry, over moderate heat, for another 2 minutes. Blend in flour, sauce, lemon juice and mushrooms, and cook all together for a final 2 minutes. Crumble up bacon and sprinkle this and parsley over livers. Serve on a hot platter. Very good with mashed potatoes or rice.

Serves 3-4.

BROWN SAUCE

(Braune Sauce)

    3 tbls. butter
    4 tbls. flour
    1 onion, chopped
    2 cups water
    1 bay leaf
    2 cloves
    2 tbls. vinegar
    salt and pepper
    paprika

Melt butter, add flour and slowly brown. Mix in onion. Add water little by little, stirring constantly. Season. Bring to a boil. Strain before serving.

CHICKEN ON RICE WITH ASPARAGUS
(Huhn auf Reis mit Spargel)

    1 5-lb. stewing chicken
    Butter Sauce (see index)
    white wine
    salt and pepper
    nutmeg
    ½ tbls. lemon juice
    1 to 2 egg yolks
    2 lbs. asparagus
    1½ cups rice

Stew chicken until tender, 1½ to 2 hours, skin if desired and cut in slices. Prepare light sauce, using chicken stock in place of water. Add wine to taste, seasonings and lemon juice. Heat chicken in sauce, adding egg yolks to thicken just before serving. Prepare rice and asparagus. Arrange rice on a platter, with chicken on top and asparagus (in piles of 4 to 6 pieces) around this. Pour sauce over it to serve.

Serves 4.

STUFFED GOOSE
(Gefüllte Gans)

    1 goose, medium size
    salt and pepper
    lemon juice
    1 tbls. flour
    2 cups water

Clean goose thoroughly. Rub with salt, pepper and lemon juice inside and out. Let stand for 2 hours. Stuff as desired (see below), sew up incision and truss. Place in a roaster, pour on hot water, cover and let it steam until it begins to fry in its own fat. The underside near the drumstick may be pierced to release additional fat. Turn goose now and then to obtain an even brown all around. Uncover and roast in 325° oven for 1 to 2 hours, depending on age of the bird. Continue to turn and baste frequently. If a deeper, crisper brown is desired, brush with melted butter. Add flour and water to the fat and season well for gravy. Skim off any surface fat before serving. Serve with Potato Dumplings (see index) or Salted Potatoes (see index) and Red Cabbage (see index), followed by stewed fruits or berries.

    stuffings: (a)
    3 rolls
    1 cup milk
    1 onion, chopped
    1 tsp. parsley, chopped
    1 tbls. butter
    heart and liver, cooked
    2 eggs, separated
    salt, pepper and nutmeg

    stuffings:

(a) Soak rolls in milk. Press dry and pluck to pieces. Sauté onion and parsley in butter. Add rolls and remove from heat. Chop heart and liver, and blend with egg yolks. Fold in beaten egg whites. Blend well with first mixture and season to taste.

(b)

1 onion, chopped
1 tsp. parsley, chopped
1 tbls. butter
heart and liver, cooked
½ cup potatoes, boiled
1 egg, beaten
cream
salt and pepper

(b) Sauté onion and parsley in butter. Add chopped heart and liver. Dice potatoes and add, together with lightly beaten egg and cream. Season to taste.

(c)

1½ lbs. chestnuts
1 tsp. sugar
1 tbls. butter
1 cup beef stock
salt

(c) Incise chestnuts crosswise. Roast in oven and remove shells. Brown sugar lightly in butter. Add chestnuts and beef stock. Season with salt and boil 20 minutes.

ROAST DUCKLING
(Gebratene Ente)

1 5-lb. duckling
salt and pepper
2 tbls. butter
1 onion, chopped
flour
2 cups beef stock

Clean duck and rub inside and out with salt and pepper. Stuff, if desired. Chop onion and add to melted butter in Dutch oven or casserole and brown duck in this on all sides. Add meat stock or water, cover and cook until done. After liquid has evaporated, turn over now and then, adding water by spoonfuls, until duck is well done and crisp.

Alternate method: Cook on top of range until *nearly* done. Remove, pour on butter and roast uncovered in 450° oven until well done. Cooking time about one hour; if stuffed, an hour and a quarter. Remove from oven.

Prepare gravy from drippings, flour and beef stock. Serve with Red Cabbage (see index) and Salted Potatoes (see index).

stuffings:
(a)

2 small rolls
1 small onion
parsley
1 tbls. butter
liver and heart, cooked
1-2 eggs
salt and pepper
nutmeg

stuffings:

(a) Soak rolls in water. Sauté finely chopped onion and parsley in butter. Add the rolls, squeezed dry, and simmer together. Chop liver and heart; add, with eggs and seasoning, to mixture.

(b)

½ cup bread crumbs
½ cup chopped nuts
½ cup sweet cream
2 tbls. butter
dash onion juice
salt and pepper

(b) Mix all ingredients in order given.

TURKEY CROQUETTES
(Truthahnkroketten)

1 cup chopped cooked turkey
⅔ cup chopped cooked ham
6 mushrooms
2 tbls. butter
1 cup beef stock
2 tbls. butter
salt and pepper
parsley
2 eggs, separated
bread crumbs
fat

Chop turkey and ham finely and mix. Chop mushrooms and sauté in butter and add. Cook beef stock until half has evaporated. Add butter, seasoning and chopped parsley and cook for 10 minutes over slow heat. Put through strainer and thicken with egg yolks. Blend meat mixture with this sauce and let cool. Shape into croquettes. Beat egg whites stiffly and dip croquettes twice, alternately, in egg white and bread crumbs. Fry in deep fat. Serve with any kind of salad.

Serves 3-4.

MEAT

PAPRIKA CUTLET WITH CREAM
(*Paprika-Rahmschnitzel*)

¾ lb. veal cutlet, 1½-inch thick
salt
2 tbls. butter
paprika
¼ tsp. flour
2-3 tbls. cream
lemon, sliced
parsley

Pound cutlet and season with salt. Fry slowly on both sides in butter for 25 minutes. Sprinkle generously with paprika, turn over once in fat and put on a warm platter. To the fat add flour and cream. Cook together briefly and pour this sauce over cutlet. Garnish with lemon slices, topped alternately with paprika and chopped parsley. Serve with rolls or dumplings, or buttered rice and a salad.

Serves 2.

WEINER SCHNITZEL

¾ lb. veal cutlet, ½-inch thick
salt and pepper
1 egg
¼ cup bread crumbs
fat
lemon
parsley

Pound cutlet, rub in seasoning. Beat egg and dip cutlet in egg and in bread crumbs. Brown in minimum amount of melted fat over low heat, 15 minutes on each side. Schnitzel must be served dry and crisp. Garnish with lemon sections and parsley. Bundles of parsley may be fried in fat until crisp to garnish. Serve on hot platter. Serve with mixed vegetables, peas, or a mixed salad.

Serves 2.

VEAL CUTLET
(*Schnitzel, naturell*)

¾ lb. veal cutlet, ½-inch thick
1 tsp. olive oil
salt and pepper
2 tbls. butter
paprika
1 lemon quartered

Soak cutlet in milk for 10 minutes. Dry, pound lightly, brush with oil and seasoning. Fry slowly in hot butter, on both sides, for about 25 minutes. When done, sprinkle with paprika. Garnish with quartered lemon. Serve with rice, potatoes or dumplings; with cauliflower, spinach or green salad.

Serves 2.

VEAL GOULASH
(*Kalbsgulasch*)

3-lb. breast of boned veal
2 onions
3 tbls. butter
1-2 tomatoes
1 cup water
salt and pepper
paprika
3 tbls. flour
extra water

Have meat cut in large cubes. Chop onions finely and brown with meat in butter. Peel and slice tomatoes. Combine with onion and meat, add water and seasoning. Cover and stew until done, about 1½ hours. Just before it is done, remove cover and let water evaporate. Sprinkle in flour and brown. Add water enough to make suitable amount of gravy. Serve with potatoes or dumplings, and a salad.

Serves 4.

VEAL KIDNEYS
(*Kalbsnieren*)

2 veal kidneys
4 tbls. butter
salt and pepper
1 tbls. flour
1 cup water

Slice kidneys and their fat. Fry in butter over strong heat until done, about 8 minutes. Season and serve. Or remove from fat, add flour and water and cook briefly. Season and pour over kidneys. Serve with mashed potatoes.

Serves 4.

STUFFED BREAST OF VEAL
(Gefüllte Kalbsbrust)
    5-6 lbs. breast of veal
    salt
    lemon juice
    4 rolls
    1 cup milk
    1 onion
    1 or 2 eggs
    parsley
    salt and pepper
    1 cup (or more) beef stock
    1 onion
    1 tbls. flour
    salt, pepper, nutmeg

Have butcher make a pocket in the meat. Rub insides with salt and lemon juice. Make stuffing as follows:

Cut up rolls and simmer briefly in milk. Cool. Chop onion and cook without browning in a little fat. Add to bread mixture. Beat egg and add, with parsley and seasoning. Mix well and stuff into pocket. Sew up.

Heat beef stock. Chop second onion and add. Cook veal in stock, covered, 1¼ hours. Turn now and then and add liquid if necessary. Or roast in moderate (350°) oven for 1½ hours. Remove from pan, add flour and seasoning and as much liquid as desired for gravy. Slice meat with a very sharp knife to prevent stuffing from crumbling. Serve with Spätzle (see index) and a green salad.

Serves 6.

SAUERBRATEN
    ½ cup vinegar
    ½ cup water
    1 onion, sliced
    salt and pepper
    1 bay leaf
    1 clove
    1½ lbs. beef (shoulder)
    1 marrow bone
    2 tbls. fat
    1 onion
    1 tomato
    sauce:
        1 tbls. flour
        vinegar or lemon juice
        pinch of sugar
        salt
        butter
        cream or wine

Cook vinegar, water, sliced onion and seasoning together for 10 minutes. Steep beef in this marinade 2 to 3 days. Drain (save liquid). Brown meat and marrow bone in hot fat. Add the onion, tomato and ½ cup of the marinade, cover and simmer on top of range for 1 hour. Turn the meat in remaining liquid so that it is coated on all sides. Carve and put on a warm platter.

For sauce, mix flour with pan liquid smoothly. Add the rest of the marinade and stir until smooth and thickened. Sauerbraten sauce calls for more ample ingredients than other sauces. Add, to taste, a little vinegar or lemon juice, a pinch of sugar, salt, a little fresh butter and a tablespoon of cream or wine. Strain and pour over meat or serve as a separate sauce. Serve with potatoes, dumplings or Spätzle (see index).

Serves 3-4.

BEEF GOULASH
(Rindergulasch)
    1 lb. beef chuck, cubed
    2-3 onions
    2-3 tbls. butter
    salt and pepper
    paprika
    1 cup water
    2 tbls. flour
    1 cup beef stock
    3 tomatoes, sliced

Chop onions and brown in butter. Add meat and seasonings. Fry meat until browned. Add water, cover, and let stew for one hour. When juice has evaporated, sprinkle with flour, brown lightly; add beef stock and sliced tomatoes and cook together briefly.

Serves 2.

BAMBERGER MEAT AND CABBAGE CASSEROLE
(Bamberger Krautbraten)

- 1 small head cabbage (about 1 pound)
- 1 tablespoon vegetable oil
- 2 medium onions, chopped
- ½ pound lean pork, cubed
- 1 pound lean ground beef
- 1 teaspoon caraway seeds
- ½ teaspoon salt
- ½ teaspoon pepper
- ½ cup dry white wine
- 1 teaspoon vegetable oil
- 3 to 6 strips thickly sliced bacon

Remove outer, wilted cabbage leaves and core. Place cabbage in a large pot of boiling water and simmer gently for 10 minutes. Remove and drain. Gently pull off 12 leaves and set aside. Finely chop the rest of the cabbage.

Heat 1 tablespoon vegetable oil; add onions, pork and ground beef. Cook until lightly browned. Drain off excess fat. Add the chopped cabbage, caraway seeds, salt, and pepper. Pour in the white wine. Cover and simmer the mixture for 10 minutes, stirring often.

Grease an ovenproof dish with 1 teaspoon of vegetable oil; line the dish with half the cabbage leaves. Spoon in the meat mixture; cover with the rest of the cabbage leaves.

Cut bacon strips in half and arrange on top. Place in preheated 350°F oven; bake for approximately 45 minutes.

Makes 4 servings.

BEEF ROLLS
(Rinderrouladen)

- 4 thin slices of beef
- salt and pepper
- 4 slices bacon
- 1 onion
- 1 tbls. parsley
- 1 tbls. mustard
- 1 tbls. flour
- 2 tbls. butter
- ½ cup water
- extra flour
- 2 tbls. cream
- salt and pepper

- paprika
- 2 tbls. beef stock

Pound beef slices and rub with salt and pepper. Cut up bacon, chop onion and parsley and mix all with mustard. Spread this on beef slices and roll up tightly. Tie with string. Dip rolls in flour and fry in butter, to brown all sides. Add water and stew for 30 minutes. When water has evaporated, turn rolls once again. Remove, untie and place on hot platter. To "Bratensatz" in pan, add flour, cream, seasonings and beef stock to make gravy. Pour over meat. Serve with Salted Potatoes (see index) and a salad.

Serves 4.

BEEF ROAST WITH MUSHROOM STUFFING
(Rostbraten mit Pilzfülle)

- ½ teaspoon salt
- ¼ teaspoon white pepper
- 2 pounds flank steak
- 1 teaspoon Dijon-style
- mustard
- **mushroom stuffing:**
  - 2 tablespoons vegetable oil
  - 1 small onion, chopped
  - 4-ounce can mushroom pieces, drained and chopped
  - ¼ cup chopped parsley
  - 2 tablespoons chopped chives
  - 1 tablespoon tomato paste
  - ¼ cup dried bread crumbs
  - ¼ teaspoon salt
  - ¼ teaspoon pepper
  - 1 teaspoon paprika
- **gravy:**
  - 3 strips bacon, cubed
  - 2 small onions, finely chopped
  - 1 cup hot beef broth
  - 1 teaspoon Dijon-style mustard
  - 2 tablespoons tomato catsup

Lightly salt and pepper flank steak on both sides. Spread one side with mustard.

To prepare stuffing, heat vegetable oil in a frypan, add onion, and cook for 3 minutes, until lightly browned. Add mushroom pieces; cook for 5 minutes. Stir in parsley, chives, tomato paste, and bread crumbs. Season with salt, pepper, and paprika.

Spread stuffing on mustard side of flank steak, roll

up jelly-roll fashion, and tie with thread or string.

To prepare gravy, cook bacon in a Dutch oven until partially done. Add the meat roll and brown on all sides, approximately 10 minutes. Add the onions and sauté for 5 minutes. Pour in beef broth, cover Dutch oven and simmer for 1 hour. Remove meat to a preheated platter. Season pan juices with mustard. Salt and pepper to taste; stir in catsup.

Serve the gravy separately.

Makes 6 servings.

OX-TAIL RAGOUT
(Ochsenschweifragout)

    1 oxtail
    water to cover
    ½ tsp. salt
    2 onions
    3 turnips
    2 tomatoes
    1 stalk celery
    2 tbls. butter
    ½ cup white wine
    1 bay leaf
    2 cloves
    salt and pepper
    paprika
    flour

Have oxtail cut in pieces the size of links of its bones. Cook 5 minutes in salted water. Dry in a strainer. Dice vegetables. Melt butter and add meat and vegetables, and fry. Add wine, seasonings, some soup stock, if necessary, to cover meat. Cover and cook 2 to 3 hours, until done. Remove meat. Add flour to juice to prepare smooth gravy. Add more wine and further seasoning, to taste. Pour over meat. Serve with Spätzle (see index) or mashed potatoes.

Serves 4.

PORK CHOPS
(Schweinekoteletten auf drierlei Art)

    4 pork chops
    salt and pepper
    1 egg, beaten
    bread crumbs
    1 tbls. butter

Here are three methods for cooking pork chops:

1. Rub chops generously on both sides with salt and pepper. Dip in egg and in bread crumbs. Fry slowly in butter until crisp and thoroughly done.

2. Season chops well and fry slowly in butter until crisp.

3. Broil chops slowly on both sides 5 inches from heat. Season well when done. Serve with Potato Salad (see index) or cooked carrots and mixed vegetables.

Serves 4.

PORK SCHNITZEL
(Schweineschnitzel)

    4-8 loin pork chops
    salt and pepper
    2 tbls. butter
    1 onion, sliced

Pound chops lightly and season. Fry in butter, with onion, on both sides, quickly over high heat. Reduce heat, cover and let simmer 20 minutes more. Serve with Salted Potatoes (see index) and vegetables.

Serves 4.

KASSELER ROAST RIBS OF PORK
(Kasseler Rippenspeer)

    2-3 lbs. smoked pork rib roast
    1 onion
    1 tomato
    1 celery knob, chopped
    1 truffle
    1 tbls. butter
    1 cup water
    1 tbls. flour
    ½ cup water
    ½ cup sour cream
    salt and pepper

Scrub the meat, then set in a roasting pan with the onion, tomato, celery, truffle, butter and water. Cover and steam for 1½ hours. When the water has evaporated, turn and brown the meat in the pan fat on all sides. Remove meat and keep it hot. Add flour and water to make gravy, add cream and, if desired, further seasoning. Strain the sauce over the roast and serve. Serve with spring potatoes, sprinkled with chopped parsley, and kale; or mashed potatoes and a green salad.

Serves 4-6.

MUTTON OR LAMB CHOPS
(Hammelkoteletten)

4-8 mutton or lamb chops
1 clove garlic
1 tbls. oil
salt and pepper
1 onion, sliced
4 tomatoes
1 tbls. flour

Rub chops with garlic, sprinkle with oil and seasonings. With slices of onion and whole tomatoes, broil at high heat for 10-15 minutes. Add flour to drippings and prepare gravy. Lamb chops may also be fried in butter. They should always be crisp on the outside, but a bit rare inside. Serve with Salted Potatoes (see index) and green beans.

Serves 4.

SMOKED HAM IN DOUGH
(Schinken in Brotteig)

1 smoked ham
Mellow Dough, Neutral (see index)

Soak ham overnight in water to cover and remove skin. Or use a ready-to-eat ham and remove skin. Dry well. Prepare dough and wrap it around ham. Bake about three hours in a fairly hot (375° - 400°) oven. To serve, cut away crust (with a very sharp knife to prevent crumbling). Slice ham and serve hot or cold, garnished with pieces of the crust.

MUTTON RAGOUT À LA BONNE FEMME
(Hammelragout Bonne Femme)

1 onion
2 tbls. butter
3 lbs. breast or neck of mutton
1 bud garlic, chopped
salt and pepper
1 tbls. flour
½ cup water
¼ cup white wine
1 tbls. lemon juice
1 tbls. ketchup or tomato sauce
½ lb. each carrots, new potatoes and green peas

Slice onion and fry lightly in butter to a golden brown. Cut mutton in large cubes, add chopped garlic and seasoning. Add to onions and fry lightly. Sprinkle with flour, add water, wine, lemon juice and tomato sauce or ketchup. Cover and cook 1½ hours. Slice carrots (or cut in strips) and add to stew. Add potatoes and cook another 15 minutes. Add green peas and cook until they are done, about 15 minutes. Serve meat on a hot platter surrounded by vegetables.

Serves 3.

MELLOW DOUGH, NEUTRAL
(Mürberteig)

1 cup flour
¼ lb. butter
4 tbls. milk
2 tbls. sugar
pinch of salt
1 tsp. baking powder

Mix all ingredients and, on a bread board, knead to a supple dough. Roll out and use as instructed in specific recipe. In view of the large butter content of this dough, it should be thoroughly cooled before baking.

LOIN OF VENISON
(Rehrücken)

1 loin of venison, 7 to 9 lbs.
salt and pepper
vinegar, or milk to cover, to soak
4 strips of bacon
1 onion, sliced
6 tbls. butter
1 cup beef stock
1 cup sour cream
1 lemon, sliced
2 tbls. flour
1 tsp. lemon juice
1 cup beef stock
1 tsp. cream
½ cup red wine

Deer meat should always be hung in a cool place to age. The longer it ages, the greater its tenderness. One to two weeks is suggested. Ribs, on the loin, may be shortened to give meat a more tractable shape. Rub with salt and pepper, wrap in a cloth soaked in vinegar and store in refrigerator overnight. Or soak overnight in milk. Lard with slivers of bacon, or wrap with sliced bacon. Fry venison, with onion, in butter until slightly brown. Add beef stock, cover and cook over low heat for ¾ hour. Uncover, baste with fat and place in a hot oven (450°) until well browned and crisp, about 15 minutes. Pour on most of the cream and keep in hot oven a little longer. Venison should remain slightly rosy inside. Pour a little of the drippings over the meat and garnish with slices of lemon. Add flour, lemon juice, beef stock, cream and wine to the remaining drippings to prepare a rich gravy, which is served in a separate gravy boat.

Serves 8-10.

VENISON FILLETS
(Rehfilet vom Grill)

>   **2 lbs. fillet of venison**
>   **¼ lb. bacon**
>   **salt and pepper**
>   **½ cup olive oil**
>   **cucumber pickles (sour)**

Cut fillets into steaks, lard with slivers of bacon, season well. Soak in olive oil, turning and then letting stand for a while so that the oil sinks in. Broil under high heat, 15 minutes on each side until well browned and tender. To serve, garnish with sour pickles. Serve with potatoes or Spätzle (see index).

Serves 3-4.

VENISON SCHNITZEL
(Rehschnitzel)

>   **4 individual steaks or cutlets of venison**
>   **salt and pepper**
>   **4 tbls. butter**
>   **2 tomatoes, halved**
>   **1 onion, sliced**
>   **1 tbls. flour**
>   **3 tbls. red wine.**

Carve steaks from leg of venison. Pound well and season. In a casserole, melt butter, add tomatoes, onion and cutlets. Cook for 10 minutes. Remove meat to a hot platter, garnish with the tomatoes. To fat add flour, more salt and pepper and wine. Strain and serve over meat. Serve with mashed potatoes, Spätzle (see index) or rice.

Serves 4.

RABBIT STEW
(Hasenpfeffer)

>   **steeping liquid:**
>   **½ cup vinegar**
>   **½ cup water**
>   **1 clove**
>   **1 bay leaf**
>   **peppercorns**
>   **1 onion, sliced**
>   **salt and pepper**
>   **2 tsp. lemon juice**
>   **1 hare or rabbit, cut up, with giblets**
>   **4 tbls. butter**
>   **4 tbls. flour**

Cook steeping ingredients together 5 minutes. Pour over meat and let soak for 2 days. Fry briefly in butter, with a little onion. Add flour and let brown. Add ½ cup of steeping liquid, cover and stew until tender, about 1½ hours. If necessary, replenish liquid.

Serves 4.

DUMPLINGS

BAVARIAN BREAD DUMPLINGS
(Bayerische Semmelklösse)

>   **10 white rolls**
>   **1-2 cups milk**
>   **½ cup bacon or ham**
>   **1 tbls. butter**
>   **1 small onion, chopped**
>   **1 tbls. parsley, chopped**
>   **3 eggs**
>   **salt and pepper**
>   **nutmeg**

Slice rolls finely and soak in lukewarm milk. Bread should be moist but not soggy. Dice bacon or ham and fry in butter together with chopped onion and parsley. Add eggs and seasonings to bread slices and combine with fried ingredients. Shape into dumplings. Cook in salt water for 20 minutes. Serve immediately.

Serves 4.

POTATO DUMPLINGS
(Gekochte Kartoffelklosse)

2 lbs. potatoes
2 cups flour
2 eggs
salt
nutmeg
2 slices bread
1 tbls. butter

Cook potatoes the day before in their skins. Next day peel and mash potatoes. Add flour, eggs and seasoning and knead to a firm dough. Cube bread and fry lightly in butter. Shape dumplings, bore a hole in each and put in several fried bread cubes. Close over the hole. Drop into boiling salted water and cook 10 to 15 minutes. Try one test dumpling in the water; if it falls apart, work more flour into the dough.

Serves 4.

SPÄTZLE

4 cups flour
3 eggs
1 cup water
1 tbls. salt

Prepare a firm dough from the flour, eggs, water and salt. Beat until it comes easily away from the sides of the bowl. Form dumplings and cook in boiling salted water. Skim them out, dip in cold water and serve on a hot platter. Spätzle may also be browned lightly in butter before serving. A favorite accompaniment to meat and vegetables.

Serves 4.

POTATOES

SALTED POTATOES
(Salzkartoffeln)

2 lbs. potatoes
1 tbls. salt

Peel raw potatoes and cut in wedges. Place in cold salted water. Cover and cook until done, about 20 minutes. Drain immediately to prevent crumbling. Replace in pot and shake around, over low heat, to dry.

Serves 4-6.

ALSATIAN FRIED POTATOES
(Pommes frites)

4 large potatoes
fat, to cover
salt, to taste

Pare raw potatoes and cut lengthwise in strips ½ inch thick. Dry thoroughly in a towel. Fry small quantities at a time in hot deep fat, using a spatula to keep pieces from sticking together. When potatoes are golden brown, remove to strainer to drain, then sprinkle with salt. *Note:* When preparing large quantities, the small initial lots may be fried lightly and stored in a strainer. Finish larger lots as above, in deep fat. It is practical to use a wire French fryer.

Serves 4.

CREAMED POTATOES
(Rahmkartoffeln)

6 potatoes
2 tbls. butter
3 tbls. flour
1 cup cream
1 tbls. parsley, chopped
nutmeg, to taste
salt and pepper

Select firm potatoes. Cook until tender. Peel and slice fairly thick. Melt butter, add flour, cream, parsley and seasoning. Heat potatoes thoroughly in this sauce. Recipe may be varied by substituting grated cheese for parsley.

Serves 4-6.

POTATO CROQUETTES
(Kartoffelkroketten)

4 large potatoes
3 tbls. butter
1 egg (whole)
1 egg, separated
salt
nutmeg
flour, as needed
1 cup bread crumbs
deep fat

Cook potatoes, peel while hot, and grate. Melt butter over low heat. Mix with potatoes, egg and egg yolk, and seasoning. Let batter stand to cool. Flour a bread board, turn out batter and form into patties, adding flour if needed. Beat egg white, dip patties in it, then in bread crumbs. Fry in deep fat until well browned.

Serves 4.

VEGETABLES

SPINACH
(Spinat)

> 1 lb. spinach
> ½ tsp. salt, in water to cover
> pinch of baking soda
> 2 tbls. butter
> 1 tbls. flour
> 1 cup or more water or milk
> cream
> ½ bud garlic, crushed
> salt and pepper

Wash spinach thoroughly and drop into boiling water. Add a dash of baking soda. Bring again to a boil and cook briefly, about 3 to 5 minutes. It is very important not to overcook spinach, as it turns brown and bitter. Strain off liquid and put spinach through a sieve. Prepare a light sauce with butter, flour, a little of the cooking water or milk. Add cream to desired consistency. Season and serve.

Serves 2.

CASSEROLE BAKED BEANS
(Bohnenkerne)

> 1 lb. dried peas or beans
> dash of salt
> 1 bay leaf
> 4 medium tomatoes, sliced
> 4 strips bacon
> 1 onion, sliced
> ½ cup cheese, grated

Soak dried peas or navy beans overnight. Cook in salted water, together with bay leaf, until soft, 2 to 3 hours. Arrange alternating layers of beans, sliced tomatoes, lightly fried bacon and sliced onions in a buttered casserole. Top with grated cheese, dot with butter and bake in hot (400°) oven until nicely browned, about 20 minutes.

Serves 4.

KOHLRABI

> 4 kohlrabi
> 1 tsp. salt
> pinch of baking soda
> 2 tbls. butter
> 1 tbls. flour
> 1 cup beef stock
> salt, pepper, nutmeg to taste
> 1 tbls. chopped parsley
> 2 tbls. cream

Remove tender leaves from stalks and cook in salted water with a pinch of baking soda. Rinse in cold water, drain well and chop finely. Pare and slice the tubers. Cook in lightly salted water until done, 25 to 30 minutes. Prepare a light sauce from butter, flour, beef stock, seasonings and cream. Add sliced kohlrabi and bring to a boil again. Either add chopped, cooked greens to this or serve separately, with greens surrounding tubers.

Serves 4.

RED CABBAGE
(Rotkraut)

> 2 lbs. red cabbage
> 1 apple
> 2 tbls. butter
> 1 bay leaf
> salt and pepper
> juniper berries
> 1 tbls. flour
> ½ cup red wine
> 1 tsp. apple or juniper jelly
> 1-2 cloves

Prepare like Bavarian Cabbage (see index) but use red instead of white wine and, to taste, add apple or juniper jelly and cloves instead of sugar and vinegar.

Serves 4.

BAVARIAN CABBAGE
(Bayerisches Kraut)

> 2 lbs. cabbage
> 1 apple
> 2 tbls. butter
> 1 bay leaf
> salt and pepper
> juniper berries
> 1 tbls. flour

½ cup white wine
sugar
vinegar

Wash and shred cabbage. Slice apple. Melt butter in pan and add cabbage and apple. Mix thoroughly. Season well with bay leaf, salt, pepper and a few juniper berries. Cook in one cup of water, more if needed, over low heat until done, about 10 minutes. When liquid has evaporated, sprinkle with flour, add wine and sugar and vinegar to taste. Serve immediately.

Serves 4.

WESTPHALIAN CABBAGE
(Kohl Westfälisch)
   1 head cabbage, approximately 2 pounds
   3 tablespoons vegetable oil
   1 teaspoon salt
   1 teaspoon caraway seeds
   1 cup hot beef broth
   2 to 3 small tart apples
   1 tablespoon cornstarch
   2 tablespoons cold water
   3 tablespoons red wine vinegar
   ¼ teaspoon sugar

Shred cabbage.

Heat vegetable oil in Dutch oven, add cabbage, and sauté for 5 minutes. Season with salt and caraway seeds. Pour in beef broth, cover, and simmer over low heat about 15 minutes.

Meanwhile, peel, quarter, core, and cut apples into thin wedges. Add to cabbage and simmer for another 30 minutes.

Blend cornstarch with cold water, add to cabbage, and stir until thickened and bubbly. Season with vinegar and sugar just before serving.

Makes 4 to 6 servings.

LEEKS
(Lauchgemüse)
   6 leeks
   ½ tsp. salt in water to cover
   2 tbls. butter
   2 tbls. flour
   ½ cup milk
   ½ cup (or more) cooking water
   salt and pepper

nutmeg
2 tbls. cream

Remove green parts from stalks, cut the rest in finger-thick slices and grate. Cook 10 minutes in boiling salted water. Drain, reserving water. Prepare a light sauce from butter, flour and milk, thin with vegetable water to desired consistency, and season. Add leeks to sauce and heat through. Add cream and serve hot.

Serves 4.

OPORTO ONIONS
(Oportozweibeln)
   4 large onions
   salted water or beef stock, to cover
   3 tbls. butter

Remove outer skins of onions. Cook in salted water or beef stock about 40 minutes. Pour on melted butter to serve.

Variation: Cook 4 large onions 20 minutes. Halve, hollow out and stuff with chopped meat. Place in greased baking dish. Add 1 cup beef stock. Sprinkle with grated cheese, dot with butter and bake in 400° oven until well browned, 20 to 25 minutes. The insides of onions may be sliced and fried for a subsequent meal.

Serves 4.

SAUERKRAUT
   2 lbs. cabbage
   3 tbls. butter
   1 onion, chopped
   apple, sliced
   salt and pepper
   1 potato, raw
   ½ cup white wine

Pluck apart cabbage and wash well. Shred. Melt butter in a fairly large pot and turn cabbage in it thoroughly. Add onion, apple and seasoning to taste. Fill pot with water. Cook until tender, about 10 minutes. Grate into this raw potato, to give a nice texture. Add wine before serving.

Variation: Instead of wine, paprika, sugar and cream may be used to season. Or champagne may be substituted for white wine. This last is particularly good when served with venison or pheasant.

Serves 4.

GLAZED CHESTNUTS
(Glasierte Kastanien)

- **1 lb. chestnuts**
- **1 tbls. sugar**
- **1 tbls. butter**
- **2 tbls. beef gravy**
- **beef stock or water**
- **salt**

Rub chestnuts with oil and bake in oven until shells crack. Shell and soak in water until skin loosens. Peel. Lightly brown sugar and butter and turn chestnuts in this mixture. Add gravy and enough beef stock (or water) to cover. Season to taste. Cover and steam until chestnuts are tender and glazed.

Serves 4-6.

SALADS AND SALAD DRESSINGS

RED BEET SALAD
(Rote Rübensalat)

- **1 lb. red beets**
- **4 tbls. vinegar**
- **4 tbls. water**
- **½ tsp. sugar**
- **2 tsp. caraway seeds**
- **1 small onion, chopped**
- **1 tsp. cloves, ground**
- **1 bay leaf**
- **salt and pepper**
- **3-4 tbls. olive oil**

Scrub beets and cook in salted water until tender. Dip in cold water, peel and slice thinly. From other ingredients, prepare a marinade, smoothing it out with oil to taste. Pour marinade over beets and let soak for several hours.

Serves 4.

ENDIVE OR CHICORY SALAD WITH ORANGES
(Endiven oder Chicoréesalat mit Orangen)

- **2 large Belgian endives**
- **1 orange, seedless**
- **½ cup sweet cream**
- **1 tbls. mustard**
- **salt and pepper**

Remove outer leaves, using only those that are white. Cut leaves in half, along center. Place on plat-

ter. Peel oranges, removing inner white skin. Shred peels and cook for 5 minutes to eliminate any bitterness. Dry and Cool. Mix cream with mustard, salt and pepper and pour this marinade over endive. Sprinkle with shredded orange peels. Slice remainder of orange and garnish salad with orange slices. (Chicory may be substituted for the endive.)

Serves 4.

POTATO SALAD
(Kartoffelsalat)

- **2 lbs. potatoes**
- **4 tbls. olive oil or bacon fat**
- **2 tbls. vinegar**
- **1 cup beef stock**
- **1 small onion, chopped**
- **salt and pepper**

Select good firm potatoes. Cook until tender. Peel and slice. When cool, sprinkle with oil or bacon fat and vinegar; add beef stock, onion and seasoning. Mix carefully and let stand overnight or for several hours. Before serving add a dash of pepper and a few drops of olive oil or beef stock.

Serves 4.

HAMBURG-STYLE FISH SALAD
(Hamburger Fischsalat)

- **1 tablespoon butter**
- **1 pound white fish fillets, fresh or frozen (cod, turbot, or haddock)**
- **½ cup hot water**
- **4 hard-cook eggs**
- **2 dill pickles**
- **1 tablespoon capers**
- **sauce:**
  - **2 tablespoons mayonnaise**
  - **2 tablespoons sour cream**
  - **2 teaspoons lemon juice**
  - **1 teaspoon Dijon-style mustard**
  - **½ teaspoon salt**
  - **¼ teaspoon white pepper**
- **garnish:**
  - **1 hard-cooked egg**
  - **4 slices canned beets**

Melt butter in frypan. Place fish in frypan and pour hot water over fish. Bring to a boil, cover, lower heat, and simmer gently for 10 minutes. Meanwhile, slice 4 hard-cooked eggs and the pickles.

(continued on p. 237)

bamberger meat and cabbage casserole (see recipe page 225)

hamburg-style (see recipe page 232)
fish salad

(see recipe page 237)
sauerkraut salad with ham

picture on opposite page: (see recipe page 225)
beef roast with mushroom stuffing

westphalian cabbage
(see recipe page 231)

235

apple cake (see recipe page 246)

(continued from p. 232)

Drain fish, cool, and cut into cubes.

Prepare salad sauce by blending mayonnaise, sour cream, lemon juice, mustard, salt, and pepper.

In a separate bowl gently mix fish cubes, egg and pickle slices, and capers. Arrange fish mixture in individual dishes and spoon salad sauce over tops. Chill for 30 minutes.

To garnish, cut remaining egg into eight pieces and chop beet slices. Arrange garnish on each serving. Serve immediately. Makes 4 servings.

CABBAGE SALAD
(Krautsalat)

1 medium head of red or white cabbage
3 tbls. oil or 2 strips of bacon, chopped
½ cup vinegar
½ cup water
salt and pepper
caraway seeds

Shred cabbage as finely as possible. Soak for 10 minutes in boiling water. Drain. Prepare a marinade with oil and seasoning and let cabbage soak in this for an hour or more. If bacon is substituted for oil, prepare marinade from vinegar, water and seasoning. Fry bacon lightly and add bacon and fat, while still hot, just before serving.

Serves 4.

SAUERKRAUT SALAD WITH HAM
(Sauerkrautsalat mit Schinken)

1 16-ounce can sauerkraut
½ pound blue grapes
6 ounces cooked ham
dressing:
   ½ cup yogurt
   ¼ teaspoon salt
   ¼ teaspoon white pepper
   1 teaspoon honey

Rinse and drain sauerkraut; chop coarsely. Wash grapes and cut in half; remove seeds if desired. Cut ham in julienne strips. Gently mix these 3 ingredients.

Blend dressing ingredients and stir into sauerkraut mixture. Marinate for 10 minutes; adjust seasoning before serving, if necessary. Makes 4 servings.

DRIED BEAN SALAD
(Kernbohnensalat)

½ lb. dried white beans
3 tbls. vinegar
3 tbls. water
1 cup beef stock
salt and pepper
1 bud garlic, crushed
1-2 strips bacon

Wash beans and let soak in water overnight. Next day, cook until tender, about 2 to 3 hours. From the remaining ingredients, except bacon, prepare a marinade. Pour this over the beans and let soak in well. Chop bacon and fry to a light brown. Just before serving, pour bacon grease and chopped bacon over beans.

Serves 4.

BEAN SALAD
(Bohnensalat)

1 lb. green beans
3 tbls. olive oil
3 tbls. vinegar
3 tabls. beef stock
1 onion, sliced
pinch of dill
salt and pepper

Slice beans lengthwise and cut in half. Cook in salted water until tender. Prepare marinade of remaining ingredients. Pour over beans and let soak in well. Additional beef stock may be added for extra juiciness.

Serves 4.

CREAM DRESSING
(Rahmmarinade)

1 tsp. mustard, prepared
1 tsp. salt
1½ tsp. confectioner's sugar
dash of pepper
1 tbls. flour
1 tsp. butter
1 egg yolk
⅓ cup vinegar
½ cup heavy cream, whipped

In double boiler, over hot, not boiling, water, beat mustard, salt, sugar, pepper, flour and butter. Add egg yolk and vinegar and continue beating until mixture thickens. Remove from heat. When cool, fold in whipped cream. This dressing may be served with any vegetable, meat or green salad.

RHINELAND DRESSING
(Rhineland Marinade)

1 tbls. powdered sugar
2 tsp. Worcestershire sauce
2 tsp. tomato ketchup
1½ tbls. vinegar
1 tbls. olive oil
½ tsp. salt
¼ tsp. mustard, prepared
dash of pepper
¼ tsp. Tabasco sauce
1½ tbls. lemon juice

Blend ingredients, in the order given, and mix well. A perfect all-around dressing for vegetable, meat or fish salad.

SAUCES, ASPIC, AND BUTTERS

SAUCE BERNAISE
(Berner Sauce)

4 tbls. white wine
3 tbls. wine vinegar
1 clove
3 shallots
1 small stem tarragon
½ bay leaf
salt
peppercorns
2 egg yolks
10 tbls. butter

Bring wine, vinegar and spices to a boil. Strain. When cool, stir in egg yolks and half the butter. Place in double boiler, over hot, *not boiling*, water and gradually add remaining butter, beating constantly until thick.

REMOULADE SAUCE
(Remouladensauce)

½ cup mayonnaise
1 tsp. mustard
1 tsp. salad herbs, chopped
1 tsp. capers
1 small pickle, chopped
cream

Blend the first five ingredients and then thin with cream to desired consistency.

HORSERADISH SAUCE
(Meerrettichsauce)

2 tbls. butter
2 tbls. flour
1 cup milk
1 small onion, chopped
a few almonds, chopped
1 tsp. sugar
pinch of salt and pepper
2 tbls. horseradish

Melt butter but do not brown. Add flour and gradually stir in milk. Add chopped onion, almonds, sugar, salt and pepper. Cook together for 15 minutes, over low heat or in double boiler. Before serving, fold in horseradish and, if desired, enrich with a little butter or cream.

CUMBERLAND SAUCE
(Cumberlandsauce)

peel of ½ orange
3 tbls. currant jelly
2 tsp. prepared mustard
2 tbls. olive oil
dash of salt
1 tbls. lemon juice

Remove white inner layer from orange peel. Chop peel finely and scald. Melt currant jelly over low heat. Add mustard and all other ingredients and stir sauce to a smooth texture. Popular with venison and other game, and with cold fish.

SAUCE RAVIGOTE
(Ravigotesauce)
2 tbls. prepared mustard
2 tbls. vinegar
2 tbls. olive oil
salt and pepper to taste
2 tbls. parsley, chopped
1 tbls. chervil, dried
2 yolks of hard-cooked eggs, chopped

Mix mustard, vinegar, oil, salt and pepper. Stir in chopped parsley, chervil and egg yolks.

BROWN BUTTER
(Braune Butter)
¼ lb. butter

Melt butter in small pan over moderate, heat, as above, but allow it to turn *light* brown.

HERB BUTTER
(Krauterbutter)
2 cups assorted herbs, chopped
2 leaves of spinach
1 shallot
1 bud garlic
juice of ½ lemon
salt
7 tbls. butter

Boil herbs briefly, drain, dry in towel and chop finely. Chop spinach leaves and shallots with garlic, lemon juice, salt and herbs. Put all through a strainer. Cream butter and add.

MUSTARD BUTTER
(Senfbutter)
1 hard-cooked egg yolk
4 tbls. butter
1 tbls. prepared mustard
1 tbls. lemon juice
salt and pepper

Press egg yolk through strainer and mix well with all other ingredients.

MOUSSELINE SAUCE
(Mousselinsauce)
2 egg yolks
1 tbls. flour
1 tbls. butter
salt and pepper
lemon juice
1 cup heavy cream, whipped

Beat egg yolks, flour, butter and seasoning to a heavy froth in top of double boiler over hot, not boiling, water. Just before serving add lemon juice to taste and fold in whipped cream.

TARTAR SAUCE
(Tartarsauce)
1 tbls. vinegar
1 tsp. lemon juice
¼ tsp. salt
1 tbls. Worcestershire Sauce
⅓ cup butter

Mix vinegar, lemon juice, salt and Worcestershire sauce in small bowl. Heat in top of double boiler. Brown butter and fold into sauce just before serving.

ASPIC
(Aspik)
2 cups white wine
2 cups water
Maggi
pinch of salt
4 tbls. vinegar
2½ envelopes gelatine in ½ cup water

Bring wine, water, Maggi, salt and vinegar to a boil. Dissolve gelatine in ½ cup water and mix with liquid. Turn out in large, shallow pan and cool. Cut into cubes.

Aspic is a fine garnish for cold meat platters, patties and salads. Aspic may also be used to prepare jellied meat: Fill individual molds (or one large mold) ½ inch deep with liquid aspic. Chill. On this put cold cuts, sliced hard-cooked eggs, pickles, tomatoes, cooked peas, beans or any desired filling. Then fill mold with liquid aspic and chill. Dip dishes in hot water and loosen edges of aspic with a knife to turn out easily.

LUNCHEON DISHES AND OTHER SPECIALTIES

RAGOUT IN SHELLS
(Ragout fin in Muscheln)
1 small ox tongue
1 onion
1 bay leaf
salt
1 sweetbread
1 cup mushrooms
4-5 tbls. butter
3 anchovies
2 tbls. flour
½ cup white wine
1 egg yolk
lemon juice
patty shells
1 cup grated cheese
extra butter
lemon slices and parsley

Cook ox tongue with seasonings for about an hour, or until skin peels off easily. Save water. Skin and dice. Blanch sweetbreads. Add mushrooms and butter and stew for 10 minutes. Chop finely. Chop anchovies and mix them and the diced tongue with the sweetbreads and mushrooms. Stir flour into wine, add one cup of cooking water. Blend with ragout and cook all ingredients together briefly. Season to taste and add some lemon juice; thicken with egg yolk. Turn out into shells. Sprinkle with grated cheese, butter and more lemon juice and bake in a hot (425°) oven until cheese is brown, 5 to 10 minutes. Garnish platter with lemon slices and parsley.
Serves 4.

PATTY SHELLS
(Pastetchen)
Laminated Dough
(see index)

Prepare dough in 4 to 6 "courses." Roll out 1/6 inch thick. Cut out 2-inch rounds, preferably with a wavy-edged cutter. Place half of these, upside down, on a wet or greased baking sheet. Form rings of the other half, by cutting out centers. Brush underside of rings with egg white, being careful egg white does not run over edges, as dough will not rise properly in such spots. The little round centers of the ring can be

used to top the filling. Brush patty and cover with egg yolk and bake in hot (400°) oven for 25 minutes, until golden brown. Fill while still hot and serve.
Makes 12-14.

POULTRY PIE
(Geflügelpastete)
1¼ lbs. poultry meat
2 tbls. flour
1 tbls. butter
1 cup water
4 eggs, separated
1 cup sweet cream
salt and pepper
1 tbls. butter
1 large onion
½ cup grated cheese
truffles

Grind meat of chicken, goose, turkey, duck, pheasant, partridge or any combination of same. Brown flour in butter, add water and cook to firm consistency. Strain, mix into meat, add egg yolks, cream and seasoning. Lightly brown in butter finely chopped onion and mix this, together with grated cheese and beaten egg whites, with previous mixture. Put in well-greased pie dish, put minced truffles on top and bake in a hot (425°) oven for 40 minutes. May be served hot or cold.
Serves 6.

LAMINATED (LAYERED) DOUGH
(Blätterteig)
2 cups flour
1 cup butter
1 tsp. salt
4 tbls. water

Cool ingredients thoroughly before using. Sift flour onto bread board, separate one-third of the flour and work all but a small piece of the butter into it. Form into a loaf and chill. Make a depression in center of remaining flour and into it add salt, the small piece of butter and, little by little, the water. Work this dough to the consistency of smooth butter until it comes away from board and hands easily. Form into a loaf, slash the top crosswise and chill. Let it stand 5 minutes, then roll out square. Place butter-dough in center of square and roll out both layers together tightly. Fold protruding edges of lower layer over upper layer and roll out again in a thin sheet. Fold this sheet over twice crosswise, so that are four layers, one on top of another. This completes the first "course." Chill the dough again and let stand 15 minutes. For the second "course," place dough on baking board with open side facing you and roll out, in one direction only, away from you. Roll gently, without excessive pressure. Again fold dough over twice to form four layers. This completes the second "course." Chill dough once more.

In specific recipes, roll completed dough out to required thickness, cut in required shape and place upside down on baking sheet. When instructed to brush with egg yolk or white, be careful it does not run over edges onto baking sheet, as this interferes with proper rising. Always bake in a hot oven.

Note: Cake bottoms are usually made in 3 or 4 courses, patties in from 4 to 6 courses.

HAM PIE
(Schinkenpastete)
> **Laminated Dough (see index) (using 1¼ cups flour)**
> **Filling:**
>> ½ lb. pork, cooked
>> ½ lb. veal, cooked
>> 1 roll
>> 1 onion
>> parsley
>> 2 eggs, separated
>> pinch of basil
>> 2 tbls. fat
>> 2 tsp. Madeira wine
>> 4 slices ham (measuring 2½ × 5 inches)

Prepare dough. Roll out one-half of the dough in a rectangle 6 by 11 inches. Fill as follows:

Grind meat. Soak roll in water and squeeze dry. Pluck apart. Chop onion and parsley. Add egg yolks (saving 1 tablespoon) and seasoning. Beat whites of eggs until stiff (saving 1 tablespoon) and fold in. Combine all ingredients (except ham). Place slices of ham on dough to within ½ inch of edges. Cover with mixture, then with other ham slices. Spread egg white on edges of dough. Roll out remaining dough and place in over all, pressing edges firmly together. Trim overlapping dough and from it form ¾-inch

strips to place criss-cross on top of pie. Brush with egg yolk and bake in a medium (375°) oven about 1 hour. Serve hot or cold.

Serves 6.

CHICKEN CROQUETTES, MACEDON
(Mazedonische Hühnercroquetten)
> 1 small onion
> 3 tbls. butter
> ¼ cup flour
> salt, pepper and paprika
> 1 cup chicken gravy
> 1 cup cooked chicken, diced
> 3 egg yolks
> ½ cup chopped mushrooms
> 2 eggs
> flour and bread crumbs
> fat

Chop onion and brown in butter. Add flour and seasoning. Blend well in gravy. Bring to a boil and add chicken, egg yolks and mushrooms. Cook 5 minutes. Cool. Turn out onto a plate and form into small elliptical cakes. Mix eggs, flour and crumbs. Dip cakes in this mixture. Fry in deep fat and let drain on a paper. Serve on a hot flat platter. Surround with peas, carrots and cauliflower rosettes. Garnish with parsley.

Serves 4-6.

POTATO PATTIES
(Kartoffelpastetchen)
> 4-5 medium potatoes
> ½ cup milk
> 1-2 tbls. butter
> salt and nutmeg
> **Filling:**
>> 1 roll
>> 2 tbls. milk
>> 1 onion
>> 1 tbls. parsley
>> 1 tbls. butter
>> ½ cup chopped roast veal
>> 3 tbls. gravy of veal roast
>> 1 egg, separated
>> salt, pepper and nutmeg

Boil and mash potatoes. Mix with milk, butter, and seasonings to make a thick batter (potato purée). Butter a baking sheet. Make 8 little round cakes from dough. With cake decorator form rims around edges and bake until light brown. Make filling as follows:

Soak roll in milk, squeeze dry, break up. Chop onion and parsley and cook in butter. Add veal, gravy, beaten yolk, beaten white and seasoning. Put in patties and bake in a medium (375°) oven until well browned.

Serves 4.

DRIED PEAS, THE BERLIN WAY
(Löffelerbsen nach Berliner Art)

1 lb. dried peas
1 onion
1 leak
1 small celery knob
1 tbls. butter
1 lb. pig's ear and snout
thyme or marjoram
salt and pepper
2 potatoes, raw, chopped fine

Soak peas overnight. Dice other vegetables and sauté lightly in butter in a fairly large pan. Add peas and fill up with water. Cook one hour, add meat, cubed, and seasoning and continue cooking until tender, 2 to 3 hours in all. To bind, add raw potatoes 20 minutes before serving.

Serves 4.

CABBAGE ROLLS
(Krautwickel)

1 head cabbage
1 lb. mixed ground meat (beef and pork)
1 egg
1 onion, chopped
1 tsp. parsley, chopped
1 tsp. butter
1 cup beef stock
1 tbls. flour
4 tbls. cream

Remove large outer leaves of cabbage, flatten out ribs and cook in salted water 2 to 3 minutes. Drain and spread out on table. Chop small leaves finely and mix with meat, egg, onion and parsley for stuffing. Spread stuffing on large leaves, roll up and tie. Fry rolls briefly in butter, pour on beef stock, cover and let simmer over low heat for 1 hour. Or simmer

for ¾ hour and bake in moderate (350°) oven for 15 minutes. Place on hot platter. Add flour and cream to pan to prepare gravy. Pour over rolls to serve. Serve with Salted Potatoes (see index)

Serves 4.

STUFFED CABBAGE
(Gefüllter Krautkopf)

1 head cabbage
1½ lbs. ground meat, mixed beef and pork
1 roll, soaked, squeezed dry and broken up
1 tsp. parsley, chopped
1 onion, chopped
1 egg
salt and pepper

Break off leaves of cabbage, flatten thick ribs, and cook in salted water 2 to 3 minutes. Drain and spread out to cool. Mix meat, roll, parsley, onion, egg and seasoning. Moisten with water. Dip a napkin in hot water and spread it out in a medium-sized bowl. Place cabbage leaves on napkin so that tips of leaves overlap in the center. Alternate layers of stuffing and leaves. Lift the four corners of the napkin and tie in a sling. Place a wooden kitchen spoon across the top of cooking pot and suspend sling from this so napkin will be nearly submerged in cooking water. Simmer for about 1½ hours. Untie napkin and turn stuffed cabbage out on a hot platter.

Serves 4.

HUNGARIAN GOULASH
(Ungarischer Gulasch-Eintopf)

2 lbs. stew beef
¼ lb. pork fat
1 lb. onions, chopped fine
salt
2 tbls. paprika
1½ lbs. potatoes

Cut up meat in rather large cubes. Melt fat in large pot and sauté onions. Salt the meat and add, letting it fry until fat is absorbed. Sprinkle generously with paprika. Pour on water to cover, cover and stew 1½ hours. Peel potatoes, cut into thin wedges, add to stew, cook ½ hour longer or until meat is tender. Add more water if necessary.

Serves 6.

KONIGSBERGER MEAT BALLS
(Königsberger Klopse)

- **1 roll**
- **1 lb. ground meat, mixed beef and pork**
- **3 potatoes, cooked and mashed**
- **2 anchovies, chopped**
- **1 egg**
- **flour, to bind**
- **3 tbls. butter**
- **2 tbls. flour**
- **1 cup beef stock**
- **capers**
- **juice of ½ lemon**
- **salt and pepper**

Soak roll in water, squeeze dry and break up. Add meat, potatoes, anchovies, egg and flour to bind. Knead mixture for 5 minutes and shape into balls. Tumble in flour and drop into salted hot water. Simmer for 12 to 15 minutes. From butter, flour and beef stock, prepare a light sauce. When smooth add capers and lemon juice. Season and bring to a boil. Let meat balls soak briefly in this before serving. Serve with Salted Potatoes (see index).

Serves 4.

STUFFED TOMATOES
(Gefüllte Tomaten)

- **12 Tomatoes**
- **Rice Filling:**
  - **2 cups rice, cooked**
  - **2 tbls. butter**
  - **tomato pulp**
  - **salt and pepper**
  - **2 tbls. cheese, grated**
  - **extra butter**
- **Cheese Filling:**
  - **2 tbls. flour**
  - **2 tbls. butter**
  - **tomato pulp**
  - **4 tbls. cheese, grated**
  - **1½ cups milk**
  - **2 eggs, separated**

Cut off tops of tomatoes and scoop out pulp. Cook pulp down, strain and blend with desired filling:

Rice filling: Mix rice, butter, tomato pulp and seasonings. Stuff tomato shells with mixture, sprinkle with cheese, dot with butter. Either steam, covered, in butter or bake in moderate (350°) oven until well browned, 30 to 40 minutes.

Cheese Filling: Brown flour in butter over low heat, add tomato pulp and cheese and moisten gradually with milk, blending well. Heat thoroughly but do not boil. Remove from heat and let cool. Stir in egg yolks, fold in beaten egg whites and stuff into tomato shells. Bake in moderate (350°) oven 30 to 40 minutes. Serve with green salad or vegetables.

Serves 6-12.

STUFFED CUCUMBERS
(Gurken, gefüllt)

- **4 medium cucumbers or 2 large cucumbers**
- **4 rolls**
- **1 cup milk**
- **2 tbls. butter**
- **1 tbls. onions, chopped**
- **1 tsp. parsley, chopped**
- **2 eggs, separated**
- **salt and pepper**
- **½ cup beef stock**
- **4 slices bacon, cooked lightly or ¼ lb. ground meat, optional**

Pare cucumbers, always cutting toward stem end. Cut in half lengthwise and scoop out insides. Soak rolls in milk, squeeze dry and pluck to pieces. Melt butter and sauté rolls, onions and parsley. Stir in egg yolks, seasoning and beef stock and fold in beaten egg whites. Stuffing may be enriched by adding crumbled bacon or ground meat, if desired.

Serves 4.

PICHELSTEINER STEW
(Pichelsteiner)

- **1 lb. meat, mixed (beef, pork, lamb)**
- **1 small head cabbage**
- **½ lb. turnips**
- **¼ lb. string beans**
- **1 celery knob**
- **½ lb. potatoes**
- **1 onion**
- **1 tsp. parsley, chopped**
- **salt and pepper**
- **paprika**
- **¼ lb. beef marrow, sliced thin**
- **butter**
- **2 cups beef stock**

Cut up meat and vegetables in fairly large chunks. Keep separate. Season well. Select a cooking pot with a tight-fitting lid. Cover bottom of pot with marrow, and on this alternate layers of meat and vegetables. Top with marrow and dot with butter. Add beef stock, cover and stew over low heat for 2 hours, or until meat is tender. Tilt or shake the pan occasionally to keep stew from sticking to bottom and burning.

Serves 4.

SCHNITZEL STEW
(Schnitzel-Eintopf)

  1½ lbs. bottom round
  1 large onion, chopped
  4 tbls. butter
  1 medium bunch carrots, sliced
  4 medium potatoes, sliced
  1½ cups beef stock
  salt and pepper
  ½ cup cream
  1 tbls. ketchup
  1 tbls. flour
  parsley

Have meat cut in 4 pieces ½ inch thick. Brown meat and onion lightly in butter. Add carrots and potatoes. Pour on beef stock, season, cover, and simmer until done, about 30 minutes. Blend cream, ketchup and flour. Add to stew and bring briefly to a boil. Garnish with parsley to serve.

Serves 4.

POTATO AND TOMATO CASSEROLE
(Kartoffeln mit Tomaten)

  2 lbs. potatoes, cooked
  1 lb. tomatoes, sliced
  3 tbls. cheese, grated
  salt and pepper
  marjoram
  1 onion, sliced and slightly fried
  butter, to dot

Peel and slice potatoes. In a buttered baking dish, arrange alternating layers of potatoes, tomatoes and grated cheese. Sprinkle with salt, pepper and marjoram. Top with cheese and fried onion rings, dot with butter. Bake in moderate (350°) oven for 30 minutes.

Serves 4.

CABBAGE WITH BACON
(Weisskraut mit Speck)

  2 lbs. cabbage
  1½ lbs. potatoes
  salt, paprika, caraway seeds
  ½ lb. bacon
  1 onion

Cut cabbage in strips and cook for 10 minutes in salted water. Peel and dice potatoes and add to cabbage. Season. Cook until potatoes are done, about 20 minutes. Drain cabbage. Chop up bacon and onion and brown together and combine with cabbage and potatoes.

Serves 4.

BAKED KIPPERS
(Bücklinge, überbacken)

  4 smoked kippers
  4 tbls. sour cream
  4 tbls. milk
  2 tbls. bread crumbs
  1 tbls. parsley, chopped
  2 tbls. butter

Place kippers in cream in greased baking dish. Add milk, sprinkle with bread crumbs and parsley. Dot with butter. Bake in a moderate (375°) oven for about 10 minutes. Serve with mashed potatoes and sauerkraut.

Serves 4.

DESSERTS AND SWEETS

DOUGH BEIGNETTE—BASIC BATTER
(Beignettenteig)

  2 cups flour
  1 egg
  2 tsp. sugar
  1 pinch of salt
  2 tbls. melted butter
  1 jigger of rum
  warm water
  fruit of your choice

It is advisable to mix this batter several hours before using. Blend all ingredients and add enough warm water to form a creamy batter. Let cool. Dip slices of apples, bananas, pineapple or other fruits in this sweet batter. Fry in deep hot fat. (For vegetables, meat or fish, prepare an unsweetened batter by eliminating sugar and rum.)

Serves 4.

CREAM STRUDEL
(Rahmstrudel)
    2 cups flour
    2 eggs
    1 tbls. butter
    ½ cup lukewarm water
    ½ tsp. vinegar
    pinch of salt
    2 tbls. butter
    2 eggs, separated
    4 tbls. sugar
    1 cup sour cream
    peel of ½ lemon, grated
    ½ lb. cottage cheese
    ¼ lb. almonds, chopped
    ¼ lb. raisins
    cinnamon
    4 tbls. butter, melted

Put flour in a bowl and make depression in the center. Into this break the eggs. Add butter, water, vinegar and salt and work until tender. Dough must be firm and have air holes in it when cut. Brush with lukewarm water. Heat a large pot and place over dough for 30 minutes. For the filling, cream butter, stir in egg yolks and sugar, add sour cream, grated lemon peel and smooth cottage cheese. Beat egg whites and fold in.

Sprinkle baking cloth with flour. Roll out dough as thin as possible; then stretch it by hand to paper thinness. Brush with melted butter. Heap on filling generously; top with chopped almonds, raisins and cinnamon. Lift baking cloth by one edge so that dough starts to roll up. Brush each turn with melted butter until dough is completely rolled up. Butter a baking sheet and carefully transfer roll to it. Press ends of roll flat. Brush entire strudel with melted butter. Bake in a hot (425°) oven 40 to 50 minutes.

Note: Strudel dough is, traditionally, pulled out by hand, by putting both hands, palm-side up under the dough and stretching as thin as possible. This is a perilous procedure for the uninitiated, so an alternate suggestion has been given: roll it out paper-thin.

APPLE STRUDEL
(Apfelstrudel)
    2 cups flour
    2 eggs, beaten
    ¼ cup water, lukewarm
    pinch of salt
    ½ tsp. vinegar
    4-5 lbs. apples, tart
    ⅓ cup sugar
    3 tbls. cinnamon
    6 tbls. butter, melted
    4 tbls. bread crumbs
    1 cup almonds or other nuts, chopped
    1½ cups raisins

Heap flour on bread board and make a depression in the center large enough to hold the beaten egg, water, salt and vinegar. Knead this to a firm dough which, when cut, will reveal air pockets. Set dough, covered, in a warm place. Peel and grate apples and sprinkle with sugar and cinnamon. Dust a cloth with flour and on it roll out dough, the thinner the better. Melt butter, mix in bread crumbs, and coat dough. Spread out apples about 1 inch high on dough, sprinkle with almonds or other nuts, as desired, and raisins. Roll dough over, in the cloth, several times to form a loaf (strudel) of several alternating layers of dough and filling. Brush finished loaf with more melted butter, put on greased baking sheet and bake in a hot (400°) oven until crust is crisp and well browned. This may be served with Vanilla Sauce (see index).

PLUM DUMPLINGS
(Zwetschgenknödel)
    3 lbs. potatoes
    5 cups flour
    4 tbls. sugar
    2 eggs, beaten
    salt
    4 tbls. butter, melted
    2 lbs. plums
    cubes of sugar
    ½ cup bread crumbs
    melted butter to dampen
    cinnamon and sugar

Cook, peel and mash potatoes. Turn out on a floured bread board. Add flour, sugar, eggs, salt and

melted butter and mix to form a firm dough. Roll out
½ inch thick and cut into pieces the size of your
palm. Remove pits from plums and replace them
with sugar cubes. Place one plum in each slice of
dough. Fold dough around plums, to cover completely. Cook in slightly salted water 5 to 8 minutes.
Mix crisp bread crumbs with melted butter. Roll finished dumplings in this and sprinkle with cinnamon
and sugar.

Serves 4.

APPLE CAKE
(Blitzkuchen mit Äpfeln)
    4 to 6 tart apples (medium size)
    2 lemons, juiced
    3 tablespoons sugar
    3 tablespoons butter
    ¾ cup sugar
    2 egg yolks (do not put 2 yolks together, as they
        will be used individually)
    ½ lemon, juiced and peel grated
    1 teaspoon baking powder
    1½ cups flour
    ¾ cup milk
    1 tablespoon rum
    2 egg whites
    1 teaspoon butter (to grease cake pan)
    1 teaspoon vegetable oil
    3 tablespoons powdered sugar

Peel apples, cut in half, and core. Cut decorative
lengthwise slits in apples, about ½ inch deep (see
picture). Sprinkle with lemon juice and sugar. Set
aside.

Cream butter and sugar together. One at a time,
beat in egg yolks.

Gradually beat in lemon juice and grated peel.

Sift baking powder and flour together. Gradually
add to batter. Blend in milk and rum. In a small bowl
beat egg whites until stiff. Fold into batter.

Generously grease a springform pan. Pour in batter
and top with apple halves. Brush apples with oil.
Bake in preheated 350°F oven 35 to 40 minutes.

Remove from pan and sprinkle with powdered
sugar. Makes 6 servings.

STUFFED APPLES
(Gefüllte Äpfel)
    4 large apples
    4 tbls. raisins
    3 tbls. sugar
    1 tsp. cinnamon
    1 tbls. bread crumbs
    4 tbls. nuts, grated
    2 tbls. butter
    extra sugar
    extra butter
    1 cup white wine

Select apples of equal size, pare them and cut off
tops. Scoop out cores carefully. Mix raisins, sugar,
cinnamon, bread crumbs and nuts. Into each apple
put first a piece of butter the size of a hazelnut, then
the raisin and nut mixture. Replace tops and set in
buttered baking dish. Sprinkle with sugar, dot with
butter and pour on wine. Bake in moderate (350°)
oven until soft, 30 to 40 minutes.

Serves 4.

SOUFFLES AND PUDDINGS

TAPIOCA SOUFFLÉ
(Sagoauflauf)
    1 cup tapioca
    3 cups milk
    pinch of salt
    2 tbls. butter
    ½ cup sugar
    2 eggs, separated
    1½ tbls. lemon juice
    1 tsp. baking soda

Soak tapioca pearls overnight. Cook tapioca in
salted milk until it thickens. Or use quick-cooking
tapioca. Let it cool. Cream butter, stir in sugar, egg
yolks and lemon juice. Combine with tapioca, and
when cool, fold in beaten egg whites and baking
soda. Bake in a greased baking dish in moderately
hot (375°) oven for 30 minutes.

Serves 4.

CHOCOLATE SOUFFLÉ
(Schokolade Auflauf)

2 tbls. butter
2 tbls. flour
¾ cup milk
3 eggs, separated
1½ squares chocolate
⅓ cup sugar
2 tbls. water, hot
½ tsp. vanilla

Melt butter, add flour. Gradually stir in milk and bring to a boil. Add egg yolks. Melt chocolate in double boiler, add sugar and water and stir until smooth. Combine the two and let cool. Fold in well-beaten egg whites and flavor with vanilla. Butter a baking dish, pour in mixture and bake in moderate (350°) oven for 25 minutes.

Serves 4-6.

NOODLE PUDDING
(Nudelauflauf)

¾ lb. broad noodles
3 eggs
2 tbls. butter
1 cup milk
¼ cup vanilla-sugar (sugar stored with a vanilla bean) or add a dash of vanilla to plain sugar

Cook noodles, rinse, drain and transfer to greased baking dish. Blend thoroughly all other ingredients and pour over noodles. Dot with butter and bake in moderate oven (350°) for 30 minutes. Serve with stewed fruits or berries.

Serves 4.

CHOCOLATE PUDDING, CHILLED
(Schokoladeflammeri)

2 cups milk
4 tbls. sugar
pinch of salt
4 tbls. cocoa
1 envelope gelatine
1 egg, separated

Heat one cup of milk and dissolve sugar and salt in it. Stir cocoa and gelatine in second cup of cold milk. Combine the two mixtures and, stirring constantly, cook together about 3 minutes until thickened. Remove from heat. Stir in egg yolk and fold in beaten white. Rinse glass dish and pour in mixture while dish is moist. Chill, then turn out on platter to serve. Serve with Vanilla Sauce (see index).

Serves 4.

BREAD PUDDING
(Brotpudding)

10 slices white bread
10 slices brown bread
6 tbls. sugar
3 cups milk
2 tbls. butter
1 tbls. flour
1 tbls. raisins, chopped
3 tbls. candied lemon peel, chopped
1 cup almonds, chopped
2 tbls. rum
confectioner's sugar

Break bread into small pieces. Dissolve sugar in milk and soak bread in this for 1 hour. Melt butter, mix with bread and blend in flour, raisins, lemon peel and nuts. Transfer to pudding form, cover, set in water and cook over moderate heat for 20 minutes. Turn out and sprinkle with rum and sugar to serve. Or serve with Vanilla Sauce (see index).

Serves 4-6.

CHERRY PUDDING
(Kirschpudding)

2¼ cups bread crumbs or zweiback, crumbled
2 cups milk
4 tbls. sugar
2 eggs, separated
3 tbls. almonds, chopped
pinch of cinnamon
1 lb. cherries, sour, pitted
1 tsp. baking powder
1 tsp. flour

Soak bread crumbs or zweiback in milk. Mix sugar and egg yolks, add almonds and cinnamon and blend well. Add this to bread crumbs. Combine cherries, flour and baking powder, fold in beaten egg whites, and add. Transfer to buttered pudding form, cover, set in water and cook over moderate heat for 1½ hours. Serve with Vanilla Sauce (see index).

Serves 4-6.

FRUIT PUDDING
(Obstauflauf)

    2 cups milk
    4 tbls. sugar
    cinnamon
    peel of ¼ lemon, grated, or dash of vanilla
    1 loaf bread
    1 lb. fresh fruit, such as strawberries, raspberries, cherries or oranges

Sweeten milk and flavor with cinnamon, lemon peel or vanilla. Slice bread and soak briefly in milk. In a greased baking dish, arrange alternate layers of bread and fruit. Bake in 375° oven for 30 minutes.

Serves 4.

CREAMS

PASTRY CREAM
(Creme Patissière)

    vanilla bean
    1 cup milk
    2 egg yolks
    1 whole egg
    8 tbls. sugar
    3 tbls. flour

Cook vanilla bean in milk about 10 minutes, remove bean. In a double boiler, beat egg yolks, egg and sugar to a froth. Stir in flour. Continue beating while gradually adding hot milk until mixture is the consistency of mayonnaise. Serve hot. Cream may be used to stuff pancakes or as the basic batter for soufflés. Fruit extracts or liqueurs may be substituted for vanilla flavoring.

VANILLA CREAM DE LUXE
(Einfache Vanillecreme)

    vanilla bean
    2 cups milk
    1 tsp. cornstarch
    4 egg yolks
    7 tbls. sugar
    1 envelope gelatine, dissolved
    1 cup cream, whipped

Cook vanilla bean in ½ cup of milk. Remove bean. To remaining milk add corstarch and vanilla-flavored milk and bring to a boil. Beat egg yolks and sugar to a froth and add. Stir in gelatine. Remove from heat and continue stirring until cream thickens. Fold in whipped cream, chill, and serve, in a glass bowl, with cookies.

Serves 4.

CHOCOLATE CREAM
(Schokoladecreme)

    1 egg yolk
    2 tbls. sugar
    1½ ozs. chocolate, grated
    3 tbls. coffee, very strong
    1 cup cream, whipped

Stir egg yolk and sugar to a froth. Melt chocolate, blend in coffee, combine with egg yolk. Beat thoroughly, fold in whipped cream, and chill. To serve, decorate with whipped cream.

Serves 2.

SWEET SAUCES

VANILLA SAUCE
(Vanillesauce)

    1 cup milk
    1 tsp. vanilla
    1 tbls. sugar
    2 egg yolks
    ½ tsp. cornstarch

Heat the milk and vanilla and then let cool. Blend sugar, egg yolks and cornstarch until smooth and stir into milk. Beat in double boiler over moderate heat until mixture thickens. Remove from heat and stir until cool.

CARAMEL SAUCE
(Karamelsauce)

    4 tbls. sugar
    1 tbls. water
    2 cups milk
    1 tbls. cornstarch
    1 egg, separated
    ½ tsp. vanilla

Brown sugar lightly in a skillet. Add water and

milk and bring to a boil. Dissolve cornstarch in water, add and cook 3 minutes. Thicken this mixture with egg yolk, flavor with vanilla and let cool. Just before serving fold in beaten egg white.

YEAST BAKING

BASIC RAISED DOUGH
(Vorteig)
> 1½ cup milk or water
> 1 yeast cake
> ½ tsp. sugar
> 4 cups flour

Scald milk and let cool until lukewarm. Dissolve yeast in milk, add sugar. Stir in enough flour to make a fluid batter, the consistency of thick pancake batter. Cover and let rise for several hours until it has doubled in bulk. This preliminary batter is called the "rising." To the rising, add the rest of the flour (and at this point any other ingredients called for in each specific recipe, such as butter, eggs, sugar, salt, flavoring and, if necessary, additional lukewarm milk). Knead and beat dough thoroughly until it is satiny and comes away from sides of bowl and off hands easily. Grease bowl, set dough in it, grease top of dough to keep it soft, cover, set in a warm place and let rise again to double its size. Form into rolls, loaves or cake, as caled for in specific recipe. Let rise 1 hour and bake in 375° oven 40 to 60 minutes. Bake rolls in 425° oven until nicely browned (about 25 minutes).

Note: This basic recipe makes 12 large rolls or 1 large loaf of bread. For bread or rolls, add ½ tsp. salt.

HAZELNUT RING
(Hazelnussring)
> 2½ cup flour
> 1 yeast cake
> 4 tbls. butter
> 3 tbls. sugar
> salt
> 1 egg
> ½ cup milk
> 1 tsp. lemon juice
> 1½ cups hazelnuts, roasted and chopped
> 4 tbls. sugar
> ½ cup sweet cream

> 1 tbls. vanilla-sugar (sugar stored with a vanilla bean)
> Vanilla Icing (see below)

Prepare yeast dough as in Basic Raised dough. Beat well and let rise at room temperature. Blend together the roasted finely chopped hazelnuts with sugar, cream and vanilla-sugar. Roll out the dough to finger thickness, spread with the hazelnut mixture, roll together and place in a ring form. Let rise again and bake about a half hour in a hot (400°) oven until nicely browned. Spread with Vanilla Icing while still warm.

VANILLA ICING
(Vanillecreme)
> 1 cup confectioner's sugar
> 1 tbls. vanilla-sugar (sugar that has been stored with vanilla bean)
> 3 tbls. water

Sift sugar, add vanilla-sugar and water and stir until it becomes thick.

CRUMB CAKE
(Streuselkuchen)
> **Dough:**
> > 1 cup milk
> > 1 yeast cake
> > 1 tsp. salt
> > 5 tbls. sugar
> > 4½ cup flour
> > 4 tbls. butter
> > 1 egg
> **Crumbs:**
> > 1 cup hazelnuts, grated
> > 1½ cups flour
> > ¾ cup sugar
> > 1 tsp. cinnamon
> > 1 cup butter, melted

Follow recipe for Basic Raised dough exactly and let rise once. Grease a baking sheet, with an inch high rim, spread dough out on sheet and let it rise once again. Combine hazelnuts, flour, sugar and cinnamon. Add melted butter, drop by drop, while kneading this mixture into crumbs. Rub crumbs between hands to obtain an even distribution and sprinkle over dough. Bake in moderate (350°) oven for 30 minutes.

French

CRAB-MEAT SPREAD
>   1 can (7½ ounces) king crab meat, drained and flaked
>   1 teaspoon prepared horseradish
>   ½ teaspoon seasoned salt
>   ¼ teaspoon lemon juice
>   dash white pepper
>   ½ cup plain yogurt

Combine crab meat, horseradish, seasoned salt, lemon juice and pepper. Fold in yogurt. Cover and chill. Use to spread on crackers or as a dip. Yields 1¼ cups

OYSTERS ROCKEFELLER
(Huîtres À La Florentine)
>   2 dozen oysters on the half shell
>   2 tablespoons chopped green onion
>   2 tablespoons chopped celery
>   3 tablespoons chopped fennel (optional)
>   3 tablespoons chopped parsley
>   ¼ pound butter
>   1 cup watercress or spinach
>   3 tablespoons bread crumbs
>   3 tablespoons Pernod or anisette
>   ¼ teaspoon salt
>   ⅛ teaspoon white pepper
>   Dash cayenne

Sauté onion, celery and herbs in 3 tablespoons butter for 3 minutes. Add watercress or spinach; let it wilt. Place this mixture, remaining butter, bread crumbs, liqueur and seasonings into blender. Blend for 1 minute. Put 1 tablespoon mixture on each oyster. Place oyster shells on rock-salt beds; dampen the salt slightly. Bake at 450°F about 4 minutes or until butter is melted and oysters are heated.

Serves 4.

QUICHE LORRAINE
>   8 ounces bacon
>   1 9-inch pastry shell, unbaked
>   1½ cups or 7 ounces Swiss cheese, natural, coarsely shredded
>   ¾ teaspoon salt
>   ¼ teaspoon pepper
>   dash of cayenne
>   dash of nutmeg
>   4 eggs
>   1½ cups half-and-half

Preheat oven to 375°F. Cut bacon into pieces and fry until brown and very crisp. Drain well. Crumble bacon into pastry shell. Sprinkle cheese over the bacon. Mix seasonings and sprinkle over cheese. Beat eggs and half-and-half together. Pour over cheese and bacon. Bake 45 minutes or until lightly browned and a knife inserted into the center comes out clean.

Serves 6.

CHICKEN-LIVER PÂTÉ
(Pâté de foie de Volaille)
>   2 tablespoons butter
>   ½ pound chicken livers
>   2 eggs, hard-cooked
>   1 package (3-ounce size) cream cheese, softened
>   1 tablespoon finely-chopped parsley
>   ¾ teaspoon salt
>   ⅛ teaspoon pepper
>   1 tablespoon cognac

Heat butter in medium frying pan. Cook chicken livers, stirring occasionally, over medium heat 10 minutes or until tender. Drain. Chop livers and eggs in food grinder (or in blender, a little at a time). With wooden spoon, work cream cheese until light and fluffy. Mix cheese into liver mixture along with remaining ingredients. Refrigerate for several hours. Serve paté with hot toast or crackers. Yields 1¼ cups.

SALMON QUICHE

pastry:
1 cup flour
pinch of salt
6 tablespoons butter
1 egg yolk
1 tablespoon lemon juice
1 or 2 teaspoons water, if needed

Sift flour and salt into bowl. Cut in butter until mixture resembles fine bread crumbs. Mix to firm dough with egg yolk and lemon juice, adding water if needed. Turn pastry onto lightly floured board; knead lightly. Roll to line base and sides of 9-inch quiche pan, approximately a 10-inch circle.

Salmon Quiche Filling
1 8-ounce can red salmon
4 strips bacon, diced
1½ cups cream
3 eggs
1 teaspoon salt
¼ teaspoon pepper
½ teaspoon paprika
2 tablespoons chopped parsley
1 tablespoon grated Parmesan cheese

Drain salmon, reserving liquid. Remove bones; flake salmon lightly. Dice bacon; fry gently until crisp. Drain well. Beat together cream, eggs, salt, pepper, paprika, parsley, cheese and reserved salmon liquid. Place salmon evenly in base of pastry shell; sprinkle bacon over. Gently pour in egg mixture. Bake at 450°F 10 minutes. Reduce heat to 350°F; cook 30 minutes more or until set in center. Slice; serve.
Serves 4-6.

ROQUEFORT CHEESE BALLS
(Amuse-Gueuleau)
¼ pound Roquefort cheese
3 tablespoons unsalted butter, softened
1 tablespoon minced green-onion tops
freshly-ground pepper to taste
2 teaspoons brandy
¼ cup bread crumbs
2 tablespoons finely-minced parsley

Mash cheese in small bowl. Beat in butter to form a smooth paste. Blend in onion, pepper and brandy.

Shape into small balls, about ½ inch in diameter. Mix crumbs and parsley. Roll balls in crumb mixture. Chill, if made ahead. Serve cheese balls at room temperature, with crusty French bread. Yields 24 balls.

BAKED CLAMS IN MORNAY SAUCE
1 pint shucked clams
dry white wine
1 recipe Basic Mornay Sauce (see Index)
2 tablespoons fine, dry bread crumbs
1 tablespoon freshly-grated Parmesan cheese
2 teaspoons chopped parsley
2 teaspoons chopped chives
Butter

Mince clams; place in saucepan. Add just enough wine to cover. Simmer about 5 minutes or until wine has evaporated. Combine clams and sauce; mix well. Spoon clam mixture into scallop shells or individual baking dishes. Blend bread crumbs, cheese, parsley and chives. Sprinkle over clam mixture; dot with butter. Place shells on baking sheet. Bake in preheated 350°F oven, 1 rack above center, 15 minutes.
Serves 8.

MARINATED MUSHROOMS
(Champignons Marines)
1 pound small whole mushrooms
marinade:
1 cup chicken broth
1 cup dry white wine
2 tablespoons fresh lemon juice
¼ cup white vinegar
¼ cup vegetable oil
1 stalk celery
1 clove garlic, peeled
¼ teaspoon rosemary
¼ teaspoon marjoram
¼ teaspoon thyme
⅛ teaspoon oregano
1 bay leaf
4 peppercorns
¼ teaspoon salt

Combine all ingredients except mushrooms in a 2-quart saucepan; bring to a boil. Simmer gently 30 minutes. Strain Marinade, pressing juice from vegetables. Return to saucepan. Add mushrooms; simmer for 5 minutes. Cool to room temperature then chill at least 4 hours, preferably overnight.

Serves 4.

BRANDY PÂTÉ

½ pound chicken livers
2 tablespoons butter
1 small onion, chopped fine
¼ teaspoon thyme
1 small bay leaf
2 ounces chopped mushrooms
3 strips crisp bacon, chopped
⅓ cup cream
1 tablespoon port
1 tablespoon dry sherry
1 teaspoon brandy
2 teaspoons salt
1 teaspoon pepper
2 tablespoons melted butter

Clean and dry chicken livers. Melt 2 tablespoons butter in pan. Sauté livers, onion, thyme, bay leaf, mushrooms and chopped bacon 7 to 10 minutes. Remove from heat; discard bay leaf. Blend mixture with cream until smooth. (A blender makes this very easy.) Push through sieve or food mill into bowl. Stir in port, sherry and brandy; season with salt and pepper. Spoon mixture into serving dish. Cover paté with melted butter. Refrigerate until butter is firm on top. This helps keep the paté moist and looks attractive. Serve paté with hot toast points or your favorite crackers. Yields 1½ cups.

SALMON PÂTÉ

1 tablespoon unflavored gelatin
½ cup hot water
1 chicken-stock cube
1 8-ounce can red salmon
¼ cup mayonnaise
2 tablespoons chopped parsley
2 teaspoons lemon juice
2 shallots or spring onions, roughly chopped
½ cup cream
1 teaspoon salt
Dash of pepper

Put gelatin, hot water and chicken-stock cube into blender. Blend at high speed 2 minutes. Add un-

drained salmon and remaining ingredients; blend until smooth. Pour mixture into lightly-greased individual molds; refrigerate until set. Unmold onto leaves of crisp lettuce. Serve with Green Horseradish Sauce.

Serves 4.

Green Horseradish Sauce
1 egg
1 egg yolk
1 teaspoon prepared mustard
½ cup chopped parsley
1 tablespoon white vinegar
salt and pepper to taste
1 cup oil
1 tablespoon bottled horseradish relish

Put 1 whole egg, egg yolk, mustard, parsley, vinegar, salt and pepper into blender; blend for 1 minute. Gradually add oil until approximately ½ cup oil has been added and mixture has thickened. Slowly pour in remaining oil. Mixture will thicken as oil is added. Add horseradish; blend a few seconds more. Refrigerate before serving. Spoon over the Salmon Pâté.

SOUPS

FRESH MUSHROOM SOUP

1 pound fresh mushrooms
2 tablespoons vegetable oil
2 scallions or shallots, minced
4 cups chicken broth or bouillon
¼ teaspoon salt
½ teaspoon lemon juice
1 lemon, sliced

Wash mushrooms and pat dry with paper towels. Chop very fine or chop small amounts at a time in blender on slowest speed. Heat oil in a frying pan and sauté scallions for about 3 minutes or until wilted. Add mushrooms; cook, stirring occasionally, for about 5 minutes. Add broth, salt and lemon juice. Bring to a boil. Reduce heat to a simmer and cook uncovered for 30 minutes. Blend finished soup in blender or press through a coarse sieve. If sieved, press hard on mushrooms to extract all the liquid. Reheat before serving. Garnish with lemon slices.

Serves 6.

FRENCH TOMATO SOUP

> 2 large onions, finely sliced
> 2 slices of bacon, chopped
> 2 tablespoon butter
> 4-6 ripe tomatoes (or 1 cup canned tomatoes) chopped
> 1 tablespoon tomato purée
> 2-3 strips of lemon rind
> 4 cups chicken stock
> 1 teaspoon sugar
> 2 tablespoon parsley
> ¼ teaspoon thyme
> 1 teaspoon basil
> garnish:
>> 1 tablespoon chopped mixed parsley and basil
>> garlic croutons

Heat the bacon pieces in a pan. When the fat has run, add the butter. When it has melted, add the onions and cook gently for 5-6 minutes until tender and golden brown. Add the tomatoes and tomato purée, lemon rind, stock, salt, pepper, sugar and herbs. Bring to a boil. Then simmer for 20 minutes or until tomatoes are tender. Put soup through a food mill or blend in electric blender. Adjust seasoning and serve hot, sprinkled with chopped parsley, basil and garlic croutons.

Serves 4-6.

MOULES MARINIÈRE

> 40-50 mussels, fresh and unopened
> 1 onion or 4-5 shallots
> 1 carrot
> 1 stalk celery
> 1 clove garlic
> 1 cup white wine
> 1 cup water
> 2 tablespoons chopped parsley
> 1 bay leaf
> a pinch of thyme
> 3 tablespoons butter
> 2½ tablespoons flour

Wash the mussels and scrub thoroughly to remove weed or sand. Knock or scrape off barnacles. Remove the beards. Examine mussels carefully, and if any are not tightly closed discard immediately, as they are poisonous if not alive when cooked. Soak the mus-

sels in plenty of cold water, as they will expel any sand from inside the shells during soaking process. Meanwhile, chop the onion or shallots, peel and chop the carrot and slice celery. Crush the garlic and add to the pan with wine, water, 1 tablespoon of chopped parsley, the bay leaf, thyme and ground black pepper. Bring to a boil and then simmer for 6-8 minutes. Drain the mussels and add to the pan. Cover tightly with a lid and simmer for 6-8 minutes, shaking the pan frequently to make sure that all mussels are covered by liquid. Remove from heat as soon as the mussels open their shells. Strain off liquid and reserve. Remove mussels from pan and carefully remove half of each shell. If serving for a party carefully remove the inner part of gristly beard; otherwise each diner can do this for himself at the table. Put the half shells holding the fish into a deep dish and keep warm. Put cooking liquid into a pan. Blend the butter and flour into a paste, and add to the liquid. Bring slowly to a boil, whisking constantly. Add the second tablespoonful of chopped parsley. Adjust seasoning and pour over the mussels.

Serves 4.

SHERRY BISQUE
(Bisque de l'xérèx)

> 1 small ham hock
> ¾ cup split green peas
> 1 bay leaf
> 6 cups beef broth
> 6 slices bacon, diced
> ¾ cup chopped onion
> 1 stalk celery, diced
> 3 tablespoons flour
> 1 8-ounce can tomato purée
> 1 cup chicken broth
> ⅓ cup sherry
> ¼ cup butter
> Freshly-ground pepper to taste

Place ham hock, split peas, bay leaf and 4 cups beef broth into 4-quart saucepan. Bring to a boil, reduce heat and simmer. Sauté bacon in frying pan until fat is rendered. Add onion and celery; cook until tender. Stir in flour; mix to blend. Add remaining 2 cups beef broth; cook until slightly thickened. Add onion mixture to split-pea mixture; continue to cook until split peas are soft, about 1½ hours. When done, remove ham hock. Purée mixture in blender or food mill. Add tomato purée, chicken broth and sherry. Add butter and pepper; stir until melted. Strain soup, if desired, before serving.

Serves 8-12.

POTATO SOUP
(Vichyssoise)

3 to 4 leeks or green onions
1 medium onion, chopped
2 tablespoons butter
2 large potatoes, peeled and diced
½ teaspoon salt
3 cups chicken broth
1 cup milk
1½ cups heavy cream
1 drop Tabasco sauce
1 tablespoon minced parsley or chives

Thoroughly clean leeks or onions, halve lengthwise, and cut into thin slices. Heat butter. Add leeks or onions; cook until transparent. Add potatoes, salt and chicken broth. Simmer mixture 35 minutes. Purée in blender or food mill; reheat. Pour in milk and 1 cup cream. Heat and stir until well-blended, but do not boil. Season with Tabasco sauce. Chill mixture. Beat ½ cup cream until stiff; fold into soup. Adjust seasonings. Serve soup garnished with chopped chives or parsley.

Serves 4.

AVOCADO CREAM SOUP

1¼ cups chicken stock
2 ripe avocados
¾ cup cream
½ cup milk
1 teaspoon salt
Dash of freshly-ground pepper

Place chicken stock in bowl; set aside. Peel avocados; remove seeds. Put chopped avocados in blender with cream and milk. Blend on medium speed until smooth. (If you do not have a blender, press avocado into a paste with a fork, then blend with cream and milk.) Put this mixture in with chicken stock; stir until smooth. (For an even finer consistency, press through a sieve.) Season with salt and pepper. Refrigerate until well-chilled. Spoon soup into bowls and enjoy.

Serves 4.

ONION SOUP
(soupe À l'oignon)

4 large onions, thinly sliced
1 tablespoon butter
1 tablespoon vegetable oil
¼ teaspoon sugar
2 tablespoons flour
6 cups beef broth
¼ cup dry white wine or vermouth
Salt and pepper to taste
4 slices French bread, cut ½ inch thick
2 teaspoons vegetable oil
1 clove garlic, peeled and cut
2 tablespoons cognac
1 cup grated Swiss cheese

In covered 4-quart saucepan or Dutch oven, cook onions slowly with butter and oil for 15 minutes. Stir occasionally. Uncover; increase heat to moderate. Add sugar; sauté onions, stirring frequently, about 30 minutes or until onions turn golden brown. Sprinkle onions with flour; stir over heat for 2 to 3 minutes. Blend in hot broth and wine; adjust seasonings. Simmer, partially covered, for 1 hour. Meanwhile, place bread slices in 350°F oven 30 minutes or until lightly toasted. Halfway through the baking, baste each slice with ½ teaspoon oil and rub with cut garlic clove. Before serving, add cognac and divide soup into ovenproof bowls or casseroles. Sprinkle ½ cup cheese in soup. Float slices of French bread on top of soup; sprinkle with rest of cheese. Bake in preheated 325°F oven 15 to 20 minutes, until hot, then set under broiler for 2 to 3 minutes, until cheese is golden brown.

Serves 4.

PUMPKIN VICHYSSOISE

1½ pounds canned pumpkin
2 leeks or large onions, sliced or chopped
¾ pound potatoes, diced
4 cups chicken stock
1¼ cups cream
1 teaspoon salt
Dash of pepper

Place pumpkin, leeks, potatoes and chicken stock into large saucepan. Bring to boil; simmer, uncovered, for 25 minutes or until potatoes are very soft and tender. Put vegetables and liquid through sieve to make fine purée. Return to pan. Add cream, salt and pepper; again bring to boil. Stir soup over low flame; simmer for 5 minutes more. This may be served hot but is usually served chilled.

Serves 4-6.

OXTAIL SOUP

1 2-pound disjointed oxtail or 2 veal tails
1 medium onion, sliced
2 tablespoons vegetable oil
8 cups water
1 teaspoon salt
4 peppercorns
¼ cup chopped parsley
½ cup diced carrots
1 cup diced celery
1 bay leaf
½ cup tomatoes, drained
1 teaspoon dried thyme
1 tablespoon flour
1 tablespoon polyunsaturated margarine
¼ cup Madeira

In a 4-quart Dutch oven, brown oxtail and onion in hot oil for several minutes. Add water, salt and peppercorns; simmer uncovered for about 5 hours. Add the parsley, carrots, celery, bay leaf, tomatoes and thyme; continue simmering for 30 minutes longer or until the vegetables are tender. Strain stock and refrigerate for an hour or more. In a blender, purée the edible meat and vegetables and reserve. Remove fat from top of stock and reheat. In a large, dry frying pan brown flour over high heat. Cool slightly. Add margarine and blend. Slowly add the stock and vegetables. Adjust the seasoning and add Madeira just before serving.

Serves 8.

SAUCES AND DRESSINGS

BEARNAISE SAUCE
(*Sauce Bearnaise*)

¼ cup white vinegar
¼ cup dry white wine
1 tablespoon minced green onion
1 teaspoon dried tarragon
3 peppercorns
3 egg yolks

1 tablespoon warm water
½ cup butter
¼ teaspoon salt

Boil vinegar, wine, onion, tarragon and peppercorns in small saucepan until liquid has reduced to 2 tablespoons. Pour liquid through fine sieve. In top of double boiler, over just simmering water, blend egg yolks and warm water until creamy. Bottom of double boiler should not touch water. Melt butter over low heat; add ½ teaspoons to yolk mixture, beating well with a wire whip after each addition. (Set bottom of pan in a cold-water bath if eggs start to look like scrambled eggs.) After some butter has been added, up to 1 teaspoon of butter can be added at one time. Leave the white residue in bottom of butter pan. After butter is added, stir in vinegar mixture and salt. Yields ¾ cups.

HOLLANDAISE SAUCE
(*Sauce Hollandaise*)

3 egg yolks
2 tablespoons lemon juice
¼ teaspoon salt
⅛ teaspoon white pepper
½ cup butter

Place egg yolks, lemon juice, salt and pepper in blender. Carefully melt butter in small pan; heat to foaming. Blend yolk mixture at top speed 3 seconds. Remove center of cover. Pour in hot butter by droplets at first, then in a thin stream. Omit the milky residue at bottom of pan. Adjust seasonings, if desired. Set jar in lukewarm water until ready to use. Reheating usually causes curdling, so prepare close to serving time. Yields ¾ cup.

BASIC BROWN SAUCE
(*Sauce Brune*)

2 onions, diced
2 carrots, diced
4 tablespoons butter
1 tablespoon sugar
¼ cup flour
2 cups beef bouillon
2 cups water
1 clove garlic, minced
2 sprigs parsley

1 bay leaf
⅛ teaspoon thyme
1 tablespoon tomato paste
¼ teaspoon salt
⅛ teaspoon pepper
1 tablespoon Madeira
2 tablespoons cognac

Sauté onions and carrots in butter for 20 minutes. Add sugar; increase heat to brown vegetables. Cook about 10 minutes, stirring very often. Do not let vegetables burn. Stir in flour; cook about 3 minutes. Add bouillon, water, garlic, parsley, bay leaf, thyme, tomato paste, salt and pepper. Bring to a boil while stirring. Reduce heat; partially cover; simmer about 1¼ hours. Strain sauce into clean pan; discard vegetables. After cooling, sauce may be frozen at this point. Just before serving, add Madeira and cognac. Yields 2 cups.

MORNAY SAUCE
1 tablespoon polyunsaturated margarine
1 tablespoon flour
1 cup skim milk
3 tablespoons grated Gruyère cheese
1 tablespoon grated Parmesan cheese
½ teaspoon Dijon mustard

Melt margarine in a small saucepan. Remove from heat and add the flour, stirring with a wire whisk. Return to a moderate heat. Add the milk gradually, stirring the mixture constantly until the sauce is thickened. Add the remaining ingredients and cook until cheese is melted. Season to taste. Yields 1¼ cups.

MADEIRA SAUCE
¼ pound mushrooms, sliced
2 tablespoons vegetable oil
3 scallions, chopped
1 tablespoon flour
1 cup beef broth or bouillon
½ cup Madeira
Salt and pepper to taste

Sauté mushrooms in hot oil until lightly browned. Remove and reserve. Add scallions and sauté briefly. Sprinkle flour in pan and stir for a minute to cook. Gradually blend in broth. (Use a wire whisk if lumps start to form.) Simmer sauce uncovered for 15 minutes, add Madeira, and simmer again for 5 minutes. Add mushrooms, and season to taste. Yields 1 cup.

FRENCH DRESSING
2 tablespoons white wine vinegar
salt
freshly ground black pepper
6-8 tablespoons olive oil

Mix vinegar with salt and pepper to taste. Add oil and beat with a fork until the mixture thickens. For a slightly thicker dressing, add a cube of ice and stir for 1-2 minutes longer, then remove the ice cube.

VARIATIONS

TARRAGON DRESSING
Add 1 teaspoon chopped fresh tarragon leaves.

CURRY DRESSING
Add ½ teaspoon curry powder and 1 teaspoon finely chopped shallots.

CAPER DRESSING
Add 1 teaspoon chopped capers, ½ clove garlic, finely crushed, and a little anchovy paste.

ROQUEFORT DRESSING
Add 3 tablespoons crumbled Roquefort cheese and blend well. Chill before serving.

MEATS

BEEF CUBES IN SHERRY
2 tablespoons shortening
2 pounds lean stewing beef, cubed
2 package onion-soup mix
1 cup sherry wine
1 can cream of mushroom soup
1 teaspoon garlic salt
¼ pound sliced mushrooms

Heat shortening in heavy pot. Brown the beef cubes on all sides. Add remaining ingredients in order given; stir well. Cover pot; simmer mixture at least 1 hour or until meat is tender to the fork. Add additional water or soup stock as needed. Serve beef over broad noodles.
Serves 4-6.

BEEF IN RED WINE SAUCE
(Boeuf Bourguignon)

> 3 tablespoons vegetable oil
> 12 small white onions, peeled
> 2 pounds lean stewing beef, cubed
> 1 tablespoon flour
> 2 cups dry red wine
> 1 cup beef bouillon
> 1 clove garlic, minced
> 1 tablespoon tomato paste
> ¼ teaspoon thyme
> 1 bay leaf
> ½ teaspoon parsley
> 1 teaspoon salt
> ½ teaspoon pepper
> ½ pound fresh mushrooms, quartered

Heat oil in a large frying pan. Sauté onions lightly; remove from pan. Add beef cubes; sauté until brown. Sprinkle cubes with flour; toss to coat meat. Cook for 2 minutes, stirring often. Add wine, bouillon, garlic, tomato paste and seasonings. Stir well, cover and simmer slowly about 3 hours or until meat is tender. Add more bouillon if necessary. The last hour of cooking, add onions. Add mushrooms the last 15 minutes. If sauce is too thin, reduce it by boiling rapidly. Adjust seasonings.

Serves 4-6.

STUFFED FILLET OF BEEF

> 1½ pounds fillet steak
> chicken stuffing
> 2 tablespoons butter
> 1 onion, chopped fine
> 2 strips bacon
> 1 chicken breast
> Enough water to cover chicken
> 1 egg
> 2 tablespoons fresh bread crumbs
> 2 tablespoons chopped parsley
> 1 teaspoon salt
> ¼ teaspoon pepper
> 8 ounces button mushrooms, sliced thin
> ½ cup dry red wine

Using small, sharp knife, cut a pocket in middle of fillet. Cut almost to edges; do not cut through. Set aside. Melt butter; sauté onion and bacon over low heat until golden brown. In another pan, cover chicken breast with water. Bring to boil; simmer for 25 minutes, until chicken is tender. Drain. Remove meat from bones; remove skin; chop chicken meat fine. Add chicken to bacon and onion mixture. Add egg, bread crumbs, parsley, salt and pepper; mix well. Press chicken stuffing firmly into pocket of steak. Place meat into greased baking dish. Bake at 350°F 40 minutes (a little less if you prefer rare meat). Surround meat with mushrooms; stir to mix in pan juices. Cook 10 minutes more. Pour wine over meat; bake another 5 minutes. To serve, slice meat and arrange it on a platter. Pour mushroom sauce over meat.

Serves 4.

STEAK DIANE

> 3 tablespoons chopped scallions
> 3 tablespoons vegetable oil
> 3 tablespoons finely-chopped chives
> 3 tablespoons finely-chopped parsley
> 1 tablespoon Worcestershire sauce
> ½ teaspoon salt
> ¼ teaspoon pepper
> 4 beef steaks, fillets, or rib-eye steaks
> ¼ cup brandy, warmed

Sauté scallions in 1 tablespoon hot vegetable oil for a minute or two. Add chives, parsley, Worcestershire sauce, salt and pepper. In second frying pan, sauté steaks with remaining 2 tablespoons hot vegetable oil until done. (Time depends on thickness of steak.) Top each steak with some scallion mixture. Flame with warmed brandy until alcohol content is completely burned. Spoon pan juices over steaks.

Serves 4.

FILET STEAKS WITH HERB BUTTER
(filets de Boeuf entrecôce bercy)

> herb butter
> > 4 ounces softened butter
> > 1 tablespoon finely-chopped parsley
> > 1 tablespoon finely-chopped chives
> > 1 teaspoon dried chervil
> > 1 teaspoon dried tarragon
> > 1 tablespoon grated shallots or onion
> > dash of pepper
> > 4 filets mignons steaks
> > 2 tablespoons vegetable oil

½ teaspoon salt
⅛ teaspoon pepper
4 lemon slices
Watercress
**French-fried potatoes (cut very thin, dried
on towels, and deep-fried)**

Make Herb Butter first by blending all ingredients. Spoon onto sheet of waxed paper; shape into a roll about 1½ inches in diameter. Chill butter in freezer while steak is prepared. Cut in 4 thick slices just before serving. Brush steaks with oil. Depending on thickness, broil about 5 minutes on each side or to desired doneness. Season with salt and pepper. Arrange steaks on preheated platter. Place 1 lemon slice on each steak; top with slice of Herb Butter. Garnish with watercress and potatoes.

Serves 4.

BEEF EN DAUBE

3 tablespoons vegetable oil
2 pounds beef stew meat
½ cup beef bouillon
1 cup dry red wine
½ teaspoon salt
¼ teaspoon dried thyme
1 clove garlic, minced
2 strips orange peel
1 pound small, whole white onions, peeled
¾ pound small mushrooms
1 teaspoon sugar
½ cup pitted ripe olives
1 10-ounce package frozen peas, thawed

In a 4-quart Dutch oven, heat 1 tablespoon of the vegetable oil and brown the meat. Pour in bouillon, wine, salt, thyme, garlic and orange peel. Cover and simmer for 1 hour or until the meat is tender. Cook uncovered for 10 minutes to reduce liquid. Meanwhile, cook the onions in boiling salted water for about 15 minutes or until just tender. Drain. Remove stems from mushrooms, slice and sauté them with the whole caps in remaining 2 tablespoons vegetable oil. Remove and add to the meat. In the same pan, sauté onions until lightly browned. Sprinkle with sugar and heat to glaze. Add to the meat. Stir in olives and peas, and simmer for 2 minutes. Remove peel.

Serves 6.

BEEF GOULASH

1 pound lean beef (round steak)
2 tablespoons vegetable oil
1 large onion, chopped
1 pound potatoes, peeled and cubed
1 green pepper, cut into strips
2 tomatoes, peeled and cut into chunks
1 clove garlic, minced
½ teaspoon caraway seeds
1 3-inch piece of lemon peel, minced
2 teaspoons paprika
½ teaspoon salt
2 cups beef bouillon

Pat meat dry with paper towels and cut into strips approximately ½ inch wide and 2 inches long. Heat oil in a 4-quart Dutch oven; add meat and chopped onion. Cook for 5 minutes or until brown. Add potato cubes and cook for an additional 5 minutes. Add green pepper, tomatoes, garlic, caraway seeds and lemon peel. Season with paprika and salt. Pour in beef bouillon, cover and simmer over low heat for 30 minutes. At the end of the cooking time, uncover and boil the liquid for a few minutes, until the liquid is reduced. Adjust the seasoning if necessary.

Serves 4.

STEAK AU POIVRE
(Pepper Steak)

2 tablespoons black peppercorns
4 pieces fillet steak, 1 inch thick
4 tablespoons butter
2 teaspoons oil
¾ cup dry white wine
2 teaspoons brandy or dry sherry
2 teaspoons butter

Coarsely crush peppercorns with rolling pin or mortar and pestle. Press crushed peppercorns into fillets on both sides. (Add more crushed pepper if needed.) Allow steaks to stand for 1 hour to absorb flavor. Heat 4 tablespoons butter and oil in pan; add steaks. Cook quickly on both sides to seal in the juices. Continue cooking until done to your preference (about 10 minutes for medium steak). Remove steaks to hot serving plate. Stir wine and brandy into same pan; bring to boil, scraping pan. Remove from heat; stir in 2 teaspoons butter. Pour over steaks.

Serves 4.

BEEF FILLET WITH SUMMER SAVORY

2 pounds beef fillet
2 tablespoons vegetable oil
½ pound mushrooms, sliced
3 small onions, sliced
1 tablespoon paprika
½ cup red wine
½ cup beef broth or bouillon
½ teaspoon summer savory
½ teaspoon salt
⅛ teaspoon pepper
1 tablespoon chopped parsley for garnish

Slice fillet into thin strips. In a large frying pan, heat oil and sauté meat over high heat. Add sliced mushrooms and onions; cook until onions have softened. Stir in the paprika, wine, broth, savory, salt and pepper. Heat to simmering. Remove meat and raise heat to reduce the sauce quickly. Pour sauce over meat, and garnish with parsley.

Serves 6.

BEEF STROGANOFF
(Sauté De Boeuf À La Parisienne)

½ pound fresh mushrooms, sliced
2 tablespoons vegetable oil
3 tablespoons butter
2 tablespoons minced green onions
½ teaspoon salt
2 pounds beef tenderloin or sirloin, cut into ¼-inch-thick strips
⅓ cup Madeira
¾ cup beef bouillon
2 teaspoons cornstarch
1 tablespoon cream
1 cup minus 1 tablespoon heavy cream
¼ teaspoon pepper
Parsley for garnish

Sauté mushrooms in 1 tablespoon hot oil and 2 tablespoon butter about 5 minutes or until lightly browned. Add onions; cook for another minute. Season with ¼ teaspoon salt. Place mushrooms in a bowl. Dry meat thoroughly on paper towels. Place 2 tablespoons butter and 1 tablespoon oil in pan; heat until butter foam subsides. Sauté beef, a few pieces at a time, 1 to 2 minutes on each side. Set sautéed beef aside in separate bowl. Pour Madeira and bouillon into frying pan; boil it down rapidly while scraping up browned particles. Reduce liquid to about ⅓

cup. Blend cornstarch with 1 tablespoon cream. Beat in remaining cream, then the cornstarch mixture. Simmer for 1 minute. Add sautéed mushrooms; simmer for 1 minute more. Sauce should be slightly thickened. Season with ¼ teaspoon salt and pepper. Adjust seasonings to taste. Add meat to sauce; heat briefly, to just below simmer, so beef will not overcook. Garnish stroganoff with parsley.

Serves 4-6.

STUFFED FLANK STEAK
(Paupiettes de Boeuf)

2 pounds flank steak, scored, or 2 round steak, thinly sliced
2 tablespoons Dijon mustard
¼ teaspoon thyme
1 egg
½ teaspoon salt
⅛ teaspoon allspice
⅛ teaspoon pepper
1 clove garlic, crushed
¼ cup dry bread crumbs
spinach stuffing
    ½ package frozen spinach, cooked and drained
    ½ cup chopped onions
    1 tablespoon bacon fat or vegetable oil
    ½ cup raw sausage meat
    6 slices bacon
    1 onion, chopped
    1 carrot, chopped
    ½ cup dry white wine
    1 can beef broth

Spread meat with mustard; sprinkle with thyme. Squeeze all water from spinach. Sauté ½ cup onions in fat or oil. Add spinach; toss. Add sausage, egg, salt, allspice, pepper, garlic and crumbs to spinach mixture. Mix well. Spread stuffing on meat; roll up jelly-roll fashion. Tie with string. Cook bacon in Dutch oven until partly done. Remove. Add meat roll to Dutch oven; brown on all sides. This takes about 10 minutes. Lay bacon over meat. Add onion, carrot, wine and broth. Bring to a simmer. Place in 325°F oven about 1 hour or until tender. Place meat on platter. Strain juices, pressing hard on vegetables. If desired, thicken with 1 tablespoon cornstarch dissolved in water. Slice meat; serve with pan juices.

Serves 4-6.

BEEF BRAISED IN BEER
(Carbonnades À La Flamande)

½ cup flour
2 teaspoons salt
¼ teaspoon pepper
3 pounds beef chuck or rump, sliced about 2 ×
    4 × ⅜ inch thick
3 tablespoons peanut oil
4 cups sliced onions
2 cloves garlic, peeled
1 bay leaf
2 tablespoons tomato paste
2 tablespoons brown sugar
½ teaspoon thyme
2 tablespoons chopped parsley
1 cup broth
2 cups beer

Mix flour, salt and pepper. Dredge beef to coat evenly with flour. Heat oil in large Dutch oven; brown the meat. Add remaining ingredients; bring to a simmer. Cover tightly. Place in preheated 325°F oven; bake for 2 hours or until meat is tender. Before serving, remove garlic and bay leaf. Serve beef with boiled potatoes.

Serves 6.

ORANGE PORK CHOPS

4 pork loin chops
1 clove garlic, crushed
½ teaspoon thyme
1 teaspoon salt
¼ teaspoon pepper
1 cup orange juice
2 tablespoons thinly-sliced orange rind
4 tablespoons oil
2 tablespoons butter
1 onion, chopped
1 carrot, diced
1 stick celery, chopped
½ cup chicken stock
½ cup dry white wine
2 tablespoons chopped parsley

Dredge chops thoroughly with garlic, thyme, salt and pepper. Combine orange juice and rind in pot; bring to boil. Remove from heat; pour over chops. Allow chops to marinate several hours or overnight. Drain chops, reserving orange marinade. Melt butter in frying pan. Add onion, carrot and celery; sauté until carrot is tender and onion golden brown. Remove mixture from heat. Place vegetables in baking dish; cover vegetables with chops. Combine reserved marinade, chicken stock and wine; pour over chops and vegetables. Cover. Bake at 400°F for 40 minutes or until chops are tender. Garnish chops with parsley.

Serves 4.

PORK WITH APPLES

2 pounds boneless pork loin, cut in 1½-inch cubes
2 tablespoons vegetable oil
4 leeks or 2 onions, sliced
2 green cooking apples, peeled, cored and sliced
1 teaspoon cumin
1 tablespoon flour
1¼ cups apple cider or apple juice
¼ cup dry vermouth
½ teaspoon salt
⅛ teaspoon freshly-ground black pepper

Brown the pork cubes in hot oil, remove from pan and reserve. Cook the leeks or onions and apples in the same oil for 5 minutes or until softened. Stir in the cumin and flour, and cook 1 minute. Transfer apple mixture to a casserole. Add pork and rest of ingredients. Cover and cook at 350°F for 1 hour.

Serves 6.

PORK WITH RED CABBAGE
(Porc Braisè Aux Choux Rouges)

4 strips bacon, diced
1 carrot, thinly sliced
1 large onion, sliced
2 tablespoons butter
2 pounds red cabbage, cut into ½-inch strips
2 tart apples, diced
1 clove garlic, mashed
1 bay leaf
⅛ teaspoon clove
⅛ teaspoon nutmeg
½ teaspoon salt
¼ teaspoon pepper
2 cups red wine
2 cups beef bouillon

3 pounds boneless roast of pork
2 tablespoons vegetable oil

Simmer diced bacon in 1 quart water about 10 minutes. Drain. Over low heat, cook bacon, carrot and onion in butter in covered ovenproof casserole 10 minutes. Do not brown. Stir in cabbage strips; mix well with other vegetables. Cover; cook slowly 15 minutes. Stir in all remaining ingredients except meat and vegetable oil. Simmer for 2 to 3 minutes on top of range. Cover; place in preheated 325°F oven. Cabbage should simmer slowly about 3 hours. Just before cabbage is finished cooking, brown pork roast in hot oil. Place pork in casserole with cabbage. Cover; continue simmering for 2 additional hours or until pork is done. Adjust seasonings.

Serves 6.

SAUERKRAUT WITH PORK CHOPS AND SAUSAGE
(Choucroute Garnie)
½ pound thickly-sliced bacon
3 cups chopped onions
2 large cans sauerkraut (2½ lbs. size) or 4 pounds bulk
2 cloves garlic, peeled
20 juniper berries (or ½ cup gin)
2 bay leaves
½ teaspoon salt
6 peppercorns
2 cups dry white wine
8 smoked pork chops or 8 fresh pork chops
2 Polish sausage, cut into 8 pieces
8 frankfurters

Cook bacon in large Dutch oven until fat is rendered. Add onions; sauté until transparent. Thoroughly rinse sauerkraut in cold water. Squeeze out moisture. Add to onions, along with juniper berries, bay leaves, salt, peppercorns and wine. Cover; bake in preheated 325°F oven 2 hours. Check for liquid; add more wine if needed. After cooking for 2 hours, add fresh pork chops. Cook for 30 minutes more. Add sausage and frankfurters. If smoked pork chops are used, cook sauerkraut 2½ hours, then add chops along with other meats. Cook another 30 to 45 minutes until all meats are done.

Serves 8.

PORK AND VEGETABLE CASSEROLE
2 tablespoons vegetable oil
1 pound lean pork, cut into bite-sized pieces
1 medium onion, chopped
2 pounds green cabbage, finely shredded
3 medium potatoes, peeled and cut into 1-inch cubes
1½ cups hot beef bouillon
½ teaspoon salt
⅛ teaspoon pepper
½ teaspoon caraway seeds
1 sprig of parsley, chopped

Heat oil in a large Dutch oven. Add meat cubes and brown on all sides for about 10 minutes. Add the onion and sauté lightly. Stir in the cabbage and potatoes. Add bouillon, and season with salt, pepper and caraway seeds. Cover and simmer for 50 minutes. Adjust seasoning if necessary. Serve garnished with chopped parsley.

Serves 4.

STUFFED ROAST PORK
(Porc À La Châtelaine)
6 pounds center-cut loin of pork
bacon stuffing
6 strips bacon, diced
2 tablespoons brandy
1 cup chopped prunes
2 cups coarse bread crumbs from French bread
1 teaspoon grated lemon rind
3 tablespoons lemon juice
1 cup chicken broth
¼ teaspoon marjoram
½ teaspoon salt
⅛ teaspoon pepper
¼ teaspoon thyme

Cut a pocket in pork roast along ribs. Fry bacon until crisp; set aside. Add 2 tablespoons brandy to chopped prunes; let stand 30 minutes. Mix bread crumbs, lemon rind, lemon juice, broth and seasonings. Add bacon, drippings and prunes with liquid. Use stuffing to fill pocket in pork. Skewer opening closed. Roast in shallow pan at 325°F about 2½ to 3 hours, until 180°F on a meat thermometer.

Serves 6.

VEAL WITH MUSHROOMS

1½ pounds veal steaks
flour for dredging meat
1 teaspoon salt
¼ teaspoon pepper
3 teaspoons flour
½ cup beef stock
½ cup cream
2 ounces mushrooms, sliced
1 tablespoon lemon juice

Pound veal steaks tender; dredge with flour seasoned with salt and pepper. Melt butter in pan; fry veal on both sides until golden brown and cooked through. Remove to warming platter. Stir 3 teaspoons flour into butter remaining in pan. Gradually add stock; continue stirring until sauce boils. Remove from flame; add cream. In separate pan, cook sliced mushrooms with lemon juice. When moisture has evaporated, remove from heat; place over veal steaks. Cover steaks with sauce; serve at once.

Serves 4.

VEAL WITH ORANGE SLICES

(Côtelettes De Veau À L'orange)

2 oranges
2 teaspoons grated orange rind
12 thinly-sliced veal cutlets
2 tablespoons vegetable oil
2 tablespoons brandy, warmed
½ cup beef bouillon
½ teaspoon salt
⅛ teaspoon white pepper
¼ cup orange juice

Grate 2 teaspoons peel from oranges. Cut away remaining peel on oranges; remove any white membrane. Slice orange into thin rounds. Place in covered baking pan in warm (200°F) oven while preparing rest of dish. In large frying pan sauté veal in hot oil until lightly browned. Add warmed brandy; flame until alcohol is completely burned off. Stir in bouillon, salt, pepper, orange juice and orange rind. Simmer, covered, for 8 minutes. Remove lid; raise heat to reduce sauce for 4 additional minutes. Serve veal on heated serving platter; cover with sauce and garnish with warm orange slices.

Serves 6.

VEAL CUTLETS WITH CHERRY SAUCE

4 lean veal cutlets, about 6 ounces each
1 tablespoon vegetable oil
½ teaspoon salt
⅛ teaspoon white pepper
¼ cup red wine
2 tablespoons evaporated skimmed milk
½ pound tart canned cherries
Parsley for garnish

Pat cutlets dry with paper towels. Heat oil in a frying pan and brown cutlets on each side for approximately 3 minutes. Season with salt and pepper. Remove cutlets from pan and keep them warm. Blend red wine and evaporated milk in pan and simmer for 3 minutes. Add drained cherries; heat through and adjust seasonings. Return cutlets to sauce and reheat, but do not boil. Arrange cutlets on preheated platter, pouring cherry sauce around them. Garnish with parsley.

Serves 4.

VEAL CUTLETS CORDON BLEU

4 thick veal cutlets
1 cup ground, cooked ham
1 cup grated gruyere cheese
garlic salt
2 tablespoons butter
2-3 tablespoons flour
2-3 tablespoons oil
1 cup white wine
½ cup chicken stock
2 tablespoons chopped parsley and tarragon
Preheat oven to 350°F

Cut a pocket in each cutlet from boneless side, being careful not to pierce the outer surface. Mix ham and cheese together, adding garlic salt and pepper. Melt 1 tablespoon butter and stir in. Stuff cutlets carefully. Do not overfill. Seal openings with tooth picks, and roll cutlets in seasoned flour. Heat oil. Add remaining butter and, when foaming, fry cutlets, taking about 3 minutes to brown each side. Place in ovenproof dish. Add stock and wine to liquid in pan and bring to boil. Stir in chopped herbs. Pour sauce over cutlets and cook in oven until veal is tender, about 20-30 minutes. Remove before serving.

Serves 4.

VEAL WITH ARTICHOKES
(Noix De Veau Aux Artechauts)

 1 clove garlic
 1 tablespoon vegetable oil
 1 pound veal round, cut into bite-size pieces and pounded
 ½ teaspoon salt
 ⅛ teaspoon pepper
 1 cup canned tomatoes
 ¼ cup sherry
 ¼ teaspoon oregano
 1 10-ounce package frozen artichoke hearts

In large frying pan sauté garlic in hot oil. Remove garlic; discard. Season veal with salt and pepper. Brown in oil. Add tomatoes, sherry, and oregano; mix well. Add artichoke hearts. Cover; simmer for 1 hour or until meat is tender.
Serves 4.

PAUPIETTES
(Veal Rolls in Sauce)

 4 veal scallops or cutlets
 ½ pound ham, finely diced
 1 clove garlic, pressed
 ½ teaspoon marjoram
 ½ teaspoon rosemary
 Salt and pepper to taste
 5 tablespoons butter
 1 tablespoon olive oil
 1 large carrot, finely chopped
 1 large onion, finely chopped
 ½ cup dry white wine
 ½ cup beef broth
 ½ teaspoon thyme
 1 bay leaf
 4 parsley stalks
 1 tablespoon all-purpose flour

Pound scallops; trim into uniform rectangles. Mince scallop trimmings. Combine trimmings, ham, garlic, marjoram, rosemary, salt and pepper; spread evenly over scallops. Roll scallops as for jelly roll; tie with string. Melt 4 tablespoons butter with oil in frying pan. Add carrot and onion; cook until golden, stirring frequently. Stir in wine and broth; add thyme, bay leaf, parsley stalks, salt and pepper. Stir to mix well; pour into baking dish. Place veal rolls in sauce; cover. Bake in preheated 350°F oven, one shelf below center, 1 hour and 30 minutes. Remove casserole from oven; lift out veal rolls to serving dish. Remove string; keep veal rolls warm. Remove bay leaf and parsley stalks from sauce; pour sauce into blender container. Process sauce until puréed. Melt 1 tablespoon butter in saucepan; stir in flour to make a smooth paste. Pour in sauce, stirring constantly; bring to boil. Reduce heat; simmer until sauce thickens. Pour sauce over veal; garnish with finely chopped parsley. Serve with boiled new potatoes or rice.
Serves 4.

BLANQUETTE DE VEAU

 2 pounds veal from shoulder or breast
 4 tablespoons butter
 1 onion
 3-4 medium carrots
 1 tablespoon flour
 2 cups chicken or veal stock
 parsley stems
 1 bay leaf
 a sprig of thyme (or ¼ teaspoon dried thyme)
 12 button mushrooms
 12 baby or pickling onions
 1 cup cream
 1 large or 2 small egg yolks
 a squeeze of lemon
 Preheat oven to 350°F

Cut veal into cubes about 1¼ inches square. Put into pan with enough cold water to cover and a little salt. Bring slowly to boil and cook for 5 minutes. Skim off the scum which rises to the surface. Drain meat and wash well with cold water. Dry. Melt 3 tablespoons of butter and cook veal cubes slowly together with quartered onion and carrots, shaking frequently and not allowing them to brown at all. Stir in flour and then add stock, parsley, bay leaf and thyme. Bring to a boil and place in oven or simmer on stove for 1-1½ hours until veal is tender. Meanwhile peel baby onions and cook in salted water for 10-15 minutes. Drain. Melt remaining tablespoon butter and cook mushrooms for a few minutes. Add to onions. Remove veal from stove and place meat in dish, adding carrots, baby onions and mushrooms. Strain cooking liquid and boil to reduce quantity slightly. Remove from heat and cool slightly. Beat egg yolks with cream, add a little hot sauce to this and strain into sauce. Add lemon juice. Do not boil under any circumstances after this point. Pour over meat and vegetables and serve at once. Serve with mashed or riced potatoes.

Serves 4-6.

BEANS WITH LAMB, PORK, AND SAUSAGE
(Cassoulet De Porc Et De Mouton)

    1 pound Great Northern beans
    6 cups water
    2 medium onions, chopped
    ½ teaspoon salt
    ¼ teaspoon pepper
    1 bay leaf
    3 whole cloves
    2 tablespoons butter
    1 tablespoon vegetable oil
    1 pound boned lamb (shoulder or leg), cut into
      2-inch chunks
    ½ pound pork, cut into 1½-inch chunks
    1 stalk celery, thinly sliced
    1 carrot, thinly sliced
    2 green onions, chopped
    ½ pound Polish sausage, thinly sliced
    1 cup red wine
    2 tablespoons tomato paste
    2 cloves garlic, minced
    3 tablespoons chopped parsley
    Dash cayenne pepper
    1 to 2 cups beef bouillon
    2 tablespoons packaged bread crumbs

Wash beans. Place beans in pan with 6 cups water. Bring to a boil; boil for 2 minutes; remove from heat and let stand, covered, for 1 hour. Add onions, salt, pepper, bay leaf and cloves to beans in their soaking liquid. Cover; cook for 1 hour. When done, drain beans; reserve liquid. Meanwhile, heat 1 tablespoon butter and oil in frying pan; fry lamb and pork until brown. Add celery, carrot, onions and sausage to meat mixture. Pour in wine; simmer for 40 minutes. Stir in tomato paste, garlic and parsley. Season with cayenne. Simmer again for 5 minutes, stirring occasionally. Add drained beans; mix thoroughly. Grease ovenproof casserole and spoon in the bean-meat mixture. Add enough bean liquid or bouillon to come to top of bean-meat mixture. Sprinkle with

bread crumbs and dot with 1 tablespoon butter. Bake in preheated 375°F oven 1 hour. Serve with chunks of French bread and red wine.

Serves 6.

BRAISED LEG OF LAMB MIRABEAU
(Gigot De Pré Salé Braise Mirabeau)

    4 pounds leg of lamb
    ½ teaspoon salt
    ⅛ teaspoon pepper
    1 quart buttermilk
    ¼ cup vegetable oil
    2 large carrots, sliced
    2 large onions, sliced
    2 cups dry white wine
    2 cups beef bouillon
    1 whole clove garlic
    4 tablespoons anchovy paste
    ¼ cup heavy cream
    1 tablespoon butter
    18 flat anchovy fillets, rinsed in cold water
    18 stuffed green olives, cut in half
    2 tablespoons fresh chopped tarragon (or 2 tea-
      spoons dried)

Rinse meat under cold, running water; pat dry with paper towels. Rub with salt and pepper. Pour buttermilk into large bowl that will hold the lamb. Add lamb; marinate for 10 hours or overnight. Drain meat; pat dry with paper towels. Heat oil in large Dutch oven. Add lamb; brown on all sides about 15 minutes. Remove to a platter. Brown carrots and onions for 2 to 3 minutes. Remove with slotted spoon to platter. Pour out browning oil. Add white wine and reduce it to half by boiling; scrape up coagulated particles. Place lamb, fattiest side up, in Dutch oven. Surround with vegetables. Pour in enough bouillon to come two-thirds of the way up the meat. Add garlic; bring liquid to simmer on top of range. Cover; place in 350°F oven 2½ hours. Turn and baste meat every half hour. Remove meat; keep it warm. Strain and degrease cooking liquid. Correct seasoning. Blend anchovy paste and cream; stir into liquid. Add butter; stir until melted. Garnish meat with anchovy fillets and olives; sprinkle with tarragon. Serve sauce separately.

Serves 8.

SAUTÉED CALVES LIVER
(Foie De Veau Sauté)

1 pound fresh calves liver, ⅜ inch thick
½ cup flour
½ teaspoon salt
⅛ teaspoon pepper
3 tablespoons butter
2 tablespoons vegetable oil
1 tablespoon chopped shallots or green onions
2 tablespoons brandy
⅓ cup beef broth

Gently remove membrane surrounding liver. Mix flour, salt and pepper. Coat liver with flour, shaking off any excess. Melt butter in large frying pan. Add oil; heat until hot. Add liver in one layer; cook over medium heat. Liver must cook 3 to 4 minutes on each side. Turn liver as needed to prevent burning. When done, liver is only faintly pink. Remove liver to heated plate; keep it warm. Add shallots to frying pan; cook until tender. Add brandy; ignite. When flame has died out, add beef broth. Boil rapidly several minutes to reduce sauce. Scrape all browned bits from bottom of pan. Pour sauce over liver. Serve liver hot with oven-browned potatoes.

Serves 4.

VEGETABLE STEW WITH LAMB

2 tablespoons vegetable oil
1 pound lean lamb, cut in bite-size pieces
1 medium onion, chopped
1 small head cabbage, shredded
1 stalk celery, sliced
2 medium carrots, sliced
1 stalk leek, sliced
6 cups hot beef bouillon
2 medium potatoes, cubed
1 small head of cauliflower, spearated into florets
1 10-ounce package frozen green beans
2 tablespoons tomato paste
½ teaspoon salt
¼ teaspoon white pepper
parsley to garnish

Heat oil in a 4-quart Dutch oven or saucepan. Brown meat for about 5 minutes. Add onion and sauté until golden brown. Add cabbage, celery, carrots, leek and hot bouillon. Bring to a boil and sim-mer for 1 hour. Add potatoes, cauliflower and beans. Continue simmering for 20 to 30 minutes until the vegetables are tender. Thin tomato paste with a little broth and add to the stew. Season with salt and pepper. Garnish with chopped parsley.

Serves 6.

LAMB STEW

1 tablespoon vegetable oil
1 pound boneless lamb, cut in 1-inch cubes
1 tablespoon flour
1 teaspoon salt
¼ teaspoon pepper
1 cup white wine
1 tablespoon tomato paste
2 cups water
1 clove garlic, minced
½ pound carrots, cubed
2 turnips, cubed
¼ pound fresh green beans, trimmed
6 small potatoes, peeled and quartered
6 small whole onions, peeled
¼ pound fresh green peas

Heat oil in a 2-quart saucepan. Brown lamb well on all sides. Sprinkle with flour, salt and pepper; stir well to coat lamb. Add wine, tomato paste, water and garlic. Bring to a simmer, cover, and cook 40 minutes. Add all vegetables except peas. Cover and cook slowly about 30 minutes, until lamb is tender and vegetables are done. Add peas and cook 8 minutes or until done.

Serves 4.

CURRY LAMB RAGOÙT

1 pound lean lamb meat
2 tablespoons vegetable oil
½ teaspoon sage
Grated rind of half a lemon
1 medium onion, chopped
2 cups beef bouillon
2 tablespoon curry powder
½ teaspoon salt
⅛ teaspoon white pepper
1 green pepper, cut in strips
1 8-ounce can sliced mushrooms
2 tomatoes, peeled and quartered

1 tart apple, peeled, cored and coarsely chopped

½ cup plain yogurt

Cut meat into 1-inch cubes. Heat oil in a heavy saucepan or Dutch oven. Add meat, sage and lemon rind; brown meat on all sides. Add onion, and sauté lightly. Drain off excess oil. Stir in bouillon, cover saucepan, and simmer for 50 minutes. Season with curry, salt and pepper. Add sliced green pepper and simmer, uncovered, for 5 minutes. Stir in drained mushrooms, tomatoes and apple. Simmer for another 5 minutes. Cool mixture slightly and gradually add yogurt to ragoût. Heat thoroughly without boiling.

Serves 4.

MUSHROOM-ONION LAMB

3 pounds boned lamb shoulder

4 carrots

2 14-ounce cans chicken broth

salt to taste

1 pound medium onions, peeled

1 pound medium mushrooms, stems removed

¼ cup butter

½ cup flour

2 egg yolks

½ cup whipping cream

2 teaspoons lemon juice

1 tablespoon finely chopped parsley

Trim excess fat from lamb; cut into ½-inch cubes. Peel carrots; quarter lengthwise; cut quarters in half. Place lamb in Dutch oven; arrange carrots around lamb. Cover with broth; season with salt. Bring to boil over high heat, removing any scum. Turn into large casserole; cover. Bake in preheated 350°F oven 1 hour or until lamb is tender. Drain broth into 3-quart suacepan. Keep lamb mixture warm. Place onions in broth; cook until almost tender. Add mushrooms; cook 7 minutes longer. Remove onions and mushrooms; keep warm with lamb mixture. Strain broth; set aside. Melt butter in medium saucepan. Add flour; cook, stirring constantly, to make light-brown sauce. Add broth gradually, stirring well after each addition; cook until smooth and thick. Combine egg yolks and cream, mixing well. Stir small amount of broth mixture into egg mixture; slowly add egg mixture to broth mixture, stirring

constantly. Place over very low heat until heated through and thickened, stirring constantly. Stir in lemon juice. Arrange lamb and vegetables on heated platter; pour sauce over all. Sprinkle with parsley; garnish with triangular-shaped croutons.

Serves 8.

POULTRY

COQ AU VIN

(Elegant Coq)

¼ pound butter

12 tiny onions

¼ pound bacon strips, cut into 1-inch pieces

4 pounds cut-up chicken pieces

½ pound mushrooms, sliced

1 clove garlic, crushed

½ cup flour

2½ cups chicken stock

⅓ cup brandy

1½ cups red wine

¼ teaspoon thyme

½ teaspoon mixed herbs

1 bay leaf

salt and pepper to taste

Heat 4 tablespoons butter in heavy, shallow pan. Add onions and bacon; cook until onions are lightly browned. Remove from pan. Add chicken pieces to pan drippings; cook until well-browned on all sides. Set aside. Add mushrooms and garlic to pan; cook until mushrooms are wilted. Remove from pan. Add remaining butter to pan drippings. Gradually stir in flour until golden brown. Remove from heat; gradually add chicken stock. Blend well. Return to heat; stir until sauce thickens. Add brandy, wine, thyme, herbs and bay leaf. Transfer chicken, vegetables and sauce to deep pan. Cover; bring to boil. Reduce heat; simmer for 30 minutes. Season with salt and pepper. Remove bay leaf. This final step can be done, covered, in 400°F oven for 40 minutes or until chicken is tender to the fork. Serve chicken with hot garlic bread and your favorite salad.

Serves 6.

COLD CHICKEN WITH BRANDIED CREAM

4 whole chicken breasts
½ cup mayonnaise
½ cup sour cream
1 tablespoon brandy
3 tablespoons cream
salt and pepper to taste
Black grapes for garnish

Boned breasts are preferred and should be cooked ahead, halved, then chilled, keeping breast meat in one piece. Mix mayonnaise, sour cream and brandy in bowl, gradually adding cream to make a good coating consistency. Extra cream may be needed. Season sauce with salt and pepper to taste. Place each chicken portion on bed of lettuce; spoon cream mixture over it. Refrigerate until ready to serve. Garnish with grapes, if desired.

Serves 4.

CHICKEN CROQUETTES

2½ pounds chicken breasts
4 tablespoons butter
2 tablespoons flour
2 teaspoons unflavored gelatin
½ cup cream
1 teaspoon salt
¼ teaspoon pepper
2 tablespoons chopped parsley
½ teaspoon dry mustard
Pinch of cayenne
2 eggs
¼ cup milk
Packaged dry bread crumbs
Oil for deep frying

Steam or boil chicken until tender, setting aside stock in which it is cooked. Remove skin and bones from chicken; chop chicken meat into small pieces. Heat butter in pan; gradually stir in flour. When well-blended, about 1 minute, remove from heat. Stir gelatin into 1 cup hot chicken stock. When dissolved, add to flour mixture. Add cream; stir until smoothly blended. Return to heat; bring to boil. When thickened, add salt, pepper, parsley, mustard and cayenne. Simmer just 2 minutes. Remove from heat; add chicken. When well-mixed, spread out on platter; refrigerate for 1 hour, until mixture is firm and set. With wet hands, shape mixture by table-spoonfuls into croquettes. Roll in dry bread crumbs. Dip into combined beaten eggs and milk. Roll again in bread crumbs. If you prefer a thicker crust, repeat egg and bread crumbs once more. Refrigerate at least 1 hour. Heat oil for deep frying; place rolls into oil. Cook until golden brown; drain on paper. Croquettes may be kept in a warming oven until ready to serve.

Serves 4-6.

JELLIED CHICKEN

3 pounds chicken parts, jointed
3 cups cold water
3 small carrots, sliced
3 stalks celery, diced
1 teaspoon salt
¼ teaspoon pepper
1 bay leaf
1 onion, chopped
2 tablespoons chopped parsley
1 tablespoon unflavored gelatin
1 tablespoon water

Joint chicken. Prepare vegetables. Place all ingredients except gelatin and 1 tablespoon water into large pot. Cover; simmer gently until chicken is all cooked, about 40 minutes. Remove from heat. Drain chicken and vegetables, reserving liquid. Remove chicken meat from bones; cut into cubes. Arrange half of cooked vegetables on greased tin. Place chopped chicken next; make final layer more vegetables. Dissolve gelatin in 1 tablespoon water. Add to 2 cups of hot, strained chicken stock. Gently pour mixture over chicken and vegetables; refrigerate until set. Unmold jellied chicken onto bed of shredded lettuce.

Serves 4-6.

ORANGE CHESTNUT CHICKEN

1 3-pound chicken
6 tablespoons butter
1 cup orange juice
½ cup chicken stock
1 teaspoon sugar
1 teaspoon salt
¼ teaspoon pepper
1 tablespoon cornstarch

Fill cavity and neck end of chicken with stuffing. Secure openings with skewers. Melt butter in baking dish. Add chicken; brush with melted butter. Bake in moderate oven, basting occasionally with pan juices, 1½ hours or until chicken is tender. Remove chicken from baking dish; keep warm. Combine rest of ingredients; add to pan juices. Stir over moderate heat until sauce thickens. Reduce heat; simmer 3 minutes. Serve sauce separately in gravy boat.

Serves 4.

chestnut stuffing
4 tablespoons butter
¼ cup chopped mushrooms
4 shallots, chopped
1 tablespoon sweet sherry
1 8-ounce can unsweetened chestnut purée
2 cups bread crumbs
½ teaspoon thyme
Salt and pepper to taste

Heat butter in pan. Add mushrooms and shallots; sauté for 3 minutes. Remove from heat. Add sherry; mix well. Combine other ingredients; stir until well mixed.

CHICKEN KIEV WITH SHERRY SAUCE
2 whole chicken breasts, split, boned and skinned
1 tablespoon chopped chives
1 tablespoon chopped parsley
½ clove garlic, minced
¼ teaspoon salt
⅛ teaspoon pepper
½ cup low-fat mozzarella cheese, grated
Toothpicks
2 tablespoons vegetable oil
1 tablespoon flour
¼ cup dry sherry
1 cup chicken bouillon or broth

Pound each chicken breast half with the flat side of a meat mallet to ¼-inch thickness. Sprinkle seasonings evenly over chicken pieces. Cover surfaces with grated cheese and roll up each half breast with cheese enclosed. Secure with a toothpick. Heat oil in a large frying pan and sauté chicken rolls until golden brown, about 8 minutes. Place in shallow baking dish. Preheat oven to 350°F. To make the sauce, stir flour into drippings in frying pan; stir until smooth. Remove from heat. Add sherry and bouillon to drippings. Return to heat and heat to boiling,

stirring constantly. Reduce sauce by boiling until slightly thickened. Spoon over chicken; cover. Bake 30 minutes. Remove toothpicks before serving.

Serves 4.

CHICKEN PROVENÇALE
4 whole chicken breasts, each approximately 8 to 10 ounces
3 tablespoons vegetable oil
½ teaspoon salt
⅛ teaspoon white pepper
1 medium tomato
5 black olives
1 clove garlic, minced
½ cup dry white wine
3 tablespoons water
¼ teaspoon instant chicken bouillon (or ½ cube)
¼ cup yogurt
Parsley for garnish

Bone chicken breasts. Heat oil in a large frying pan and fry chicken breasts, approximately 15 minutes, until they are golden brown and completely cooked. Season with salt and pepper. Arrange on a preheated platter and keep warm. Peel and chop tomato; slice olives. Add tomato, olives and minced garlic to pan drippings. Pour in wine and water; stir in dry bouillon. Bring to a boil and simmer uncovered for 8 minutes. Cool sauce slightly and gradually add yogurt. Warm sauce over low heat if necessary. Pour sauce over chicken breats; garnish with parsley.

Serves 4.

BROILED CHICKEN WITH MUSHROOMS
1 3-pound chicken
3 tablespoons polyunsaturated margarine, melted
2 onions, cut into quarters
2 tablespoons polyunsaturated margarine
½ pound mushrooms, stemmed
1 teaspoon salt
½ teaspoon pepper
2 tablespoons cognac

Split chicken in half and brush with 3 tablespoons melted margarine. Broil 5 inches from heat for about 20 minutes. Brush with margarine every 5 minutes. Do not allow the skin to burn or blister. Meanwhile, sauté onions for 5 minutes in 2 tablespoons margarine. Add mushrooms and cook another 5 minutes. Season with salt and pepper. Pour cognac over vegetables and set ablaze. When chicken is cooked, split each piece in two. Arrange vegetables on platter with chicken.

Serves 4.

CHICKEN IN RED WINE

4 whole chicken legs
2 teaspoons salt
1 teaspoon paprika
¼ teaspoon thyme
1 bay leaf
¾ cup dry red wine
1 cup water
½ cup tomato juice
1 teaspoon salt
¼ teaspoon pepper
chopped parsley for garnish

Separate chicken into thighs and drumsticks, or keep whole, according to your preference. Mix salt and paprika; rub well into chicken pieces. Broil chicken until browned evenly on both sides. Remove from broiler. Place in ovenproof dish. Add thyme, bay leaf, wine and water. Cover; put in 400°F oven 1 hour or until chicken is tender. Place chicken on warming dish. Pour juices into small pan. Add tomato juice, salt and pepper; heat until all flavors blend. Pour sauce over chicken; garnish with parsley.

Serves 4.

CHICKEN TOURANGELLE

1 4-pound stewing chicken
2 large onions, quartered
2 cups chicken stock
6 to 8 medium mushrooms
½ cup dry white wine
½ cup whipping cream
Salt and freshly-ground pepper to taste
Grated rind of ½ orange
2 cups mashed potatoes
2 tablespoons toasted sliced almonds

Place chicken, onions and stock in roasting pan; cover. Bake in preheated 325°F oven 2 hours or until chicken is tender. Remove chicken from roasting pan; cool until easily handled. Remove skin and bones from chicken; cut chicken into serving pieces. Arrange on heated platter; keep warm. Cut stems from mushrooms; cut caps in half. Add mushroom caps and stems to liquid in roasting pan; bring to boil over high heat. Boil until liquid is reduced to 2 cups. Stir in wine and cream; boil until reduced to 2 cups liquid. Season with salt and pepper; stir in orange rind. Pour sauce over chicken. Place mashed potatoes in pastry bag with large writing tube affixed; pipe around chicken mixture. Sprinkle potato mixture with almonds.

Serves 6.

STUFFED CHICKEN BREASTS WITH SHERRY SAUCE

(Suprêmes De Volaille Farcis À L'Xérès)

2 whole chicken breasts, split, boned, and skinned
4 tablespoons butter
1 tablespoon chopped chives
1 tablespoon parsley
½ clove garlic, minced
½ teaspoon salt
⅛ teaspoon pepper
4 slices Swiss cheese
2 tablespoons vegetable oil
2 tablespoons flour
1 cup water
¼ cup dry sherry
2 teaspoons chicken-seasoned stock base

Pound each half chicken breast with flat side of meat mallet to ¼-inch thick. Form butter into 4 balls. Roll balls in mixture of chives, parsley, garlic, salt, and pepper. Place 1 seasoned ball on each slice of Swiss cheese. Place cheese on chicken breasts; roll so butter is completely enclosed. Secure with toothpicks. Heat oil in frying pan; brown the chicken rolls about 8 minutes. Place into covered shallow baking dish. Preheat oven to 350°F. To make sauce, stir flour into drippings in pan; stir and heat until smooth. Remove from heat. Mix water, sherry and stock base. Stir into drippings; heat to boiling, stirring constantly. Spoon sauce over chicken; cover. Bake for 30 minutes. Remove toothpicks.

Serves 4.

CHICKEN VOL-AU-VENT

2 whole chicken breasts
4 tablespoons butter
3 tablespoons flour
1 cup chicken stock
¾ cup cream
salt and pepper to taste
2 ounces grated cheddar cheese
1 7-ounce can champignons (small mushrooms)
3 shallots, chopped
1 tablespoon chopped parsley
2 teaspoons dry sherry
1½ teaspoons prepared mustard
4 patty-shell cases (vol-au-vents)

Cook chicken breasts in boiling water until meat is tender. Reserve stock. Remove bones and skin; cut meat into 1-inch pieces. Melt butter in pan; stir in flour. Remove from heat. Gradually add chicken stock and cream, stirring until combined. Return to heat; allow sauce to thicken. Season with salt and pepper; simmer for 2 minutes more. Add grated cheese, sliced mushrooms, shallots, parsley, sherry and mustard. Stir until cheese has melted. Add chicken pieces; heat through over low flame. Warm the patty shells in moderate (350°F) oven until hot. Spoon chicken mixture into patty shells. Garnish with chopped parsley or dill if desired.

Serves 4.

CHICKEN VERONIQUE
(Poulet Veronique)

⅓ cup flour
½ teaspoon salt
⅛ teaspoon freshly-ground pepper
1 3- to 4-pound broiler-fryer, cut up, or 6 pieces chicken
¼ cup vegetable oil
¼ cup dry white wine
⅓ cup orange juice
4 tablespoons honey
¼ teaspoon salt
1 tablespoon chopped parsley
2 teaspoons grated orange rind
1 cup halved seedless green grapes
Orange slices

Mix flour, salt and pepper. Dredge chicken in flour mixture. Shake off excess flour. Heat oil in large fry-ing pan or Dutch oven. Brown chicken pieces on all sides. Drain off oil, if desired. Add wine, juice, honey, salt, parsley and orange rind. Cover; simmer over low heat 45 minutes until chicken is done. Remove chicken to serving platter. Add grapes to pan juices. Heat gently 2 minutes to heat grapes. Pour sauce over chicken. Garnish with orange slices and additional green grapes.

Serves 4-6.

POACHED CHICKEN WITH VEGETABLES
(Poularde Bouillie À L'anglaise)

1 small onion
2 cloves garlic, peeled
3 sprigs parsley
1 teaspoon tarragon
1 3-pound chicken
1½ cups dry white wine 1 cup chicken broth
1 teaspoon salt
4 carrots, peeled
4 small turnips, peeled and quartered
4 small leeks, cleaned and blanched 5 minutes in boiling water (green onions may be used)
2 tablespoons flour
½ cup heavy cream
2 egg yolks
2 to 3 teaspoons horseradish

Place onion, garlic, parsley and tarragon in cavity of chicken; truss. Place chicken in large Dutch oven. Add wine, broth and salt; bring to a boil. Cover; place in preheated 325°F oven. Bake chicken 45 minutes. Add vegetables. Cover; Bake for 30 minutes longer. When chicken and vegetables are done, remove to serving platter. Whisk flour into cream. Skim any fat from pan juices. Beat in cream; heat until thick. Add small amount of gravy to egg yolks, then add egg yolks to pan. Stir and heat through. Add horseradish. Serve sauce with chicken.

Serves 4.

GOOSE EN DAUBE

1 goose, wild or domestic
1 cup diced bacon
1 cup chopped shallots or mild onions
2 cloves garlic
several parsley stalks
a sprig of thyme

2 sprigs basil (or teaspoon dried basil)
1 large or 2 small bay leaves
2 cleaned and washed pig feet if available (or 2 teaspoons gelatine added after cooking)
¼ cup brandy
2-3 cups red wine
2 cups water or more if necessary to cover bird
3-4 tablespoons flour mixed to a thick paste for sealing casserole
Preheat oven to 290°F

Put goose into a thick fireproof casserole with lid, on top of a layer of mix bacon, onion and all other ingredients, sprinkling the rest over the top. Pour in all liquids, which should cover bird. Cover with lid and seal this with a paste made from flour and water. Cook in oven for about 4½-5 hours. When dish has cooled, break seal and remove goose. Carve all meat and put slices in large dish. Strain cooking liquid off all pieces of vegetables etc; skim off any fat and check seasoning. If no pig feet were included, dissolve 2 teaspoons gelatine in hot liquid. Pour this liquid over goose and put in refrigerator to set. Serve cold with endive and orange salad, and hot potatoes. (This method can also be used to cook duck or chicken, but cooking time is shorter.)

Serves 6-8.

DUCK WITH ORANGE SAUCE
(Canard À L'orange)

1 6- to 7-pound duck or 2 3- 4-pound ducks
½ teaspoon salt
⅛ teaspoon pepper
orange sauce
   2 tablespoons sugar
   2 tablespoons vinegar
   Brown sauce (see Index for recipe, but omit Madeira and cognac)
   2 tablespoons frozen orange-juice concentrate
   1 teaspoon lemon juice
   1 tablespoon cornstarch
   1 tablespoon Madeira
   2 tablespoons cognac
   2 tablespoons Grand Marnier
   2 oranges, sectioned

Clean duck; remove giblets. Sprinkle cavity with salt and pepper. Truss; scald with boiling water to open pores so fat will drain out during cooking. Also make small knife slits through skin in thigh, back, and lower breast areas. Roast both sides of duck at 425°F for 1 hour. Reduce heat to 325°F; cook 6- to 7-pound duck 1 more hour or 3- to 4-pound duck 30 minutes more. If duck is not browned sufficiently, increase heat to 425°F for a few minutes. Meanwhile, make Orange Sauce. Combine sugar and vinegar; boil briefly to caramelize (brown). Cool, add Brown Sauce, and heat to dissolve. Stir in orange and lemon juices; simmer for 8 to 10 minutes. Thicken slightly by mixing cornstarch with Madeira and adding to sauce. Simmer for 1 to 2 minutes. Finish sauce with cognac, Grand Marnier and orange sections. When duck is roasted, let stand about 10 minutes before carving. Spoon some hot sauce over carved duck; serve rest of sauce separately.

Serves 4.

CURRIED TURKEY

3 turkey legs and thighs, cut at joint into serving pieces
2 tablespoons seasoned flour (add ½ teaspoon salt and ¼ teaspoon pepper)
2 onions, sliced
3 tablespoons vegetable oil
1 apple, peeled, cored and chopped
2 tablespoon curry powder
2 cups chicken broth
1 tablespoon lemon juice
2 tablespoons chutney
4 tomatoes, chopped

Coat turkey pieces with seasoned flour. Sauté onions in hot oil until soft in a large frying pan or Dutch oven. Add turkey pieces and fry until golden brown. Stir in chopped apple and curry powder. Cook 2 minutes. Add broth, lemon juice, chutney and tomatoes; mix well. Cover and simmer for 1 hour or more. Cooking time will vary according to the size of the turkey pieces.

Serves 6.

FISH

LENTEN MACKEREL

4 medium tomatoes, skinned
1 small onion, thinly sliced
4 peppercorns
2 strips lemon peel
4 thick mackerel or snapper steaks
leaves of 4 small sprigs thyme
leaves of 2 sprigs fennel
Salt to taste
½ cup fish stock
½ cup dry white wine

Slice tomatoes. Arrange tomato and onion slices in well-buttered, shallow baking pan. Add peppercorns and lemon peel. Arrange mackerel steaks over tomato mixture. Sprinkle with thyme and fennel leaves; season with salt. Pour stock and wine into baking pan; cover. Bake in preheated 325°F oven 20 to 25 minutes or until mackerel flakes easily when pierced with a fork. One-half teaspoon powdered thyme and 2 teaspoon dried fennel may be substituted for thyme and fennel leaves.

Serves 4.

CABILLAUD AU GRATIN

1 pound potatoes
4 tablespoons butter or margarine
2 tablespoons light cream or milk
1 egg
1½ pound cod fillets
2 tablespoons dry white wine
2 teaspoons lemon juice
2 tablespoons flour
1 small package frozen shrimps
½ cup grated Gruyère cheese
milk
Preheat oven to 450°F

Cook the potatoes in boiling salted water, drain thoroughly and dry over low heat. Add 2 tablespoons butter, cream and beaten egg; whip until fluffy. Put the fish into a skillet with the wine, lemon juice and enough salted water to barely cover. Poach for 15 minutes. Drain carefully and retain the stock. Flake the fish coarsely, removing any skin. Make a sauce with the remaining 2 tablespoons butter, flour and 1 cup of the fish stock. Add the shrimp and cheese. Season to taste. Put the fish into an oven dish, add enough sauce to moisten and cover with the potatoes. Brush with a little milk and bake for about 30 minutes or until the potato crust is brown. Serve any remaining sauce separately, thinning it (if necessary) with a little of the fish stock.

Serves 4-5.

POACHED FISH
(Filets De Poisson Pochés Au Vin Blanc)

5 cups boiling water
2 medium onions, sliced
1 carrot, chopped
1 stalk celery
4 sprigs parsley
1 bay leaf
2 tablespoons salt
1 lemon, sliced
2 cups dry white wine
8 fish fillets or 1 3- to 4-pound whole dressed fish
2 tablespoons butter
2 tablespoons flour
½ cup heavy cream
1 egg yolk
2 tablespoon lemon juice

In 3-quart saucepan, combine water, onions, carrot, celery, parsley, bay leaf, salt and lemon. Bring to a boil. Reduce heat; simmer for 15 minutes. Add wine; simmer 15 minutes longer. Strain liquid. Cool to lukewarm. Place fresh fillets in bottom of greased casserole. Cover with stock. Bring just to simmer on the range. Cover tightly; place in preheated 325°F oven. Cook fish 10 to 15 minutes, until done, or simmer on top of stove. If poaching a whole fish, first wrap in cheesecloth. Then place fish in large shallow pan, such as a French fish poacher; cover with liquid. Cook fish at simmer about 10 minutes per inch of thickness. Remove from heat; leave fish in broth while preparing sauce. To prepare sauce for fish, melt butter in small pan. Add flour; stir to blend. Add 1 cup of the poaching liquid. Cook, stirring constantly, until thickened. Mix cream and egg yolk. Stirring rapidly, add cream and lemon juice to sauce. Keep sauce warm. Pour over fish.

Serves 8.

FISH STEAKS SEVILLE

⅓ cup chopped green pepper
¼ cup chopped onion
1 clove garlic, minced
2 tablespoons vegetable oil
1 16-ounce can tomatoes
2 teaspoons chili powder
½ teaspoon salt
¼ teaspoon pepper
1 bay leaf
1 teaspoon cornstarch
1 tablespoon water
2 pounds fresh or frozen halibut steaks

Sauté green pepper, onion and garlic in hot oil until softened. Add tomatoes, chili powder, salt, pepper and bay leaf. Simmer for 5 minutes. Blend cornstarch with water and gradually stir into the hot sauce. Cook, stirring constantly, until thickened and bubbling. Arrange fish steaks in a greased baking dish. Pour the sauce over the fish. Bake in a preheated 350°F oven for 30 minutes or until the fish is done. Lift the fish from the pan with a spatula.

Serves 4-6.

COQUILLES SAINT JACQUES

1½ cups sauterne
2 pounds fresh scallops
½ pound medium mushrooms. sliced
6 green onions, finely chopped
6 tablespoons butter
3 tablespoons water
1 tablespoon finely-chopped parsley
1 tablespoon lemon juice
¼ cup all-purpose flour
2 egg yolks
¼ cup whipping cream
½ teaspoon salt
⅛ teaspoon freshly-ground pepper
2 cups mashed potatoes

Bring sauterne to boil in medium-size saucepan; add scallops. Reduce heat; simmer 3 minutes or until scallops are tender. Drain; set aside. Reserve broth. Combine mushrooms, onions, 2 tablespoons butter, water, parsley and lemon juice in saucepan. Cover; simmer about 10 minutes, stirring occasionally. Melt remaining butter in saucepan. Stir in flour; cook, stirring constantly, until lightly browned. Stir in reserved broth slowly; cook, stirring constantly, until

thickened and smooth. Remove from heat. Combine egg yolks and cream; beat well. Add part of hot sauce to egg mixture very slowly, beating constantly with whisk. Beat egg mixture into remaining sauce. Season with salt and pepper. Stir in mushroom mixture, then scallops. Spoon evenly into 8 scallop shells or small ramekins. Pipe mashed potatoes around shells. Place shells in jelly-roll pan. Bake in preheated 400°F oven 15-20 minutes or until potatoes are lightly browned. Serve immediately.

Serves 8.

SEAFOOD STEW

(Bouillabaisse)

2 tablespoons vegetable oil
2 onions, chopped, or 3 leeks, sliced
4 cloves garlic, crushed
2 fresh tomatoes, peeled and diced
3 tablespoons tomato paste
2 cups bottled clam juice
4 cups chicken bouillon
1 tablespoon salt
⅛ teaspoon pepper
¼ teaspoon saffron
½ teaspoon thyme
1 bay leaf
6 sprigs parsley
Grated rind of 1 orange
seafoods
1 2-pound lobster and/or other shellfish, such as clams, mussels (with shells), scallops, crab or shrimp
2 pounds assorted white fish fillets, such as sea bass, perch, cod, sole, flounder or red snapper
Chopped parsley for garnish

Heat vegetable oil in large saucepan or Dutch oven. Sauté onions or leeks several minutes, until translucent. Add remaining sauce ingredients; simmer 45 minutes. Prepare seafoods by cooking lobster. (Place in large kettle of boiling, salted water 10 minutes.) Break claws and tail from body; crack claws; cut tail into 1-inch chunks. Remove black vein from tail pieces; leave shell on meat. Wash and cut fish fillets into 2-inch pieces. Add lobster and firm-fleshed fish (sea bass, perch, etc.) to boiling sauce. Boil rapidly 5 minutes, then add tender-fleshed fish, such as clams, scallops, sole or cod. Boil another 5 minutes. Lift seafoods out as soon as cooked; keep them warm in soup tureen or platter. Boil liquid 10 minutes to reduce. Strain liquid through coarse sieve into tureen, mashing through some of the vegetables. Garnish with parsley.

Serves 6.

FRIED TROUT GRENOBLE
(Truites Grenobloise)

    4 freshwater trout, fresh or frozen (each about
       ½ pound)
    juice of 1 lemon
    salt
    5 tablespoons flour
    ½ cup vegetable oil
    ¼ cup butter
    1 slice dry bread, crumbled
    2 tablespoons capers
    1 lemon, sliced
    Parsley sprigs for garnish

Thoroughly wash fish; pat dry with paper towels. Sprinkle with half the lemon juice; let stand 5 minutes. Salt trout inside and out; roll it in flour. Heat oil in frying pan. Add trout; fry for 5 minutes on each side or until golden. Remove fish carefully with slotted spoon; discard oil. Melt butter in same frying pan. Return trout to pan; fry for 5 minutes on each side. Remove; arrange on preheated platter. Add bread crumbs to butter; cook until browned. Pour over trout. Sprinkle rest of lemon juice over trout. Top with drained capers. Garnish with lemon slices and parsley sprigs.   Serves 4.

SCALLOPS WITH MUSHROOMS
(Coquilles St. Jacques À La Parisienne)

    1½ pounds scallops
    ½ cup butter
    1 cup dry white wine
    ½ teaspoon salt
    ⅛ teaspoon pepper
    1 green onion, minced
    4 tablespoons flour
    1 cup heavy cream
    1 cup milk
    ½ pound fresh mushrooms, sliced
    Drops of lemon juice
    Salt and pepper to taste

    1 tablespoon cognac
    2 tablespoons butter
    6 scallop shells or pyrex dishes
    Roe for garnish (optional)

Wash scallops well in slightly-salted water to remove all grit. Drain and dry on paper towels. Cut scallops in half or quarters to make them bite-size. In medium saucepan, bring ½ cup butter, wine, ½ teaspoon salt, ⅛ teaspoon pepper and onion to simmer. Add scallops; return to simmer. Cover; simmer slowly 5 minutes. Remove scallops with slotted spoon; set aside. Boil pan liquids; reduce to just the butter. Add flour; cook, stirring, for 3 minutes. Stir in cream, milk, mushrooms and lemon juice. Salt and pepper to taste. Over medium heat, cook until thickened, stirring frequently. Add cognac. Blend two-thirds of sauce with scallops. Grease shells or dishes. Divide scallop mixture between them. Cover with rest of sauce. Dot with 2 tablespoons butter. Just before serving, place in preheated 400°F oven; heat about 10 minutes or until sauce is bubbling. Garnish with roe, if available.

Serves 6.

HERB-STUFFED TROUT WITH SAUCE

    6 dressed fresh trout
    2 bay leaves, halved
    1 small shallot, thinly sliced
    4 peppercorns
    2 or 3 sprigs parsley
    1 teaspoon salt
    ½ cup wine vinegar
    ½ cup water
    1½ cups soft bread crumbs
    1 egg, beaten
    2 tablespoons freshly-minced parsley
    1 tablespoon chopped chives
    Salt and pepper to taste
    Melted butter
    1 tablespoon capers
    1 small lemon, cut into sections

Remove heads and tails from trout; bone without cutting in half. Place in shallow glass container. Combine bay leaves, shallot, peppercorns, parsley and 1 teaspoon salt; sprinkle over trout. Mix vinegar and water; pour over trout. Marinate in refrigerator overnight. Drain; reserve marinade. Combine crumbs, egg, 1 tablespoon parsley and chives in bowl; salt and pepper to taste. Mix well. Stuff trout cavities with dressing; brush trout with melted butter. Arrange trout in shallow baking dish; cover lightly with aluminum foil. Bake in preheated 375°F oven about 20 minutes or until trout flakes easily. Strain reserved marinade; place in small saucepan. Stir in capers, remaining parsley, lemon sections and marinade mixture. Heat through. Arrange trout on serving dish; pour sauce over.

Serves 6.

LEMON TROUT WITH PARSLEY JELLY

    4 fresh dressed trout
    ½ cup dry white wine
    2 tablespoons vegetable oil
    1 small onion, sliced
    ½ cup chopped green onions
    ½ bay leaf
    ½ teaspoon salt
    ½ teaspoon thyme
    3 peppercorns
    Juice of 1 lemon
    3 cups fish stock
    1 tablespoon butter
    2 envelopes unflavored gelatin
    3 tablespoons minced parsley

Place trout in buttered, shallow baking dish. Combine wine, oil, onion slices, green onions, bay leaf, salt, thyme, peppercorns, lemon juice, fish stock and butter in medium-size saucepan; bring to boil. Simmer for 15 minutes. Strain; pour over trout. Cover with aluminum foil. Bake in preheated 350°F oven about 20 minutes or until trout flakes easily when pierced with a fork. Remove baking dish from oven; lift out trout. Remove skins from just below heads to just above tails, then place trout in deep platter. Soften gelatin in ½ cup cold water; stir into hot liquid in baking dish until dissolved. Add parsley; mix well. Pour over trout. Cool; chill until firm. Garnish with canelled lemon slices.

Serves 4.

SOLE WITH MUSHROOMS
(Sole Bonne Femme)
    1 cup fresh mushrooms
    2 tablespoons minced shallots
    2 tablespoons chopped parsley
    ½ teaspoon salt
    Dash pepper
    1½ pounds sole fillets
    ½ cup dry white wine (more, if needed)
    2 tablespoons flour
    2 tablespoons butter
    2 to 4 tablespoons heavy cream

Mix mushrooms, shallots, parsley, salt and pepper. Place in greased, flat baking dish. Place fish over mushrooms. Add enough wine to cover bottom of dish. Bring to a simmer. Cover with foil. Place in preheated 350°F oven 15-20 minutes, until fish is opaque. Remove fish; keep it warm. Mix flour and butter. Boil the juices remaining from fish until they are reduced by one-half. Beat in flour-butter mixture; cook until thickened. Add juices that have drained from fish and enough cream to make a medium sauce. Pour sauce over fish.

Serves 4.

FLOUNDER À L'ORANGE
    1 teaspoon salt
    Dash pepper
    2 tablespoons orange juice
    1 teaspoon grated orange rind
    2 tablespoons vegetable oil
    1½ pounds flounder fillets, cut into 6 serving
        pieces
    ⅛ teaspoon nutmeg

Combine salt, pepper, orange juice, orange rind and vegetable oil. Place fish in an oiled, shallow pan and pour sauce on top of fish. Sprinkle with nutmeg and bake in a preheated 350°F oven for 20-30 minutes.

Serves 6.

SOLE WITH TOMATOES
(Sole Duglére)
    1 pound tomatoes, peeled, seeded and chopped
        (about 1½ cups)
    2 tablespoons minced shallots
    2 tablespoons minced parsley
    ½ teaspoon salt
    dash pepper
    1½ pounds sole fillets
    ¾ cup dry white wine
    ¼ cup water or clam juice

2 tablespoons butter or margarine
2 tablespoons flour
½ teaspoon sugar
3 to 4 tablespoons heavy cream

Mix tomatoes, shallots, parsley, salt and pepper; place in bottom of greased, flat baking dish. Place fillets over tomatoes. Add wine and water; bring to simmer on the range. Cover with aluminum foil. Place in preheated 325°F oven 13-15 minutes, until fish is opaque. Remove fish to serving dish; keep it warm. Boil juices until mixture is reduced to about one-half. Mix butter and flour. Stir into juices; cook until thickened. Add sugar, cream and juices drained from fish on platter. Pour sauce over fish.

Serves 4.

STUFFED FILLETS OF SOLE
(Filets De Sole Farcis)
shrimp stuffing
    2 tablespoons minced shallots or green onions
    2 tablespoons butter or margarine
    ½ pound mushrooms, sliced
    2 tablespoons chopped parsley
    ½ pound tiny shrimp, cooked and cleaned
6 fillets of sole
2 tablespoons butter
2 tablespoons flour
1 cup dry white wine
½ cup heavy cream or half-and-half
¼ teaspoon salt
2 tablespoons brandy
½ cup grated Swiss cheese

Cook shallots in 2 tablespoons melted butter until transparent. Add mushrooms; cook until all liquid has evaporated. Add parsley and shrimp. Place about 2 tablespoons stuffing on large end of each fillet. Roll up fillets; place in greased, flat baking dish (12 × 8 × 2 inches). Melt 2 tablespoons butter; mix with flour. Add white wine; cook until thick. Stir in cream, salt and brandy. Add any remaining stuffing to sauce. Pour sauce over fillets. Bake in preheated 400°F oven about 20 to 25 minutes, until fish is done. Sprinkle with Swiss cheese the last 5 minutes of baking. The top should be golden brown.

Serves 6.

FISH STEAKS WITH SHRIMP SAUCE
4 fish steaks (each 6 to 8 ounces)
Juice of 1 lemon
½ teaspoon salt
¼ teaspoon white pepper
2 tablespoons polyunsaturated margarine
1 medium onion, sliced
1 tablespoon chopped parsley
½ cup dry white wine
½ cup beef bouillon
6 ounces fresh mushrooms, sliced
¼ pound frozen cooked shrimps
1 tablespoon lemon juice
¼ cup plain yogurt
Lemon slices and parsley for garnish

Wash fish, pat dry and sprinkle with lemon juice, salt and pepper. Heat margarine in a frying pan, add fish and onion. Brown fish for 5 minutes on each side. Sprinkle with parsley, pour in white wine and simmer for 5 minutes. Remove fish to a heated platter and keep them warm. Add bouillon to frying pan and bring to boil. Add mushrooms and simmer slowly for 8 minutes, stirring often. Add shrimps and simmer for 2-3 minutes. Season sauce with lemon juice and stir in yogurt. Heat thoroughly, but do not boil. Adjust seasonings. Pour over fish steaks and garnish with lemon slices and parsley.

SALMON STEAKS WITH HOLLANDAISE SAUCE
(Filets De Saumon Hollandaise)
¼ pound fresh small mushrooms
1 tablespoon butter
½ cup white wine
6 tablespoons water
½ teaspoon salt
⅛ teaspoon white pepper
4 salmon steaks, each about 6 to 8 ounces
Juice of ½ lemon
1 recipe Hollandaise Sauce (see Index)
8 ounces fresh oysters
1 4½-ounce can deveined shrimp
1 ounce truffles, sliced (optional)

Clean mushrooms; cut into thin slices. Heat butter in frying pan. Add mushrooms; sauté for 3 minutes. Add ¼ cup wine and the water. Season with salt and pepper; simmer for 10 minutes. Meanwhile, rinse salmon steaks under cold running water; pat dry.

Sprinkle with lemon juice. Let stand 5 minutes. Strain mushrooms, reserving juice. Set mushrooms aside. Add mushroom juice to frying pan. Add rest of wine. Bring to a boil; add salmon steaks. Cover; simmer over low heat 20 minutes. While salmon is cooking, prepare Hollandaise Sauce. Keep it warm. Remove salmon steaks with slotted spoon to preheated platter. Keep them warm. Add oysters to simmering stock. Heat about 5 minutes or until edges begin to curl. Add shrimp; just heat through. Remove; drain. Spoon around salmon steaks. Pour Hollandaise Sauce over salmon. Garnish with reserved reheated mushrooms and truffle slices if desired.

Serves 4.

FRIED DABS WITH TARTAR SAUCE

4 whole dabs or small flounder fillets
All-purpose flour
2 eggs, beaten
Fine dry bread crumbs
2 hard-boiled eggs, finely chopped
1 tablespoon freshly minced parsley
1 cup tartar sauce

Wash dabs; pat dry. Coat dabs with flour, shaking off any excess; dip into beaten eggs. Coat generously with bread crumbs, patting crumbs into egg coating firmly. Fry dabs in deep fat at 375°F until brown on both sides. Drain on paper toweling; arrange on heated serving platter. Sprinkle with eggs, then parsley. Serve dabs with tartar sauce and French bread.

Serves 4.

SALMON MOUSSE
(Mousse De Saumon)

2 tablespoons gelatin
1½ cups fish stock, from poaching fish (or 1½ cups bottled clam juice)
½ cup mayonnaise
1 tablespoon lemon juice
1 1-pound salmon steak, cooked, boned and mashed, or 2 cups canned salmon
1 tablespoon Madeira
¼ teaspoon salt
⅛ teaspoon white pepper
½ cup heavy cream, whipped
Lemon or cucumber slices for garnish

Sprinkle gelatin over ½ cup cold stock, then heat stock to dissolve gelatin completely. With wire whisk, beat in mayonnaise and lemon juice. Cool until slightly thickened. Fold in salmon and Madeira. Add salt and pepper to taste. Gently fold in whipped cream. Pour into oiled 2-quart fish mold. Chill until set. Unmold mousse to serve. Garnish with lemon or cucumber slices. Makes a 2-quart mold.

Serves 8-12.

SHRIMP-FILLED BRIOCHE

½ pound fresh shrimp
½ cup minced celery
1 small cucumber, peeled and diced
½ cup cooked green peas
½ cup mayonnaise
2 teaspoons lemon juice
3 or 4 drops hot sauce
Salt and pepper to taste
1 brioche, hollowed-out

Cook and clean shrimp; chill. Combine shrimp, celery, cucumber and peas in mixing bowl. Combine mayonnaise, lemon juice and hot sauce. Add shrimp mixture; toss carefully. Season with salt and pepper; pack into brioche shell. Wrap tightly in foil; refrigerate until ready to serve.

Serves 4.

EGG DISHES

ONION PANCAKES

1 cup flour
Pinch of salt
1 egg, beaten
1¼ cups milk

Sift flour and salt into bowl; make well in center of dry ingredients. Combine egg and milk; gradually add to flour. Mix to smooth batter. Heat griddle or frying pan; grease lightly. Pour 2 or 3 tablespoons mixture into pan to form fairly large pancake. Loosen edges of pancake with knife; when lightly browned underneath and bubbling in center, turn and brown other side. Repeat this process, making 1 pancake at a time until all batter is used, about 8-10 pancakes.

onion filling

    6 tablespoons butter
    3 large onions, finely chopped
    3 tablespoons flour
    1⅔ cups milk
    1 teaspoon salt
    Dash of pepper
    ½ teaspoon dry mustard
    Pinch of nutmeg
    8 ounces grated cheddar cheese

Heat butter in pan; sauté onions until tender. Add flour; stir until well mixed. Remove from heat. Gradually add milk; stir until combined. Return to heat; stir until sauce boils and thickens. Reduce heat; add salt, pepper, mustard and nutmeg. Mix well; simmer 5 minutes, stirring occasionally. Stack pancakes on ovenproof dish, layering each with onion sauce and some grated cheese. Top last pancake on stack with grated cheese only. Bake whole stack in hot (450°F) oven 10 minutes or until cheese is golden brown. Cut stack into wedges to serve.

Serves 4.

CHEESE SOUFFLÉ
(Soufflé Au Fromage)

    4 tablespoons butter
    3 tablespoons flour
    1 cup milk
    ½ teaspoon salt
    Dash pepper
    ¼ teaspoon dry mustard
    1 cup shredded sharp cheddar or Swiss cheese
    4 eggs, separated
    ¼ teaspoon cream of tartar
    1 tablespoon Parmesan cheese or fine bread
       crumbs

Melt 3 tablespoons butter in 1-quart saucepan. Stir in flour; heat for a few minutes. Add milk all at once. Cook and stir over medium heat until mixture thickens. Stir in salt, pepper and mustard. Add cheese; cool slightly. Beat in egg yolks. In medium-size bowl beat egg whites until frothy. Beat in cream of tartar; continue beating egg whites until soft peaks form. Stir ¼ of egg whites into cheese sauce. Gently fold in remaining whites. Prepare a 1½- or 2-quart soufflé dish by greasing with 1 tablespoon butter and dusting with Parmesan cheese. Pour soufflé into dish;

bake in preheated 375°F oven 25-30 minutes. Soufflé is done when it is puffed and golden and looks slightly dry, not shiny. Serve soufflé at once, with a sauce if desired.

Serves 4.

SAVORY BREAD OMELET

    3 eggs
    Salt and pepper to taste
    1½ teaspoons finely-chopped fresh parsley
    1 tablespoon butter
    ½ cup fried croutons
    2 tablespoons grated Parmesan cheese

Beat eggs lightly with fork. Season with salt and pepper; add parsley. Beat again. Melt butter in 9-inch omelet pan until butter just begins to brown around edge. Add egg mixture; reduce heat. Lift around edge with fork or spatula; tilt pan to allow egg to run underneath. Cook until browned and set on bottom but top is still moist. Sprinkle croutons to within 1 inch of edge; sprinkle with 1 tablespoon cheese. Flip over; slide onto heated plate. Sprinkle with remaining cheese. Serve immediately.

Serves 1-2.

OMELET WITH CHICKEN LIVERS

    2 tablespoons butter
    ½ cup finely-chopped onions
    ½ pound chicken livers, quartered
    ½ cup beef consommé
    ¼ cup sherry
    ½ cup half-and-half cream
    ½ teaspoon salt
    Pepper to taste
    1 French omelet
    Fresh parsley, finely chopped

Melt butter in medium-size saucepan over medium heat. Add onions and livers; cook, stirring occasionally, until browned. Add consommé and sherry. Simmer about 20 minutes or until livers are tender. Remove livers with slotted spoon; keep them warm. Add cream slowly to pan juices stirring constantly. Increase heat; cook until sauce is thick and creamy. Season with salt and pepper. Prepare French omelet in usual way; turn out onto heated platter. Pour sauce over omelet. Arrange livers over top; sprinkle with parsley. Serve at once.

Serves 2-3.

SHRIMP OMELET
  ¼ cup chopped mushrooms
  1 teaspoon oil
  6 shallots or spring onions, chopped
  2 stalks celery, chopped
  1 pound shrimp
  8 eggs
  1 cup bean sprouts
  1 teaspoon salt
  ¼ teaspoon pepper
  1 tablespoon oil

Wash and chop mushrooms. Cook in hot oil until tender. Drain. Chop onions and celery fine. Shell, devein and chop shrimp. Beat eggs slightly. Add shrimp, shallots, celery, mushrooms, bean sprouts, salt and pepper. Mix lightly. Heat oil in large frying pan. Pour in enough omelet mixture to make 5-inch omelet. Several individual omelets can cook at same time. When firm on one side, turn and cook other side. Stack finished omelets on warming plate while cooking rest of omelets. Serve with sauce spooned over.
  Serves 4.

  sauce
    1 cup chicken stock
    1 teaspoon sugar
    2 teaspoons soy sauce
    1 tablespoon cornstarch
    ¼ cup cold water

Combine stock, sugar and soy sauce in saucepan; bring to boil. Mix cornstarch with cold water; add to saucepan. Mix well, stirring until mixture boils and thickens.

BASIC OMELET AND FILLINGS
(Omelettes)
  2 eggs
  2 tablespoons water
  ¼ teaspoon salt
  Dash of pepper
  1 tablespoon butter

In small bowl, mix eggs, water, salt and pepper with a fork. Heat butter in 8-inch omelet pan until just hot enough to sizzle a drop of water. Pour in egg mixture. Mixture should start to set immediately. With spatula, draw cooked portions from edge to-ward center, so that uncooked portions flow to bottom. Tilt pan as you do this, and slide pan back and forth over heat to keep mixture from sticking. Add filling, if desired. While top is still moist and creamy looking, fold in half or roll with spatula. Turn out onto plate with a quick flip of the wrist. Omelets will take about 2 minutes from start to finish.
  Serves 1.

  omelet fillings
    cheese—1-2 tablespoons grated Swiss or
      Parmesan cheese
    herbs—1 tablespoon minced fresh herbs,
      such as parsley, chives or tarragon
    other fillings—2-3 tablespoons sautéed
      ham or chicken livers, cooked shrimp or
      crab, cooked asparagus tips, etc.

PIPERADE
  3 tablespoons olive oil
  1 green pepper, seeded and thinly sliced
  1 onion, peeled and finely chopped
  1 tomato, peeled, seeded and chopped
  1 clove garlic, crushed
  1 teaspoon salt
  ⅛ teaspoon freshly-ground black pepper
  6 eggs

Heat the oil in a skillet, add the green pepper and onion, and sauté until the vegetables begin to soften. Add tomato, garlic and seasoning, and simmer until the ingredients are soft and mushy. Add the lightly beaten eggs and stir just enough to mix with the vegetables. Cook for a few minutes until the eggs are just set. Serve with toast or on thin sautéed slices of ham.
  Serves 4.

VEGETABLES

CRISP POTATO BALLS
  2 pounds potatoes, mashed
  4 tablespoons butter
  3 strips bacon, finely chopped
  4 shallots, chopped
  4 ounces grated cheddar cheese
  1 ounce grated Parmesan cheese
  1 teaspoon salt

¼ teaspoon pepper
2 eggs, beaten
½ cup milk
2 cups bread crumbs
Oil for deep frying

Heat butter in pan; add bacon. Fry until crisp. Add bacon and butter mixture to mashed potatoes. Add shallots, grated cheeses, salt and pepper. Mix well. Take tablespoons of potato mixture and roll into balls with floured hands. Combine beaten eggs and milk. Coat each potato ball with egg mixture; roll balls in bread crumbs. Repeat egg and bread crumbing to give a firm coating. Deep fry a few balls at a time in hot oil until golden brown and crisp. Drain well; keep balls warm until all are fried.

Serves 4-6.

STUFFED ARTICHOKES
4 artichokes
2 lemons
2 cups chicken stock

Remove stalk from artichoke, cutting across base with sharp knife. Slice ½ inch off top leaves. Trim outer leaves with scissors, ½ inch from tips. Rinse under cold water. Cut lemon into slices ½ inch thick. Place lemon and artichokes in chicken stock that has come to boil. Reduce heat; simmer for 15 minutes until leaves can be pulled out easily. Remove from pan; turn upside down to drain.

anchovy filling
4 tablespoons butter
1 medium onion, chopped
1 clove garlic, crushed
2½ cups bread crumbs
1 2-ounce can anchovy fillets, drained, finely chopped
3 tablespoons chopped parsley
½ teaspoon salt
Dash of pepper
1 cup sour cream
1 tablespoon grated onion
1 teaspoon grated lemon rind
½ cup grated Parmesan cheese

Melt butter in frying pan. Add chopped onion and garlic; sauté until onion is tender. Add 2 cups bread crumbs, stirring until bread crumbs are golden brown. Remove from heat. Add anchovy fillets, parsley, salt and pepper. Pull leaves gently away from artichoke tops so that centers show. Spoon breadcrumb mixture into openings. Combine sour cream, grated onion and lemon rind; spoon over artichokes. Top with ½ cup crumbs and cheese. Stand artichokes in 1 inch water in baking dish. Bake in 400°F oven 15 minutes or until tops are golden brown.

Serves 4.

BROCCOLI CASSEROLE
1 package frozen broccoli
1¼ cups milk
3 eggs, lightly beaten
½ teaspoon salt
½ teaspoon nutmeg
½ cup grated cheese

Preheat oven to 350°F. Cook broccoli in small amount of boiling water 3 minutes; drain. Pour milk into small saucepan; bring to boil. Cool to lukewarm. Mix eggs with salt and nutmeg. Add milk and cheese, beating constantly. Pour into greased baking dish; add broccoli. Bake for 30-40 minutes or until knife inserted in center comes out clean. Must be served hot.

Serves 3-4.

POTATOES À L'ALSACIENNE
¼ cup butter
1 small green cabbage, cored and coarsely chopped
2 large onions, chopped
6 potatoes, cooked, peeled and sliced thin
¼ cup flour
1 can (13¾ ounces) chicken broth
2 cups shredded Bonbel or St. Paulin cheese

In large saucepan, heat butter and sauté cabbage and onions till wilted. Place cabbage, onions and potatoes in shallow 3-quart casserole. Stir flour into butter and pan juices, and slowly stir in chicken broth. Stir over low heat till sauce bubbles and thickens. Pour sauce over vegetables. Sprinkle top of casserole with cheese. Bake at 350°F for 45 minutes till brown and bubbly.

Serves 6.

CAROTTES À LA CREME
(Carrots in Cream Sauce)
> **6 to 8 large carrots, about 1½ pounds**
> **2 tablespoons butter**
> **Salt and freshly-ground pepper to taste**
> **½ cup heavy cream**

Trim and peel the carrots, and, using a sharp knife or a slicer, cut the carrots into thin slices, about ⅛-inch thick. There should be about five cups. Heat the butter in a heavy, deep skillet and add the carrots. Salt and pepper to taste. The skillet must have a thick bottom because the carrots will cook without liquid and otherwise will burn. Cover closely and cook 8 minutes. Stir and shake the skillet as the carrots cook. When the carrots are tender, add the cream. Cook about 8-10 minutes longer or until the carrots are tender but not mushy. The sauce should be slightly absorbed and somewhat thickened.

Serves 4.

POMMES ANNA
> **2 pounds potatoes**
> **½ cup melted butter**
> **¼ cup grated onion**
> **Salt and white pepper to taste**

Peel potatoes; cut into paper-thin slices. Brush bottom and sides of 6½ × 3-inch soufflé dish generously with butter. Arrange potatoes, overlapping slices, around sides of soufflé dish to form a firm wall; place an overlapping layer of potatoes in bottom of dish to cover. Brush lightly with butter; sprinkle lightly with onion, salt and pepper. Repeat layers until all ingredients are used; cover lightly with foil. Bake in preheated 400°F oven 30 minutes. Remove foil; bake 30 minutes longer or until top is well browned. Unmold potatoes onto heated serving platter.

Serves 6-8.

CAULIFLOWER WITH MORNAY SAUCE
> **1 large head cauliflower**
> **Freshly-grated bread crumbs**
> **⅓ cup melted butter**
> **Basic mornay sauce**

Wash and trim cauliflower, then separate into florets. Place in vegetable steamer; steam until tender. Arrange around edge of baking dish. Sprinkle liberally with bread crumbs. Drizzle butter over bread crumbs. Spoon Mornay Sauce into center of baking dish. Broil until crumbs are slightly browned. Serves 4-6.

> **basic mornay sauce**
> > **1 cup white sauce**
> > **2 tablespoons butter**
> > **1 cup grated Parmesan cheese**

Prepare white sauce; remove from heat. Cut butter into small pieces. Stir Parmesan cheese and butter into white sauce, beating with wooden spoon until butter is melted. Amount of salt in while sauce may be decreased if desired because Parmesan cheese sometimes imparts a salty flavor.

TOMATO FLAN
> **pastry**
> > **1 tablespoon butter**
> > **1 cup flour**
> > **Pinch of salt**
> > **1 egg yolk, lightly beaten**
> > **1 tablespoon lemon juice**

In bowl, cut butter into combined flour and salt. When mixture resembles fine bread crumbs, add egg yolk and lemon juice. Add 1 to 2 teaspoons water if needed to make dough hold together. Turn pastry onto lightly-floured surface; roll to 10-inch circle (will fit bottom and sides of 9-inch pie pan). Line pan with pastry; refrigerate 1 hour.

> **tomato filling**
> > **2 medium onions, chopped fine**
> > **3 sticks celery, diced**
> > **2 tablespoons butter**
> > **1 pound tomatoes, peeled and chopped**
> > **1 teaspoon salt**
> > **¼ teaspoon pepper**
> > **1 clove garlic, crushed**
> > **1 teaspoon sugar**
> > **2 eggs**
> > **1 cup cream**
> > **1 tablespoon grated Parmesan cheese**
> > **¼ teaspoon Worcestershire sauce**
> > **Pinch of nutmeg**

Sauté onion and celery in melted butter until onion is transparent. Add tomatoes, salt, pepper, garlic and sugar; bring to boil. Reduce heat; simmer until mixture has thickened, about 30 minutes. Allow to cool. Combine eggs, cream, cheese, Worcestershire sauce and nutmeg; mix well. Spoon cool Tomato Filling into pastry shell; gently pour over egg mixture. Bake 10 minutes at 425°F. Reduce heat to 350°F; bake 20 minutes more or until mixture is set in center.

Serves 6.

POTATO-GARLIC SCALLOP
(Gratin De Pommes De Terre À L'ail)
- 1 clove garlic
- 4 tablespoons butter
- 4 cups thinly-sliced potatoes (¼ inch thick)
- 1 cup grated Swiss cheese
- 1½ cups hot milk
- 1 teaspoon salt
- ⅛ teaspoon pepper

Cut garlic in half; rub over inside of 2-quart baking dish. Using 1 tablespoon butter, thoroughly grease casserole. Spread half of potatoes in dish. Cover with half of cheese. Add remaining potatoes; top with cheese. Mix milk, salt and pepper. Pour over potatoes. Dot with remaining 3 tablespoons butter. Bake in preheated 375°F oven 45-60 minutes. Reduce heat or add more milk if potatoes become dry before they are tender. When done, the top should be nicely browned.

Serves 4-6.

SPINACH CASSEROLE
(Spinach À La Nice)
- 2 pounds spinach
- 1 tablespoon olive oil
- 2 clove garlic, minced
- ½ teaspoon salt
- ⅛ teaspoon pepper
- ⅛ teaspoon ground nutmeg
- 4 eggs
- ¼ cup heavy cream
- **Butter to grease dish**
- 2 tablespoons dried bread crumbs (packaged)
- 1 tablespoon butter

Thoroughly wash spinach; drain. Heat oil in large Dutch oven or saucepan. Add garlic; cook for 1 minute. Add spinach; cover; steam for 3 minutes. Season with salt, pepper and nutmeg. In small bowl, beat eggs and cream until well blended. Stir in spinach. Grease ovenproof dish with butter; spoon in spinach mixture. Sprinkle with bread crumbs; dot with butter. Place in preheated 425°F oven. Bake spinach about 15 minutes or until lightly browned.

Serves 6-8.

ZUCCHINI AND TOMATO CASSEROLE
(Courquettes Et Tomates À La Provençale)
- 2 tablespoons vegetable oil
- 1 small onion, chopped
- ½ clove garlic, minced
- 2 zucchini squash, sliced
- 2 tomatoes, peeled, or 1 cup canned tomatoes
- ½ teaspoon salt
- ½ teaspoon basil
- ¼ teaspoon black pepper
- 2 tablespoons grated Parmesan cheese

Heat oil in heavy frying pan. Sauté onion and garlic. Stir in zucchini; cover; cook until vegetables are tender. Add tomatoes, salt, basil and pepper. Continue cooking, uncovered, until mixture is well-blended, about 10 minutes. Sprinkle with grated cheese. Place under broiler a few minutes to brown the top.

Serves 4.

GREEN PEAS BONNE FEMME
- ¼ pound Canadian bacon, cut in 1-inch pieces
- 1 tablespoon polyunsaturated margarine
- 3 cups fresh green peas/ 6 small white onions, peeled
- **Inner leaves of lettuce head**
- ½ cup water
- ½ teaspoon salt
- ¼ teaspoon pepper
- ½ teaspoon sugar
- 1 tablespoon finely-chopped parsley

Fry bacon in margarine until lightly browned. Add peas, onions, lettuce, water, salt, pepper and sugar. Cover and cook for 10 to 15 minutes or until peas are tender. When peas are done, drain remaining liquid. Sprinkle with parsley before serving.

Serves 6.

DESSERTS

STRAWBERRY GÂTEAU

    4 egg whites
    ⅛ teaspoon salt
    1¼ cups very fine sugar
    1 cup ground pecans
    1 teaspoon vinegar
    ½ teaspoon vanilla
    4 dessert spoons black coffee
    filling:
        1 pound strawberries
        2 cups whipped cream
        1 can Eagle Brand milk
        6 squares plain chocolate

Beat egg whites and salt until stiff. Gradually add sugar and beat until meringue consistency. Fold in remaining ingredients. Put into two greased and floured eight-inch springform pans. Bake in 350°F oven approximately 35 minutes. Release sides of pans. Cool on bottom of pan. After cake has cooled, prepare the chocolate by cooking the Eagle Brand milk and chocolate in a double boiler until thick and of icing consistency. Remove from burner and cool. Remove gâteau from base of pan and place a layer of meringue on serving plate. Spread with layer of chocolate and top that with a layer of strawberries. Top this with ¾-inch to 1-inch layer of whipped cream. Prepare the second layer separately but in the same way as the first. Then place the second layer on top of the first. Refrigerate for several hours or overnight. Garnish with strawberries and serve.
    Serves 8-10.

CHOCOLATE MOUSSE
(Mousseline Au Chocolat)

    8 ounces semisweet chocolate pieces
    2 tablespoons water
    ¼ cup powdered sugar
    ½ cup unsalted butter, softened
    6 eggs, separated
    1 tablespoon dark rum
    ½ teaspoon vanilla
    2 tablespoons sugar

Melt chocolate and 2 tablespoons water in double boiler. When melted, stir in powdered sugar; add butter bit by bit. Set aside. Beat egg yolks until thick and lemon-colored, about 5 minutes. Gently fold in chocolate. Reheat slightly to melt chocolate, if necessary. Stir in rum and vanilla. Beat egg whites until foamy. Beat in 2 tablespoons sugar; beat until stiff peaks form. Gently fold whites into chocolate-yolk mixture. Pour into individual serving dishes. Chill at least 4 hours. Serve with whipped cream if desired.
    Serves 6-8.

DESSERT CROISSANTS
(Croissants À La Gelée De Groseilles)

    4 tablespoons apricot jam or red currant jelly
    3 tablespoons water
    6 hot croissants, freshly made or reheated
    1 tablespoon corn syrup
    1 teaspoon cognac
    1 teaspoon lemon juice
    About ¼ cup powdered sugar

Boil jam or jelly with 2 tablespoons water 1 minute. With pastry brush, coat hot croissants with mixture. Boil corn syrup and 1 tablespoon water 1 minute. Off heat, add cognac and lemon juice. Stir in enough powdered sugar to make a thin paste. Spread over jam coating. Serve croissants while warm.
    Serves 6.

PASTRY CREAM
(Crème Pâtissière)

    ⅔ cup sugar
    3 egg yolks
    ⅓ cup flour
    1½ cups boiling milk
    1 tablespoon butter
    ⅓ cup ground almonds (optional)
    ¼ teaspoon almond extract (optional)
    1 teaspoon vanilla

In small bowl, beat sugar and egg yolks until mixture forms a ribbon on the surface, which slowly dissolves when beaters are lifted. Gradually beat in flour; beat until smooth. Slowly add hot milk, beating constantly. Pour mixture into 1-quart saucepan; cook over low heat until mixture thickens, stirring constantly. Add butter, almonds and extracts. Cool Pastry Cream. Use for tarts or other desserts. Keeps several days, but must be refrigerated. Yields 2 cups.

MOLDED ICE CREAM
(Bombe Glaćee)

1 quart coffee ice cream, softened
¾ cup chopped nuts
1 quart chocolate ice cream, softened
1 pint vanilla ice cream, softened
2 tablespoons brandy
2 ounces unsweetened chocolate, melted and cooled
¼ cup light corn syrup
1 egg

Line 2-quart bowl or mold with heavy-duty aluminum foil. Blend coffee ice cream with ½ cup nuts. Line mold with coffee ice cream. Freeze until firm (about 1 hour). Use softened chocolate ice cream to form second layer, leaving a deep hole in center. Freeze until firm. Blend vanilla ice cream and brandy. Fill hole; smooth bottom of mold. Freeze several hours. Turn out ice cream onto cold tray. Carefully remove foil; return to freezer. Combine chocolate, corn syrup and egg; beat for 4 minutes. Working quickly, spread frosting over molded ice cream. Garnish with remaining ¼ cup nuts. Slice to serve.

Serves 8.

CHERRY PUDDING CAKE
(Clafoutis)

2 cups pitted black cherries, fresh, or 1 1-pound can Bing cherries, drained
2 tablespoons cognac or brandy
2 tablespoons sugar
1 cup milk
⅓ cup sugar
3 eggs
2 teaspoons vanilla
½ teaspoon almond extract
⅛ teaspoon salt
1 cup flour
Powdered sugar

Place cherries in small bowl; pour brandy over them. Stir in 2 tablespoons sugar; set aside. In blender container, place remaining ingredients, except powdered sugar, in order listed. Blend on high 1 minute, or beat all ingredients to form a smooth batter. Pour ¼ of batter into 9-inch pie pan (2 inches deep). Place in 350°F oven about 2 minutes, until batter is set. Place cherries on top of batter; add any cherry juice and remaining batter. Return to oven; continue to bake for 45 minutes, until a knife inserted in center can be withdrawn clean. Sprinkle cake generously with powdered sugar. Serve cake warm.

Serves 6-8.

Jewish

SABBATH AND HOLIDAY RECIPES

CARROT TZIMMES

5 large carrots
5 medium white potatoes
3 medium sweet potatoes
2½ to 3 pounds beef brisket
1 teaspoon salt
½ cup sugar (more if desired)
Water
1 small onion (optional)
2 tablespoons flour browned with
2 tablespoons chicken fat or vegetable shortening

Scrape and cut carrots into thin rounds, or dice. Pare and cut white potatoes into quarters. Pare and cut sweet potatoes into 1-inch thick rounds. Sear the brisket of beef in pot to be used for cooking, turning frequently until evenly browned. Add the vegetables, salt and sugar. Water to cover about 1 inch over all should be used as frequently as required during the cooking process until the meat is tender enough to pierce with a fork. Cook over low heat after bringing to a bubble boil. Cooking time required is from 2½ to 3 hours. Do not stir contents of pot. To prevent possible sticking, shake the pot occasionally.

If an onion is used for additional flavor, it should be left whole, with 1 or 2 cuts at the root end to permit the flow of juice, and removed before it becomes too mushy. Honey may be substituted for sugar.

When the liquid has been reduced by half, turn into a baking pan or casserole. Add an *einbren* or thickening, made by lightly browning flour in hot melted shortening and stirring in some of the liquid from the tzimmes. Shake the casserole to distribute the thickening. Then bake in over for 30 minutes at 350°F. or till brown on top.

Serves 6.

TZIMMES OR DRIED FRUITS
(Balkan Style)

½ pound each medium prunes, dried apricots, peaches, pears, seeded raisins
1 cup long grain rice (brown rice may be used)
½ cup honey
½ teaspoon salt
¼ teaspoon cinnamon
1 quart boiling water

Rinse dried fruits and drain well. Use a colander for best results under running hot water. Combine with rice and add the other ingredients in the order listed. Cook over moderate heat, preferably on an asbestos pad, covered for the first 5 minutes or until it reaches boiling point. Reduce heat to a slow simmer for the next 15 to 20 minutes or until rice is tender and the liquid in the pot almost entirely absorbed. Shake the pot occasionally to prevent sticking, or add a little boiling water if necessary. Serve hot or cold.

Serves 6.

Variation 1: Turn into a casserole, dot with butter and brown lightly under broiler flame just before serving. This dish may be served cold.

Variation 2: Lightly brown 2 tablespoons flour in 2 tablespoons butter and add after turning into casserole. This adds a customary tzimmes thickening and many more calories.

MATZO BRIE OR FRIED MATZO

2 eggs
½ cup liquid (milk or water)
¼ teaspoon salt
Dash of cinnamon
2 matzos
3 tablespoons shortening

Beat eggs, add liquid, salt and seasoning, and break the matzo into this mixture. Stir well and turn into melted fat in a well-heated frying pan. Cover. Cook over moderate heat about 10 minutes or till browned on under side. Turn and brown, uncovered, for about 3 minutes. Serve hot, plain or with a sprinkling of sugar and cinnamon, applesauce or honey.

Serves 2.

MEAT ROSSEL BORSHT

1½ pounds brisket of beef
4 cups cold water
1 onion
2 bay leaves
3 cups beet sour (rossel)
Salt and pepper to taste
Lemon juice (optional)
Sugar to taste
6 egg yolks

Cook the meat, onion, bay leaves, in water at a slow boil until meat is tender when pierced with a fork. Add the other ingredients, except egg yolks, and boil 15 minutes longer. Serve hot with 1 beaten egg yolk per serving (depending on taste), for thickening, and garnish with parsley, sliced hard cooked egg and plain boiled potato.

Serves 6.

BAKED MATZO-VEGETABLE SCALLOP

3 matzos
1 large onion, sliced
4 whole tomatoes, medium sized
½ teaspoon salt
Dash of pepper
1 teaspoon sugar
3 tablespoons chicken or goose schmaltz
½ cup soup or water (if needed)

Grease generously a 9 × 9 × 2" baking dish and cover the bottom with thinly sliced onion. Break one matzo into sections and arrange over onions. Cover with slices of tomato, sprinkle with salt, pepper and sugar and top with sections of the second matzo. Cover with the remaining onion slices and top with the third matzo. Cover and bake 30 minutes at 350°F. Remove cover and if the top layer of matzo is not softened, add ½ cup soup or water. Continue to bake until lightly browned on top. Serve with meat or fish meal.

Serves 4.

Variations can be made by adding sliced eggplant, green peppers or shredded cabbage between layers of matzos.

PASSOVER EGG NOODLES

4 eggs
4 tablespoons cold water
1 tablespoon matzo cake flour
Dash of salt

Beat eggs slightly, adding the other ingredients to make a very thin batter. Beat well until smooth. Pour in a thin stream on a well-greased frying pan, starting at the center and tilting the pan to distribute evenly. Cook over moderate heat until lightly browned on under side and turn out on a tea towel, bottom side up, to cool while the second edition is poured and cooked. Roll up each thin pancake and cut into thin strips or noodles. Drop into boiling hot soup (clear chicken soup) just before serving.

Serves 6 to 8.

GRATED POTATO KNAIDLACH

3 large raw potatoes and
1 cup cooked, mashed potatoes
2 eggs
2 tablespoons chicken fat
½ teaspoon salt
Dash of pepper or cinnamon
½ cup matzo meal
1 tablespoon onion juice

Pare and grate potatoes. Squeeze out as much liquid as possible by pressing with the hands. Combine with the rest of ingredients, mixing thoroughly. The mixture should be firm enough to form into balls. More matzo meal may be added if necessary. Shape into balls the size of walnuts and drop into rapidly boiling salted water, cooking for about 1 hour over a moderate heat after the last ball is dropped in. Drain and serve in clear soup or as dumplings in stew, chicken fricassee or meat gravy.

Serves 6 to 8.

MATZO MEAL PANCAKES
(Crisp and Light)

3 eggs
½ cup cold water
¼ teaspoon salt
1 cup matzo meal
1 grated onion, medium size
Melted shortening or oil for deep frying

Beat eggs and combine with cold water, salt, ⅔ of

the grated onion and enough matzo meal to make a stiff batter that will drop from the spoon. Heat shortening in a heavy frying pan and add the remaining piece of onion for flavor. Drop batter from spoon to form round cakes and fry till brown before turning over to brown on under side. Lift out one at a time and drain thoroughly before serving with applesauce, mixed dried fruits compote, cranberry sauce or just plain with meat or cheese dishes.

Yields 12 to 14 pancakes.

SCALLOPED MATZOS
(Milchig)
    4 eggs
    6 matzos
    1 pound cottage cheese
    2 tablespoons butter, melted
    ½ teaspoon salt
    1 tablespoon sugar
    ½ teaspoon cinnamon optional
    ¼ cup raisins

Beat 2 eggs till light and break the matzos into quarters which can be dipped into the eggs. Let stand while you blend the other 2 eggs and seasonings with the cheese. Butter a casserole or pudding dish. Arrange alternate layers of matzos and cheese in the dish. Bake ½ hour at 350°F. or till nicely browned. Serve with stewed fruit or plain. An excellent luncheon dish.

Serves 6 to 8.

BANANA PUDDING
    2 large tart apples, grated unpared
    2 tablespoons lemon juice
    ½ cup sugar
    3 egg yolks
    ½ cup matzo meal
    ¼ teaspoon cinnamon
    ¼ teaspoon nutmeg
    2 large bananas for topping
    3 egg whites
    ⅛ teaspoon salt
    2 tablespoons sugar
    Dash of grated lemon rind

Combine grated apple and lemon juice. Beat sugar and egg yolks till creamy and add by stirring in quickly, and alternately with matzo meal to which

spices have been added. Grease a pudding dish and turn in this mixture. Bake at 325°F. approximately 35 minutes, till set. Turn out on serving plate and top with sliced bananas. Beat egg whites with salt and sugar till thick and spread on top just before serving.

May be eaten cold without topping of bananas and beaten egg white meringue. A dusting of sugar and cinnamon may substitute for egg topping.

Serves 6.

CHEESE PUDDING
    4 matzos
    Lukewarm water
    1 pound dry cottage cheese
    4 eggs
    2 cups milk
    1 lemon, grated rind and juice
    ¾ cup sugar
    1 teaspoon salt

Soak matzos in lukewarm water. Drain and press extra moisture out carefully so as not to break the matzos. Generously butter square deep cake pan. Put 1 matzo on bottom of pan, spread with ⅓ of the cheese, put on another matzo and spread with cheese till 3 matzos are used. Cover top with fourth matzo. Beat eggs slightly. Add milk, lemon, sugar and seasoning. Pour over the matzo and cheese. Bake in oven at 375°F. for 1 hour. Can be served hot or cold.

Serves 8.

NUT CAKE
    9 eggs, separated
    1 lemon, grated rind and juice
    9 tablespoons sugar
    1 cup finely ground almonds
    2 tablespoons matzo cake flour

Beat egg yolks till light colored and creamy. Fold in grated lemon rind and then lemon juice, a little at a time, till combined. Beat egg whites, adding sugar gradually, till the mixture is stiff. Fold the second mixture into the first with an over and over stroke, adding the finely ground nuts in the final few strokes. Sprinkle the flour over the top and fold in very lightly. Turn the mixture into an ungreased spring form and bake at 325°F. for 45 minutes or till lightly browned. This cake must not be disturbed during the baking process if you want it to rise to its maximum height. When done, press lightly with the forefinger in center to make sure it is not sticky, before removing from the oven.

Makes a large size cake.

PASSOVER PUFFS

½ cup shortening (vegetable,
    salad oil or butter)
1 cup water
1 cup matzo cake flour
1 cup matzo meal
2 tablespoons sugar (optional)
6 eggs, spearated
1 tablespoon lemon juice
1 teaspoon salt

Bring shortening and water to a boil in a deep saucepan. Remove from heat and stir in matzo cake flour and matzo meal, with sugar added if desired. Stir till smooth. Beat egg yolks till creamy and stir in till blended. Add lemon juice. Beat egg whites, with salt, stiff but not dry and fold into the mixture, which should be cool. Drop batter from teaspoon or tablespoon about 2 inches apart on a lightly greased cookie sheet and bake at 350°F. for 15 minutes or till lightly browned and puffed. The puffs should double in diameter, be hollow like cream puffs but not quite as light. Let cool before filling through a slit in top or side.

Filling may be preserves, stewed dried fruits or whipped cream to which sugar has been added to suit the taste. Chopped nuts may be added to any of the mentioned fillings in any quantity suitable to the occasion.

Yields approximately 24 large or 48 small puffs.

HOMEMADE CHALLAH
(for Sabbath and Holidays)

8 cups flour
1 tablespoon salt
1 tablespoon sugar
4 tablespoons vegetable shortening
2 cups hot potato water
2 packages yeast
3 eggs
Pinch of saffron *added to hot liquid

Sift flour and salt into a large mixing bowl. Mix sugar and shortening with the hot liquid. If potato water is not available, use plain hot water. When cooled to lukewarm, dissolve the yeast in some of the liquid and stir into the flour to make a sponge in the center of the bowl. Cover and let rise 30 minutes. Add slightly beaten eggs to the sponge and stir in remaining liquid to make a dough. Turn out on a floured board and knead thoroughly until smooth and elastic. The dough should not stick to hand or board. Return to mixing bowl, brush top with shortening or dust with flour, cover, and let rise in a warm place until approximately double in bulk. Knead on floured board for 10 minutes and shape into coils for round loaves. Or, cut in half and divide each into 3 to make braided or twist loaves. Place on greased or floured baking sheet and let rise again till about double in bulk. Brush with egg yolk and water and bake 15 minutes at 400°F., reduce heat to 375°F. and bake for 45 minutes or till nicely crusted and light brown on bottom.

Yields 2 loaves.

* Saffron is an herb used in baking to lend a yellow color and fragrance. It is closely associated with the fragrant spices of the "Psumim" or Spice Box used on Sabbath and holidays. It can be purchased in any food shop or drug store.

BAGEL

3 cups flour (plus 3 tablespoons for kneading
    board)
1½ teaspoons salt
2 tablespoons sugar
1 package yeast
⅔ cup lukewarm water
3 tablespoons salad oil (or shortening)
1 egg
4 quarts boiling water to which add 2 table-
    spoons sugar

Sift dry ingredients together into a deep mixing bowl. Dissolve yeast in ⅓ of the lukewarm water. Add oil or melted shortening to remainder of warm water and stir into dissolved yeast. Make a well in the center of flour mixture and stir in the liquid, adding slightly beaten egg when half the liquid has been used. Stir briskly to form a ball of dough and knead on a lightly floured board two minutes. Return dough to mixing bowl, smooth side up, and punch down three times. Cover and let rise at room temperature 15 to 20 minutes, or until the dough has come to top of bowl. Knead again on board till smooth and elastic as for rolls. Divide dough into 12 equal portions. Form into lengths not more than ¾ inch thick, pinching ends together. Place on a floured cookie sheet and slip under broiler flame 3 minutes. Drop each bagel into rapidly boiling water in a deep kettle and cook over moderate heat 15 to 20 minutes. Skim out and place on a cookie sheet. Bake at 375°F. for 10 minutes then increase heat to 400°F for 5 to 6 minutes or till bagels are browned and crust golden brown and crisp, approximately 15 minutes.

Yields 12.

Variations are made by sprinkling bagels with poppy seed or coarse salt before baking.

RECIPES FROM ISRAEL

PATLIJAN BOEREG
(An Egyptian Eggplant Specialty)

This is a popular dish in Israel, especially with Jews from Near Eastern countries. It is prepared as follows:

> 1 large eggplant
> Salt to taste
> ¼ cup flour
> ¾ cup oil
> 3 eggs
> ½ pound dry pot cheese
> 1 teaspoon minced parsley
> 1 tablespoon lemon juice

Cut unpared eggplant into ¼-inch thick slices or rounds. Salt lightly and let stand approximately half an hour. Pat each slice dry, dust lightly with flour and fry in hot oil till nicely browned on both sides. Pour off surplus oil, leaving the fried eggplant slices in bottom of frying pan. Remove half the fried eggplant to a plate. Beat 2 eggs, add dry cheese and 1 teaspoon minced parsley and spread over the eggplant slices in the pan. Cover with remaining fried eggplant, and cook over low heat for 3 to 5 minutes. Beat remaining egg till light and frothy. Lift cover and pour beaten egg over top layer of eggplant. Let cook uncovered till set. Garnish with parsley or a sprinkling of lemon juice. Serve hot.

Serves 4.

SAUTÉED SQUASH
> 1 pound squash (small green variety)
> ⅛ teaspoon salt
> 3 tablespoons fine cracker crumbs or matzo meal
> 3 tablespoons hot melted shortening
> 3 tablespoons sugar
> Pinch of cinnamon

Cut into ¼-inch thick rounds (unpared squash) or lengthwise into ¼-inch thick slices. Sprinkle with salt very lightly and roll each piece in crumbs or matzo meal. Sauté in hot melted shortening on both sides of slices till tender and lightly browned. Sprinkle with sugar and cinnamon as cooked slices are removed from pan to baking dish. Return to hot frying pan and cover till serving time or heat in moderate oven 5 to 10 minutes. This dish is frequently served cold.

Serves 4.

MOUSSAKA
(Armenian Eggplant and Meat)

This dish is also popular with Jews from the Near East.

> 1 pound ground lamb, mutton or beef
> Salt and pepper, or paprika to taste
> 1 eggplant
> ⅔ cup tomato paste
> ½ cup dry bread crumbs or browned borgoul (wheat grits)

Season meat to taste and press down into the bottom of a greased casserole or baking dish. Slice unpared eggplant into thin rounds and arrange over meat. Top with tomato paste, cover with bread crumbs or borgoul. Cover tightly and bake 30 minutes at 350°F. Remove cover and let brown on top, approximately 10 minutes.

Serves 4.

DRIED APRICOT SOUP
> 2 cups dried apricots
> 3 cups cold water
> 3 tablespoons sugar or 1 tablespoon honey
> ¼ teaspoon cinnamon
> Dash of nutmeg
> 1 teaspoon lemon juice
> Pinch of salt

1 cup light cream and
1½ cups milk or
1¼ cups evaporated milk and
1¼ cups water
3 egg whites or grated lemon rind

Stew apricots in cold water over simmer flame in a covered pot 30 minutes. Put through a sieve or fruit press. Yields approximately 2 cups purée. Add sugar or honey, cinnamon, nutmeg, lemon juice and salt while hot. Just before serving, hot or cold, stir in cream and milk or diluted evaporated milk and heat but do not boil. Top with a little grated lemon rind or float teaspoonfuls of beaten egg white on top of each serving, using 3 egg whites for the above amount.

Serves 6.

VEGETABLE MEAL-IN-ONE
(Sephardic Recipe)

1 cup diced green beans
1 cup diced carrots
1 cup diced eggplant
1 cup stewed or 1½ cups sliced fresh tomatoes
1 teaspoon salt
4 tablespoons butter or other shortening
4 eggs, well beaten
2 cups cooked rice, drained, tightly packed

Wash and drain diced vegetables. Combine and add tomatoes, sprinkle with salt and stir once or twice. Butter baking dish or casserole and turn in vegetable mixture. Melt remaining shortening in a saucepan and drizzle over top of vegetables. Pour beaten eggs over top and bake 25 to 30 minutes at 350°F. or till eggs are set. Serve with mounds of cooked rice around or underneath.

Serves 5 or 6.

Variation: Substitute cooked fine noodles or macaroni for rice.

BALUK PLAKKI
(A favorite dish among Jews from Turkey)

3 pounds cleaned fish (any firm-fleshed fish can be used)
½ cup oil, butter or vegetable shortening
Salt to taste
2 large onions
4 large tomatoes (or 1 cup strained, canned)
1 cup boiling water

Parsley and/or fresh mint
Lemon wedges (optional)

Prepare the fish as for broiling. Rub inside and outside with oil and salt lightly. Broil under low heat turning when inner side is brown, then brown outer side. Place the fish in a long baking dish, cover with sliced onions and tomatoes or the strained canned tomato. Sprinkle lightly with salt and bake 20 minutes at 400°F. Then add 1 cup boiling water and baste. Bake 5 to 10 minutes longer. Serve either hot or cold, garnished with parsley and/or fresh mint. Wedges of lemon may be added.

Serves 6.

DA-VO-OD BASHA
(Near East Dish)

4 small eggplants
½ pound chopped lamb or mutton
Salt to taste
½ cup tomato purée or 1 cup stewed tomatoes
2 tablespoons vinegar
2 tablespoons brown sugar (approximately)

Cut unpared eggplant lengthwise and scoop out seed sections. Chop seed sections with the meat and season to taste with salt. Return to eggplant halves, pressing down into the cavities and mounding up slightly. Arrange in a baking pan, add tomato purée and vinegar sweetened to taste. Bake 20 to 30 minutes at 350°F. or till the eggplants can be pierced with a fork.

Serves 4.

DOLMA
(East Europeans call this dish Holishkes or Praakes)

Cabbage leaves
Boiling water
3 large tomatoes
3 green peppers, cut lengthwise
1½ pounds chopped meat (lamb preferred)
Salt to taste
½ cup borgoul or brown rice
Lemon juice or vinegar to taste
Brown sugar as required

Cover cabbage leaves with boiling water and let stand till wilted and soft. Cut stem ends from tomatoes and peppers and remove seeds. Add tomato centers to meat, season to taste then add the borgoul or rice. Fill the drained wilted cabbage leaves with the meat mixture and tuck in the ends. Fill tomatoes and peppers. Arrange the cabbage rolls among the stuffed tomato and pepper halves in a casserole or deep baking dish. Add lemon juice, sugar and enough water to prevent sticking to bottom of dish. Cover and cook over low heat 30 to 40 minutes or till gravy has formed. Uncover and cook 10 to 20 minutes longer or till nicely browned on top.

Serves 6.

FAGGOT SALAD
(Probably referring to the Spanish Inquisition)

    1 cup tiny Brussels sprouts
    1 cup cauliflower florets
    Salt
    1 cup cubed cooked liver, beef or chicken
    2 tablespoons shortening
    1 cup sliced mushrooms
    4- to 6-inch lengths of celery stalks
    6 pickled gherkins, cut lengthwise
    Lettuce, shredded
    Salad dressing or mayonnaise

Cook the sprouts and cauliflower florets separately in a minimum of salted water until tender. Drain well. Broil liver before cutting into cubes. Sauté the sliced mushrooms. Arrange the celery stalks on shredded lettuce, then the sliced gherkins (or slice lengthwise any pickled cucumbers on hand), and next add the Brussels sprouts and cauliflower. Add the cubed liver and top with mushrooms. Either pass the salad dressing or add it carefully just before serving.

Serves 4.

ASHOURAH
(A dessert familiar to Near Eastern Jews)

    1 cup seeded raisins, chopped fine
    1½ pounds sugar
    ¼ cup water
    ¼ cup each chopped toasted almonds, walnuts
      and hazel nuts
    1 pound borgoul or brown rice
    Salt
    1 teaspoon rosewater or almond extract
    1 teaspoon cinnamon or nutmeg

Boil sugar and raisins in ¼ cup water till bubble stage is reached. Remove from heat and add nuts.

Cook borgoul in slightly salted cold water to cover and drain when tender. Stir into the raisins and nuts mixture, cook about 5 minutes. Fold in the flavoring. Serve a heaping spoonful of this mixture over more nuts and top with an almond. Add a sprinkling of cinnamon or nutmeg if desired.

Serves 6 to 8.

SARMI
(Called Sarmali in the Balkan Countries)

This is a favorite dish among Jews from Armenia, Turkey and the Near East.

    8 grape leaves the size of a hand
    Boiling water
    4 large onions, diced or chopped
    Vegetable shortening or oil
    1 cup rice
    ⅓ cup cut or chopped seeded raisins
    Salt to taste
    Parsley

Wash grape leaves and cover with boiling water till the leaves are wilted. Drain well. Fry onions in shortening till light brown and transparent. Add washed rice and raisins and stir well over reduced heat for 2 minutes. Add salt to taste. Let cool before placing a spoonful of the mixture in the center of each leaf and rolling up, tucking in the ends or forming into a tightly-wrapped ball. Arrange neatly in a heavy skillet, add water to cover and let simmer 30 minutes. Water may be added if necessary to prevent sticking. Slip under broiler flame to brown if desired. Serve with matzoun, yogurt or sour cream topping, hot or cold and garnish with parsley.

Serves 4.

KATAIYIFF
(A sweetmeat classic with Turkish Jews)

    1 pound fine noodles
    Salt
    4 tablespoons butter or other shortening
    1 cup slivered almonds or hazel nuts
    1 cup honey (approximately)

Cook noodles in slightly salted water till tender and drain thoroughly. Pack into a shallow oblong pan and when cold and caked, turn out and cut into squares. Arrange on a well-greased baking sheet and cover each slice with nuts. Pour honey over each piece and bake 20 to 30 minutes at 350°F. Serve with a sprinkling of nuts on each and drizzle more honey over the nuts. It is a bit sticky, but delicious.

BREAKFAST

APPLE FRITTERS

2 eggs, separated
½ cup water
1 cup flour
1 tablespoon melted butter or oil
1 tablespoon lemon juice or wine
¼ teaspoon salt
4 large apples (pared, cored and sliced)
Flour
¼ cup lemon juice
½ cup sugar

Beat the egg yolks till light yellow. Add water and stir in flour. Combine the lemon juice and melted butter or oil and blend into batter mixture. Beat egg whites stiff, add salt, and fold into the batter.

Dip each apple slice in flour, then dip into the batter. Lift out with a fork and fry in deep fat until a delicate brown on both sides. Drain on paper and serve with lemon juice and sugar dusted on top.

Yields 20 fritters.

EGG ROLLS INTERNATIONAL

1 cup flour
¼ teaspoon salt
3 eggs
⅔ cup milk or water
1 tablespoon melted shortening

Sift together flour and salt. Beat eggs till light. Stir or beat in dry ingredients alternately with liquid till a smooth batter is formed. Melt shortening on frying pan and add to batter. Pour batter in a thin stream on to greased pan, tipping to distribute over entire surface evenly as possible. Cook over moderate heat till lightly browned on under side. Turn bottom side up on a kitchen towel. Spread with filling, roll up like jelly roll, tucking in both ends. When all rolls are made, brown under broiler flame or in well-greased frying pan. Cut rolls in half to facilitate handling. Serve hot.

Yields 6 rolls or 12 halves.

EGGS NEAPOLITAN

2 tablespoons butter
1 cup fine crumbs (bread or cracker)
6 tablespoons mushroom sauce
6 eggs
Salt to taste
Pepper to taste

Butter the inside of individual ramekins and sprinkle with crumbs. Add a tablespoonful of sauce then break into each 1 egg and sprinkle with salt and pepper. Cover with crumbs and set the ramekins in a shallow pan of hot water. Bake at 350°F. until the yolk of egg is set, approximately 10 minutes.

Serves 6.

DAIRY AND MEATLESS MEALS

CHEESE KREPLACH

Dough
Pinch of salt
Flour enough to make a stiff dough as for noodles (See Index, Noodle Dough)
1 egg
1 tablespoon cold water

Make a well in the center of sifted flour and salt and add egg and water. With a fork stir together to make the noodle dough. Roll out to ⅛-inch thickness, cut into 2½-inch squares and fill each with the following cheese mixture:

Cheese Filling for Kreplach
1 pound dry cottage cheese
2 egg yolks or 1 whole egg and 2 tablespoons sour cream
¼ teaspoon salt
Sugar and cinnamon to taste (if served with sour cream)
Or dash of white pepper (if served with hot milk)

Drop prepared kreplach into rapidly boiling water, one at a time. Cook, covered for 10 minutes. Uncover and reduce heat for 5 minutes. Drain. Drizzle with additional butter and brown under broiler flame. Serve with cream cheese and sour cream.

Serves 4 to 6.

CHEESE BLINTZES

2 eggs
½ cup sifted flour
¾ cup water (or milk and water)
1 tablespoon melted butter
Pinch of salt

Make a thin batter of beaten eggs, flour added alternately with the liquid while beating with a fork, then working in the melted butter and salt until smooth. Heat a heavy frying pan and butter well before pouring in a thin stream of batter, starting at center and tilting pan to spread the mixture evenly across the bottom. Reduce the heat as soon as you begin pouring on the batter to achieve a well-baked pancake layer for the first blintze. As soon as the underside is lightly browned, turn out on a double layer of kitchen towel, browned side up. Start the second blintze layer, buttering the pan before pouring batter. While the second (and successive) blintzes are baking on the frying pan spread the browned side just turned out with the following mixture:

Filling for Cheese Blintzes
1 pound cottage cheese (or cream cheese)
1 egg yolk
2 tablespoons sugar
Dash of salt
Dash of cinnamon (or few drops of vanilla)

Mix with a fork to a spreadable consistency. Spread evenly and roll up each blintze, tucking in at the ends. Cut in two, and when all are filled and rolled up, and cut, fry them in butter until nicely-browned on both sides. Serve with sour cream, stewed berries, cherries, rhubarb, or compote of prunes and dried apricots.

Yields 12 blintzes if a 10-inch frying pan is used Serves 4 (three per serving).

CHEESE AND NOODLE RING
(*Shevuoth Dish*)

3 cups boiled noodles
Salted water
1½ cups cottage cheese or half this amount and
   ½ cup cream cheese
2 eggs
½ teaspoon salt
Dash of pepper

3 tablespoons dry cracker crumbs
3 tablespoons butter

Boil broad noodles in salted water 7 to 10 minutes. Drain and rinse with hot water. To 3 cups boiled noodles add 1½ cups cottage cheese or ½ cup each cottage cheese and cream cheese. Add salt, pepper and eggs. Turn into a well-buttered ring mold, sprinkle with cracker crumbs and bake at 375°F. for 30 minutes or till lightly browned on top.

Serves 4.

Variation: Turn into a buttered heavy frying pan and cook over moderate heat 5 minutes, stirring lightly to prevent sticking. Brown more cracker crumbs in hot melted butter and sprinkle on top.

GOLDEN GLOW

½ cup yellow corn meal
2½ cups boiling water
½ teaspoon salt
½ pound American Cheddar cheese
½ cup milk
1 tablespoon butter
¼ teaspoon paprika

Make a mush of the cornmeal, by stirring it gradually into rapidly boiling salted water and stirring constantly until the mush leaves sides of saucepan. Or, cook over boiling water 30 to 40 minutes. Pour into a shallow pan. When cold, cut into small squares.

Melt cheese in top of double boiler. Add milk gradually, stirring constantly to blend.

Arrange layers of mush and cheese mixture in a buttered baking dish and sprinkle with paprika. Bake 20 minutes at 350°F. or until lightly browned on top.

Serves 4.

GRATED POTATO KUGEL

6 medium potatoes
1 onion
3 eggs
½ teaspoon salt
¾ cup flour (approximately)
Dash of white pepper (optional)
4 tablespoons shortening

Grate raw pared potatoes, squeeze out excess liquid and grate onion into the pulp. Add eggs, salt and as much flour as necessary to make a batter that will drop from the spoon. Heat shortening in baking pan and fold into batter. Turn batter into greased baking pan. Bake 30 to 40 minutes at 375°F. or till nicely browned and crisp at edges.

Serves 4 to 6.

RICE AND NUT CROQUETTES

    3 tablespoons butter or margarine
    4 tablespoons flour
    ½ teaspoon salt
    Dash cayenne
    1 cup milk
    2 teaspoons grated onion
    ½ teaspoon dry mustard
    2 cups boiled rice
    1 cup chopped pecans or other nuts
    Fine dry bread crumbs
    1 egg
    1 tablespoon water

Melt fat, blend in flour, salt and cayenne. Add milk. Cook, stirring constantly, over a low flame till mixture is very thick. Add onion and mustard. Cool. Add rice and nuts. Add additional salt to taste. Chill.

Shape into 10 or 12 balls and roll in crumbs. Blend egg with 1 tablespoon water. Coat croquettes well with egg and dip again into crumbs. Fry in deep hot fat (380°F—a cube of bread turns light brown in forty seconds) till brown. Drain on unglazed paper. Serve with tomato sauce.

Serves 5 to 6.

LOKSHEN KUGEL
(Basic Recipe)

    ½ pound broad noodles
    2 quarts boiling water
    1 teaspoon salt
    2 eggs
    3 tablespoons sugar
    ¼ teaspoon cinnamon or 1 tablespoon lemon
      juice
    ⅛ teaspoon salt
    4 tablespoons shortening
    ½ cup chopped seedless raisins
    ¼ cup chopped almonds (optional)
    3 tablespoons bread crumbs

Drop noodles in rapidly boiling salted water and cook till tender. Drain in a colander, pouring hot water through to rinse well. Beat eggs with sugar, cinnamon, salt, and add the noddles. Melt shortening in the baking dish and add to mixture. Turn half the mixture into greased baking dish, sprinkle with raisins and nuts, and add remainder. Top with crumbs and bake 45 minutes at 400°F.

Serves 4 to 6.

Variation 1: Substitute 1 cup thinly sliced tart apples for raisins, or combine equal amounts of each.

Variation 2: Use chopped greben (cracklings) and chicken or goose fat for shortening.

Variation 3: Substitute 1 cup finely cut dried prunes for other fruit, with or without nuts. Add lemon juice and ¼ teaspoon grated rind.

MACARONI WITH MUSHROOMS

    ½ pound macaroni
    1 quart boiling water
    Salt
    1 onion, sliced
    2 tablespoons butter or oil
    ½ pound fresh mushrooms or 1 can mushrooms
    Salt and papper to taste
    1 tablespoon dry crumbs
    1 cup milk

Boil macaroni in salted water till tender. Drain. Brown onion in shortening, add mushrooms and sauté. Combine with macaroni. Add seasoning to taste. Turn into buttered casserole, top with dry crumbs and add milk. Bake 30 minutes at 350°F. or till browned on top.

Serves 4 to 5.

Variation: Substitute boiled or roasted chestnuts for mushrooms.

EGGPLANT STEAK WITH ONIONS

    1 eggplant
    1 teaspoon salt
    2 eggs, beaten
    1 cup bread crumbs
    4 tablespoons oil or shortening
    2 tablespoons grated cheese
    1 tablespoon minced parsley
    1 large onion

Slice the eggplant in rounds ½-inch thick. Do not peel. Salt the slices lightly and allow to stand for 30 minutes. Drain or wipe each slice dry. Dip in beaten egg then in crumbs and fry till brown on both sides. Serve with grated cheese and minced parsley. Cut the onion into rounds and fry till light brown. Serve with the eggplant steaks.

Serves 4 or 5 (depending on size of eggplant).

HOMEMADE NOODLE DOUGH
(Basic Recipe)
        2 cups sifted flour (approximately)
        2 eggs
        2 or 3 teaspoons cold water

Sift flour into mixing bowl or on kneading board. Make a well in the center. Add eggs and combine with a fork adding spoonfuls of water as necessary to form a ball of dough that is compact but not hard. Knead dough until as smooth and elastic as possible. Roll out on a lightly floured board. Use the rolling pin from the outer edges toward the center, turning the board as necessary in order to achieve easier rolling. When dough is rolled *evenly thin* through the whole round, let stand 10 to 20 minutes in order to dry so that it will not stick together when rolled up. Roll up lightly. Use a sharp knife to cut fine. Shake to loosen and spread noodles on lightly floured cloth. Let dry at room temperature. Store in jars when dried. *Do not try to make noodle dough in damp weather, especially, if you are a novice at it.*
Uses for Homemade Noodle Dough:

It may be cut fine and used with clear chicken or meat soup. The dough may be cut into broad noodles and used with cheese or other combinations and for kugel.

When cut into 1-inch squares and pinched together like bowknots, the noodles are called shpaetzlen (see recipe below for complete instructions). These are used for soups and goulashes.

Noodle dough can also be used for making kreplach filled with cheese or chopped and seasoned cooked meat, liver, or chicken. (See Index for kreplach recipes.) Rolled out dough must not be dried out before cutting into 2½- to 3-inch squares for filling.

Recipes using homemade noodle dough are given below.

Shpaetzlen are like the scalloped, bow-knot, dried noodles that can be bought in packages. They can be made at home, minus the scalloped edges, by cutting the noodle dough as soon as it is rolled out. Cut into 1-inch squares and pinch together with thumb and forefinger. Let dry about a half hour before dropping one by one into rapidly boiling salted water. Cook over moderate heat about 10 minutes after the last one has been dropped in. Skim out with a perforated spoon or drain thoroughly in a colander.

SOUPS

BEET BORSHT
        4 medium size beets and tops
        1 onion, peeled
        4 cups boiling water
        1 tablespoon salt
        ½ cup mild vinegar or ¼ cup lemon juice (or ¼ teaspoon citric acid crystals)
        3 tablespoons brown sugar (or to taste)

Cut tops from beets two inches from the roots. Scrub beets thoroughly, cover with cold water and boil 15 minutes or until tender enough to pierce with a toothpick. While beets are boiling, wash leaves and chop fine in a wooden bowl. The stems may be used, too. Strain the liquid from beets into a bowl or soup pot. Slip skins from beets and grate them, using a fine grater. Grate onion into grated beets. Add this to the strained beet juice, boiled water and chopped beet tops. Add salt and bring to a quick boil. Reduce heat and cook 5 minutes. Add vinegar sweetened to taste with brown sugar. Or sour salt crystals dissolved in ½ cup beet soup and sweetened to taste with brown sugar. Cool and chill in closed jars. Add a boiled potato, 3 tablespoons diced cucumber and 1 heaping tablespoon sour cream to each plateful just before serving. If you have fresh dill, use it for garnish.

Serves 6 to 8.

Variation 1: Add 1 hard-cooked egg diced or sliced, to each serving in addition to or in place of the other garnish.

Variation 2: For a fleishig (meat) borsht, use diced or grated cooked beets with 1½ to 2 pounds brisket of beef. Cook 1½ hours or until meat is tender. Add the same ingredients including tops and seasoning 15 minutes before serving. Thicken hot borsht by stirring in 1 egg yolk per serving. Add boiled potato. Or substitute garnish of sliced hard cooked eggs.

Variation 3: Cook 1 cupful diced rhubarb with borsht and omit vinegar or lemon juice.

Variation 4: For a delicious summertime cooler, serve strained meatless beet borsht (with or without rhubarb), in tall glasses topped with fresh mint after thickening with a little sour cream.

Variation 5: A borsht cocktail that is delicious on a hot summer day is made by adding sparkling water or lemon soda to strained chilled borsht.

KRUPNIK

¾ cup pearl barley

6 cups water or vegetable juice

1 onion or 2 leeks, cut fine

1 carrot, grated

1 small turnip, grated, or ½ cup mushrooms (dried or diced fresh)

1 stalk celery, diced fine

4 tablespoons butter

Salt and pepper

Sour cream as desired for thickening and topping

Cook barley over moderate heat in half of the vegetable juice or stock. When tender add the other ingredients and remaining liquid. Season to taste with salt and pepper and cook 15 to 20 minutes or until vegetables are tender. When ready to serve thicken with sour cream and top with a little of same. A bit of minced parsley adds a festive look.

Serves 6.

RUMANIAN BEAN SOUP WITH TAYGLACH
(Egg Drops)

Soup

1 quart cold water

1½ cups dry lima beans

1 teaspoon salt

1 onion

2 tablespoons chicken fat, oil, vegetable shortening or butter

Tayglach

1 egg

2 tablespoons flour

a pinch of salt

Soak beans in cold water to cover, overnight preferably, but at least three hours. Drain. Add fresh cold water and salt. Cook over moderate heat in a covered pot 45 minutes or till beans are tender. Drain. Add fresh cold water and salt. Cook over moderate heat in covered pot 45 minutes or till beans are tender. Drain, reserving liquid. Reduce beans to pulp, through strainer or food press.

Add the bean pulp to liquid. There should be about 1 quart of thickened soup. Thin with boiled water if you wish, and add diced brown onion. Bring to a boil and drop from the tip of a spoon the tayglach or egg drops made by combining to a paste the beaten egg, flour and salt, one at a time while the soup is at moderate boiling point or bubbling slightly. After the last egg drop is put in, turn down heat and let cook 5 to 7 minutes.

Serves 4.

FISH CHOWDER

1½ cups diced raw potatoes

1½ cups water

1½ cups milk

2 cups flaked leftover fish (boiled, broiled or baked)

Salt and pepper to taste

2 tablespoons butter

1 tablespoon flour

Minced parsley

Boil potatoes in water till tender. Add milk, fish and season to taste. Blend flour in hot melted butter and thin into a smooth paste with 3 tablespoons of liquid from pot. Cook 5 minutes longer and serve. Garnish with minced parsley.

Serves 6.

Variation: Canned salmon or tuna fish may be substituted.

CHERRY SOUP WITH EGG DROPS

Soup

1 quart stemmed and pitted cherries (canned or fresh)

1 tablespoon lemon juice

2 tablespoons sugar (more with sour cherries)

1 quart cold water

Pinch of salt

Egg Drops (Minute Dumplings)

1 egg

¼ cup cold water

3 tablespoons flour

Pinch of salt
Pinch of nutmeg

If soup is to be served hot, then prepare the egg drops first. Beat egg well. Stir in water then add flour, salt and flavoring and beat virorously with a fork or spoon till smooth. Bring the combined soup ingredients to a boil and drop the egg mixture from the tip of a teaspoon into the rapidly boiling soup. Cook for 5 minutes and the dumplings will rise to the top when done.

If soup is to be served iced, do not cook it with the egg drops. After bringing soup to a boil and cooking for 5 minutes, let it cool. Then chill it in the refrigerator in a glass jar for at least 2 hours before serving. Just before serving, cook the egg drops in slightly salted water, using the same procedure as above. Drain them well before adding to the soup. A spoonful of sour cream may be added to each serving, stirred in or floated on top.

Serves 6 to 8.

BAVARIAN KARTOFFEL KLEISS
(Mashed Potato Dumplings)

4 boiled potatoes, mashed
2 eggs, slightly beaten
2 slices toast, crushed or like amount of cracker meal
Salt and pepper to taste
1 teaspoon cornstarch
1 teaspoon minced parsley
Dash of nutmeg or cinnamon (optional)

Combine ingredients in the order listed and form into balls the size of hazelnuts or walnuts. Drop into rapidly boiling salted water one at a time. Lift out as soon as they rise to the top, using perforated spoon. Add chicken fat or other shortening and brown lightly in a frying pan. Serve with soup or meat gravy.

Serves 6.

SOUP NUTS
(Mandlen)

3 eggs
2 tablespoons salad oil
1 teaspoon salt
2 cups sifted flour

Beat eggs slightly, add oil and salt while beating. Stir into sifted flour gradually to make a dough stiff enough to handle. Form into pencil thin rolls on a floured board or between the palms of both hands. Flatten slightly and cut into quarter- or half-inch pieces. Bake on a cookie sheet or in a shallow baking pan at 375°F. for 10 minutes until nicely browned. Shake the pan or stir occasionally to brown evenly on all sides. When cold and dry these mandlen may be stored for several days and heated before serving in clear soup or with meat gravy.

Serves 6 to 8.

Variation: Drop the mandlen into hot melted shortening and cook like doughnuts until nicely browned and crisp. Skim out with a perforated spoon as soon as brown. It is best to drop in only as many as will not crowd the pan and skim out as fast as browned. Drain on paper towels. Reheat by enclosing in a paper bag twisting top to close and placing in a preheated, 350°F. oven for 5 minutes.

MOTHER WOLFF SOUP

2 pounds lean beef
½ pound marrow bones
4 quarts cold water
1 large onion
1 cup each diced potatoes, diced carrot, celery, yellow or white squash, green beans, peas (fresh or dried), parsnips and 1 cup canned tomato sauce
½ cupful dried lima beans
¼ cup each rice, barley, yellow split peas
Salt and pepper to taste
½ cup uncooked fine noodles
½ cup minced parsley or dill

Boil meat and bones in water, skim carefully, then add all ingredients except noodles. Cover and simmer 2 hours. Season with salt and pepper to taste, add noodles and boil 10 minutes longer. Serve hot, garnished with parsley or fresh dill. This is a very hearty soup, full of vitamins and minerals. May be stored in a covered dish in the refrigerator for several days. If too thick, add boiling water and reheat.

Serves 8 to 10.

FISH

BAKED WHITE FISH WITH TOMATO SAUCE

4 pounds whitefish
Salt
2 tablespoons flour
1 onion
1 green pepper
1 clove garlic
4 tablespoons butter or oil
1 No. 2½ can tomatoes
1 tablespoon lemon juice
1 teaspoon brown sugar
Salt and pepper to taste
Minced parsley

Remove scales and head from fish. Split in half and salt inside and outside. After 20 minutes, wash and dry fish portions and dust with flour.

Mince onion, garlic and green pepper and sauté in hot shortening in the baking dish to be used. Place fish on top and cover with tomatoes. Add sugar dissolved in lemon juice and bake 20 to 30 minutes at 375°F. Serve from the baking dish. Sprinkle with salt and pepper and garnish with parsley.

Serves 6 to 8.

GEFILTE FISH
(Basic Recipe)

3 pounds fish (any firm-fleshed fish, preferably yellow pike, carp, buffalo, or any combination of these)
Salt (as required)
2 large onions, 1 diced
2 eggs
Pepper to taste (optional)
1 large carrot, sliced
2 stalks celery, diced
2 slices white bread, soaked and squeezed
Parsley
Cold water to cover

Skin and bone the fish, leaving skin attached to bones of each part or cut. After the whole fish has been dressed and sectioned, salt evenly skin-bone cuts to be stuffed. Let stand in a covered glass bowl in the refrigerator while chopping the filleted parts or flesh. Grate in one onion, add eggs, salt and pepper to taste, and soaked bread if desired as a "stretcher."

If no bread is used, add 2 tablespoons cold water and combine thoroughly. Wet the hands and return pulp to bones, covering with the attached skin. Place the head bones and diced vegetables in the bottom of a deep pot. Place filled fish sections neatly on top, add cold water to cover. Cover pot. Bring to a quick boil, remove cover and turn down heat, keeping the fish at a slow boil 1½ to 2 hours. The liquid should be reduced by half. When cool, remove to a platter carefully, to retain shape of each section. Strain the liquid over the fish or into a separate bowl. Chill thoroughly before serving, using the carrot for garnish. The jelled sauce may be cut and served separately or as an additional garnish.

Serves 4 to 6.

Variation 1: Grate a raw carrot into chopped filleted fish after grating in an onion. Add the ingredients as listed. After forming and arranging balls or filled sections in cooking pot, add 1 carrot thinly sliced.

Variation 2: Place bones, head and skin removed in the process of filleting fish on the bottom of pot. Arrange several stalks of celery across and arrange fish balls on top to make removal easier when cooked. The bones and skin add flavor to the fish sauce. Discard bones after removing fish and straining sauce.

Variation 3: Form 3-inch patties of pulp, dip in fine crumbs and fry. Or bake 12 to 15 minutes at 375°F.

Variation 4: Remove all bones from skin cuts and fill with chopped fish pulp as in basic recipe.

HALIBUT RING

2 pounds halibut
Cold water to cover
½ cup diced celery
2 small carrots, diced
1 tablespoon grated onion
1 tablespoon lemon juice or vinegar
1 teaspoon salt
¼ teaspoon pepper (optional)
2 eggs, separated
1 cup whipped cream
Parsley
Green pepper strips and carrot strips (as many as desired)

Simmer fish in water 3 minutes. Add prepared vegetables and seasonings. Cover and cook 10 to 15 minutes or until fish is firm but tender when tested with a fork. Let cool. Lift out fish and remove skin and bones. Purée vegetables after straining through a colander. Beat eggs separately and combine, folding in whipped cream. Arrange pepper and carrot strips in any desired formation in a well-buttered ring mold and turn in the beaten egg and cream mixture carefully and evenly. Arrange fish in this and add purée, distributing as evenly as possible without disturbing decorative vegetable strips at bottom of mold. Set in a pan of boiling water and bake 30 to 35 minutes at 375°F. or till set. Lift from hot water container and invert serving plate over ring mold. Turn quickly to unmold. Garnish with parsley and more green pepper and carrot strips. Add lemon wedges if desired. May be served cold.

Serves 6 to 8.

SWEET-SOUR FISH

4½ to 5 pounds trout or pickerel
Salt
2 cups vinegar
½ cup water
½ cup brown sugar
3 tablespoons butter
¼ teaspoon each cinnamon and cloves
4 onions
6 lemons, sliced
1 cup seedless raisins
¼ cup blanched and sliced almonds
3 egg yolks
Salt as required

Clean fish and remove the head. Cut into 2½-inch cuts and salt lightly. Cover and let stand in the refrigerator for 2 hours. Boil together water, vinegar, sugar, raisins, almonds, butter and seasonings until raisins are puffed. Arrange sliced onions in the bottom of the cooking pot. Wash and clean the head, removing gills and eyes. Place over onions. Rinse fish and arrange neatly around the head. Cover with cold water. Add half the sliced lemons and boil 15 minutes, then add other ingredients. Cook over moderate heat 45 minutes. When cool, lift the pieces of fish out and arrange on a platter deep enough to hold at least 1-inch depth of liquid. Cook contents of pot 10 minutes.

Strain the gravy. Stir into beaten eggs. With a fork remove some of the raisins and almonds and use as a garnish with remainder of sliced lemon. Chill.

Serves 8 to 10.

BAKED SALMON STEAKS

2 pounds salmon, fresh or quick frozen, (cut ¾ to 1 inch thick)
2 tablespoons melted butter or oil
2 onions, sliced (optional)
1 cup milk
½ teaspoon salt
¾ cup fine cracker or dry bread crumbs
Dash of white pepper (optional)
Lemon wedges for garnish

Melt the shortening in shallow glass baking pan in oven while preparing the fish steaks. If onions are to be used, arrange the slices in bottom of pan. Dip the steaks in milk (or water) to which salt has been added, then roll in crumbs to which pepper has been added. Place the salmon steaks on top of sliced onions and bake, uncovered, 15 to 20 minutes at 475°F., turning up the heat for 2 minutes just before serving. The fish should be golden brown on top and easily pierced with a fork. Transfer to a heated serving platter or serve in the baking dish, garnished with lemon.

Serves 4 to 6.

BAKED FISH CAKES
(Basic Recipe)

1 cup flaked or chopped fish (fresh, quick frozen or canned)
1 cup dry bread crumbs
2 cups milk
4 tablespoons butter
⅛ teaspoon salt and pepper, mixed
4 eggs
2 tablespoons melted butter for greasing pans

Flake or chop the fish very fine. Combine bread crumbs, milk, 4 tablespoons butter and salt and pepper. Cook in top of double boiler 10 minutes. Stir in fish. Beat eggs till light and stir into the hot mixture. Remove from heat. Grease 8 custard cups or medium size muffin pans with hot melted butter, and turn in the fish and crumb mixture. Bake 30 minutes at 350°F. or till firm and lightly browned on top. Unmold. Serve with Creole sauce, horse-radish, lemon sauce, mushroom sauce, Cream of Mushroom Soup, heated, or tomato sauce.

Serves 4.

Variation 1: Drop the fish and crumbs mixture on a well-greased baking dish, 2 inches apart each way. Bake as in basic recipe.

Variation 2: Substitute 1½ cups leftover baked, broiled or cooked fish, boned and chopped, for the amount in basic recipe. Bake as above.

Variation 3: Fry fish and crumbs mixture like pancakes, using ⅓ cup of oil or melted vegetable shortening in a heavy frying pan. Turn the cakes as soon as brown on under side and brown on other side. Drain on paper towels. Serve with sour cream.

FINNAN HADDIE SCALLOP

1 onion
3 tablespoons butter or salad oil
3 medium size potatoes, pared and sliced thin
1 pound finnan haddie (smoked haddock)
Milk (approximately 1 cup)
2 tablespoons minced parsley

Slice or dice onion and spread over bottom of a glass casserole. Add 2 tablespoons shortening and about ⅓ of the sliced potatoes. Cut portions of finnan haddie should be placed over the layer of potato slices and topped with a second layer of potatoes. If you have any of the fish left, cut it into thin strips and place in a sunburst design, topping with remainder of potato slices.

Add milk slowly from the side of casserole to half way up. Cover with crumbs and dot with shortening or drizzle with remaining oil. Cover and bake at 375°F. for 45 to 50 minutes or till potatoes are tender. Remove cover and brown under broiler flame. Sprinkle with minced parsley and serve hot.

Serves 4.

RUSSIAN HERRING BALLS

(Kotleti Sledziowe)

5 herrings, filleted
1 onion, finely diced
3 tablespoons butter or oil
3 small hard crusted rolls, grated (1 cup, approximately)
2 eggs
½ cup cracker crumbs

Dash of pepper (optional)
Melted shortening for frying

Chop herring fillets. Brown onion in hot butter and stir in grated rolls (or equivalent in dry bread crumbs). Beat eggs and blend in as soon as onion and crumbs are cool. Add to chopped herring. If more moisture is required, a few drops of lemon juice or cold water may be added. The mixture should be thick enough to mold into balls the size of walnuts. Roll each ball in cracker crumbs, seasoned with pepper if desired, and fry in hot melted shortening till browned on all sides.

Serves 6 to 8.

HERRING SALAD

(Gehackte Herring)

1 large prepared herring, filleted
2 hard cooked eggs
1 tart apple, pared
1 small onion (optional)
2 tablespoons lemon juice of 3 tablespoons vinegar
2 tablespoons salad oil
2 tablespoons sugar (or to taste)
3 tablespoons dry bread or cracker crumbs
Dash of pepper (optional)

Chop herring fillets and eggs to a smooth pulp. Grate in apple and onion. Add lemon juice or vinegar and oil. Taste and add sugar. Stir in dry crumbs and add pepper. Cover and refrigerate ½ hour.

Serves 2 to 4 as an appetizer, or 6 to 8 spread on crackers or thinly sliced toasted cuts of bread for canapes.

VARIETY MEATS

CHOPPED CALF'S OR BEEF LIVER

(Basic Recipe)

Slice liver 1 inch thick and broil 5 to 10 minutes or till light brown on both sides. Remove veins and skin. Put through food chopper using fine cutting blade. Or chop to a smooth paste in a wooden bowl.

For each pound of liver fry ¼ cup finely diced onion in ¼ cup hot melted schmaltz or other shortening till nicely browned and add to liver paste with salt and pepper to taste. Use a fork for mixing till smooth. The fat as well as fried onion is added.

Variation 1: To each pound of liver add 2 hard cooked eggs before chopping.

Variation 2: To basic recipe add ½ cup peanut butter and blend well.

CHOPPED CHICKEN LIVER

Combine broiled chicken livers, hard cooked eggs and greben. Run through food chopper, season to taste with salt, pepper, celery salt or garlic salt, and add chicken or goose fat, or salad oil. Use as canapé spread. Top with tiny bits of pimento or green pepper, minced parsley or water cress, or sliced stuffed olive. Or press into a well-greased mold. Unmold on shredded mixed greens and garnish.

BROILED SWEETBREADS

Prepare sweetbreads for cooking like any other meat. Cover with cold water to which 1 tablespoon vinegar has been added. Cook over moderate heat 20 minutes and drain. Remove membrane as soon as cool enough to handle. Slice ½ inch thick. Place slices in a shallow glass baking pan, dot with shortening, dust lightly with salt, pepper and paprika and slip under broiler for 10 minutes or till lightly browned. Serve hot or keep hot in heated oven till serving time.

Two pairs of sweetbreads of beef will serve 4.

BRAINS WITH EGG SAUCE

1 set beef or calf's brains
Boiling water to cover
1 onion, diced or sliced thin
1 green pepper, diced
1 tomato, skinned and diced
1 cup hot water
¼ teaspoon salt and pepper
Dash of ginger
2 eggs
2 tablespoons lemon juice
1 tablespoon cornstarch
1 tablespoon cold water

Cover brains with boiling water and cover for 5 minutes. Drain. Remove membrane. Place brains, un-cut, in a saucepan and add vegetables, hot water, salt, pepper and ginger. Cover and cook over moderate heat 30 to 35 minutes. Lift out brains and put the sauce through a coarse strainer. There should be about 1 cup of sauce. Return sauce to saucepan and stir in well-beaten eggs and lemon juice. Blend cornstarch with cold water and add. Cook over low heat, stirring till smooth. Add the brains and cover. Simmer 10 minutes.

Serves 4.

STUFFED KISHKE
(Beef Casings—also called Stuffed Derma)

Beef casings purchased from the butcher shop are only partially cleaned. Casings have to be washed in cold water and scraped free of fat. It is best to have casings cut to 12-inch lengths for easier facility in handling for cleaning and stuffing. For final rinsing, use lukewarm water, turning casings inside out. Sew together one end of each length and fill with the following mixture:

Stuffing for Each 12-Inch Length of Casing
1 cup flour
½ cup chopped beef suet (fat from casings may be used)
1 small onion, grated
⅛ teaspoon salt
Dash of pepper
2 tablespoons fine bread or cracker crumbs

Combine ingredients in the order listed. Stir well in a shallow bowl. Place the sewed up end of casing in the center of flour mixture and begin stuffing by turning in the end with the mixture as you proceed to fill the entire length of casing. The casing should not be stuffed too full as the filling expands and the casing shrinks during cooking process. Tie or sew up and rinse free of flour mixture that has adhered to outer surface. Plunge into boiling water for 1 minute. This helps shrink casing. It is ready to be tucked into the midst of a Tzimmes (See Index) or placed with meat of any kind to be roasted or stewed.

Stuffed Kishke may be roasted with chicken, duck, goose or turkey. Or, it may be roasted independently on a bed of sliced onions to which schmaltz and grebenes have been added. Roast 1½ to 2 hours at 350°F. or till nicely browned.

SWEET-SOUR HEART

2 veal or 1 beef heart, cut into cubes
4 tablespoons hot melted shortening
1½ cups stewed fresh or canned tomatoes
½ cup vinegar
4 tablespoons water
4 tablespoons brown sugar
2 tablespoons flour
2 tablespoons hot melted shortening
1 teaspoon salt
Dash of paprika (optional)

Sauté heart in hot melted shortening 5 to 10 minutes over moderate heat. Add tomato, vinegar, water and sugar. Cover and simmer 35 to 40 minutes or till beef heart is tender enough to pierce with a fork. Brown flour in hot melted shortening in a separate saucepan and stir in some of the gravy from heart combination till smooth. Cook 5 minutes. Combine and taste. Add salt and paprika. Cook 5 minutes longer before serving.

Serves 6.

BEEF, LAMB AND VEAL

SAUERBRATEN

1 cup cider vinegar
½ cup cold water
6 bay leaves
1 teaspoon peppercorns
1 tablespoon mustard seed
½ cup brown sugar
4½ to 5 pounds brisket, first cut
2 cloves garlic, minced
2 large onions, sliced fine
½ cup seeded raisins
8 to 10 gingersnaps
1 cup concentrated tomato sauce (canned)

Make a marinade of vinegar, water, bay leaves, peppercorns, mustard seed and brown sugar. Place meat in this and keep well covered in the refrigerator overnight. Lift meat from marinade and sear quickly in a preheated heavy pot. Add garlic, onions, raisins and gingersnaps. Cover and cook over moderate heat 30 minutes. Reduce heat and simmer 2½ to 3 hours. Add tomato sauce and ½ cup of the marinade. Cook 10 minutes.

Serves 8.

STEWED STEAK

(Chuck, Flank or Rib)

1½ to 2 pounds steak
Flour for dredging
3 tablespoons shortening
1 large onion, sliced or diced
1 carrot, shredded or thinly sliced
1 cup diced celery
1 green pepper, thin strips (optional)
1 cup canned or stewed tomatoes
1 tablespoon vinegar or lemon juice
1 tablespoon brown sugar
½ cup hot water
Salt and pepper

Cut steak into serving portions and dredge with flour. Melt shortening in a heavy frying pan. Add steak and fry 3 to 5 minutes on each side. Add vegetables, vinegar, sugar and water to cover the meat. Cover and cook over moderate heat 15 to 20 minutes. Reduce heat and simmer 10 to 15 minutes uncovered. Test with a fork for tenderness. The steak should be turned and cooked for 5 to 10 minutes longer if not tender enough at this point. Add salt and pepper to taste before serving.

Serves 4 to 6.

SWEET-SOUR BEEF AND CABBAGE

2½ to 3 pounds brisket of beef or short ribs
2 pounds cabbage, shredded or chopped
1 teaspoon salt
1 onion, diced fine
¾ cup vinegar
½ cup brown sugar
½ cup seeded raisins
2 tablespoons cracker crumbs or flour
2 tablespoons shortening

Sear meat in pot in which it is to be cooked, over moderate heat. Sprinkle cabbage with salt. Let stand while preparing onion. Squeeze out liquid from cabbage, add onion and stir into the pot, moving seared meat to one side. When cabbage and onion are lightly browned, add the remaining ingredients except crumbs or flour and shortening. Cover pot and cook over reduced heat 1 hour. Lift cover and turn meat. If additional liquid is needed, add ¼ cup of boiling water at a time. The cabbage should be light brown and the meat beginning to be tender when pierced with a fork. Reduce heat and simmer 45 minutes longer. Thicken with crumbs or browned flour and shortening 10 minutes before serving time.

Serves 5 to 6.

SHORT RIBS OF BEEF STEW
(Basic Recipe)

   3 pounds short ribs, bones cracked
   3 tablespoons flour
   3 tablespoons melted shortening
   1 onion, diced
   1 carrot, diced
   1 cup diced celery
   Salt and pepper to taste
   1 cup canned tomato sauce

Ribs may be cut apart before dredging in flour. Brown quickly in hot shortening and add onion. Stir 2 minutes over moderate heat. Add carrot and celery, taste and add salt and pepper if desired. Cover and cook 30 minutes over moderate heat. Uncover and add tomato sauce diluted with water if desired. Cover and simmer 1 hour.

Serves 4.

POT ROAST WITH CIDER

   2 cups cider
   2 tablespoons molasses
   2 large onions, sliced thin
   1 clove garlic, minced
   2 bay leaves
   ⅛ teaspoon each ginger and allspice
   4 to 4½ pounds chuck or brisket (first cut)
   3 tablespoons shortening
   3 tablespoons flour
   ½ teaspoon salt
   Dash of pepper (optional)

Make a marinade of cider, molasses, onions, garlic, bay leaves and spice. Place the meat in this, cover and let stand in the refrigerator overnight. Turn and keep in marinade until ready for roasting in a heavy pot or pressure cooker. Melt shortening in pot. Lift meat from marinade and dust with flour, salt and pepper. Sear meat in hot melted shortening, turning once or twice to brown all parts. Add the marinade and cook over moderate heat 2 hours. Reduce heat and simmer 30 minutes.

Serves 8 to 9.

HOLISHKES
(Meat filled cabbage leaves, also called Praakes and Galuptzi, depending on locale)

   1 pound chopped beef
   ¼ cup uncooked rice
   1 egg
   1 onion, grated
   1 carrot, grated
   ¼ teaspoon salt
   10 or 12 cabbage leaves
   ¼ cup lemon juice, vinegar or ⅛ teaspoon citric acid crystals
   ½ cup brown sugar
   1 cup tomato sauce, canned
   Water to cover

Combine chopped meat, rice and egg. Grate in onion and carrot. Add salt. Blanch cabbage leaves by covering them with boiling water for 2 or 3 minutes. Drain cabbage leaves. Place a ball of the meat mixture in the center of each cabbage leaf and roll up, tucking in the ends securely. Place close together in a heavy frying pan, add the other ingredients and enough water to cover. Cover tightly and cook over moderate heat 30 minutes. Reduce heat and simmer 20 minutes. Bake in the oven 20 minutes at 350°F. to brown on top, turning once to brown under sides. Hot water may be added in small quantities if necessary during the baking period.

Serves 4 to 5.

CORNED BEEF AND VEGETABLES
(Called New England Boiled Dinner)

   2 pounds corned beef
   Cold water to cover
   1 onion, diced or sliced
   4 medium size beets, pared and diced
   4 medium size carrots, scraped and sliced or diced
   1 pound cabbage, shredded or cut into sections
   4 medium size potatoes, pared and quartered
   2 tablespoons shortening
   2 tablespoons flour

Cover corned beef with cold water. Cook in a deep kettle over moderate heat 1 hour. Add vegetables, cover and cook 35 to 45 minutes. Test meat for tenderness, and if necessary, continue cooking 10 to 15 minutes longer till meat is tender. Melt shortening in a saucepan and brown the flour, stirring constantly.

Stir in 1 cup of the sauce from kettle and cook 5 minutes. Add to the cooked corned beef and vegetables and shake the pot gently to distribute evenly. Cook 5 minutes. Serve hot.

Serves 4 to 6.

FRESH BEEF TONGUE

A 4 to 4½ pound fresh beef tongue
Cold water to cover
1 clove garlic, minced
1 onion, sliced
2 bay leaves
10 peppercorns
1 scant teaspoon salt
Vegetables to be Added
   ½ cup diced carrots
   ½ cup diced celery
   3 onions, sliced
   4 cups strained liquid

Combine all ingredients and bring to a brisk boil. Reduce heat and simmer 1½ hours. Remove tongue from liquid, remove skin and trim away parts from base. Strain the liquid and reserve. Place the vegetables in a roasting pan. Top with trimmed tongue and add strained liquid. Cover and bake approximately 2 hours at 300°F. or till tender.

Serves 8.

BEEF TONGUE ORIENTALE

A 4 to 4½ pound fresh beef tongue
Cold water to cover
1 large onion, diced
2 cloves garlic, minced
2 bay leaves
2 tablespoons vinegar or lemon juice
2 tablespoons sugar
2 tablespoons honey or corn syrup
1 cup seedless raisins
¼ teaspoon ginger or 6 gingersnaps
Thickening for Sauce
   2 tablespoons cornstarch
   2 tablespoons cold water

Cook tongue in water to cover over moderate heat for 30 minutes. Add onion, garlic and bay leaves. Cover and continue cooking 30 to 45 minutes. Test with a fork. If tender, lift out tongue to a plate. Strain liquid. Remove skin from tongue and trim away ex-cess fatty part at base of tongue. Return skinned tongue to liquid. Add vinegar, sugar, honey, raisins and ginger. Cover and simmer 45 minutes. Test again for tenderness. If not soft enough to pierce easily at center of top, cook 15 to 20 minutes longer. The sauce may be thickened with 2 tablespoons cornstarch mixed with cold water and added to the gravy after lifing out tongue. Cook gravy 5 to 10 minutes, stirring once or twice.

Serves 8.

STUFFED PEPPERS
(Basic Recipe)
[Called Ardei Implut in Rumania and other Balkan countries]

Six 5-inch sweet green peppers
Boiling water for blanching
1 pound chopped beef
¼ cup uncooked rice or ½ cup cooked rice or
   bread crumbs
1 onion, grated
1 carrot, grated
½ teaspoon salt
Dash of pepper
2 eggs
Water to cover
Sauce
   1 cup tomato purée
   ½ cup water
   3 tablespoons vinegar, or lemon juice
   3 tablespoons brown sugar
   ⅛ teaspoon paprika
   ½ cup raisins (optional)

Cut away stem end of peppers. Remove seeds. Blanch and invert to drain while preparing the meat mixture for filling. Combine all ingredients except water. Mix thoroughly. Stuff peppers compactly and even with the top. Stand upright in a casserole and cover with water. Bake 45 minutes at 350°F. Remove cover and increase heat to 400°F. for 15 minutes.

Cook sauce on top of stove, stirring continuously till thick, approximately 10 minutes over moderate heat. Add to the peppers in casserole, turn off heat. The heat of the oven is sufficient to lightly brown tops of pepper stuffing and cook sauce with liquid in casserole.

Serves 6.

LAMB STEW
(Basic Recipe)

> 3 pounds breast or shoulder of lamb, cut up
>
> 3 tablespoons hot melted shortening (schmaltz preferred)
>
> 2 large onions, diced
>
> 1 large carrot, diced or sliced
>
> 1 large parsnip, diced or sliced
>
> 2 medium white turnips, pared and diced
>
> 1 cup finely cut green beans
>
> 1 pound potatoes, pared and cubed
>
> 1 cup finely cut celery and leaves
>
> 2 tablespoons minced parsley
>
> ¼ teaspoon powdered garlic
>
> 1 teaspoon salt
>
> ¼ teaspoon paprika

Braise the meat in hot melted shortening in the pot in which it is to be stewed. Add diced onion and as soon as light brown, add the remaining ingredients in the order listed. Cover pot and cook over low heat, allowing 25 minutes per pound. Shake the pot once or twice during the stewing time to prevent sticking. Water that adhered to vegetables provides sufficient moisture to form a rich gravy.

Serves 4 to 5.

PITCHA
(Calf's Feet Jelly—also called Sulze)

> 2 calf's feet, cleaned and sawed to fit pot
>
> Cold water to cover
>
> 1 onion
>
> 1 clove garlic
>
> 3 bay leaves
>
> 1 teaspoon peppercorns (optional)
>
> Salt to taste
>
> 2 tablespoons lemon juice or
>
> ½ cup vinegar
>
> 3 hard cooked eggs, sliced
>
> Sliced lemon for garnish or parsley

Cook feet in water 10 minutes. Skim and add onion, garlic, bay leaves, peppercorns. Cook over reduced heat for 1 hour. Skim again, Simmer for 3 hours or till bones stand away from gristle and meat. Strain. Cut usable meat and gristle into fine cubes. Add to strained liquid. Taste and add salt if necessary. Add vinegar. Cook 5 minutes after bringing to a quick boil. Turn into an oblong glass dish about 2 inches in depth. Let cool until partly jelled. Place some egg slices on the top and stand remaining egg slices upright inside the dish along the sides. Chill in refrigerator. When completely jelled and firm to the touch, unmold on serving plate. Cut into squares if desired. Garnish with parsley and/or lemon. Chicory, shredded lettuce or watercress makes a nice base on which to serve this dish as an appetizer.

Serves 4 to 6.

Variation 1: Add 1 wine glass of sherry before turning into dish or other mold. Do not stir the wine in while hot.

Variation 2: Add 2 egg whites, stiffly beaten with a pinch of salt, after straining the liquid into a bowl. Put aside gristle and meat particles for later addition. Cook over moderate heat combined liquid and beaten egg whites for 20 minutes or till clear. This makes a clear jelly. When cool, add sherry without stirring. Place the gristle and meat bits in the bottom of mold or dish and add the clear jelly. Chill. Use sliced hard cooked eggs for garnish.

BONED VEAL SHOULDER POT ROAST
(Basic Recipe)

> 4½ to 5 pound boned shoulder
>
> 3 tablespoons hot melted shortening, chicken schmaltz preferably
>
> 1 cup diced onions
>
> 1 large carrot, diced
>
> 1 cup diced celery
>
> 2 bay leaves
>
> 10 peppercorns
>
> 1 clove garlic, diced fine
>
> 1 teaspoon salt
>
> ¼ teaspoon paprika

Sear meat in hot melted fat in roasting pot or Dutch oven. Lift out meat and add the other ingredients. Stir 1 or 2 minutes over moderate heat or till onions begin to soften. If possible, place a perforated rack over the vegetables and place the pot roast on it. Add enough water to come ½ inch over vegetables, approximately 1 cup. Cover and cook over moderate heat 2½ hours. Reduce heat and simmer 20 minutes uncovered. Thicken gravy with an einbren made of 2 tablespoons flour browned in 2 tablespoons melted shortening and ½ cup of gravy from pot stirred in till smooth. Cook 5 minutes. Lift out meat and rack, combine thickening with gravy and vegetables in the pot. Put gravy with vegetables through a coarse strainer for smooth gravy. Or serve unstrained over sliced pot roast.

Serves 6 to 7.

Variation 1: Substitute 1 cup cider for water. Do not use perforated rack in pot. Turn pot roast once or twice during the first hour of cooking. Slice meat when done and return to pot for 10 minutes before serving.

VEAL STEAKS
(Bombay Style)

4 veal shoulder steaks ½ inch thick (approximately 8 oz. each)
1 clove of garlic
4 tablespoons flour
⅛ teaspoon salt and pepper
4 tablespoons hot melted shortening
1 large onion, sliced or diced

Rub meat with cut clove of garlic. Dredge with flour seasoned with salt and pepper. Reserve 1 tablespoon melted shortening. Brown steaks on both sides in 3 tablespoons hot melted shortening in a heavy frying pan. Remove steaks from pan. Wipe pan with a paper towel and add reserved tablespoon of fat. Sauté onions till light yellow, return browned steaks to pan and add:

Sauce

1 No. 2 can tomatoes (including juice)
4 tablespoons canned tomato paste
½ teaspoon salt
1 teaspoon brown sugar
1 teaspoon curry powder
½ teaspoon thyme or poultry seasoning
1 teaspoon soy sauce
4 medium size canned pimentos, diced or cut in strips

Cover and simmer 45 minutes or till steaks are tender. Arrange steaks on a heated platter and pour gravy over. Garnish with parsley.

Serves 4.

POULTRY

DUCKLING WITH A BLUSH

A 4½ to 5½ pound duckling, prepared and disjointed
2 cloves garlic
3 tablespoons flour
⅛ teaspoon each celery salt, onion salt, paprika
3 tablespoons chicken schmaltz or other shortening
2 cups stewed fresh cranberries or 1 tall can whole cranberry sauce

Rub each piece of duck with garlic. Combine flour and seasoning. Roll each piece of duck with flour mixture till well coated. Melt fat in bottom of casserole and add duck pieces. Top with cranberry sauce, cover and bake 45 to 50 minutes per pound at 325°F.

Serves 5 to 6.

BREAD CRUMB DRESSING
(Basic Recipe)

1 large onion, diced
4 tablespoons chicken schmaltz
3 stalks celery, diced fine
½ large green pepper, diced fine
½ cup shredded carrot
½ cup thinly sliced fresh or canned mushrooms
3 cups grated stale challah or other bread
2 eggs
½ teaspoon powdered garlic
1 teaspoon salt
Dash of ginger, paprika and white pepper

Sauté onion in hot melted schmaltz for 2 minutes before adding celery, green pepper and carrot. Stir while cooking over moderate heat 5 minutes. Add bread crumbs and mushrooms and stir for 1 minute over increased heat. Beat eggs in a bowl. Add the cooked mixture in frying pan and stir well. Add seasoning as soon as cool. If the mixture is too dry, ½ cup of hot water or chicken soup may be added, stirring well.

Yields an amount sufficient for stuffing a 5½- to 6-pound fowl. For stuffing turkey or large goose, double amounts of all ingredients.

Variation 1: Add ½ cup finely cut dry prunes to basic dressing.

Variation 2: Add ½ cup thinly sliced or diced apple and a dash of cinnamon or nutmeg, 1 tablespoon lemon juice, 2 tablespoons sugar.

Variation 3: Add ½ cup diced roasted chestnuts to basic dressing and/or variations.

GEFILTE HELZEL
(Basic Recipe)

1 cup flour
⅛ teaspoon salt
¼ cup chopped uncooked chicken fat or melted shortening
2 tablespoons grated onion
Dash of nutmeg (optional)

Combine all ingredients listed. Sew up the small end of chicken neck and fill ¾ full. Sew up other end. Wash with cold water then pour boiling water over. This will bring a smoothness to skin. Cook with other food or place in roasting pan with the bird. Remove thread at both ends before slicing for serving.

For stuffing the necks of geese or turkey, double or triple the amount of ingredients according to size of neck skin.

CHICKEN PILAF

1 cup rice, brown or white
2 cups chicken stock or cold water
½ teaspoon salt if water is used
1 medium size onion, chopped or diced
2 tablespoons schmaltz or vegetable shortening
2 cups diced cooked chicken, white meat
Diced cooked gizzard
1 cup tomato juice or thin sauce
4 tablespoons hot melted schmaltz

Rinse rice and drain. Cook in chicken stock or water in double boiler until the liquid has been absorbed. The rice should be tender when pressed between finger and thumb. Sauté onion in schmaltz and add diced chicken and sliced gizzard as soon as light brown. Stir lightly 1 minute over moderate heat. Add cooked rice and tomato juice. Turn into a well-greased pudding dish, topping with remaining hot melted shortening. Bake 20 to 30 minutes at 350°F. or till lightly browned on top.

Serves 4.

CHICKEN PAPRIKA WITH RICE

1 large onion, diced
4 tablespoons schmaltz
A 4½ to 5 pound chicken, sectioned
2 tablespoons flour
¼ teaspoon salt
Boiling water
1 cup uncooked rice
1 teaspoon salt
Dash of garlic salt
½ teaspoon paprika

Sauté onion in hot melted shortening till light brown. Dredge sections of chicken in flour seasoned with ¼ teaspoon salt. Brown each piece in pan in which onion has been cooked, pushing onion to one side. Add boiling water to cover, adding a little at a time. Add rinsed rice and seasoning, cover tightly and simmer 1½ hours. Turn into a casserole or baking pan and bake 30 minutes at 325°F. It should have absorbed all the gravy and be lightly browned on top. The rice should be puffed and brown.

Serves 6.

CASSEROLE OF TURKEY LEFTOVERS

2 cups diced cooked turkey
2 cups diced boiled potatoes
1 cup cooked or canned peas
1 large raw carrot, shredded
1 onion, diced
3 tablespoons schmaltz or other shortening
3 tablespoons finely cut celery
1 green pepper, cut in strips
1 cup water

Place diced turkey in bottom of a casserole. Top with potatoes and peas and add shredded carrot. Brown onion in melted fat and add celery and pepper, stirring 1 to 2 minutes. Place this mixture in casserole by pressing down in the center and stirring lightly. Add water. Cover and bake 20 minutes at 350°F. Uncover and bake 10 to 15 minutes longer or till lightly browned on top.

Serves 4.

SAUCES

HOLLANDAISE SAUCE

2 egg yolks
½ cup butter or margarine
1 tablespoon lemon juice
¼ teaspoon salt
Dash of cayenne
½ cup boiling water

Add egg yolks one at a time to melted butter in top of double boiler over hot water, blending each thoroughly. Add lemon juice. Cook over hot water till thick stirring constantly till smooth. Just before serving add seasoning and boiling water gradually, stirring and beating constantly to keep consistency smooth.

Yields ¾ cup.

Variation 1: Stir in gradually 1 tablespoon sherry just before serving.

Variation 2: Blend in a little anchovy paste for fish salad.

Note: Should Hollandaise Sauce separate, beat in more lemon juice and 1 or 2 tablespoons boiling water drop by drop, stirring till smooth.

WHITE SAUCE
(Basic Recipe—Milchig)

2 tablespoons butter
1 tablespoon flour
1 cup milk
¼ teaspoon salt
Dash of white pepper

Melt butter in saucepan over low heat. Blend in flour but do not brown. Add milk gradually, stirring till smooth. Cook 3 minutes. This makes a sauce thin enough to pour over or cook with vegetables.

Yields 1 cup.

Variations:

Medium White Sauce can be made by doubling the amount of flour and using part cream or ¾ cup evaporated milk and ¼ cup water. Use for creamed vegetables, fish and scalloped dishes.

Thick White Sauce can be made by blending 4 tablespoons butter with 4 tablespoons flour. Add 1 cup milk or ¾ cup evaporated milk.

Cheese Sauce can be made by adding ¼ to 1 cup grated cheese to either Medium or Thick White Sauce. Season with celery salt or onion salt and use with vegetables, fish and egg dishes.

Curry Sauce can be made by adding 1 teaspoon curry powder to Medium White Sauce. ⅛ teaspoon garlic salt or powdered garlic and/or ½ teaspoon minced onion may be added.

Caper Sauce can be made by adding 1 tablespoon capers to basic recipe or variations.

Brown Sauce can be made by melting butter until brown, blend in flour. Stir till as brown as desired. Do not scorch. Proceed as in basic recipe. For meat meals, substitute vegetable shortening, chicken fat or oil for butter, and thin out with soup stock or gravy.

Lemon Sauce can be made by adding 1 teaspoon lemon juice to basic recipe for White Sauce.

VEGETABLES

SPICED GREEN BEANS

1 pound green beans
2 tablespoons vinegar or lemon juice
Brown sugar to taste
1 clove garlic
1 bay leaf
Dash of allspice

Cut beans diagonally or lengthwise. Cook in very little water 5 minutes, in a covered saucepan. Add the other ingredients, cook 3 minutes longer. Remove garlic and bay leaf. Serve hot or cold. Excellent with cold meats or fish.

Serves 6 to 8.

CREAMED MASHED BEETS

3 cups cooked, mashed beets
1 tablespoon lemon juice
½ teaspoon salt
½ cup heavy cream or sour cream
½ cup crumbs
1 tablespoon butter

Cooked or canned beets, drained, put through the ricer may be used. Add lemon juice and salt, fold in sour cream or stiffly beaten heavy cream. Top with crumbs and dot with butter. Slip under broiler flame to brown lightly and serve hot.

Serves 4.

GINGER BEETS

1 tablespoon flour
1 tablespoon shortening
½ cup beet liquid
2 cups cooked beets, cut in strips
1 tablespoon lemon juice or vinegar
2 tablespoons brown sugar
¼ teaspoon salt
1 teaspoon ground ginger
¼ teaspoon dry mustard (optional)

Blend flour and shortening and brown lightly. Add beet liquid and stir till smooth. Add the other ingredients. Cook 3 to 5 minutes. Fine with lamb, veal or fish meals.

Serves 5 or 6.

BROCCOLI FLORETS

1 onion
1 clove garlic
2 tablespoons oil or vegetable shortening
3 pounds broccoli
1 teaspoon salt
2 tablespoons lemon juice
1 cup water

Use tender parts of stems with the flower or head. Cut stems into ¼-inch rounds, and separate the heads into florets. Brown diced onion and garlic in shortening. Remove the garlic. Add broccoli, salt and lemon juice and water. Cover and simmer 15 to 20 minutes. Garnish with boiled or roasted chestnuts.

Serves 6 to 8.

CABBAGE IN SOUR CREAM

1 medium head cabbage (3 to 3½ pounds)
½ cup cold water
2 cups sour cream
2 tablespoons butter
½ cup flour
½ cup mild vinegar
½ cup sugar
Salt to taste

Shred cabbage and add water. Cook in frying pan for 5 minutes. Drain off excess liquid. Add sour cream and butter. Blend flour, vinegar and sugar and stir in. Cook 3 minutes longer. Add salt.

Serves 6.

CARROT AND TURNIP

6 young carrots (approximately 1 pound), diced
6 young white turnips, diced
Water
½ teaspoon salt
¼ teaspoon sugar
2 tablespoons butter or other fat
Dash of paprika
Greens (tender tops of carrots and turnips) cut fine

Wash carrots and turnips after removing tops. Do not scrape or pare them. Dice, then cover with cold water, add salt and sugar and cook in a covered pot 6 to 8 minutes or till tender. The liquid should be reduced by half. Turn into a large bowl and mash with a fork. Add the melted shortening and serve hot, heaped up in a vegetable dish or in individual portions, garnished with greens and a sprinkling of paprika. Or form into balls and garnish.

Serves 4 to 6.

CORN FRITTERS

2 cups cooked corn kernels
2 eggs
½ teaspoon salt
½ cup flour
½ cup milk or water
Shortening for frying

Beat eggs, add salt, flour and liquid to make a smooth batter. Add corn kernels and drop by the spoonful in deep hot melted shortening. Fry till nicely browned on both sides. Drain well.

Serves 4.

CORN O'BRIEN

2 cups corn, cooked
1 onion
1 large green pepper
2 tablespoons butter
1 tablespoon flour
½ cup milk
¼ teaspoon salt
Dash of white pepper

Cut corn from cob or use canned whole kernals. Dice onion and green pepper. Sauté in butter till lightly browned. Blend in flour, stirring lightly 1 to 2 minutes, add milk slowly to blend smooth. Add cooked corn and season to taste. Cook 3 minutes. If uncooked corn kernels are used, sauté with browned onion and pepper before adding milk in which flour has been blended smooth. Cook over low heat 5 to 10 minutes till corn is tender.

Serves 4.

Variation: To serve with meat, omit butter and milk. Use vegetable shortening or chicken fat and add soup stock or water.

CAULIFLOWER WITH BROWN RICE

 1 cup brown rice
 1 quart water
 1 teaspoon salt
 2 tablespoons butter or vegetable shortening
 1 head cauliflower (trimmed)
 1 tablespoon lemon juice
 2 tablespoons bread crumbs
 1 tablespoon minced parsley

Boil rice in salted water, in double boiler 30 minutes till tender. Drain well, return to upper part of boiler and let steam till dry. Add 1 tablespoon butter. Cook whole cauliflower in very little water in a tightly covered pot. Lemon juice and salt should be added after boiling starts. Boil 5 minutes, or till tender. Drain. Place the whole head of cauliflower on serving platter, dot with remaining butter. Surround with rice and top with crumbs. Sprinkle with minced parsley.

Serves 4 to 6.

SCALLOPED KALE

 1½ pounds kale
 1 onion, diced
 2 tablespoons butter
 ½ cup grated cheese
 ½ cup dry crumbs
 1½ teaspoons salt
 1 cup thin white sauce (See Sauces)
 2 hard cooked eggs

Cut away fibrous stems and wilted tops from kale. Wash well. Drain. Chop or cut fine. Cook in a tightly covered pot over moderate heat 8 to 10 minutes. Sauté onion in butter till light brown. Combine cooked kale with onion and turn into a casserole or baking dish. Top with grated cheese mixed with

crumbs. Bake 15 minutes at 375° F. Pour on white sauce and garnish with sliced cooked eggs.

Serves 4.

EGGPLANT SALAD
(Russian Style)

Remove stem and peel. Slice, cut into cubes. Cook over moderate heat in very little water 5 minutes or till transparent. Drain, chop and add sliced or diced hard cooked eggs, lemon juice or vinegar, salt and pepper to taste. Add minced or sliced onion, sliced black radish, black olives or minced parsley as garnish.

MUSHROOMS À LA RUSSE

 4 cups sliced fresh mushrooms
 1 heaping tablespoon flour
 ¼ teaspoon salt
 1 cup sour cream
 1 teaspoon onion juice or
 2 tablespoons chopped chives or green onion tips
 Generous dash of paprika

Do not peel fresh mushrooms but cut away the woody, fibrous stem section. Slice from the top down as thin as desired. Wash in slightly salted water and drain well. Enough water will cling to the slices to form sufficient steam. Place in saucepan or heated frying pan and cook over low heat 3 to 5 minutes. Rub the flour and salt with a little sour cream until smooth then stir into the remaining sour cream. Add to steamed mushrooms, stirring lightly to combine, then add the onion juice or chives. Cook 1 minute longer and serve hot on toast or Holland rusks. Garnish with a dash of paprika or a few bits of parsley.

Serves 4.

PARSNIPS

This root vegetable is very flavorful when young and tender. It should be scraped like carrots, cut lengthwise into quarters, and soaked in salted cold water 5 minutes before cooking. Allow 2 slender parsnips per serving, if fairly large. Cook parsnips 10 minutes in just enough water to prevent sticking. Add melted butter or schmaltz.

MINTED GREEN PEAS
   2 cups shelled fresh peas or 1 tall can
   ¼ teaspoon salt
   Few grains of sugar
   ½ cup cold water
   2 tablespoons chopped fresh mint leaves
   1 tablespoon butter

If canned peas are used, heat with liquid from can. If quick frozen peas are used, follow directions on the package. For fresh peas, add cold water, salt and sugar and cook in tightly covered saucepan 5 to 7 minutes over moderate heat. Or 2 minutes in Pressure Cooker. Just before serving add butter and chopped mint, shake the pan to distribute evenly.

Remember when marketing that it takes about 3 pounds unshelled peas to serve 4.

STEWED OKRA AND TOMATOES
   1 pound okra
   1 cup tomatoes, stewed
   2 tablespoons butter, oil or chicken fat
   1 tablespoon lemon juice
   1 tablespoon brown sugar
   ½ teaspoon salt
   Boiling water

Remove stems and tips from pods. Wash and drain. Slice pods if large. Add boiling water to barely cover and cook 15 minutes. Add the other ingredients and cook 5 minutes longer.
Serves 4.

CREAMED ONIONS
   8 medium size white or yellow onions
   Cold water to cover
   ¼ teaspoon salt
   3 tablespoons butter
   3 tablespoons flour
   1½ cups milk
   4 tablespoons grated cheese, sharp or mild
      cheddar type
   Dash of paprika (optional)

Peel onions and cut away root and stem ends. Cover with cold water, add salt and bring to a quick boil. Reduce heat and cook, uncovered, 20 to 25 minutes or until the onions are tender enough to pierce with a toothpick. Drain. Make a cream sauce by melting butter in a saucepan and rubbing in the flour till smooth. Stir in milk and cook over moderate heat 5 to 8 minutes, stirring constantly till thick. Add grated cheese and stir till smooth. Remove from heat. Add the cooked onions. Heat before serving. Add a dash of paprika for color if desired.
   Serves 4.
   Variation: White pickling onions 1 inch in diameter may be used, allowing 4 to 6 per serving. Proceed as in basic recipe.

POTATO GOLD
   4 medium potatoes, sliced
   4 medium carrots, diced
   1 medium onion, diced
   2 tablespoons butter or vegetable shortening
   2 tablespoons milk (or soup stock)
   Salt and pepper to taste

Cook potatoes and carrots together in about 2 inches of water in a tightly covered saucepan. When tender, press through a potato ricer, colander or coarse sieve. Brown onion in shortening and combine, adding milk or soup stock and seasoning. Remove from heat. Mix or beat well. Mound up the Potato Gold and garnish with a sprig of parsley.
   Serves 6.

POTATO-CHEESE PUFFS
   1½ cups mashed potatoes (hot or cold)
   3 tablespoons hot milk
   ½ cup grated cheese (or dry pot cheese)
   2 eggs, separated
   1 teaspoon salt
   ¼ teaspoon paprika
   1 tablespoon finely chopped green pepper (or
      parsley)
   1 small grated onion (or 1 tablespoon juice)
   2 tablespoons melted butter

Beat mashed potatoes with milk. Add egg yolks to cheese and beat till fluffy. Combine other ingredients. Fold in stiffly beaten egg whites and melted butter. Drop in small mounds on a well-greased cookie sheet and bake 20 minutes at 350° F. or till nicely browned. Excellent with a fish or vegetable dinner.
   Serves 6.

SWEET POTATOES WITH CHESTNUTS

2 pounds sweet potatoes, pared
1 pound chestnuts
½ cup brown sugar
¼ cup water
½ cup bread crumbs
2 tablespoons butter or substitute

Slice sweet potatoes in 1-inch thick rounds. Boil 5 minutes in enough water to cover, adding ¼ teaspoon salt and covering the pot while boiling. Remove the shells from chestnuts and parboil at least 10 minutes. Drain and remove brown skins. Drain water from sweet potatoes, saving ¼ cup to mix with brown sugar and shortening. Arrange layers of sweet potato rounds and chestnuts in a baking dish or casserole, add the sugar mixture, top with crumbs and bake 30 to 40 minutes at 350° F. till brown.

Serves 6.

Yam is the name for the Southern sweet potato which is less dry and much sweeter than the lighter colored ones. Both varieties can be used in these recipes.

LATKES

(Grated Potato Pancakes)
6 medium size potatoes
1 onion
2 eggs
½ cup flour
1 teaspoon salt
Vegetable shortening or oil for deep frying

Pare and grate potatoes into a mixing bowl. Squeeze out liquid. Peel and grate onion into potatoes. Add eggs, flour and salt and stir to make a smooth batter that will drop heavily from the spoon. Heap the shortening in a heavy frying pan using enough to cover the pancakes amply. Drop the batter from a spoon into the hot shortening, making pancakes 3 inches from a spoon into the hot shortening, making pancakes 3 inches in diameter. Fry over moderate heat until brown on the underside, turn to brown. Lift out and drain off excess fat on paper towel. Pancakes fried in deep fat should be puffed and crisp.

Serves 4 to 6.

Variation 1: Use same mixture in greased shallow baking pan (8'' × 12'' cookie pan), bake 45 minutes at 350° F. or until nicely browned. Cut into squares and serve hot.

Variation 2: Add ½ cup well-chopped greben to grated potato batter. Substitute fine matzo meal for flour and fry as in basic recipe.

Variation 3: Turn either basic recipe or Variation 2 into well-greased small muffin pan and bake 45 minutes at 350°F.

GREEN PEPPER SAUTÉ

6 large green or red sweet peppers
¼ cup vegetable shortening
Salt and pepper

Core and cut peppers in eighths. Cover with boiling water and cook 3 minutes. Drain and sauté in hot melted shortening until lightly browned.

Serves 4 to 6.

SWEET-SOUR SPINACH

1 pound spinach
1 large onion
2 tablespoons shortening
2 tablespoons flour
½ cup cider vinegar
2 tablespoons brown sugar
1 teaspoon salt
1 cup drained canned tomatoes

Wash and drain spinach. Shred or chop leaves and stems. Brown diced onion in shortening. Stir in flour and blend till light brown. Add vinegar in which sugar has been dissolved. Add salt. Stir till smooth. Add tomatoes and chopped spinach and cook 3 minutes.

Serves 4.

ACORN SQUASH

Cut halves through stem end. Remove seeds. Add 1 teaspoon butter, dust with salt and paprika and bake 40 to 60 minutes at 375° F. or till tender.

Variation 1: Boil halves in salted water to cover till tender. Drain and brush the inside with melted butter or other shortening. Bake 10 minutes to brown. Or, slip under the broiler.

Variation 2: Fill baked or boiled halves with cooked diced beets, creamed white onions, boiled rice or creamed spinach with grated cheese topping.

TOMATOES, STUFFED AND BAKED

6 tomatoes
1 cup chopped meat (leftover or fresh)
½ cup boiled rice or bread crumbs
Salt and pepper to taste
¼ teaspoon poultry seasoning
1 tablespoon onion juice
1 tablespoon fat

Slice off stem ends of tomatoes, scoop out centers and invert tomatoes to drain. Make a stuffing of meat, rice and seasonings and add the scooped out part of tomatoes if desired. Press enough into each tomato to fill, make small balls to place on top of each, dot with a little fat and bake 30 minutes at 375° F., or till tender and the tops browned. Serve from the baking dish.

Serves 6.

Variation: Use any other stuffing such as rice and cheese; bread crumbs, eggs and cheese; canned salmon and rice or bread crumbs; cooked soybeans and cheese.

TOMATO FRITTERS

4 slightly under-ripe tomatoes
1 egg
¼ cup water or milk
¾ cup flour
¼ teaspoon salt
Melted shortening

Cut tomatoes into thick slices and dust with flour. Make a batter of beaten egg, salt, flour and liquid. Dip tomatoes in batter and fry in deep hot melted shortening till nicely browned on both sides.

Serves 4.

YELLOW TURNIPS
(Rutabagas)

Prepare like white turnips. These are good mashed, creamed or made into Tzimmes. Because these are a little more tough fibered than young white turnips, they require longer cooking. They have a much stronger flavor, too. But they are full of vitamins B and C, so be sure to include them in the diet. Cook 20 to 30 minutes in salted water to cover.

Allow ½ pound per serving.

TURNIPS

Select young, small size white turnips. Pare and slice or dice. Cook 5 minutes in a minimum of salted hot water or till tender. Drain and mash with butter or other shortening. Serve hot.

Allow ½ pound per serving.

VEGETABLE LOAF

2 tablespoons melted shortening
1 cup diced or chopped onion
1 cup minced celery
1 cup grated raw carrots
1 cup finely ground English walnuts (or mixed nuts)
1 cup dry whole wheat or rye bread crumbs
1 teaspoon each salt and poultry seasoning
2 eggs
1 cup evaporated milk or cream
1½ cups tomato or mushroom sauce

Cook onions in hot melted shortening till light brown and add vegetables, nuts, crumbs and seasonings. Sauté. Beat eggs and stir in cream. Combine both mixtures and turn into a well-greased loaf pan or shape into balls or patties for individual portions. Bake at 350° F. 40 to 45 minutes or till nicely browned. Turn out loaf and serve with tomato sauce or fresh mushroom sauce. Or, use a can of cream of mushroom soup, heated just before serving. Garnish with sliced hard cooked eggs or cooked green peas around the loaf.

Serves 4 to 6.

LEGUMES AND GRAINS

BAKED BEANS
(Basic Recipe)

2 cups navy beans
½ teaspoon salt
1 onion
4 tablespoons shortening
¼ tablespoon molasses
½ cup tomato sauce

Beans should be soaked in cold water for several hours or overnight. Drain, cover with fresh cold water, add salt and onion and cook over moderate heat until the skins of beans fill out and beans begin to soften enough to crush between thumb and forefinger. Add molasses and tomato sauce. Turn into a casserole, cover and bake 1 to 1½ hours at 325° F. Uncover and bake 10 to 25 minutes longer till reddish brown on top.

Serves 4 to 6.

Variation 1: Use tenderized navy beans (marked on package). These do not require soaking. Cook as above.

Variation 2: Add 1½ to 2 pounds brisket of beef to the ingredients listed. Omit shortening. Cook over low heat 1½ hours, then add molasses and tomato sauce just before turning into casserole, leaving the fat part of meat exposed. Bake 1 to 1½ hours at 300° F.

Variation 3: Black-eyed round beans or red kidney beans may be substituted.

BOILED SOYBEANS
(Basic Recipe)

½ cup soybeans per serving
⅛ teaspoon salt
Cold water to cover
Onion (optional)

Cook till tender and serve whole, with or without liquid, with butter or grated cheese added while hot.

Variation 1: Mash or put through potato ricer and add butter or other shortening.

Variation 2: Drain cooked soybeans and add ¼ cup tomato sauce, Creole sauce, fried onion rings. Slip under broiler flame to brown lightly.

KASHA
(Basic Recipe)

1½ cups coarse buckwheat groats
2 egg yolks
3 to 4 cups boiling water
1 teaspoon salt
1 onion, diced
4 tablespoons shortening

Heat a heavy frying pan over moderate flame and add groats. Stir to prevent too rapid browning or scorching. Stir in beaten egg yolks and continue stirring till groats are egg coated and dry. Add water gradually, stirring steadily. Add salt. Cover and reduce heat for 10 to 15 minutes or till the grains are tender. If necessary to prevent sticking, more boiling water may be added, a little at a time. The groats should have doubled in bulk before adding browned diced onion and fat in which it has been prepared while the groats were being cooked.

Turn cooked kasha into a shallow baking dish and bake 10 minutes at 350° F. or till nicely browned.

Yields 3 cups.

Variation: Spread groats in a thin layer on bottom of a shallow baking pan. Brown in the oven at 350° F. approximately 10 minutes, stirring once or twice. Beat eggs in a bowl and stir in browned groats. Return to hot oven to dry, leaving oven door open, and stirring 2 or 3 times to prevent scorching. Cook in boiling salted water as directed in basic recipe and combine when tender with browned onion, chopped greben and same amount of fat.

KASHA-VARNITCHKES

1 cup coarse buckwheat groats
2 egg yolks
4 cups boiling water
1 teaspoon salt
4 tablespoons chicken fat or butter
1 cup cooked noodle squares or bow-knots

Brown the groats in a heated heavy skillet or frying pan, stirring constantly to prevent burning. Stir in the egg yolks till grains are coated. Add the hot water slowly, stirring constantly. Add salt. Cook till tender over moderate heat. Add shortening and cooked noodle squares. Turn into a casserole and brown under broiler flame till nicely and evenly browned. Serve with meat gravy or plain.

Serves 3 or 4.

SWEET-SOUR LENTILS

1½ cups lentils
1 quart cold water
2 tablespoons butter or vegetable shortening
2 tablespoons flour
¼ teaspoon salt
Juice of 1 lemon (a bit of grated rind)
2 tablespoons sugar

Cook lentils in cold water 45 minutes to 1 hour or till tender. Drain, reserving liquid. Heat shortening in saucepan and add flour, stirring till deep brown. Add some of the liquid strained from cooked lentils, stirring smooth. Add salt, sugar and lemon juice and rind. Cook 1 minute before adding to lentils. Turn into a casserole and bake 15 minutes at 350° F., or till the liquid has been absorbed. Garnish with minced parsley or sprinkle with paprika and serve hot.

Serves 4.

PEAS AND RICE CASSEROLE

1 cup rice (brown or converted)
3 tablespoons butter or substitute
2 cups peas, fresh, frozen or drained canned
½ teaspoon salt
1 tablespoon sugar
3 cups boiling water

After washing rice under running water and draining it thoroughly, add to the melted shortening in a heated, heavy frying pan. Stir constantly until lightly browned. Add peas, salt and sugar and stir in gradually the boiling water. Cook only 5 minutes uncovered, then turn into a casserole. Cover and bake at 350° F. for 45 minutes. Uncover, and if rice is tender, place a few strips of cheddar cheese on top. Bake until cheese is melted. Or, slip under the broiler flame long enough to melt the cheese and brown lightly on top.

Serves 4 to 6.

NAHIT WITH RICE
(Rumanian Style)

1 cup cooked nahit
¼ cup rice
3 cups water
1 teaspoon salt
½ cup honey
¼ cup brown sugar

Combine and cook over moderate heat 20 to 30 minutes or until rice is tender. Turn into a casserole. Bake at 400° F. for 15 minutes or till nicely browned on top.

Variation: Cook chick peas with 2 pounds brisket of beef and an onion 1½ hours or till meat is tender. Remove onion, add an einbren and brown in the oven, with or without adding honey and sugar.

Rice. There are several varieties on the market. The directions on package include proportions of liquid and grains, in accordance with the variety. A general and basic rule is to use 4 cups water to 1 cup rice.

Brown rice is the unpolished variety that is advocated by nutritionists. *Converted,* long grain rice, retains most of the original vitamin content. *Polished rice* is the least desirable variety. *Wild rice* is in the luxury class.

NAHIT
(Basic Recipe)

Soak dry chick peas in cold water to cover 10 to 12 hours. Drain, rinse in cold water. Add fresh water to come 2 inches over top. Cook in a covered pot 30 to 45 minutes, add salt to taste and continue cooking uncovered till tender. Drain, dust lightly with salt and serve hot or cold.

VIENNESE RISI BISI

1 cup rice
2 teaspoons salt
Few drops of lemon juice
1 cup canned or fresh peas
6 cups boiling water
3 tablespoons oil, butter or schmaltz
1 onion, diced fine
Minced parsley

Cook rice in salted water, (adding lemon juice for whiteness) over moderate heat 30 minutes or until tender. Drain rice and add peas. If fresh peas are used, return rice and peas to pot and cover well, allowing the steam to tenderize peas. Top of a double boiler is fine for the purpose.

Brown diced onion in shortening and stir into the rice and peas, using two forks.

Serves 5 to 6.

SALADS AND SALAD DRESSINGS

BASIC SALAD MARINADE

½ cup salad oil (corn, peanut or soy bean)
¼ cup olive oil (optional)
½ cup lemon juice or wine vinegar
3 tablespoons brown sugar
Dash of salt and pepper
¼ teaspoon paprika
Clove of garlic (cut and left in Marinade)

Combine all ingredients in a tightly covered bottle or jar and shake well. Beat when prepared in advance and chilled. Yields approximate;y 1½ cups. Store in refrigerator.

Variation: For *Fish* or *Meat Salads,* add horseradish, a dash of curry, and/or minced parsley and green pepper.

For *Vegetable* or *Egg Salads,* add onion juice or grated onion, minced parsley, chopped pickle relish, chopped stuffed olives.

For *Fruit Salads,* add well-mashed cream cheese mixed with sour cream, light cream, evaporated milk and/or pineapple juice to taste. Add confectioners' sugar as desired and a few drops of almond extract.

For *Greens Salads,* add grated Parmesan or Roquefort cheese.

A POPULAR RUSSIAN DRESSING

Add to Basic Salad Marinade chopped cucumbers, mixed pickles, olives, chili sauce and a dash of cayenne or Worcestershire sauce.

BOILED SALAD DRESSING

3 egg yolks
1 tablespoon flour
1 teaspoon dry mustard
¼ teaspoon salt
¼ teaspoon paprika
1 tablespoon sugar
¼ cup vinegar or lemon juice
¾ cup cold water
2 tablespoons butter or oil

Beat egg yolks slightly. Stir in the mixed dry ingredients. Blend water and vinegar and add a little at a time, stirring to blend smoothly. Cook over hot water until thickened and stir in butter or oil after removing from heat. Chill before using.

Yields 1½ cups.

Variation 1: Thin with sour cream, whipped cream or evaporated milk before using.

Variation 2: Thin with cider, pineapple juice or onion juice.

AVOCADO SALAD

1 package orange or lemon gelatin
1½ cups water
1 avocado, mashed
3 ounces cream cheese
½ cup mayonnaise
½ green pepper
¼ cup celery heart
Pinch of salt
Few drops onion juice

Dissolve gelatin in 1 cup hot water, then add ½ cup cold water. Combine avocado with cheese and mayonnaise. Dice pepper and celery. Add seasonings and combine with gelatin. Turn into 9-inch square pan. Cut into 1-inch cubes when firm. Serve on a nest of shredded lettuce.

Serves 6.

MOLDED BEET SALAD

2 cups beet juice
2 packages lemon gelatin
1½ cups water
1 cup shredded or grated cooked beets
½ pound cream cheese
1 cup whipping cream or evaporated milk (chilled)

Heat beet juice. Dissolve gelatin in boiling water and add beet juice and grated beets. Whip chilled evaporated milk with a rotary beater. Add cheese and beat a few minutes together. Combine. Chill in cup molds. When set, unmold on lettuce or other salad greens.

Serves 6 to 8.

CHANNUKAH CANDLE SALAD

2 bananas
4 slices canned pineapple
4 orange gumdrops
4 strips green pepper
Lettuce
Mayonnaise

Cut bananas in half and remove tips. Stand upright in pineapple centers. Top with gumdrop to represent flame. Pour a little mayonnaise from tip of each candle to represent melted wax. Arrange strip of pepper for handle, making a loop fastened into pineapple at base of candle.

Serves 4.

Variation: Cut red apples in 2 without paring and remove cores. Set a half banana into center to represent candle, top with gumdrop and pour mayonnaise down side of candle.

CARROT AND GREEN PEPPER SALAD

1 cup shredded raw carrots
¼ cup mayonnaise or salad dressing
1 medium size green pepper, diced or chopped
3 walnuts coarsely chopped
Salad greens (lettuce, chicory, escarole, parsley)

Combine shredded carrots with dressing, chopped nuts and green pepper. Serve on mixed greens on individual salad plates. Top with dressing.

Serves 4.

CUCUMBER IN LIME GELATIN

1 package lime gelatin
1 cup boiling water
1 large cucumber
1 cup grated raw carrot
1 cup finely chopped cabbage
1 cup chopped apple
¼ cup chopped nuts or peanuts
½ cup canned shredded pineapple
Salt to taste
Shredded salad greens

Dissolve gelatin in boiling water. Grate unpared cucumber, combine with carrot, cabbage, apple, nuts, drained pineapple and salt to taste. Combine with gelatin. Turn into a ring mold rinsed in cold water. Chill till firm. Unmold and serve on shredded salad greens marinated with dressing. This salad may be turned into individual molds.

Serves 8.

BLACK MAJESTY SALAD

24 large prunes
1 cup cream or cottage cheese
½ cup chopped nuts
Mayonnaise (½ cup approximately)
8 slices canned pineapple
1 small head lettuce

Soak prunes. When soft, remove pits and drain well. Combine cheese, nuts and 1 tablespoon each mayonnaise and pineapple syrup. Stuff centers of each prune with cheese mixture. Arrange 3 prunes on each slice of pineapple. Chill at least a half hour before serving. Arrange on shredded lettuce on serving plate or as individual salads.

Serves 8.

FROZEN BANANA SALAD

Two 3-ounce packages cream cheese
¼ teaspoon salt
½ cup mayonnaise
2 tablespoons lemon juice
½ cup canned crushed pineapple
2 medium size bananas
½ cup coarsely chopped walnuts
½ cup thinly sliced maraschino cherries
1 cup whipped evaporated milk

Mash cheese in a mixing bowl, adding salt, mayonnaise and lemon juice. Combine with the other ingredients in the order listed, folding in whipped milk last. Turn into freezer tray and freeze till firm. Unmold on a bed of shredded salad greens. Garnish with sliced bananas, maraschino cherries, chopped nuts or fresh berries.

Serves 8.

PINEAPPLE-CHEESE RING
(With Whipped Cream)

1 package lemon or lime gelatin
½ cup boiling water
1 cup pineapple juice
1 cup cream or evaporated milk
½ pound cream cheese
½ cup chopped almonds
½ cup minced green pepper
½ cup mayonnaise
Dash of salt
1 cup canned crushed pineapple, drained
Green pepper slices
Mint leaves, water cress, shredded lettuce

Dissolve gelatin in boiling water and add the pineapple juice. Cool while preparing the rest of the ingredients. Chill and whip cream (or evaporated milk) and combine with well-mashed cheese. Add all the other ingredients except green pepper slices and greens and stir in cold gelatin mixture. Turn into a rinsed ring mold and chill in the refrigerator till set about 2 hours. When ready to serve, dip bottom of ring in hot water and invert on serving plate. Garnish with green pepper slices or strips and greens. In center of ring place a tall stemmed compote dish of salad dressing. Cut the ring and serve like cake, spooning some of the dressing over each serving.

Serves 8.

Dressing #1—Combine 1 cup sour cream with 2 tablespoons lemon juice or pineapple juice and sweeten to taste with confectioners' sugar.

Dressing #2—Beat 3 ounces cream cheese with ½ cup pineapple juice till smooth, using rotary beater. Add 1 tablespoon lemon or orange juice and enough honey to taste, Add finely chopped almonds or pecans if desired.

DESSERTS

LEKACH
(Traditional Honey Cake)
  6 eggs, or 4 eggs plus ½ cup coffee
  1 cup sugar
  1 cup honey
  2 tablespoons salad oil or melted shortening
  3½ cups flour
  1½ teaspoons baking powder
  1 teaspoon baking soda
  ¼ teaspoon ground cloves
  ½ teaspoon each allspice, cinnamon
  ½ cup each raisins, chopped nuts
  ¼ cup finely cut citron
  2 tablespoons brandy

Beat eggs, adding sugar gradually while beating until light and creamy. Stir in honey and shortening. (The 6-egg recipe makes a cake of finer texture.) If using eggs and coffee, dilute honey with hot coffee before combining. Sift together all dry ingredients and add nuts and fruit before combining with first mixture. Add brandy last. Turn into a greased, paper-lined rectangular pan and bake at 310° F. for one hour. Invert and allow cake to cool before removing. When ready to serve, cut into squares or diamond shapes.

LEBKUCHEN
(Traditional Recipe)
  4 eggs
  1 pound brown sugar
  3½ cups flour
  1 teaspoon baking powder
  2 teaspoons cinnamon
  ¼ teaspoon allspice
  ¼ cup shredded citron

  ¼ cup chopped walnuts or almonds

Beat eggs and sugar till creamy. Sift dry ingredients and stir in. Blend in the chopped nuts and citron. Spread the dough to ½-inch thickness on a wax-paper-lined baking sheet. Bake in a moderate oven (350° F.) about 30 minutes. Cover with a thin frosting made of confectioners' sugar and water before cake is cool. Cut into squares or oblongs. Keep 1 week before serving. Keep in a well-covered jar.

NUT AND RAISIN HONEY CAKE
(Traditional Holiday Cake)
  2 eggs
  1 cup sugar
  ½ cup salad oil
  ½ pound honey
  2 tablespoons brandy
  2 cups flour
  2 teaspoons baking powder
  ½ teaspoon baking soda
  ⅛ teaspoon salt
  ½ cup seedless raisins
  ¼ cup chopped nuts
  ½ cup hot coffee

Beat eggs, adding sugar while beating till smooth and creamy. Stir in oil till smooth, add honey and brandy and beat with spoon till well blended. Sift dry ingredients together and add raisins and nuts. Combine with creamy mixture, adding a little coffee while stirring to a smooth batter. Turn into a wax-paper-lined baking pan 8" × 11" × 2" and bake at 350° F. for 1 hour. If browned at edges and light brown on top the honey cake is done. Test by inserting a toothpick in center. If toothpick comes out dry, remove cake from oven to cool. Cut into slices 1½ inches wide, then diagonally to make diamond shapes.

MANDELBRODT
  3 eggs
  ½ cup sugar
  1½ teaspoons baking powder
  1½ cups flour
  ½ cup finely chopped blanched almonds

Beat eggs and sugar until thick. Sift the flour and baking powder, and add the almonds. Combine mixtures and pour the batter into a well-greased narrow loaf pan. Bake in a moderate oven 40 to 45 minutes at 350° F. When cold, cut into ½-inch slices.

Yields approximately 24.

PURIM KICHLACH

1 cup sugar
1 cup melted shortening or salad oil
4 eggs
4 cups sifted flour
3 teaspoons baking powder
½ teaspoon salt
¾ cup lukewarm water or milk
¾ cup poppyseed

Cream sugar and shortening. Add one egg at a time, beating or stirring well after each addition. Sift dry ingredients and add poppyseeds. Combine both mixtures, adding a little of the liquid as you mix to a stiff dough. Roll out on lightly floured board to ¼-inch thickness. Cut with a fluted cutter into triangles 2½ inches in size. If no fluted cutter is available, use a knife for cutting into squares then fold from opposite corners to make triangles. Brush cookies with diluted egg yolk and sprinkle with a few poppyseeds after arranging them on a greased and lightly floured cookie sheet. Bake for 12 to 15 minutes at 375° F.

Yields 50 to 60 cookies.

REFERENCES

RENDERING CHICKEN OR GOOSE FAT
(Schmaltz)

Cut fatty skin and other fat clusters into small pieces. Cover with cold water and cook in a heavy kettle or frying pan, uncovered until the water has almost entirely evaporated. Reduce heat and add diced onions, allowing one onion to each cupful of fat. A clove of garlic adds flavor. Also, when rendering a large quantity of fat, the addition of a few slices of raw potato will help clarify the fat. The fat is done when the onion is nicely browned, also the potato, and the cracklings are dry and crisp. Let cool slightly before straining to separate cracklings from clarified schmaltz.

Cracklings are called *greben* or *grebenes* and make excellent additions to mashed potatoes. *Grebenes* also enhance chopped liver dishes. Use some finely chopped cracklings for fillings in Knaidlach mit Neshomes, Mashed Potato Croquettes, and Poultry Stuffings. Cracklings have been called "Jewish Popcorn." To store for Passover use, separate from rendered schmaltz and cover with ¼ inch layer of melted rendered fat in glass jars, jelly glasses or glazed stoneware. Cover with muslin when cold, then adjust covers. Store in cool place till wanted for use.

CHOWCHOW

4 quarts chopped or cut green tomatoes
6 diced cucumbers
4 large onions, diced
4 red peppers (sweet), chopped
4 red peppers (hot), cut fine
2 cups diced celery
3 cloves garlic, minced
1 cup salt
1 quart pickling vinegar
1½ cups brown sugar
2 tablespoons dry mustard
½ teaspoon ground allspice
½ teaspoon cinnamon

Combine vegetables, garlic and salt. Let stand overnight in a crock or wooden bowl. In the morning, drain off all liquid. Add vinegar, sugar and seasonings. Cook until vegetables are tender, stirring occasionally. Pack in sterilized pint jars and seal.

Yields 10 to 12 pints.

APPLE AND RAISIN CHUTNEY

4 quarts apples, peeled
2 onions, peeled
1 clove of garlic
1 cup seeded raisins
5 cups vinegar
¼ cup white mustard seed
2 tablespoons ground ginger
1 pod hot red pepper
1 cup brown sugar

Chop apples, onions, garlic and raisins. Add ½ of the vinegar. Cook until soft. Add remaining ingredients. Cook until thick, stirring occasionally. Pour into hot sterilized jars and seal at once.

Yields 8 to 9 pints.

Scandinavian

THE SMÖRGÅSBORD

THE SMÖRGÅSBORD

Often the first thought that comes to mind for a traveler through the Scandinavian countries is the traditional smörgåsbord. No one can see the tables laden with herring, salmon, caviar, varieties of bread, and thin-sliced meats and not carry the taste-bud memories for the rest of his life.

The word smörgåsbord means bread-and-butter table. Needless to say, there is more than just bread and butter on the table. It is a tastefully arranged buffet of many different foods — so many as to challenge and defeat even the heartiest of appetites. What a delightful way to be defeated, though, for just as the eater is more than satisfied, a fresh, clean plate is brought to him and there are still more delicacies to try.

Common to all smörgåsbords, whichever Scandinavian country you are in, is the center table on which all the food is attractively displayed for your gourmet pleasure.

The open-faced sandwiches so prevalent in Denmark may have their origin from Viking feasts. They may be a modern evolution from a long time ago when rounds of bread were used instead of plates. They are eaten today with a knife and fork and offer a limitless variety of simple and elaborate fare. A sandwich may be as simple as thin apple slices with jelly on a thin slice of buttered bread — or as elaborate as smoked salmon on white bread with scrambled eggs on top, served hot. The variety is endless and depends on the creativity of the cook. The smörgåsbord can be a group of appetizers offered prior to a large meal. Anchovy sticks, liver loaf, and Swedish meatballs, to say nothing of the many combinations of herring and other delicacies from the sea, all have their place on such a table. If you indulge too heavily in this type of smörgåsbord, however, you may not want anything after it. Scandinavian appetizers are filling.

Hot main dishes can be included on a smörgåsbord. Pastry-covered meat loaf, beef roll, and ham rolls are always popular. The array of hot and cold vegetables, fruits, and salads can be as elaborate as you want to make it.

MUSTARD MARINATED SMELT
4 servings

This is an intriguing, spicy and quite economical dish. Often, as in this dish, the smelt is eaten raw (so is matjes herring or any other pickled herring). Don't let that deter you. Marinated smelt is well worth the effort and a very good appetizer. Served with hot boiled potatoes it becomes a small entrée.

1 lb fillets of smelt
marinade:
    1⅔ cup water
    ⅔ cup pickling vinegar
    1 tbsp salt
dressing:
    ½ cup mustard
    4 tbsp vinegar
    ½ cup oil
    2 tbsp sugar
    ½ tsp coarsely ground pepper
    ½ cup chopped fresh dill

The smelt will probably be frozen. Let it thaw and skin it; peel off a little piece of the skin with a sharp knife, grasp it with a piece of paper towel and pull; it should come off easily. Cut fillets in halves. Mix marinade and pour over fish in a large bowl. Marinate in refrigerator over night. Mix ingredients for dressing. Drain fillets and layer them with dressing in a widemouthed jar or crock. Chill for at least 24 hours before serving.

MEATBALLS
4 servings

Meatballs used to be made of a mixture of ground beef and ground lean pork, sometimes with the addition of ground veal. If you want to make classic meatballs, you may have to grind your own pork. But ground lean beef by itself will do very nicely too.

Meatballs are a simple dish. There are no herbs, no fancy sauces, no sour cream, no tomatoes. If they are served on a smörgåsbord or as an appetizer they can be either cold or hot. As a main dish they can be served with gravy made from the drippings in the pan with an addition of stock, bouillon cubes or soy sauce. The smaller the meatballs, the finer they are. For a smörgåsbord they're usually the size of a quarter, or smaller.

Cook small meatballs about 5 minutes, larger ones about 8 minutes. Roll meatballs with your hands. If you keep your hands wet and put the finished meatballs on a moistened cutting board, they're easy to handle. There is a trick to frying them and keeping them round. The butter should be hot. Don't fill the skillet more than two-thirds full. Shake frequently so that the meatballs roll around in the hot butter and are browned on all sides.

Turn heat down and let them cook through. If you fry a lot of meatballs, the skillet may have to be washed (and thoroughly dried) between every two or three batches. Meatballs freeze very well. If you make gravy, the gravy should be frozen separately.

1 lb ground meat (beef and pork mixed or beef only)
1 egg
1½ tsp salt
dash of pepper
dash of allspice
⅓-½ cup unseasoned bread crumbs
¾ cup table cream or milk
1 medium-sized onion
butter

Peel and grate onion. The grated onion can be fried or used raw, as you prefer. Raw onion gives a somewhat stronger taste. Soak bread crumbs in cream. Mix meat, egg, spices and grated onion. Add bread crumbs to meat mixture, and stir well. Roll meatballs and fry in a generous amount of hot butter.

STUFFED EGGS
4 hard-boiled eggs
1 tbsp butter
3 tbsp Scandinavian caviar
salt
pepper
garnish:
  parsley
  tomatoes
  lettuce

Cut eggs into halves crosswise or lengthwise. Remove yolks carefully and put whites aside. Mix egg yolks, butter and caviar and stir until smooth. Season to taste. Force through pastry bag into whites. Decorate each egg with a sprig of parsley. Arrange on platter of lettuce leaves and garnish with sliced tomatoes.

BIRD'S NEST
1 raw egg yolk
2 tbsp capers
3 tbsp chopped onion
1 small can (3 oz) Scandinavian anchovy fillets, finely chopped
3 tbsp pickled beets, finely chopped
3 tbsp parsley, finely chopped

Place a small glass upside down on a plate. Arrange capers in a ring around the glass, then add rings of chopped onions, anchovies, beets and parsley. Remove glass and slide the raw egg yolk into the middle. Serve immediately — the egg yolk dries if it's left standing. To eat, mix the ingredients on the plate and spread on a piece of bread.

MUSHROOM-FILLED TOMATOES
8 medium-sized tomatoes
salt
pepper
stuffing:
  2 tbsp butter
  ½ lb chopped mushrooms, fresh or canned
  1 cup liquid, table cream and stock (if canned mushrooms are used)
  salt
  pepper

1 tbsp dry sherry
2 tbsp grated cheese

Preheat oven to 375°. Wash tomatoes and cut off the top. Scoop out the center and sprinkle the inside with salt and pepper. Melt butter and sauté mushrooms over low heat. Season. Stir in flour and add liquid gradually. Simmer 5 minutes, stirring. Season and add wine. Place tomatoes in buttered baking dish and fill with creamed mushrooms. Sprinkle top with cheese. Bake for about 15 minutes or until golden brown.

DILLED HERRING

4 fillets of salt herring
1 cup finely-chopped onion
4 tbsp chopped dill
marinade:
    ¾ cup pickling vinegar
    ¾ cup water
    ¾ cup sugar
    5 grains of pepper

Soak fillets in water for about 8 hours. Boil vinegar, water, sugar and pepper for marinade and cool. Cut fillets into ½" pieces. Layer herring, onion and dill in a widemouthed jar. Cover the fish with marinade, Marinate in refrigerator for 1 day.

DANISH HERRING SALAD
6-8 servings

Put fillets in cold water overnight, rinse and dry before using.

4-6 fillets of salt herring
2 medium-sized potatoes, boiled and cold
2 pickled beets
1 sour pickle
2 medium-sized tart apples
1 small red onion
dressing:
    2 tbsp butter
    2 tbsp flour
    1⅓ cup table cream
    2 tbsp juice of pickled beets
    1 tsp mustard
    ½ tsp pepper
    sugar

garnish:
    2 hard-boiled eggs
    parsley

Start by making the dressing. Melt butter and blend in flour over low heat. Slowly stir in table cream. Keep stirring till sauce has thickened, then simmer for 3-4 minutes. Remove from heat and add vinegar, mustard and salt (plus a little bit of sugar if you like). Cool. Now peel apples and potatoes. Chop all the ingredients and mix into cold dressing. Serve in a bowl, garnished with sliced hard-boiled eggs and sprigs of parsley.

HERRING SALAD FROM NORWAY
4 servings

4 fillets of matjes herring
3 carrots
2 onions
6 medium-sized potatoes, boiled and cold
dressing:
    2 tbsp vinegar
    ⅓ cup oil
    salt
    pepper

Peel and wash carrots and cut them into thin slices. Peel potatoes and slice them thin. Peel and slice onions. Cut herrings into 1" pieces. Layer potatoes, carrots, onions and herrings in a deep dish and pour dressing over them. Chill for several hours.

CREAMED SHRIMP
4 servings

1 tbsp butter
3 tbsp flour
2 cups half and half
1½ cup cooked, chopped shrimp
salt
pepper
2 tbsp finely-chopped dill

Melt butter over low heat and stir in flour. Add half and half. Simmer and stir over low heat until the sauce thickens. Season and stir in shrimp.

MARINATED HERRING
4 servings

> **4 large fillets of fresh herring**
> **brine:**
> > **4 cups water**
> > **⅔ cup coarse salt (kosher salt)**
> > **4 tbsp sugar**
> **marinade:**
> > **1⅓ cup pickling vinegar**
> > **2 cups water**
> > **1½ cup sugar**
> > **1 tbsp whole allspice**
> > **1 tsp whole pepper**
> > **½ tsp ground pepper**
> > **2 tsp dill seeds**
> > **1 tsp whole cloves**
> > **4 onions**
> > **1 leek (or 3 spring onions)**

Wash fillets and drain. Boil ingredients for brine and cool. Pour brine over herring fillets and chill for 2 days. Remove fish from brine, wash and drain. Mix ingredients for marinade and boil. Cool. Put herring fillets and sliced onions and leek into a crock or deep dish and pour cold marinate over them. Fish may have to be weighted to stay in marinade. Use a small plate and a jar filled with water or a small clean rock. Marinate in refrigerator for 3 days before serving.

PICKLED HERRING
The classic marinated herring, a must on every Scandinavian smörgåsbord and Christmas table.

> **4 fillets of salt herring**
> **1 piece horseradish, about 1″ long**
> **1 carrot**
> **2 red onions**
> **2 bay leaves**
> **2 tsp allspice**
> **2 tsp mustard seeds**
> **2 small pieces dried ginger or 2 tsp ground ginger**
> **marinade:**
> > **¾ cup pickling vinegar**
> > **⅔ cup water**
> > **1 cup sugar**

Soak herring overnight. Wash, drain and cut into 1″ pieces. Boil water, vinegar and sugar for marinade and cool. Peel horseradish, carrot and onions, and cut into thin slices. Layer herring with onions, carrots, horseradish and spices in a tall widemouthed jar or crock. Cover the fish with marinade. Marinate in refrigerator for 1 day. Fresh horseradish may be hard to find. A tablespoon of ready-made grated horseradish can be sprinkled between the herring layers instead.

LIVER PATÉ
> **1 lb pork liver**
> **½ lb fat back**
> **1 red onion**
> **6 fillets of Scandinavian anchovies**
> **1 tsp ground cloves**
> **1 tsp ground black pepper**
> **1 tbsp salt**
> **2 eggs**
> **3 tbsp butter**
> **3 tbsp flour**
> **1⅔ cup milk**

Preheat oven to 400°. Grind liver and fat back finely, together with onion and fillets of anchovies. Mix in lightly-beaten egg yolks and spices. Melt butter over low heat and blend in flour. Slowly stir in milk. Cook and stir until thickened and smooth. Cool. Stir into liver mixture. Whip egg whites stiff and carefully fold into mixture. Pour into well-greased loaf pan, set the pan into a larger one of hot water and cook for about 1 hour or until done.

BREAKFAST

DANISH OMELET
4 servings

A hearty breakfast dish, which combines the main products of Danish agriculture: pork, eggs and cream. It can also be served on a smörgåsbord.

> **6 slices of salt pork (if you can't find salt pork, bacon will do)**
> **2 tomatoes**
> **2 raw potatoes**
> **6 eggs**
> **⅓ cup table cream**
> **salt**
> **pepper**

1 bunch of spring onions or chives

Fry salt pork and drain on a piece of paper towel. Peel potatoes, cut into small cubes, and fry in pork drippings for 7 minutes or till tender. Pour off excess fat. Mix potatoes together with pork and add sliced tomatoes. Beat eggs and cream with a fork, season with salt and pepper, and add to pan. Shake the skillet and tilt it a little, or stir with a fork, so the omelet cooks evenly. When it's done, slice spring onions thinly and sprinkle them on top. Serve straight from the skillet.

PANCAKES WITH BACON
4 servings

    1½ cup milk
    2 eggs
    ⅓ cup flour
    ½ lb bacon or salt pork

Beat eggs and milk and stir into flour to make an even batter. If you use bacon, sauté slices slowly until they are crisp. Drain them on paper towel and crumble them. Pour off the bacon fat and use it for frying pancakes. If you use salt pork, cube the piece before frying, or cut the slices into smaller pieces.

Heat a skillet, using about 1 tsp bacon fat for each pancake, and 1-2 tbsp fried bacon or salt pork. Pour a thin layer of batter, tip the skillet and let it spread evenly over the bottom. Cook the pancake over moderate heat. When it is brown, turn it and brown the other side. The smaller the skillet, the easier the pancakes are to cook and turn. Serve with cranberry sauce or jelly for a rich breakfast dish.

MEAT

DILLED LAMB OR VEAL
4 servings

This is a favorite Swedish stew. It should be seasoned with coarsely chopped fresh dill, but dried dill leaves out of a jar will give a similar flavor. Scandinavian lamb is a lean meat. If the lamb you buy is fat, the meat should be boiled a day ahead and cooled in the stock. The fat will rise to the surface and harden, and is easy to lift off. Otherwise you get a very fatty dish.

    2½ lb lamb or veal shoulder or breast
for every 2 cups of water:
    2 tsp salt
    5 grains of pepper
    1 bay leaf
    1 onion
    dill (use the stalks, keep the tiny leaves for the sauce)
sauce:
    1 tbsp butter
    3 tbsp flour
    2 cups stock
    1 egg yolk
    ¼-½ cup table cream
    1-2 tbsp lemon juice or cider vinegar
    3 tbsp chopped dill

Pour cold water over the meat so that it is barely covered. Boil and skim. Now add spices, sliced onions and dill, cover and simmer until meat is tender, about 1 hour.

Melt butter and stir in flour. Stirring constantly over low heat, add 2 cups of strained stock and continue to cook slowly until the gravy is thickened. Add table cream to smoothen it, or 1 egg yolk diluted in a few tablespoons of cream. Season with salt, pepper and lemon juice or vinegar to taste and add chopped dill. Cut meat into bite-sized pieces (discard some of the bones) and heat in gravy. Serve with rice or boiled potatoes.

LAMB AND CABBAGE STEW
4 servings

    2 lb lean lamb shoulder or breast
    1 medium-sized cabbage
    3 tbsp butter
    salt
    10 grains of pepper
    2 bay leaves
    1-2 cups water
    chopped parsley

Shred cabbage and cut meat into bite-sized pieces. Brown in butter, season with salt, pepper and bay leaves, and add water so that the mixture is barely covered. Cover and simmer until meat is tender, about 1½ hours. Check seasoning, sprinkle with parsley and serve with boiled potatoes.

LAMB STEW FROM FINLAND
4 servings

2 lb lamb shoulder or breast
8 medium-sized potatoes
2 carrots
1 bunch of spring onions
salt
pepper
thyme
2 cups water
chopped parsley

Cut meat into bite-sized pieces. Peel and slice potatoes and carrots. Peel and slice onions. Layer vegetables and meat in a pot, season with salt, pepper and thyme and pour in enough water so that the meat is barely covered. Cover and simmer until meat is tender, about 1 hour. Check seasoning and serve sprinkled with chopped parsley.

DANISH MEAT PATTIES
6 servings

1½ lb ground lean pork
1 finely chopped onion
salt
pepper
dash of allspice
3 eggs
3-4 tbsp flour
1½ cup table cream
butter
1½ cup stock (made from bouillon cube and water)
1-2 tsp soy sauce

Stir eggs with flour and 1 cup of cream. Work this mixture into ground meat together with chopped onions and spices. Let rest for about half an hour. The mixture should be firm enough so that you can make patties. If it is too firm you can add a little water.

Make thin patties about the size of your palm and fry them in hot butter, a few minutes on each side. They should be well done. Remove them. Stir remaining cream and stock into the frying pan. Season with soy sauce. Strain the gravy. Serve the meat patties with gravy and boiled potatoes. Buttered spinach is often served together with them.

SCRAPPLE

4 lb veal shank, neck or breast
8 cups water
1 tbsp salt
½ tbsp whole pepper
1 tsp whole allspice
1 bay leaf
2 whole cloves
1 onion
To season scrapple:
    salt
    pepper
    pickling vinegar
    2 tbsp gelatin

Put meat in a large pot and add water, spices and sliced onion. Boil until quite tender. Strain, reserving liquid. Cut meat from bones and cut into small pieces or grind it coarsely. Strain stock once more, add meat and heat. Season well with salt, pepper and pickling vinegar. Dissolve gelatin in a few tablespoons of cold water and stir into meat mixture. Pour into one large or several small molds and chill.

DANISH CURRIED MEATBALLS
6 servings

1½ lb ground lean pork
1 onion
salt, pepper
1⅓ cup half and half
3 eggs
3 tbsp flour
4-6 cups stock (made of bouillon cube and water)
curry sauce:
    1 chopped onion
    1 tart apples, chopped
    3 tbsp butter
    2 tbsp curry
    3 tbsp flour
    2 cups stock (use the stock in which the meatballs were cooked)
    1 cup half and half
    salt, pepper

Chop onion and mix into ground meat. Beat eggs together with flour and half and half, season with salt and pepper, and mix into ground meat. Heat stock. Roll small meatballs and simmer in stock, 7-8 minutes.

Sauté chopped onion and apple in butter. Add curry and sauté for a few minutes. Stir in flour and, when well blended, add stock and half and half. Stir over low heat until well combined and thickened. Season to taste and heat meatballs in sauce. Serve with boiled rice.

SAILOR'S BEEF STEW
4 servings

1 lb lean stewing beef in bite-sized cubes
salt
pepper
bay leaf
2 tbsp butter
2 onions
5-6 medium-sized potatoes
1½ cup stock

Slice onions and brown them. Brown meat and season well with salt and pepper. Peel and slice raw potatoes. Butter the bottom of a heavy pan and layer potatoes, meat, onions and seasoning. The bottom and top layers should be potatoes. Add stock (of beef bouillon cube) and cover. Simmer for 1-1½ hours.

For stronger flavor, try using 1 cup of stock and ½ cup of Danish beer. But don't be too generous with the beer; more than ½ cup gives the stew a bitter flavor.

ROLLED STEAKS
4 servings

A good, spicy, old-fashioned beef casserole which used to be served as a Sunday dinner. It's not as complicated as it may sound; to roll and secure the meat is not difficult, and if a roll or two comes undone, the gravy will taste even better for it.

1 lb sandwich steaks, thin slices of top round
(or other thin slices of beef)
1 small piece fat back
2 sour pickles
twigs of parsley
2 onions
2 carrots
1 celery stalk
1 bay leaf

a pinch of thyme
a pinch of allspice
2-3 tbsp butter
1 tbsp flour
1 cup table cream
2 tsp tomato purée
1 cup stock

Cut meat into pieces about the size of your hand— large enough to be filled and rolled, small enough to make one serving each. Cut fat back into thin strips. Season them with salt, pepper and allspice. Cut pickles into strips, chop onions and carrots coarsely.

Put 1-2 strips of seasoned fat back, 1 strip of pickle, about 1 tsp onion and 2 tsp carrot on each piece of meat. Roll meat and secure with toothpicks.

Brown meat carefully in a frying pan, using about 1½ tbsp butter. Sauté onions and carrots in remaining butter in a heavy pot with a well-fitted lid. Dust with flour, stir in stock and continue stirring until sauce has thickened. Season with thyme and tomato purée. Put meat rolls into gravy and simmer very gently (they'll come undone otherwise) until they are tender, 15-40 minutes, depending on the quality of the meat. (You can pour a few tablespoons of water into the frying pan, heat it, and add this to the meat in the pot.) When the meat is tender, add about ½ cup cream, heat and serve.

MEAT LOAF
4 servings

Prepare Meatball mixture, see index (onions
can be omitted), mixing in an additional ¾
cup milk or water
2 onions
2 tbsp butter
4 medium-sized tomatoes
½ cup grated cheese

Preheat oven to 375°. Peel and slice onions and sauté slowly in butter until almost tender. Butter a baking dish and layer meat and onions, topping with meat mixture. Cover top with sliced tomatoes and sprinkle with grated cheese. Bake for approximately 50 minutes. Cover with foil if top gets brown before meat is done. Hot meat loaf is usually served with potatoes and a salad. It's delicious cold and sliced for sandwiches.

SWEDISH HAMBURGER
4 servings

1 lb ground beef
    2 boiled potatoes
    1 egg
    1 cup milk
    salt
    pepper
    ½ cup chopped pickled beets
    2 tbsp chopped onion
    2 tbsp chopped capers
    butter

Peel boiled potatoes and mash them with a fork. Mix into ground meat together with egg and seasoning. Add beets, onion and capers, and stir well. Make hamburger patties and fry in butter or broil to taste. Swedish hamburgers are sometimes served topped with a fried egg.

BEEF WITH HORSERADISH
4 servings

This is a classic Scandinavian way of preparing inexpensive cuts of beef; they are boiled with vegetables and spices which enhance the taste of the meat.

    2-2½ lb chuck or brisket of beef
    for every quart water:
        1 carrot
        1 small parsnip
        1 small piece celery root
        1 chopped onion
        1 tbsp salt
        5 whole allspice
        1 bay leaf
    sauce:
        1½ tbsp butter
        2 tbsp flour
        1 cup beef stock
        1 cup milk
        salt
        pepper
        2-3 tbsp grated horseradish

Place meat in kettle and barely cover with water. Bring to boiling point and skim. Add vegetables, bring to boiling point and skim. Add salt, allspice and bay leaf, and simmer for about 2 hours or until meat is tender.

Melt butter in saucepan. Add flour and stir until well blended. Gradually stir in stock and milk. Simmer 5 minutes, stirring occasionally. Season. Add grated horseradish. Don't boil sauce after adding horseradish or flavor will be bitter.

KARELIAN STEW
6 servings

A very simple, hearty stew that gets its flavor from the mixture of various meats. It takes 2 hours to cook but takes care of itself during most of that time.

    1 lb chuck
    1 lb veal (shoulder or breast)
    1 lb lean pork (picnic shoulder or shoulder butt)
    1-2 tbsp salt
    coarsely-ground pepper
    2 bay leaves
    2 onions
    hot water

Preheat oven to 375°. Cut meat into bite-sized pieces, season well and arrange in a deep ovenware dish or pot. Put the fat pieces on top. Add sliced onions. Add hot water so that it barely covers the meat. Cover and cook for about 2 hours. Remove lid for the last half hour of cooking. Some of the water should be reduced, making a nice gravy, and the meat on top should be slightly browned.

STUFFED CABBAGE
6 servings

    1 head of cabbage, about 3 lb
    water
    salt
    stuffing:
        4 tbsp rice
        ½ cup water
        ¾-1 cup milk
        ¾ lb ground meat, preferably ground beef and ground lean pork mixed
        salt

pepper
½ cup milk
butter
2 tbsp syrup
¾ cup hot stock
1 tsp cumin

Trim stem and outer, damaged leaves from a head of cabbage and boil 5-10 minutes: You'll need approximately 2 quarts of water. Drain and cool so that cabbage can be handled, then carefully peel off leaves. Prepare stuffing: Wash rice and pour into boiling water. Cook till water is almost evaporated, then add milk; cover and simmer over low heat until rice is very tender. Cool.

Preheat oven to 375°. Mix rice and meat, add a little more milk to a soft mixture and season well with salt and pepper. Put about 1 tbsp of stuffing in the middle of each cabbage leaf and roll tightly, tucking in the edges. Place them close together in a buttered baking dish. Dot each roll with a little butter, some cumin and syrup. Pour stock into dish and bake till cabbage is brown and very tender, about 45 minutes.

Remove cabbage rolls to a serving dish and keep them hot. Add some more stock if there is too little left at the bottom of the baking dish, and season well. Cream can be added. For a thick gravy, melt 1 tbsp butter, stir in 2 tbsp flour and add stock (and soy sauce), stirring constantly over low heat until sauce has thickened. Season well and pour over cabbage, or heat stuffed cabbage very carefully in the gravy. Stuffed cabbage is usually served with boiled potatoes or rice and lingonberries. Cranberry sauce will also do well. For variety the cabbage rolls can be cooked with thin strips of bacon. Roll a strip of bacon around each cabbage roll before putting it into the baking dish. Don't add any additional salt. Cook and serve according to above recipe.

SCANDINAVIAN HASH
4 servings

A well-made Scandinavian hash is a treat — in spite of the fact that it's made of leftovers. It was probably invented by a thrifty housewife; today it's served even in first-class restaurants. The hash is supposed to be well browned and not mushy. To achieve this, onions and potatoes have to be browned separately. The more varieties of leftover meat you mix into it, the better it tastes. If you take care to cube the potatoes neatly, the hash will also look good. Often the hash is served with a fried egg or a raw egg yolk per person.

2 onions
2-3 tbsp butter
6-8 boiled, cold potatoes
1½ cup cooked leftover meat (roast beef, pork roast, pork chops, leg of lamb, ham)
salt
pepper
chopped parsley for garnish

Chop onions. Cube potatoes and leftover meat. Sauté onions until nicely browned. Remove from skillet. Sauté potato cubes. Mix in meat and reheat onions, season well with salt and pepper, and garnish with chopped parsley.

LIVER HASH FROM FINLAND
4 servings

The liver for this old-fashioned recipe has to be ground. You can grind it yourself in a meat grinder or put it through a blender.

1 lb baby beef liver
5 cups milk
1 cup rice (choose a variety with round, short kernels, not the long Carolina rice)
1 onion
2 tbsp butter
3-4 tbsp syrup
⅔ cup raisins
salt
pepper
marjoram

Pour rice into the cold milk, heat slowly and simmer until the rice is soft, about 25 minutes. Let the mixture cool. Preheat oven to 375°. Chop onion and fry in butter until it is transparent but not browned. Mix liver, syrup, raisins and onions into the rice. Season with salt, pepper and marjoram. Cook the rice and liver mixture in a buttered dish for about 1 hour. Serve with cranberry jelly and melted butter.

BRAISED GOOSE
8 servings

> **1 goose 10-12 lb**
> **1 lemon**
> **salt**
> **pepper**
> **2 cups good chicken stock**
> **stuffing:**
> > **tart apples**
> > **pitted prunes**
> **gravy:**
> > **degreased juices from the goose, plus stock to make about 2 cups liquid**
> > **1 tbsp cornstarch**
> > **2 tbsp brandy**
> > **soy sauce**
> > **red currant jelly**

Preheat oven to 300-350°. Season goose with salt and pepper and rub inside and out with lemon. Pare and quarter tart apples and stuff goose with a mixture of apples and pitted prunes. Secure the opening with small skewers and a criss-crossed string, and tie the ends of the drumsticks together so the legs will be close to the body. Place on a rack in a roasting pan and pour stock into pan. Roast for approximately 4 hours or until done. (Figure 20-25 minutes to the pound.) Leave oven door slightly ajar for the last 10 minutes of cooking.

Carefully pour off all the drippings before goose is completely done. Degrease as much as possible. Thicken with cornstarch in a few tablespoons of cold water or stock. Season well with salt, pepper, brandy, a teaspoon of soy sauce or a little bit of red currant jelly. Braised goose is served with boiled or fried potatoes, stewed prunes (they can be simmered in a little bit of wine), stewed apple halves or apple sauce and red currant jelly.

VEGETABLES

DANISH SPICY RED CABBAGE

This is mainly Christmas food, to be served with glazed ham or spareribs. It tastes very good with pork roast, with sausage and even with turkey. Spicy red cabbage can be made weeks before Christmas and frozen. It freezes very well and is good reheated, though it may get a little bit more mushy in the process.

> **2-3 heads of red cabbage**
> **2 onions**
> **4 tart apples**
> **¾ cup cider vinegar**
> **½-1 cup brown sugar**
> **lard, ham drippings or butter**
> **6 cloves**
> **1 bay leaf**
> **3 grains of allspice**
> **salt**
> **1-2 cups red wine or cranberry juice**

Shred cabbage. Peel and slice onions. Sauté in lard, ham drippings or butter in heavy pot. Add cured, peeled and quartered apples and spices. Season with sugar and vinegar to taste and add enough red wine or cranberry juice to moisten cabbage thoroughly. Cover and simmer over low heat until cabbage is very tender, 1½ hours or more. Check seasoning. It's a matter of taste how spicy you want the cabbage.

STEWED HOCKS WITH CABBAGE
6 servings

This is a simple, inexpensive and very rich meal to serve on a chilly day. It takes 2-2½ hours to prepare, but once it's stewing in the pot it needs little or no supervision.

> **1 large head of cabbage**
> **2 large onions**
> **4 slices of salt pork**
> **butter or lard**
> **4 cloves**
> **¼-½ cup brown sugar**
> **2 tbsp cider vinegar**
> **salt**
> **pepper**
> **2 small pork hocks**
> **2-4 cups water**

Trim stalk and discard outer leaves of cabbage, then shred it finely. Sauté salt pork over low heat in large pot. Remove pork slices and sauté shredded cabbage in drippings. Add 1-2 tbsp butter or lard if there aren't enough drippings. Peel onions, stick cloves in them and add to cabbage. Stir over low heat until it is evenly browned. Sprinkle with salt, sugar, pepper and add vinegar and water. Add pork hocks and slices of salt pork; cover and simmer till meat is done, 1½-2 hours. Peeled potatoes can be added to the pork hocks for the last half hour of cooking.

CABBAGE PUDDING
4 servings

> **1 medium-sized cabbage**
> **butter or shortening**
> **salt**
> **pepper**
> **bay leaf**
> **stuffing:**
> > **see Stuffed cabbage**

Preheat oven to 400°. Trim off stem and outer, damaged leaves of cabbage. Quarter, then shred cabbage and sauté covered over low heat for approximately 15 minutes. Season well with salt, pepper and bay leaf. Prepare stuffing according to recipe for Stuffed cabbage. Butter a baking dish. Cover with a layer of cabbage. Spread stuffing and top with the remaining cabbage. Dot with butter and bake for about 1 hour or until the meat is cooked and the cabbage nicely browned. Serve with boiled potatoes and lingonberries or cranberry sauce.

ROAST POTATOES

> **6 baking potatoes small enough to fit in a deep spoon**
> **3 tablespoons melted butter**
> **1 teaspoon salt**
> **2 tablespoons bread crumbs**
> **2 tablespoons Parmesan cheese (optional)**

Preheat the oven to 425°F.

Peel the potatoes and put them in cold water to prevent discoloring. Put 1 potato in the deep spoon and slice it down to the edge of the spoon, making the slices about ⅛ inch apart. The spoon will prevent you from cutting through the potato. Return the sliced potato to the cold water and slice the others in the same manner. Drain the potatoes and pat dry. Put the potatoes, cut-side-up, in a large buttered baking dish. Baste them with some of the melted butter.

Sprinkle them with salt and cook them for 30 minutes in the preheated oven.

Now sprinkle the bread crumbs over each potato and baste them with the remaining melted butter. Continue to cook the potatoes for another 15 minutes or until they are golden brown and tender. Parmesan cheese may be added 5 minutes before the potatoes are done. Makes 6 portions.

MASHED POTATOES

> **3 medium-sized potatoes**
> **water**
> **salt**
> **1 tbsp butter**
> **¼ cup milk**
> **2 egg yolks**
> **salt**
> **pepper**
> **dash of nutmeg**

Peel potatoes and boil in salted water until soft. Drain. Mash thoroughly or put through a blender. Add butter; gradually add milk and work until smooth. Add egg yolks and beat until light and fluffy. Season.

POTATOES À LA HASSELBACKEN
4 servings

These baked potatoes are easy to prepare but very good and quite unusual. In Sweden, where the dish originated, it's often served as a party variation of the dinner potato.

> **8-10 medium-sized potatoes**
> **salt**
> **3 tbsp butter**
> **4-5 tbsp grated cheese**
> **unseasoned bread crumbs**

Preheat oven to 450°. Peel potatoes and slice, but not all the way through, so that the bottom still is one piece. The easiest way of doing this is to put one potato at a time on a large spoon. Slice: the concave spoon keeps the knife from cutting all the way through the potato. Put them into a buttered baking dish. Melt remaining butter and brush on potatoes, sprinkle with salt, bread crumbs and grated cheese. Bake until done, about 1 hour. Serve from baking dish.

POTATO DUMPLINGS
4 servings

Potato dumplings cannot be made from an American baking potato like an Idaho. The dough won't keep its shape and dissolves in the water. Any other kind of mature potato will do fine. If you're hesitant, make a small amount of dough and test-boil.

8 medium-sized potatoes
¾ cup flour
1 egg
½ lb bacon or Canadian bacon
1 onion
salt
pepper
allspice
butter

Peel and boil potatoes and mash them. Cool. Mix in egg and flour to make a soft dough. Season with salt and pepper. Chop onion and sauté in butter. Cube Canadian bacon and sauté. If you use ordinary bacon, fry in slices until it is crisp. Drain and break into pieces. Mix onion and bacon, and season with allspice. Roll dough into 2″ wide roll, cut into 2″ long pieces. Put about 1 tbsp of onion and bacon mixture into the center of each piece and form them into balls. Drop balls into gently boiling salted water and boil for 10-15 minutes. Drain them well. Serve with melted butter or lingonberries.

CREAMED POTATOES
4 servings

These potatoes are good with bacon, salt pork or sausage: very often they are served together with smoked fish.

2 tbsp butter
2 tbsp flour
1⅔ cup milk
salt
pepper
dash of nutmeg
4 tbsp chopped parsley
6-8 boiled potatoes

Melt butter over low heat and stir in flour. Add milk stirring constantly until sauce thickens and continue simmering for 4-5 minutes. Season with salt, freshly-ground pepper and a dash of nutmeg. Add cubed boiled potatoes and heat. Serve sprinkled with parsley.

Variation

Creamed potatoes can be made from raw cubed potatoes. Combine butter, seasoning, 6 cubed raw potatoes, and 1½ cup heavy cream in a double boiler, cover and simmer very slowly until potatoes are tender and sauce has thickened. Garnish with chopped dill. This variation has a finer taste but is also more complicated and more expensive to make.

MASHED POTATOES-RUTABAGA
4 servings

1 rutabaga, about 1 lb
4-6 medium-sized potatoes
3-4 cups stock
salt
5 grains of pepper
5 grains of allspice

Peel rutabaga and slice. Put into boiling stock together with coarsely crushed pepper and allspice. Depending on the saltiness of the stock, you may have to add salt. Cook for 20 minutes. Now add peeled and sliced potatoes, cover, and continue boiling until rutabaga and potatoes are very tender. Drain and reserve stock. Put vegetables through a blender; add stock a little at a time until the mixture has the consistency of fluffy mashed potatoes. A piece of butter can be stirred in to enhance the taste. Serve with corned beef, sausage or cured ham.

SWEDISH POTATO PANCAKES
4 servings

8 medium-sized potatoes
2 eggs
1 tsp salt
butter or lard to fry them in

Peel potatoes and grate them coarsely. Mix with 2 eggs and salt. Fry pancakes, the size of an ordinary pancake (about 4″ in diameter). Serve potato pancakes with bacon and lingonberries or cranberry sauce.

BROWN BEANS
4 servings

> 1⅔ cup kidney beans
> 4 cups water
> ½ tbsp salt
> 4 tbsp syrup or brown sugar
> 1-3 tbsp vinegar

Wash and soak beans overnight in salted water. Boil in the same water until tender, 1-1½ hours. Stir from time to time and add more water if necessary. Season with brown sugar, vinegar and salt. The beans should be mild, and slightly sweet and sour. Brown beans are served with fried salt pork or with meatballs and are a traditional Scandinavian dish.

DANISH SAUERKRAUT
4-6 servings

> 1 can (1 lb) sauerkraut
> 2 onions
> 4 whole cloves
> 1 tsp coarsely-crushed caraway
> 3-4 tbsp water or white wine

Strain sauerkraut and rinse it with cold water. Chop 2 onions. Simmer sauerkraut for about 30 minutes together with onions and spices. Keep the sauerkraut covered. If it looks dry, add a little water or a few tablespoons white wine.

In Denmark this sauerkraut is often served with "kassler," smoked pork loin, which has been cooked separately. You can add 1 smoked pork chop per person and simmer them with the sauerkraut. They should be done within 15 minutes. Serve with boiled potatoes and mustard.

SALADS AND DRESSINGS

PICKLED CUCUMBER

This old-fashioned cucumber salad used to be served with the traditional veal roast for Sunday dinner. Fortunately the pickled cucumber salad is good with Rolled steaks (see index) and with any cold meat, with ham, meatballs, and even hamburgers.

> 6 cucumbers, about 3 lb
> 3 tbsp dill seeds

> 1⅔ cup sugar
> 4 tbsp salt
> 2 tbsp mustard seeds
> 1⅔ cup pickling vinegar
> 2 cups water

Mix sugar, salt, mustard seeds, vinegar and water, and stir until sugar is completely dissolved. Wash cucumbers and slice thinly. Layer cucumber slices with dill seeds in widemouthed jars, pour the vinegar mixture over them and cover with foil. Store in refrigerator. Will keep 2-3 weeks.

HORSERADISH CREAM
To serve with duck, cold fish in aspic, cold salmon.

> ½ cup whipping cream
> ½ tbsp vinegar
> 1 tsp sugar
> 1 tbsp grated horseradish (or the same amount prepared horseradish from a jar)

Whip cream until it is thick but not stiff. Mix in other ingredients. Chill and serve. Horseradish cream is sometimes served frozen, almost like serving a spicy ice-cream with your cold fish. If you want to try it, whip cream until it is almost stiff, add other ingredients and freeze in a tray. Spoon into a bowl and serve.

OLD-FASHIONED DRESSING

Scandinavia has interesting salad dressings. They are sometimes served with cold, boiled or marinated fish, but will taste good with any of your favorite salads.

> 1 hard-boiled egg yolk
> 1 raw egg yolk
> 2 tbsp mustard
> 1 tsp vinegar
> salt
> pepper
> 1 cup whipped cream

Mash hard-boiled egg yolk and cream together with raw egg yolk, mustard and spices. Carefully fold in whipped cream. Serve cold.

ucia bread (see recipe page 355)   lefser (see recipe page 356)

fishballs (see recipe page 341)   Picture on next page: the smorgasbord   333

fish soup (see recipe page 343

roast potatoes (see recipe page 330)

HERRING SALAD
10 servings

- 4 fillets of salt herring
- 8 medium-sized boiled potatoes
- 2 large tart apples
- 6 pickled beets
- 1 onion
- pepper
- beet juice
- ¾-1 cup whipping cream
- garnish:
  - 2 hard-boiled eggs
  - parsley

Soak herring overnight. Peel potatoes and apples. Cube all ingredients finely and mix together. Add beet juice and pepper to taste. (Medium stiff, whipped cream is sometimes added to the salad. It makes for a more mild, creamy taste.) Rinse a bowl with cold water and firm down salad. Chill for several hours, then unmold on a platter. Garnish with sliced hard-boiled eggs and parsley.

SHELLFISH SALAD
4 servings

A shellfish salad is often served on a smörgåsbord or as a party dish for a light supper.

- gently mix:
  - 1½ cup chopped shrimp or crabmeat
  - 1 can (4½ oz) well drained mussels
  - 1½ cup sliced raw mushrooms
  - 1 cup tiny sweet peas (if canned, drain well)
  - ½ cup cubed cucumber
  - 2 hard-boiled eggs
- dressing:
  - ¼ cup vinegar
  - ½ cup oil
  - salt
  - coarsely-ground pepper
  - 2 tbsp finely-chopped dill

Pour the dressing over the salad mixture and refrigerate for a few hours. Serve salad on a bed of crisp, coarsely-cut lettuce and garnish with slices of hard-boiled eggs.

FISH

MARINATED SMELT
4 servings

- 15 leftover stuffed fillets of smelt
- marinade:
  - 1¾ cup pickling vinegar
  - 1¼ cup water
  - ½ cup sugar
  - 1 tsp crushed allspice
  - 3 sliced onions
  - bay leaf
  - dill

Boil vinegar, water, sugar, allspice and bay leaf. Cool. Layer smelt, sliced onions and dill and pour marinade over. Marinate overnight. Serve cold with crisp bread and butter.

BROILED SMELT
4 servings

- 2 lb smelt
- 2 tbsp salt
- herb butter:
  - 2 oz. butter
  - 4 tbsp finely-chopped parsley and dill
  - 1 tbsp lemon juice
  - salt
  - pepper

Wash and drain (thawed) smelt and season with salt. Broil over coal fire or a grill. The fish is supposed to be dark brown to almost black on both sides. Serve immediately — it's best when it's really hot. Herb butter and baked potatoes are served with it.

Work butter until soft and mix in other ingredients. Chill before serving.

STUFFED SMELT FILLETS
4 servings

Fried stuffed smelt is usually served with mashed potatoes. The stuffed smelt is excellent cold, and is often served as a snack on crisp bread together with mayonnaise. Leftover cold smelt can also be marinated.

1 lb fillets of smelt
butter and oil
bread crumbs
salt
pepper
stuffing:
    1. chopped parsley, lemon juice
    2. chopped dill, tomato purée
    3. chopped chives
    4. finely chopped onion and tomato purée

Sift bread crumbs on a piece of paper towel and spread out half the fillets of smelt, meaty side up. Sprinkle with salt and put about ½-1 tbsp of any one stuffing on each fish. Cover with remaining smelts, skin side up; sprinkle with salt and sift bread crumbs over them. Fry in a mixture of oil and butter until golden brown on both sides. The breaded fish can also be broiled. Broil about 3 minutes on each side.

GRILLED EEL
4 servings

This is a very old recipe from southern Sweden, easily prepared on any outdoor grill.

1 eel of 2-3 lb
salt (preferably coarse, kosher salt)

Clean eel but do not skin. Rub with salt and refrigerate for 6-8 hours. Heat coals in an outdoor grill. When they're red hot they should be covered with finely-cut branches to give the eel a smoky, woodsy flavor. Wash eel, dry it with a paper towel and put it on the grill. Cook until it is dark-brown all around. Serve hot with slices of lemon and buttered baked potatoes. The meat is white, tender and delicious, the smoked-grilled fish a gourmet's treat.

SMOKED EEL

If you'd like to try smoked eel, but can't find it at a store, it's easy and fun to smoke the fish yourself. Pick large eels—the larger the better. Clean them but don't skin them. For smoking, any old metal can like a clean garbage can or an old oil drum will do. Put a few holes in the bottom of the can, turn it upside down, and hang the eels inside, fastening them with wire or rope. Light a charcoal fire, put a few bricks around it, and set the metal can on the bricks. Put wet branches on the coal; preferably cedar; used to add flavor to the fish. Keep the fire going but keep smothering it with wet branches: the fish needs smoke and heat.

Eel which is about 2″ in diameter should take 3 hours to smoke. When the fish is ready, it's golden colored on the outside and the meat is a snowy white. Have ready several handfuls of salt, preferably coarse (kosher) salt. Pack the warm fish in salt and leave it till the following day.

To serve: scrape off salt, cut into bite-sized pieces and enjoy. Smoked eel is often served with very soft scrambled eggs or buttered spinach.

FISH AU GRATIN
6 servings

2 lb fillets of sole, flounder or pike
salt
dash of pepper
3 tbsp lemon juice
1 tbsp butter
4½ oz can mussels or the same amount coarse-
    ly-chopped shrimp
sauce:
    2 tbsp butter
    1 tbsp flour
    1½ cup fish stock and light cream
    2 egg yolks
    2-3 tbsp cold butter
    salt
    dash of pepper
    2 tbsp grated cheese

Preheat oven to 425°. Sprinkle fillets with salt and pepper. Place in buttered baking dish, pour lemon juice over, dot with butter. Cover with aluminum foil and bake for 10 minutes. Remove from oven and cool. Pour off fish stock. Garnish with shrimp or mussels.

Melt butter in saucepan, stir in flour gradually, add fish stock and cream. Simmer 5 minutes. Remove from heat and stir in egg yolks and cold butter. Heat but do not boil, stirring constantly. Remove from heat and stir until thick. Season. Pour over fish.

HERRING WITH ONION SAUCE
4 servings

Salt herring was the mainstay of Scandinavia's diet during the winter months until the turn of the century. Rye flour makes the fish crusty and gives it a particular flavor. The onion sauce, which is surprisingly mild, goes very well with the salty fish.

6 fillets of salt herring
rye flour or unseasoned bread crumbs
butter and oil
onion sauce:
    3 large onions
    2 oz butter
    3 tbsp flour
    2 cups milk, or milk and cream mixed
    salt, pepper

Wash fillets of herring and soak overnight. Drain well on paper towel and bread with rye flour (or unseasoned bread crumbs). Fry in a mixture of oil and butter until golden brown on both sides. Keep hot and make onion sauce.

Slice onions and sauté slowly in butter. Blend in flour and add milk, stirring constantly over low heat until sauce has thickened. Season, but be careful with the salt; the herring will be quite salty. Serve with boiled potatoes.

HERRING BALLS
4 servings

2 fillets of salt herring
4 medium-sized potatoes
⅔ cup cooked, leftover meat
1 onion
1 tbsp cornstarch
3-4 tbsp milk
a few turns on your pepper mill (or a dash of ground pepper)
4 tbsp bread crumbs
butter

Soak fillets of herring for 8 hours or overnight. Boil potatoes (do not peel them) and let them cool. Peel cold potatoes and put them through a blender together with dried herring fillets and leftover meat. The mixture should be coarsely ground, not puréed. Stir in cornstarch and milk. Season with pepper, no salt should be needed. Form mixture into balls, the

size of a walnut. Roll them in bread crumbs and fry them in butter until they are hot and nicely browned. Serve with a salad and boiled potatoes.

SALT HERRING AU GRATIN
4 servings

Salt herring au gratin becomes quite juicy with a rich custard. The potatoes retain some of their crunchiness and the herring gives it just the right amount of saltiness.

3 fillets of salt herring
2 finely-chopped onions
2 tbsp butter
6 large potatoes
5 eggs
1⅔ cup milk
½ tsp coarsely-ground pepper

Soak herring fillets 8 hours or overnight. Boil potatoes (do not peel them) and let them cool. Rinse and dry herring fillets and cut them into small pieces. Peel potatoes and slice them thinly. Cook onions in 1 tbsp butter until they are tender but not browned. Preheat oven to 375-400°. Butter a deep ovenware dish. Layer potatoes, chopped onions and herring, with potatoes as a bottom and top layer. Mix eggs and milk, season with pepper and pour this custard over the potatoes. Cook for 40 minutes. Serve with browned butter and a salad.

QUENELLES FROM NORWAY
4 servings

Well-made quenelles are a treat—airy and light and succulent. They're also time-consuming to make; if you take the trouble to make them at all, you may as well use fresh fish. If you buy fish whole and have it cleaned, take home bones, heads and fins to use for the stock. If the fish is already cut into fillets, you can buy some inexpensive fish for your stock or simply use salted water.

1½ lb fillets of haddock, cod or whiting
2 tsp salt
½-1 tsp ground pepper
dash of nutmeg
1 egg white
1 tbsp cornstarch or potato flour
1 cup milk

1 cup whipping cream
fish stock:
    4 cups water
    heads, fins and bones of fish
    1 quartered onion
    1 sliced carrot
    salt
    whole pepper (1 clove)

Cut fish into small pieces and put through a blender. It should be pureed. Work the fish into a smooth paste and gradually and carefully add 1 egg white and the cornstarch.

FISH IN ASPIC
4 servings

Fish in aspic is a common dish in Scandinavia. Mainly it's mackerel which is prepared in this fashion, but eel and other kinds of fish may also be used. Shellfish or shrimp are sometimes added to the mold for looks and taste. It's an excellent party dish, prepared in advance, and it's both good looking and good to eat. Serve with a mayonnaise or tartar sauce, with hot rolls and a salad.

stock:
    for every 4 cups water, take:
    1 tbsp salt
    2 tbsp vinegar
    3 grains whole pepper
    2 tbsp gelatin for every 3½ cup of stock
    5 grains allspice
    1 bay leaf
    2 tbsp coarsely-chopped dill

Rinse fish and cut into 2-3″ pieces. Mix ingredients for stock. Boil stock for 10 minutes, correct seasoning; it should have a good, strong, somewhat sour taste. Simmer fish until tender, but do not let it boil. Mackerel should be done in less than 10 minutes. Remove from stock. Strain stock. There should be about 3½ cups. If there isn't enough, add water, lemon juice or a little bit of vinegar. Soak gelatin in ¼ cup cold stock. Dissolve in heated stock.

Chill until it begins to thicken.

Skin fish and remove bones, but leave it in large pieces. Put a layer of aspic in a wet mold, arrange pieces of fish on top, garnish with dill, pieces of celery, shrimp or thin slices of carrot. Pour a layer of aspic over fish. Repeat until mold is filled. The last layer should be aspic. Chill. Unmold and serve.

PIKE WITH HORSE-RADISH
4 servings

1 pike, 2-2½ lb
1 tbsp salt
4 cups water
1 tbsp salt
1 onion
5 grains of pepper
parsley
sauce:
    2-3 oz butter
    grated horseradish
garnish:
    parsley
    1 lemon

Have fish cleaned and scaled. If the head is left on (that's how it's usually served in Scandinavia), the gills must be cut out. Rub fish with salt inside and out, and leave for 10 minutes. Boil water, salt, pepper, parsley and sliced onion. Simmer pike gently for 20 minutes or until done. Strain and garnish with parsley and sliced lemon. Melt butter, blend in grated horseradish to taste (and season with a little lemon juice), Serve with boiled potatoes.

CREAMED PERCH
4 servings

This is a simple, classic recipe for perch. Supposedly it was invented at Blå Porten, The Blue Gate, a Stockholm restaurant famous in the 1890s.

4 medium-sized perch, about 2 lb
2 tbsp butter
2 tbsp flour
1 cup water and table cream mixed
2 tsp salt
dash of pepper
1 bay leaf
dash of thyme
parsley and/or dill

Have fish scaled and cleaned. Ordinarily it is used whole, with the head left on. If you don't want to bone the fish at the table you can use perch fillets instead.

Season fish with salt and pepper and put a generous amount of parsley and/or dill inside. Butter a pot and put the fish in, stomach down, backs up; pack them close together so they support each other. Gradually add cold water and cream to flour until it becomes a thin paste. Pour over fish. Add bay leaf and thyme. If you are using fillets, add parsley and/or dill. Cover and simmer gently. Shake or tilt pot from time to time so the fish doesn't burn. Whole fish is done in 10-15 minutes, fillets in 5-7 minutes. Serve with baked or boiled potatoes.

BACALAO CASSEROLE
6-8 servings

1 lb salt dried cod
6—8 medium-sized raw potatoes
4 medium-sized onions
¼ fresh Spanish pepper pod
⅔ cup tomato purée
¾ cup oil
¾ cup water
garnish:
    2 tomatoes
    2 tbsp chopped parsley

Rinse fish and soak 2 days, changing water a few times. Remove skin and bones, and cut fish into small squares. Peel potatoes and slice. Peel and slice onion and parboil a few minutes. Layer in deep saucepan or heavy kettle: potato slices, fish, onion, pepper and tomato purée. Pour in oil and cold water. Cover and simmer carefully 45 minutes or until potatoes and fish are tender. Do not stir, but shake pan occasionally. Serve hot, garnished with tomato slices and chopped parsley.

FISHBALLS

2 pounds cod fillets
4 teaspoons lemon juice
1 can sardines in oil
3 tablespoons butter
Dash of pepper
1 large onion, finely chopped
½ bunch parsley
½ bunch fresh dill
2 eggs, beaten
2 rolls, crumbed
4 teaspoons aquavit

Parsley for garnish
lemon slices for garnish
batter:
    2 eggs, beaten
    4 tablespoons bread crumbs
    Oil for frying

Rinse the cod fillets under cold water and dry them on paper towels. Cover fillets with lemon juice and let them sit for 5 minutes. Next, put the cod and the sardines through a food chopper. Reserve the sardine oil for future use.

Cream the butter in a large bowl. Add the fish and pepper. Add the onion, parsley, and dill. Last, put in 2 beaten eggs, the sardine oil, rolls, and the aquavit. Mix well and season to taste.

With wet hands form the mixture into balls that are pressed somewhat flat. Dip the balls into the 2 beaten eggs, then dust them with bread crumbs. Heat a generous amount of oil in a frypan. Fry the fishballs for about 15 minutes or until they are golden brown.

Serve the fishballs garnished with parsley and slices of lemon.

Makes 6 servings.

BAKED LUTFISH
4-5 servings

Lutfish is dried ling, a variety of codfish, which is lye-cured and then soaked in water for several days. It's a Scandinavian specialty, a reminder of ancient customs. Lye-curing was a way of preserving in the old days when there were few ways to keep food. The tradition of eating lutfish for Christmas is a Catholic one. Even though the Scandinavian countries have officially been Protestant ever since the fifteen hundreds, lutfish is still a Christmas tradition in the majority of Scandinavian homes.

4 lb lutfish
2 tbsp salt
1 tbsp butter
cream sauce:
    4 tbsp butter
    3 tbsp flour
    2 cups table cream
    salt
    pepper

Preheat oven to 400°. Sprinkle fish with salt and put it skin side down in a buttered baking dish. Cover with aluminum foil and bake for 30-40 minutes. Pour off water before serving. Remove foil and serve with melted butter and/or cream sauce, salt, pepper, ground allspice, mustard, boiled potatoes and sweet peas.

Melt butter over low heat and blend in flour. Slowly stir in cream. Cook and stir over low heat until thickened and smooth, about 5 minutes. Season. Add about 1 tbsp of cold butter for better flavor.

MARINATED SALMON
6-8 servings

  2 lb or more fresh salmon (not frozen); pick a piece from the middle of the fish where it's thick

  for every lb fish:
  2-3 tbsp salt
  2-3 tbsp sugar
  10 grains coarsely-crushed pepper
  ⅔ cup cut fresh dill

Scrape fish clean with a knife and dry on paper towel. Do not wash. Cut the fish open along its back ridge: remove backbone. Rub fish (both the meat and the skin side) with salt and sugar. Sprinkle with coarsely-ground pepper. Cover the bottom of a shallow pan with dill and put one piece of fish on top, skin side down. Cover meat side with dill, place other piece of fish on top, skin side up. The thick part of the upper fillet will now be resting on the thin part of the bottom fillet, exactly opposite to the way the pieces were originally joined. Cover with remaining dill. Marinate in refrigerator at least 48 hours.

Marinated salmon will keep in the refrigerator for a week. To serve: Scrape off pepper and dill and cut salmon into thin slices, without cutting all the way through the skin. This way the fish is skinned before serving. (Thin strips of skin from marinated salmon are sometimes broiled and served as a garnish along with the fish.)

Traditionally marinated salmon is served with toast and butter, lemon wedges, or a special sauce (see index). Sometimes marinated salmon is served as an hors d'oeuvre. If the salmon is to be eaten as an entrée, allow 4-5 oz per person; allow 2-3 oz if it is served as hors d'oeuvre.

SAUCE FOR MARINATED SALMON
Sufficient for 2 lb fish

  1 tbsp vinegar
  2 tbsp sugar
  6 tbsp mustard (pick a sour variety or use Dijon mustard)
  ⅔ cup oil
  2 tbsp finely-chopped fresh dill

Mix vinegar, sugar and mustard. Gradually add oil one drop at a time while stirring constantly, just as if you were making a mayonnaise. Stir in dill.

How to marinate other fish

Any fat fish can be marinated in the same fashion as salmon. Mackerel is often served marinated in Scandinavia. The fish must be fresh, though, not frozen or thawed.

FISH SOUFFLÉ
4 servings

  1 lb cleaned cod or haddock
  2 cups water
  1 tbsp lemon juice
  1 tsp salt
  5 grains of pepper
  cream sauce:
    2 tbsp butter
    3 tbsp flour
    1¼ cup fish stock
    dash of nutmeg
    3 eggs
    2 tbsp chopped parsley

Preheat oven to 350°. Simmer fish slowly in water seasoned with lemon, salt and pepper. Strain, reserve stock and reduce it to about 1¼ cup. Melt butter, stir in flour and add reduced fish stock, stirring constantly until sauce has thickened. Remove from heat and stir in 3 beaten egg yolks with nutmeg, parsley and fish in small flakes. Season well. Cool.

Beat egg whites until stiff and fold them lightly into the fish misture. Pour into a well-greased soufflé or other dish with straight, high edges. Bake until firm, 45-60 minutes. Serve the soufflé with brown butter or with chilled spiced butter.

NORWEGIAN FISH MOUSSE

6 servings

- 1½ lb fillets of haddock, cod or pike
- 2 tbsp salt
- 1 tsp pepper
- dash of nutmeg
- 1½ tbsp cornstarch
- 1⅓ cup milk
- 1½ cup table cream

Dry fish fillets and put them through a blender. Work purée until it is smooth. Stir in cornstarch and seasoning, then gradually add milk and cream. The mixture should be like an even, heavy cream. Check the seasoning. Preheat oven to 375°.

Pour mixture into a buttered and breaded pudding mold, 8″ in diameter. Cover mold with aluminum foil. Put a deep baking dish into the oven and fill it to about ¾ with boiling water. Place the pudding mold in the hot water and cook 45-60 minutes or until the mousse is set. Check the water a few times and add more if needed. Unmold carefully on a hot platter and garnish with parsley, sautéed mushrooms or shrimp. Serve with browned butter or shrimp sauce.

SOUPS

BEEF BROTH

4 servings

- 2 lb beef shank
- 6 cups cold water
- 2 tsp salt
- 5 grains of pepper
- 2 cloves
- 5 medium-sized potatoes
- 1 large carrot
- 1 turnip
- 2 leeks or onions or a bunch or spring onions
- parsley

Cover meat with cold water and bring slowly to a boil. Skim well. Season, cover and simmer gently for 45 minutes. Now add sliced potatoes, carrot, leeks or onions. Continue simmering until meat and vegetables are done. (Meanwhile prepare dumplings, see below). Remove meat, discard any fat, cut into bite-sized pieces, and put back into the broth. Check seasoning. Serve with dumplings and chopped parsley.

DUMPLINGS

4 servings

- 1½ tbsp butter
- 4 tbsp flour
- 1⅔ cup milk
- 2 egg yolks
- 2 tbsp grated cheese
- a dash of grated cardamon or a drop of almond flavoring

Melt butter over low heat and blend in flour. Add milk, stirring constantly until sauce has thickened. Remove from heat. Beat together egg yolks and 1-2 tbsp milk, add a little of the sauce to this mixture and blend well. Return this mixture to the rest of the sauce and cook over low heat, stirring vigorously until sauce is hot, thick and well blended. Stir in cheese and cardamon or almond flavoring. Let cool.

Bring 4-6 cups of salted water to a rapid boil. Reduce heat. Gently drop dumplings the size of a quarter into the hot water and simmer for 4-5 minutes. Remove, drain and serve in the broth. The seasoning—cardamon or almond—together with beef broth is unusual and interesting.

FISH SOUP

- 1 pound fish fillets
- 2 tablespoons lemon juice
- 2 tablespoons aquavit
- Chives
- 4 onions, peeled
- 1 leek
- 2 carrots
- 4 to 5 medium potatoes
- 3 slices bacon
- 4 cups beef broth or meat stock
- Pinch of saffron
- ½ teaspoon basil
- 1 bay leaf
- Salt and pepper to taste
- Parsley for garnish

Drain the fish fillets and cut them into 1-inch pieces. Put them into a deep dish. Add the lemon juice and aquavit, and cover.

Finely chop the chives and peeled onions.

Cut the leek in half and then into pieces.

Peel and dice the carrots and potatoes.

Dice the bacon and put it into a pot, cooking it until it is just transparent. Add the onions and chives and cook for 3 minutes more. Let this mixture steam. Add the leek, carrots, and potatoes; steam for 1 minute more. Pour in the meat stock and add the saffron, basil, and bay leaf. Cover and cook for 15 minutes. Then add the fish mixture with its liquid and simmer slowly for 5 minutes more. Season the soup with salt and pepper.

Serve the soup in bowls or in a tureen. Garnish with parsley. Makes 4 to 6 servings.

MUSHROOM SOUP
4 servings

> ½ lb fresh mushrooms
> 2 tbsp butter
> salt
> pepper
> 2 tbsp flour
> 5 cups stock and mushroom juice
> ⅓ cup whipping cream
> ½ tsp lemon juice
> 1-2 tbsp Madeira or sherry
> 1 tsp grated onion

Rinse mushrooms and cut into slices. Cook mushrooms in their own juices until soft. Strain off cooking liquid. Add butter and sauté mushrooms over low heat. Season. Sprinkle flour oven them and add liquid. Simmer for 5 minutes. Add cream and lemon juice. Wine and grated onion can also be added. Taste for seasoning.

SALMON SOUP
4 servings

> ½ lb fresh salmon
> ½ lb potatoes
> 4 cups water
> ½ cup chopped onion
> 1 cup whipping cream
> 3 tbsp chopped dill
> salt
> pepper
> allspice
> 2 tbsp butter

The original recipe calls for fish stock. If you buy fresh salmon you can have it cleaned, but take home bones, fins and skin, and boil them in 4 cups of water. Season with a piece of celery, salt, pepper, one sliced onion and some dill. The soup tastes good even if you don't start with preparing a fish stock but use 4 cups of plain water.

Peel and slice potatoes. Boil them together with chopped onions, salt, pepper and a few grains of coarsely-crushed allspice, until they are very tender. Clean and wash salmon and cut it in bite-sized pieces. Put them in the soup and simmer gently until they are done. Add cream, dill and seasoning. Heat. Add 2 tbsp butter just before serving.

NETTLE SOUP
4 servings

> 6 cups tiny nettles
> 6 cups chicken stock
> 3 tbsp flour
> 1½ tbsp butter
> salt
> pepper
> ½ tsp crushed aniseeds or fennel
> 1 tbsp chopped chives

Clean nettles; remove wilted leaves and coarse stems. Rinse very well. Blanch in 1 cup salted water. Strain, reserving liquid, and put through a mixer. If should be a coarse purée—don't grind them too finely. Melt butter over low heat and blend in flour. Add stock, stirring constantly. Add liquid from nettles together with ground nettles and season. Serve with a poached egg in each plate, or with hard-boiled quartered or sliced eggs.

YELLOW PEA SOUP
4 servings

> 1⅔ cup dried yellow peas
> 2 quarts water
> ½ lb lean cured ham or pork
> 1 onion
> marjoram
> salt

Prepare Yellow pea soup as you would Split pea soup (see below) but season with marjoram instead of thyme. Hot mustard is usually served with the ham. Both soups can be prepared in large quantities and frozen.

SPLIT PEA SOUP
4 servings

   1⅔ cup split peas
   2 quarts water
   ½ lb lean cured ham or pork
   1 onion
   2 carrots
   thyme
   salt

Wash peas and soak in 2 quarts of water over night. Bring to a rapid boil and skim. Chop onion, slice carrots and add to peas together with seasoning and meat. Cover and simmer gently until peas and meat are done, 1-1½ hours. Remove meat, cut it into small pieces and put them back into the soup. Check seasoning before serving.

KALE SOUP
4 servings

This hearty green soup used to be frequent winter food and is still quite popular all over Scandinavia.

   2 lb kale
   2 cups water
   1 tsp salt
   4 tbsp chopped chives or onion
   1 tbsp butter
   1½ tbsp flour
   4 cups pork stock plus cooking liquid from kale
   salt
   pepper

Wash kale leaves well and drain. Cook in salted water for 10 minutes or until soft. Strain, reserving liquid. Chop kale and chives finely or put through a mixer. Melt butter, add flour and stir until well blended. Add stock, stirring, and simmer 5 minutes. Add kale and chives and reheat. Season. Serve with poached eggs or hard-boiled eggs cut in half.

BROWN CABBAGE SOUP
4 servings

   1 large head of cabbage
   2 oz butter
   1 tbsp brown sugar
   4 cups stock
   1 tsp salt

   ½ tsp crushed pepper
   ½ tsp crushed allspice
   parsley

Shred cabbage. Melt butter in heavy pan and sauté cabbage over low heat. Stir constantly until cabbage is nicely browned. Add sugar and spices, cover and simmer gently for about 30 minutes. Add stock and continue simmering until cabbage is very tender. Sprinkle with chopped parsley before serving.

This soup is often served with small meatballs called "frikadeller." Prepare half a batch of Meatballs (see index). Boil 6 cups of salted water. Turn down heat and boil meatballs gently for 6—8 minutes. Remove, drain and put them in the soup. They can also be boiled directly in the cabbage soup, but will cloud the stock.

FINNISH CUCUMBER SOUP

   ⅓—½ cup butter
   1 small chopped onion
   4 medium-sized cucumbers
   3 tbsp flour
   6 cups chicken stock
   dash of pepper
   2 egg yolks
   1 tbsp dry sherry
   1 cup table cream
   3 tbsp chopped parsley

Melt butter in saucepan and add onion and peeled and sliced cucumbers. Simmer for 10 minutes, stirring frequently. Sprinkle with flour and mix well. Gradually add chicken stock and pepper and simmer another 10 minutes, stirring constantly. Beat soup until smooth. Beat egg yolks, sherry and cream. Gradually stir into soup. Season and add parsley. Cucumber soup is served chilled.

SUMMER VEGETABLE SOUP
4 servings

For Scandinavians this soup is a great summer treat—once upon a time it was made with the first tender vegetables from their gardens, which they'd been waiting for all spring. Today vegetables of any kind are available all through the year. But the soup remains a favorite; it has a mild, slightly sweet taste.

1 bunch of tiny fresh carrots
1 stalk of celery
1 bunch of spring onions
1 cup fresh green peas
1 small head of cauliflower
salt
4 cups milk
2-3 tbsp butter
½ cup table cream
½ cup chopped parsley

Clean vegetables, slice carrots, celery, and onions and break cauliflower into small pieces. Blanch vegetables in 1 cup salted water. Reserve liquid. Melt 2 tbsp butter, blend in flour and add milk, stirring constantly over low heat. Add vegetables and the water they were blanched in. Season with salt; stir in cream and remaining butter and garnish with chopped parsley. Vegetables should be crisp and barely done. An extra dot of butter in each plate will enhance the flavor of the vegetables.

FRUIT SOUP
4 servings

½ lb mixed, pared fruit
5 cups water
lemon
1 piece cinnamon
⅓ cup sugar or more, depending on tartness of fruit
2 tbsp cornstarch

Simmer fruit with sugar and cinnamon until tender. For apples, pears, strawberries and other sweet fruit, add juice from ½ lemon and a piece of lemon rind. Thin cornstarch with ¼ cup cold water, let soup come to a rapid boil and stir in cornstarch mixture. The soup can be served hot or cold.

DESSERTS

SWEDISH APPLE CAKE
4 servings

This is a very old-fashioned dessert. Traditionally confectioner's sugar used to be sprinkled in a pattern on top of the cake. To make the pattern, cut a piece of stiff paper in the shope of the bottom of the pan. Now fold this rounded sheet of paper three times, so that it's folded in eighths. Cut holes, squares and crescent shapes into the layers of paper. Unfold. You should have an even, lacy-looking pattern. Place on cool cake and sift confectioner's sugar over it. Remove pattern carefully.

2 cups unseasoned bread crumbs or cracker crumbs
3 oz butter
1⅔-2 cups tart apple sauce
confectioner's sugar

Preheat oven to 400°. Butter a ring mold (with removable rim). Reserve about ½ tbsp butter. Sauté bread crumbs lightly in remaining butter. Put a layer of bread crumbs on the bottom of the pan, spread apple sauce on top, add another layer of bread crumbs, spread another layer of apple sauce, and top with bread crumbs. Bake for 30 minutes. Serve warm or cold, sprinkled with confectioner's sugar. Custard sauce (see index) is usually served with it.

SCANDINAVIAN CHEESE CAKE
4 servings

6-7 oz cottage cheese (small curd)
2 eggs
¾ cup table cream
1 tbsp sugar
½ tsp vanilla
3 tbsp chopped almonds

Preheat oven to 425°. Beat eggs lightly with cream. Put cheese through a sieve or through a blender and mix in other ingredients. Pour into buttered ovenware dish and cook for 15-20 minutes. Serve hot with fruit preserve (and whipped cream).

WIZARD'S PUDDING
6 servings

3 egg whites
1 cup lingonberry or cranberry preserve
½ tbsp vanilla
2½ tbsp sugar

Beat egg whites until stiff. Add preserve, vanilla and sugar, and beat vigorously until very light and fluffy, using electric mixer. Serve with milk.

RHUBARB PIE
4 servings

Pie crust with egg:
1 cup flour
3 tbsp sugar
1 egg yolk
4 oz. butter
1 egg
Rhubarb filling:
   1 lb rhubarb
   ½ cup sugar or more depending on taste
   1 tbsp cornstarch

Mix flour and sugar and cut in butter. Add egg yolk and gather into a ball. Cool for about 1 hour. Preheat oven to 425°. Roll out ⅔ of the dough and line bottom and sides of a pie dish. Bake for 10 minutes. Remove from oven. Clean and cut rhubarb in 1" long pieces. Mix with cornstarch and sugar and fill into pie shell. Roll remaining dough into strips and weave a lattice work on top of the filling. Brush with egg and bake for another 20 minutes or until done. Serve lukewarm with whipped cream.

DANISH FRUIT PUDDING
4 servings

1 lb strawberries
2 tbsp sugar
⅓ cup water
1½ tbsp cornstarch

Clean berries and rinse in a colander. Drain well. Mash with sugar and bring to a quick boil. Thin cornstarch with water and pour into hot strawberries, stirring constantly. Bring to another quick boil and remove from heat. Pour into a bowl and chill. (Sprinkle about 2 tbsp sugar on top to keep surface soft.) Serve cold with table cream.

CUSTARD SAUCE
4 servings
   ¾ cup table cream
   1-2 tsp vanilla
   3 egg yolks
   2 tbsp sugar
   ¾ cup whipping cream

Heat table cream. Beat egg yolks and sugar until mixture is foamy. Beating continuously, pour hot cream over mixture. Pour into double boiler (or simmer over low heat) and continue beating until mixture has thickened. Let cool and stir from time to time. Stir in vanilla. Whip cream and fold gently into the sauce. Serve chilled.

APPLE CAKE

3 eggs
1½ cup sugar
3 oz butter
⅔ cup milk
1¾ cup flour
2½ tsp baking powder
4 tart apples
4 tbsp brown sugar
2 tsp cinnamon

Preheat oven to 400°. Grease and flour a round baking pan or bread it with unseasoned bread crumbs (the way it's usually done in Scandinavia.) It gives the cake a slightly crusty surface. Peel apples and slice thinly. (Drip a little lemon juice oven them if you're not using them immediately so that they don't turn brown.) Beat eggs and sugar until foamy. Melt butter, add milk and heat. Pour the hot mixture over the eggs. Mix flour with baking powder and add to egg mixture. Pour into pan. Arrange apple slices on top and sprinkle with brown sugar and cinnamon. Bake for 30 minutes or until done.

ROYAL MERINGUES
4 servings

Meringues:
4 egg whites
½ cup sugar
Garnish:
   2 ripe bananas
   chocolate syrup
   1¼ cup whipping cream

Preheat oven to 225°. Make meringues: beat egg whites (with an electric beater) until foamy. Add 1 tbsp sugar at a time and continue beating until the mixture stands in stiff spikes and the bowl can be turned upside-down. Drop mixture on ungreased cookie sheets and bake for 45 minutes or until dry. Let cool on cookie sheets for about 5 minutes before removing them.

Arrange cool meringues on a platter together with sliced bananas. Cover with whipped cream and garnish with chocolate syrup. Serve at once.

CARAMEL CUSTARD
4 servings

caramel:
1 cup sugar
3 tbsp boiling water
custard:
1⅔ cup table cream
1 cup milk
2 tbsp sugar
1 tsp vanilla or grated rind of ½ lemon
4 eggs
15 blanched almonds

Melt sugar in skillet over low heat until light brown syrup forms. Stir occasionally with wooden spoon until all lumps are gone. Slowly add boiling water and simmer until smooth. Coat bottom and sides of heated ring mold with caramel. Preheat oven to 300°.

Boil cream, milk and sugar in skillet used for preparing caramel. Remove from heat and add vanilla or lemon rind. Beat eggs in bowl and pour the hot milk mixture over, beating vigorously. Pour mixture into caramel-coated mold. Place deep oblong baking pan in oven and fill with hot water. Place mold in the water and bake for 45 minutes, or until custard is set. Chill, unmold and garnish with almonds.

GINGER PEARS (PRESERVE)

Pears should be barely ripe. Use seckels, the small, sweet, early variety
For every 2 lb of pears you'll need:
2 cups water
2 cups sugar
3 pieces of dried ginger

Boil sugar, water and ginger to a light syrup, 5-10 minutes. Peel pears and cut them in half lengthwise. Remove seeds. Use a teaspoon and not a knife, otherwise it's difficult not to cut into the pear. Simmer pears very gently over low heat until they are transparent. They should keep their shape, which means that the heat has to be very low. It will take about 1 hour or slightly longer.

Remove pears and put them into crocks. Boil syrup until it has thickened slightly, another 10 minutes, and pour it over the pears. Cool and cover. Keep preserve in a cool and dry place. It will keep for almost 1 year. Traditionally it was served as a Sunday dessert together with whipped cream or table cream. It tastes very good together with ice cream.

PRUNE SOUFFLÉ
4 servings

6-7 oz pitted prunes
⅓ cup brown sugar
3-4 tbsp chopped almonds
1 tbsp cornstarch
4-5 egg whites

Preheat oven to 325°. Chop prunes and mix with almonds and sugar. Beat egg whites stiff. Sprinkle cornstarch on top, then gently fold in prune mixture. Pour into well-buttered soufflé or other ovenware dish with high, straight sides. Cook for 30 minutes. Serve hot with chilled table cream or vanilla ice cream.

FLUFFY BERRY PUDDING
4 servings

2 cups water
1 cup sweetened raspberry or cranberry juice
½ cup cream of wheat

Boil water and juice. Gradually sprinkle cream of wheat into liquid beating vigorously to prevent lumps. Simmer for 5 minutes, stirring occasionally. Remove from heat and pour into mixer or large bowl. Beat well until cold and very fluffy. Pour into serving dish. Cool in refrigerator for ½ hour. Serve with milk or cream.

WAFFLES
8 waffles

In Sweden the right time to eat waffles is in the spring. They are often served on March 25, the feast of the Annunciation, called "Marie Bebådelse," a Catholic holiday. Sweden has been Protestant since the fifteen hundreds, yet in some way or another has preserved many catholic holidays—even if only for eating waffles.

¾ cup water
1¼ cup flour
1¼ cup whipping cream
2 tbsp butter

Stir flour and water to make an even batter. Stir in melted butter. Whip cream and fold into flour mixture. (Use a wide-mouthed pitcher for mixing the batter so that it's easy to pour on the waffle iron. If you mix the batter in a bowl, use a large wooden spoon or ladle for pouring it on the iron.)

Heat a waffle iron. If you have an electric one, the indicator will tell you when it is ready to use. If the iron is properly broken in it shouldn't need any grease. Pour the grid surface about ⅔ full of batter. Close the lid and wait about 4 minutes. If you try to open the iron and it resists, that means the waffle is not quite done. Cook about 1 minute more and try again. Cook waffles 2-3 minutes on each wide.

PANCAKES
4 servings

Pancakes are best directly from the pan. In Scandinavia they are served with fresh berries mashed with sugar or with jam or jelly or with lingonberry preserve. If you omit sugar in this recipe, the pancakes can be used with meat or vegetable fillings. They are delicious filled with creamed spinach and ham, then broiled with grated cheese on top. These pancakes come close to the famous French crepes—the large thin pancakes—which, depending on the filling, are served both as a main dish and as a dessert.

2 eggs
1 cup flour
2½ cup milk
a pinch of salt
2 tsp sugar

Beat eggs with a little of the milk. Stir in flour and beat to an even mixture. Add remaining milk and stir in salt and sugar. If your griddle is well broken in it will need to be buttered only once or twice while you're cooking these pancakes.

Melt about 1 tsp of butter in griddle; pour batter, using a ladle, and tilt griddle so that it is evenly coated with a thin layer of batter. When bubbles appear on the surface, lift carefully with a spatula to see

if cakes are browned. Turn only once. Fold or roll pancakes and keep them hot. Stir batter while cooking cakes so that the flour doesn't sink to the bottom of the bowl.

Plättar
are tiny pancakes, made from the same batter as the larger ones. You need a special griddle, called "plättlagg" in Swedish. The "plättar" are usually served stacked—a stack of 8 is a normal serving.

PANCAKE FROM FINLAND
6 servings

4 eggs
½ cup sugar
1⅔-2 cups whipping cream
¾ cup flour
2 tbsp butter

Preheat oven to 425°. Beat eggs and sugar until foamy. Fold in flour. Whip cream and fold into egg mixture. Add melted butter. Pour batter into buttered skillet or ovenware pan and bake for about 20 minutes or until set. Serve warm with raspberry jam or other fruit preserve.

BAKED GOODS

GINGERBREAD COOKIES
150 cookies

2 sticks butter
¾ cup sugar
⅔ cup syrup
2-3 tbsp cinnamon
1 tsp ground cloves
1 tsp ground cardamon
1 tbsp ground ginger
1 cup chopped almonds
1 tsp baking soda
4 cups flour

Prepare dough a day in advance. Melt butter in large pan over low heat. Remove from heat. Add sugar, syrup, spices, baking soda, almonds and about 3½ cup of flour. Knead dough on floured board until it is smooth and gradually work in remaining flour. Roll dough into rolls, 2″ in diameter. Chill overnight. Preheat oven to 350°. Slice rolls into thin cookies and put on greased cookie sheets. Bake for 10-12 minutes.

DANISH ALMOND COOKIES
25 cookies

These traditional Danish cookies are very rich. They're excellent with ice cream or with a cup of coffee after dinner. They keep very well.

> **1 lb almond paste**
> **½ tsp almond flavoring**
> **1-2 egg whites**
> **icing:**
>> **⅓ cup confectioner's sugar**
>> **½ tsp lemon juice**
>> **egg white**

Preheat oven to 350°. Grate almond paste and mix in almond flavoring and egg whites. The mixture should be like a semi-soft dough. Roll into 1″ thick rolls, about 2″ long. Pinch one side to give them their characteristic triangular form. Bake for 6-8 minutes. The cookies should have a little bit of color but should be soft inside. Mix sugar, lemon juice and egg white for the icing (or use commercial icing). Fill icing into paper or canvas bag and make a fine zig-zag pattern over the cookies.

OATMEAL COOKIES
40 cookies

> **1⅔ cup oatmeal**
> **1 cup flour**
> **⅓ cup sugar**
> **1⅔ stick butter**

Mix flour and oatmeal with sugar and cut in butter. Gather to a dough and chill for 1 hour. Preheat oven to 360°. Roll cookies about the size of a quarter, put them an inch apart on greased cookie sheet (they need room to expand while cooking). Press down on them lightly with a fork and bake for about 8 minutes.

RAISIN COOKIES
120 cookies
> **1 stick butter**
> **¾ cup confectioner's sugar**
> **2 eggs**
> **¾ cup flour**
> **⅔ cup finely-chopped raisins**
> **3 tbsp brandy, rum, unflavored aquavit or vodka**

Pour brandy over raisins and let them marinate for 1 hour. Preheat oven to 375-400°. Cream butter and sugar until the mixture is light and foamy. Add eggs and flour, then add raisins and their liquid. Drop cookies (using two teaspoons) about the size of a nickel on well-greased cookie sheets. Space them generously. Bake for 8-10 minutes. Remove from cookie sheets while they're still hot. Let cool.

FINNISH COOKIES
50 cookies

> **6-7 oz butter**
> **⅓ cup sugar**
> **2 oz grated almonds**
> **1⅔ cup flour**
> **½ tsp almond flavoring**
> **1 egg**
> **3-4 tbsp sugar**
> **3-4 tbsp chopped almonds**

Work butter until soft. Stir in sugar, grated almonds, almond flavoring and flour; form into a ball. Chill dough for 1 hour. Preheat oven to 350°. Roll dough into rolls ⅓-½″ thick and cut them into 2″ long cookies. Brush with beaten egg and sprinkle with sugar and chopped almonds. Bake on greased cookie sheets for 6-8 minutes or until golden colored.

COOKIES FOR UPPÅKRA
50 cookies

> **1⅔ cup flour**
> **⅓ cup cornstarch or potato flour**
> **⅓ cup sugar**
> **6-7 oz butter**
> **1 egg white**
> **3-4 tbsp sugar**
> **3-4 tbsp chopped almonds**

Mix flour and sugar and cut in butter. Form a smooth ball. Chill dough until firm. Preheat oven to 350°. Roll out dough ⅛″ thick. Cut round cookies, 2-2½″ in diameter. Fold off-center so that the lower edge is showing. Brush with egg white and sprinkle with sugar and almonds. Bake on greased cookie sheets for 8-10 minutes. The cookies can also be filled with jam, usually raspberry preserve is used.

VANILLA RINGS
50 cookies

1¾-2 cups flour
⅓ cup sugar
1 tbsp vanilla
6-7 oz butter
1 egg yolk

Mix flour and sugar and cut in butter. Add egg yolk and vanilla and gather dough into a ball. Cool in refrigerator for 30 minutes. Preheat oven to 350°. Grease a cookie sheet. Force dough through a pastry bag with a wide notched metal tip and make round cookies directly on the cookie sheet. Bake for 10 minutes or until golden brown.

DANISH APPLE COOKIES
20 double cookies

1⅔ stick butter
1 egg
⅔ cup sugar
1½ tsp baking powder
2½ cup flour
tart apple sauce

Preheat oven to 425°. Cream butter, add egg and sugar. Sift flour with baking powder and add to butter mixture. Roll out dough about ⅛″ thick, cut round cookies with cookie cutter or glass. Place on greased cookie sheets and bake for 6 minutes or until done. Cool. Spread half the cookies with tart apple sauce, put the other cookies on top as though you were making sandwiches. Sprinkle with confectioner's sugar.

FARMER'S COOKIES
60 cookies

2½ cup flour
1 tsp baking soda
¾ cup sugar
2 tbsp syrup
⅓ cup chopped almonds
1⅔ stick butter

Mix flour with baking soda, sugar and almonds. Cut in butter, add syrup and gather into a dough. Knead for a few minutes, divide into three parts, and roll into rolls 1½-2″ in diameter. Chill. Preheat oven

to 375-400°. Slice rolls into cookies about ¼″ thick. Place on greased cookie sheets and bake for 8 minutes.

NORWEGIAN CUSTARD CAKES
24 pastries

1¼ cup flour
⅓ cup sugar
1⅔ stick butter
filling:
        approximately 2 cups vanilla custard, see index

Mix flour and sugar and cut in butter. Gather dough into a ball and chill for 1 hour. Preheat oven to 400°. Butter 24 individual muffin cups or small pastry pans. Roll out ⅔ of dough, line cups, fill with about 1 tbsp of vanilla custard. Roll out remaining dough and place top crusts on each pastry. Press down the edges. Bake for 20 minutes or until done. Let cool for a few minutes, then unmold carefully. Serve cold, sprinkled with confectioner's sugar.

LACE COOKIES
25 cookies

3 eggs
2 tbsp sugar
¾ cup table cream
1½ cup flour
2 tbsp grated lemon rind
sugar to sprinkle them with
oil or shortening for deep-fat frying

Beat eggs until light and foamy, add sugar and beat for another couple of minutes. Fold in cream, flour and grated lemon rind. Heat fat for deep-fat frying to 400°. Use a pastry bag and squeeze lacy cookies into the hot fat. Try to get the cookies as round as possible and about 3″ in diameter. Bake golden brown, remove and drain on paper towel. Sprinkle with sugar before serving.

ALMOND TARTS
35 tarts

⅔ cup butter
⅓ cup sugar
1 egg yolk

½ cup ground, blanched almonds
1½ cup flour

Cream butter and sugar until light and fluffy. Add egg yolk, almonds and flour, and mix thoroughly. Chill dough for 1 hour. Preheat oven to 325°. Use your thumbs to coat the inside of small fluted tins with dough. Put flour on your thumbs so the dough doesn't stick to them. Bake for 10 minutes or until light brown. Turn upside down on plain board. Bang tins lightly against board, to make sure that the tarts don't stick. Cool before removing tins. Serve plain or filled with jam and whipped cream.

AMBROSIA CAKE

2 eggs
⅔ cup sugar
4 oz butter
⅔ cup flour
icing:
   ¾ cup confectioner's sugar
   2 tbsp water
   1 tsp lemon juice
   4 tbsp chopped, candied orange peel

Preheat oven to 400°. Beat eggs and sugar until foamy. Melt butter and stir into egg mixture. Add flour. Pour batter into buttered cake pan and bake for about 30 minutes. Stir confectioner's sugar and lemon juice until smooth. Spread evenly over cold cake and sprinkle with orange peel.

TOSCA TORTE

2 eggs
⅔ cup sugar
¾ cup flour
1 tsp baking powder
2 tbsp table cream
1 stick butter
frosting:
   ½ stick butter
   ⅓ cup almonds
   3 tbsp sugar
   1 tbsp flour
   1 tbsp table cream

Preheat oven to 325°. Beat eggs and sugar until the mixture is light and foamy. Sift flour with baking powder and add to egg mixture. Melt butter over low heat and let cool. Add cream and melted butter to batter. Butter and flour a round cake form or frying pan with high sides. Pour batter into pan and cook until it is half-done, about 15-20 minutes.

Meanwhile chop almonds. Combine all ingredients for frosting in a small pan, stirring constantly. Heat until butter is melted and surface begins to bubble. Pour this mixture over the half-done cake and continue baking it until it is done, another 15-20 minutes. Total baking time: about 40 minutes.

SPICE CAKE

2 eggs
⅔ cup sugar
2 tsp cinnamon
1 tsp ginger
1 tsp cloves
1¼ cup flour
2 tsp baking powder
3 oz butter
⅔ cup sour cream

Preheat oven to 350°. Beat eggs and sugar until light and foamy. Stir in spices. Mix flour and baking powder and add to egg mixture. Melt butter and blend into batter together with sour cream. Pour into greased and floured baking pan. Bake for 45 minutes or until done.

ROYAL POTATO CAKE

3 oz butter
¾ cup sugar
3 eggs
3½ oz boiled, cold potatoes (2 medium-sized potatoes)
2 tsp cream of wheat
⅔ cup almonds

Preheat oven to 350°. Grate potatoes or put through a blender. Beat sugar and butter till light and foamy. Add egg yolks and grated potatoes, together with grated or finely chopped almonds. Beat egg whites until stiff and fold into batter together with cream of wheat. Pour batter into well-greased and floured round cake pan and bake for 20-30 minutes or until done. Let cool for 10 minutes before reversing it on a platter. Dust with confectioner's sugar. Can be served warm together with cold whipped cream, vanilla or lemon custard, or ice cream.

SUN CAKE

3 eggs
1 cup sugar
1 cup flour
1 tsp baking powder
5 oz butter
½ cup almonds

Preheat oven to 350°. Beat eggs and sugar until foamy. Mix flour and baking powder and add to egg mixture. Melt butter and stir into batter. Pour into buttered and floured cake pan. Chop and split almonds into halves. Sprinkle almonds over cake and bake for about 40 minutes.

KINUSKI TORTE

Very light sugar cake:
4 eggs
¾ cup sugar
⅓ cup flour
1 tsp baking powder
3 tbsp potato flour or cornstarch
vanilla custard:
    1¼ cup table cream
    2 egg yolks
    2 tbsp sugar
    1 tbsp cornstarch
    2-3 tsp vanilla
kinuski topping:
    2 cups table cream
    1 cup sugar
    ⅓ cup aight syrup
    3 tbsp butter
    1 tsp vanilla

Preheat oven to 400°. Beat eggs and sugar until white and foamy. Mix flour and cornstarch with baking powder and add to egg mixture. Pour into greased and floured round cake pan and bake for 30 minutes or until done. Let cool. Cut into three layers and fill with vanilla custard and tart apple sauce.

Combine cream, egg yolks, sugar and cornstarch in top of double boiler. Beat constantly and simmer until mixture has thickened. Let cool and stir from time to time so that the custard is smooth. Add vanilla to taste.

Combine cream, sugar and syrup, and simmer gently over low heat till sheeting stage (220°) or until a few drops of the mixture form a soft ball when dropped in cold water. Add butter and vanilla. Pour hot over cake and let cool.

CARDAMON MUFFINS
20 muffins

½ stick butter
1 egg
⅔ cup sugar
⅓ cup table cream
1 tsp baking powder
1-2 tsp ground cardamon
¾ cup flour

Preheat oven to 300-350°. Melt butter and let it cool. Beat egg and sugar until the mixture is foamy. Sift or mix flour with baking powder and cardamon. Add half of this mixture to egg and sugar. Add cream. Blend in remaining flour, then carefully add cool butter. Fill batter to ⅔ in buttered and floured muffin tins. Bake for 12-15 minutes. Let cool a few minutes, then remove from tins. The muffins are best while they're still warm, but they contain so much moisture that they can also be reheated.

SWEET YEAST BREAD
48 small buns or 3-5 loaves

The basic ingredients are simple: ordinary, not self-rising flour, yeast, sugar, milk, and margarine or butter. But there is a wealth of different recipes. For special occasions the buns or yeast breads can become quite elaborate. They may contain eggs, lots of butter, raisins, cardamon, cinnamon, candied fruit or orange peel, cream instead of milk, and even saffron.

If you've never made yeast bread, it may seem like an awesome undertaking. Actually it's quite easy. There are two kinds of yeast: fresh (or compressed) yeast and dry powdered yeast. Fresh yeast comes in cakes and should be dissolved in liquid that's about 85°. Powdered yeast requires a temperature of 110-115° for dissolving. If the liquid is too hot, the yeast bacteria will die; if it's too cold, the yeast won't dissolve.

Yeast bread doesn't rise immediately: it takes time for the yeast bacteria to multiply. It can take anywhere from 40 minutes to 2 hours, depending on the temperature of the room: the higher the temperature the faster the dough will rise. If the room where you are working is cool, you can place the bowl containing your dough into a larger bowl filled with warm water. Yeast dough rises more rapidly at high altitudes and has to be watched carefully.

2 oz yeast
2 cups milk
1 stick butter
⅓ cup sugar
2 tsp ground cardamon
1 egg
5½-6 cups flour
1 egg to brush them with
sprinkle with:
    sugar (and chopped almonds)

Melt butter over low heat. Add milk and heat to 85°. Crumble yeast in a large bowl. Pour lukewarm milk over yeast and stir until it is completely dissolved. Add sugar, cardamon and 4 cups flour. Now add egg and gradually work in another cup of flour. Work dough until it begins to leave the sides of the bowl. Sprinkle a few tablespoons of flour on top of dough, cover bowl with a towel and let rise until it is double in size—40 minutes to 1 hour.

Punch down dough with a wooden spoon and knead on a floured board until it is smooth and shiny—about 5 minutes. Shape into buns, loaves etc. Let rise again until the buns or loaves have doubled in bulk. Brush with lightly beaten egg and sprinkle with sugar and almonds. Bake loaves for 20 minutes at 375-400°. Bake buns ar 475-500° for 5 minutes.

YEAST BREAD WITH APPLES

½ batch yeast dough, see index
4 medium-sized tart apples
1 lemon
1 tbsp cinnamon
⅓ cup sugar
⅓ cup chopped almonds
or 6 oz almond paste

Preheat oven to 375-400°. Prepare yeast dough. Roll it and put it into a buttered shallow baking dish. Peel and pare apples, cut them into thin slices and arrange them on top of the dough. Sprinkle with lemon juice, cinnamon, sugar and almonds, or with grated or chopped almond paste. Cook for 25 minutes.

CINNAMON BUNS
50 buns

Prepare dough according to recipe for sweet yeast bread (see index)

Filling:
1 stick butter
⅔ cup sugar
2-3 tbsp cinnamon
brush with:
    1 egg

Preheat oven to 475-500°. When dough has risen once, punch it down, turn it out on a floured board and knead it a few times. Roll out half the dough at a time to a rectangle, ⅛-¼" thick. Spread with butter, sprinkle with sugar and cinnamon and roll it into a roll. Cut slices, about 1" thick and put them into paper cups, cut side up. Let rise on cookie sheets, brush with beaten egg and bake for 7 minutes or until nicely browned.

LENTEN BUNS
10 buns

These large buns are made only during the weeks before Easter. They're cut in half and put together again with a filling of whipped cream and almond paste and eaten on a soup plate together with hot milk and cinnamon. If this seems too exotic to you, the yeast dough recipe is a particularly good one: you can make smaller lenten buns, fill them and eat them for dessert with a cup of coffee.

2 oz yeast
¾ cup table cream
1 stick butter
4 tbsp sugar
1 tsp ground cardamon
½ tsp almond flavoring
1 egg
3 cups flour
brush with:
    1 egg

Preheat oven to 475-500°. Crumble yeast in large mixing bowl. Melt butter over low heat, add cream and heat mixture till 85°. Pour over yeast and stir until it is completely dissolved. Add sugar, cardamon, almond flavoring, egg and about half the flour.

Beat the dough, adding remaining flour a little at a time. (Reserve a few tablespoons of flour to flour the board.) The dough should be smooth and begin to leave the sides of the bowl. Sprinkle a table spoon of flour over the dough, cover it with a towel and let rise until it has doubled in bulk, 40 minutes to 2 hours.

Punch down dough, then knead it on a floured board until it is very smooth. Shape it into ten large (or more smaller) buns. Put them on greased cookie sheets and let them rise till double size. Brush with lightly beaten egg. Bake for 8-10 minutes.

LUCIA BREAD

St. Lucia of Syrakus was a young Christian murdered in the Middle Ages. The young maiden is traditionally remembered in Sweden by the baking of this bread for her holiday on December 13.

1 package dry yeast
½ cup lukewarm milk
¼ cup sugar
3 to 4 cups flour
1 egg
½ teaspoon saffron
½ teaspoon salt
4 tablespoons butter
Extra flour for kneading
1 egg yolk for glazing
Dried currants for garnishing

Dissolve the yeast in 2 tablespoons of milk which has been heated to lukewarm. Mix this with the sugar, flour, egg, and 2 more tablespoons of milk to make a dough. Cover the dough and place it in a warm spot to rise for 15 minutes.

Put the saffron into a bowl with 4 tablespoons of milk. Add the salt. Melt but do not heat the butter. Pour this over the saffron mixture. Add this mixture to the risen dough and knead thoroughly until the dough does not stick to the bowl. Cover the dough and again place it in a warm spot to rest for 30 minutes. If necessary or desired, knead and let it rise again.

On a floured board roll out the dough to ½ inch thick. Shape it into rolls about 8 inches long. These can then be worked into shapes of spirals, pretzels, or crosses. Place them on a greased baking sheet. Glaze them with the beaten egg yolk and dot them with dried currants. Bake them at 425°F for about 15 minutes.

Serve the Lucia bread warm with plenty of butter and hot coffee. Makes about 24 pieces.

WHOLE WHEAT BREAD
1 bread

1⅓ oz (2 cakes compressed) yeast
1¼ cup milk
½ stick butter
1 tsp salt
2 tbsp syrup
2⅓ cup whole wheat flour
1½ cup all purpose flour

Crumble yeast in a large bowl and dissolve in a few tablespoons of cold milk. Melt butter over low heat. Remove from heat and add remaining milk. Now pour this lukewarm mixture into the bowl. Add salt, syrup and whole wheat flour. Gradually add all purpose flour. Beat dough until it is smooth and begins to leave the sides of the bowl. Sprinkle about 1 tablespoon flour on top, cover and let rise until it has doubled in bulk, 30 minutes to 1 hour, depending on the temperature of the room.

Preheat oven to 400°. Grease a loaf pan. Punch down dough, turn it out onto a lightly floured board and knead it until it is smooth. Roll it into an even loaf and put it in the pan. Let rise until it has doubled in bulk. Bake for 40 minutes or until done. Brush the hot bread quickly with cold water. Let it cool a few minutes, remove it from the pan, wrap it in a kitchen towel and let it cool.

LUCIA BUNS
20 buns

Lucia buns are made for the feast of St. Lucie on December 13. St. Lucie is a Catholic saint, a martyr from the 10th century who was blinded rather than betray her faith. How she came to be celebrated in Scandinavia no one knows for sure. Some say she was really a goblin queen worshipped long before the arrival of Christianity. Another story has it that the blinded maiden is a symbol of inner light, making her an appropriate saint to remember when the winter days are short.

At any rate, St. Lucie celebrations are cherished all over Scandinavia. The feast of St. Lucie is both solemn and commercial, funny and serious. The morning of the feast children get up very early and wake their parents with candles and buns. Young girls dressed in white walk in procession through homes, offices, hospitals and schools. They wear a wreath of fir or lingonberry twigs decorated with candles on their heads. Every town chooses one girl to represent St. Lucie.

The deep yellow Lucia buns are appetizing to look at and good to eat. They contain saffron, an exotic spice. Their odd shape is an ancient one. Similarly shaped breads may have been used in sun or fertility rites in a pre-Christian era.

> ½ tsp saffron
> 1 package of yeast
> 1 cup milk
> 1 egg
> 1 stick butter
> ⅔ cup sugar
> ⅓ cup raisins
> 3¾-4 cups flour

Saffron gives all most of its flavor if it is ground. If you own a mortar, grind the fine threads together with 1 tbsp of sugar. You can also crush the saffron on a plate, using a table knife. Mix it with a little bit of sugar; the saffron threads are so fine that they'll stick to a knife or a plate, unless they are first mixed with some other ingredient.

Melt the butter over low heat. Pour the milk into the butter and heat the mixture to 85°. Crumble yeast in a large mixing bowl. Pour a little bit of the milk mixture over the yeast and stir until it is completely dissolved. Add the remaining milk. Now add saffron, sugar and raisins. Beat an egg lightly and mix it into the milk. Then gradually add flour. How to proceed from here, see index for basic recipe for yeast dough. When the dough has risen once and you've punched it down, shape Lucia buns (see picture) and let rise again. Brush with beaten egg and bake them for about 8 minutes in a hot oven, about 500°.

LEFSER

> 3 or 4 potatoes
> ¾ cup cold water
> 1 teaspoon salt
> 3 cups rye flour
> 1 cup wheat flour
> Extra flour for kneading

Peel, wash, and dry the potatoes. Grate them into a large bowl. Add the water, salt, and the flours, and mix well. Let the dough stand covered overnight.

The next day, on a flour-covered board, roll out the dough very thin. Cut it into circles about 6 inches round. Place the rounds at least 1 inch apart on a greased baking pan. (This amount of dough will cover 3 pans.)

Bake at 400°F for 6 minutes. Then turn the lefser and bake it for 6 more minutes.

Serve the lefser fresh with plenty of butter. Makes 12 pieces.

Mexican

SALADS

ADELITA'S CHRISTMAS SALAD
YOLK SALAD DRESSING
- **8 hard-boiled yolks**
- **3 T. olive oil**
- **6 T. claret**
- **2 T. dry mustard**
- **1 finely chopped green onion**
- **⅛ t. pepper**
- **¼ c. vinegar**
- **1 t. salt**
- **1 t. sugar**

Method: Hard boil eggs, 6 min. at least. Mash yolks. Combine with the olive oil, claret, mustard, onion, and pepper. Let stand half an hour. Strain. Add vinegar, salt and sugar. Taste to correct seasoning. Refrigerate until needed. (10 minutes).

CHRISTMAS SALAD
- **For each person:**
- **Lettuce leaves**
- **Large tomato slice**
- **Guacamole**
-    ***or***
- **Minced onion**
- **Round avocado slice**
- **Pomegranate seeds (optional)**
- **Yolk Salad Dressing**
- **Radish rose**

Method: On a large saucer or bread and butter plate, arrange one or more lettuce leaves. Place large tomato slice in center. Place avocado slice on tomato. Fill center of avocado slice with guacamole or minced onion. Pour Yolk Salad Dressing over the mound, and sprinkle with pomegranate seeds. Adorn with a radish rose at side. Time: about 15 minutes for 6 people.

ACAPULCO AVOCADO SALAD
- **3 T. olive oil**
- **3 T. vinegar**
- **1 t. salt**
- **½ t. black pepper**
- **1 t. chile powder**
- **4 green onions, finely sliced**
- **4 medium tomatoes, peeled and diced**
- **2 t. finely minced parsley**
- **4 avocados**
- **1 c. papaya cubes (optional)**

Method: Mix oil, vinegar, salt, pepper, chile powder. Cut tomatoes and onions into a bowl and mix well. Add parsley. Halve avocadoes lengthwise and discard seeds. With a spoon carefully remove most of the meat, being careful not to puncture shells; break up large pieces, and toss the avocado with the tomato mix and dressing. If desired, add papaya cubes also. Chill shells and salad. To serve, spoon salad into shells. Not counting refrigeration, total time: 25 min.
Serves 8.

BREADS & CAKES

PAN DULCE
- **bread sponge:**
- **2 t. sugar**
- **¾ c. lukewarm water**
- **1 yeast cake**
- **1 c. sifted flour**
- **¼ t. salt**
- **remaining ingredients:**
- **¾ c. sugar**
- **1 T. shortening, melted**
- **2 eggs, room temperature, beaten**
- **3 c. flour, sifted**
- **1 to 2 c. flour, sifted**

Method: In a medium-sized bowl dissolve sugar in lukewarm water, add yeast cake, crumbled, and stir until completely dissolved. Add the flour and salt and beat well. Cover the bowl with a cloth and stand it in a warm place (not hot), to rise until double in bulk, about an hour. In large mixer bowl cream the sugar and shortening and add the well-beaten eggs; then gradually add two cups of flour, until thoroughly mixed. Add the third cupful to the bread sponge, and mix well. Add the sponge to the mix in large bowl and beat and stir together with a large spoon. Cover with a cloth and again place in warm spot to rise until double, about an hour. Do not let stand too long; it becomes bitter. Now put 1-½ cups of flower in sifter, although you may not need it all. Flour bread board (or table top) and turn dough out on it. With a quite moist dough, such as this, it is better first to turn it with a spatula. Fold over the dough and sift some flour over it, folding over again with spatula, and continue flouring and folding until more easily handled. Then with floured hands knead thoroughly. To knead, lift the edge of dough farthest from you, fold it to meet the edge nearest you, press down with heels of your hands to weld the edges together, flip dough around so that an unwelded edge becomes bottom edge and knead and punch together, stretch out and continue kneading and punching and folding until dough becomes elastic and silky and no longer sticks to hands or board—incorporating more flour and flouring board as necessary. This takes 5 to 7 minutes. Shape into half-round ball, flat side down. With sharp knife, slice it through once, then directly across first slice, slice again, to make four pieces. Divide these lengthwise, to make eight; then divide the eight to make 16. Using flour on your hands, quickly dip each cut edge into flour on the board, and shape each segment into a round bun. Have two cookie sheets ready. As each bun is shaped, flour its bottom thoroughly and place it on cookie sheet. Leave plenty of space between buns, and arrange 8 to each sheet. Top with Pan Dulce topping (recipe follows). Cover with a cloth and let rise again in warm place until double in bulk, one hour. Bake at 400° until nicely browned on top, approx. 20 minutes. These burn easily, so watch them during last five minutes. When done, turn oven off and let them cool in the oven. Including rising time: 4 hours. Makes 16.

PAN DULCE TOPPING
- ¼ c. shortening
- ¼ c. sugar
- ¼ t. salt
- 1 t. cinnamon
- ¾ c. flour

Method: Cream together shortening, sugar, salt, cinnamon. Add the flour and mix until crumbly. Mixture may be sprinkled over the whole bun, and left rough. If you like this easiest method, first brush milk lightly across the bun to make the topping adhere. Another way: With a sharp knife, slash across the bun to make a slight indentation, and move knife to open it a little—about ½ inch deep. Take a tablespoonful of topping in palm of hand and squeeze it tightly. This should give it a nice shape, plump in the middle and tapered at each end. Press into the indentation. Cinnamon may be omitted.

GORDITAS
- 2 c. Masa Harina
- 2 T. melted shortening or cooking oil
- 1 t. salt
- 1-½ c. boiling water
- Cooking oil for frying

Method: Most supermarkets now carry Masa Harina, the dehydrated masa. Thoroughly mix the Masa Harina, oil, salt, and boiling water. If not rushed, let dough stand for 10 to 20 minutes, to firm. Shape into round, patty-like cakes, the size of uncooked biscuits. Heat ½ inch of shortening in a large pan and fry them until golden brown on both sides, about 3-4 minutes to a side. Use a pancake turner. Time, without standing: approx. 20 min. Makes 16.

PAN DE ADRIANA
- 4 c. flour
- ¾ c. sugar
- 1 c. milk (room temperature)
- ½ yeast cake or ½ pkg. dry yeast
- ½ c. ground almonds
- 4 eggs (room temperature)
- 1 t. anise
- 1 c. lard or butter at room temperature
- 1 c. flour

Method: Sift flour and sugar into a large mixing bowl. Heat milk to lukewarm and dissolve the yeast in it. Stir into flour and sugar. Add almonds, eggs and anise, and beat well with a large spoon. This is too stiff for the mixer. When well-blended, add softened shortening and continue blending with your hand. Squeeze and press together until smooth and even. Place flour in sifter and sift half of it onto bread board. Spread it and empty dough onto flour. Knead and thump and lift dough as described in *Pan Dulce* recipe, until none sticks to board or hands, and most of the flour, or all, has been used. Butter two loaf pans (9 × 5 × 3). Divide dough into two equal parts and shape two loaves. Place in pans and set in a warm place to rise, covered with cloth. Let rise until double, 3-½ to 4 hours. Bake in 350° oven 50 to 60 minutes. This attractive golden bread is delicious, served hot or cold. Two loaves. Time, including 3-½ hour rising time: 4-¾ hours.

EGGS

EGGS WITH CHORIZO
4 links chorizo, or 1 cupful if homemade
1 T. cooking oil
8 eggs

Method: Peel chorizo. In a large pan heat just enough oil to prevent sticking. Fry the chorizo, crumbling it with fork as it fries until it is well-browned, about 10 minutes. If it has released too much fat, reduce to 2-3 tablespoonsful. Break eggs into a bowl, beat slightly with a fork, pour into the chorizo and continue cooking and stirring over medium heat until scrambled to desired consistency. (7-10 min.) These are excellent with hot tortillas or with gorditas. Time: 20 min.

Serves 4-6.

HUEVOS RANCHEROS
4 T. cooking oil
1 c. red or green chile sauce, warmed
8 eggs
Salt

Method: In a large pan, heat cooking oil. In a smaller pan, heat chile sauce. When the oil is hot, break each egg into a saucer and slide it from saucer into hot oil, reducing heat to keep from burning. Fry until whites are well set (hasten this by spooning fat over them.) Remove eggs to warmed deep plates, and pour one or two tablespoonsful of sauce over each. If you wish, pass additional heated sauce. Serve with plenty of hot tortillas. If you use cold sauce, it should be at room temperature, not refrigerator cold, or it will chill the eggs. Time: Approx. 10 minutes.

Serves 4.

INDIAN DISHES

CORN TORTILLAS
2 c. "masa"
or
2 c. Masa Harina
1-½ c. warm water

Method: If you can buy your "masa" already made from a tortilla factory in your vicinity, you need nothing else—unless the masa has grown too dry in which case add a little hot water to make it malleable. Otherwise, use Masa Harina. This is dehydrated "masa" made by the Quaker Oates Company, and I am forever grateful to them for thus making my cookbook possible; before the advent of Masa Harina unless you had a source of masa near at hand it was impossible to indulge in making many recipes described in this book. In a medium bowl, place two cupsful of Masa Harina, and pour the warm water into it. Combine well to make a smooth stiff dough. Shape dough into balls the size of a large walnut. (About ten minutes.) Let stand 20 min. if you have time. It makes them less sticky. Wet and wring out thoroughly two non-terry clean dishtowels. (Or substitute waxed paper.) Spread one on bread board. Place about 3 balls on it, well apart, cover with the second cloth, and roll out as thin as you can without breaking them. It takes practice. Remove to griddle and do the next few. A second method, is to substitute a small smooth board for the rolling pin. Press it down with a firm even pressure on one ball of dough at a time until a perfectly shaped tortilla is formed. Very lightly grease griddle, reduce heat to medium, and bake tortillas on it quickly. When the flat surface of the tortilla ballons up, or begins to blister, turn the tortilla quickly to bake until it ballons or blisters again. About three minutes to each side. Mexican tortilla makers always turn their tortillas with their fingers, so skillfully they never burn them, but for non-Mexican a pancake turner is better. Time (without standing): about 30 min. Makes 12.

LAZY ENCHILADAS

1 can tomato soup
3 eggs
1 t. salt
2 T. chile powder
½ c. grated Romano cheese
½ c. finely sliced green onions
Cooking oil
1 dozen fresh tortillas
Lettuce finely sliced

Method: In blender or mixer, combine tomato soup, eggs, salt and chile powder. Prepare cheese and onions and mix together in small bowl. In large pan over medium heat, heat the oil. Start with 3 tablespoonful and add as needed. It requires about 1 T. per tortilla. Dip tortillas quickly into the soup and egg sauce, and fry 1-½ min. on each side—only until egg is cooked. Remove tortilla to platter with lettuce on it, sprinkle down the middle with onion-cheese, roll up and resprinkle with same mixture. If desired these may be made ahead and kept hot in warm oven for 15 to 20 min., then transferred to their lettuce bed. Time: 30 min.

Serves 6.

ENCHILADAS VERDES

1 head iceberg lettuce
1 large onion
2 green onions
¾ c. grated dry white cheese
2 bottles La Victoria Green Taco Sauce
1 c. cream
1 egg
1 t. salt
1-1½ c. cooking oil
24 tortillas

Method: On a large platter arrange half the lettuce, coarsely sliced. Slice large onion, soak in salt water

½ hour. Drain, dry with paper towels and separate into rings. Finely chop green onions and mix with large onion in bowl. Place cheese in another bowl. Mix taco sauce, cream, egg and salt and warm, but not to point of cooking the egg. In a large pan heat the cooking oil (about ½ inch at a time). Quickly fry as many tortillas as the pan will hold, dipping them first into egg sauce, sliding them into pan and turning them over in the same order of putting them in—they should be limp, not crisp. When the last is turned, remove the first and dip into warm sauce, being sure both sides are coated. Place on paper plate, sprinkle with cheese and onion, fold, slide onto lettuce and continue with second tortilla. If you add a tortilla to the pan each time you take one out, and turn them also as you take out, you run less risk of getting them toasted. Don't let oil run out, nor drain it; they have to be a little greasy to be good. When they cover the lettuce, sprinkle all with cheese and onion and lettuce; then start the second layer on top of them. If any chile mixture remains, pour it over the last enchiladas before sprinkling with all remaining onion, cheese, and lettuce. Serve at once. Time without soaking of onion; about 45 minutes, the first time; with practice, 25-30.

Serves 6-12.

SOPA DE TORTILLA

1 dozen tortillas
½ c. cooking oil
1 large onion, minced
Garlic if desired, finely minced, or use ¼ t. garlic salt
1 large tomato, peeled and crushed
¼ t. orégano, *or* 1 t. finely chopped fresh mint, *or* 1 t. chile powder
1 t. salt
¼ c. grated dry white cheese, Romano and/or Parmesan
2 hard-boiled egg yolks
1-2 T. butter

Method: Cut tortillas in fourths, and fry in hot cooking oil over medium heat only long enough to turn them golden. Remove them and keep them hot. In the same oil used for frying tortillas, fry onion and garlic until limp, add tomato, orégano, mint or chile and salt. In well-greased double boiler top, layer tortillas alternately with sauce and dry cheese; finish with sauce and cheese. On top put a garnish of egg yolks pressed through a sieve, and dot the whole with butter. Cover. Cook over boiling water 30 minutes. Time: 1 hour, 8 min.

Serves 4-6.

BAKED TACOS
    12 tortillas
    3 T. cooking oil
    1 lb. Munster, Jack, Monterey or panela cheese
    1 4-oz. can green chiles
    1 c. sour cream

Method: Grease baking dish. Preheat oven to 350°. Heat shortening over medium flame. Slice 12 strips of cheese. Slice four chiles into 3 strips each, or six chiles into 2 strips each. Dip each tortilla in hot oil, place on paper plate, put a strip of cheese and a strip of chile in it, roll up and place in baking dish. When first layer is finished, sprinkle lightly with salt and make second layer on top, salt, etc. Bake 15 min. Serve with or without sour cream on each taco. You may, if you wish, ladle the cream over the tacos and bake it with them. It's excellent either way. Time: 30 min.

Serves 4-6.

HOW TO MAKE TAMALES

The traditional wrapping for tamales is corn husks, in Mexico called Hojas, which simply means leaves. Some have been handled so carefully that the only preparation needed is a soak in *hot hot* water; but some have corn silk. The best way is to plunge them into very hot water until cool enough to handle, placing a large platter over them to hold them down. The hojas become soft and pliable. Clean them of cornsilk, and scissor off wormy parts. Leave husks in clean hot water until nearly time to use them. Dry between paper or dish towels in dozens as required—2 or 3 dozen each time. Husks broken or too narrow are torn lengthwise into "strings" (about ½ inch wide) for tying up the tamales.

If husks are not obtainable, use aluminum foil cut in pieces about 8 × 10. In Yucatan and Colombia, they use banana leaves. Banana leaves, after cutting in sections, must be boiled briefly before using to make them pliable and prevent splitting. If you use any of these untraditional wrappings, tie them with string. Rubber bands are great, too! If you use waxed paper, use double thickness.

Method of making: Take a corn husk, or if small, two husks and overlap them, to form a shape about 6 × 8 across, and the normal length of the husk. Spread dough over it, leaving exposed about an inch from bottom and three inches from top. Place a slightly mounded tablespoonful of filling on the dough, including some of the liquid. Fold the right section of husk over the middle, and the left to slightly overlap the right; fold up the bottom. Bend the top down toward the middle, and securely tie the resulting package. In Mexico it is general practice to tie each variety in its own pattern for easy identification when serving. For instance, chicken tamales may have a string around each end; beef tamales only one string around the middle. Little sweet tamales almost invariably are made like little purses—the dough placed in the middle of the husk, right edge folded over, left edge folded over, and the top and bottom folded to meet at the top and there be gathered together and tied firmly like a bag pudding. Some space should be left for tamales to expand, which they do while steaming. Steaming time: 1 to 2 hours. When tamales are small and have dough very thinly spread, they may be done even before the hour is up. The thinly spread are the very best. But most of us are inexperienced, and a doughy tamale is not as good as one that has really firmed up, so to be on the safe side, give them 1-½ hours and then break one open to find out what is happening. If you make many, for 10 people or more—you need a large steamer.

Some cooks put a little baking powder in their tamale dough to make it lighter. Some use hot water instead of hot broth, in which case salt must be added, too. Hot broth usually is salted. After mixing the dough, cooks who are very particular about having tamales fine and light beat it for a long time—and here a mixer helps.

BEEF FILLING FOR TAMALES
  ¼ c. cooking oil
  1-½ lb. chopped or ground beef, or chuck or round cut in very small cubes
  1 large onion, minced
  2 large tomatoes, cubed
  1 small bottle olives (any kind except ripe)
  1 can green chiles, or chile powder—1-5 t., or 1 large red chile, deveined, seeded, and ground
  10-15 sprigs parsley, minced
  ½ t. orégano, rubbed between palms
  2 large carrots, cubed
  1 large potato, peeled and cubed
  3 zucchini, cubed—all 3 vegetables dice-sized
  Garlic: (optional) 1-4 cloves
  Fruta en vinagre: 5 or 6 pieces, if obtainable
  Salt and pepper

Method: In a very large pan, in ¼ c. cooking oil, over high heat, stir and fry beef and onions together until beef is browned, about 10 minutes. Reduce heat and add tomatoes, olives and their liquid, chopped chiles; the whole can makes what I call mildly hot tamales, but this only if you extract all seeds. If you use Gebhardt's chile powder, add one teaspoonful only, and after filling is cooked, if too bland, cautiously add teaspoon by teaspoon (dissolved in pan juices) stirring in and tasting until it suits you. Add parsley, orégano, carrots, potato and zucchini, all in small cubes, ¼ to ½ inch wide . . . and garlic. Cover and cook until vegetables are well done and hash is not too juicy. The mix should be juicy otherwise tamales will be dry. The level of liquid should be slightly reduced below level of solids. Taste to correct seasoning. Time: 1 hour.

DOUGH FOR BEEF TAMALES
  recipe for prepared masa:
    6 c. prepared masa
    Water to soften slightly
    2 c. shortening, lard preferred
    1 t. salt
  Recipe for Masa Harina
    3 c. Masa Harina
    1 c. shortening
    3 c. boiling broth (beef preferred) or hot water
    1 t. salt

Method: Heat the shortening with the broth or water and salt, but not if you use prepared masa. Beat it into the Masa Harina. You may use the mixer. If you use prepared masa, work the shortening into it—make it easier by having it at room temperature—then add the salt and only enough hot water to make the masa spreadable. It should be like peanut butter at room temperature in summer. Time: 15 minutes. Makes 50-60 tamales.

FILLING FOR CHICKEN TAMALES
  1 3 lb. chicken
  1 bay leaf
  1 t. salt
  ¼ c. cooking oil
  1 large onion, minced
  1 #2-½ can tomatoes
  10-15 sprigs parsley
  Pinch of saffron
  ¼ t. orégano
  ¼ c. raisins
  ½ c. blanched almonds
  3 carrots cubed small
  3 zucchini cubed small
  1 or 2 small pickled green chiles (optional; but they do make the tamales taste good!)
  1 small bottle green olives, any kind, or ½ c.
  ½ t. cumin seed, ground
  ½ t. coriander seed, ground
  Additional chile powder or chiles as desired.

Method: Put chicken to cook in a large pot with water to cover, bay leaf and salt. Boil until well done, about 45 min. In Mexico the bones are left in it. I remove them; it makes eating the tamales easier and less messy to handle. Deboning chicken usually takes from 20 min. to ½ hour. Reserve the chicken broth for the tamale dough. While chicken boils, in a very large pan heat ¼ c. cooking oil, fry the onion until golden (3 min.); add the tomatoes, well-crushed, the parsley (stems discarded, leaves minced), saffron, orégano, raisins, blanched almonds, carrots, zucchini, salt. If you use the little pickled chiles, even though whole, this may be seasoned enough for you, although it's almost a certainty it will need more salt. Tomatoes are great salt-consumers and so is cornmeal. Simmer the mixture 10 minutes, then taste. If too bland, add moistened chile powder until it suits. A good combination is about ½ t. red hot New Mexican or Cayenne chile with a tablespoonful or two of bland paprika. Simmer uncovered until all the vegetables are tender and mixture well thickened, about 25 min. more. Makes 50-60 tamales. Time: 1 hour.

DOUGH FOR CHICKEN TAMALES

4 c. Masa Harina
3 c. chicken broth, boiling
1 c. lard
1 t. salt (unless broth is salted)

Method: Mix together and beat well. Makes 50-60 tamales.

FILLING FOR PORK TAMALES

2 lbs. pork spare-ribs, farmer style (have butcher separate them and cut into 2 inch lengths)
1 t. salt
1 bottle green taco sauce

Method: Boil spare-ribs in water to cover with 1 t. salt until tender. If desired, add one or two cloves of garlic. When well-done, drain spare-ribs and mix with taco sauce. It is not necessary to remove bones from the meat. Neither is it against the rules. Time: 1 hour. Makes 20-25 tamales.

DOUGH FOR PORK TAMALES

3 c. Masa Harina
2 c. pork broth, boiling
1 c. lard, room temperature
1 t. salt

Method: Mix together. Beat well. Time: 10 minutes. Makes 20-25.

SWEET TAMALES

4 c. Masa Harina
1 c. sugar
1 t. salt
3 inches stick cinnamon, crushed
2 c. lard, room temperature
Boiling water to make soft dough, about 4 c.
1 c. raisins
1 c. blanched almonds, whole or halved
Red vegetable coloring

Method: Mix the Masa Harina, sugar, salt, cinnamon, and add the lard and boiling water; stir and beat until dough is soft but not runny. Add raisins and almonds and beat them in with a spoon. Cool for ease in handling. Just before putting dough into husks, stir in a few streaks of vegetable coloring—about ⅛ teaspoon—do not mix in, stir only a few times, to make dough streaky. Use about a soup-spoonful of dough to each small tamale. Time: 20 minutes. Makes 40 tamales.

WARNING: While the fillings can only improve by being made a day or so before, the doughs never should be made more than an hour or two before cooking, and should be kept warm and spreadable.

FISH

MARINATED FISH

2 lbs. good white fish, boned, fileted
1 large onion, thinly sliced
2 long canned green chiles (Ortega)
4-6 small dried red peppers
2 buds of garlic
1 t. salt
20 to 40 small wild or bitter oranges—they yield very little juice, so 1 grapefruit and lemon or limes may be used instead.

Method: In large pan heat water to boiling, gently add fish fillets; reduce heat but keep bubbling for 15 minutes. Slice onions and separate rings. Juice oranges; and in a small pan simmer the red peppers in just enough water to cover. Drain filets and discard water. Blenderize the red chiles and the water in which they cooked with the garlic and salt. In a large bowl with cover, alternate layers of fish slices, sliced or minced green chile, and red chile mixture, until all the filets are used. Strain the fruit juice over all, or remove the seeds and leave the fruit particles. Make sure fish is totally covered. Refrigerate 24 hours before serving. To serve, drain off sauce and arrange fish attractively on lettuce leaves. This is always served cold; it makes a pleasing dish. Without soaking time: 20 minutes.

Serves 8-10.

RED SNAPPER A LA VERACRUZ

1 attractive red snapper 4 lbs.
Salt, flour, cooking oil
1 clove garlic, minced
1 t. salt
2 large onions, chopped
2 T. parsley, minced
4 large canned or fresh tomatoes
1 bay leaf
2 slices lemon
½ c. stuffed olives (4 oz.)
¼ t. pepper

Method: Be sure all the scales are removed from fish; wipe it gently inside and out with a damp cloth. Dry. Score sides of fish three or four times with a sharp knife. Salt and flour the fish. Heat sufficient cooking oil (about ½ inch in a large pan, olive oil preferred) and then fry the fish over medium heat, first on one side then the other, until golden brown. (About five min. to each side.) The fish will be half-cooked. Transfer it to a well-greased baking pan or roaster, and cover to keep warm. Make sauce: Pour off excess oil from pan in which fish fried, leaving about ⅛ cupful. Reheat, and fry the garlic, salt and onion until the onion is golden. Add tomatoes, parsley, bay leaf, lemon, olives, and pepper. Bring to a rapid boil; reduce heat and simmer 10 to 15 minutes, crushing tomatoes with a spoon. Pour sauce over fish, and set the pan over low heat to season and simmer another 10 or 15 minutes; or place in 350° oven for the same length of time. Time: 45 min.

Serves 8-10.

MEATS

KIDNEYS IN WINE

1 lb. beef kidneys
2 lemons
2 T. cooking fat
1 large onion, minced
2 c. tomato pulp
1 t. finely minced parsley
3 T. green olive bits
¼ t. pepper
1 t. salt
¼ c. sherry

Method: Wash kidneys. Remove fat. Slice kidneys thin and pour the juice of two lemons over them. Stir well. Let stand one hour at room temperature. Drain and dry with paper towels. In large pan, heat the cooking oil, add the onions and cook until transparent, 3-5 minutes. Add kidneys, stir and turn until browned. Cover and reduce heat. Buzz tomatoes in blender and add with the parsley and olives to the kidneys. Simmer until thick, about 10 minutes. Add sherry, stir again, cover and simmer three minutes more. Serve at once. Total time: 1-½ hours.

Serves 4.

TONGUE WITH PRUNE SAUCE

1 large beef tongue (2-½ to 3 lbs.)
2 bay leaves
8 peppercorns
1 t. salt
1 lb. prunes
1 stick cinnamon
¼ c. sugar
¼ c. red dry wine
½ head lettuce, coarsely sliced

Method: Cover tongue with cold water in a large pot. Add bay leaves, peppercorns and salt. Bring to a boil. Reduce heat and cook, covered, for 2 to 2-½ hours—until fork easily penetrates meat at large end. Drain tongue and cool 10 minutes. Reserve liquid for soups. With a sharp knife, remove fat and gristle from large end. Slit skin on bottom of tongue lengthwise. Loosen skin at large end by easing knife under it, and peel it off. The skin removes like a glove when this is done correctly. Discard fat, gristle, bones and skin. Cut in half-inch thick slices. Time: 2-¾ hours.

Prune sauce: Soak prunes in water to barely cover for an hour. When plump, add cinnamon and sugar, and if needed, more water. Bring to boil. Cover, reduce heat and simmer until prunes are tender and syrup thick, about 20 minutes. Remove, drain, and reserve liquid. Discard cinnamon and prune seeds. Mash pulp. Blend in wine and enough of prune liquid to make sauce the consistency of boiled custard. Or place prunes in blender with wine and buzz, adding prune liquid by tablespoonful until right consistency is reached. With seeded prunes and blender, about 3 minutes. Otherwise, 10. Cut lettuce in half and slice one half in ½ inch slices; separate into shreds. Arrange on a large platter. Accommodate whole or sliced tongue on lettuce. Pour prune sauce over tongue, or pass in a gravy-boat to let each serve himself. Total time: 3 hours.

Serves 8.

CHORIZO

    1 lb. ground beef
    1 lb. ground pork (unseasoned)
    3 cloves garlic crushed with 1 t. salt
    ½ t. orégano, finely crushed
    1-3 t. New Mexico chile powder (very hot)
    1 t. coriander, ground
    1 t. cumin, ground
    1-½ t. cayenne pepper (fiery)
    1 t. pepper
    1 t. salt
    ½ c. vinegar
    ½ c. sherry

Method: Place the meats in a large bowl. Grind the garlic and salt in a mortar, add the orégano and seeds and spices, and blend with the garlic. Work in the additional teaspoonful of salt. Add the vinegar and sherry and stir until well blended. Pour all this over the meats and work it in with your hand to mix thoroughly. Be sure to mix very thoroughly, because the vinegar and sherry "cure" the meat and prevent spoilage. Cover with cloth and stand bowl in a cool place until the next day. Divide into serving portions and shape them like fat weiners. Wrap each in a piece of saran wrap. Freeze all you do not plan to use soon. Store the rest in a covered jar in your refrigerator. Let season for at least three days before using. Time: 20-25 minutes. Two pint jars if packed solid without shaping.

MEAT ROUNDS

    1 lb. ground round
    2 large potatoes, peeled and boiled
    1 t. salt
    ½ t. pepper
    2 eggs
    ¼ c. bread crumbs
    ½ c. cooking oil

    1 lettuce, sliced
    2 stalks celery, thinly sliced
    2 tomatoes, sliced
    2 hard-cooked eggs, sliced
    Parsley

Method: Place meat in bowl, mash and add the potatoes, two T. of crumbs, salt and pepper. Mix well with hand. Shape into thin patties, about five inches across—makes 8. Beat egg whites stiff, still beating add yolks, one at a time; remove, and dip patties first into egg batter and then into crumbs. Heat cooking oil and fry patties until browned on both sides, about 7 minutes to a side. Slice lettuce and celery and toss with 3 T. olive oil, sprinkle with 2 T. vinegar and toss again. Spread salad mixture on a large platter. Slice each tomato and each egg into four slices. Arrange fried patties on lettuce, top each with a slice of tomato and a slice of hard-boiled egg. Decorate with parsley sprigs. Serve. Time: 50 min.

Serves 4.

LOIN OF PORK WITH ORANGE SAUCE

    1 large pork roast 5-6 lbs.
    ½ lb. raw ham, cubed
    6 sweet oranges, juiced, or 1 can frozen concentrate
    1 t. salt
    1 t. pepper
    1 T. Worcestershire sauce
    1 c. dry red wine, or cider vinegar, or cider
    1 c. blanched almonds
    ½ c. raisins
    1 t. instant coffee
    Boiling water as needed

Method: Lard the loin with the ham cubes. Press them in as firmly as possible. (About 20 min.) Place roast in deep roasting pan and cover with the juice (reconstituted if not fresh), salt and pepper. Let stand at least an hour; turn over once. Add wine and Worcestershire sauce. Cover and bake at 350° until very tender, allowing 25 to 30 minutes per pound. Thirty minutes before serving, place the almonds and raisins in blender with some of the pan juices and thoroughly grind them, adding the coffee. Pour over the roast and stir into pan juices. If too thick, thin with a little boiling water. Cover and continue cooking. Thirty minutes later the sauce should have the consistency of a thick gravy. If too thin, grind a slice of bread and add to thicken, stir well and cook about 5 min. more.

Serves 12-15.

LIVER AND RICE

4 T. cooking oil
½ lb. liver
½ lb. rice
1 clove garlic
1 dry red chile pepper or 1 T. chile powder
1 bay leaf
1 pinch of orégano
1 t. salt
1 brown onion, minced
3 c. hot broth or water

Method: Heat the oil and brown the liver, garlic, chile, bay leaf, orégano, salt and onion. Add the rice. Add the hot water or broth. Remove to a well-buttered casserole and bake in a 350° oven an hour, or more if you want it thicker. Time: 1 hour, 10 min.

Serves 4.

SPARERIBS IN GREEN CHILE

Method: To each 3 or 4 lbs. of spareribs allow one bottle of La Victoria green (or red) taco sauce. Allow about ½ lb. per person if using this recipe as the main course. If following this complete menu, two ribs per person will do. Buy them farmer style, with plenty of meat. Ask the butcher to chop them into two inch lengths, or do it yourself with a cleaver and sharp knife. Wash to remove any bone splinters. Dry. Heat oven to 350°. Place ribs in a large covered baking pan. If ribs are lean, add a little cooking oil at bottom of the pan. Bake for an hour, or until brown. Uncover and cook ten minutes more. Remove pan from oven and cover ribs with chile sauce. Return to oven for 10 minutes more—15 if sauce is very cold—until sauce bubbles. The meat should be very tender, the fat practically turned to "cracklin's," and the sauce thick. Serve with hot tortillas. Time: 1 hr. 15 min.

PORK CHOPS GRILLED À LA YUCATAN

6 pork chops
Sour orange juice to cover, or orange and lemon juice mixed, or grapefruit juice
½ t. pepper
2 cloves garlic crushed with 1 t. salt
Cooking oil for frying
1 pkg. forzen peas, boiled
1 T. butter
6 sprigs parsley, finely minced

Method: Soak chops in fruit juice, pepper, and garlic salt. Be sure meat is completely covered. Soak two hours (or more). Cook and drain peas. Preheat oven to 450°. Drain chops and dry with paper towels, brush with lard or oil, and broil ten minutes on each side, about four inches from broiler, until done. Fry peas in the butter. Remove chops to serving dish, arrange peas around them, and sprinkle with the parsley. Time (without marinade time): 20 minutes.

Serves 6.

TONGUE WITH BANANA

1 tongue, boiled and peeled (2-½ to 3 lbs.)
1 large brown onion
2 large tomatoes
½ t. cinnamon
¼ t. cloves
1 t. salt
¼ t. orégano
1 T. vinegar
4 T. cooking oil
2 T. raisins
1 T. capers
3 half-ripe bananas, peeled, each in four chunks
3-4 sprigs parsley

Method: Boil tongue until tender, usually 1-½ to 2 hours—once in a while one is tough and takes much longer. It is ready when a fork goes easily into it. Reserve liquid for other recipes. Let tongue cool, to handle easily. Slit outside skin down the center lengthwise underneath the tongue. Now with small sharp knife peel off all outer membrane—it should come off easily as a glove. Remove excess fat, gristle, bones. Slice tongue and keep it warm. In blender buzz onion, peeled and quartered, tomatoes, cinnamon, cloves, salt, orégano and vinegar. Heat oil and pour the tomato mixture into it. Simmer ten minutes. Add the raisins, capers, tongue and bananas. Cover tightly, and simmer ten minutes more. Serve on a large platter with minced parsley sprinkled over it, and parsley sprigs surrounding it. Time, after boiling tongue: 25 minutes.

Serves 8.

PICADILLO

¼ lb. ground beef
¼ lb. ground pork, *unseasoned*
2 T. cooking oil
½ c. finely minced onion
1 c. tomato, chopped
2 zucchini, finely diced
1 carrot, finely diced
1 medium potato, finely diced
A pinch of orégano
Salt and pepper to taste

Method: Mix together the beef and pork, and cook in the heated cooking oil with the onion, stirring and breaking up meat while it cooks so that it is well frizzled. Add the tomato, zucchini, carrot, potato, orégano (rubbed between your palms), and salt and pepper to taste. Cover and simmer until thick, 20 to 30 minutes. Cool. Stuff into peppers, to serve at once; or to cool, refrigerate, and serve later.

BREADED OX-TAILS

1 ox-tail
1 t. salt
½ t. ground cloves
¼ t. cumin (ground)
¼ t. pepper
¼ t. marjoram
¼ t. thyme
2 cloves of garlic, finely minced
1 c. vinegar
2 c. bread crumbs

Method: Allow one ox-tail to each three consumers and ask your butcher to separate the bones. The day before serving, grind the salt and all the spices and garlic together, then blend with the vinegar in a deep bowl and add the oxtails. Stir to make sure each piece is drenched and refrigerate; turn over

with a spoon three times during next 24 hours. Empty all into a cooking pot, and add only such water as may be needed to cover the meat. Bring quickly to a boil, reduce heat, cover and simmer until tender. Remove and cool in its liquid. Drain. Add ¼ t. salt and ¼ t. pepper to crumbs and stir to mix well. Cut pieces of aluminum foil large enough for thorough wrapping of each piece of meat. Butter foil, and sprinkle with crumbs. In remaining crumbs, roll each piece of meat to coat well, lay each on a piece of foil, and wrap carefully. Under 400° broiler, broil each package about 15 min. on each side. Serve in foil. Exclusive of soaking time: approx. 1 hour.

Serves 6.

PIGS' FEET IN ESCABECHE

Pigs' feet (allow 1 to each serving.)
2 bay leaves
2 carrots
1 t. salt
1 egg for each 2 feet
1 t. flour for each egg
½ t. salt
¼ to ½ c. shortening
2 c. red or white wine, dry
¼ c. vinegar
1 T. sugar
1 t. cinnamon
½ t. ground cloves
2 T. toasted sesame seeds

Method: Cook the pigs' feet in water with bay leaves, carrots, and 1 t. salt, until tender (2 hrs.) Remove from water, cool, and discard all bones. Toast sesame seed in small pan over heat, stirring. Pin together pieces of pigs' feet with toothpicks, to be removed before serving. Make chunks about 2 × 2. Beat egg whites until stiff, add yolks slowly, one at a time; still beating slowly add flour. Season with salt. Dip chunks in this batter, and fry until golden on all sides in the heated oil (about ½ inch deep in pan). Remove from pan. There should be about 2 tablespoonsful of oil left; if it looks like less, add some. Add wine, vinegar, sugar and spices to this fat. Bring to boil, return pigs' feet to pan, reduce heat, cover pan. Simmer five minutes. Sprinkle with toasted sesame seed and serve at once. Time: 3 hrs. 35 min.

Serves 8.

SWEETBREADS WITH CHILE SAUCE

2 lbs. sweetbreads
Salt, pepper
¼ c. olive oil or butter
½ to 1 c. green chile sauce

Method: Soak the sweetbreads for an hour in fresh salted water. Drain. Drop them in boiling water, reduce heat and boil gently 5 minutes. Remove and drain. Dry with paper towels. Cut sweetbreads in cubes and sprinkle lightly with salt and pepper (use shakers). Heat the oil or butter, and sauté sweetbreads until golden; add chile sauce and simmer until the sauce begins to bubble. Omitting soaking time: approx. 20 minutes.

Serves 6 adequately, four generously.

TRIPE WITH CHORIZO AND GARBANZOS

1 to 2 lb. tripe
Lemon juice or vinegar
1 veal knuckle
1 c. ham bits or 2 ham hocks
2 links chorizo, peeled
2 cans garbanzo (chick-peas)
2 cloves of garlic crushed with 1 t. salt
1 green bell pepper, deveined, seeded, sliced; or
   1 can chiles verdes sliced
3 cloves of garlic
½ t. salt
⅛ t. cumin seed, ground
A pinch of saffron
8 coriander seeds, ground
1 slice of French bread, about 2 inches thick,
   soaked in 1 c. broth with ¼ c. vinegar

Method: Wash tripe in hot water, rub with lemon juice of vinegar. Place to boil in a five quart saucepan, with veal knuckle, ham, chorizo, garbanzo with its liquid, lemon juice, garlic salt, and peppers: add water to cover. Boil for ½ hour. Extract tripe and cut into one inch squares, return to pot and continue simmering 1 to 1-½ hours longer, until tender. Grind the additional garlic and salt with the cumin, coriander, and peppercorns. Add to pot. Soak the bread in a cupful of the broth from pot with the vinegar, then blenderize and add to pot. (Add a little additional hot water if needed.) Simmer an additional 15 minutes. Serve with lemon wedges, coarsely chopped lettuce, finely sliced green onions, and chile sauce, each in its own bowl. Time: 2 hrs. 15 min.

Serves 10.

POULTRY

TURKEY MOLE

1 turkey, 10-15 lbs.
2 8-½ oz. jars La Victoria Mole Poblano

CHICKEN MOLE

1 large chicken
1 8-½ oz. La Victoria Mole Poblano

Method: Boil fowl in water to cover until tender (1 hour for chicken, 1-½ to 2 for turkey), adding a bay leaf, onion, few cloves of garlic, any or all, as you wish. When fowl is tender, drain, reserving liquid. When cool enough to handle, debone. Cut meat in bite sizes. In very large saucepan, empty the mole; add some of the liquids from pot and stir over medium flame. Add more liquid as needed until all the sauce is the consistency of a good thick gravy, neither like library paste, nor runny. Add meat and about ½ cupful of additional broth, stir well and simmer five minutes. Serve with plenty of hot tortillas. Mole sauce also comes in small cans, dehydrated, but is not as good as the moist kind in jars. Chicken recipe serves approx. 8; turkey recipe, 10-15 . . . more if there is much additional food. Time for sauce: approx. 10 minutes.

ROAST GOOSE OR TURKEY

To prepare fowl, wipe it carefully inside and out with clean damp cloth. Rub with salt. Examine for overlooked pin feathers and singe them off with a lighted match or candle; pluck dark ends of other overlooked feathers with tweezers. Allow 1 lb. of uncooked turkey for each 2 people.

APPLE DRESSING

½ lb. prunes, pitted
½ lb. blanched almonds, halved
10 green apples (pippins) peeled, cored, and
   slightly cooked in
¼ lb. butter (1 stick)
½ lb. pound cake, crumbled

1 t. sugar
1 t. salt
¼ t. pepper
½ t. nutmeg, fresh grated
2 c. cooking sherry (or apple cider)

Method: Boil prunes till soft and discard pits. Or buy pitted prunes and soak in water to barely cover until plump. Blanche shelled almonds by pouring boiling water on them; let stand five minutes, then pop them out of their skins. Slice in halves lengthwise. Prepare apples and cut in bite sizes. Warm butter over low heat in a large pan, and sauté apples until transparent and tinged with gold. Add cake crumbles (not crumbs!), almonds, prunes, sugar, salt, pepper, nutmeg, and sherry. Mix and stir. Cool. (1 hour.) Stuff fowl with this mixture, sew up openings, and roast without peaking. Bake 3-½ to 4 hours for a turkey 6-8 lbs. 7 to 8-¼ for one 20-24 lbs., (before stuffing). Add about 1-¼ hours for each extra four lbs. When well done, leg should be easy to move back and forth. Young goose, 30 min. per lb. 300° oven.

ROAST DUCK À LA MARIA

Preliminary step, for wild ducks only: Stuff a large onion into the body cavity of each duck, and parboil in boiling water for ½ hour. Remove from liquid, drain, cool, discard onions and dry the ducks.

STUFFING *(for one duck)*
2 parboiled medium potatoes, peeled and diced finely
2 carrots, parboiled, diced small
2 turnips, parboiled, diced small
2 raw zucchini, diced small
1 medium onion, chopped fine and fried in 2 T. butter
1 or 2 small red peppers
Bacon strips

Method: Parboil potatoes, carrots, and turnips; peel and dice very small-about ½ inch. Peel and chop onion fine and fry in hot butter until transparent. Remove and discard stems on peppers. Break peppers into small bits. If you object to hot seasonings, let them stay whole, but warn eaters to watch for them and discard them. But do include them; they impart a special flavor to the stuffing. Add onion, peppers, and thin sliced zucchini to the other vegetables. Wash and chop fine the giblets and add to stuffing, and mix with 1 teaspoonful of salt. If domesticated duck, wash inside and out and dry with paper towels; salt and pepper all over, inside and out. Stuff the body cavity with the vegetable mix, and sew. Then stuff as much as possible into the neck skin cavity and either sew it up or fold the large flap of neck skin over the opening and tie it down with a stout cord around the duck's body. Very lightly grease roaster and place duck in it. Arrange strips of bacon lengthwise over breast-side of body, and secure with toothpicks at each end, to discard before serving. Use two smaller strips to fasten across the long ones. Cover and roast in preheated 300° oven 2 hours. Reduce heat to 150°, and cook ½ hour more. Then remove roaster lid and bake yet another ½ hour . . . a total of three hours. Time: 3 hrs. 45 min.

Serves 4.

POMEGRANATE CHICKEN
1 large tender stewing hen
¼ c. cooking oil
1 medium can tomatoes, sieved
1 c. chicken broth
¼ t. ground cloves
¼ t. pepper
¼ t. cinnamon
Pinch of saffron
¼ c. blanched almonds
¼ c. raisins
1 c. Malaga wine
Seeds of 1 pomegranate
Avocado (optional)

Method: Disjoint chicken. Heat oil and lightly fry chicken until brown on all sides. (30 minutes.) Add tomatoes, broth, spices, almonds and raisins. Cover, reduce heat. Boil gently till meat is tender and sauce thickened (25 minutes). Add wine, simmer 5 minutes more. If sauce is soupy, quickly grind 1 or 2 slices of white bread in blender and add to thicken. Remove to platter, pour sauce around it, and sprinkle with pomegranate seeds. Garnish with avocado slices. 1 hour.

Serves 6.

CHICKEN IN ORANGE SAUCE

Chicken, about 3 lbs., disjointed
Salt, pepper
3 T. butter
½ c. blanched almonds
½ c. seedles raisins
¼ t. nutmeg
1 t. salt
¼ t. pepper
¼ t. cinnamon
¼ t. cloves
1 small can pineapple chunks, drained, or fresh chunks
2 c. fresh or frozen reconstituted orange juice
2 T. flour

Method: Sprinkle the chicken with salt and pepper. Brown the chicken in the heated butter (medium flame) add the almonds, raisins, nutmeg, salt, pepper, cinnamon and cloves, pineapple and orange juice. Cover and simmer about 40 minutes. Mix the flour with a very little cold water until smooth, and put through a sieve into the pan juices. Cook and stir until thick, about 5 minutes longer. Time: 1 hour, 20 min.

Serves 4-6.

SHERRIED CHICKEN BREASTS

8 chicken breasts
¼ c. butter (½ stick)
½ c. sherry
4 medium onions, minced
1-2 cloves garlic, finely minced
4 T. parsley, minced
1 bay leaf
3 eggs well-beaten
1 c. bread crumbs
Sauce:
    2 T. butter
    2 T. finely sliced little green onions
    2 T. flour
    1 t. grated lemon peel
    2 c. chicken consommé
    ¼ c. sherry

Method: Over medium heat, fry the chicken breasts in butter until they are well-browned on all sides. Add sherry, onions, garlic, parsley and bay leaf and cover pan. Cook chicken until tender. (20 min.) Remove from heat and discard bay leaf. Remove chicken from sauce to cool until easy to handle, about 15 minutes. With a sharp knife, slit between breast and bone structure, creating a pocket which is stuffed with the drained mixture from pan. If necessary fasten with toothpicks to remove before serving. Beat egg whites stiff; still beating add one yolk at a time. Place crumbs in a shallow bowl. Dip chicken breasts first into egg and then into crumbs. Place on well-buttered cookie sheet, bone-side down, and slide them under 450° broiler for about 5 min., or until browned. Do not turn. Sauce: Melt 2 T. butter in medium sauce pan, add onions and flour, and stir together until onions are transparent and flour blended in. About 3 min. Add the consommé and cook till thick, stirring often—about 5 minutes. Add lemon peel and sherry, stir well, and let thicken again, about 3-5 min. more. Pour over chicken breasts and serve. Time: 50-55 min.

Serves 4-8. (2 to a person, or 1 to a person.)

CHICKEN À LA BELLA MULATA

1 large stewing hen
Water to cover
1 t. salt
½ c. cooking oil
½ lb. pork backbone or spare ribs
¼ c. unblanched almonds
2 thick slices French Bread
2 cloves garlic ground with 1 t. salt
1 medium onion, chopped
4 tomatoes, peeled and chopped
15 sprigs of parsley, minced
1 t. ground cinnamon
½ t. ground nutmeg
½ t. ground cloves
½ t. pepper
1 T. chile powder (mild or hot)
1 t. cumin seed, ground
1 t. coriander seed, ground
1 c. sherry

Method: In a four or five quart sauce pan, boil the disjointed hen with water to barely cover, and 1 t. salt, until well-done. In a very large pan, heat ½ c. cooking oil and fry the pork until nicely brown on all sides. Push to one side and fry the almonds until brown, then the bread. Blenderize almonds and bread. Add remaining oil to the pan. Crush garlic and salt together and fry with the onion until transparent; reduce heat and add tomatoes, parsley, cinnamon, nutmeg, cloves, pepper, chile powder, cumin and coriander seeds. Add almonds and bread, and a cup of chicken broth. Simmer until thick. Add the chicken to the sauce, and if necessary, another half cup or cup of broth. Simmer 25 minutes, or until thick, covered. Then add the sherry, cover, and simmer three minutes more, until it begins to bubble. Serve at once. Time: 1 hour.

Serves 6-8.

GREEN CHICKEN

2 young fryers, disjointed
¼ c. cooking oil
2 T. olive oil
1 t. salt
1 c. water
1 finely minced clove of garlic
4 T. finely minced onion
1 slice of white bread
6 sprigs parsley, finely minced
4 T. cooked peas
1 c. cooked peas

Method: Wash chicken and dry with paper towels. Heat cooking oil and fry chicken golden brown. Add water and salt, cover, reduce heat and simmer until tender, (abt. 45 min. for frying and simmering). In a second pan heat olive oil and fry onion and garlic until golden, about 5 min., push aside and fry bread on both sides. Blenderize the onion, garlic bread, and 4 T. cooked peas, with a little water from the peas . . . about two tablespoonful. Add with the whole peas to the chicken and simmer until thick, about 5 min. more. Serve. Time: 45 min. to 1 hour.

Serves 8.

MOUNTAIN TURKEY

½ large turkey, or 1 small turkey
6 pork chops, deboned & cut into bite sizes
2 cloves garlic, crushed with 1 t. salt
½ t. pepper
½ t. orégano, rubbed between palms
4 c. Masa Harina
2 t. salt

8-10 c. turkey broth
½ lb. butter

Method: Place the turkey and pork in your largest cooking pot, or perhaps your roaster. Add water to cover. Add the garlic, pepper, and orégano. Bring to a rapid boil, reduce heat, cover and cook until turkey is tender (2 hrs.) Keep the meat covered with water throughout cooking; if you need to add water, be sure it is hot. Remove turkey and meat and keep them hot. Measure the remaining broth. Return ten cupsful to the pot. In a bowl moisten the Masa Harina with 4 c. of cold water. Cornmeal, wet thoroughly with cold water, will not lump when added to boiling water. Bring broth again to a boil, empty the Masa Harina, salt, and butter into it, and stir and stir. Taste to correct seasoning. When it becomes very thick, empty half onto a large platter. Distribute the turkey over it, and the pork over the turkey. Empty the rest of the cornmeal over the first layers. Let set 5 minutes before serving.

SAUCES

HOT CHILE SAUCE

Chiles (red, green, yellow) ½ to 1 c.
1 c. tomatillos
1-2 cloves of garlic
1 to 1-½ t. salt
Cilantro (Chinese parsley; coriander herb) to taste (optional)
Limewater (optional)

Method: For this recipe, use fresh chiles, red for red sauce, green for chile verde sauce. Grind together in your blender the drained tomatillos with chiles, first removing the chiles' stems, seeds, and inside white membranes. Add a clove or two of garlic—if you wish. Add salt to taste. If you can find cilantro, add that too, discarding tough stems, until its flavor is noticeable. For a truly hot sauce use a cupful of chiles for each cup of tomatillos; use only a few chiles to begin, taste, and add more as you may wish.

RED CHILE SAUCE

2-6 red chiles
2 large tomatoes
½ large onion, minced
1-2 cloves garlic
1 to 1-½ t. salt
¼ to ½ t. orégano
1 T. lime water

Red chile sauce is as easily made, and is more often used with eggs. Remove chiles' stems, seeds, and inside white membranes. Grind the chiles with one or two large tomatoes, add half an onion finely chopped, garlic if wanted, and salt. Add a pinch of orégano and a tablespoonful of lime water. The quanitity of each ingredient is best determined, as with the green sauce, by the cook. Roughly speaking, use half a cupful of red chiles to two large tomatoes—and you will soon know if you prefer more or less chile.

Either of these raw chile sauces is excellent for Huevos Rancheros. A third sauce, used almost as often, is cooked:

Cooked Chile Sauce: Make the red chile sauce. Heat two tablespoonsful of cooking oil, pour the red sauce into it, and simmer ten minutes. Use hot over the eggs. The other two sauces are used, cold, and the contrast of cold sauce with hot egg is rather pleasant.

NUT SAUCE

½ c. unblanched almonds
½ c. walnut or pecan meats
¼ c. water
¼ t. salt
1 t. sugar
⅛ c. salad oil
⅛ c. vinegar

Method: Blenderize nut meats with the water, salt and sugar. Add the oil and vinegar and buzz half a minute more. Spoon over the peppers. Time for Chiles with Nut Sauce: 1 hour 15 min.

Serves 6-8.

SOUPS

AVOCADO SOUP

4 tortillas
4 T. cooking oil
4 avocados, finely cubed
½ bunch watercress, 1 inch lengths
1 brown onion, minced
1-½ c. tomatoes, cubed (or canned, well crushed)
6 c. beef broth or consommé (or use 6 c. boiling water and 6 chicken or beef bouillon cubes)

Method: Slice tortillas once across middle, then stack and cut in ½ inch strips. Heat two tablespoonsful cooking oil. In this fry the tortillas until golden brown over medium heat. (About 5 min.) Keep them warm. Peel and cube avocados. Discard hard stems of cress and cut the cress into 1 inch lengths. Heat remaining oil, buzz onion and tomato in blender and pour into hot oil. Reduce heat and simmer mixture until thick (10 min.). Heat beef broth in large saucepan. Pour tomato mixture into heated broth; add salt and pepper to taste. Boil rapidly 15 minutes. Place tortillas, avocados and cress in a large tureen; pour boiling broth over them and serve at once. Total time: 40 min.

Serves 8.

VEGETABLE SOUP

2 T. cooking oil
1-½ c. tomato pulp
1 large brown onion, minced
8 c. beef broth (save from recipe below, or use bouillon cubes)
3 turnips, cubed
3 carrots, sliced thin across
½ c. peas
1 c. string beans, 1 in. lengths, or ½ pkg. frozen string beans, French style
2 T. tapioca

Method: Heat oil, add tomato pulp and onion buzzed together in blender; simmer until thick, about 10 minutes. Add to the beef broth with all the vegetables. Season to taste with salt and pepper. If broth is unseasoned, this will take about two t. salt, ½ t. pepper. When boiling starts, sprinkle in tapioca gently. Reduce heat and cook about ½ hour more, until vegetables are tender and tapioca transparent. Time: 45 min.

Serves 8.

ARTICHOKE SOUP

8 artichokes or 1 can (14 oz.) artichoke hearts
1 large onion
2 quarts milk
3 T. butter
2 T. flour
1 t. salt
¼ t. pepper
2 egg yolks
1 c. oyster crackers

Method: Wash artichokes thoroughly. Remove and discard outer leaves. Scrape "choke" from the hearts, cut hearts in halves. Peel and slice the onion. Buzz hearts and onion with ½ cup of milk in your blender. Heat the butter, add the flour and stir to a paste; then add the artichoke mixture. Stir until thick, about five minutes. Heat the rest of the milk and add the artichoke mixture; stir well, and season with salt and pepper to taste. Lightly beat the egg yolks and mix a little of the heated soup with them, then add yolks to the soup. Stir well. Serve with oyster crackers sprinkled over the top. Total time: approx. 25 minutes.

Serves 8.

BEEF AND POTATOES

10 c. water
3 lbs. top round
3 medium potatoes, boiled, peeled, cubed
3 T. cooking fat
1 slice of bread
½ c. peanuts without skins (or 4 T. peanut butter)
1 clove garlic, finely minced
1 large onion, finely minced
2 c. tomato pulp
3 whole cloves
1 t. cinnamon
2 t. salt
½ t. pepper

Method: In a five quart pot bring water to a rapid boil and plunge in the meat, add the washed un- peeled potatoes. Reduce heat and simmer gently un- til beef is tender, about two hours. When potatoes are done (test with fork) after first 20 min., remove them, peel and dice. While meat cooks, heat oil in a small pan. Fry the bread and peanuts until golden, then buzz them in your blender, adding a little broth if necessary, along with the garlic, onion, tomatoes, cloves, cinnamon, pepper and salt. Return to the pan in which the bread and peanuts fried and simmer until thick, about ten minutes. When the meat is tender, remove and slice it. In a large pan place two cups of the broth, add the tomato mixture, the meat slices, and the potatoes. Bring to a rapid boil, cover, reduce heat and simmer an additional ten minutes, or until sauce thickens. Should it be too watery still after fifteen minutes, quickly grind and add another slice of bread, stir well and simmer only long enough to rectify the wateriness—4 or 5 minutes. Approx. 2 hours 20 minutes, including boiling.

Serves 8, generously.

FOAM SOUP

½ c. butter (¼ lb.)
1 c. flour
1 t. baking powder
6 t. grated Romano cheese
3 eggs
4 c. chicken or meat broth
1 can tomato soup *or* 1-½ c. tomato juice (depending on whether you want soup thick or clear)
⅛ t. orégano
¼ t. pepper

Method: Melt butter. Blend in flour, baking pow- der and cheese. Remove from heat. Beat egg whites until very stiff. Still beating, add one yolk at a time, being sure each blends in before adding the next. Still beating slowly, add flour and cheese mixture, a little at a time. (10 minutes.) Heat the broth and combine tomato soup (or juice) with it. Add orégano and pepper. When boiling, drop in egg and cheese mix, a teaspoonful at a time. Makes 16. (10 minutes.) Cover tightly, reduce heat so mixture won't boil over, and cook 10 minutes. Sever in large tureen, as soon as done. Time: 30 min.

Serves 8.

CAPIROTADA

1 loaf French bread (1 lb.—the long kind, about two feet)
½ c. cooking oil
4 c. water
4 large tomatoes, peeled and cubed, or 1 #2-½ can tomatoes
1 large onion, minced
2 c. sugar
5 cloves
1 stick cinnamon (abt. 3 in.)
4-6 tortillas
¼ c. blanched almonds, halved
¼ c. raisins
½ c. grated dry cheese—Romano or Parmesan

Method: Cut loaf in half through center lengthwise, between upper and lower crusts. Cut halves into four or five inch sections. In a large pan heat cooking oil and quickly fry top and bottom of bread; try not to burn it. You may need more oil; the bread soaks it up hungrily. Grease a large (17 × 12 × 2-½) pan with butter; grease tortillas on *both* sides and cover the bottom of the pan with them (prevents sticking.) Arrange the fried bread in the pan. In two quart pot, bring the water, tomatoes, onion, sugar, cloves, and stick cinnamon well crushed, to a boil. Reduce heat slightly, and boil vigorously until reduced to half, about an hour. Pour syrup over bread in pan, being sure that each piece is well covered, then sprinkle with raisins and almonds and grated cheese. Cover with aluminum foil, and bake in preheated 350° oven 20 minutes; remove foil, and bake 5 minutes more. Total time: approx. 1 hour, 45 min. Serves 10 amply, 12 to 14 adequately.

POTATO SOUP

3 large potatoes, peeled and grated
¼ c. cooking oil
2 c. tomato pulp
1 large onion, minced
2 T. cooking oil
3 c. broth, meat or chicken
¼ c. grated dry white cheese—Romano or Parmesan

Method: Peel and coarsely grate potatoes, plunge into salted water for ten minutes. Remove and dry with paper towels. Heat ¼ c. cooking oil and fry the potatoes to golden brown: about ten minutes. Drain excess grease and keep potatoes warm in a large tureen. Blend the tomato and onion. Heat the 2 T. oil and in it simmer the tomato mixture until thick, about ten minutes. Heat broth, add tomato mixture, and boil 15 minutes. Add grated cheese, and pour over the potatoes. Serve at once. Time: 55 minutes. Serves 8.

ZUCCHINI SOUP

6 large tender zucchini
1 quart whole milk
4 T. butter
1 t. salt
½ to ¾ t. black pepper
Oyster crackers (optional)

Method: Wash whole zucchini and parboil unpeeled in water to barely cover, until fork-tender, about ten minutes. Remove zucchini and discard stems. Crush zucchini roughly with fork or potato masher. Leave some lumps. Return to cooking water, with milk, butter, salt and pepper. Bring to boiling point. Serve. Similar to oyster soup, this takes equally well to oyster crackers or crisp soda crackers. Time: 20 min. Serves 6.

WHITE BEAN SOUP

2 c. white beans
3 strips of bacon
2 c. tomato pulp
1 brown onion, minced
1-½ t. salt
¼ t. pepper
2 slices bread
2 T. butter

Method: Soak beans overnight. Cook in same water three hours, or until tender. If more water is needed to keep beans covered, be sure it is boiling. Drain beans; return liquid to pot. Blenderize beans a cupful at a time, adding some of their liquid to make blending easy. Return to pot. Fry bacon until crisp, and drain. Reserve the fat. Buzz the tomato and onion in the blender. Heat two tablespoonful of the bacon fat and simmer the tomato mixture until it thickens, about ten minutes. Add to soup. Cut the bread into small cubes, heat the butter, and fry the bread, stirring, until golden—3 to 5 min. Add with crumbled bacon to soup and serve at once. Time, exclusive of soaking beans: 3 hrs. 25 min.

Serves 8.

OXTAIL SOUP

1 oxtail
2 qts. water
2 c. cooked and ground garbanzo, or 1 15-oz. can, drained
¼ c. cooking oil
1 t. salt
1 medium onion, finely minced
¼ t. pepper
½ to 1 T. finely minced parsley
Lemon wedges and/or chile sauce

Method: Place oxtail in water to boil. When it comes to a boil, reduce heat, and cook until meat is tender—at least two hours. Cool. Pick meat from bones and discard bones and excess fat. Return meat to broth. If you cook the garbanzos yourself, soak them overnight. Change waters and boil until tender and easily crushed between fingers. Drain. Buzz in blender with a little of the broth. Add garbanzos to meat. Heat cooking oil and fry onion until golden brown, and add. There should be about eight cups of soup; if necessary, add a little hot water. Season with salt and pepper. Bring to boiling point, add parsley, and serve, passing lemon wedges and chile sauce to enhance flavors. Time: With canned garbanzo, 2-½ hours.

Serves 8-10.

CARROT SOUP

1 large onion, minced
½ medium can tomatoes or 2 tomatoes, diced
4 to 6 large carrots
4 to 6 c. water or consommé
¼ c. cooking oil

Method: Mince onion, dice tomatoes. Wash carrots and remove any imperfections. Place water or consommé to boil. Sauté onion in heated oil until tender and transparent; add tomatoes and simmer until thick. Add tomato mixture and carrots (whole, unpeeled) to broth, or boiling water. When carrots are fork-tender, remove and crush them roughly with

a fork and return to soup. Salt and pepper to taste. Time: 30 min.

Serves 8.

LENTIL SOUP

6-8 c. water
1 c. big lentils (½ lb.)
2 T. cooking oil
2 c. tomato pulp, canned if fresh
1 large onion, minced
3-5 tender zucchini
2 large, or 3 medium, underripe bananas
1-2 t. salt

Method: In large pot put cold water and lentils on high heat. When boiling starts, reduce heat to medium. Cook two hours. At end of 1-½ hours, heat cooking oil, fry onion until transparent, add tomato and cook 10-15 min. Empty into soup. If water level has reduced greatly, add enough hot water to insure 6-8 c. broth. Slice zucchini into soup. Remove both ends of bananas and slice, unpeeled, in thin rounds into soup. Cover and continue gently boiling until serving time; add salt, taste, stir well and serve. Time: 2 hours.

Serves 16.

CREAM OF CORN SOUP

4 egg yolks
1 qt. milk
4 T. cornstarch dissolved in ¼ c. cold water
4 T. butter (optional)
2 c. tender young cooked corn or 1 can cream style
2 canned green chiles (Ortega)
1 t. salt
¼ t. black pepper
¼ to ½ t. fresh ground nutmeg

Method: Beat yolks into milk in double boiler top over boiling water. Stir often. Blenderize corn and chiles, and add to milk and egg. Add cornstarch. Stir until mixture coats the spoon, in 5 to 7 minutes. Do not overcook or it will separate. Pass through sieve to remove unwanted particles, return to pot, add salt, butter, pepper and nutmeg. When again hot, serve with croutons. Time: 15-20 minutes.

Serves 8.

CALDO ACAPULCO

soup:

2 T. cooking oil

1 medium onion, finely minced

2 c. tomatoes, diced

6 sprigs cilantro (Chinese parsley; coriander herb) or pinch of orégano

4 c. boiling water or consommé

noodles:

½ c. Masa Harina

1 t. chile powder

½ t. salt

⅛ c. cooking fat

½ c. water

Method: Heat the oil and gently sauté the onion until golden. Add tomatoes and simmer until thick, 10 minutes. Buzz the mixture in your blender or press through sieve. Add cilantro, stems discarded, finely minced. Bring consommé to a boil, add tomato mixture. Let it simmer while you make the noodles: Sift the Masa Harina, chile powder, salt and baking powder, or simply stir them in a bowl with a spoon. Add water a little at a time and stir thoroughly; you want a stiff dough. Pat dough into thin tortillas, about 3 inches across. Spread on bread board to dry for ½ hour. Slice into strips ½ inch wide. Heat remaining cooking fat; fry strips golden brown. Keep hot and add to soup at the moment of serving. Time: 45 min.

Serves 6.

FRIJOL SOUP

4 to 6 c. pinto or pink bean broth

1 to 2 c. puréed beans

2 T. cooking oil or bacon fat

1 large onion, minced

2 c. tomatoes, peeled and puréed or chopped

½ t. orégano or 2 or 3 sprigs of parsley minced fine, or both

Croutons, 2 T. for each serving, or large slice of French bread fried, for each serving, 2 T. butter for each slice

Grated Romano and/or Parmesan cheese

Method: Follow recipe for cooking frijoles. Drain and measure 6 c. broth to return to pot. If you don't have enough, add hot water to extend broth. Purée beans in blender and add to pot. Heat cooking oil or fat, sauté the onion until transparent, add tomatoes and simmer ten minutes, until thick. Add orégano, rubbed between your palms, or parsley. Now add tomato mixture to soup. Bring to boil, reduce heat, and continue boiling gently about 5 minutes. Serve. Place croutons of fried bread in serving bowl, or individual soup bowls, and pour soup over them. Time, exclusive of bean cooking time: 20 min.

Serves 10.

CHONA'S ALBONDIGAS

caldo:

6-8 c. water

1 large soup bone

¼ to ½ head cabbage, in wedges

1-2 large onions, quartered

1 tomato, cubed

10-15 sprigs cilantro (Chinese parsley) or parsley

2-3 cloves garlic

½ can garbanzo (optional)

salt to taste

albóndigas:

1 lb. chopped beef, or

½ lb. ground round and ½ lb. ground pork, unseasoned

6 sprigs fresh mint, stem discarded, finely minced or

½ to 1 t. orégano, rubbed between palms

¼ c. rice

1 egg

1 t. salt

Method: Make classic Mexican soup—caldo—in 5 to 8 qt. pot. In it put the water and soup bone, bring quickly to a boil, add all the other ingredients listed in the first column, reduce heat and let boil gently until meat on bone is tender. For the albóndigas, combine the two meats (if you use pork also) in medium bowl, punch hole in center and into hole put the mint, rice and egg, then mix and squeeze by hand until ingredients are combined. Add salt and work again. Shape balls size of a large walnut. Drop into the boiling soup about ½ hour before serving time; cover pot. Serve albóndigas with hot French bread, hot tortillas, or both; also pass lemon wedges, chile sauce, and bananas to add to the soup if desired. Time: 1 hour.

Serves 8.

SOPA DE JOCOQUE

  2 c. cooking oil or bacon drippings

  2 large onions, minced

  1 or 2 cloves garlic, finely minced

  1 #2-½ can tomatoes, crushed

  2 dozen fresh corn tortillas

  1 lb. Cheddar cheese, ⅛ in. thick slices

  4 oz. can Ortega green chiles, sliced in strips

  4 oz. can pimentos, sliced

  1 qt. buttermilk

  Salt, as desired (about 1 T.)

Method: Preheat oven to 350°. Grease liberally a large pan (17 × 11-½ × 2-½). Heat oil or drippings and sauté the onions and garlic, add the tomatoes and cook until mixture thickens, about 10 minutes. Place a layer of tortillas in the bottom of the pan. You have to tear some of them in halves or quarters to cover the bottom. Place a slice of cheese on each tortilla and parts of slices on torn sections; sprinkle all heavily with sauce, lightly with salt; distribute a strip of chile and one of pimento as you did the cheese; pour buttermilk over all to cover thinly. Repeat the operation until all the tortillas are used, cover with all of the leftover sauce, cover with all the buttermilk, and arrange the prettiest slices of cheese, chiles and pimento in a pleasing design on top. Place aluminum foil over the pan and tuck in the edges to seal. Bake one hour. Remove foil during last ten minutes to allow light browning. Time: 1 hour, 25 min. Serves 6 heartily, unless used as a substitute for rice or potatoes at a big meal: then it serves 12.

POTATO-BALL SOUP

  potato-balls

   ¼ lb. potatoes

   ½ t. grated nutmeg

   2 T. butter

   1 egg

   4 T. butter

  soup

   1 medium onion, minced

   2 T. butter

   1 medium tomato, well-chopped

   1 chile verde, chopped

   ¼ t. nutmeg

   4 hard-boiled egg yolks, mashed

   4 to 6 c. hot meat or chicken broth, or consommé

Method: Boil, peel and mash the potatoes. Mix with nutmeg, 2 T. butter, and egg. Between two spoons, shape into about 18 balls the size of a walnut, and fry in 4 T. butter until brown. Keep them warm. Soup: In remaining butter, fry the onion until transparent; add tomato, chile verde, nutmeg and yolks, and simmer until the tomato is cooked, about 15 minutes. Add to the hot broth. Add potato balls and serve at once. Time: 1 hr.

Serves 6-8.

TOMATO SOUP

  6 large ripe tomatoes, or 1 #2-1/2 can tomatoes

  ½ lb. chopped ham, raw

  4 c. chicken or beef broth

  1 pkg. frozen young peas, or 1 small can French peas

  Salt, pepper, to taste

Method: Boil tomatoes until tender in the least possible amount of water; or use canned. Press through sieve to remove skin and seed, or buzz in blender. Fry ham, which should have some fat, until well browned. Combine tomatoes with broth in a large pot, add ham, bring to a boil. Reduce heat. Simmer 15 min. During the simmering add peas, and salt and pepper to taste. Total time: 30 min.

Serves 6.

ZUCCHINI-TOMATO SOUP

  4 to 8 tender zucchini (6 to 7 inches)

  Water to cover

  2 T. butter

  1 T. onion flakes

  2 cans tomato soup

  ¼ t. pepper

  Oyster crackers or croutons

Method: Boil zucchini until tender in water to cover in a 3-4 qt. pot, about 10 min. Remove zucchini, and crush roughly. Return to water in pot (there should be about 4 cups). Add soup and stir thoroughly. Heat butter and sauté onion flakes until golden. Add with pepper to the soup. When it boils again, serve. This is very good with oyster crackers or croutons. Time: 25 min.

Serves 8.

WINE SOUP

    2 T. olive oil or butter
    1 small onion, finely minced
    2 T. flour
    1 medium tomato, peeled and chopped
    5 c. chicken or meat broth, heated
    3 hard-boiled eggs, quartered
    2 t. salt
    ½ t. pepper
    2 slices bread
    2 T. butter
    1 c. red wine or claret

Method: Heat oil or butter, add onion and fry over medium heat until golden. Blend in flour until smooth, then add tomato. Cover tightly and simmer 10 min. Add tomato mix to heated broth; reduce heat and simmer ten minutes more. Add salt and pepper; taste to correct seasoning. Cut bread into cubes. Heat the butter, and fry the bread, stirring, until it has browned nicely. About 3 min. for two slices. Add the fried bread, the eggs and wine to the soup and serve at once. Time: 25 min.

Serves 8.

POOR MAN'S SOUP

    6 slices dried bread
    ½ c. olive oil
    1 T. cooking oil
    1 medium onion, minced
    1 clove garlic, minced
    1 c. chile sauce, red or green
    1-½ c. milk
    ½ c. soft cheese, white, Provolone, cottage, goat
        cheese Munster or Jack
    Salt to taste

Method: Spread the bread slices out to dry an hour or two before you begin. Cube bread slices. Heat olive oil and fry the cubes, stirring constantly to prevent burning, until golden brown. Remove to a bowl and keep them warm. In the same pan heat the cooking oil and fry the onion and garlic until transparent. Add chili sauce and milk, and bring quickly to a boil. Add the cheese. Stir only until cheese begins to melt; then divide croutons into small bowls and pour the soup over them. This is very rich—hence the small bowls. The chile may be decreased to ½ cupful or

less, and milk increased to compensate. Time: about 20 min.

Serves 6.

RICE STEW

    3 c. chicken broth
    1 c. rice
    ½ c. cooked ham, cubed
    1 link chorizo, peeled and sliced, or Polish
        Kohlbase, or ½ c. home-made chorizo
    Salt (only if needed)

Method: Heat chicken broth to boiling, add rice, and half of the ham and the chorizo. Reduce heat, cover tightly, and simmer 20 min. or until rice is tender. Taste, and add salt if needed. Grease a casserole. Place half the rice in it, the rest of the meats mixed together, and cover with remaining rice. Cover and bake 30 min. at 350°. Time: 55 min.

Serves 6.

VEGETABLES

VEGETABLE SOUFFLE

    2 medium-sized carrots
    1 small turnip
    2 medium-sized zucchini
    3-4 cauliflower florets
    1 c. peas
    5 eggs
    3 T. flour
    3 T. Cheddar cheese, grated
    ½ c. cream
    3 T. bread crumbs

Method: Preheat oven to 350°. Slice vegetables very thin. Florets should be about ½ cup. Peas may be canned. Cook the vegetables (except peas) together in ½ cup water, with tight lid on utensil so that they steam more than boil. At end of 15 minutes, add fresh peas. If peas are canned, drain them. At end of 5 more minutes, drain vegetables thoroughly; reserve water to make soup. While draining, separate whites of eggs into large mixer bowl, yolks into smaller one. Beat whites very stiff. Beat yolks stiff, and still beating, add flour, cheese, and cream. Mix all vegetables into the yolk mixture. Liberally butter a two quart casserole; press crumbs firmly into the butter. Combine yolk mixture with whites, pour into casserole, and bake, uncovered, in a large pan with water in it, for an hour. Serve in the casserole. Time: 1-½ hours.

Serves 6-8.

TURNIPS WITH MILK
   8 medium-sized turnips
   ⅛ lb. butter (½ stick)
   2 T. flour
   1 c. milk
   ½ t. salt
   ⅛ t. freshly ground pepper
   ½ to 1 t. freshly grated nutmeg

Method: Boil turnips until tender. Cooking time depends on size. When fork easily goes into largest turnip, they're done. Peel, slice into cubes about ½ inch square. Melt butter over medium heat. Blend in flower, add milk and seasonings, and stir until thick (5 min.) Taste to correct seasoning. Add turnips, and serve. Time: 25 min.

Serves 8.

POTATOES WITH RICOTTA
   6 medium potatoes, peeled
   2 T. cooking oil
   1 clove garlic, finely minced
   1 t. salt
   1 can minced green chiles (Ortega)
   ¼ lb. ricotta cheese or Mexican requesón

Method: Boil potatoes in water to cover until tender, about 20 minutes. Drain well. Slice in thin slices. Peel and finely mince garlic. In a large pan, heat the oil. Add garlic, reduce heat and simmer 3 min. or until garlic is transparent. Add potatoes. Add chiles with their liquid, and salt. Stir well, cover, and simmer for ten minutes. Stir several times to prevent sticking. If very dry, add one or two tablespoons of very hot water. Taste to correct seasoning. Stir in cheese, remove to serving dish and serve at once. Time: about 40 minutes.

Serves 8.

CORN PATTIES
   sauce
      1 T. cooking oil
      1 small green onion, sliced thin
      2 canned green chiles, minced
      1 can tomato soup, undiluted
      ½ lb. fresh cheese (Jack or Muenster preferred) finely chopped
   patties
      4 ears of tender corn
      4 T. sour cream
      2 eggs
      3 T. flour
      ½ c. cooking oil

Method: Heat cooking oil, add onion. When onion is transparent, add the chiles and soup; stir and simmer 10 min. Keep warm. Prepare cheese, but do not add. To make the patties, clean corn thoroughly and slice from ears. Use potato-peeler; slice half way down the cob very lightly to remove tops of kernals, then again go over it with a heavier stroke until all the grains yield their edible portions—then repeat with the second half. Blenderize corn. Transfer to mixer and beat in the cream, eggs, and flour. Heat the oil and drop the mixture in by tablespoonsful. Brown well on both sides, about 2-3 min. to each side. Place in deep dish to conserve heat. Reheat tomato sauce, add cheese, stir well and pour over the patties. Makes 20. Time: 25 minutes.

Serves 8.

CARROTS COOKED IN MILK
   6 to 8 medium carrots
   1 c. evaporated milk
   1 t. sugar
   ½ t. pepper
   1 t. salt
   3 T. butter

Method: For fast cooking, select nice tender young carrots—crisp ones, with tips that do not bend flexibly. Wash but do not peel. Slice very thin in rounds. Grease a quart and a half casserole, place carrot slices in it, cover with milk, add sugar, pepper, salt and butter. If needed, supply a little more milk. Bake covered at 450° until tender, ½ hour.

Serves 6.

STUFFED ZUCCHINI

12 tender zucchini
½ lb. soft white cheese, Jack, cream or Muen-
ster cut in strips to fit zucchini
2 eggs
1 t. salt
½ t. pepper
2 t. flour
Fat for frying

Method: Parboil zucchini in boiling salted water for five minutes. Cut in halves, carefully remove centers with spoon, place strips of cheese in halves and fill with zucchini pulp, then fasten each two halves together with toothpicks, to remove before serving. Beat whites of eggs very stiff, still beating add yolks, slowly, one at a time; then salt, pepper, and flour. Heat oil for frying (about ½ inch in pan). Dip zucchini in egg batter and fry until well browned on both sides. Time: 20-25 minutes.

Serves 4-6.

ASPARAGUS WITH ALMOND SAUCE

1 bunch new asparagus, or 1 large can aspara-
gus tips, or 1 pkg. frozen asparagus
⅛ c. cooking oil or butter
10 unpeeled almonds
4 little green onions, minced
1 large onion, minced
2 slices dark whole wheat bread (best, but white
serves)
2 sprigs parsley
½ c. water
1 t. salt

Method: Wash asparagus and snap off woody ends of stalks. Cook until tender. A large coffee pot is ideal for cooking asparagus—put in enough water to boil the hard ends, and let rest of stalks steam. (15 min.)

Sauce: Heat shortening and fry almonds to a dark brown. Remove almonds and in same fat fry the bread until golden on both sides. You may have to add more shortening. Remove bread and set pan aside. Grind bread and almonds together, with ½ c. water. Return pan to heat, replenish oil or butter if needed, and gently sauté the finely minced onions (include some of small onions' green stalks) until transparent (3-5 min.) Add the bread and almond mixture, minced parsley, and salt. Bring to a quick

boil, reduce heat and simmer 10 minutes, or until thick. Serve very hot over well-drained asparagus. Time: 40 min.

Serves 6.

BANANAS IN WINE

6 red cooking bananas, or underripe bananas,
peeled, cut in half, and halved lengthwise
¼ c. butter (½ stick)
½ c. sugar
1 c. red wine

Method: In a large pan heat butter over medium heat. Fry banana slices on each side until they brown. Time depends on size and variety of bananas, state of ripeness, and heat applied. Probably 25 minutes. Place slices fried first in deep bowl to conserve heat, and when all are fried, add the sugar to the pan and stir briskly until all the sugar melts (be careful not to burn). When sugar has caramelized, add the wine (if you warm it first it will sputter less.) Turn heat low and return all bananas to the pan to simmer until the sugar melts into the wine; 15 min. or less—then remove bananas again to deep, warm serving dish and pour the syrup over them. Serve at once. Time: 30 min.

Serves 6.

EGGPLANT ACAPULCO

1 large eggplant
1 large brown onion, minced
1 clove garlic, minced
2 sprigs parsley, minced
3 T. butter
1 c. bread crumbs
6 T. grated Romano cheese
⅛ t. pepper, ½ t. salt

Method: Slice eggplant in half lengthwise. Soak halves one hour in salted water. Remove and plunge into boiling water, cover, and parboil ten minutes. Remove, drain, cool. Peel and mince the onion, garlic and parsley (omit stems). Heat butter and sauté the onion, garlic and parsley until onion is transparent (7 min.). Measure ¾ of the crumbs into a bowl, and mix in the onion mixture. Carefully remove eggplant pulp to leave shells about ½ inch thick. Chop pulp and combine with the crumbs, 3 T. of the cheese, salt and pepper. Butter a casserole and arrange the shells in it. Fill shells with eggplant mixture, mounding well; combine remaining cheese and crumbs and pat over the tops of the mounds. Bake in 350° oven until crumbs are nicely browned (20 min.). Time exclusive of soaking: 45 min.

Serves 2 generously.

POTATOES PARADISE

6 medium potatoes, boiled, peeled, mashed
½ c. butter (1 stick)
½ c. sugar
½ c. grated white dry cheese (Parmesan, Romano)
1 c. milk
4 eggs, beaten
1 t. salt
½ t. pepper
½ c. bread crumbs

Method: Slowly and in the folowing order stir into the mashed potatoes the butter, sugar, cheese, milk, beaten yolks, salt and pepper, then fold in stiffly beaten whites. Liberally butter a casserole and pat all the bread crumbs into the butter. Pour in the potato mix and place in the oven at 350° in a large pan of hot water. Bake 1 to 1-½ hours until golden on top and firmly set (test it as you might a cake). Run a spatula around edge of potatoes, and unmold carefully onto a large platter. Time: 1 hr. 45 min. to 2 hrs. 15 min.

Serves 8-10.

PEAS WITH LETTUCE

⅛ lb. butter (½ stick)
½ head iceberg lettuce, chopped
1 pkg. frozen peas
½ t. sugar
¼ t. pepper
½ t. sweet basil
½ c. beef or chicken broth or consommé
¼ c. red wine (dry)

Method: Melt butter in bottom of casserole with cover in which you will cook and serve this. Add lettuce, peas, sugar, pepper, basil, and broth. Cover and simmer over low heat until broth is absorbed, about 20 min. Add wine, cover and cook 3 minutes more, and serve. Time: 25 minutes.

Serves 6.

COLACHE

1 t. butter or cooking oil
1 large onion, finely minced
1 c. string beans, in inch lengths, or ½ pkg. frozen string beans
2 large peeled tomatoes, cubed, or 1 to 1-½ c. canned tomatoes, crushed
5 zucchini, sliced in rounds
1 chile verde, chopped
4 ears corn, cut from ears, or 2 cans whole kernal, or 1 can cream style
1 t. salt
¼ t. pepper

Method: Heat the butter and cook the onion until golden. Add string beans, zucchini, chile, tomatoes and corn, cover and simmer until vegetables are tender, about ½ hour. Add salt and pepper. Taste to correct seasoning. Use low heat and stir several times, but do not cook dry. Time: 35 min.

Serves 8.

LENTILS IN ESCABECHE

4 large onions, peeled, sliced, with rings separated
1 c. vinegar
¼ c. olive oil
1 t. salt
1 clove garlic
¼ t. pepper
2-6 tiny red peppers
1 lb. largest lentils
Water to cover
Salt
2 T. olive oil

Method: Prepare onions in escabeche the day before. Slice onions and separate into rings, then put to soak in the vinegar, olive oil, salt, garlic, pepper and peppers. If you do not care for hot peppers, leave them whole; if you enjoy chiles, break them into tiny bits. The following day boil the lentils 1-2 hours, or until tender. Boil gently to keep them whole. Do not salt until they are thoroughly done. Add salt to taste. Drain, and reserve liquid for soup. Place drained lentils on a large platter, with some depth. Drain the onions and spread them over the lentils. Sprinkle with 2 T. olive oil. Time: 2 hours.

Serves 10-12.

GREEN CORN CASSEROLE

3 ears of tender young green corn or 1 can cream style corn (large)
1 c. milk, evaporated preferred
1 t. sugar
1 t. salt
1 inch stick cinnamon
3 eggs, separated

Method: Slice tender young corn from ears, or use a large can of cream style corn. Cook in milk barely to cover, with sugar, salt and cinnamon, 15 minutes over low heat. Stir to prevent sticking. Beat egg whites until stiff, add yolks one at a time, still beating. Discard cinnamon stick. Gently fold corn mixture into the eggs. Pour into a well-buttered 6 cup casserole. Set in pan of hot water and bake at 350° until golden brown and firm about 1 hour. Serve in casserole. Time: 1 hour, 20 min.
Serves 8.

DROWNED CAULIFLOWER

2 large onions
1 large cauliflower
2 cloves garlic
1 t. salt
2 T. cooking oil
½ c. seeded green olives
1 avocado, peeled, seeded, in strips
½ t. orégano
2 T. olive oil
4 to 6 chiles serranos (buy canned; very hot peppers!)

Method: Boil big onions about 20 minutes, until tender. Cut in half through stem end and separate into "petals." At the same time but not in same pot parboil cauliflower. When tender, drain it and carefully separate into florets. Cut the large florets in half through stem and blossom, as the more seasoning they absorb, the better they taste. Dry with paper towels. Mince garlic and rub with the salt to a paste in a mortar. In large pan heat cooking oil and sauté the garlic paste until golden. Push to one side. Add florets to heated oil, and sauté over medium heat until golden. Turn often to prevent burning. Remove to a casserole or pretty bowl, arranging them stem downward. Drizzle remaining garlic and oil over them. Sprinkle with onion petals, olives, and avocado slices. Rubbing orégano between your palms, sprinkle it on the florets. Drizzle with olive oil. Arrange chiles serranos around bowl. Time: 45 minutes.

Serves 8.

STUFFED CHAYOTES

4 or 5 chayotes (large)
½ lb. cooked kid or lamb, shredded (pork and ham also good)
1 small onion, minced
4 T. butter
2 eggs
1 c. crumbs
1 t. Salt
½ t. pepper

Method: Allow one chayote for each two people. Drop chayotes into boiling water and boil till fork-tender, 15-20 minutes. Drain and cool. Slice lengthwise into halves. With spoon scoop out pulp and seeds, leaving shell about ½ inch thick. Be careful not to break it. Chop the pulp and seeds with the shredded meat. Mince the onion, heat the butter, and fry the onion until golden (6 min.). Add to the chayote mixture with the two eggs, whites and yolks separately beaten to stiffness, half the crumbs, salt and pepper. Mix well and fill the shells, mounding the mixture. Pat remaining crumbs over tops. Bake in 350° oven until nicely browned, 20-25 min. Serves 8-10. If chayotes are not in season, large zucchini may be successfully used.

ARTICHOKES IN ESCABECHE

10 to 12 small artichokes
½ c. olive oil
1 c. vinegar
1 t. salt
1 large onion, sliced thin
½ t. pepper
½ t. orégano
2 bay leaves
2 cloves garlic

Method: Prepare this several days before use. Select tiny artichokes, the completely edible kind. Hearts of older artichokes, or canned hearts, may be used instead. Boil artichokes until just tender. Drain. In olive oil, sauté the onion, salt, pepper, orégano

and bay leaves until onion is golden; add the artichokes and sauté five minutes more. Then add the vinegar and garlic. Place all in a covered utensil or jar. To serve, drain off the sauce, which may then be used to flavor olives or for salads. Time: 20 minutes.
Serves 6-8.

CHILES IN NUT SAUCE

Try to obtain long green mildly hot chiles poblanos; or use 2 4-oz. cans of Ortega's whole Green Chiles. If you use fresh chiles, roast them ten minutes in a hot oven. Remove and wrap in a towel to steam 10 minutes. Unwrap, slit lengthwise, remove all seeds and interior white membrane. Try not to break the peppers. Place them, whether canned or steamed, in a bowl and cover with vinegar to steep at least six hours. Drain, stuff with Picadillo Filling and top with Nut Sauce. 2 cans of chiles verdes serve 6 people.

MACARONI WITH SPINACH

3 T. cooking oil
1 lb. macaroni
2 T. cooking oil
1 large onion, minced
1 clove garlic, finely minced
2 medium tomatoes, finely chopped
1 pkg. frozen spinach, or 1 bunch fresh spinach, boiled 3 min.
4 c. chicken or meat broth or consommé
2 t. salt, ½ t. pepper
½ c. grated dry white cheese (Romano, Parmesan, or both)

Method: In large deep pan, heat cooking oil. Break macaroni into two-inch pieces and fry in the oil until golden brown. Drain. In the same pan heat the 2 T. of cooking oil, add onion and garlic and fry until golden. Add tomato, reduce heat and simmer, crushing tomato as it cooks. When sauce thickens (about 10 min.) add the spinach, cooked, drained and chopped; then the macaroni. Barely cover with boiling water or stock, add salt and pepper, cover and reduce heat. Simmer until liquid is absorbed—about 25 min. Remove to large platter, sprinkle heavily with cheese, and serve. Total time: 45 minutes.
Serves 12.

SCRAMBLED CARROTS

4-5 carrots, boiled
2 T. cooking oil
3 large onion, minced
1 medium tomato, minced
2-4 eggs
½ t. salt

Method: Slice cooked carrots into thin disks. Heat oil. Brown onion in oil, add tomatoes and carrots, and cook gently until sauce begins to dry, about 10 minutes. Break eggs into bowl, add salt, stir quickly with fork and pour over the carrots. Stir and cook until dry, 5 to 10 minutes. Serve at once.
Serves 6-8.

CABBAGE WITH CREAM

1 medium to large cabbage, cut into wedges
Salted water to cover
1 c. cream, sweet or sour, as preferred
½ t. pepper
½ t. nutmeg fresh grated
4 T. butter (½ cube)

Method: Cut cabbage into quarters, then cut into strips. Bring salted water to a rapid boil in a large saucepan. Drop in cabbage, cover, and boil fast until tender, 6 to 10 minutes. Drain thoroughly. Add cream (room temperature), pepper, nutmeg, and butter. Rapidly heat through. Taste to correct seasoning. The nutmeg should be plainly perceptible. Serve at once. Time: 15 min. One medium cabbage serves 4.

STRING BEANS IN EGG SAUCE

4 T. butter
4 sprigs parsley, finely minced
1 pkg. frozen French style string beans
1 egg yolk
⅛ c. vinegar
½ t. salt or sugar

Method: Melt butter, add parsley (discard stems). Sauté over medium heat until parsley wilts, about 3 min. Add frozen beans, cover, and sauté over slow heat. Stir once or twice to speed deicing. When beans are tender (20 min.) beat yolk into vinegar, add to beans, stir well, and stir and cook until yolk is set—but no longer. About 5 min. Taste, and if necessary, season with salt or sugar. Time: 30 min.
Serves 4.

CAULIFLOWER IN GUACAMOLE

    1 large cauliflower

    guacomole:

        2 avocados

        1 medium tomato, chopped fine

        1 medium onion, chopped fine

        La Victoria Green Taco Sauce

        Salt

        Chinese parsley (cilantro) or mint, or orégano

Method: In a large lidded pan, heat water to boiling, add cauliflower stem side down, cover and cook until tender (15-20 min.). Drain thoroughly, upside down.

Guacamole: Peel, seed, and crush avocados with a fork, leaving some lumps. If not for immediate use, save a seed. To roughly mashed avocado pulp, add the tomato and onion. Add chile sauce cautiously, tasting until it meets your requirements, salt to taste, add the herbal seasoning you prefer, again to taste. For this recipe the cauliflower is served hot with room temperature or cold guacamole, as a vegetable; both may be served cold as salad. Arrange cauliflower in center of a platter, surrounded by lettuce leaves; ice with guacamole, heavily. Sprinkle a handful of ruby-red pomgranate seeds over the whole to enhance the effect. Time: 35 minutes.

Serves 8.

CALABACITAS

    6-8 zucchine

    3 T. butter

    1 medium onion, minced

    1 tomato, peeled and crushed

    ½ t. salt

    ¼ t. pepper

    ¼ t. orégano, if desired

Method: Wash but do not peel zucchini. In a large pan over medium heat, melt the butter, add the onions, cover, and simmer until onion is transparent, 3-5 minutes. Remove stems from zucchini and rapidly slice or cube zucchini into the pan. Add tomato, salt, pepper and orégano. If the tomato is very dry, add ¼ c. hot water. Cover and cook 20-30 minutes, until zucchini is tender. Time: 35 minutes.

Serves 6.

GREEN CHILE TURNOVERS

    Masa Harina, 2 C.

    Cheese, dry white grated, ¼ c.

    Salt, ½ t.

    Cooking oil, 2 T.

    Boiling water, 1-½ c.

    Jack cheese, strips ½ in. wide and abt. ¼ inch thick

    Green chiles, Ortega, 3-4, each in 4 strips

    Oil for cooking

Method: Mix Masa Harina, dry cheese and salt; add cooking oil and water to make a thick but spreadable dough. Divide into 12 portions, shape into balls, and press each between two pieces of waxed paper with a flat board, applying even pressure. On each tortilla, place a strip each of cheese and chile, and using bottom piece of waxed paper to help, fold over the tortilla, press edges together. In a large pan heat ¼ inch of cooking oil and fry the turnovers until golden brown on each side. Serve at once with a sauce of ½ c. sour cream and ½ c. green taco sauce, blended. Time: 45 min.

Serves 12 turnovers.

BOILED POTATOES
(Mexican style)

Peel even, regular-sized potatoes. Place in saucepan with a well-fitting lid with 1 t. salt and ½ c. water. Cover pan tightly. Bring water to a boil; reduce heat and continue cooking until potatoes are thoroughly done, shaking the pan occasionally to prevent sticking. This takes about half an hour—it depends on size of the potatoes. Serve with plenty of butter and pepper.

ONIONS IN VINEGAR

Select large Bermuda or red onions. Peel and slice as thinly as possible. Use a bowl with tight-fitting lid, and cover the onions with equal parts of water and vinegar, 1 t. salt, ½ t. orégano, and a good pinch of pepper, at least ½ teaspoonful. Lift and stir to separate rings and distribute marinade evenly (15-20 min.). Cover, and place in refrigerator for at least six hours before serving. Drain well. Save the vinegar to use in salad dressings or to pour over meat as a tenderizer.

PICKLED CHILES

Pack chiles in a sterilized quart jar, preferably green chiles, long and thin or small and plump. Fill jar ¾ full of vinegar and finish filling with water; add a tablespoonful of salt, and a generous pinch of orégano. Make lid tight, and ripen a few weeks in any cool place—the vinegar preserves the chiles so refrigeration is not mandatory. If you wish, stab the chiles through and through with a large needle before pickling.

BEVERAGES

ROMPOPE

1 pint milk (evaporated)
1 c. sugar
2 T. ground blanched almonds
3 inches stick cinnamon, crushed
2 egg yolks
1 c. brandy
2 drops nutmeg essence or essence of cloves

Method: Bring milk with the sugar, almonds, and cinnamon to a boil. Boil five minutes, stirring to dissolve sugar. Cool twenty minutes; beat in the egg yolks. Strain. Add the brandy and essence of nutmeg or cloves. Pour into a bottle and refrigerate. Serve in small cups or liqueur glasses. Time: about 15 min.

ANISETTE

Method: Boil together four cups of sugar and four cups of water until syrupy (25-30 min.) Cool. Have ready two wine bottles (fifths). Pour half the syrup in each. When wholly cold, finish filling with vodka. Add 60 drops of essence of anise or a teaspoonful of anise flavoring. Time: 2 hours 10 min.

ATOLE

Atole is made plain or salted, but far more often sweetened and flavored. Some of its many flavors; pineapple, strawberry, almond, vanilla, tamarind, blackberry, cinnamon.

STRAWBERRY ATOLE

Use 1 basket of strawberries, hulled, washed, crushed, and follow directions for pineapple atole.

CINNAMON ATOLE

5 c. milk
1 stick cinnamon, finely slivered
½ c. Masa Harina
¼ c. sugar
1 c. water

Method: Put milk and cinnamon in pot to boil over high heat. In a medium-sized mixing bowl, stir together the Masa Harina and sugar, add the water and stir until smooth. When milk boils, pour the Masa mixture slowly into the milk, so that boiling is not slowed, stirring all the while. Reduce heat slightly and continue stirring to prevent sticking. When mixture reaches the consistency of thin boiled custard—about 5 minutes—remove and cool about five minutes, then serve at once. If you wish, strain it. If you like it sweeter, add more sugar. Time: 15 min.
Serves 8-10.

PINEAPPLE ATOLE

Instead of cinnamon, use 1 small can of crushed pineapple. Follow above recipe omitting cinnamon, but do not add pineapple until after the mixture has thickened and been removed from heat—it curdles if pineapple is added too soon.

DESSERTS

PINEAPPLE FLAN

1 c. pineapple juice
½ c. sugar
6 eggs
¼ c. sugar for caramelizing (optional)

Method: Cook the pineapple juice and sugar to a syrup by boiling hard and stirring five minutes. Beat eggs until very light and stiff. Pour two tablespoonful of the syrup into a one quart baking dish and turn to coat the bottom and sides (or if you wish caramelize the additional sugar and use this instead.) Pour remaining syrup into beaten eggs, and briefly beat again. Pour into baking dish. Set in pan of hot water and bake in preheated 350° oven 45 minutes to 1 hour. Cool. Cover and refrigerate. Best when made day before serving. Run knife around edge of flan and unmold on platter to serve. Total time: 1 hour.
Serves 6.

CHOCOLATE FLAN

1 oz. (1 square) bitter chocolate
¼ c. water
2 c. evaporated or well-boiled milk
6 egg yolks
1 T. vanilla
1 c. sugar

Method: Preheat oven to 350°. Set large pan of water in oven, with mold in pan. Use an oval baking casserole, 1-½ quart size. In double boiler top, over hot water, melt chocolate in ¼ c. water. Add to the milk beaten with the yolks and vanilla and ½ c. sugar. Beat well. Caramelize ½ c. sugar over high heat in a small saucepan, stirring hard. When sugar begins to melt, reduce heat and continue stirring until sugar has all melted and is a light tan. Do not burn—it turns bitter. Pour it into the bottom of the mold, and tilt to cover the bottom. Pour the chocolate mixture into the mold. Bake one hour. Cool thoroughly. (Make it the day before use and let it firm in refrigerator.) Slide spatula around upper edge of custard to loosen; place a large platter with some depth over the casserole, and invert carefully. Let mold remain about fifteen minutes so all the caramel sauce can drip down. Preparation time: about 15 min.
Serves 6.

ORANGE BASKETS

6 large oranges
2 slices canned pineapple
2 ripe bananas
½ c. sugar
½ c. strawberries, sliced
1 c. whipping or all purpose cream
1 T. powdered sugar
½ t. almond extract
6 large strawberries

Method: Fine big navel oranges are the best for this recipe; others will do. Wash oranges thoroughly in hot soapy water and then in cold to remove any traces of sprays, unless you know they are from unsprayed trees. Dry well. Cut a round segment off the bottom. Excavate all the pulp you can, using potato peeler, small sharp knife, and spoon; discard white membranes. Clean out shell. Place pulp in a mixing bowl and combine with the sliced pineapple and bananas and sugar. Gently fold in sliced strawber-

ries, avoiding crushing them. Fill the rinds with this mixture. Whip the cream, add powdered sugar and almond extract a second or two before beating ends. If desired, tint this cream pale pink with vegetable coloring. Heap the orange baskets, with spoon or decorating tube. In center of each place one whole strawberry. Refrigerate two hours. Time (less refrigeration) 35 min.
Serves 6.

OLD-FASHIONED DESSERT

¾ c. sugar
½ c. water
4 whole cloves
½ c. sherry
6-8 cake slices (pound, sponge, any plain cake)
5 egg yolks

Method: Boil sugar, water and cloves together for five minutes. Cool. Add sherry. While syrup cools, arrange cake slices on a large platter and pour half the sherry-syrup over them. Try to arrange the slices like petals of a flower on a large round platter, their ends meeting toward the center, leaving a hole about three inches across. Between cake slices long segments of large peaches or nectarines are placed). Now slightly beat yolks, pour a little syrup into them and stir, empty into the remaining syrup and stir over medium heat until mixture coats the spoon (5 min.). Pour over the cake, making sure each slice gets its share. Garnish as desired. Serve hot or cold. Time not including time to make cake: 15 min.
Serves 8.

ICE CREAM WITH CAJETA

1 can sweetened condensed milk
1 small can crushed pineapple
1 qt. vanilla or coffee ice cream

Method: Place condensed milk, intact—don't even remove label—in water to cover and boil two hours. Be sure to keep can completely covered throughout boiling. Cook completely. Punch hole in one end of can, remove the other end, and slice out into bowl. Drain pineapple and mix with the cajeta. Use as topping for ice cream.
Serves 8-10.

COCONUT SWEET

    1 7-oz. can coconut
    2 c. milk
    1-¾ c. sugar
    1 stick cinnamon
    3 egg yolks
    2 T. butter
    ¼ c. sliced unblanched almonds

Method: Place one cup of the milk, the sugar and the cinnamon over moderate heat in a large pan; when it begins to boil, add the coconut and stir until coconut looks transparent. Add the yolks beaten with the rest of the milk, and stir constantly "until you can see the bottom of the pan"—that is, until a wide swath of pan appears every time you move the spoon through the mixture. Butter a large platter. Empty the mixture on it, sprinkle with the almonds, and cool. Serve hot or cold, as you wish. Time: 20 min.

Serves 10-16 small portions.

TIDBITS FOR THE CARDINAL

    cake:
        4 eggs, separated
        ½ c. sugar
        ¼ c. corn starch
        ¼ c. cake flour
        1 c. sherry
    syrup:
        2 c. sugar
        1 c. water

Method: Preheat oven to 350°. In large bowl beat 4 egg whites very stiff. In small bowl, beat yolks until lemony, add sugar and continue beating. When stiff, add slowly, by tablespoonsful, the corn starch and cake flour. Carefully fold yolk mixture into beaten whites. Place in well-buttered pan (8" × 8" × 2"). Bake 15 min. Turn off oven, slightly open door, and allow cake to cool in oven to prevent falling. When cold, cut into 16 squares. Arrange in a pretty bowl and slowly saturate with sherry. This requires about 1 cupful. Make syrup by bringing water and sugar to boil, and cook 5 minutes. Cook before pouring over cake. Refrigeration makes it even better. Time: 35 min.

Serves 8.

CHONGOS

    1 quart milk
    2 egg yolks
    2 junket tablets (rennet)
    ¾ to 1 c. sugar
    1 inch stick cinnamon, splintered

Method: In a 2 qt. pot heat the milk quickly to lukewarm; while it warms, beat the yolks in mixer or blender. Stir them into the milk, and add the rennet dissolved in 1 T. of water. (Junket tablets are hard to find unflavored; if your supermarket doesn't yield them, try the drugstore.) Stir hard briefly, and pour into deep pan or pot about 8" × 10", and 3" or more deep, or pot about 8-10 in diameter. Let set without moving until firm. Slice into squares with knife (16 squares). Sprinkle sugar and cinnamon over it and place over low heat to barely simmer 2 hours, or until curds have slightly-cheese-like consistency, (taste a small bit) and syrup thickens. Serve in attractive dish. Not counting time in firming: about 7 minutes.

Serves 8.

MARQUESOTE

    6 egg whites
    2 c. whipping or all purpose cream
    1 c. powdered sugar
    ½ c. cake flour
    1 t. vanilla

Method: Heavily butter a square pan (8 × 8 × 2). Heat oven to 250°. Beat whites until very stiff. Beat cream stiff, and add sugar to it a little at a time, folding it in until all the sugar is used. Now fold the whites into the cream mixture by the large spoonful, very carefully, alternating with spoonsful of the 3-times-sifted flour, and the vanilla. Work as lightly and gently as you can. Pour into the buttered pan and bake about 1-½ hours, until pale golden on top. At the end of the time, open the oven door cautiously and look; if golden, test with thin sharp knife; if it comes out clean, cake is done. If in doubt, give it more time. When satisfied that it is done, close door very gently and let it cool where it is. Cold, cut it into lady finger strips to serve. The bottom is jellylike; the top like meringue. Time: 2 hours.

Makes 16 fingers.

ZARA'S ICE CREAM

1 can evaporated milk
2 egg whites, beaten
1 small jar maraschino cherries (4 oz.)

Method: Blend milk (chilled in refrigerator) and cherries and their liquid in blender, only for a moment or two: cherries should not be too well blended. Thoroughly whip egg whites, fold in cherry mixture. Freeze to desired consistency. If you like a stronger flavor, add from ½ to 1 t. almond extract. Time: 2-½ hours.
Serves 6.

PINEAPPLE SHERBERT

1 c. pineapple juice
1 can crushed pineapple
¼ c. sugar
Juice of ½ lemon
4 egg whites, well beaten

Method: Combine pineapple juice, pineapple, sugar, and lemon juice. Stir to dissolve sugar. In freezer pans, freeze to a mush, 1 to 2 hours (you'll have to watch it). Remove and beat in your mixer. Return to refrigerator, beat the egg whites very stiff, then combine the pineapple mush with the stiff egg whites and return to freezer again. 1-2 hours more. Preparation time, exclusive of freezing time: about 10 minutes.
Serves 8.

NIÑO ENVUELTO

½ c. melted butter, cooled
5 eggs
½ c. sugar
¾ c. flour
Prune or peach jam

Method: Melt and cool butter. Beat yolks and whites separately until stiff. Combine and still beating, slowly add sugar, sifted flour, and melted butter. On baking sheet place waxed paper. Butter paper. Spread dough about ½ inch thick over the paper. Bake at 350° about 50 min.-1 hour. When cake tester comes out clean, remove cake from oven and roll up quickly, paper and all. Wrap in a towel. Let rest 15-20 min. Unwrap, carefully loosening paper, but leav-ing it under the cake. Spread the cake with jam, re-roll, discarding waxed paper. Roll entire cake in powdered sugar. Cut off both ends for neat appearance. Slice about one inch thick to serve. This Mexican jelly roll—"Bundled-up Baby"—is particularly good with coffee.
Serves 12-15.

ORANGE CUP

This simple, easy-to-make mixture is a delightful *aperitif* before meals, or may be used as a finale, as here. Allow one fine orange per person. Peel and segment fruit, remove all membranes; break each segment into bite sizes. For each orange allow 3 to 4 fresh mint leaves, minced fine. Allow 2 T. honey to each. Combine honey and mint leaves and pour over the oranges, stir well, and chill. Serve in attractive glass bowls or stemware. Time: 10-15 min. for 6.
Serves 6 generously, 8 adequately.

TIPSY APPLES

6 good cooking apples
2 c. sugar
Juice of ½ lemon
½ stick cinnamon, slivered
2 c. dry red wine

Method: Peel and core apples, placing in cold water with lemon juice to prevent discoloring. Remove to ovenproof casserole with lid. (You can make one of aluminum foil.) Fill apple cavities with sugar and pour remaining sugar over them. Sprinkle with slivered cinnamon. Pour wine around apples. Cover and bake at 250°, 2 hours at least. Serve warm (not hot), or chilled, with cream or without.
Serves 6.

PRUNE JAM

1 lb. prunes, pitted preferred
1-½ c. water
1-½ c. sugar
1 inch stick of cinnamon
1 lemon peeled, slightly rubbed with grater

Method: Bring all ingredients to a boil, and cook ten minutes. Remove, and discard peel, cinnamon, and prune pits. Blenderize prunes, adding syrup a tablespoonful or two at a time, only until mixture becomes a thick paste. Time: 12 min.

LEMON BANANA CLOUD

4 egg whites
½ c. sugar
3 very ripe mashed bananas
Grated rind of 1 lemon
1 t. vanilla

Method: Beat egg whites until very stiff. Still beating, add sugar in slow dribbles, banana pulp, also slowly, grated rind and vanilla. Pour gently into buttered casserole and bake at 350° until set and brown on top—20-30 min. Serve cold. Better if made the day before serving. Time: 30 minutes.
Serves 6.

NEÁPOLITAN SNOW PUDDING

2 c. milk
½ stick cinnamon, slivered
⅓ c. sugar
3 T. blanched, well-ground almonds
6 egg whites
1 lemon rind, grated

Method: Boil milk with cinnamon and sugar for 10 minutes; add almonds and boil 5 more minutes. Stir to prevent sticking. Cool. To unbeaten egg whites, add the lemon rind and strained milk; stir all together well and bake in a buttered mold set in a pan of hot water in 350° until firm when shaken and beginning to be golden on top (45 min.). Chill before serving. Total time, about 1 hour. Serves 6. Serve with Pudding Sauce

PUDDING SAUCE

2 c. water
2 c. sugar
6 egg yolks
1 c. orange juice

Method: Make syrup by boiling the sugar and water together five minutes after reaching boiling point. Cool 15 minutes. Beat the yolks and orange juice together in mixer, add to the syrup, and cook again on medium heat stirring constantly until mixture coats the spoon—approx. 15 minutes. To serve, have pudding and sauce well chilled. Run a thin knife around pudding to loosen it, and invert on a large platter. Pour the sauce over and around it. You may prefer to reduce the sugar for the sauce to 1-¾, 1-½, or even 1 cup instead of 2—it is a very sweet syrup! If this reduction is made, it must be given more cooking time before it becomes syrupy. Time: 35 min.
Serves 6.

ALMENDRADO

1 T. gelatine (1 env.)
¼ c. cold water
5 egg whites
½ c. sugar
1 c. almonds, blanched and ground
½ t. almond extract
Red and green food coloring

Method: Soften gelatine in cold water and set cup in hot water over low heat to dissolve. Beat egg whites stiff but not dry. Still beating, slowly dribble in the sugar, almond extract, and gelatine, until the mixture peaks. Transfer ⅓ to another bowl. Gently sprinkle ground almonds over the remaining ⅔, and fold them in gently. Place half of this in a second small bowl. Carefully color the mixture in one bowl a delicate green, and that in the other red, using only enough tint to make the color definite. Line a loaf pan (8-½ × 4-½ × 3) with waxed paper, let some overlap ends of pan, to ease removing of dessert. Spoon the green layer into the pan, smooth it; spoon in the white layer and smooth; and follow with the red layer. Chill in refrigerator at least six hours. "Almonded" is the literal translation of *almendrado*. The colors are those of the Mexican flag. Slice gelatine in inch-thick portions to serve. Preparation time: 20 minutes. Serves 6. Top with custard cream.

CUSTARD CREAM

1 pint milk (2 c.)
5 egg yolks
¼ c. sugar
Pinch of salt
1 T. vanilla

Method: Mix milk, yolks, sugar and salt in the top of a double boiler over boiling water, and stir constantly. When mixture coats the spoon (about 15 min.) remove and cool about 15 min. more. Press through a sieve to remove hard bits of egg white. Beat in vanilla and cool. Chill in refrigerator. Beat the "crust" in before serving. Time: 15 min.
Serves 6.

APRICOT CREAM

1 can apricot halves, or 2 c. fresh fruit, peeled and seeded
1 c. whipping cream
½ c. apricot liquid from can
½ c. sugar (if you use fresh apricots, increase sugar to ¾ c., cream to 1-½ c.

Method: Chop fruit fine, but leave some lumps. Whip the cream and combine with the fruit, liquid, and sugar. Pour into freezer pans and set in freezer. Ready in 2-3 hours. Makes 2 icecube trays full.

Serves 8-12.

ALMOND VANILLA PUDDING

3 pints milk, scalded (or use evaporated)
3 egg yolks
½ c. blanched almonds
1 c. sugar
2 t. vanilla
1 pkg. gelatine dissolved in ½ c. cold water

Method: Place milk, yolks, almonds, sugar and vanilla in top of double boiler over hot water until mixture coats spoon, stirring occasionally. Dissolve gelatine in cold water and set in small pan of hot water until it becomes transparent; stir into the other mixture and cool. Chill before serving. Time: ½ hour.

Serves 6-8.

ADELITA'S MERENGADO

4 c. milk
1 c. sugar
1 stick cinnamon, crushed
Rind of 1 lemon, grated
4 egg whites
1 t. anise flavoring
¼ c. sugar

Method: Combine milk, 1 c. sugar, cinnamon and lemon rind in large sauce pan, and bring rapidly to a boil. Lower heat and simmer 5 minutes. Strain. Cool. Beat the egg whites until stiff, then add the ¼ c. sugar, very slowly, still beating. Add anise flavor to the milk, and carefully fold in the whites, avoiding breaking them up. Freeze several hours until set.

This is a refreshing and delightful summer sherbert. In addition to the anise flavoring, you may add a teaspoonful of almond flavoring. In summer leave this snowy looking dessert cooly ungarnished, or decorate it only with a cool green leaf or two: mint, nasturtium, or lemon verbena. In winter try a sprinkle—very light—of instant cocoa, a dash of cinnamon, or a whisper of instant coffee. Time, including freezing time: 2-½ to 3 hours.

Serves 6.

PAPAYA AND ORANGE DESSERT

2 papayas
4 large oranges

Method: Make this 3 or 4 hours before serving. Cut papaya in half lengthwise, discard seeds, peel papaya and cut into neat cubes. Peel oranges, remove as much white membrane as possible, segment and remove remaining membrane and seeds, divide orange into bite sizes and stir into the papaya cubes. When oranges are properly sweet, nothing more is needed. If acid, dribble some honey over the fruit or sprinkle with sugar. Refrigerate. Serve in pretty glass cups or bowls, and enjoy. Preparation time: 10-15 min.

Serves 8.

Index